The Haunted Study

THE HAUNTED STUDY

A Social History
of the English Novel 1875–1914

PETER KEATING

'No one has the faintest conception of what I'm trying for,' he said to me, 'and not many have read three pages that I've written; but I must dine with them first – they'll find out why when they've time.' It was rather rude justice perhaps; but the fatigue had the merit of being a new sort, while the phantasmagoric town was probably after all less of a battlefield than the haunted study.

Henry James, 'The Death of the Lion' (1894)

Secker & Warburg
London

First published in England 1989
by Martin Secker & Warburg Limited,
Michelin House, 81 Fulham Road, London SW3 6RB
© 1989 by Peter Keating

British Library Cataloguing in Publication Data

Keating, Peter
  The haunted novel: a social history of the English
  novel 1875–1914.
  1. Fiction in English 1837 – Forms   Novels   Critical
  studies
  I. Title
  823'.009

ISBN 0 436 23248 0

Set in 11/13pt Ehrhardt
Printed and bound in Great Britain
by Richard Clay Ltd, Bungay, Suffolk

Contents

Preface

'Whoever seriously occupies himself with literature will soon perceive its vital connexions with other agencies,' Matthew Arnold observed in his preface to *Mixed Essays* (1879). That perception, regarded by Arnold as axiomatic, has not seemed so obviously true to many of the literary critics and theorists who have led the way in the academic professionalisation of literary studies in the twentieth century, even though in other respects they have often looked back to Arnold as an inspirational guide. The main trend of twentieth-century literary criticism has been to establish itself as an autonomous discipline, cut off from and independent of other 'agencies': in that process literature's connections with social history have been particularly, and surprisingly, neglected.

By the end of the nineteenth century there was already a sharp division in academic approaches to the study of English literature. Historians formed the dominant group. They stressed the importance of knowledge, information, facts, chronology, biography, social and political context. In contrast, literary critics scorned such fact-gathering as irrelevant to the student's true task which was to develop taste, sensibility, fine discrimination. There was no intrinsic reason why these two approaches should have been kept apart from each other, but social pressures on the academic study of English literature – a topic examined in the final chapter of the present book – gave priority to the critics. Their victory over the historians was swift and devastatingly complete. Literary history was not quite annihilated, but its survival (along with that of textual scholarship) was tolerated only grudgingly. Most unrepentant literary historians turned to the monograph. Others found in Marxism a strong ideological resistance to the separation of literature and history. Whether this situation will be changed substantially by the recent growth of interest in literary theory is still uncertain. At present, several of literary theory's proliferating strands are even more aggressively ahistorical than the literary

criticism they are displacing, though the position of theoretical
Marxism has become strengthened, and some branches of feminism
have been attracted to history as a means of retrieving from
obscurity those women writers for whom literary criticism could
find no place. Allowing for exceptions such as these, the study of
literature in the present century has been, in effect, de-historicised.

Literary criticism's most complete victory was over the wide-
ranging surveys compiled by late Victorian literary historians. Even
now, anyone needing to consult a history of nineteenth-century
literature that offers reliable information on the range and variety
of writers working at any given time (and, of course, indications of
the ways in which those writers and their work are related) is still
likely to turn either to the standard books by such turn-of-the-
century historians as George Saintsbury, Oliver Elton, A. W.
Ward, Hugh Walker, and Ernest Baker, or to a small number of
more recently published histories, the method of which varies little
from that of the earlier models. What makes the continuing
unadventurousness of this kind of literary history so surprising is
that while the British contribution to literary theory over the past
twenty or so years has been slight, the achievements of social
historians in Britain – often inspired by Marxism but by no means
exclusively so – have been impressive. Remarkably little attention
has been paid by students of literature to these developments in
social history and other related areas of research such as historical
sociology, even though it is here that many of literature's
'connexions with other agencies' are most significantly to be found.

The structuring of the seven chapters that make up the present
book requires a brief explanation. Each chapter is centred on one
topic or theme and explores various aspects of it; in each chapter,
literature and history are interrelated, though in varying ways and
proportions according to the nature of the material being presented;
all of the chapters are organised on a chronological basis, and each
of them covers the whole period. In addition, the opening and
closing chapters are, as their titles indicate, connected to each other in
a different manner. The first chapter is primarily descriptive. Taking
as a starting point Trollope's decision in 1875 to write his autobiography, it outlines the changing business of literature in the period,
and focuses on the social and economic position of novelists. In the
final chapter, much of the same material is re-examined, though
interpretatively rather than descriptively, and with the main focus on

the social and economic position of readers. The book can therefore
be read as either a continuous narrative or as a series of interrelated
narratives, though the full argument of the book is intended to be
cumulative. I felt that only with this kind of method would it be
possible to attempt to do justice to the many different ways in which
literature and history are inextricably connected, and, through an
accumulation of those demonstrated connections, offer an historical
explanation of the emergence of modernist fiction in Britain.

I am conscious of owing an immense debt to the social, economic,
cultural and literary historians who have written on various aspects
of this period: without their work it would not have been possible for
me to adopt the kind of interdisciplinary approach that I have. This
debt I have tried to acknowledge in the notes which are used not only
to identify sources but also to indicate further reading on particular
topics: the alternative – a very substantial and unwieldy secondary
bibliography – would, I felt, be of doubtful value to the reader. The
notes are not intended to be complete, but even so, in a book that
encroaches on so many different academic territories there are bound
to be omissions and over-simplifications which are accountable to me.
In the notes I have made few references to works of literary criticism
and theory. This is partly due to the type of material I am dealing
with, but more substantially to the historical approach I have taken
to a number of issues which are frequently discussed or mentioned
by critics and theorists. To those writers whose view of literature is
irredeemably ahistorical my findings are unlikely to matter one way
or another: to those with an interest in history, it will, I hope, be
clear where the connections I am making are complementary to
theirs and where there is disagreement. To have been constantly
taking up such issues with individual critics would have changed into
something entirely different the book I wanted to write.

I would like to express my gratitude to the Society of Authors
and the British Library for permission to quote from material in
the archives of the Society of Authors; the Travel and Research
Committee of Edinburgh University for financial help; the Hunt-
ington Library, San Marino, California, for appointing me to a
visiting fellowship in the summer of 1978; the National Library of
Scotland, Edinburgh, where so much of the research for this book
was carried out; and, above all, to Valerie Shaw for her unfailing
help and encouragement in all sorts of ways.

Peter Keating

Introduction

'I suppose things have changed?' she said.
  'Never was such an age of transition.'
  She wondered what to. Mr Ramage did not know. 'Sufficient unto
me is the change thereof,' he said, with all the effect of an epigram.

H. G. Wells, *Ann Veronica* (1909)

In literary and cultural studies, the most common description of the period of time covered by this book is 'age of transition': it is used to evoke an indeterminate stretch of some thirty or forty years, bounded on the one side by the achievements of 'the Victorians' and on the other by those of 'the Moderns'. In so far as such a description allows the period a mood of its own – lodged precariously, as it is assumed to be, between two distinct phases of creativity – that mood is invariably seen as one of confusion and uncertainty. Wells's Mr Ramage wants to get Ann Veronica onto the saucy subject of the 'New Woman'. That was certainly a prominent aspect of the transition, but so, it can seem, was everything else. The comprehensive nature of this 'swift transition' was influentially expressed by the historian G. M. Young:

> A sense of vagueness, of incoherence and indirection, grows
> on us as we watch the eighties struggling for a foothold in
> the swirl and wreckage of new ideas and old beliefs.[1]

Equally influential has been Raymond Williams's similar classification of the years from 1880 to 1914 as an 'interregnum', though Williams is more negative, and considerably less historical, than Young in finding that – with the idiosyncratic exception of T. E. Hulme – the writers of the period did not represent 'anything very new' but rather 'a working-out of unfinished lines, a tentative redirection'.[2] Similar terminology and attitudes are to be found in many other studies of the period.[3]

In addition to (and often working against) the concept of the whole period as one of transition, there are various popular sub-divisions. 'The Nineties' and 'Fin de Siècle' are the most well-established, though 'The Edwardians' have also often been seen as inhabitants of a relatively fleeting age of transition, neither quite Victorian, nor Nineties, nor Modern. Recently, Samuel Hynes has argued that rather than be subsumed within a broader unit of time, the Edwardian Age should be acknowledged as a distinct 'literary period' with 'a beginning, a middle, and an end, a consciousness of its own separateness from what went before and what followed, and a body of literature that expresses that consciousness'.[4] And, hovering over many of these attempts at periodicity is the long-running critical debate on when exactly 'Modernism' can be said to begin, or, sometimes, whether it can ever be said to have begun at all.

Of course, periodicity itself itself has been attacked as fostering an artificial sense of what historical processes involve· all 'ages', it is argued, are 'ages of transition'. Allowing for the degree of self-evident truth in this stance, and putting to one side the not inconsiderable practical problems its application poses for the historian, it still seems reasonable to assume (at least as far as literature is concerned) that there are (1) periods of time when imaginative writers feel closely involved in, and sometimes commit-ted to, the main social and political tendencies of their age; (2) certain events – whether political or intellectual – which are felt as so disruptive that they make it impossible for imaginative writers to accept the dominant values and attitudes held by their immediate predecessors; and (3) periods of time when imaginative writers feel either set apart from, or aggessively opposed to, the formative political and social tendencies of their age. The last two of these three propositions are applicable to the late nineteenth and early twentieth centuries, and their conjunction is largely responsible for the popularity of the transition label.

This is not, however, a type of classification that has simply been imposed retrospectively by historians and critics. The late Victor-ians themselves were intensely conscious of their transitory state. By 1909, as Wells (though not Mr Ramage) realised, the perception that the age was one of transition had become commonplace. It was a realisation that could provoke uncertainty, confusion, pessimism, even apocalyptic gloom – the moods most usually emphasised in literary studies of the period. But, alternatively, it could inspire pride, excitement and eager anticipation. The primary causes of late Victorian insecurity – that 'swirl and wreckage of new ideas and old beliefs', to re-quote G. M. Young – were both political and intellectual. Out of the twin forces of electoral reform and Darwinism a new kind of society would emerge. Everyone who thought about the situation knew that, and many of them understood that the form the new society would take was still to be determined. Conservatives, Liberals, Fabians, Marxists, Socialists, Anarchists, and perhaps most important of all, the economic and cultural manipulators of the emergent mass-market, were in no doubt that they were in transition: it was on what exactly they were in transition to, and how they planned to get there, that they disagreed. In 1888 Bernard Shaw was invited to address the British Association, and in a fit of Fabian enthusiasm he suggested the topic '*Finishing* the Transition to Social Democracy'. On reflection he dropped the word 'finishing' because, being 'in the middle of the transition', there might still be some way to go. Eventually he dropped most other words in the original title as well, and the talk, as published in *Fabian Essays* (1889), became simply 'Transition'.[5]

For a politically-conscious theorist like Shaw – as for many other theorists and activists of different political persuasions – the task ahead was nothing less than the total reconstruction of British society, but as the process of extending the franchise was already well under way it was easier to advance a societal model than to convince the constituent parts of that model that their interests were identical. Some commentators did not see a problem here at all, so obviously were the working classes coming into their own. This was not a conviction held only by Socialists and Marxists. The pioneer social psychologist Gustave Le Bon, for example, was expressing a very widely-held belief indeed when he claimed that although 'the modern age represents a period of transition and anarchy' it was clear that for the first time in human history 'the crowd' would determine the future: 'The divine right of the masses is about to replace the divine right of Kings.'[6] There were, however, many different ways in which 'the masses' could be helped to attain, or prevented from attaining, their inheritance. There were also other forms of social reconstruction in which the importance of the working-class cause was acknowledged but not given the priority allowed to it by Le Bon, Socialists and Marxists.

Humanists saw themselves as in transition to a secular state in which, once freed of supernatural sanctions and rewards, totally new kinds of ethical codes would be formulated and put into operation. Feminists saw themselves as in transition to a sexually liberated state in which, once freed of legal and familial restraints, their full potential – and therefore that of a majority of the British population – would be revealed in unprecedented and unpredictable ways. Educationalists saw themselves as working towards a future in which universal literacy would effect an almost inconceivable cultural transformation of the entire nation. Scientists pointed to the even more miraculous, magically unknowable, transformation that their technological wizardry could eventually bring about. Not all of these interests were, of course, incompatible with each other, but no one of them was able to establish a dominant formative influence on the new society: more characteristic were splits and divisions, competing pressure groups, and proliferating theories. As H. G. Wells noted in 1911: 'The ideas go on – and no person or party succeeds in embodying them.'[7] In practice, there were almost as many different kinds of transition as there were groups of people committed to the reform of specific problems. Out of these diverse activities there emerged the social and cultural fragmentation that has characterised Britain ever since.

It is the continuous twentieth-century struggle with issues initiated or reformulated by the late Victorians that most effectively undermines the 'age of transition' and 'interregnum' labels. Late Victorian writers were not waiting passively for a new age to emerge: they were in active rebellion against virtually everything the previous generation represented and were desperate to create new forms and structures to replace those they had destroyed. Nor is it sensible – except, perhaps, in very limited formalist terms – to believe that a new phase of stability (literary or otherwise) came out of the supposed transition. Most late Victorian Utopian visions were either blurred by, or absorbed within, the overwhelming force of democratic consumerism. Other dreams and aspirations did not necessarily collapse, though the early optimism did, with the result that a great deal of later energy has had to be directed to various kinds of ideological re-activation. This is most strikingly apparent in many recent neo-Marxist literary and historical studies of the nineteenth and twentieth centuries. What they offer is an analysis of failure, an obsessive concern with the question, what went wrong? Related attitudes are to be found elsewhere. It is, for example, unlikely that the 'New Women' of the 1890s would be surprised by many of the issues raised in recent feminist studies: they would, however, almost certainly be astonished that those issues are still a matter of passionate debate in the 1980s. The conviction that within fifty or sixty or one hundred years, the uncertainties, inconsistencies, and incongruities of the age would have been rationalised away is to be found in many strands of late Victorian literature: the length of time needed for the transformation to cease being a prophecy and become an actuality may have varied, but that it would happen within a discernible time span was held as certain.[9] This was something quite different from the mid-Victorian trust in the concept of progress. The mid-Victorians had survived their own traumatic 'age of transition' and were prepared to settle for a long process of amelioration. They did not realise that their children and grandchildren would be in such a hurry to confront a new phase of disruptive change.

Novelists were to play crucial parts in that disruption, but they did not initiate it or in any fundamental way dictate its terms. Like many other groups of people, they were generally eager to break from the immediate past, hopeful that great things would eventually emerge from the transition, and, at the same time, unsure what was going to happen or how it might come about. 'The mind,' Hardy wrote, employing an archetypal image of transition, was 'adrift on change, and harassed by the irrepressible new.'[10] In spite of his total difference of emphasis, Hardy was claiming much the same as Max Nordau, the implacable enemy of all manifestations of modernism, who yearned for a future time when great artists would once again make beauty the object of their endeavours and seek to inspire mankind. 'Meanwhile,' Nordau complained, 'interregnum in all its terrors prevails.'[11] For Hardy and Nordau those terrors were primarily the result of an apparently unstoppable spirit of intellectual and artistic enquiry, though for many of the novelists whose careers were beginning in the final decades of the century, the terrors of an age of transition were as much economic as intellectual. The business of literature was also 'adrift on change' and being forced to come to terms with 'the irrepressible new'.

Part One

TAKING SIDES

Chapter One

Novelists and Readers

'I mean, mother, that I am going to give up my post at Brimage and
Waring's and that I shall try another line of life altogether. I shall try
to live by literature.'

Walter Besant, *All in a Garden Fair* (1883)

'If my calculation of 40,000 words (now set up) is correct (and I
cannot be very far wrong) then I've written up to the value of £100
advanced me by Mr B'wood. I would be glad – if at all feasible – to
have £20 further on acct/. I am ashamed to everlastingly proclaim my
destitution – and weary of the thing itself.'

Joseph Conrad to David S. Meldrum, 17 December 1899

On 15 December 1874 Anthony Trollope wrote to the publisher
Nicholas Trübner telling him of his plan to visit Australia and
suggesting that Trübner commission a series of 'twenty letters'
which would describe the 'social condition of the people' in
Australia and other countries visited on the way.[1] There was
nothing unusual in such an arrangement. Trollope was the most
widely-travelled of Victorian novelists and, whether his journeys
were on official business for the Post Office or simply made out of
personal curiosity, he rarely missed an opportunity to earn some
extra money by writing about them. This particular journey,
though, carries a slight air of mystery. In one sense it was strange
that Trollope should have been making it at all. It was only three years
since he had visited Australia to attend the wedding of his younger
son Fred who was a sheep-farmer in New South Wales. On that
occasion Trollope had travelled with his wife and cook. They stayed
for eighteen months and Trollope published a series of travel articles

in the *Daily Telegraph* as well as what he himself described as a
'dull and long' book about their experiences.[2] Now, in spite of the
exhaustion of the earlier visit, he was determined to go back. This
time he was to travel alone: the main reason once again was Fred.
'I believe I can give him a helping hand by going out,' Trollope
explained to John Blackwood: 'I can see what money I can advance
him out of my small means, and settle certain things with him.'[3]

Trollope left England on 1 March 1875. A few days earlier he
had delivered to Frederic Chapman the manuscript of *The Prime
Minister*. While at sea he completed another novel, *Is He Popenjoy?*
In Australia he began writing *The American Senator* which he
finished on his way back to England. He also sent Trübner the
twenty travel letters which were published in the *Liverpool
Mercury*, and some time before arriving home in October 1875 he
began writing his autobiography. The manuscript was completed
by 30 April 1876 when Trollope wrote a letter to his elder son
Henry, bequeathing to him all rights in the autobiography and
requesting that it be published as soon as possible after Trollope's
death. The manuscript and the letter were then put to one side:
Henry was not even told of their existence until two years later.[4]
Trollope died in November 1882 and, following his instructions
precisely, Henry arranged for *An Autobiography* to be published.
The manuscript showed that Trollope had occasionally added
pieces to it, but it remained substantially the work he had written
seven years earlier on his return from Australia.

Nobody knows why a man like Trollope, who gloried in
projecting himself as blunt and straightforward in literary matters,
should have behaved so secretively over this particular manuscript,
though he had been worried by bad health in 1874 and he probably
believed that he had only a short time to live: the *Autobiography*,
like the visit to Fred in Australia, was Trollope settling up with
life. The literary form that settlement took involved no startling
revelations about his contemporaries or about his own inner life: it
focused on his working methods and his attitude to the Art of
Fiction. There have been many attempts by criti s to extricate
Trollope from the damage *An Autobiography* did to his posthumous
reputation: his motives have been variously ascribed to his bluff
honesty, undue modesty, over-subtle creative imagination. More
persuasively, it has been argued that by the mid-1870s Trollope
was acutely aware that his popularity was in decline and that in

writing his autobiography he was striking back at the critics.[5] Explanations such as these, however, are too defensive. *An Autobiography* was an assault, not a defence: its peculiar tone, strategy and effect were carefully calculated. It takes perhaps a modern practitioner in the tradition of Trollope to recognise fully the degree of calculation involved. 'His more important statements about himself as a novelist,' J. B. Priestley has written, 'though not untrue, were deliberately provocative. He was doing something more than merely blurting out the truth. He was flying in the face of current prejudice. In effect he was deciding that he might as well be hanged for a sheep as for a lamb.'[6]

The animal image that Trollope himself favoured was that of the tortoise, moving slowly, steadfastly, ploddingly forward to defeat the flamboyant, unreliable hare.[7] Writing by the clock, so many hours per day, so many pages per hour, so many words per page, he allowed nothing to interrupt the regular flow, not business nor holidays, not even travel by sea as he tells us at the most unromantic moment of this aggressively unromantic account: 'More than once I left my paper on the cabin table, rushing away to be sick in the privacy of my stateroom.'[8] Just as the fable of the hare and the tortoise aimed to inculcate values of steadfastness and slow dedication which were finally rewarded, so Trollope, the literary tortoise, emphasised the rewards that came to him. He had worked towards a great moral end, regarding himself as a preacher of sermons in which entertainment and instruction combined to make 'virtue alluring and vice ugly'.[9] In the kind of phrase that was to echo derisively through late Victorian criticism, he announced proudly: 'I do believe that no girl has risen from the reading of my pages less modest than she was before.'[10] There were material as well as spiritual achievements to record, and Trollope set out the sums he had received for each of his books and carefully added them up. By the time he wrote his autobiography the total came to £68,959 17s 6d. 'I look upon the result,' he commented, 'as comfortable, but not splendid.'[11]

It is crucial to the strategy of *An Autobiography* that Trollope rarely appears to be denigrating himself. Occasionally he loses balance and sounds boastful rather than honest, but usually he displays pride in his books, critical discrimination when discussing them, and an insistence that they have been written to the best of his capabilities. Of slipshod work he is scornful: it is craftsmanship he is talking about, as in the most notorious of his comparisons, a 'shoemaker' or a 'tallow-chandler' understands the term.[12] As J. B. Priestley says, it is the 'emphasis' of *An Autobiography* that prevents us from accepting it as just another bland, self-congratulatory chronicle.[13] None of Trollope's great contemporaries would have denied the necessity for regular, hard work if their novels were to be written. It was of Dickens, not Trollope, that a first-hand witness was speaking when he said: 'No humdrum monotonous task could ever have been discharged with . . . more business-like regularity than he gave to the work of his imagination or fancy.'[14] In many instances Trollope's contemporaries earned more from their novels than he did: from *Middlemarch* alone George Eliot is estimated to have earned £9,000, three times the amount Trollope received for his most lucrative novels. Nor would they have disagreed strongly with the novelist's social role being classed as similar to that of a clergyman. Trollope would have been familiar with similar statements by Thackeray, the contemporary novelist he most admired, and he would have approved of Charlotte Brontë's warm tribute to Thackeray as being 'the first social regenerator of his day'.[15] Nor would Dickens and Eliot, different as they are from each other in virtually every way, have found it possible to countenance any aesthetic of fiction that did not allow a central social function to the novelist.

An Autobiography was Trollope's idiosyncratic recognition that not only was he about to die but that the great age of Victorian fiction would go with him. From the grave he would assert the stolid and socially responsible decency of Victorian achievement and taunt the coming generation to do as well. It is unlikely that he had in mind any specific novelists. He was, rather, sensing the changing mood of the 1870s and, as his novels of the period demonstrate, setting the certainties of a dying age against the moral and artistic chaos to come. The 'novelists of the present day' whose work he considers in *An Autobiography* belong in spirit and reputation to the earlier period. Of these, Dickens, Thackeray, Charlotte Brontë, Charles Lever and Bulwer Lytton were already dead: George Eliot, with *Daniel Deronda* (1876) still to be published when Trollope was drafting his memoir, died in 1880, two years before Trollope himself. Of the other novelists he mentions, Wilkie Collins and Charles Reade were entering the last phases of their popularity, and Disraeli was to cause one more temporary sensation with the publication of *Endymion* (1880), for which he was reputed to have received the largest sum ever paid to a novelist for a single work. Only Rhoda Broughton, who was known personally to Trollope, belonged firmly to a younger generation than his own. In all of this Trollope was not being blind to what was going on around him. He might have mentioned Meredith, who had been publishing fiction since 1856 but was still to enter the most remarkable phase of his remarkable career, or Hardy, whose third novel *Far from the Madding Crowd* (1874) was being enthusiastically reviewed. With these exceptions there were not many signs in the mid-1870s that worthy successors to the great Victorians were about to emerge. The best English novel of 1875 was Trollope's own *The Way We Live Now*. Apart from that, the publishing lists were dominated by minor works from Victorian favourites – Reade and Collins, Mrs Henry Wood, Mrs Craik, Mrs Oliphant, R. D. Blackmore and Harrison Ainsworth.

The books of 1875 that were to have, indirectly, the most significance for the future of English fiction were published in Boston. They were Henry James's first collection of short stories, *A Passionate Pilgrim and Other Tales* and his first novel *Roderick Hudson* which did not appear in an English edition until four years later. It was also in 1875 that James moved from America to Europe, choosing first Paris and then London as the base from which he would set about transforming the quality and status of modern fiction. The view of England offered in *The Way We Live Now* is of a country in a state of decay, dominated socially by an upper class that has surrendered all moral responsibility, and manipulated by dishonest foreign speculators. For the decadent sons of an exhausted aristocracy – those 'mashers', drunkards and stage-door 'johnnies' who were to feature so prominently in late Victorian popular fiction and music-hall songs – the moral code of their gambling club becomes representative of England's crisis:

> 'By George,' said Dolly, as he filled another pipe and ordered
> more brandy and water, 'I think everything is going to come
> to an end. I do indeed. I never heard of such a thing before
> as a man being done in this way . . . I feel as though there
> were no good in hoping that things would ever come right.'[16]

Literature too is seen as part of the general malaise through Lady Carbury's ambition to build a career 'not by producing good books,

but by inducing certain people to say that the books were good'
and her refusal to believe that 'anything like real selling praise is
ever given to anybody, except to friends'.[17] That kind of cynicism
is the direct opposite of Trollope's own belief in literary merit
making its way in the world. *The Way We Live Now* has been well
described as a novel about the 'treason of the gentlemen of
England', with the lonely, ineffectual, and childless Sir Roger
Carbury trying vainly to maintain standards in an otherwise
corrupt country-house world.[18] This was the same world that
Henry James, his choice of a home about to be made, contemplated
from a London hotel. He was also to become eventually a severe
critic of upper-class decadence, and he was to regard Trollope as
the type of naive novelist who would be made redundant by the
new artistic sophistication. But on 1 November 1875 his idealism
had still to be tested. He was independent and in Europe. 'Dear
People all,' he wrote to his family in America, 'I take possession of
the old world – I inhale it – I appropriate it!'[19]

At almost the same moment as the young Henry James laid
breathless claim to his literary property, Trollope was beginning to
write the first draft of his autobiography. Whether or not it was
directed consciously at the Iconoclasts, Aesthetes, Naturalists,
Realists, and Neo-Romantics who were to dominate British fiction
for the next forty years, *An Autobiography* hit at them with
shocking accuracy. Nothing could have been more calculated to
infuriate them than this self-portrait of a good and successful
novelist; totting up his money, much of which had been earned
part-time; glorying in his foxhunting and card-playing; offering his
novels as sermons and himself as a preacher; arguing for the
craftsmanship of the shoemaker rather than the mystical inspiration
of the Artist; and urging the young literary aspirant to follow the
example of the tortoise.

There are, of course, important qualifications to be made to the
portrait, and Trollope makes some of them. He is careful to point
out that earning a living from literature is a distressingly precarious
business and that failure is a far more common experience than
success.[20] These convictions he tended to pursue in his neglected
short stories which abound with dreamy unpractical young men
hawking their unsaleable wares around the weary, eminently
practical, editors and publishers of London.[21] Trollope's own table
of earnings shows that he served a thirteen-year apprenticeship

before he received as much as £600 for a three-volume novel,
and throughout his life his personal instinct was to discourage
others from trying to follow his example. If they insisted on a
career in literature then *An Autobiography* would show them how it
could be done, and offer an example more likely to repel than
encourage. Trollope's usual business method was to sell a novel
outright to a publisher. Providing the sum was large enough – and
the most he ever received for a single novel was £3,200 – he was
spared what he called further 'bargaining'.[22] His early unhappy
experiences with half-profit contracts had convinced him that it
was better to take a large lump sum, and get on with writing
another novel, than to take a relatively small advance and risk
earning either much more or nothing at all. To the young Thomas
Hardy he admitted that most of his money came from 'the early
and costly editions' of his books, though he also added, with a
shrewd glance at what was to become a crucial issue for late
Victorian writers: 'There can be no doubt that the royalty system is
the best, if you can get a publisher to give you a royalty, and if you
are not in need of immediate money.'[23]

The full royalty system, by which an author receives an agreed
percentage of the published price of every copy of a book sold, and
therefore retains a direct financial interest in the success or failure
of his work, was hardly known in Britain before the 1880s, though
the term 'royalty' was used in a slightly different sense. In its
modern form, the royalty system came from America.[24] British
commentators acknowledged that it offered a fairer deal to authors
than other kinds of publishing agreements, and there was an active
campaign for it to be adopted in Britain. It was adopted, but only
gradually, and at first as simply one possible option among several.
As late as 1892 the issue was still regarded as sufficiently
controversial for the literary agent A. P. Watt to be asked in an
interview if he believed in 'selling books on the royalty system'.[25]
The casualness with which the system was introduced into Britain,
and the confusion it often caused, can be illustrated by some
negotiations carried out by the publishing firm of Cassell. Cassell's
reputation had been based largely on the publishing of moral tales
and periodicals, but in the 1880s they decided to expand into the
fiction market. Their decision in 1888 to begin publishing three-
volume novels, just six years before the practice was generally

abandoned, must rank as one of the worst business judgments of the decade.[26] On the other hand, their publication of one-volume adventure stories selling at 5/- each was far-sighted and highly profitable, with Robert Louis Stevenson's *Treasure Island* appearing in 1883, and Rider Haggard's *King Solomon's Mines* in 1885.

Treasure Island had been serialised in the periodical *Young Folks* late in 1881: Stevenson received a total payment of £30. The story was rewritten and recommended to Cassell by W. E. Henley who negotiated terms on Stevenson's behalf. It was accepted and Stevenson, delighted with the news, told his parents that he was to be paid £100 for it ('A hundred jingling, tingling, golden, minted quid').[27] From a slightly later letter to Henley it is clear that Stevenson thought the book had been sold outright ('Really, £100 is a sight more than *Treasure Island* is worth').[28] In fact it was an advance covering the first 4,000 copies, the equivalent of a 10% royalty. He was to receive £20 for each subsequent 1,000 copies sold (a slightly reduced royalty) and other terms in the contract covered possible American sales.[29] Two years later Haggard discussed with Cassell the terms for *King Solomon's Mines*. He was offered the choice of selling the book outright for £100 or taking a straight 10% royalty on the published price. His total earnings from his two earlier novels had come to only £50, and he therefore replied that he would take the £100. But while the contract was being drawn up a clerk in Cassell's office whispered to him, 'Mr Haggard, if I were you I should take the royalty.'[30] He took the advice and the royalty. Cassell accepted Haggard's change of mind and seem to have made no objection to drawing up a new contract. Thirty-one thousand copies of *King Solomon's Mines* were sold in the first year alone, bringing Haggard more than £750.[31] *Treasure Island* was a less spectacular success, but twelve thousand copies had been sold by 1886, and Cassell had paid Stevenson £272 10s 0d.[32] Both novels continued to sell well year after year and to bring regular sums of money to their authors.

As these negotiations are in many respects typical of changes taking place between authors and publishers in the 1880s it is worth looking more closely at the attitudes of the participants. Both novelists were to become very successful financially, yet at this early stage in their careers both would quite happily have signed away, for relatively small sums of money, all financial rights to their work. It is clear that neither Haggard nor Stevenson really knew what a royalty was: both assumed that a publisher would expect to buy the copyright of a book and that the author had little or no say in the matter. Henley, an experienced man-of-letters, did realise the possible advantages of keeping a financial interest in a book and pressed for it on Stevenson's behalf: Cassell's office clerk also understood what might be at stake and intervened to help Haggard. The publisher cannot be accused of dishonesty, though he was certainly not going to put himself out to stop the inexperienced authors from making a wrong decision. But for Henley, Stevenson would presumably have been offered £100 for the copyright, as indeed he thought he had been. Two years after Stevenson's negotiations, and a sign of rapidly changing times, Haggard was asked to choose between a royalty and outright sale, but with no advice on which course might be more advantageous to him, and with the temptation of much-needed money being held out to influence his decision. This sounds like sharp practice if not dishonesty, as the publisher was fully aware that if he succeeded in buying the copyright and the book sold well, then he would have no legal obligation to share any profits with the author. If called upon to justify his part in such negotiations – and publishers were increasingly challenged in just this way – he might have pointed out that publishing is a commercial business, with all of the financial investment coming from the publisher; that the author was perfectly happy with his lump-sum payment; that as the author would not be asked to return any money in the event of the book making a loss it was unreasonable of him to expect a share in possible profits; and, anyway, when entering a business transaction an author should know what he is doing.

As far as Stevenson and Haggard are concerned there was not even the consolation that if these particular negotiations had not turned out happily they would at least have gained wisdom from an unfortunate experience. Throughout his life Stevenson remained notoriously slapdash about publishing agreements and relied on an ill-assorted group of advisers to help him out, while only a few years after being so lucky over *King Solomon's Mines*, Haggard was again selling the copyright of his novels and bitterly regretting his foolishness.[33] The greatest danger for the publisher in such negotiations was of possibly losing a highly lucrative long-term investment in an author in order to gain an immediate, uncertain profit. Stevenson saw no reason to hold a grudge against Cassell. In

1886 he sent them *Kidnapped*, for which he received an advance of £150 and a 15% royalty.[34] But Haggard, resentful at the thought of the income he might have lost on *King Solomon's Mines*, took his subsequent best-sellers *Allan Quartermaine* and *She* to Longman, and did not return to Cassell for nearly twenty years. He also included in *Mr Meeson's Will* (1888) a satirical portrait of a publishing house that was so obviously based on Cassell that it almost provoked an action for libel.[35]

The attractiveness of a standardised royalty system, accepted by everyone involved in the publication of a book, sounds obvious enough. It would serve to check unscrupulous publishers, protect unpractical authors, give both sides an interest in a book's success, and therefore improve relations between publishers and authors. To H. G. Wells, writing in 1903, reforms such as these seemed so urgently desirable that he called for legislation to forcibly prevent an author from selling the copyright of his books.[36] Less extreme demands for a standardised form of publishing contract based on the royalty system recur throughout the period. Publishers and authors were both aware of its possibilities, but putting it into operation was more a matter of luck than reasoned agreement. For many years publishers tended to regard a royalty as a reward to be paid once an author had proved his commercial worth: authors tended to say they were obliged to connive at this attitude if they wished to see their work in print. The resulting arbitrariness, unfairness, sheer silliness and constant resentment can be seen from a few individual examples, ranging from authors who could barely scrape a living from fiction, through authors who earned very comfortable livings, to the spectacular best-seller. All of them shared the conviction that at some point in their careers they had been tricked by publishers, and the argument that their own naivety was just as much to blame merely increased the bitterness.

When George Gissing had completed his classic study of poverty-stricken authorship *New Grub Street* (1891) he took it immediately to Smith, Elder and sold the copyright to them for £150, ignoring not only the financial potential but even the message of his own book.[37] Hall Caine, looking back over his life in 1908, stated: 'So far as I am able to judge, taking the earnings of plays and books together, it is not improbable that as much money has come to me . . . as ever came to any one not now living, who followed the profession of the pen.'[38] It is a remarkable boast, but it did not prevent him from feeling as resentful as Gissing towards publishers. Caine was never to forget taking his first novel to a publisher and having it returned to him without comment by the office boy: instead of giving him 'a word of cheer' the publisher had made him 'drink the waters of Morah'.[39] When he did succeed in selling a novel the copyright went to Chatto and Windus for £75: his second novel went to the same publisher for £150. Once Caine had developed more business sense and realised his remarkable earning power he was careful to see that no more of his novels went to the same publisher.[40] In 1886 Conan Doyle was offered £25 for the copyright of *A Study in Scarlet*, the novel in which Sherlock Holmes made his first appearance. He asked for some kind of royalty instead and was told by the publisher: 'We shall be unable to allow you to retain a percentage on the sale of your work as it may give rise to some confusion. The tale may have to be inserted together with some others in one of our annuals.'[41] Twenty-six years later Doyle signed an agreement with The Eclair Film and Cinematograph Co. giving them the rights to make films of the Sherlock Holmes stories, only to find that another film company had already purchased the rights of *A Study in Scarlet*. On the advice of the Society of Authors, Doyle offered Eclair £25 compensation, exactly the same sum he had received for the book in the first place.[42] In 1894 Conrad sold the copyright of his first novel *Almayer's Folly* to T. Fisher Unwin for £20. Unwin informed Conrad that only if he wished 'to share the risk of publication' could he also 'participate in the profits', and then listed the familiar arguments why Conrad could not possibly expect more than £20 for his book.[43] Unwin also promised better terms for the next book and kept his promise, though that did not prevent Conrad from despising him, dubbing him EPL (the 'Enlightened Patron of Letters'), and moving to a more sympathetic publisher as soon as he could. One year after his traumatic interview with Unwin, Conrad was asked for advice by a friend who was about to go through the same experience. He replied:

> The proposal to share expenses is made to everybody – as a
> matter of course – but in my case he offered alternative
> terms to buy right out. (For a song.) Be cautious. You know
> what is in his mind and you may work out some
> arrangement.[44]

'Be cautious . . . and you may work out some arrangement': it expresses with great neatness the distrust that was now accepted as normal in relations between publishers and authors. The alternatives offered by Unwin to Conrad were actually worse than those which Cassell had presented to Haggard ten years earlier, while Trollope's advice to Hardy, another ten years further back, that he should take a royalty if he could get a publisher to give him one and if he was not in need of immediate money, begins to sound like dreamy idealism. There were some publishers who were willing to turn that dream into reality: William Heinemann, for instance, who was a newcomer to publishing and eager to attract young authors. It was Heinemann who helped create Hall Caine's fortunes by suggesting that instead of buying the copyright of *The Bondman* (1890) for the £400 that Caine wanted, it would be more sensible of him to accept an advance of £300 against future royalties.[43] Heinemann behaved even more generously to Sarah Grand, buying the copyright of *The Heavenly Twins* (1893) for £100 because he admired the book but could not see it being a commercial success. When it became one of the hits of the year he drew up a new contract which allowed royalties to Sarah Grand and sent her a cheque for the £1,200 due to her: it has been estimated that *The Heavenly Twins* earned a total of £18,000 for the previously unknown author.[46] Gissing also noted a change in publishing attitude when in 1891 he met A. H. Bullen who was a partner in the recently established firm of Lawrence and Bullen. Bullen offered terms for Gissing's new novel on an advance and royalty basis, and gradually broke down Gissing's habitual gloom by a mixture of fair-dealing and flattery. When Bullen wrote that while he hoped eventually to make a profit out of Gissing's novels the 'privilege' of publishing them made up for any loss, Gissing copied Bullen's letter into his diary and commented: 'Was ever struggling author thus addressed? Replied to the good fellow.'[47]

Because of the importance attached by the late Victorians to the royalty system they often managed to make it sound as though most earlier writers of any artistic value had been the victims of wily publishers: Dr Johnson vainly seeking a patron, Milton receiving only a few pounds for *Paradise Lost*, Scott writing himself to death – these tales of authors who were to attain legendary fame in spite of being scorned or betrayed by publishers were told and retold with salutary relish in late Victorian Grub

Street. That the more immediate past did not yield a comparable batch of great writers in financial difficulty was explained away either by denying the greatness of such writers or by disdainful reference to their worthless pandering to popularity. They were tradesmen, not artists. Hadn't Trollope shamelessly admitted as much? What these charges against the early and mid-Victorians tacitly acknowledged was that fundamental, though barely comprehended, changes were taking place in the marketing of fiction, as in virtually every other aspect of British life. The royalty system became symbolic of a new kind of individual freedom that would release authors from the compromises and concessions that had inhibited the mid-Victorians, just as the mid-Victorians themselves had sometimes seen their own phase of marketing as a release from eighteenth-century aristocratic patronage. The trouble was that individual freedom, unless backed by some kind of general agreement or legislation, led to the kind of arbitrary, chance, or totally unfair negotiations between authors and publishers that have just been described. It also meant that each author would need to take a new kind of gamble on the reading public expressing an interest in his work. The author was to be enfranchised as the working-class voter had recently been but at the same time he was claiming the status of the politician: the royalty system was his equivalent of the ballot-box. Through it he would receive a vote of confidence and popular success, or be rejected and enter the wilderness.

The changes taking place were real enough, but they were not, of course, sudden or definite. The mid-Victorian author trying to sell a first novel had also been at the mercy of the publisher: he would often be expected to sell the copyright and, then as later, be told that once he had begun to make a name his financial prospects would improve. It was even likely that he wouldn't find a publisher who was that generous. The practice of the author paying for first publication, or contributing to the expenses, was common until the end of the century: Hardy, Gissing, and Galsworthy were just three of the late Victorian novelists who started their careers in this way. And although the modern royalty system did not exist in the mid-Victorian period, it was still possible for an established author to agree terms with a publisher which amounted to much the same thing, as the prolonged negotiations which George Henry Lewes carried out with Blackwood for George Eliot indicate. For *The Mill on the Floss* (1860) Eliot received £2,000 to cover an edition of 4,000 copies (the equivalent of a 30% royalty) and payment at the same rate for all copies sold above that number: in addition she received royalties on the subsequent, cheaper editions of the novel, amounting to 25% on the 12/- two-volume edition and 20% on the one-volume 6/- edition. For *Middlemarch* (1871–2) which was published originally in an experimental eight parts, Lewes held out for a 2/- royalty on each 5/- part, the equivalent of 40%.[48] The financial arrangements for *Middlemarch* were unusual in almost every respect, but the method adopted for *The Mill on the Floss*, with a lump sum to cover a specified level of sales and extra payments for further copies sold, was, apart from the special generosity with which Eliot was treated, a familiar mid-Victorian practice. A popular variation was for the publisher to buy the copyright of a novel for a specified number of years and allow it to revert to the author once that time had lapsed. This meant that an author who found himself with a long-selling novel was able to benefit by negotiating reprints or cheap editions. Dickens, adopting a method that was largely used only for the publication of much cheaper forms of fiction, managed to avoid some of these contractual problems by publishing originally in monthly numbers and negotiating volume publication separately.[49] Even the outright sale of copyright, as with Trollope, could be regarded as sensible if the price was high enough. Thackeray tended to share that view. In 1859 he agreed terms with Smith, Elder for a new novel. He was to receive £350 for each of twelve monthly instalments (a total of £4,200) while the publisher would take all profits from editions in book form in Britain, Europe and America: in this instance, though, Thackeray was in a position to earn some extra money because profits from subsequent cheap editions were to be shared equally between author and publisher.[50] As Royal A. Gettmann has shown, even the generally-distrusted 'profit-sharing' or 'joint-account' agreements might be balanced in favour of the author and worth signing if he had already proved the commercial value of his work: in such circumstances the upper hand was his.[51]

The special conditions of the mid-Victorian fiction market – allowing for Dickens as a phenomenal exception – were created by the artificially high price of novels and the dominance of the circulating libraries. Novels were usually first published in three volumes and priced at 10/6d per volume, a total of 31/6d per novel:

they came to be called three-deckers after the triple-decked
battleship.[52] The formal price of a three-decker, however, hardly
mattered because few readers ever bought new three-volume
novels: they borrowed them from circulating libraries which, in
turn, negotiated large discounts with the publishers, so that the
average amount at which a three-decker changed hands was
probably less than half the official retail price. From the mid-
nineteenth century, the largest and most influential of the circulating libraries was Mudie's Select Library, founded in 1842. Many
smaller libraries were absorbed or driven out of business by
Mudie's, though some – among them Mitchell's, Day's, Gawthorne
and Hutt, Douglas and Foulis and the London Book Society – did
survive, and there were many small local circulating libraries
throughout Britain which continued to flourish. But Mudie's only
serious national rival was W. H. Smith, a library offshoot of the
railway bookstall business, that specialised in one-volume reprints
of novels rather than three-deckers. Mudie's predominance persisted until early in the present century when the growth of public
libraries began to force changes in the system, though not, as might
have been expected, by drawing large numbers of readers away
from circulating libraries, but rather by giving a new kind of social
status to a library subscription. This trend was initiated by Boots
in 1900, and followed by, among others, The Times Book Club
and prestigious London stores like Harrods.

The minimum subscription to Mudie's was £1 1s 0d a year
which entitled a reader to borrow one volume at a time: for £2 2s 0d
he could borrow four volumes, and so on up to one hundred
guineas. It was therefore possible for an individual, a family or
group of families, a provincial library, mechanics' institute, or
business firm, to take out an appropriate subscription. The
individual who could afford the £2 2s 0d subscription was able to
read in a year as many three-deckers as he could manage for little
more than the official price of one of them. Mudie's great success
rested on the low subscription (which undercut other circulating
libraries) and the large scale of his book purchases (which meant an
instant profit margin for the publisher and the virtual right to huge
discounts). A publisher who tried to hold out against Mudie's
terms could do so effectively only if he had a book which Mudie
felt he had to buy. This happened sometimes, though not very
often.[53] Nor did competition from other circulating libraries often

provoke Mudie into raising his prices: his orders were usually
much greater than theirs and competition to their disadvantage. It
was more common for publishers to show themselves desperate for
Mudie's favour (while often abusing him privately) because that
was the only way to balance their accounts. Later in the century
the relationship was more conspiratorial. When Mudie's became a
limited-liability company in 1864, half of the shares were immediately bought by publishers who from now on would be
haggling with Mudie for discounts on over-priced novels and at the
same time drawing a dividend from Mudie's profits.[54]

For the novelist, the number of novels taken by the circulating
libraries was crucial because it served to establish his market worth
and increased his negotiating power. In modern best-selling terms
the figures seem absurdly small, but the artificially high price of
novels, and the security which a large order from the libraries
entailed, made possible the substantial advances to popular writers.
This was what Trollope meant by saying that most of his money
came from 'the early and costly editions' of his books. The novelist
who was capable of writing readable novels without ever attaining
any special popularity or distinction but with the circulating-
library market strongly in mind also benefited from the system.
The provision of a bland staple diet for Mudie subscribers became
a standard criticism of the libraries: it was what the *Daily News* had
in mind in 1871 when it described England as a 'Paradise of
inefficient and unknown novelists'.[55] But the collaboration between
publishers and circulating libraries did have positive features.
Apart from helping to give comfortable incomes to the greatest
novelists of the age (which in itself was more than the early
twentieth century was able to manage), it could ensure a regular, if
not glamorous income for a conscientious author, and provide
(often at the cost of a copyright) the opportunity for a talented
newcomer to make a bid for fame. On the other hand, there has to
be set the damage a circulating library could do to a writing career
by refusing to take or circulate a particular novel. The adjective
'select' in Mudie's title had been carefully chosen to reassure timid
subscribers that they had nothing to fear from the books they
ordered, and the moral control that the word 'select' promised was
continuously exercised: W. H. Smith followed a similar policy.
There were occasional attempts to ban individual novels, but direct
action of this sort was of far less importance to the general tone of

Victorian fiction than the financial threat that the circulating libraries could always use to bring publishers into line. It was publishers rather than librarians who advised or forced authors to play safe, though it was the libraries that usually took the blame.

All of the complaints against the tyranny of the circulating libraries and the three-volume novel that were to be associated with the late Victorian reaction were perfectly familiar to the mid-Victorians themselves. There were attempts throughout the period to market one-volume novels, to bypass the libraries and encourage the development of a book-buying rather than a book-borrowing attitude in the reading public, but with little success apart from adventure, religious, and juvenile fiction – which was anyway traditionally published in one-volume form.[56] For most publishers and readers the one-volume novel was the 6/- reprint which appeared after the three-volume first edition had enjoyed an unchallenged run for a period of time agreed between the publisher and Mudie: or it was a reprint of longer-established works which were marketed primarily on Smith's railway bookstalls. Sales of these reprints were large and provided a valuable additional source of income to whoever owned the copyright, hence the significance of mid-Victorian contracts which leased the copyright of a novel for only a specified period of time or level of sales. It was in these areas that the argument against the artifically maintained high price of fiction and in favour of cheaper novels sold direct to the public seemed overwhelmingly proved: yet the three-volume novel continued to thrive. It did so, as John Sutherland has pointed out, 'for the dullest of literary reasons – because it was commercially safe'.[57] And just as the circulating libraries had sustained the life of the three-decker, and carried the major publishers along with them as long as it suited their commercial purposes, so they decided, without consulting the publishers, when it should die.

On 27 June 1894 Mudie's and Smith's announced that from the beginning of the following year they would pay no more than 4/- (less the usual discounts) per volume for fiction, and that the publishers must agree not to issue cheap editions of books purchased by the libraries until one year after publication. It was an ultimatum. These were, Mudie's insisted, 'the only terms upon which it will be possible in the future to buy books in any quantity for library use'.[58] The two main aims of the ultimatum were to render the publication of three-volume novels uneconomic, and to

encourage publishers to issue new fiction in single-volume form.
Both aims were quickly successful. The number of three-volume
novels published in 1894 was 184; this fell to 52 in 1895, 25 in
1896, and 4 in 1897.[59] The new single-volume novels were priced
at 6/- (taking over the traditional price of the one-volume reprint of
the three-decker) and this remained in effect until after 1914.
There were arguments for and against the libraries' ultimatum in
newspapers and trade journals, but there was little the publishers
could do. For years they had been surrendering to terms dictated
by Mudie; for years the three-decker had been mocked and abused.
But the publishers clung unadventurously to it when authors,
booksellers, critics, and even the circulating libraries themselves
knew that it had served whatever usefulness it once had. Guinevere
Griest makes the important observation that during the last quarter
of the nineteenth century defences of the three-decker appeared
'almost exclusively' in the magazines owned by publishers and in
the *Publishers' Circular*.[60] There was, however, one spirited attempt
to test the nerve of the circulating libraries, when Simpkin,
Marshall Hamilton, Kent and Co. published in 1895 M. E.
Braddon's *Sons of Fire*, a new, three-volume novel at 31s 6d, and
announced that no cheap edition would appear for one year. It was an
imaginative choice for a test case, Miss Braddon being not only one
of the most popular novelists in Britain but also an outspoken admirer
of the three-decker. The circulating libraries responded by banning
it. Miss Braddon, realistic and professional as always had 'three
completed unpublished one-volume novels ready in her desk'.[61]

The reasons given by the circulating libraries for their action
pointed, ironically, to the growing public demand for fiction. Too
many three-volume novels were being written, and as the active life
of most of them was short, the libraries faced serious difficulties in
disposing of surplus stock. This problem was not new: the libraries
had always maintained lucrative sales departments to sell three-
deckers cheaply once there was no longer a demand from
borrowers. So established was this practice that publishers had
watched the price announced by the libraries for second-hand
copies to decide whether it was worth bringing out a 6/- reprint.[62]
But by the 1880s market forces were expanding so fast and
changing so much that libraries and publishers could no longer
collaborate effectively. It was not only the rapid appearance of one-
volume reprints after the first publication of a three-decker that

fixed the three-volume novel as an anachronism: discontent was being expressed from all the participants in the book trade. There had been a substantial increase in the number of cheaply-priced one-volume adventure stories and thrillers of the kind made popular by Haggard and Stevenson, and a dramatic change in the number of periodicals which gave a central place to fiction but which were no longer controlled primarily by book publishers. Booksellers had always complained at the way the three-decker took business away from them, and they now faced the new worry of competition from public libraries. Many young novelists, determined to challenge what they regarded as the moral and artistic timidity of their predecessors, were increasingly resentful at the attempts by librarians and publishers to impose a mechanical and largely arbitrary form onto fiction. Publishers themselves were becoming divided between the long-established firms whose prosperity had been built on the three-decker and a generation of younger publishers who were eager to adapt to new conditions. In this atmosphere of uncertainty and change, the first concerted effort to direct circumstances rather than be swept along by them came, surprisingly, from the authors who in 1883 began planning to turn themselves into a society.

The full title was The Incorporated Society of Authors.[63] This was usually abbreviated to The Society of Authors, though it was popularly known as 'Besant's Society', a recognition of how closely the cause of authors' rights was associated with one man. 'In the beginning was Walter Besant,' states the opening sentence of G. H. Thring's unpublished account of the Society, and the mythic status this grants Besant is perfectly just.[64] He was one of the twelve founder-members who met together on 28 September 1883 to draw up the Society's three main objectives:

1. The maintenance, definition and defence of literary property.
2. The consolidation and amendment of the laws of domestic copyright.
3. The promotion of international copyright.[65]

On 18 February 1884 a public meeting was called to elect a Council and Management Committee. Besant was the first Chairman of the Society and apart from a short break in 1886 he served in that capacity until his retirement in 1893. When the Society's magazine the *Author* began publication in May 1890 it was edited and often largely written by Besant. He was the Society's figurehead, its chief publicist, and for many years its main source of financial support. His attacks on publishers as parasites who lived on the hard labour of authors, and built up highly profitable businesses in which they personally took no financial risks worth mentioning, ensured publicity in every major periodical and newspaper in Britain: as publishers counterattacked the publicity expanded, with Besant defending his point of view in countless letters and articles. Until the emergence through the Society of other popular writers like Anthony Hope, Hall Caine, and Bernard Shaw, who were able to take over the public leadership, Besant was virtually alone. The day-to-day business of the Society was handled by a series of dedicated secretaries, notable S. Squire Sprigge and G. H. Thring, both of whom became acknowledged authorities on the business of literature.[66] Besant was also conscious of the need to bring into connection with the Society writers whose names would carry literary prestige. Tennyson was persuaded to accept the presidency in 1884: 'With him at our head,' Besant noted later, 'we were from the start accepted seriously.'[67] Tennyson was followed as president by Meredith, Hardy, and J. M. Barrie. Vice-presidencies were accepted by, among others, Matthew Arnold, Wilkie Collins, T. H. Huxley, Charlotte Yonge and Max Müller.

If Besant himself could not give literary distinction to the Society, he did possess assets which were just as valuable. His recent novel *All Sorts and Conditions of Men* (1882), which tells a romantic story of the dreary East End of London being culturally transformed by the building of a Palace of Delight, had associated him in the public mind with the philanthropic and Settlement work in the East End which came to symbolise a new kind of social concern during the last two decades of the century.[68] His work for The People's Palace, which was popularly believed to have been inspired by Besant's novel, paralleled his work for the Society of Authors. He founded a *Palace Journal* to encourage working-class literary talent, launched a plan for a Palace library of twenty thousand volumes, and wrote tirelessly to draw attention to the East End, making himself, in the process, a pioneering urban historian of some distinction.[69] He was known as someone who was socially responsible, honest, and deeply concerned about the quality of working-class life. To this image, was added a secure popularity as a writer of historical and social-conscience romances. Early attempts to discredit the Society of Authors tried to portray its members as mere tradesmen, vulgar and greedy, destroying the dignity of literature and ruining relationships between authors and publishers. Besant delighted in such charges, knowing full well that his own motives were above selfish consideration. He never exaggerated his literary ability, admitted proudly that hard work had earned him a good income from his writings, and focused attention on the sufferings of less fortunate authors. Writers, he claimed repeatedly, tended to be foolishly ignorant of their most basic commercial rights and were taken advantage of by unscrupulous money-grabbing publishers. They therefore needed to be protected on two sides – against their own failings and against the publishers' wily manipulation. This was the dual function that the Society would serve. It was not the first time that British authors had tried to combine. There had been several unsuccessful earlier attempts, stretching back to the eighteenth century: closer to hand, there was the more promising example in France of the Société des Gens de Lettres which had been founded in 1837 and was one of Besant's inspirational models.[70] Financial help for authors was available in Britain from the long-established Royal Literary Fund, Royal Society of Literature, and the Civil List. Welcome as awards from such organisations were to needy authors, they invariably carried a taint of charity or patronage: they epitomised literary failure.[71] Besant was very much in favour of public recognition for authors – far too much, his critics claimed – and he strongly supported pensions for authors in need, but both were only acceptable to him as manifestations of a predominantly successful literary community. His view was that if the business of literature could be organised fairly, and authors allowed their due rights, then charity would disappear.

It was to take about six years for Besant's aggressive publicity to persuade a sufficient number of authors that they needed him or his Society. In its first year of existence membership grew from the original twelve to sixty-eight. Two years later there were one hundred and fifty-three members paying the £1 1s 0d annual subscription. It was nowhere near enough and at this point it looked as though the Society would go bankrupt: presumably Besant's own money prevented this happening. In 1887 dramatic publicity was gained from a well-attended conference and the publication of its proceedings as *The Grievances Between Authors and Publishers*, though in the following year membership was still only two hundred and twenty. Then suddenly everything changed. According to Thring, 1889 marked the turning-point in the Society's fortunes: from that date 'there was no looking back'.[72] Membership had risen to three hundred and seventy-two: two years later that figure had almost doubled. In 1892 it rose again, to eight hundred and seventy-two, and then increased steadily until 1911 when it passed two thousand.

These increases in membership, which turned the Society of Authors from a tiny band of largely unknown figures into a pressure-group of considerable influence, cannot be explained simply in terms of Besant's relentless propaganda: nor does it mean that authors were gradually converted to his belief that most publishers were crooks. The sudden leaps of membership indicate moments when external events encroached even on the solitary, often isolated, lives of individual writers, forcing them to acknowledge their possible need of some kind of solidarity with their fellow-writers. In 1886, at its lowest financial point, the Society began to centre its attention on just one of its original aims – the campaign to persuade America to accept a Copyright Act. It was a wise decision. American 'piracy' had provoked the anger and contempt of British authors throughout the nineteenth century. If the American government was to agree to abide by the laws of international copyright – as, with some qualifications, it did in 1891 – then American publishers and readers would have to pay for British books instead of stealing them, and there would be created, as Besant never tired of pointing out, the largest English-reading audience the world had ever known. It was an argument capable of reaching the consciousness of all but the most hopelessly unpractical author. Also in the late 1880s a less welcome form of external pressure began to be felt by writers with the formation of the National Vigilance Association and the prosecution of Henry Vizetelly: here again the feeling that professional support might be needed if censorship developed was undoubtedly a factor that encouraged many hitherto uncommitted authors to turn to the Society, as yet more were to do in the early years of the twentieth century during The Times Book Club 'war' and the renewed fears of censorship, this time by both the circulating and public libraries.

While these various moments of crisis help to explain sudden leaps in membership, the main reason for the Society's growing authority was the rapid expansion and diversification of the literary market. The possibilities of earning money from writing had never before been so varied, and an increasing number of people were keen to take advantage of them. T. H. S. Escott went so far as to claim: 'Most moderately well-educated people nowadays are actual or potential authors. They have dabbled in literature for purposes of pleasure or profit, they have published a book, or they have written magazine or newspaper articles.'[73] H. G. Wells was no dabbler. He viewed with professional relish the opportunities now open to aspiring authors: 'New books were being demanded and fresh authors were in request. Below and above alike there was opportunity, more public, more publicity, more publishers and more patronage.'[74] But if it was easier to get a start, it was more difficult to find one's way in a market that was so bewilderingly complex that it could be comprehended and made to yield a decent living only by a writer who could afford the time to make a special study of it. This is the point made by Jasper Milvain against Edwin Reardon in *New Grub Street*: 'I am learning my business. Literature nowadays is a trade. Putting aside men of genius, who may succeed by mere cosmic force, your successful man of letters is your skilful tradesman.'[75] It was not necessary to condone Milvain's self-seeking to recognise the truth contained in his analysis of the situation. *New Grub Street* was reviewed enthusiastically by Besant who claimed that the 'fidelity' of Gissing's 'portraits' made him 'shudder'.[76] In response, Andrew Lang replied that he also was 'a dweller in Grub Street' and he didn't know anyone 'who resembles these unhappy *râtés*': it was simply Gissing's morbid realism that led him to ignore the 'jolly' and 'plucky' writers who were everywhere to be found in the literary world.[77]

It is significant that these two successful late Victorian men-of-letters should have disagreed so totally over whether the writers in *New Grub Street* were true-to-life. Lang, as usual, was taking the chance to assert the superiority of Romance over Realism, but in doing so he also revealed the splits and factions, the cliques and exclusive groupings, that were already dividing up the new market. Milvain was 'realistic' in the sense that Besant used the term. He was an instantly recognisable portrait of a familiar type of literary middleman, and no serious late Victorian writer – realist or romantic – would have wanted to follow his road to success. But then, neither Reardon nor Gissing provided an attractive alternative model of how to live by literature in an age of unprecedented opportunities. Besant's shudder was caused not by Milvain's self-seeking, but by Reardon's commercial ignorance. It was to help avert such personal disasters that Besant had founded the Society of Authors, and this was to be done by teaching Reardon how to sell his manuscript sensibly, not by urging him (as Milvain does) to write differently.

The intense competiton that a Reardon faced in this rapidly expanding market can be seen from the amount of fiction being published. At the end of 1875 the *Publishers' Circular* announced that it had been, 'a very good, in the sense of having been a very productive, year, and a decided improvement on 1874.'[78] The number of new 'adult' novels recorded as being published in that year was 644, as compared with 516 in the previous year: in addition there were also 188 'juvenile' works of fiction published, representing a slight drop on 1874. This trade 'improvement' was not maintained. In the next ten years – including a freakish leap to 607 in 1879 – the average number of new adult novels appearing each year fell to 429, while the average number of juvenile works actually increased substantially to 470. Then in 1886 the number of adult novels rose sharply to 755 and marked the inauguration of a boom that, with occasional variations, was to continue until just before the First World War. In 1887, recording a total of 762 new adult novels, the *Publishers' Circular* observed tartly: 'Novels keep up their average of more than two *per diem*, Sunday included.'[79] Worse was to come. By 1894, the year when the circulating libraries announced the death of the three-decker because they could no longer keep up with the amount of fiction being published, 1,315 new adult novels appeared, an average of 3.5 per day, 'Sunday included'. At the same time the *Publishers' Circular* decided that in future there would be little point in trying in their yearly tables of books published to separate adult and juvenile fiction. This was partly because, 'from the mere title it is frequently impossible to tell whether a work of fiction is intended for the young or not', but also for the more flattering reason that 'so-called juvenile works are nowadays so well written, that often they suit older readers quite as well as those for whom they are primarily intended.'[80] The change in classification was not caused by a continuing increase of juvenile over adult fiction. As we have seen, in the early 1880s the number of works of juvenile fiction was temporarily greater than that for adults, but from 1886 this trend was once again reversed. Taking the adult/juvenile combined totals for the years 1895 to 1914, the average number of new novels published per year was 1,618 (or 4.4 per day). There were two peak years when the total rose considerably above this average: in 1897 the total reached 1,960 (5.3 per day) and in 1906 it rose to a staggering 2,108 (or 5.7 per day).

The *Publishers' Circular* always acknowledged the difficulties involved in compiling truly reliable tables, but it also insisted that the statistics were 'as exact as possible' and that 'every book that enters the Row or Stationers' Hall Court, and that is really published, we endeavour to chronicle.'[81] However, these figures cannot be taken at face value. In spite of the improved quality of juvenile fiction – an acknowledgment that allowed, say, Stevenson and F. Anstey the 'adult' recognition they had already received from readers – many 'works of fiction' would have been bound tracts, didactic tales, and Sunday-School 'prize' or 'reward' books: they fell into the category that trade journals now increasingly referred to as 'goody-goody'. The careful qualifying phrase covering every book 'that is really published' indicates another problem – the large amount of cheaply-produced, usually paper-covered fiction that would not have been included in the *Circular*'s calculations. It was also correct, as the *Bookseller* pointed out when challenging the totals given in the *Publishers' Circular* for 1889, that returns from provincial publishers were particularly unreliable.[82] The following year the *Bookseller* admitted that its own listings fell 'far short of the total of works issued, as scores of works annually escape our efforts to catalogue them'.[83] When these factors are taken into account, it is reasonable to assume that the figures given above for the number of novels being published annually in volume form are underestimates, and that the underestimation would be very considerable if reprints (which are not included in these figures) were taken into account.

Even so, the high figures for new novels still give hardly any true indication of the actual amount of fiction being written and published: that can only be approximated by considering the growth of newspapers and periodicals in the second half of the nineteenth century. The immediate economic causes of this phase of expansion were new technological developments in printing and communication, and mid-Victorian free-trade legislation which repealed the Advertisement Duty in 1853, Stamp Duty in 1855, and Paper Duty in 1860. The total number of different newspapers and periodicals published during the Victorian period is largely a matter of conjecture: according to the classification employed, the estimated total varies between twenty-five thousand and fifty thousand.[84] Representative contemporary statistics were published annually in the *Newspaper Press Directory*. As with new novels, the figures cannot be accepted as complete, though the trends they indicate seem correct. In 1875 the *Directory* listed a total of 1,609 newspapers published in the British Isles. This number increased steadily, year by year, with a slight falling off during the period 1907–12, to stand at 2,504 in 1914. In 1875 the number of weekly, monthly and quarterly magazines was given as 643. Here again there was a steady, though more spectacular increase to 1,298 in 1885; 2,081 in 1895, and to 2,531 in 1903 when the *Directory* changed its method of classification, making it impossible to follow through to 1914, though the upward trend was probably not halted in any significant way. Each year the *Directory* also estimated how many of the magazines were of 'a decidedly religious character'. These figures show an increase from 240 in 1875 to 534 in 1903. This is generally in keeping with newspapers and non-religious magazines, though the rate of increase is slower and, when considered in relation to that of magazines as a whole, can be considered to represent a substantial decline. The falling proportion of religious magazines demonstrates the growing secularisation of British literature. In 1875 37% of all periodicals listed were predominantly religious in tone: by 1903 it was 21%.

Although the most substantial expansion of the periodical market occurred in the 1890s, and therefore paralleled the similar boom in novels, the pattern of growth was different and it had begun in the middle years of the century, when, as John Gross has noted, 'the tempo of journalism accelerated sharply'.[85] This was first apparent in a group of periodicals that set out to bring the long-established quarterlies up to date. They were self-consciously intellectual, covered a wide range of topics, and featured articles rather than 'reviews'. Some of these articles were signed by the writers, thus challenging the quarterlies' theoretical code of anonymity and introducing a personal note into journalistic

debates. They were generally cheaper than the quarterlies, appeared monthly or weekly, and appealed to a largely middle-class
and university-educated readership. They brought to periodical
literature not so much a seriousness of purpose – that was already
amply represented – but rather a determination to establish
between themselves and their readers common principles and
standards on the major political, moral, religious, and cultural
issues of the day. The *Saturday Review* (1856) led the way. It was
followed by the *Cornhill* (1860), *Fortnightly* (1863), *Contemporary*
(1866), *Academy* (1869), *Nineteenth Century* (1877), and *National*
(1883). Serialised fiction had its part to play in some of these
periodicals, but it was tolerated rather than welcomed, or it was
selected for its obvious superiority, as in the *Fortnightly* where
fiction meant Meredith. The main intention was, as Thackeray
explained to Trollope about the *Cornhill*, 'the getting out of novel
spinning, and back into the world'.[86] It was not always possible to
live up to that ideal. Just over twenty years, and several changes of
editor later, Mrs Oliphant noted that James Payn had taken over
the editorship of the *Cornhill*: 'He means to make it more popular –
that is, to have more fiction in it.'[87]

This change of emphasis brought the *Cornhill* more in line with a
group of rival periodicals which gave a central place to serialised
fiction, and supporting roles to informative articles, short stories, and
poetry. Some of these were publishing-house magazines such as
Macmillan's (1858), *Tinsley's* (1867), *Longman's* (1869), and *Murray's*
(1887): others relied on the names of popular authors to draw readers,
notably Mrs Henry Wood's *Argosy* (1865) and M. E. Braddon's
Belgravia (1866). But with or without a special selling-point, the same
kind of 'monthly miscellany' (as Edmund Yates subtitled *Time* in
1879) was reproduced in dozens of periodicals. It was the 'miscellany'
type of periodical that was to have such a spectacular success in the
1890s. What made the later periodicals seem very new was their
format rather than content. They became slightly larger to emphasize
their difference from books, and everything was illustrated, at first by
line engravings and then, from the mid-1890s, by photographs. One
of the earliest of the new-style periodicals was the *English Illustrated*
(1883), though it was the *Strand* (1891) that set the pattern for the
decade. It was followed by, among others, the *Idler* (1892), *Pall Mall*
(1893), *Windsor* (1895), *Pearson's* (1896), *Temple* (1896), *Harmsworth
Monthly Pictorial* (1898), *John Bull* (1906), and *Nash's* (1909).

Most of these weekly and monthly periodicals relied for their success on the combination of a relatively cheap price and high-quality production to attract a large number of readers. Another group of new-style periodicals, in an attempt to reach even greater numbers of readers, discarded any interest in quality of content or format, and lowered their prices still further, to 2d, 1d, or even $\frac{1}{2}d$. The pioneering late Victorian periodical of this kind was George Newnes's *Tit-Bits* (1881) which offered its readers innocuous paragraphs, snippets or 'tit-bits' of entertaining information, together with ingenious competitions, on cheap paper and closely packed into tight columns that made it look, ironically, like a miniature version of *The Times*. An early enthusiastic contributor of paragraphs to *Tit-Bits* was Alfred Harmsworth, who took it as the model for his own penny weekly *Answers* (1888) and, seizing upon the logic of the incipient mass market, for numerous other cheap papers aimed at carefully defined groups of readers – *Forget-Me-Not*, 'a high-class penny journal for ladies'; *Home Chat* for the housewife; *Comic Cuts* for the toddler. There was something for everyone, or at least for everyone who could go to make up a commercially viable aggregate. Harmsworth was a manipulator rather than an initiator of trends: the proliferation of cheap periodicals was already under way before he brought his special business skills to work on it. So was the corresponding movement of newspapers into the cheap market. First the halfpenny evening papers in the 1880s – the *News*, *Echo*, and most influentially, the *Star*; and then the halfpenny dailies – Harmsworth's *Daily Mail* (1896), Arthur Pearson's *Daily Express* (1900), and Harmsworth's *Daily Mirror* which failed when it first appeared in 1903 as a paper 'written by gentlewomen for gentlewomen', before assuming its more familiar role in the following year.

Of course, not all of the possibly 50,000 different Victorian newspapers and periodicals were concerned with fiction: many of them were directed at local, professional, or specialist interests. But when considering the growing market for writers in this period it is important to stress the total number of periodicals because a very large proportion of them did contain a fictional component. Religious, family, and children's magazines had traditionally carried fiction: they continued to do so, and sometimes revealed an astute understanding of market forces. The *Boy's Own Paper*, for example, was started in 1879 by the Religious Tract Society with the intention of drawing boys away from the penny-dreadfuls and towards more 'healthy' literature. The RTS examined the various boys' magazines already available on the market before deciding on their own format, with the result that the 'healthy' fictional offering in the first number of *BOP* was not, as might have been expected, a goody-goody tale, but 'My First Football Match' by 'An Old Boy', a pseudonym for Talbot Baines Reed whose school stories estabished both *BOP* and a new fashion in school stories.[88] This high standard of fiction was not matched by the *Girl's Own Paper* (1880), mainly because, being for girls, a different kind of inculcation was regarded as appropriate. Even so, Charles Peters, the first editor of *GOP*, was determined that 'the sisterhood' would receive, along with the 'best advice' and the 'best information', the 'most readable fiction' available.[89] The new illustrated monthlies accepted that fiction was their main selling point, and, as we have seen, the more intellectually ambitious periodicals often gave in to their readers' wish for entertainment in the form of serialised fiction. *Tit-Bits*, *Answers*, other cheap magazines, the evening newspapers and later the mass dailies, all contained serial fiction, short stories or dramatised sketches. Specialist periodicals were eager to commission appropriate stories. Socialist periodicals such as *Commonweal* and *Justice* serialised, respectively, William Morris's *News from Nowhere* and H. J. Bramsbury's *A Working-Class Tragedy*, thus maintaining a tradition established by Chartist papers of the 1840s. A radical, free-thinking periodical like *The New Life* (1902) serialised a radical, free-thinking Utopian novel; cycling periodicals published stories about cycling; Society journals included, among the glitter and gossip, smart stories in dialogue of the type made popular by Anthony Hope's *The Dolly Dialogues* (1894). Even the *Author*, with plenty of real-life stories of authors' sufferings to hand, used fiction to demonstrate more forcibly the woeful experiences of authors in the clutches of devious publishers. The widespread feeling that without fiction almost any periodical would be at a serious disadvantage in the market-place was expressed by W. T. Stead, introducing the *Review of Reviews* in 1890. Every editor of a new periodical at this time was virtually obliged to announce his arrival by justifying his existence, and Stead, a master publicist and apologist for the new commercialism, had taken care to circularise in advance a large number of public figures whose views on his great idea he now published in facsimile. The *Review of Reviews* was to be the busy man's periodical, which meant the periodical for the man who was too busy to read the periodicals. It would consist of extracts from and summaries of all the other periodicals so that the reader could keep in touch with what was going on without too much contact with the printed word. The problem was, as Stead recognised, that 'three-fourths of periodical literature consists of fiction' and if the *Review of Reviews* could not find some way of dealing with this – it being 'impossible to summarise serials' – then it would not be a true 'mirror of its contemporaries'. His solution was to include in each number 'a condensed novel, with its salient features and best scenes intact', promising that 'it will often be the best foreign novel of the month'.[90] Stead kept his word, providing immediately ten-page 'condensations' of Mark Twain's *A Yankee at the Court of King Arthur* and Tolstoy's *The Kreutzer Sonata*. There were also many attempts to accommodate the public appetite for fiction with periodicals which dispensed with everything but fiction. This policy worked most successfully where it was already well established – in the vast number of cheap romantic novelettes aimed primarily at working-class women – but there were also attempts to extend the formula to a more middle-class readership with periodicals like *Chapman's Magazine of Fiction* and *The Magazine of Fiction*, both of which began publication in 1895.

Some of the humbler items of fiction that were now to be found in so many periodicals functioned simply as fillers and were no doubt often written by members of the editorial staff. A far larger proportion came from an incalculable number of professional and semi-professional writers whose literary pretensions reached no higher than the satisfaction of undemanding readers.[91] But the seized opportunity to earn some money by writing while nursing high literary ambitions was also part of the scene. Viewed retrospectively, and conscious of the cultural fragmentation to come, the associations and conjunctions between novelists and periodicals at this time can appear startling. Conrad, Woolf and Joyce all submitted work to, and had it turned down by, *Tit-Bits*.[92] Arthur Morrison began his career by writing sketches for bicycling magazines, and was commissioned by *Tit-Bits* to write a story for one of its treasure-hunt competitions.[93] The young H. G. Wells, like the young Alfred Harmsworth, wrote anonymous paragraphs, at 2/6d a time, for several of the new periodicals.[94] One of the best of Hardy's short stories, 'The Melancholy Hussar of the German Legion', was first published in the *Bristol Times and Mirror*, and among the family offerings of the first number of the *English Illustrated Magazine* was Henry James's subtle appreciation of Matthew Arnold.

In one area, the insatiable demand for periodical fiction was largely responsible for bringing about an important and lasting change in the attitudes of British writers. When the first number of the art periodical *Black and White* appeared in 1891 its editor announced: 'For the present there will be no serial stories: but a complete short story by an eminent writer, English or foreign, will appear in each number.'[95] The editor obviously felt that he was being rather daring in doing without a serial, though he was not sufficiently courageous to dispense with fiction entirely. What is significant about the announcement is the emphasis placed on short stories, and the conviction that 'eminent writers' could be found to produce them: such a policy would have been unthinkable only ten years earlier. Even the term 'short story', when used to define a distinctive literary form, was virtually unknown at that time in Britain. It was first coined by the American critic Brander Matthews in an article in the *Saturday Review*, July 1884, and justified in several other articles before being presented as a full-blown theory *The Philosophy of the Short-story* (1901). Matthews's idiosyncratic spelling of 'Short-story' was a deliberate attempt to set it apart from stories which merely happen to be short, the meaning usually given by British authors before the 1880s. In addition to arguing for the short story as a distinctive form, Matthews was also, with the examples of Poe and Hawthorne in mind, keen to assert in this particular area the superiority of American over British literature. It was the appearance of Stevenson and Kipling that forced Matthews to acknowledge that this situation had changed, though as both of these British authors were strongly influenced by the American short story his original argument was hardly invalidated. Matthews's campaign for a recognition that the short story was different from the novel, not only in length but in kind, was quickly effective. His definition of the short story, which was taken directly from Poe and stressed 'the effect of totality' and 'unity of impression', was widely accepted. It was a genuine victory. Poe and Hawthorne had never used the term short story, preferring instead to call their work 'tales', as Kipling and

James also did. Stevenson tended to use the terms 'story', 'short story', and 'tale' interchangeably. He was still doing so as late as 1891 when he offered, in words that echoed those of Poe, his famous comments on a short story:

> The dénouement of a long story is nothing; it is just a 'full
> close', which you may approach and accompany as you please
> – it is a coda, not an essential member in the rhythm; but
> the body and end of a short story is bone of the bone and
> blood of the blood of the beginning.[96]

It was this kind of theoretical interest that was to turn the short story into one of the most admired and successful literary forms in modern fiction, and, like the mid-Victorian three-decker, it was to achieve its high status in the face of bland and formula-ridden commercialism. British authors were late starters, as Matthews said: they could absorb the influences of American, French and Russian masters of the short story, and even experience some of those influences through the presence among them of Henry James who had been writing highly original short stories since the 1860s. They were also willing to accept the conceptualising of Brander Matthews. But it is doubtful whether any of this would have mattered, except to a very small number of dedicated authors, if the market had not been so desperate to fill periodical columns with fiction that, as H. G. Wells noted, 'no short story of the slightest distinction went for long unrecognised': his own short stories, he claimed, were only written at the prompting of C. L. Hind, the editor of the *Pall Mall Budget*.[97] Even Gissing, who normally held fastidiously aloof from journalistic pressures, gave in to editorial pleas from Clement Shorter for short stories written in bulk:

> He will be 'exceedingly glad' to have 6 stories from me for
> the Eng. Illustrated, at 12 guineas each, I to keep the
> American rights. Moreover, he hopes I shall be able to dine
> with him shortly, and would like to 'see more of' me.
> Evidently he thinks me of some commercial value. I replied,
> saying that I would do the stories, and that he should have
> all the serial rights, as I can't sell the American myself.[98]

The number of short stories Gissing wrote in the 1890s was a major factor in the raising of his earnings to a reasonable level for the first time in his career. Conrad too received flattering approaches from editors:

Today I heard from the *Cornhill*. A letter signed by Charles
L. Graves writing by desire of the Editor. Asks for short
stories. Serials full up to 1899 (I will be dead before then).
Short stories at £1 1s 0d per 500 words (that is one page).
Very nice letter.[99]

Conrad's literary conscience in such matters was so intense that he
could make Gissing sound like a pot-boiling hack, yet even he
could not resist the feeling that short stories might be a quick way
of earning some much-needed money. The editor of the *Cornhill*
received his story, and in addition Conrad managed to produce
enough further stories to make up the volume *Tales of Unrest*
(1898) for Fisher Unwin. They were a torment to write and
confirmed Conrad in his belief (shared fervently by James) that
stories, short or long, should be the length that their imaginative
creation demanded, no more and no less. It was for this reason
that James felt so strongly about the 'blessed *nouvelle*', looked
admiringly to the very different publishing situation in France, and
welcomed the founding of the *Yellow Book* in 1894 because its
editorial policy was that the appropriate length of a story should be
decided by the author.[100] Reviewers were now beginning to
distinguish between short stories which were simply fillers of
periodical space and those which were striving for special artistic
effects. 'This is, we believe, Mr Gissing's first essay in a new art,'
an anonymous reviewer of *Human Odds and Ends* (1897) noted:
'Truth to say, some of the contents of this volume are not stories at
all, they are the raw material of fiction, sketches and studies, mere
scraps and suggestions, without the unity and finish that in its way
the *conte* no less than the *roman* demands.'[101] At a more
commercial level, the brevity of the short story suited the
commonly-expressed editorial belief that periodical readers were
becoming incapable of sustaining interest in the written word for
any length of time: the short story was also cheaper to commission
and easier to handle than serials. At the turn of the century Arnold
Bennett estimated that each of the illustrated magazines used on
average more than sixty short stories a year, and that estimate
covers only a tiny segment of the total market.[102]

It was the first periodical publication of a short story that earned
money for most authors. A number of stories then gathered
together in volume form would bring a further fee, if only a small
one: it was simply a commercial exercise. But there was also a

developing tendency, in accordance with the artistic seriousness
with which the short story was now being taken, to give such
collections a greater degree of formal unity. Either way, the
transition of a short story from an item in a periodical to an item in
a book could involve complicated negotiations. Conrad discussed
with Unwin the length of his stories, their marketing, and how
many more words he needed to write, in a resentful mood that
disclosed clearly enough that he was working off an advance paid to
him for volume rights.[103] George Moore's correspondence with
Unwin was, in comparison, ebullient, with Moore excited by both
the fluid market situation and the series of stories that were to
make up *The Untilled Field* (1903). Sometimes he would send to
Unwin a story to publish 'in your magazine' or to place in another
magazine, while at other times he would flaunt the offers he was
getting from rival publishers:

> About a week ago I got a letter from New York offering me
> £20 for a short story. I declined not thinking it enough. I
> generally get £40. This little fact will cause you to lick your
> chops. £200 for twelve short stories, all rights including serial
> and American Tauchnitz! My dear Unwin you would clear
> the whole matter off with American serial rights.[104]

Financial considerations did not, however, deflect Moore's concern
with the unified book that would eventually develop out of the
stories, wherever they were first published. 'The book is a perfect
unity,' he told Unwin, 'and I hope it will not be reviewed as a
collection of short stories.'[105]

For Moore, Gissing and Conrad, as for very popular authors like
Ouida and Marie Corelli, the short story was, no matter how
conscientiously they fulfilled their publishing contracts, secondary
to the novel in their writing lives. But there were other authors
whose literary careers were built almost entirely on this 'new' art
form. The Aesthetes of the Nineties were particularly attracted to
the short story, finding in it the perfect form to express their
melancholy, tired view of life: it became the prose equivalent of the
lyric poem, interchangeably so for Ernest Dowson, or a genuine
alternative for Frederick Wedmore and Hubert Crackanthorpe
whose best work epitomises Chesterton's perception that the
modern interest in the short story was 'a sign of real sense of
fleetingness and fragility ... We have no instinct of anything
ultimate and enduring.'[106] That the short story was for such

writers commercially unprofitable reinforced the value of its artistic fragility: even at this early stage there could be heard the common twentieth-century complaint that short stories do not 'sell'.[107] There was, however, some strong evidence to the contrary. For Bret Harte – the creator of the cowboy story and of a theory about the origins of the short story very different from that of Brander Matthews – the popularity in Britain of his archetypal American stories became, literally, a lifeline. Desperate to stay in Europe, and deprived of his post as American Consul in Glasgow, Harte teamed up with the literary agent A. P. Watt: between them they managed to provide periodicals in Britain and America with a regular supply of wild-West stories which were then published in volume form.[108] George Egerton's was a very different kind of career, though it too was built on the short story. In *Keynotes* (1893) and *Discords* (1894) she employed the short story to write about the inner experiences of women, making it perhaps, at this particular moment when women writers were urgent to assert their literary independence from men while generally lacking a coherent ideology that would help them to do so, a favoured literary form, a view supported by a contemporary of Egerton's like Ella D'Arcy and the slightly later Katherine Mansfield. At no other period in Britain would the degree of fame and money that came to Conan Doyle from the Sherlock Holmes stories have been possible: Doyle always regretted that the popularity of Holmes prevented readers from recognising the greater merit of his historical novels. He may have been right, but Doyle's reputation was fixed for ever by the special conjunction of the *Strand Magazine*, his own mythopoeic imagination, and the mind of a fictional detective that could work out ingenious puzzles within the space of 9,000 words. Kipling also regretted his inability to write a full-length novel that displayed anything like the quality of his short stories, and he was inclined, one suspects, to feel that his writing was influenced permanently by his early experience of writing stories as fillers for the *Civil and Military Gazette* in Lahore, though it is as probable, as Valerie Shaw has noted, that the even earlier experience of Browning's dramatic monologues had as binding an influence upon him.[109] Whatever the sources of his genius, he remains to the present day the only British writer of indisputably major status whose reputation rests almost entirely on his short stories.

To the demand by periodicals of every shade and variety for serial-novels and short stories, there must be added a new kind of competition from provincial newspapers which began in the early 1870s. As a well-informed observer noted in 1890, the *feuilleton* had 'long been an indispensable feature of French journalism' though ignored by newspaper editors in Britain: but now 'there is hardly a weekly newspaper in the land that does not run stories, and whose editor does not regard fiction as his sheet anchor.'[110] These comments were prompted by the death of William Tillotson whose family firm, based in Bolton, had pioneered the syndication of fiction. Tillotsons was not the only 'Fiction Bureau' – its principal rivals were The National Press Agency and The Northern Newspaper Syndicate – but the name became synonymous with the practice, as Mudie's was for circulating libraries and McClure's for syndication in America. Michael Turner fixes as the starting point for the Tillotsons' interest in fiction the founding of the *Bolton Weekly Journal* in 1871 which included an anonymous serial *Jessie Melville*. Two years later they announced that they would be serialising 'An Original Story by that Greatest Living Novelist Miss Braddon', the 'very great cost' of which they offered as 'an earnest of the determination to make the Journal in every sense acceptable to its readers'. As Turner points out, the heavy outlay on Braddon's novel coincided with the launching of the two new Tillotsons newspapers. It was a fairly obvious step not only to continue the serialisation of works by 'Eminent Novelists' (as the Tillotsons authors were always described) but to make a further profit by selling the fiction rights to other newspaper chains.[111] It was an extension of the already well-established practice of news syndication.

The success of Tillotsons indicates more graphically than any other single factor the enormous market for fiction in the last two decades of the nineteenth century, with the cheap provincial press reaching many readers who were unaffected by changes in the circulating libraries or by the metropolitan monthlies and weeklies. It is impossible to say how justified the claim was that a serialised novel in a provincial newspaper substantially increased circulation figures, but nobody seemed eager to dispute it. The editor of the *Sheffield Weekly Telegraph*, dissatisfied with the fiction offered by the syndicates, decided to choose his own authors according to their ability to write 'good beginnings' and announced as the result of his policy that the circulation of his paper had increased from 30,000 to 230,000.[112] If circulation began to fall, editors would sometimes try to improve things by running a second serial simultaneously. The quality of much of the syndicated fiction was so low that even in these boom conditions it never attained the dignity of being reprinted in hard covers. There were, however, local compensations available. The popularity of some serials was so great in certain areas of the country that they would be re-run if a newspaper's circulation needed a boost, while a local author could attain a degree of fame that nationally-renowned novelists might envy. 'William Black, James Payn, Walter Besant, and even Miss Braddon (whom we find fairly popular), cannot hold up a candle to David Pae,' announced one editor of a provincial newspaper.[113]

If many of the suppliers of syndicated fiction are now totally forgotten, circulating-library favourites like Hall Caine, Ouida, Edna Lyall, Besant and Haggard, were strongly in demand, and there was a spattering of more impressive names, including those of Bennett, Wells, and, most notably, Hardy. For the novelist, the main advantage of syndication was money. A serial in a provincial paper might increase a novelist's general selling power, but probably not by a great deal. A Tillotsons contract usually covered only serial rights, leaving the novelist free to negotiate other forms of publication separately. In this sense it was comparable to other standard sources of additional income from a novel, such as a Colonial or a Tauchnitz edition, though, depending on the author's reputation, considerably more lucrative.[114] The prices paid by Tillotsons ranged from the £50 which Amelia E. Barr received for her 70,000 word serial *A Sister to Esau*, to the £1,300 which Besant received for the 156,000 words of *Herr Paulus*. In addition to serials, Tillotsons were bulk buyers of short stories and 'storyettes': at Christmas they sent out to newspaper offices a 'supplementary supply of stories and feature material'. In 1901, they claimed to syndicate each year 30 full-length serials and more than 300 short stories.[115]

The amount of fiction being published in book form, paperback, periodicals and newspapers was becoming so difficult to comprehend that even Besant began to display signs of weariness. In 1895 he observed:

> The number of magazines and journals of which the contents are almost altogether, or wholly devoted to fiction, is bewildering. A new venture is promised to begin this month with the

> opening chapters of eight new novels. Heavens! Imagine the
> simultaneous swallowing of eight opening chapters, and then
> waiting for a week for the next eight second chapters.[116]

It is understandable that dedicated novelists like Gissing and James
should have complained constantly that most of this fiction was
not, in any literary sense, fiction at all. Although such complaints
do now begin to take on a new kind of cultural significance, they
would not have been totally unfamiliar to earlier generations of
writers, whether the Dunces of the original Grub Street or the
producers of formula-fiction for Mudie's. But while writers are
necessarily responsible for the quality of their own work, they do
not (except in a very special sense) create the market in which that
work must find its commercial place if they expect to make a living
by it. This distinction was fundamental to Besant's reasoning.

He insisted that the first of the Society of Authors' 'Ten
Commandments' must be directed at persuading writers that they
had a right to a fair share in what was their own 'property':

> Literary property is a very real thing. It is as real as property
> in land, houses, mines or any other kind of property. Hun-
> dreds of people live upon its proceeds in great luxury, plenty
> and comfort. Thousands of people live upon it by thrift and
> carefulness.[117]

Besant's approach was commonsensical rather than theoretical.
Here, he is answering charges that it is vulgar for an author to
think of his books in terms of 'property' by counter-charging that it
is ridiculous for an author to watch middlemen living well from
literature while he himself – the producer of their wealth – struggles
to survive. It has been said of Besant that 'he offers the Darwinian
norm on which the novel is built' as though he is arguing solely
from the criterion of commercial success, but he does nothing of
the kind.[118] The terminology Besant used and the ambitions he
held out as possible to authors were often materialistic, but the
underlying argument was closer to socialist than capitalist thinking
of the time. In urging that authors should unite to oppose the
unfair practices of publishers, the Society of Authors was at one
with the wider changes in the 1880s and 1890s that saw the growth
of trade unionism among groups of workers who had hitherto
lacked the power or will to organise themselves. No less than the
dockworkers and matchgirls, authors were being urged to gain

strength for a battle against their 'employers', the publishers and editors. The ultimate aim of the Society, once recruitment was complete, was the establishment of a great co-operative from which parasitic middlemen would have been removed by placing the means and control of production entirely in the hands of the authors who would receive back the full profits their books earned.[119] Enemies of the Society were eager to point out, and rightly so, that if it succeeded it would be, in all but name, a trade union.[120]

It was to gain precisely this kind of strength for the Society that Besant would have opposed the attitudes of a Gissing or James. They not only mulishly persisted in not earning as much as they deserved from their works, but weakened the solidarity of writers by refusing to recognise that 'literary property may exist quite independently of literary worth':

> Now, in these columns [the *Author*] we are not critics: we
> take the low line – it may be very low, but it is useful – of
> considering literary property alone, apart from literary
> worth.[121]

Such an approach was not only 'useful', it was crucial if the Society was to serve any practical function at all. By taking the 'low line' it emphasised that in the complexities of the modern literary market what all writers, of whatever quality, shared was the need to make a living. If the Society could successfully formulate certain principles and practices to govern relations between publishers and authors then all writers, according to their market value, would benefit. The best-selling author would make even more money: the author who was concerned with the literary rather than the commercial value of his work would be provided with sufficient financial backing to allow him to continue writing in conditions of relative comfort; the industry of the unpretentious supplier of the lower strata of the market would be rewarded proportionately; while the writer who still managed to slip through the co-operative net would be helped by a pension scheme. It was an idealistic plan, but it was not selfishly Darwinian.

If Besant's emotional sympathy fell on any particular groups of authors it was on the virtually anonymous providers of entertainment or instruction for hundreds of thousands of readers of cheaply produced novels, whether religious in tone or romantic, and on the literary aspirant who longed, often in vain, to see his work in print. The best-selling author was rewarded with material comfort and flattering publicity in the new periodicals; the good, unpopular author obtained some consolation from the praise of discerning critics and the belief (rightly or wrongly held) that his books would continue to be read after his death. In both cases, these authors could gain from their own experience or turn to the Society for help. But the unpublished author and the writer of didactic novels and penny novelettes were unlikely to become rich or respected; nor did they expect to obtain professional advice. Besant saw them as the real victims of commercialism. They were, he claimed, drawing on his East End experiences, the 'wage slaves' of modern publishing: their employers were 'sweaters'.

The chance to speak on behalf of the wage slaves came in 1890 when the Society for the Promotion of Christian Knowledge announced that the profit made by their literature department the previous year stood at £7,660 and asked for suggestions that would sustain them in their role as 'the literary handmaid of the Church of England'. Besant asked writers who had worked with the SPCK to give him details of their earnings, and on the strength of the information he received, offered the SPCK a helpful suggestion. It was: 'Thou shalt not cheat the author while buying his work from him. Thou shalt not pay the workmen a price which will reserve for thyself the principal profit.' The cases instanced by Besant included the outright purchase by the SPCK of a 'small bio-graphical work' for £12 which sold 7,000 copies; and someone who had written ten works of history and fiction for the SPCK for an average of £50 per volume. On the assumption that a minimum sale of 6,000 could be expected, Besant estimated that the author of these ten works had been paid a total of £415 while the SPCK had made £2,739 profit on them. To these commercial considerations there was added the charge that organisations such as the SPCK could only function by sweating 'unknown and obscure' authors, most of whom were women.[122] The mixture of precisely calculated sums and moral fervour was characteristic of Besant's method: its purpose was to provoke opponents to an incriminating response. The SPCK obliged.

Before the official reply came, 'a Bishop' wrote to the *Author* claiming that there was no reason 'to suppose that the publishing department of the SPCK act otherwise than other publishers.'[123] Besant, glorying in an unfamiliar role, replied that that amounted to a slur on decent publishers. Then, switching to a more familiar argument, he claimed it was well known that no publisher took any commercial risks and the SPCK with its guaranteed outlets and ready market was, therefore, in an even stronger position than other publishing houses, yet still paid its authors at a lower rate than anyone else. The official SPCK response hardly improved matters by claiming that, 'the payments made are certainly as high as, and probably higher than, those offered by other publishers for the same class of literature.'[124] For Besant this was only an admission that there were in existence even harsher sweaters than the SPCK. To the argument that the SPCK gave away, in the name of Christianity, large numbers of their books, Besant simply pointed to the equally large profits they themselves had announced. But the greatest self-damage inflicted by the SPCK came from their attempt to refute Besant's sums; through their self-justification we get a rare glimpse of what must have been a very substantial group of authors, mainly women, throughout the Victorian age, who earned from writing pitiful amounts of money.[125] Some of these writers did not live entirely on their earnings, and Besant would have said that such a defence was irrelevant; others would have written out of a sense of religious duty, and commercial considerations did not therefore apply. And although it is true that some of these publications were little more than thin paper tracts, the material issued by religious publishing houses included small, beautifully printed novelettes; medium-length biographies and histories; and full-scale novels which (apart from their didactic intent) were barely distinguishable from their secular equivalents: many of them were especially suitable as prize or reward books. The sales of such books could be phenomenal. In 1903 alone, at a point when the sales of religious books were beginning to decline, the Religious Tract Society circulated 14 million copies of their publications.[126]

Answering Besant's specific cases, the SPCK pointed out that they had paid £12 12s 0d, not £12 for the 'small biographical work' and that it had sold 5,520 copies. As many of these copies had been given away or sold at reduced rates, they had made only £57 8s 11d profit. By profit, Besant pointed out, the SPCK were resorting to the old trick of meaning what was left 'after the whole expenses of their establishment are met'. In the course of their refutation, with no apparent understanding of what they were admitting, the SPCK gave their version of the earnings of the woman who claimed to have written ten works for them at an average of £50 per volume. In fact, she had written twenty books of varying length. In 1871 she had received £25 for a novel of 50,000 words, and in 1876 £10 for a novel of 75,000. Altogether the SPCK had paid her £716 2s 0d. Besant had clearly been exaggerating and the woman mild in her complaint.[127] It is an easy enough calculation to show that on the SPCK's figures she had received an average of approximately £35 per book, or, as those books had been spread over a period of thirty years, £24 per year. The SPCK's final jibe that she must have been content or she wouldn't have gone on writing for them was the classic justification of the sweater.

The SPCK were, however, undoubtedly correct to claim that their low payments to authors were in line with what some other publishers paid for 'the same class of literature': what separated them from secular sweaters, and made them a welcome target for the Society of Authors, was their high moral tone and a captive market that made it unlikely, though not impossible, that their authors would branch out into more profitable fields of writing.[128] The writers of penny novelettes, it was estimated, received between £2 10s 0d and £10 for stories of 30,000 words, which 'are sold by hundreds of thousands. They cost to produce a small fraction under a halfpenny, they realise to the publisher a small fraction over a halfpenny.'[129] The constantly changing editors and titles of these novelettes suggest that any publishing profit on them was short-term: the authors involved in their production are even more obscure than those employed by the SPCK. When Edwin Brett, well-known for his boys' stories, became editor of a series of novelettes in 1886, he boasted to his readers that the stories would be by 'the very best of the new writers of fiction'. His named authors were: Alice Gunter, Wray Lindsay, Sapphire, Effie Raleigh, and Pauline Brontë.[130] If the experiences of 'Rita' are reliable, then even when one of these penny novelette writers managed to make the transition to full-length novels she remained at the mercy of publishers who expected her, with some justice in this instance, to have no business sense at all. Rita's narration of how John Maxwell – Miss Braddon's husband – pressured her into parting with the reprint rights of six of her novels for the total sum of £50 is unpleasant even by the standards of the age.[131] A few years later she sold the cheap-edition rights of her novel *Peg the Rake* (1894) to Hutchinson for £65. The book was still selling when she wrote her memoirs in 1936: the last published sales figures, she claimed, were 184,000.[132] Rita was at least sensible enough to realise that if she was ever to be free to write what she wanted then she needed professional help. When Tillotsons sold the 'second serial rights' of one of her stories without consulting her, she persuaded the Society of Authors to go to court on her behalf. She was awarded £125 damages.[133]

There was, however, one group of writers who were more vulnerable, and often considerably more pathetic, than the writers of novelettes. These were the unpublished, and perhaps unpublishable. The SPCK claimed that every year it received unsought, 'thousands of MSS of small stories which are offered without condition for the Society's approval and for publication'.[134] Besant had hoped that the Society of Authors would be able to provide an advice service for budding authors, but gave up in despair at the low quality of the material received: he estimated that only 3% of manuscripts submitted to publishers was actually publishable.[135] In one of its fiction competitions, *Tit-Bits* offered a £1,000 prize for the best serial submitted: the winning entry, chosen from 20,000 entires, was by Grant Allen, a professional writer.[136]

So common were literary competitions – run by either periodicals or publishers – that when Conrad noticed that Zack's novel *On Trial*, then being serialised in *Blackwood's*, dealt like his own *Lord Jim* with the subject of 'honour', he launched a rather heavy joke at William Blackwood:

> I hope nobody will suspect Maga of having started a 'literary' competition for the best story on the State of Funk and that Zack and I rivalize for the possession of a nickel-plated chronometer or a lathe and plaster palace, or whatever other 'literary' rewards are now going in the great world of democracy.[137]

Perhaps Conrad had forgotten that not all that many years earlier he himself had entered 'The Black Mate' in just such a competition run by *Tit-Bits*: but he might have been expected to know that the contestants in a literary competition were likely to take it very seriously indeed. It was important not just because it could bring them fame and possibly fortune, but because it would turn them into published authors. No longer would they have to suffer rejection slips or the scornful comments of publishers' readers, and they would be saved from sinking down into the underworld of the late Victorian book market where the aptly-named 'vanity publishers' dwelt.

Strictly speaking, vanity publishing should cover all authors who were willing to pay to see their work in print, including those now-famous authors who had paid for their first novels to be published. The 'vanity' of, say, Gissing and Hardy was justified by their subsequent careers: they paid to help establish themselves, to display publicly the talent they knew they possessed. But for large numbers of would-be authors the talent existed only in their imaginations, and it was this that distinguished them from Gissing and Hardy. Otherwise, they shared the same longing to see their names in print. Vanity publishing was not, then, simply a matter of shady dealing. There was no reason why a vanity publishing house should not operate openly, providing that it kept within the law and did not pretend to be something it wasn't. A perfectly sensible author who was anxious to see his book in print and knew that it was likely to have a very limited sale, might, quite reasonably, pay to have his ambition realised. Many reputable as well as vanity publishers were happy to handle this kind of book. But there was also a flourishing trade in literary vanity which at its lowest was a direct swindle, and at its best, sharp practice. In the early 1880s, for example, the London Literary Society advertised regularly in trade journals. The novels it published were prominently displayed, together with the names of authors and quotations from reviews. Everyone knew that LLS authors paid for their novels to be published, but this in itself was not an unusual practice, and it must have been comforting for potential clients to see that the LLS's advertisements listed several works by its more successful authors. Outwardly there was little to distinguish this particular organisation from other publishers: the way it functioned only became apparent in 1888 when it was declared bankrupt. It was owned and run by just one man, John Playster Steed, who in 1880 had advertised for aspiring writers to join a society that would publish books by its members: two thousand people responded, each with a subscription of £1 1s 0d. With that healthy capital sum, Steed was able to maintain a decent public image for eight years. His authors paid £60 to cover the cost of publication, various additional expenses, and received falsified accounts. Steed's favourite technique was to charge for 2,000 copies of a novel while actually printing only a quarter of that number.[138] A more common method was for a vanity publisher to establish a firm with a small office, handsome note-paper, a name like The Charing Cross Publishing Company or the Authors' Alliance, and solicit manuscripts through newspaper advertisements. Negotiations would usually take place by letter, though meetings between would-be authors and phoney publishers were occasionally arranged. Sometimes the companies sponsored cheaply-produced magazines of their own in which they printed poems or stories paid for by the authors: sometimes, they would simply take the money and run. These men were no more than confidence tricksters, applying age-old methods to the booming book market. They had no connection with genuine publishing houses and were hounded by the Society of Authors. Even when the Society had enough evidence to proceed against crooked publishers, it was the nature of literary vanity that the victims were rarely willing to admit their foolishness publicly. The breakthrough came in 1891 when a vanity author with the unbelievably appropriate name of Mr Swindells was persuaded to take legal action to retrieve money paid to William James Morgan. The Society gave evidence against Morgan and contributed to the costs of the prosecution. Mr Swindells was awarded £500.[139] The case encouraged the Public Prosecutor to take further action, this time against the 'International Society of Literature, Science and Art' which was only the most recent name of a firm that had been operating for years. At the head of the company was Sir Gilbert Campbell, though William Morgan was again involved together with three other men. The Society of Authors once more handed over to the prosecution the evidence it had spent years gathering. Campbell was sentenced to eighteen months hard labour, Morgan to eight years penal servitude: the other men involved also received prison sentences.[140]

The Society of Authors and genuine publishers alike were delighted when con-men such as these were exposed, but there was a more subtle and less obviously crooked form of vanity publishing that they could do little about. This was encouraged by publishers themselves who could not be accused of actual swindling; they *did* publish the books they contracted for, the author *did* see his name on a title page and read the reviews. The author got, in other words, what he paid for and nothing that he wasn't willing to pay for: if there was any profit it went to the publisher. There is no way of estimating what proportion of novels published came under this category, but it was undoubtedly substantial. As one literary adviser told his students: 'All publishers are more or less willing to publish books at their authors' sole or partial risk.'[141] An author who felt he had been made a fool of, or felt he had made a fool of himself, under this kind of system was even less likely to announce the fact than someone who had been openly robbed. There is, however, at least one fully detailed account available by Arthur Hamilton. It was published anonymously in 1879 as *The Confessions of a Scribbler*.

Hamilton's novel was first serialised in a provincial newspaper, the fifty-three chapters being spread over eight months. He received £20 and a good deal of local praise. Sure that his novel was good enough to succeed in book form he wrote to London publishers, taking their addresses from literary journals, drawing their attention to the novel and making it clear that he would expect to retain the rights in it. He received no replies. He then changed his letter to enquire about the terms the publishers offered for novels, and still received no reply. He then wrote asking publishers to send him the 'terms' on which they would publish his novel. There was an immediate response, but Hamilton who, as his original letter indicates was up on the current advice never to sell a copyright, hesitated. All of the publishers he had written to so far were reputable firms, but they had shown no interest in him unless he was willing to contribute to costs. He then saw an advertisement for a vanity publisher and was genuinely thrilled by its tone:

> Here was the long sought-for found at last. I could tell it at once. Here was a gentleman who *would* look at a manuscript were it sent to him, and who would, moreover (astonishing condescension!) give it his PROMPT ATTENTION.[142]

He signed a contract which committed him to paying £105 'the whole of your risk and expense in this matter', though he did have to contribute a further £30 for 'trade expenses'. Out of the proceeds of the sale, the publisher will first deduct any costs above the £105 paid by Hamilton, and then the author will receive a staggering 90% of 'the actual profits'. Each stage of his gradual disillusionment is detailed with obvious honesty and some top-heavy irony – the advertisements he has paid for which never appear; a few reviews in obscure periodicals and a 'vituperative' review in the *Athenaeum*: the realisation that he has no right to examine the publisher's

accounts; the vague and long-delayed answers to his letters by a publisher who is not now so eager to correspond; the eventual admission
that sixty-three copies of the novel have been sold; and, finally, an
account which shows that he owes the publisher £13 0s 3d.

Hamilton's novel was probably of little worth and it was foolish
of him to get caught up with a vanity publisher, though he clearly
possessed enough common-sense and self-awareness to turn the
unhappy experience into a readable book. Many authors in a
similar situation would not have been capable even of that. Every
aspect of Hamilton's dealings with his publisher can be found
duplicated in the *Author*, especially the money paid for non-
existent advertisements and accounting charges for 'hidden expenses': these were common complaints of Besant's that particularly
irritated publishers. Hamilton's story also illustrates, of course, the
yearning of many thousands of amateur authors to share in the
cultural and financial prestige accorded to a successful novelist at a
time when the novel was both the major literary form and the
dominant source of entertainment. Its full significance is, however,
only apparent when it is considered in relation to the other
experiences of authors already given here. From novelists of the
finest quality like James and Conrad, through a writer of penny
novelettes like 'Rita' to the self-financed Hamilton, the sense of
living in a state of constant crisis is always present. Hardly any
writer seems capable of managing his own affairs or of understanding how he stands in relation to any other author. Mid-Victorian
novelists were able to make qualitative and self-judgments with a
confidence that writers at the end of the century could only believe
came from cynicism. Of course, then as now, there were third-rate
novelists convinced they were under-valued; reviewers who claimed
for eternity novelists who would be forgotten within a month; and
writers like Dickens and George Eliot whose genius did not
prevent them from keeping a watchful eye on their sales figures.
But in harmony with these attitudes went a degree of tolerance
that was to be a matter of envy to later generations: it was what
Virginia Woolf described as writing with the age behind you.[143]
Trollope understood that he was not as great a novelist as Jane
Austen and Thackeray, and settled for being second-rate, knowing
full well that in such company second-rate was hardly degradation;
Dickens might have noted that G. W. M. Reynolds was attracting
more readers for his penny serials than he himself was for his

monthly parts, but it was not a cause for sleepless nights; Eliot
could mock 'silly novels by lady novelists' without feeling that their
temporary success threatened her existence. But by the 1890s, this
kind of tolerant confidence had been replaced by anger, bewilderment, or the semi-serious envy that Woolf was eventually to
express so memorably in her essays on the mid- and late Victorian
authors she admired. One of these authors, George Gissing, wrote
in 1891:

> Three 'enormous reputations' have been made in England
> during the past year or so; Rudyard Kipling, Hall Caine, and
> J. M. Barrie. These are fortunate men; I wish my receipts
> from literature were one quarter of what each of them
> earns.[144]

Gissing is beginning to sound much in need of Besant's advice that
literary and commercial considerations should be kept firmly apart,
though it would, perhaps, be fairer to say that like almost every other
novelist of the time he was becoming worn out by his struggle to
attain and hold a place in a literary market of unprecedented
opportunity and complexity. To middlemen the sufferings of a
Gissing were incomprehensible. In 1895 the *Publishers' Circular*
announced: 'It is safe to say that at no period in the world's history
were novelists so well looked after as they are today.'[145]

No doubt the *Publishers' Circular* had the Society of Authors
strongly in mind when making that bland judgment: if so, it was
allowing the Society more power than it actually possessed. The
difficult formative period had been survived and membership was
increasing year by year, but there was a worrying uncertainty about
the Society's ultimate aims and function. Individual authors
attracted by Besant's publicity and recognising from their own
experiences the essential truth of his charges against publishers
naturally wanted to know what they would gain by taking out
membership, as Edna Lyall did in 1887:

> I have read with great interest the accounts of the conference
> held by the Incorporated Society of Authors. Having suffered
> very much from lack of good advice and from my own
> ignorance of business matters and lack of the bargain-making
> faculty I feel very anxious to know more about the society.
>   Will you kindly let me know what are the duties and

advantages of membership, and also whether I should be
eligible as a member.[146]

She was eligible for membership because she was a published
author. It was a publicity bonus for the Society that her novels
were very popular, and her application would have been particularly
welcome because she was a woman writer: at the conference which
Edna Lyall read about, Edmund Gosse had drawn special attention
to women as one of the groups of writers most open to
manipulation by publishers and editors.[147] Women took an active
interest in the Society from its earliest days, though they were not
admitted to its ruling Council until 1896. The immediate 'advantage' someone like Edna Lyall derived from membership was the
access it allowed to the massive amount of information about the
business of literature being collected by the Society. In the
Society's manuals and in the pages of the *Author* she could
examine different types of publishing contracts, with the possible
benefits and snags of each carefully outlined; make herself exceptionally well-informed on such matters as the costs of production
and the relative earnings of author and publisher on all sorts of
books; and learn from the experiences of other authors. She could
obtain free advice from the Society's solicitors on the legal aspects
of contracts, though the Society would not negotiate contracts
directly on her behalf. At a more informal level, she was able to
learn from the Society secretary which publishers and editors were
not to be trusted.

The 'duties' of membership were really inseparable from its
'advantages'. First and foremost was the need to attain solidarity:
'Remember always,' members were urged, 'you are fighting the
battles of other writers, even if you are reaping no benefit for
yourselves.'[148] Giving advice and help to individual authors was
less important than speaking on matters of principle affecting all
authors if the Society was to establish itself as the centre of
authority on all matters relating to literary business in Britain. It
was for this reason that so much attention was given initially to
gathering information. Every time a newspaper referred approvingly
to the Society's policy on some particular issue, and every time a
representative of the Society was called upon by the courts to
explain what exactly was involved in plagiarism or vanity publishing, public authority was enhanced. This was most apparent on the
questions of international and domestic copyright. There was

already an attempt under way to reform the existing mess of copyright legislation when the Society was formed, and, as we have seen, Besant gave the matter top priority. Society representatives were sent to the Berne convention on international copyright in 1886, and to the subsequent conventions to revise the Berne treaty held in Paris (1896) and Berlin (1910). The Society also took the lead in the long-running campaign to persuade America to subscribe to international copyright law which culminated in the limited success of the Chace Act of 1891 and its more effective extension in 1909, and there were other, smaller victories to record in the reform of Colonial copyright. The campaign to change the law on domestic copyright culminated in the Act of 1911 which, by recognising the rights of an author and his heirs to the copyright of his works for up to a period of fifty years after the author's death, was a triumphant vindication of the Society's insistence that authors should never dispose of their copyrights, and its belief that at a commercial level a book was no less a piece of property than a house or land.[149] Through negotiations such as these, based on solid research and moral fervour, the Society was able to fix itself in the public mind as the automatic point of reference on all aspects of the business of literature.

Not all the publicity, however, worked to the Society's advantage. Its repeated attacks on the wealth of publishers, with details of publishers' wills printed in the *Author* and compared with those of hard-up authors, and on the Civil List for squandering its resources on the undeserving widows of army generals and public servants rather than helping to relieve poverty-stricken writers, would have carried more weight if the Society could have demonstrated its own concern in a more tangible public form than the technicalities of literary business. Its promised Pension Fund was established, though it was pitifully inadequate.[150] And while the ideal of the Society turning itself into a co-operative publishing venture was never lost sight of entirely, there was no serious attempt to make it a reality. The Society did, however, find enough money to hold large-scale dinners and to open an Authors' Club. Both institutions provoked charges that the Society was little more than a self-congratulatory, self-seeking group of materialistic writers. While it was not difficult to refute such insults, the damage they did lingered on. There were more hurtful rebuffs as well. When the Nobel Prizes were set up in 1901, the Swedish Academy announced that it would seek recommendations on the award from official organisations throughout the world: the Society of Authors was shocked to find that it was not regarded as Britain's official spokesman. A committee was immediately established to make recommendations, but, as Thring later commented, 'they seemed to have no effect on members of the Swedish Academy'.[151] Compensation on this issue came in the form of the award of the 1907 Nobel Prize for Literature to Kipling, a committed member of the Society. The curious attempt in 1909 to set up a British Academy of Letters, independently of the Society, looked like another snub, and this time from writers who should have considered themselves loyal allies.[152] On the other hand, the Society's call for more public honours to be awarded to authors was answered by Lord Rosebery in 1895 when the first of the modern literary knighthoods went to Besant for his 'services to the dignity of letters'. It was rightly regarded as conferring distinction on the Society as much as Besant personally, and a banquet was held to celebrate the event. The publicity was welcome, but it did not help dissuade critics from observing cynically that some Authors were doing rather well out of their Society.

One other common accusation made against the Society during its early years – that it had forced trade-unionism onto one side of a professional relationship that had traditionally rested on a personal trust – became redundant in the 1890s as first booksellers and then publishers followed the example of the authors and began to combine. The London Booksellers' Society was founded in 1890 and expanded five years later into the more effective Associated Booksellers of Great Britain and Ireland.[153] Later in 1895 the publishers elected a committee to begin drawing up rules for the formation of a Publishers' Association. It met formally for the first time in March 1896: fifty-eight members were enrolled that year, an additional ten by 1900, and in 1910 membership stood at ninety-three.[154] Like authors, the booksellers and publishers were responding to the growing complexity of the market by trying to establish common principles and practice. Booksellers were concerned at the number of their members being forced out of business, and at the way the massive expansion of periodicals and newspapers had brought into being the corner stationer's shop which would happily stock popular and cheap books as a sideline, thus drawing off the most lucrative trade from specialist booksellers.

Publishers were worried by the aggressiveness of the Society of Authors and the uncertainty of what would happen to book prices and sales now that the circulating libraries had killed off the three-decker. They were also conscious that the changing nature of the book market was attracting new ambitious publishers who were challenging the houses which had dominated the mid-Victorian scene. Longmans, Murray, and Macmillan adapted successfully and were leading supporters of the Publishers' Association, but Chapman and Hall, Smith Elder, Bentley, and Tinsley were struggling to survive. Among the new houses which were to be influential in publishing fiction during this period were Hodder and Stoughton (1868), after William Robertson Nicoll joined the firm in 1884; Chatto and Windus (1876); Swann Sonnenschein (1878); Hutchinsons (1880); T. Fisher Unwin (1882); John Lane and Elkin Matthews began in 1887 the partnership that was to lead to the Bodley Head; Methuen (1889); Heinemann (1890) closely followed the same year by the revival of Constable; Edward Arnold (1891); Lawrence and Bullen (1891); Grant Richards (1897); Duckworth (1898); Eveleigh Nash (1902); Sidgwick and Jackson (1908); Mills and Boon (1909) who were at first so far away from the reputation they now have for specialising in romantic novelettes that in 1912 they considered publishing Joyce's *Dubliners*; and Martin Secker (1910).

The immediate cause of the booksellers combining was their discontent with the mid-Victorian 'free trade' policy on book prices.[155] The large discounts allowed on the price of new books had led to competitive underselling and reduced profit margins which booksellers claimed were destroying the trade. The favoured solution was for book prices to be controlled, with a trade discount going to booksellers but not to the public: it was a system that could function effectively only if publishers were willing to co-operate in taking action against those booksellers who continued to undersell. Most publishers were uninterested in the scheme until Frederick Macmillan demonstrated that what he called 'net' books could be published successfully. Using an economics textbook as a test case in 1890, Macmillan reduced what would have been the book's normal price, fixed a trade discount on that, and threatened to boycott any bookseller who tried to sell the book at a still lower price. By 1894 Macmillan was publishing one hundred net books a year and had taken action against a recalcitrant bookseller. Other publishers followed suit and a Net Book Agreement came into operation on the first day of the new century.[156] Although it did not apply to new novels, which the public continued to buy at a discount, the significance of the agreement in this context is that throughout the protracted negotiations the support of the Society of Authors was regarded by the publishers as crucial. The Society's initial response was to reject the proposals and assert their faith in free trade as authors had done in the 1850s, but this brought them into conflict with their traditional allies the booksellers rather than their traditional enemies the publishers, and under pressure a modified set of proposals was accepted.

It involved the kind of authoritative recognition the Society most wanted, and in this case the pleasure was enhanced by dealing as an acknowledged equal with other professional bodies. The first major test of the Net Book Agreement, and of the professional alliance, came with the formation of The Times Book Club in 1905. Using American marketing experts and its own prestigious name *The Times* offered free membership of the Book Club to anyone taking out an annual subscription to the newspaper. At first some publishers were happy to negotiate large sales of books to *The Times* at special trade discounts: when the booksellers objected they were assured that *The Times* had agreed to abide by the Net Book Agreement. Trouble began when *The Times* advertised 'the greatest sale of books that has ever been held' and justified their action with the argument that books were being kept at artificially high prices by publishers and booksellers. As was noted earlier, it had long been a familiar practice of the circulating libraries to sell copies of books second-hand once they had served their loan purposes, and a minimum period of six months was generally accepted. But *The Times* hardly bothered to pretend that the books were second-hand and also bought up large numbers of remainders which they advertised as 'unspoilt copies'. The discounts offered to the public were huge, with recently-published 6/- novels being sold for 9*d*. Technically the Net Book Agreement remained intact, though its spirit was outrageously flouted by *The Times*. As it became clear that books were being undersold simply to boost the newspaper's circulation, those publishers who had previously welcomed the Book Club turned angrily against it. Each side accused the other of trying to establish a trade monopoly, *The Times* being charged in addition with acting as a cover for an

American takeover of British publishing. The Society of Authors once again put aside its traditional free-trade policy in order to confront the threat posed by *The Times*.[157] The position of authors was conveyed neatly by a Lewis Carroll parody:

> 'Monopoly,' the Book Club said,
>   'Is what we chiefly need,
> To swamp the crowd of Publishers
>   And Booksellers, indeed.
> Now, if you're ready, Authors dear,
>   We can begin to feed.'
>
> 'But not on us,' the Authors said,
>   Turning a little blue;
> 'After such kindness, that would be
>   A dismal thing to do.'
> 'The chance is fine,' the Book Club said,
>   'You'll get a good review.'[158]

Authors, publishers, and booksellers united against *The Times* in a 'book war' that lasted for three years. They refused to co-operate with the Book Club or to advertise in *The Times*. In retaliation, *The Times* employed its letters column ruthlessly to advance its own case, and insisted that whenever its *Literary Supplement* reviewed a book from one of the boycotting publishers the review should carry a note urging readers interested in buying the book to help defeat the 'Publishers' Trust' by waiting until it appeared in the Book Club's monthly catalogue. Peace was declared when Alfred Harmsworth, now Lord Northcliffe, bought *The Times* in 1908. The Book Club agreed to accept the terms of the Net Book Agreement and worked out an acceptable definition of 'second-hand'. American mass-marketing was held at bay, in publishing at least, for a little longer.

Although the book war demonstrated that it was possible for the Publishers' Association and the Society of Authors to work in harmony when they recognised an issue of common concern, relations between the two organisations remained tense, largely because of an attempt to improve the situation that went badly wrong. In his inaugural address as the first president of the Publishers' Association in 1896, C. J. Longman expressed the hope that the Association would give priority to improving relations with authors and suggested the drafting of standardised publishing contracts as a means of removing a main cause of discontent.[159] The model contracts were drawn up by a sub-committee of the Association and in 1898 copies were sent to the Society of Authors. They were published in the *Author* where Besant and Thring took them to pieces, clause by clause. Pointing out that this was the product not of 'individual grabbers' but the 'collective wisdom' of publishers, Besant demonstrated how all the proposals were weighted against the author and in favour of the publisher. 'There remains one more method,' he concluded sarcastically, 'that of giving the publisher the books printed and bound.'[160] For once Besant had a strong outside ally. 'No wonder Sir Walter Besant is jubilant,' the *Athenaeum* announced, and in an article as damning as Besant's said of the draft contracts that 'one would almost think that they were a caricature by an embittered author of the demands of the typical publisher.'[161] Kipling's letter of support was brief, to-the-point, and typical of the attitude of many authors:

> I have seen the draft contracts. Nothing that you, or the
> *Author*, or the whole Society has ever done to, or said about,
> the publisher will condemn him half as thoroughly as his
> own notions of fairness set forth for him, by his own lawyer,
> in his own way. Can one say more than that?[162]

It was in many respects the moment of Besant's greatest triumph. The Publishers' Association kept quiet and in his Annual Report for 1899 the president, John Murray, referred to the contracts and implied that they represented guidelines for discussion with the Society. He added loftily: 'The Society, however, took another view of the case, and have, we believe, issued a very severe criticism of the drafts.'[163] It may be that the publishers did not regard the draft contracts as final, though it is unlikely that they could have regarded them simply as discussion documents without making this clear to the Society. The most damaging aspect of the whole affair was, as R. J. L. Kingsford has said, that 'the possibility of two-sided discussion was missed'.[164] And Besant's triumphant dissection of the model contracts must have played a large part in dispelling whatever willingness there was among the publishers to clarify points of difference. His abrasive approach had served the Society well while it was struggling to establish itself and while its target was the individual publisher: subtler

methods and a determination to negotiate might just have brought a
more positive response from the newly-formed Publishers' Association which had at least expressed a wish to improve relations. It is also
possible that the Society lost more at that particular moment than the
chance of a 'two-sided discussion': in reasserting its hostility to the
publishers it had won a moral victory, but lacked the power to pursue
the advantage it had temporarily gained. The publishers regarded
the Society's great victory as though it had never occurred.

There were other factors which tended to restrict the power of the
Society to formulate and promote policies generally acceptable to
its members: these were built into the nature of the Society itself
and were, therefore, more damaging than the indifference of
publishers. The problem can be illustrated by one of the anecdotes
the Society used to attract new members:

> We received a letter at these offices a short time since, in
> which one eminent author said that he would rather be
> cheated than do sums. This seems to us quite intelligible, but
> the question is, 'would he rather be cheated than have sums
> done for him?' [165]

The answer to that question was not the simple 'yes' the Society
expected. What authors were increasingly demanding was not that
the sums should be done for them, but that the whole business side
of literature should be taken off their hands, and there were now
coming into existence specialist literary agents who were willing to
do this. Besant's own publishing contracts were negotiated by A.
P. Watt: he contributed an appreciative letter to one of the self-
advertising volumes which Watt occasionally had printed. As
Besant's message that publishers were crooks and authors dupes
began to take effect, an increasing number of authors followed the
example of the leader of the Society and employed literary agents.
It seemed a perfectly sensible step. The nearest the Society came to
being directly involved with literary agency was in 1889 when it set
up an Authors' Syndicate: it existed precariously only for a short
while, uncertain whether it was an integral part of the Society or
merely a distant, tolerated appendage. It was run by William
Morris Colles, and offered to handle the business of members of
the Society, especially on matters of syndication: fees were not
charged, though expenses were deducted from any commission

obtained. Colles was an early and enthusiastic member of the Society, the author of several of their pamphlets, but the Syndicate ran into trouble when Colles tried to set himself up independently as a literary agent, bringing into conflict his personal business interests and those of the Society. The Syndicate collapsed, and while the details are not fully clear, the Society seemed happy to extricate itself from the connection.[166] If Colles had been more reliable it is possible that the Society might have looked more sympathetically at the question of literary agency, but as things turned out Besant and the Society were, in principle, opposed to literary agents: here was one issue on which the Society and publishers were curiously in agreement.

The explanation of this damaging ambiguity was that the Society saw itself ideally as superseding the need for all middlemen, including literary agents. In Besant's view, even publishers were no more than men who bound and distributed an author's property. Besant justified his personal preference for commission publishing with the claim that this method turned the publisher into an employee of the author: his business use of A. P. Watt could be explained away in similar terms. This was how the literary agent could be kept in his true, subordinate place. But other kinds of publishing contracts allowed too much power to the agent: they also encouraged the agent to act for publishers as well as authors, thus weakening the Society's determination to put authors in a position of control over publishers. The Society was willing to gather information, communicate it to authors, speak on their behalf, do their sums, give evidence in court, and bolster up the ultimate dream of an author's co-operative, but it would not negotiate contracts for individual authors. To do so would lessen its stature as a centre of literary authority. The Society would not, in other words, provide the service that authors felt most in need of. In standing firm on the issue of literary agency the Society lost a much-needed source of income, for the literary agent took a continuing 10% of an author's earnings from the books the agent had handled, while the Society relied entirely on annual subscriptions. Being a member of the Society did not prevent an author from also employing an agent: indeed, the new kind of business awareness fostered by the Society actually encouraged authors to do so. Inevitably there were conflicts of loyalty. Unless an author was deeply committed to the wider principles of authorship, it was

natural that he should often feel closer to an agent who, at best, not
only increased his earnings and took over negotiations with
publishers, but might also act as personal adviser, banker, and
even, ironically, as an intermediary between his client and the
Society of Authors. Elinor Glyn applied for membership of the
Society when she was angered by unauthorised American dramatisa-
tions of her novels, but she refused to deal directly with the
secretary of the Society and insisted that all correspondence should
be through her literary agent Curtis Brown.[167] When *The Rainbow*
was suppressed in 1915, D. H. Lawrence was urged to join the
Society. He did so. Asked by the Society's secretary for details of
the police action against *The Rainbow*, Lawrence suggested he
should ring J. B. Pinker who would explain what was going on.[168]
In cases such as these, the Society found itself dealing not so much
with one of its own members, but with a literary agent on behalf of
one of *his* clients: it was becoming difficult to decide where exactly
true authority lay in matters of literary business. The Society
complained constantly about authors who only applied for membership when they were in trouble and then let their subscriptions
lapse. It was a justifiable complaint, and its main cause lay in the
greater appeal to the author of the literary agent. As Arnold
Bennett noted perceptively, though with slight exaggeration, the
Society of Authors 'against immense obstacles has performed
wonders in the economic education of the creative artist . . . The
literary agent, against obstacles still more immense, has carried out
the details of the revolution.'[169]

There was nothing new in authors relying for help on close
friends or legal advisers, a relationship that traditionally had
fulfilled many of the functions of literary agency: Dickens and
Forster, George Eliot and Lewes, are familiar mid-Victorian
examples, and this type of informality did not disappear with the
professionalisation of literary advice in the late Victorian period. A
publisher's reader (who was himself becoming a regular and
necessary part of the literary scene) might, like Meredith, work
part-time for just one firm in order to supplement his low earnings
from fiction; but a reader like Edward Garnett was able to make
this his main source of income and combine it with the more
disinterested roles of artistic adviser and talent-spotter. Garnett
fulfilled these various functions with legendary success: he was, in
effect, an author's reader as well as a publisher's reader.[170]

Magazine editors and popular book-reviewers were also often in powerful positions to encourage and promote types of fiction they admired. A particularly interesting example of the way that an employee of a publishing firm could encourage and help an author to such an extent that it is impossible to decide whether what is involved is business or friendship, can be seen with Conrad and David S. Meldrum. Meldrum was 'literary adviser' to Blackwoods and a novelist in his own right, a humble one as he was well aware. Meldrum's letters and memoranda to William Blackwood, the head of the firm, went far beyond the understandable wish to obtain the work of a good, relatively unknown writer. He urged Conrad's genius on Blackwood, warned of the attempts of other publishers to 'entice' him away, and supported Conrad's pleas for money with the argument that in this instance 'popularity' was irrelevant: to publish *Heart of Darkness* and *Lord Jim* in *Blackwood's Magazine* should be regarded as an honour which could only be rewarded by the gratitude of posterity.[171] Meldrum's advocacy was based firmly on his understanding that at this point in time a writer of Conrad's genius was almost bound to need protecting against financial collapse. Impractical Conrad may have been, but, Meldrum told Blackwood, this was not the same old story of 'easy-going and extravagant' young authors:

> I find it no difficulty to understand Conrad's position. It
> surprises me that he can get along at all. His long story costs
> two years' work. He *may* get £400 out of it, not more. And
> we see what he does besides his long story – two or three
> short ones each year, bringing in at the most £100. That
> means that his total income from his work doesn't exceed
> £300 . . . I think it very splendid of him to refuse to do any
> pot-boiling and hope, for him and for ourselves too, that it
> will pay him in the long run.[172]

Conrad gave his trust in return for Meldrum's sympathetic admiration. His unreasonable requests for further advances on work still not completed were tested out on Meldrum before being submitted formally to William Blackwood. Conrad either did not know, or chose not to know, that by the time his letter reached Blackwood, Meldrum had prepared the way for its reception, urging that the money be made available and a 'kind' reply sent to the desperate author. In spite of his skills as an intermediary, Meldrum could not provide the comprehensive financial service that Conrad needed.

In 1899 Conrad had been approached by J. B. Pinker who offered
to take over his business affairs. He replied: 'My method of writing
is so unbusinesslike that I don't think you could have any use for
such an unsatisfactory person. I generally sell a work before it is
begun, get paid when it is half done and don't do the other half till
the spirit moves me.'[173] Pinker had been warned, but he
persevered and took control of Conrad's precarious career.

Other kinds of informal advisers could contribute to the chaos
that Conrad hoped to climb out of by turning to a professional.
Robert Louis Stevenson surrounded himself with a bewildering
array of helpers and consultants, which included friends, relatives,
and several experienced men of letters, while J. M. Barrie existed
in a class all by himself. During his early days in London Barrie
seemed endlessly able to supply the journalistic market with slight,
well-paid articles, and completely incapable of understanding why he
should open a bank account, let alone employ an agent. His
method, which he relinquished only when forced to do so, was to
forward cheques to a close friend who paid them into his own
account and sent cash to Barrie as and when it was demanded:
'You might send me the money in gold in a registered envelope. The
odd shilling can wait. Banknotes are a nuisance here.'[174] When
Barrie did eventually engage professional help he became one of
the relatively rare cases of an author being swindled by an
agent.[175] Unless an author could draw on the help of a well-
informed friend, it was usually the publisher himself who had to be
trusted for advice and encouragement, and that immediately raised
the possibility of a clash of financial interests. Some publishers
took very seriously the need to encourage developing talent,
investing in a promising author's future in just the way that
Meldrum advised Blackwood to do with Conrad; and just as
certainly there were authors who, sensing their growing commercial
worth, deserted the publisher who had nurtured their talent for
another who was willing to pay more money. But occasional acts of
generosity or abuse on either side could not alter the overwhelming
feeling that the relationship was too arbitrary, with publishers
holding financial control and exercising a form of patronage that
authors increasingly resented. What the author needed was professional expertise placed at his, rather than the publisher's, disposal,
and, as James Hepburn observes, in the middle years of the
century an important part of the appeal of vanity publishers –

before they were hailed as the most villainous of a generally
dishonest breed – was that they advertised themselves as 'the
friend of authors known and unknown' and sponsored writing
manuals and guides from which the literary aspirant might at least
learn something.[176]

The professional literary agent promised to take the author out
of this atmosphere of uncertainty and distrust by offering, in return
for a percentage of money earned, a specialist knowledge to match
that of the publisher. No longer would an author be forced to
accept a publisher's word for the size of an imprint or the precise
number of copies of a novel covered by a stipulated royalty; for his
entitlement to a share in subsidiary rights or a cheap or American
edition; for the amount that had or had not been spent on
advertising and production. The agent would also take upon
himself any unpleasantness that might develop during negotiations:
this was, in the minds of many authors, his greatest service.
Nothing confirmed his worth more than the fact that from the
beginning he aroused the active hostility of publishers, who saw his
direct intervention as an even greater threat than the advisory
function of the Society of Authors. 'One thing is certain,' an
authority on literary business wrote in 1899, the literary agent 'has
entirely broken down the friendly relations formerly existing
between author and publisher.'[177] That had been the standard
criticism of literary agency for many years, but it was publishers
rather than authors who professed to believe it. Some publishers
tried to ignore the literary agent: others took the line that had
already failed with the Society of Authors and portrayed him as the
author's enemy. In an article on the 'hardships of publishers'
William Heinemann announced that he had refused to read a
manuscript 'which came to me through an agent – an honest one to
wit – simply because he demanded an advance on royalties for a
new work by a hitherto unsuccessful author'.[178] The attitudes
there are characteristically complex. Although in favour of the
royalty system, Heinemann's indignation was vented on another
controversial issue of the day – the payment of an unearned
advance to a 'hitherto unsuccessful author'. He was unable or
unwilling to see that in the professional atmosphere of late
Victorian Grub Street the two issues were becoming inseparable,
unless, of course, the author had a reliable alternative source of
income. The implication made in passing, that most literary agents

are dishonest, served to enforce the underlying message that if this particular author had not been misled by his agent's greed then the manuscript might well have been considered sympathetically. Interpreted less charitably, it meant that an 'unsuccessful' author should willingly place himself under the commercial patronage of the publisher, and it was precisely this kind of attitude that was encouraging authors to turn to agents for help. The rise of the literary agent was one of the factors – together with the high wages demanded by printers' unions, and the formation of authors into a 'trades union' – that Heinemann blamed for the 'hardship' being suffered by late Victorian publishers: the solution he favoured was for publishers also to form themselves into a 'brotherly band'.[179] This, as we have seen, they did in 1896 with the formation of the Publishers' Association.

Unionisation, however did nothing to lessen the agent's appeal. When A. P. Watt was asked in an interview if it invariably followed that success for a publisher meant success for the author, he replied: 'O yes, always, if he's a client of mine.'[180] That was the kind of confidence authors wanted placed at their disposal. It also irritated publishers, and served to raise false hopes in incompetent writers. If the talent or commercial potential was not there in the first place, it could not be supplied by an agent, though it was widely felt that agents were responsible for the booming of worthless bestsellers and for encouraging greedy authors to play interested publishers off against each other. The element of truth in such charges could not be expected to influence authors who now believed, overwhelmingly, that the literary agent was an indispensable ally in their battle for survival. By the turn of the century most British novelists of any commercial or artistic standing had had some experience of employing an agent. They ranged from already established authors like Meredith, Hardy, and James; through the hopelessly unpractical Gissing and Conrad, and the pushy Wells and Bennett; to a naive, much put-upon writer of romantic novelettes like Rita. In a euphoric mood following his elopement with Frieda Weekley and the publication of *Sons and Lovers* in 1913, Lawrence looked to a literary agent to place the stories and novels which he expected would sustain his and Frieda's life of exile, while at the other end of the earnings scale, even M. E. Braddon, whose publisher husband John Maxwell had been legendary for his hard business sense, felt after Maxwell's death that she could not do without the advice of a professional agent.[181] The literary agent had established a permanent place for himself in a remarkably short space of time. According to James Hepburn, the 'first nameable agents known to be true agents' were A. M. Burghes and A. P. Watt.[182] Both were active around 1880, and Watt possibly as early as 1875 when he was acting on behalf of his friend George MacDonald. Colles's Authors' Syndicate was formed in 1889, J. B. Pinker's agency in 1896, and Curtis Brown's in 1899. By 1914 there were more than thirty advisory agencies and syndicates of various kinds advertising their services in trade journals.

The Society of Authors and literary agency were the main indicators that literary advice had become a marketable commodity, but they did not have the field to themselves. Coinciding with their growth of influence came the publication of literary handbooks, manuals, guides, reference works and periodicals. Foremost among these publications were the volumes compiled by Sprigge and Besant for the Society of Authors – *The Cost of Production* (1889) and *The Methods of Publishing* (1890) – together with the Society's more specialised pamphlets; the monthly numbers of the *Author* from May 1890; and Besant's *The Pen and the Book* (1899). These were by no means the first advisory books on literary business to appear, but the comprehensive range of information they contained, and the way they spoke unequivocally for authors and against publishers, established entirely new standards. Rival publications were jealously scrutinised by Besant and Sprigge. Percy Russell's *The Author's Manual* (1890) received a heavily sarcastic review in the *Author* in which it was pointed out that Russell had earlier written a similar guide for the crooked London Literary Society: the situation was aggravated because Digby, Long, the publishers of *The Author's Manual*, were one of the houses often criticised by the Society of Authors.[183] Neither these criticisms nor the general uselessness of Russell's latest manual as a practical guide could prevent it from being reprinted throughout the period, so great was the demand from literary aspirants for any kind of advice. Some of the manuals – Leopold Wagner's *How to Publish* (1898), for example, and Arnold Bennett's *How to Become an Author* (1903) – did provide useful information, but elsewhere much of the advice being offered was little more than belletristic chat. It was widely assumed that the only person who could possibly bring himself to

write such a manual was a failed author, an assumption used
skilfully by Gissing in *New Grub Street*. 'Now that's one of the
finest jokes I ever heard,' Milvain says of Whelpdale: 'A man who
can't get anyone to publish his own books makes a living by telling
other people how to write!'[184] Whelpdale's literary advice service
is not, however, important in itself: it signifies a practical
imagination that is eventually to create a fortune by pandering to
the taste of the 'quarter-educated'. In this scheme of things literary
manuals were seen as part of the market trash. Just as it took a
failed author to write a manual, so it was convenient to believe that
the only person likely to buy one would be beyond help. As H. G.
Wells said of Bennett's *How to Become an Author*: 'It's quite the
best book in its way and it's a 'orrible way. It will, thank God! be
not of the slightest use to any human being.'[185] That reliable
information was badly needed by many authors, and not just by the
unsuccessful and the hopeless, is demonstrated by the career of *The
Literary Year Book*. It began in 1897 and was at first severely
criticised for the arbitrary nature of the information it contained.
The problem was that it didn't quite know what kind of book it
was trying to be: addresses of publishers and literary agents
mingled with eassay-length surveys of the year's publications and
photographs of fashionable authors. The publishers of the *Year
Book* took notice of the criticism, appointed a new editor, and year
by year gave a greater amount of space to solid information. In
1902 it was renamed *The Writers' Year Book* and in 1906 *The
Writers' and Artists' Year Book*: to the present day it remains the
handbook to which aspiring writers are most likely to turn for
reliable information on market requirements and rates of pay.

There was also a growing market for books which presented the
opinions or advice of contemporary writers on various subjects,
directly or indirectly connected with literature. Most of these books
were collections of articles, interviews, or paragraphs which had
already been published in periodicals and newspapers. Representative of this kind of popular, and popularising, bookmaking
are: Jerome K. Jerome (ed.) *My First Book* (1894); H. D. Traill
(ed.) *Among My Books* (1898); William Stead Jr (ed.) *Books and
How to Read Them* (1905); Helen Black, *Notable Women Authors of
the Day* (1906), and similar books which came directly from
publishers or newspapers without an editorial credit, such as
Letters on the Simple Life (1905) and *Homes and Haunts of Famous*

Authors (1906). By their very nature these books not only satisfied a public interest in the views of authors, but also provided advice, example and indirect encouragement to anyone ambitious for literary fame. *The Art of Authorship* (1890) edited by George Bainton served similar purposes, but less innocently: it was the result of an elaborate confidence trick. Bainton had written to a large number of well-known authors asking for their advice on 'composition and public speech', so that he could use the information verbally to help teach young men to get on in the world. A surprising number of authors replied, and, Bainton claimed, their words were so valuable that he decided they deserved to be given a 'more permanent form'. He added a running commentary to the authors' letters, divided them into chapters, composed an unctuous introduction, and published the book. Gissing, Meredith, Hardy, Corelli and Caine, together with dozens of other writers, suddenly discovered that they were part-authors of what was, in effect, a literary manual. Bainton was probably not motivated by a desire to make money: it is more likely that he longed to see his name on the cover of a book, to become associated in some way with genuine authors, those marvellous beings who, he drooled, 'give dignity and sweetness to other lives, living again "in minds made better by their presence"'.[186] Romanticism was just as strong an element as cynicism in the late Victorian literary market-place. Demythologising was also prominent, with exposés and inside stories of every area of the book world. Arthur Hamilton's *Confessions of a Scribbler* has already been mentioned, and to it there should be added George Moore's *Confessions of a Young Man* (1886); John Strange Winter's *Confessions of a Publisher* (1888); the anonymous 'Confessions of a Publisher's Reader' which appeared in *Tit-Bits* in 1890; Arnold Bennett's *The Truth About an Author* (1903) which was also first published anonymously; Gissing's *The Private Papers of Henry Ryecroft* (1903); and Percy Vere's *Confessions of a Literary Free-Lance* (1913). Once again, it is easy enough to see the influence of the Society of Authors in this stripping of the bookman down to the basic economic facts of his existence, as it is also possible to see the counterbalancing romantic tendency that would soon, in many cases, be all that the novelist had left to justify his nakedness.

The literary manuals, handbooks and confessions made up only a tiny fraction of the space given to authorship in newspapers and

periodicals: it was all part of what Henry James described as 'the
mania for publicity which is one of the most striking signs of our
times'.[187] When the narrator of *The Aspern Papers* tracks down
Miss Bordereau to Venice, he is surprised to learn that this
wonderful link with the age of Romanticism is still alive, but even
more surprised that nobody seems to know about her:

> It was a revelation to us that it was possible to keep so quiet
> as that in the latter half of the nineteenth century – the age
> of newspapers and telegrams and photographs and
> interviewers.[188]

The monthly and weekly illustrated periodicals constantly drew
attention not only to the opinions of popular and temporarily
fashionable authors, but also to their homes, habits, looks, and
personal habits. As the American invention of the personalised
interview spread to Britain, and as it became increasingly possible
to use photographs rather than line engravings in periodicals and
newspapers, what anyone connected with books did or looked like
became newsworthy. To avoid this rampant publicity, it was
necessary to hide away, or keep 'quiet' like Miss Bordereau. But
while that might be desirable, and just possible, for the now aged
mistress of a long-dead poet, it could mean disaster for a novelist
who needed to earn his living. Even if he was sufficiently confident
in his work to hide away and get on with it, there was no guarantee
he would succeed in keeping quiet. Sooner or later a journalist, or
towards the close of this period a 'researcher', would track him
down. As press visibility became the order of the day, the value of
personal privacy increased, and the problems this caused could
apply to both popular and unpopular authors, though in rather
different ways. Ethel M. Dell and Conrad, for instance, shared a
distaste at having their photographs published in the press. Dell's
reticence led to a frantic desire by editors to obtain a snapshot of
her and unintentionally heightened public interest in her work:
Conrad's reticence was accepted as confirming his artistic superiority.[189] It is a small, characteristic instance of the confusion of
values that was built into the burgeoning press coverage of
authorship. One way out of the problem had already been shown
by the intellectual weekly and monthly periodicals established in
the 1860s. They included literature among their concerns, but gave
no special prominence to it. Trade journals covering every aspect

of books – authorship, publishing, bookselling and librarianship – were strongly established, but they also, within their specialist areas, were comprehensive. What was now felt as desperately needed were periodicals that would bring to bear on literature a powerful sense of critical discrimination, separating off the trivial from the profound, the ephemeral from the permanently valuable.

Until very nearly the close of the nineteenth century, the most respected literary periodical of this kind in Britain was the *Athenaeum*. It had been founded as long ago as 1828, was published weekly, cost threepence, contained no illustrations, and claimed to cover within its densely packed columns the latest developments in 'literature, science, and the fine arts'. It included book reviews, well-informed articles on the book trade, and a prestigious correspondence column, but no fiction. Its nearest rival was the *Academy*, which dated from 1869, was also a threepenny weekly and had adopted a similar format to that of the *Athenaeum*, but gave more attention to scholarly and educational issues. The only other comparable periodical was the now unjustly forgotten *Literary World* which was founded in 1868 and directed at a less professional market: it was aptly described by Arthur Waugh as 'a penny *Athenaeum*'.[190] However reliable the *Athenaeum* and *Academy* were, it was impossible for them not to appear anachronistic among the proliferating periodicals of the 1890s. That they seemed aggressively old-fashioned when set against the *English Illustrated, Strand*, or *Pearson's* was only to be expected and may not have mattered very much, but they looked hardly less staid when compared with nearly every other periodical of the time. What effectively fixed the format of the *Athenaeum* and *Academy* as irretrievably out-of-date was the appearance of the first number of the *Bookman* in October 1891. It was founded and edited by William Robertson Nicoll, who was already editor of the successful *British Weekly*. He knew the market well and consciously planned for his new sixpenny monthly to compete with the illustrated periodicals and to satisfy a well-defined market demand:

> My experience is that there is a great class of literary
> aspirants whose wants are met in no way. Then a great many
> like to know about books and to be guided, but they don't
> wish it more than once a month, and they can't wade
> through reviews like the *Athenaeum* and *Academy*. Who can
> read a complete number of either?[191]

As those sentiments indicate, there was more than a touch of Gissing's Whelpdale about Nicoll, but it would be unfair to pursue the comparison too far: the differences between them were more significant. Whelpdale had wanted periodical literature to be lowered to meet an assumed maximum standard of mass semi-literacy. Nicoll wanted to tempt out of that undifferentiated mass those readers who wished to learn more about, and were capable of appreciating, true literature: it was not unrelated to the cultural salvage policy already being planned by educational institutions. Under Nicoll's general editorship, though effectively run by a series of sub-editors, most notably Arthur St John Adcock, the *Bookman* attempted to combine the characteristic qualities of *Tit-Bits*, the *English Illustrated*, and the *Athenaeum*. There were paragraphs of gossipy news about books and authors; sharply worded advice for young writers who wished to submit their work for criticism; handsome illustrations; full-length surveys of writers, living and dead; and a good deal of trade news, both serious and facetious. Nicoll's mission to use the periodical to promote good literature remained firm: the book reviews were often excellent, and there could have been few important writers of the time who did not contribute to, or have their work discussed in, the *Bookman*. But it was the frothier, popularising aspects of the periodical that made it suspect, and its commercial success seemed to confirm the suspicion. What was really against the *Bookman* was that it had tried to do too much. Nicoll believed that, given a little encouragement, far more readers could be drawn to literature: the new tendency was to hang on to the few who were already around.

On 19 October 1897, almost six years to the day since the *Bookman* had first appeared, *The Times* announced solemnly that it was publishing a new periodical, *Literature*, in order to fill a serious gap in the market. It would appear weekly, be edited by H. D. Traill, cost 6*d*., and strive to be 'an impartial and authoritative organ of literary criticism and a comprehensive and trustworthy medium of literary intelligence'. This was to be achieved, as Traill made immediately clear in his editorials, by employing criticism to differentiate between the 'better authors' and the 'rubbish-heap of incompetence'.[192] *Literature* survived for just over four years, though its ambition to become an Arnoldian focal-point of critical discrimination in a world of collapsing educational standards faded some time before its actual end. It succumbed to the turn-of-the-century literary disease of belletrism, while the *Bookman*, secure in its more comprehensive attitude to literature, continued to flourish. The values that had originally inspired *Literature* were not, however, allowed to lapse. The periodical's title was united with that of the *Academy*, and the early spirit of *Literature* was immediately taken up again by *The Times*, with the issue of its own Saturday *Supplement*, beginning 17 January 1902. This time the attempt to establish 'an impartial and authoritative organ of literary criticism' was pursued more rigorously. The same year saw the start of *T. P.'s Weekly*, which was little more than a pennyworth of rambling anecdotes about literature, mainly from T. P. O'Connor himself, though it was a periodical capable of producing the occasional surprise, as when it serialised *Nostromo* in 1904. Two further entrants into this area of the periodical market were the *Book Monthly* (1903) and *Mainly About Books* (1907). In the opening years of the twentieth century, literary criticism was still primarily a journalistic activity, its three principal moods – the austere, the belletristic, and the chatty – being typified by the *Times Literary Supplement*, *Bookman* and *T. P.'s Weekly*. Virtually all periodicals and newspapers now carried news about authors, and many of them featured book reviews: there was also a growing scholarly press.[193] But when the urgent mood of critical discrimination signalled by *Literature* and the *TLS* was taken up, it tended to be by periodicals which were not exclusively concerned with literary criticism. The critical call by Ford Madox Ford as the founding editor of the *English Review* in 1908 was very much part of the new tradition, though the work featured in his periodical was more strikingly imaginative than critical; and, as Britain began to catch up on the years of European intellectual experimentation it had largely ignored, the 'critical' spirit of the time was just as much typi- fied by the Nietzsche-inspired *New Age*, revived under the editorship of A. R. Orage from 1907; the socialist *New Statesman* (1913); and the feminist *Freewoman* (1911) which swiftly changed its name to the *New Freewoman* (1913), and then to the *Egoist* (1914) which, a portent for the future, toned down its political concerns in favour of a mixture of critical aggression and new imaginative literature.

It is possible to see several kinds of separation and affiliation at work in this periodical literature. Fundamental to everything else was the desire to distance all literature that was worthy of the name from the debased reading-matter being produced for mass entertain-

ment. Virtually everyone was agreed on that: when a dissenting
voice, like William Robertson Nicoll's, was raised, compromise was
immediately interpreted as debasement. There was, however, no
agreement on a solution to the problem. One camp, typified by
Literature and the *TLS*, argued for the development of a stern
discipline of literary criticism that would have as its purpose the
guardianship of imaginative literature. On the other hand, Ford,
through the *English Review* and Pound through the *Egoist*,
regarded the modern critical spirit and the new literature as
inseparable because both drew on common inspirational sources.
From this point of view, criticism was an ally rather than a
protector of literature: it could function as manifesto, defence, or
even explication as long as the point being made had an immediate
relevance to the work of literature or fine art that stood beside it in
the same periodical. It was the closeness of this relationship that
distinguished the 'little' magazine from the commercial miscellany,
and its singleness of purpose that restricted it – often defiantly so –
to a coterie interest. *The Yellow Book* (1894–7) has come to be
regarded, almost automatically, as the archetypal late Victorian
'little magazine', though in many respects it barely qualifies for the
description. It was a substantial, hardbacked, handsomely produced, and (at 5/-) a rather expensive quarterly. In comparison with
what was going on outside its pages at this time, and excepting a few
important short stories, much of the fiction and poetry in *The
Yellow Book* was undistinguished: its criticism, however, tended to
be of a higher quality, and dominating everything else was the
extraordinary artwork of Aubrey Beardsley, which gave the
periodical its reputation for defiant, anti-social Aestheticism. The
Yellow Book's principal rival was the *Savoy* (1896), and its
attempted successor the *Dome* (1897), both of which survived for
only a few numbers. After the failure of these periodicals, and a
large number of similar publications in the 1890s, commercial
considerations tended to be put completely aside. Such representative 'little' magazines as the *Green Sheaf* (1903), *Arrow* (1906),
Neolith (1907), *Rhythm* (1911), *Blue Review* (1913) and *Blast*
(1914), were not expected to run for many issues or to attract more
than a few readers who were not already converts to the particular
views advanced. Like their Pre-Raphaelite prototype, the *Germ*
(1848), they had become manifestos.[194]

*

Until the last two decades of the nineteenth century, Victorian fiction displayed little interest in the work, lives, careers, business transactions or social status of novelists. While self-portraiture was an accepted, even expected, mode for painters and poets, the Victorian novelist did not feel that his artistic or professional development was a suitable subject to explore in fiction, even though he was often forcefully present in his work to comfort, guide, or criticise his readers on virtually every other area of modern life. The fullest mid-Victorian fictional studies of the development of a novelist are Thackeray's *Pendennis* (1848) and Dickens's *David Copperfield* (1850), in neither of which is the theme of artistic development given any degree of convincing centrality. Victorian reasoning on this issue was no doubt based on the conviction that too great a concentration on the self would have risked a fatal weakening of the novelist's social function, and it was outside fiction – in letters, lectures, essays, or studies of fellow writers – that novelists expressed their personal thoughts on the art and commerce of fiction: Trollope was behaving in a character- istically mid-Victorian manner when he reserved his opinions on such matters for his short stories, lectures and autobiography. There are many reasons why this situation changed so decisively. The widespread admiration of late Victorian novelists for French novels like Balzac's *Illusions perdues* and Flaubert's *L'Education sentimentale*, in which literary ambition is ruthlessly analysed, was a major factor: closely related was the growing self-consciousness of novelists about what they felt as the hitherto neglected artistry of their profession. The cult of aestheticism – once again profoundly influenced by France – encouraged an introspection of the kind that mid-Victorian novelists had struggled consciously to keep at bay, and there were many other late Victorian novelists who were not strongly drawn to aestheticism but whose distrust of the changes taking place in British society drove them increasingly into themselves.

In contrast to these various attitudes, there was a mood of excitement at the expanding market for fiction, an exhilaration at the range of commercial opportunities now available to the professional writer. Publicity, in this particular area, fed on publicity. As Besant's propaganda on behalf of authors was taken up and debated in periodicals and newspapers, and as public interest in authorship developed in the ways already examined

here, the novelist became a familiar character in fiction of every
type and quality, from elegant trifles like Henry Harland's *The
Cardinal's Snuff-Box* (1900), through Mary Cholmondeley's sensational *Red Pottage* (1899) and Florence L. Barclay's high romance
The Rosary (1909), to Marie Corelli's block-busting *The Sorrows of
Satan* (1895) and Oliver Onions's subtle collection of ghost stories
Widdershins (1911). The painter had not been as neglected as the
novelist in earlier fiction, but towards the close of the century he
too began to feature more prominently as a fictional character. This
was partly a reflection of novelists' growing interest in theories of
synesthesia, though that particular interest was itself part of the
more comprehensive assertion that the writing of novels, once it
could rid itself of the degrading connection with popular entertainment, was an activity worthy of comparison with that of the poet,
musician, sculptor or painter. In the campaign to attain artistic
respectability, the painter was the novelist's natural ally and the
role he was called upon to play in fiction was often one of
surrogacy. Henry James was especially influential in this development. There is, he claimed in 1884, a 'community of method of the
artist who paints a picture and the artist who writes a novel'.[195]
The focal point of James's stories and novels of the artistic life
moves knowledgeably, and in some respects arbitrarily, between
fiction and the visual arts, while the protagonist of *Roderick Hudson*
(1875), the novel which more than any other can be seen as
heralding the late Victorian neo-Romantic obsession with the
Artist, is a sculptor. As far as the general reading public was
concerned the link between novelist and painter centred less on
shared artistic problems or theories than on the wildly unconventional, and often morally disreputable, lives that 'Artists' were
commonly supposed to lead. British precedents for 'bohemianism'
were to be found mainly among the Romantic writers of the early
nineteenth century, and, nearer to hand, among the Pre-Raphaelites
and Aesthetes: novelists did not figure prominently in this kind of
company – something, it would often have been felt, that was
greatly to their credit.[196] The principal mythopoeic source,
however, for the application of the word 'bohemian' almost
exclusively to the lifestyle of people with artistic talents or
temperaments, was Henry Murger's *Scenès de la vie de bohême*
which was first published in Paris in 1847 and successfully
dramatised as *La Vie de Bohême* two years later. The new usage

was widely adopted in Britain, with Thackeray probably leading the way in 1847 in attributing Becky Sharp's 'wild, roving nature' to her parents, who 'were both Bohemians, by taste and circumstances'.[197] Mid-Victorian critics and novelists would often have been familiar with the realities of French Bohemian life, but it was Murger's safer idealisation that held the attention of the public, and, to a surprising extent, that of novelists as well. Even the self-conscious emulation of French bohemianism by British Aesthetes in the 1880s could not quite escape Murger's influence: Gilbert and Sullivan in *Patience* and George du Maurier in his *Punch* cartoons had no difficulty transforming artistic rebelliousness into something socially quaint, precious, and funny. On a more serious level, George Moore's *Confessions of a Young Man*, for all its precocious daring, was in many respects Murger brought up to date for an easily-shocked British public. Early in 1890 Gissing began work on the novel that would eventually become *New Grub Street*: he called the first draft 'A Man of Letters'. Five days later he was reading *La Vie de Bohême* for, he claimed, the twentieth time.[198] He was possibly not exaggerating: the presence of Murger can be sensed in *New Grub Street* whenever Reardon, Milvain, Biffen and Whelpdale meet to discuss literature, recall earlier struggles, or gossip about the literary scene. The late Victorian canonisation of Murger was, however, still to take place. In 1894 one of the publishing sensations of the year was George du Maurier's *Trilby*, a novel which drew on du Maurier's own experiences as an art student in Paris and on *La Vie de Bohême*.[199] The following year the popularity of *Trilby* was further enhanced by a stage adaptation with Beerbohm Tree playing the part of Svengali. While reading public and theatre audiences were being entertained by the bohemian adventures of British painters and singers in Parisian garrets, Oscar Wilde, the real-life epitome of Aestheticism in Britain, was being arrested, tried, publicly humilated, and sent to prison. In 1896 Puccini's opera *La Bohème*, an adaptation of *La Vie de Bohême*, was first performed in Turin. The following year *La Bohème* was performed in an English translation, first in Manchester and then at Covent Garden: it was called *The Bohemians*.

The bitter-sweet garret life portrayed by Murger, du Maurier and Puccini did not feature prominently in the many novels about novelists which were published in Britain from the early 1880s onwards. Instead, attention focused on the commercialisation of literature, or what James described ironically as 'the modern poetry of numbers'.[200] James's principal contribution to this theme took the form of a series of short stories, beginning with 'The Author of Beltraffio' (1884) and 'The Lesson of the Master' (1888), and then, after a gap of several years in which his attitude towards the business of literature was being bitterly sharpened by his experiences in the commercial theatre, such stories as 'The Private Life', 'The Real Thing', 'Nona Vincent', 'The Middle Years', 'The Death of the Lion', 'The Coxon Fund', 'The Next Time', 'The Figure in the Carpet', 'John Delavoy', and 'The Real Right Thing', all of which appeared originally in periodicals in the 1890s. The literary world of James's stories is phantasmagoric, a cultural battlefield on which insensitive editors, philistine wives and unscrupulous interviewers, journalists, reviewers and best-selling novelists seek to impose personal humiliation and artistic degradation on any truly serious writer with whom they come in contact. Like Gissing in *New Grub Street*, the only romance that James finds in such a world lies in the isolated, lonely, dedicated pursuit of artistic perfection. In theory, this ideal was subscribed to by most novelists of the time: it was on the issue of whether any form of compromise with the market was possible that they divided. Given the apparently ever-increasing demand for fiction and the widely varying taste of readers, there seemed no good reason why the writing of novels shouldn't be regarded as a job like any other, with the individual novelist enjoying a degree of success proportionate to his ability, temperament, or understanding of market forces. Far from being a degradation, the commercialisation of literature was exciting, an adventure, a challenge, its various branches each contributing something distinctive to an employment that offered the possibility – though no more than that – of a financial reward and social status equal to those traditionally associated with the established professions. This was the line pursued by Besant, and appropriately enough it was Besant who gave it a fictional form in *All in a Garden Fair* (1883), a tortuous modernised fairy-tale which drew admiring comments from writers as far removed from Besant as Kipling and Gissing.[201] Later novels which offered a similar glamorised view of the commercial opportunities of literature were J. M. Barrie's *When a Man's Single* (1888), James Payn's *A Modern Dick Whittington* (1892) and Arnold Bennett's *A Great Man* (1904). In spite of some well-meant warnings on the poverty that can confront literary aspirants, Barrie's novel is a celebration, in a sub-Murger manner, of the ease with which money could be earnt by anyone capable of supplying paragraphs and articles on nothing-in-particular to the newspapers. The moment when Rob Angus's bohemian apprenticeship is rewarded with the post of a leader-writer at £800 per year is characteristic of the novel's tone:

> 'You suit me very well, Angus,' the editor said. 'You have no
> lurking desire to write a book, have you?'
>   'No,' Rob answered; 'since I joined the Press that ambition
> seems to have gone from me.'
>   'Quite so,' said Mr Rowbottham, his tone implying that
> Rob now left the court without a stain upon his character.
> The editor's cigar went out, and he made a spill of a page
> from 'Sonnets of the Woods', which had just come in for
> review.[202]

A comparable scene in James or Gissing would be scathingly ironic, but in Barrie even the cynicism seems unconscious. At least James Payn was clear-eyed about the way he earned his living. For thirty-five working years, he stated, his 'pen' had brought him a yearly average of fifteen hundred pounds.[203] It was not a boast. Anyone with medium intelligence and an industrious disposition could do the same: as the title of one of the last of Payn's many novels proclaimed, the modern Dick Whittington should aspire to become not Lord Mayor of London, but a successful novelist:

> Lawrence Merridew was no genius. He was only a clever
> young fellow, with a decided taste for light literature. Neither
> fame nor fortune (to be called such) was within his reach,
> nor did he ever attain to them. But like scores, if not
> hundreds of his fellows, he made in time considerable way in
> the calling he had chosen for himself: probably a larger
> income than he would have realised in any other recognised
> and (so-called) safer profession for which he had no bent . . .
> And then the pleasure of it![204]

Bennett's Henry Knight doesn't even have a 'decided taste for light literature', though he does have a father whose hobby is writing pseudonymous letters to newspapers, and it is from him, presumably, that Henry inherits his popular touch. Aided by adoring relatives, a business-like literary agent, the agent's glamorous and knowledgeable typist, and by tactical publishers, Henry Knight is transformed into a phenomenally best-selling novelist, without

having the slightest idea how it has all been achieved: 'Ah, that gift!
That gift utterly puzzled him. "I just sit down and write," he
thought. "And there it is! They go mad over it."'[205] No doubt
Bennett was being ironic about this 'great man', but in the light of
his own career and his later reputation with younger novelists, the
irony is hardly convincing. More than any other novelist of the
time Bennett represented the spirit of compromise between Art
and the market. He wanted to have, and to a certain extent
managed to get, everything. On the one hand the serious student of
French fictional theories, the author of *Anna of the Five Towns*,
The Old Wives' Tale, and 'The Death of Simon Fuge', his short
story that almost matches those of James for subtle understanding
of the ambiguous place of the artist in modern society. And, on the
other hand, the swashbuckling conqueror of the commercial market
who could announce to his literary agent, 'You don't yet realise
what an engine for the production of fiction you have in me,' and
to his friend George Sturt: 'I believe I could fart sensational fiction
now.'[206]

For Besant, Payn, Barrie and one half of Bennett, compromise
was a policy decision, taken as either a way of buying time to write
more serious fiction or as a path to a comfortable livelihood. But in
most of the fiction about the artistic life, compromise represents
failure, the collapse of ambitions, an inability to nurture the stoical
personal resolve and lofty disregard of commercialism that were
now regarded as the serious artist's indispensable qualities. Several
of James's short stories pursue this theme; so do *New Grub Street*,
Kipling's *The Light that Failed* (1890), George Moore's *Vain
Fortune* (1890), Leonard Merrick's *Cynthia* (1896), George Paston's
A Writer of Books (1898), and Bennett's *A Man from the North*
(1898). The austerity with which the self must be given up entirely
to the work is explained by Dick Heldar in *The Light that Failed*:

> 'You must sacrifice yourself, and live under orders, and never
> think for yourself, and never have real satisfaction in your
> work except just at the beginning, when you're reaching out
> after a notion.'
> 'How can you believe all that?'
> 'There's no question of belief or disbelief. That's the law,
> and you take it or refuse it as you please. I try to obey, but I
> can't, and then my work turns bad on my hands.'[207]

It is usually marriage that turns the work bad on the artist's hands by weakening his resolve and driving him into the market-place: sexual satisfaction is placed at the top of the list of sacrifices which the serious writer must make if he is to 'live under orders'. Humphrey Kent's experience in *Cynthia* is representative. With a 'literary', though not a 'popular', success achieved, he is determined to establish himself among the leading novelists of the day, and he knows how this has to be done: 'Damn it, I mean to be true! I *won't* sell my birthright for a third edition!' [208] Marriage to pretty, suburban and 'unliterary' Cynthia forces him into contact with some less idealistic areas of the literary world. Simply because his success is 'literary' and not 'popular' he can no longer expect the advance on royalties that would enable him to write the books he wants to write, and in order to support his wife and child he works first as the editor of a shabby periodical and then as a 'ghost' writer for a popular woman novelist: the editors who turn down stories by Humphrey Kent are eager to accept the same stories when signed by Eva Deane-Pitt.

Like many such novels and stories, *Cynthia* is closely related to the literary 'confessions' and 'memoirs' mentioned earlier in that much of its effect comes from the exposure of literary commercialism, though this is done with little personal bitterness. The solution, after all, is clear to most of these aspiring artists, and if they fail it is their own fault: they should have kept clear of both marriage and the market-place. Richard Larch, Bennett's 'man from the North', surrenders his literary ambitions so completely that the girl he plans to marry doesn't even know of them: 'It would be impossible to write in the suburban doll's house which was to be theirs. No!' [209] *A Writer of Books* by 'George Paston' (a pseudonym for Emily Morse Symonds) is unusual in that the aspiring novelist is a woman, but the difficulties she encounters with publishers and editors are little different from those of Humphrey Kent and Richard Larch. Determined to try her 'fortune in literature', Cosima Chubleigh takes what was now regarded, in life and fiction, as the first essential step, and moves from the provinces to London. She has enough money to keep herself for two years. If it doesn't work out, she announces with the typical independence of the New Woman, then she can become a 'clerk or a shop girl'. [210] She doesn't actually do that, but her literary career is a disaster. She lives economically in a boarding-house, works hard, and listens to all the advice given to her: the problem is that she is quite unable to live on the money she can earn from writing novels. The £1 17s 8d she receives on a half-profits agreement for her first novel is little more than the cost of one week's lodging, and she soon comes to realise that even with higher sales and more favourable terms she will not be able to survive. She learns that without 'exceptional luck' she will be unable to earn a living from fiction until she has 'made a name', and that she is unlikely to do that until she has 'brought' out five or six fairly successful novels.[211] It was a fact of literary life that had to be faced not only by the fictional Cosima Chubleigh, but by many of the most important real-life novelists of the age. The next generation of novelists would try to solve it by concentrating entirely on the development of the Artist and dispensing entirely with commercialism. Stephen Dedalus and Paul Morel are Artists alright, but they have nothing to do with publishers, editors, agents, syndicates, literary advice manuals, unearned advances, or royalties: they are not even shown writing books.

Meanwhile, all the evidence of a booming market seemed to suggest that there was plenty for everyone, that no talent would go unrewarded or unrecognised, and that the best was still to come. In 1887, at the 'Grievances' conference, Besant had shared with the delegates 'a beautiful dream'. It was a dream of the future, but not 'of the far distant future – after my time, but in the time of my children perhaps, and my grandchildren certainly.' What Besant's literary grandchildren could look forward to was a world containing more than four hundred million English-speaking people, all educated 'more or less'. They would all read journals and books. Servicing their needs, there would be a 'great army of men and women':

> These men and women belong to a great society called the
> Society of Authors, which has branches all over the habitable
> globe; each branch a centre of light and leading, so that not a
> town or a village all over Great Britain, America and
> Australia, but has its local secretary, and is in correspondence
> with the central office.

The one thing that Besant's dream did not tell him was whether the central office of this world-wide society of writers and readers was to be 'in Chicago or London'.[212] That, however, was not one of the more urgent problems exercising the minds of novelists.

Eleven years after Besant's dream, Cosima Chubleigh was drawing her £1 17s 8d half profits and recognising the justice of the advice that if her next novel did well it might bring her thirty or forty pounds. Five years further on, Henry Ryecroft, mellowed by retirement and a small inheritance, looked back on a life devoted to authorship. Anyone who encourages a young men or woman to turn to 'literature' for a living, he decided, 'commits no less than a crime':

> Hateful as is the struggle for life in every form, this rough-
> and-tumble of the literary arena seems to me sordid and
> degrading beyond all others. Oh, your prices per thousand
> words! Oh, your paragraphs and your interviewings! And oh,
> the black despair that awaits those down-trodden in the
> fray.[213]

Part Two

CHANGING TIMES

Chapter Two

The Prevailing Sound of the Age

'You're rather early-Victorian,' replied Sybil, who by this term was
wont to signify barbarism or cruelty in art, letters, morality or social
feeling.

George Gissing, *The Whirlpool* (1897)

Whenever I open a paper and see Death of a Great Victorian, I thank
Heaven there's one more of them gone.

W. Somerset Maugham, *Of Human Bondage* (1915)

'The newspaper this morning tells me that Queen Victoria died last
night, at Osborne, at 6.30,' George Gissing recorded on 23 January
1901: 'The end has been certain for several days. Wrote to Walter
and to Mother.'[1] Not many of the Queen's subjects would have
taken the news so phlegmatically: the immediate response of J. A.
Hammerton was probably more typical. Learning of Victoria's
death from newspaper bill-boards, he claimed to have 'felt that all
the world had changed in an instant of time ... For a moment or
two the mind was unwilling to accept the truth.' Hammerton soon
recovered and, as a committed journalist, began to look for a news
angle on the event. He found it in the 'flood of prose and poetry'
which commemorated the late Queen. He estimated that more than
three thousand elegiac poems had been published 'in the press of
Britain and the colonies alone', a selection of which he collected
together in an elegant anthology 'bound in white linen, each page
printed with a purple border and a purple book-mark sewn in the
binding'. Hammerton readily admitted that his initial feeling of
disbelief was only temporary: it was a 'sort of anaesthesia', and

'with the proclamation of King Edward VII it was surprising how quickly we came out of it, looking eagerly forward to a new kingly era'.[2] His feelings were echoed in the music hall:

> Father's going to change his socks and Auntie have a bath,
> On the day King Edward gets his crown on.[3]

In spite of our habit of labelling periods of English Literature with the names of Kings and Queens, there is no sound reason why the accession or death of a monarch should affect imaginative literature in any but local ways, like the production of Hammerton's anthology. There was a marked relaxation of social manners in the Edwardian age, together with an intensification of various kinds of intellectual and artistic concern and an escalation of domestic and international tensions, all of which were to have profound consequences for modern literature: but none of them was initiated by Edward's accession. As far as the social history of the English novel is concerned, the year 1901 is of little significance. The origins of Edwardian change and disaffection lie thirty years back in the nineteenth century. They are not buried or distant, vague factors that may or may not have exerted an oblique influence on individual writers. Nor are they 'literary background', elements that can be separated from artistic achievement as though imaginative literature has no living connection with the immediate world it strives to interpret. They are very much foreground – forces and events that serve, in the act of shaping the nature of a particular phase of society, to close certain options for writers and open others. It is primarily a matter of what is felt by writers at any given time as possible or impossible for them, something that Virginia Woolf recognised in a brilliant defence of her own modernist art: 'The tools of one generation are useless for the next.'[4]

Needing the stability that a firm date can seem to give, Woolf settled on 1910 as the year, and even December as the month, when 'human character changed'. The meticulously precise reference is probably to the First Post-Impressionist exhibition in London which ran from November 1910 to January 1911, though that hardly lessens the outrageousness of the claim, as Woolf, of course, well understood. She was careful to stress that this change had not been 'sudden and definite' – like a chicken laying an egg – but the result of a long process in which Samuel Butler and

Bernard Shaw played conspicuous parts, and in which literature was merely one element among many:

> All human relations have shifted – those between masters and
> servants, husbands and wives, parents and children. And
> when human relations change there is at the same time a
> change in religion, conduct, politics and literature.

These words were written in 1924. Around her Woolf could hear 'the sound of breaking and falling, crashing and destruction . . . the prevailing sound of the Georgian [or Modern] age'.[5] Crashing with everything else were whatever scraps of Victorianism that had survived the First World War, their literary obituary being offered in countless books, ranging from Lytton Strachey's elegant debunking in *Eminent Victorians* (1918) and *Queen Victoria* (1921) to the ferocious, flailing abuse of Richard Aldington's *Death of a Hero* (1929).

The anti-Victorianism that is so characteristic of the 1920s reveals complex motives. At different times it is an explanation of, or a justification for, the radically changed mood of modern literature; an accusation of blame for the war; an angry cry against sexual frustration caused by Victorian inhibition and prudery; horror at the continuance of a mass poverty which had been created and condoned by the Victorians; annoyance at a lingering religiosity that science and the Great War should have finished off once and for all; and, rarely absent entirely from these areas of discontent, a bemused nostalgia for an artistic and social stability that once was and is no more. For the near-sighted, one focal point became the Edwardian Garden Party which, as many historians have since pointed out, was not much fun for the vast majority of the uninvited. The principal target was the collective image referred to variously as 'the Victorians' or 'Victorianism' that G. M. Young was to dismantle so influentially. These terms were not used by detractors to indicate everyone who lived during, or everything that belonged to, the whole of Victoria's reign: nor was the derisory mood of anti-Victorianism simply a post-war phenomenon. Hostility was directed, almost exclusively, at the early and mid-Victorians: Young clearly had this in mind when he settled on the years 1830 to 1865 as the period of time to be covered by the original version of his great apologia.[6] To be a late Victorian was to escape the contempt directed at the earlier generations, and there were good reasons for this discrimination, as the case of Virginia

Woolf illustrates. In 1910, when human character changed, Woolf
was twenty-eight years of age: she had been nineteen when Queen
Victoria died, but never for a moment did she think of herself as a
Victorian. That title was reserved for her father, Leslie Stephen,
and the aunts she was to write so much about: nor did it apply to
her own contemporaries or the generation that immediately
preceded them. When Woolf wanted to dissociate the work of
Lawrence, Joyce, T. S. Eliot and herself from that of Wells,
Bennett and Galsworthy, she did not accuse them of being
Victorian. That would have been too great an insult: it would have
denied them the distinctive, influential place they had earned, and
Woolf was careful to be fair to them, in historical terms at least:

> To drop metaphor, I think that after the creative activity of
> the Victorian age it was quite necessary, not only for
> literature, but for life, that someone should write the books
> that Mr Wells, Mr Bennett, and Mr Galsworthy have written.
> Yet what odd books they are! [7]

By fixing as post-Victorian or Edwardian these three novelists
who were all born in the mid-1860s (and were, therefore, fifteen or
sixteen years older than herself), Woolf was able to define the
special nature of the modernist movement and at the same time
maintain the close connection it had with anti-Victorianism. She
adopted a similar attitude to several other near-contemporary
writers she admired – Gissing, Butler, Hardy, James. They come
'after the creative activity of the Victorian age': they are, to use the
more recent classification, modern (of their time and often
crucially necessary to it) but not yet modernist (committed
exponents of radically new artistic methods appropriate to an age of
collapsed values). Virginia Woolf was naturally more concerned
with modernism than with the process that led to it: when Leonard
Woolf attempted a similar analysis of anti-Victorianism he gave
greater attention to its early stages and, in doing so, made explicit
what his wife implied. The literary 'protagonists' of the 'revolt
against bourgeois Victorianism' he listed as 'Swinburne, Bernard
Shaw, Samuel Butler in *The Way of All Flesh*, and to some extent
Hardy and Wells': Ibsen, the philosopher G. E. Moore, and the
late novels of James were given as additional influences. 'Thackeray
and Dickens,' on the other hand, 'meant nothing to us or rather
they stood for an era, a way of life, a system of morals against

which we were in revolt.' Leonard Woolf was evoking the 'exhilaration' of being a student at Cambridge in 1903 and realising that the revolution was already well under way:

> We found ourselves living in the springtime of a conscious
> revolt against the social, political, religious, moral, intellectual,
> and artistic institutions, beliefs and standards of our fathers
> and grandfathers. We felt ourselves to be the second generation
> in this exciting movement of men and ideas.[8]

If the various writers belonging to that first generation referred to by Leonard Woolf are 'in transition', the chroniclers of an 'interregnum' (as in one very obvious sense they are), they also belong inescapably to the process that leads to modernism, and their contributions to that process are characteristically iconoclastic. 'Breaking and falling, crashing and destruction' is as much the 'prevailing sound' of late Victorian Britain as it was to be of the 1920s. Even the First World War could be viewed, in this particular context, as a horrifying, apocalyptic climax that confirmed rather than caused a radical change in values. It was this that Virginia Woolf recognised as she looked back from 1924 to her symbolic turning-point. She would have had little difficulty in agreeing with Samuel Hynes that 'virtually everything that is thought of as characteristically modern already existed in England by 1914'.[9]

That 'virtually everything' includes many of the social and aesthetic influences that were to shape the work of the three greatest modernist novelists in Britain – Woolf, James Joyce, and D. H. Lawrence. In 1914, Woolf was thirty-two years of age and already had an established reputation as a book-reviewer and essayist. Her first novel, *The Voyage Out*, on which she had worked for many years, was published in 1915, though the novels which established her as a leading modernist were post-war. In this respect her career was slightly different from those of Joyce and Lawrence. Joyce was the same age as Woolf. The short stories making up *Dubliners* were first sent to the publisher Grant Richards in December 1905 and accepted by him for publication two months later, though they were not to appear in print until 1914. A similar period of delayed publication was suffered by *A Portrait of the Artist as a Young Man*. Its moment of conception is dated by Richard Ellmann as 7 January 1904 when Joyce 'wrote off in one day, and with scarcely any hesitation, an autobiographical story that mixed admiration for himself with irony. At the suggestion of his brother Stanislaus he called it "A Portrait of the Artist".'[10] Over the next two years this sketch was expanded into the novel *Stephen Hero* which remained unpublished, and this in turn was extensively re-written as *A Portrait of the Artist as a Young Man*, first serialised in the *Egoist*, 1914–15. The early chapters of *A Portrait* date back to at least 1909 and most of the book was probably completed two years before its serialisation. Even *Ulysses*, the novel which more than any other marked the formal overthrow of Victorian realism, was begun before 1914, and according to Ellmann, was being planned by Joyce seven years earlier.[11] Parts of *Ulysses* were serialised in *The Little Review* in 1918: the completed work first appeared in volume form in Paris in 1922. Lawrence was three years younger than Joyce and Woolf and had no difficulty publishing his early work – ironically so, considering the later controversies. By 1914 he had published three novels, *The White Peacock* (1911), *The Trespasser* (1912) and *Sons and Lovers* (1913): his collection of short stories *The Prussian Officer* was published in 1914. He had already announced as 'nearly finished' a new novel *The Sisters* which would eventually be divided into two and rewritten as *The Rainbow* and *Women in Love*.[12] The first of these novels was published in 1915 and immediately suppressed: *Women in Love* was completed in October 1916, though not published for a further five years.

The familiar critical habit of classifying these three writers as modern, with James and Conrad sometimes added as honorary precursors, involves separating them not only from an older, established generation they were reacting against – an activity common enough in literary history – but from near and actual contemporaries as well, some of whom are not notably less important as novelists than those who are regarded as superseding them. The proliferation of classifying labels (for both authors and sub-divisions of time) demonstrates the confusion. Hardy and Gissing are 'in transition'. Conrad is an 'early modern' according to some accounts and an 'Edwardian' according to others. Galsworthy has become the very type of 'Edwardian' novelist though the completed version of *The Forsyte Saga* was first published in 1922, the same year as *Jacob's Room* and *Ulysses*. Oscar Wilde belongs to 'the Nineties', but Gissing, Hardy and James, who published much of their best work in the 1890s, do not. These curious forms of discrimination (of which Woolf's punctilious dismissal of the Edwardians is symptomatic) are not brought about entirely by the anti-historicism of professional literary critics: they are built into the process of emergent modernism and have no precise equivalents in early or mid-Victorian literature. The explanation lies partly in the special nature of the modernist response – that permanent state of formal experimentation which manifests itself within an author's work not as traditional development or change but as an unstoppable reaction against the self; and partly in the unusually prolonged period of gestation or 'transition' that modernism seems to have required.

'We were full of experiments and reforms,' Virginia Woolf recalled, remembering the mood of her Bloomsbury circle in 1904: 'We were going to do without table napkins ... we were going to paint; to write; to have coffee after dinner instead of tea at nine o'clock. Everything was going to be new; everything was going to be different. Everything was on trial.'[13] That youthful mood of a whole world in transformation, with old habits and values to be thrown aside and an incalculable range of new options to choose from, can be duplicated again and again during the last thirty years of Victoria's reign. It is to be found in all areas of Britain, in other English-speaking countries, in vastly different class settings, and it is related not only to literature, but to religion, morals and politics as well. It could be Lawrence nerving himself to break away from Eastwood and Croydon ('With *should* and *ought* I have nothing to do'); Stephen Dedalus in turn-of-the-century Dublin ('You talk to me of nationality, language, religion. I shall try to fly by those nets'); or George Moore in Paris twenty years earlier practising the autobiographical mode and very similar language in an even more self-conscious manner in an attempt to 'shake himself free from race and language and to recreate himself as it were in the womb of a new nationality'.[14] It could be Wells inspired by T. H. Huxley at South Kensington in 1884 and spending 'the most educational year' of his life, or Well's semi-autobiographical Remington looking back, like Leonard Woolf, to his days at Cambridge: 'We were not going to be afraid of ideas any longer, we were going to throw down every barrier of prohibition and take them in and see what came of it.'[15] Or Gissing in a London slum, answering a newspaper advertisement in 1878 inserted by 'a student of ancient and modern literature, a free-thinker in religion, a lover of art in all forms, hater of conventionalism', finding through that advertisement a friend to talk with and reproducing the experience in *The Unclassed* (1884); or Yeat's 'tragic generation' of the 1890s in 'revolt against Victorianism' and turning their London pub into a French café; or Robert Louis Stevenson and Charles Baxter as students at Edinburgh University twenty years earlier drawing up the constitution of a debating society with its first rule, 'Disregard everything our parents have taught us.'[16] It could be Walter Pater in Oxford insisting that, 'not the fruit of experience but experience itself is the end . . . What we have to do is to be for ever curiously testing opinion and courting new impressions, never acquiescing in a facile orthodoxy of Comte or of Hegel or of our own'; or Waldo in Olive Schreiner's *Story of an African Farm* (1883) being advised, 'We of this generation are not destined to eat and be satisfied as our fathers were; we must be content to go hungry.'[17] It could be Samuel Butler, one of the first imaginative writers to appreciate the significance of Darwin, reading the *Origin of Species* on a sheep farm in New Zealand and writing the early chapters of what was to become *Erewhon* (1872) in which Victorian values are turned topsy-turvy, initiating a distinguished tradition of late Victorian and early twentieth century anti-Utopias. Answering the negativism that that tradition was soon to reveal, there is the hero of *News from Nowhere* (1890) who, returning one night from 'a brisk conversational discussion' at the Socialist League on 'what would happen on the Morrow of the Revolution', finds himself in a world in which there is no longer any need for debate, the problems and horrors of Victorian Britain having been swept away and replaced by a Marxist Utopia.[18] H. G. Wells wanted to see a rather different kind of Utopia established in Britain, though in 1901 his destructive enthusiasm was as great as Morris's: 'I shall talk treason at the R.I. I'm going to write, talk, preach revolution for the next five years.'[19] Everywhere, from the 1870s onwards, there is not simply a questioning of fundamental beliefs – that is even more characteristic of the mid-Victorians – but an air of denigration and mockery, a determination to reject mid-Victorian values and take a chance on what comes next. In mood, it ranges from Gilbert and Sullivan's Aesthetes who 'lie upon the daisies and discourse in novel phrases' of their 'complicated' states of mind, to Lawrence's witches' coven:

The talk was very often political or sociological, and interesting,

curiously anarchistic . . . Everything seemed to be thrown
into the melting pot, and it seemed to Ursula they were all
witches, helping the pot to bubble. There was an elation and
a satisfaction in it all, but it was cruelly exhausting for the
new-comers.[20]

From Butler, and to a lesser extent Gilbert and Sullivan, there
descends one of the most immediately palpable signs of literary
revolt – the resurgence of satirical interest in paradox and epigram
that Oscar Wilde was to refine into a way of life. During the early
Victorian period the irreverence that paradox and epigram are so
fitted to express had been driven underground by the self-conscious
seriousness of the age. The last of the early Victorians to succumb
had been Thackeray who explained his change of attitude to Mark
Lemon, the editor of *Punch*: 'A few years ago I should have
sneered at the idea of setting up as a teacher at all . . . but I have
got to believe in the business and in many other things since then.
And our profession seems to me as serious as the Parson's own.'[21]
Thackeray was rejecting his earlier career as an irreverent satirist of
society and acknowledging that Regency values had no useful role
to play in the establishment of Victorianism. The fascination with
paradox and epigram later in the century reversed the pattern of
Thackeray's experience. Now it was the moral earnestness of the
Victorians that had to be overthrown, and that task would be
achieved by turning Victorian morality upside down and inside out
to demonstrate the importance of being earnest which, of course,
meant not being earnest while remaining Ernest. Here, as at so
many other points, the satire of Wilde and Butler connects:

> Theobald had proposed calling him George, after old Mr
> Pontifex, but strange to say Mr Pontifex overruled him in
> favour of the name of Ernest. The word 'earnest' was just
> beginning to come into fashion [c.1835] and he thought the
> possession of such a name might, like his having been
> baptised in water from the Jordan, have a permanent effect
> upon his character, and influence him for good during the
> more critical periods of his life.[22]

It was nobody's intention to dethrone earnestness permanently. At
times Wilde comes near to sacrificing his art to the belief that 'In
matters of grave importance, style not sincerity, is the vital
thing.'[23] But there is a seriousness of purpose behind this attitude,

as there is behind much of Wilde's social criticism, his dandified
image of the artist, and the aesthetic principles he imported from
France. In Butler, paradox was intended at first to espouse
Darwinian ideas, then later, as he came to feel betrayed by Darwin,
an alternative evolutionary theory. Chesterton placed paradox at
the service of Catholicism: Shaw practised irreverence in the name
of Socialism and the Life Force. If a developed sense of ridicule
distinguished this particular group of writers, what they shared
with nearly every other novelist in Britain from about 1880 was the
conviction that before their own artistic purposes could take root
and flourish they needed to dissociate themselves from Victorianism. The seriousness of this kind of linguistic challenge was
early recognised. Welcoming the prison sentence given to Wilde in
1895, the *Daily Telegraph* expressed the hope that it would serve as
a deterrent to, among others, 'novelists who have sought to imitate
the style of paradox and unreality'. [24]

Not that anti-Victorianism possessed any one central, coherent
point of focus. At its most extreme it could be foolishly general. When
Leonard Woolf talks of participating in a 'conscious revolt against
the social, political, religious, moral, intellectual, and artistic
institutions, beliefs and standards of our fathers and grandfathers',
his dislike of the Victorians is so inclusive that he seems to have
wiped out even his own base of attack, as though he yearns to stand
naked in a world emptied of all social forms. It is unlikely that he
meant to imply that, though Birkin in *Women in Love* certainly does,
and indeed more: his apocalyptic vision embraces, with a certain
amount of relish, a world swept clean of 'foul humanity' himself
included, leaving 'the trees and the grass and birds'. [25] It is almost as
desolate as the future bleak landscapes visited by Well's time-traveller, or the longing for total annihilation affected by Dorian Gray:

> '*Fin de siècle*', murmured Lord Henry.
> '*Fin du globe*', answered his hostess.
> 'I wish it were *fin du globe*', said Dorian with a sigh. 'Life is
> a great disappointment.' [26]

For those who refuse the temptations of self-indulgent aestheticism,
choosing instead to confront modern problems, life often proves no
more satisfying than it is for Dorian Gray. At the close of Gissing's
greatest novel of working-class life, *The Nether World* (1889),
Sidney Hewett and Jane Snowdon, their ambitions and hopes

destroyed, are set against yet another late Victorian wasteland, this time the London slums:

> Where they abode it was not all dark. Sorrow certainly
> awaited them, perchance defeat in even the humble aims that
> they had set themselves; but at least their lives would remain
> a protest against those brute forces of society which fill with
> wreck the abysses of the nether world.[27]

To 'remain a protest' is something, though not much, in a society governed by intractable 'brute forces'. It is, however, more comfort than Jude Fawley and Sue Bridehead can derive in *Jude the Obscure* (1895), the most harrowing of all late Victorian expressions of the belief that mid-Victorian social connections have been replaced by discordant contrasts.[28] Jude and Sue are 'pioneers', ahead of their time and painfully aware of the fact, and, perhaps intended as demonstrations of Hardy's insistence that the view of life informing his novels is one of 'evolutionary meliorism' rather than blank pessimism.[29] But it is never clear what exactly Jude and Sue are pioneers of, or what exactly they are evolving towards, though it is clear that everything in the world around them is wrong – the marriage laws, their family backgrounds, educational opportunities, religion, sexual relationships, paternity, even the ancient struggle between 'flesh and spirit' is advanced as being somehow the fault of Victorianism. 'When people of a later age look back upon the barbarous customs and superstitions of the times that we have the unhappiness to live in, what *will* they say!'[30]

The shortest answer to Sue's rhetorical question is that nobody in a 'later age' was to be as horrified by, or as damning of, Victorianism as the late Victorians themselves. Remington's denunciation in Well's *The New Machiavelli* is characteristically complete:

> The Victorian epoch was not the dawn of a new era; it was a
> hasty trial experiment, a gigantic experiment of the most
> slovenly and wasteful kind . . . the nineteenth century was an
> age of demonstrations, some of them very impressive demonstra-
> tions, of the powers that have come to mankind; but of
> permanent achievement what will our descendants cherish? It is
> hard to estimate what grains of precious metals may not be
> found in a mud torrent of human production on so large a scale,
> but will anyone, a hundred years from now, consent to live in
> the houses the Victorians built, travel by their roads or railways,
> value the furnishings they made to live among or esteem, except

for curious or historical reasons, their prevalent art and the
clipped and limited literature that satisfied their souls? [31]

That is not one of Wells's most perceptive prophecies. Within
considerably less than half a century there was to be established an
army of scholars, linked by academic networks throughout the
world, who seemed little interested in anything but the Victorians.
The houses, railways and furnishings mocked by Wells, were to
become objects of fashionable admiration, while the 'clipped and
limited literature' that satisfied Victorian souls was being hailed,
uncontroversially, as an achievement rivalling that of the Elizabethans.
That Wells should have been so spectacularly wrong is an indication
of how deeply entrenched anti-Victorianism had become by this
time. Remington's outburst is offered as axiomatic: he doesn't sound
unduly aggressive or wilfully shocking. He doesn't really expect
anyone to disagree with him. The Victorian age is already well in the
past, buried beneath the mud-torrent it created, and Britain is ready
for a Wellsian reconstruction on rational, scientific lines.

What is apparent in all of these cases is the way that
responsibility for present discontent is cast back upon the mid-
Victorians. The 'experiments' that Remington sees as typifying the
nineteenth century may have been 'gigantic', but they have, none
the less, failed. Their waste and slovenliness have been dumped on
a later generation, a mess of unanswered questions from great
failed experiments which now demand reactivation or, more
commonly in the literature of the period, make pointless, even
impossible, any action other than self-preservation or self-indulgence. In this, if in little else, Remington is at one with Sidney
Hewett, Jane Snowdon, Jude Fawley, Sue Bridehead and Dorian
Gray. The time-traveller excludes himself from this company not
because he conjectures about what the future may hold – Jude and
Sue are just as fond of doing that. Nor because he translates desires
into action – as Dorian Gray also does. But because he seems
unable to conceive of human life as anything but a continuum, and
therefore as a process that contains meaning stretching out beyond
the present. He is shocked to learn from his travels that a
continuum is not necessarily the same thing as progress. He learns,
in other words, that the Victorians had got it all wrong.

In so far as anti-Victorianism functioned on a coherent,
comprehensive level, it can be seen as a complete rejection or

reformulation of all of those key concepts governing mid-Victorian thought – Free Trade, Progress, Self-Help, Respectability, Christian Duty – that historians like G. M. Young, Asa Briggs and W. L. Burn have defined so lucidly.[32] H. G. Wells was not the only novelist attracted to the idea of cataloguing the great changes that had occurred between mid- and late Victorian England. In *The Old Wives' Tale* (1908) Arnold Bennett employed specific details of social and political change as one way of charting the development of time, as when Mr Critchlow and Mrs Baines stand by John Baines's death-bed:

> They knew not that they were gazing at a vanished era. John
> Baines had belonged to the past, to the age when men really
> did think of their souls, when orators by phrases could move
> crowds to fury or pity, when no one had learnt to hurry,
> when Demos was only turning in his sleep, when the sole
> beauty of life resided in its inflexible and slow dignity, when
> hell really had no bottom, and a gilt-clasped Bible really was
> the secret of England's greatness. Mid-Victorian England lay
> on that mahogany bed. Ideals had passed away with John
> Baines.[33]

Bennett did not share his friend H. G. Wells's faith in man's ability – once he was rid of the chaotic mess of Victorianism – to move forward in a condition of reasoned progress. But his equally strong conviction that man's life was governed by ideals that were both deeply-held and unattainable, made him no less perceptive a chronicler of an age in which mid-Victorian England had been rendered distant by the rise of Socialism, the decline of Evangelical fervour, and the commercial manipulation of a mass society. While Bennett implies the presence of these new forces by stressing how alien they would have been to John Baines, Hubert Crackanthorpe evoked a lost stability by cataloguing the ills of a late Victorian present:

> Tomorrow for the first time he was to speak in the Lords:
> sardonically, he bethought himself of the dreary lack of
> humour of English politics . . . of the age grown strangely
> picturesque; of the rich, enfeebled by monstrous ease; of the
> shivering poor, clamouring nightly for justice; of a helpless
> democracy, vast revolt of the ill-informed; of priests striving
> to be rational; of sentimental moralists protecting iniquity; of
> middle-class princes; of sybaritic saints; of complacent and
> pompous politicians; of doctors, hurrying the degeneration of
> the race; of artists discarding possibilities for limitations; of

press-men befooling a pretentious public; of critics, refining
upon the 'busman's' methods; of inhabitants of Camberwell
chattering of culture; of ladies of the pavement, aping the
conventionality of nonconformist circles.[34]

It was out of the clash between mid-Victorian idealism and the
reality of the late Victorian inheritance that there developed the now
received image of the Victorians as hypocrites. Unless they could be
regarded as innocent to the point of imbecility, how else were the
blatant contradictions in their lives to be explained? How could they
believe in the teaching of Jesus and brutally beat their own children;
idealise their wives as angels in the house yet tolerate, and often use, the
prostitutes who made up a sizeable proportion of city populations;
speak proudly of the vast industrial wealth of Britain while the poor
were dying in the streets; boast of the progress of the nation when few
children had access to any education that took them beyond the barest
literacy; talk of sustaining democratic rights when only upper- and
middle-class male property-holders had a direct say in the election of a
government? Out of apparent contradictions such as these the typical
Victorian emerged not only as a hypocrite, but also as a middle-class
hypocrite, which, in an age so conscious of the growing power of
Socialism, was often seen as more than doubling the offence.

While the aesthetes and decadents tried to shock the middle
classes out of their supposed complacency by outrageous behaviour,
and the realistic novelists, in Wilde's brilliant epigram, held up a
mirror so that Caliban could rage at his own reflection, it was the
satirists who carried anti-Victorianism to victory.[35] As the principal
charge focused increasingly on hypocrisy (whether the specific
wrong attacked was political, social or literary), verbal wit and
satirical ridicule became the most telling weapons available. Drama
does not come within the scope of this study, but the important
roles played by Shaw and Wilde in the mockery of Victorianism
must at least be acknowledged. Many of Shaw's early plays
dramatise the theme of Victorian hypocrisy as a way of life, while
Wilde's *The Importance of Being Earnest* can be read as a sustained,
affectionate wholesale undermining of Victorian values. Lady
Bracknell, outwardly determined to uphold the social code appropriate to her status and inwardly willing to surrender everything
if the price is high enough, established herself immediately as the
very type of Victorian grotesque. When Jack Worthing, alien in
every possible respect from the late Victorian social conscience,

believes not only that Miss Prism is his mother but that she is unmarried, he speaks in the tones and clichés of the outraged late Victorian feminist, male or female:

> Unmarried! I do not deny that is a serious blow. But after all
> who has the right to cast a stone against one who has
> suffered? Cannot repentance wipe out an act of folly? Why
> should there be one law for men, and another for women.
> Mother, I forgive you.[36]

And when Miss Prism herself insists, indignantly, that her lost three-volume novel was a worthy and orthodox literary achievement ('The good ended happily, and the bad unhappily. That is what Fiction means'), there could hardly have been a young author hearing such a statement who did not applaud both the relevance of the charge against mid-Victorian fiction and the ridiculousness of the attitude for his own generation.[37]

Author after author, bitterly or humorously, in fiction or from life, recorded memorable instances of what Arthur Waugh called the 'poisonous complacency' of the Victorians.[38] Typical of a whole class of religious bigots is Mrs Remington who 'had been trained in a hard and narrow system that made evil out of many things not in the least evil', and no small part of the popularity of *Dr Jekyll and Mr Hyde* (1886) was its sympathetic portrayal of a man who wished to 'wear a more than commonly grave countenance before the public' but was forced to conceal his pleasures and commit himself to 'a profound duplicity of life'.[39] Chesterton remembered a 'solemn friend' of his grandfather, who every Sunday would walk the streets carrying a prayer-book, but with no intention of going to church. When asked the reason for this curious behaviour, he replied, with uplifted hand: 'I do it, Chessie, as an example to others.'[40] Beatrice Webb, lacking Chesterton's taste for the bizarre, could still record of the father she loved: 'He attended church regularly, took the sacrament and prayed night and morning. It seems incredible, but I know that, as a man, he repeated the prayer taught him at his mother's lap – "Gentle Jesus, meek and mild, look upon a little child."' Webb's warning that this story might seem incredible did not stop her from going on to explain to her younger readers just how normal such behaviour was: 'No one of the present generation realizes with what sincerity and fervour these doctrines were held by the representative men

and women of the mid-Victorian middle class.'[41] Considered in these
terms Philip Gosse was extreme rather than representative, but the
portrait of him by his son Edmund in *Father and Son* (1907) is one of
the finest, and slyest, expressions of anti-Victorianism.

In most respects, Philip Gosse did not qualify automatically as a
grotesque. He was a true believer, a literalist, and a man of some
standing in the intellectual world. He was not a hypocrite: nor was
he selfish, cruel, nor, apart from being misguided in the way he
attempted to reconcile Christianity and Science, a fool. There are
moments of deep emotional intensity in *Father and Son*, as when
the widowed, isolated, natural scientist becomes suddenly aware of
the loneliness of his young son:

> Sometimes, when the early twilight descended upon us in the
> study, and he could no longer peer with advantage into the
> depths of his microscope, he would beckon me to him
> silently, and fold me closely in his arms. I used to turn my
> face up to his, patiently and wonderingly, while the large,
> unwilling tears gathered in the corners of his eyelids.[42]

Philip Gosse's life is dedicated to comprehending the wonders of
God's creation and he weeps for the impossibility of his task. It is
not despair or doubt. He is no Robert Elsemere or Mark Rutherford
searching for new religious directions: all is there before him, in the
Bible or under the microscope, if only he is granted the power to see.
It is the son's incomprehension that gives the book its specialness,
his disbelief that the father can really be so simple-minded and
unconsciously cruel. The publication of *Omphalos* (1857) which was
to 'smoothly open the lock of geological mystery' reveals Philip
Gosse as ludicrously out of touch with modern thought, and the
moment when he seizes the Christmas pudding from the servants'
table, runs down the garden with it and hurls 'the accursed thing' on
the dust-heap, turns him into a figure of wild folly.[43] The sufferings
the son undergoes make up a catalogue of familiar complaints
against the Victorians – the long dreary Sundays; the inability of his
parents to realise how dreadful it is for the young boy to be the
solitary companion of his mother as she dies slowly and stoically
from cancer; the religious priggishness that is encouraged in him;
the foolishness of the father joining his son in prayer to ask God
whether an invitation to a local children's party might be accepted;
the paternal fear that reading imaginative literature could lead, like
eating Christmas pudding, to eternal damnation.

Father and Son and *The Way of All Flesh* are now often linked together in critical studies, and the two books do clearly have much in common, not least a blend of barely diluted autobiographical reminiscence and fictional techniques. But there are also significant differences between them. It is, for example, one of the oddities of the period that the novel which more than any other fixed for early twentieth-century writers the image of their Victorian predecessors as canting hypocrites, was not written by someone who belonged to their own generation. Butler began writing *The Way of All Flesh* (1903) in the early 1870s. He completed the manuscript ten years later and, to use V. S. Pritchett's simile, left it lying in his desk like a bomb timed to go off after his death and 'blow up the Victorian family'.[44] Examination of that particular aspect of Butler's influence must be postponed for the moment, but there is more to *The Way of All Flesh* than its dismantling of the family unit. Like Edmund Gosse, Butler blames the repressive ethos of the family on a religion that he regards as totally discredited, and fixes evolutionary theory as the main agent of liberation. But Gosse admits to no satirical purpose: he is writing an unadorned 'document . . . a record of educational and religious conditions which, having passed away, will never return'.[45] Butler, on the other hand, is openly satirical, full of unconcealed resentment at the damage done by Victorianism. Philip Gosse is misguided and unconsciously cruel: Theobald Pontifex is a sadist and hypocrite. It is important to the evolutionary design of *The Way of All Flesh* that we should see Theobald's relationship with *his* father before Theobald's son Ernest overturns the pattern: Butler knew full well that the forces moulding Victorianism were at work long before Queen Victoria came to the throne. From Old George Pontifex descends the violence, mean-mindedness and 'will-shaking' that are to keep Theobald in line but are to have less power over Ernest. The hated characteristics of the earlier generations are conveyed in a series of memorable vignettes. Old Mr Pontifex dropping the bottle of Jordan water on the cellar floor, and immediately, 'with his usual presence of mind' gasping out 'a month's warning' to the butler; the Miss Allabys playing cards to decide which of them is to marry Theobald; the gluttonous headmaster Dr Skinner, author of a great work of theological scholarship, *Meditations upon the Epistle and Character of St Jude*, a book 'so exhaustive that no one who bought it need ever meditate upon the subject again – indeed it exhausted

all who had anything to do with it'; Theobald, on one of the
Sundays his family dreaded so much, beating the young Ernest for
being unable to pronounce a simple word properly:

> 'I have sent him up to bed,' said Theobald, as he returned to
> the drawing-room, 'and now, Christina, I think we will have
> the servants in to prayers,' and he rang the bell for them,
> red-handed as he was.[46]

Ernest himself is not allowed to escape unmarked by the
Pontifex inheritance. While at university it even seems for a while
that he will become as hypocritical as his father and grandfather.
Butler demonstrates the danger in one of the most irreverent
passages of the book. Ernest, inspired by a visiting preacher,
decides to 'give up all for Christ – even his tobacco':

> Tobacco had nowhere been forbidden in the Bible; but then
> it had not yet been discovered, and had probably only
> escaped proscription for this reason. We can conceive of St
> Paul or even our Lord himself as drinking a cup of tea, but
> we cannot imagine either of them as smoking a cigarette or a
> churchwarden. Ernest could not deny this, and admitted that
> Paul would almost certainly have condemned tobacco in good
> round terms if he had known of its existence. Was it not then
> taking rather a mean advantage of the Apostle to stand on his
> not having actually forbidden it? On the other hand, it was
> possible that God knew Paul would have forbidden smoking,
> and had purposely arranged the discovery of tobacco for a
> period at which Paul should be no longer living. This might
> seem rather hard on Paul, considering all he had done for
> Christianity, but it would be made up to him in other ways.
>   These reflections satisfied Ernest that on the whole he had
> better smoke, so he sneaked to his portmanteau and brought
> out his pipes and tobacco again. There should be moderation,
> he felt, in all things, even in virtue.[47]

Ernest has thoroughly learned what was now considered the
Victorians' natural ability to offer high-sounding justification for
indulging in whatever worldly pleasures attracted them, and even
then having to 'sneak' off to enjoy themselves. There is also the
tendency to make a simple decision a matter of tortuous soul-
searching, and the explaining away of anything that might make an
uncomfortable challenge to life: Ernest's line of reasoning is almost
certainly intended by Butler as a parody of those believers,

including Philip Gosse, whose refusal to accept the obvious truth of evolutionary theory led them into fantastic alternative explanations of why the species differed from each other or how fossils came into existence. But it is the subject and the way it is treated that are characteristic of the late Victorian period and inconceivable at any earlier time in the nineteenth century. If a novel, published without fuss, and indeed slow to develop into the cult book it did become, could joke so facetiously about St Paul, and offer an image of Christ smoking a cigarette, then Victorianism really was on the way out.

Not that it ever disappeared entirely. In 1908 W. L. Courtney observed: 'It is odd, if we think of it, with what whole-hearted energy we despise the Victorian era,' and he pointed to a number of recently published books which defended the Victorians.[48] It was, though, a very self-conscious and ineffective counter-revolution, typified by J. Comyns Carr's *Some Eminent Victorians*, one of the books Courtney refers to. Carr pronounces himself 'an impenitent Victorian', and admits that holding the views he does he must be 'prepared to endure with patience the pitying tolerance, or even the indulgent rebuke, of the men who herald the younger generation'.[49] It was to be some years before he and his contemporaries were to receive any patience or tolerance in return.

Although it is perfectly appropriate to describe *The Way of All Flesh* as lying in Butler's desk like a bomb timed to go off after his death, it must also be said that the impact it had was local and predominantly social. While Butler's iconoclasm could be welcomed, by Virginia Woolf among others, as an essential weapon in the struggle to escape the inhibiting pressure of Victorianism, it was also a quality to be necessarily replaced once its liberating purpose had been fulfilled. Butler's future reputation was fixed, and limited, by the success with which he had carried out his task of demolition. Not only had he finally smashed the popular image of the Victorians as pious, respectable, earnest and devoted to the family: he had erected an alternative, and equally distorted, view of them as devious, hypocritical and self-seeking. The job was done, at least for turn-of-the-century writers. When it was later taken up by Lytton Strachey, the anti-Victorianism was more distanced and calculating, offered in the guise of a pseudo-Wildean belief that 'ignorance is the first requisite of the historian'.[50] Still later historians were to find Butler guilty of a similar ignorance of the true nature of Victorian life, but that is not the impression given by *The Way of All Flesh* which owes so much of its impact to Butler's tone of personal affront at the indignities heaped upon him: what he leaves out is of little importance compared with the vindictive passion of what he includes. There were writers who admired *The Way of All Flesh* so much that they refused to see it as a local achievement. Bernard Shaw took the relative neglect of Butler as an opportunity to inform the English that they 'do not deserve to have great men', and berated critics of his own plays for their 'cacklings about Ibsen and Nietzsche' while ignoring a closer and more potent influence: 'I now point out Samuel Butler, and trust that in consequence I shall hear a little less in future of the novelty and foreign origin of the ideas which are now making their way into the English theatre through plays written by Socialists.'[51] It was just of Shaw to acknowledge Butler's view that moral progress was dependent on financial security as the source of his own similar argument in *Major Barbara*, but it was wrong of him to depreciate the part played by ideas of 'foreign origin' in anti-Victorianism. Of all writers of the period, Shaw, the self-appointed and brilliantly successful British spokesman for Ibsen and Wagner (and to a lesser extent Nietzsche) should have known better.

For those British novelists whose work began to be published from 1880 onwards, there was hardly a single 'idea', felt as immediately fresh and vitally important to their literary or artistic ambitions, that could be claimed as indigenous: virtually everything came from abroad. The situation was significantly different for novelists whose reputations were established by about 1880 or who had begun publication relatively late in life. Meredith, in this respect, as in many others, is uncharacteristic in that throughout his life he had spoken against the insularity of Victorianism: he lived long enough to see his feelings triumph among a younger generation of novelists and to hear himself hailed as an inspirational rare example of a writer who had not allowed his work to be corrupted by mid-Victorian philistinism. In comparison it was possible for William Hale White, who was roughly the same age as Meredith, though fifty years old before he published the first of the 'Mark Rutherford' books in 1881, to appear anachronistic among novelists of the 1880s in his enthusiastic admiration for George Eliot and Wordsworth and in the way he tended to set his novels back in the 1840s. Much the same can be said of the degree of importance attached by Hardy to the thought of John Stuart Mill. Even Darwinism, the most profoundly influential British contribution to the changing intellectual climate of the late nineteenth century, was not for younger novelists the source of metaphysical torment that it was so strikingly for Hardy: nor did it provide for them the kind of intellectual justification that so delighted Butler. It had settled down to enjoy what Chesterton aptly described as 'a very widespread though an exceedingly vague victory'.[52] This is not, of course, to say that evolutionary theory no longer provoked interest or controversy. On the contrary, there is hardly an area of literature or social history in which its influence was not felt – in sociology, theology, politics, and imperialism: in the novel of childhood, natural life, and Empire; in science fiction and fantasy; it was one of the factors that caused Marie Corelli to rage against the decadence of modern life; without Darwinism, Marlow's journey through the Congo in search of Kurtz, and Lawrence's vision of the Brangwyn generations, would not have taken the forms they do.

The diffused nature of Darwinism or evolutionism, the way it produced so quickly both a particular view of the world and a terminology to describe that view, indicates an unusual degree of readiness for so radical a theory. Even allowing that *On the Origin of Species* (1859) marked a culminating point in a lengthy period of scientific and historical investigation rather than a sudden overthrow of deeply held beliefs, the speed of its acceptance remains surprising. Alvar Ellegard has demonstrated that: 'By the end of the 1860s Darwin's name, and the terms of Evolution and Natural Selection had been established firmly in the minds of the public at large,' and this judgment is borne out by the widespread acceptance of Darwinism by late Victorian novelists.[53] The objections of a Marie Corelli seem crazily out of place in a world so swiftly adapting itself to Darwinian terminology, while H. G. Wells, the only major novelist of the time positively inspired by evolutionary theory, reinforces, in his enthusiastic acceptance, the recognition of it as a new starting-point, and – something shared by many other writers whether they were excited by evolutionary theory or not – the main intellectual justification for rejecting so many habits and customs of the recent past. Even then it was not always Darwinism itself that exercised the minds of novelists: it tended to enter

British fiction as a re-import, returning to its native land in various guises and modifications, fitting itself easily into Schopenhauerian pessimism, French naturalism, and Nietzschean élitism.

It was to France that British novelists looked for fictional models which would lead them away from the simple-minded hypocrisy of the mid-Victorians. 'In the nineties,' Bennett noted, 'we used to regard *Une Vie* with mute awe, as being the summit of achievement in fiction.'[54] Another British novelist might have selected a different author and novel, but they would almost invariably have been French. The principal charges against the Victorian novel were put decisively by Henry James in his 1884 article 'The Art of Fiction', written in answer to a lecture by Walter Besant which had carried the same title. James sees Victorian fiction as having suffered from a 'moral timidity' caused by its being addressed 'in a large degree to young people', and from it not being 'what the French call *discutable*. It had no air of having a theory, a conviction, a consciousness of itself behind it.' It was, James decided, '*naïf*'.[55] The reversal of Victorian moral timidity was to be no easy task. Four years after 'The Art of Fiction', attempting to describe the 'sense *par excellence*' which Maupassant speaks for 'with extraordinary distinctness and authority', James could barely bring himself to say what that 'sense' was: he doubted whether even a mention of it would be allowed in an English periodical. Eventually he fixes the adjective 'sexual' to sense, but with a nervousness that has no irony in it.[56] James's own extraordinary 'distinctness and authority' emerge in his discussion of the less dangerous question of fictional form. Against the Victorian 'pudding' view of fiction, with its implied mixture of good things, often irrelevant to the whole experience but nice for the taster, he sets an organic theory learnt from the great nineteenth-century French tradition:

> A novel is a living thing, all one and continuous, like any
> other organism, and in proportion as it lives will it be found,
> that in each of the parts there is something of each of the
> other parts.[57]

James was certainly aware that form was not an end in itself, as his critical essays on Flaubert and Maupassant make clear enough, but he tends to allot to it an importance that serves to excuse other weaknesses, and, in so far as James is criticising the limitations of British and American fiction by praising the virtues of the French, form does take first place. Of Maupassant's short stories he says: 'Sometimes the grimace is very droll, sometimes the wound is very horrible; but in either case the whole thing is real, observed, noted, and represented, not an invention or a castle in the air.'[58] It is the Anglo-Saxon novelist who has discarded reality and substituted empty dreams. Of *Madame Bovary*, in spite of his conviction that the heroine of the novel lacked sufficient depth and dignity for the role Flaubert assigns her, he writes:

> The form is in *itself* as interesting, as active, as much of the
> essence of the subject as the idea, and yet so close is its fit
> and so inseparable its life that we catch it at no moment on
> any errand of its own. That verily is to *be* interesting – all
> round; that is to be genuine and whole.[59]

By contrast the Anglo-Saxon novel is flabby and shapeless, lacking structure, given over to digressions and moral purpose, unintelligent. As so often with James his public pronouncements are elegantly oblique: blunter comments (making much the same point) were conveyed privately, as in this letter to W. D. Howells from Paris in 1884:

> I have been seeing something of Daudet, Goncourt and Zola;
> and there is nothing more interesting to me now than the
> effort and experiment of this little group, with its truly infernal
> intelligence of art, form, manner – its intense artistic life.
> They do the only kind of work today that I respect; and in
> spite of their ferocious pessimism and their handling of
> unclean things, they are at least serious and honest. The
> floods of tepid soap and water which under the name of
> novels are being vomited forth in England, seem to me, by
> contrast, to do little honour to our race.[60]

James's criticism of Victorian fiction and his obsession with organic form were widely shared. One result of 'The Art of Fiction' was a friendship between James and Stevenson which helped in a small degree to break down James's view of British philistinism. Stevenson's 'A Humble Remonstrance' takes friendly issue with James, and his own work (as both men realised) was totally different from that of James, but the ideal of organic form (even though Stevenson was rarely to attain it) is passionately advocated: 'From all its chapters, from all its pages, from all its sentences, the well-written novel echoes, and re-echoes its one creative and controlling thought.'[61] From novelist after novelist there came demands to break away from shapeless Victorian fiction and strive instead for greater tightness of narrative structure and authorial impersonality, to confront, in spite of James's constant warnings to the contrary, Art instead of life. 'Is it artistically strong? Is it good as a picture,' Waymark asks of his novel in Gissing's *The Unclassed*; 'There was a time when I might have written in this way with a declared social object. That is all gone by. I have no longer a spark of social enthusiasm. Art is all I now care for, and as art I wish my work to be judged.'[62] Even Lawrence who despised the 'accurate-impersonal school of Flaubert' praised Balzac's *Eugénie Grandet* as being 'as perfect a novel as I have ever read. It is wonderfully concentrated; there is nothing superfluous, nothing out of place.'[63] Lawrence's admiration for the perfect structure of *Eugénie Grandet* was shared by James and Bennett: Balzac's daring technique of revealing Eugénie's true personality not through her own actions but by a delineation of the hereditary factors that have made her the woman she is provided a direct model for both James's *Washington Square* and Bennett's *Anna of the Five Towns*. Conrad too, struggling to write his first novels, turned away from the fiction of his adopted country and looked to France for inspiration: 'I have studied *Pierre et Jean* – thought, method, and all – with the profoundest despair. It seems nothing, but it has a technical complexity which makes me tear my hair.'[64] Even Miss Braddon, generally despised in this context as too concerned with the market-place to have any worthwhile interest in fictional form, studied the French novel and applied the lessons learnt from it to her own work.[65] By the time Stephen Dedalus offered his view of the artistic personality as refining itself out of existence and claimed that the artist 'like the God of the creation, remains within or behind or beyond or above his handiwork', he was speaking within a well-established tradition in British fiction.[66]

The mid-Victorians had been fully aware of the early stages of French 'realism', and they had, characteristically, absorbed the controversial nature of a Balzac, George Sand or Flaubert; taking an occasional hint rather than succumbing to an overwhelming influence, confident in the greater relevance of their own work to their own society.[67] Henry James, coming to Britain from outside as the mid-Victorian period was drawing to a close, was uniquely positioned to evaluate the joint influence upon him of the English and French novel, to balance the lessons that his own art could learn from Jane Austen and Balzac, Thackeray and Flaubert. But even he was not prepared for the impact on Britain of Zola and Naturalism. Zola's naturalistic theories were first advanced in the preface to the second edition of *Thérèse Raquin* (1868), then in a preface to the first of the Rougon-Macquart novels *La Fortune des Rougon*, and more systematically in *Le Roman expérimental* (1880). Zola never denies the role of 'invention and genius' in the novelist's work, but he sees this as a matter of directing observed phenomena, what he calls the 'mechanism' of facts which reveal 'man in his individual and social action'. The task of the novelist is compared with that of the scientist and surgeon. He too carries out an experiment or operation: 'We must operate with characters, passions, human and social data as the chemist and physicist work on inert bodies, as the physiologist works on living bodies.'[68] Where the scientific novelist most differs from the surgeon is that his analysis is concerned with the formation of human behaviour as well as its physiological manifestations, and this means dealing above all with the formative power of heredity and environment.

Zola's stress on the objectivity of the novelist and on the inevitable outcome of his fictional 'experiments' did not separate him markedly from Balzac and Flaubert: it was the sensational results of those experiments and his hardly less sensational theoretical claims that did this. Most British novelists treated Zola's theories warily, though they provoked ecstasy in George Moore:

> The idea of a new art based upon science, in opposition to
> the art of the old world that was based on imagination, an
> art that should explain all things and embrace modern life in
> its entirety, in its endless ramifications, be, as it were, a new
> creed in a new civilisation, filled me with wonder, and I
> stood dumb before the vastness of the conception, and the
> towering height of the ambition.[69]

For a few years in the 1880s Moore was Britain's leading public spokesman for naturalism, Zola's 'ricochet' as he himself described his role.[70] He made naturalism a central issue in his battle with the circulating libraries, and in his early novels, most notably *A Mummer's Wife* (1885), he closely followed French naturalistic principles. Few other British novelists were so slavish in their admiration for naturalism as the young Moore, and there was no one eager to follow it through in the manner of Zola, but this does not mean, as critics sometimes argue, that it had little lasting effect in Britain. On the contrary, allowing that the British versions were modified for the reasons given by James, and that French realism or naturalism was not necessarily the same thing as Zolaism, its influence was strongly felt throughout this period, so much so that its eventual rejection in favour of different narrative methods became one of the main distinguishing marks of modernism in British fiction. As we have seen, Woolf's separation of the Edwardians, and Georgians was justified by the need to move beyond a fiction based on documentary realism, and she observes that two of the writers she wishes to claim as Georgians – Forster and Lawrence – only qualify because they have put aside that part of their early work that involved a 'compromise' with the materialism of the Edwardians.[71] Joyce is not included in this particular judgment but he could well have been. The irony with which Stephen Dedalus's Flaubertian definition of the artist is treated in *A Portrait* takes its affectionate tone from Joyce's acknowledgment of how important naturalism had been to him when writing *Dubliners* and *Stephen Hero*. Elsewhere, the influence of naturalism is observable in Gissing and Hardy; Kipling's Indian and soldier stories; a number of short-story writers of the 1890s like Frederick Wedmore, Hubert Crackanthorpe and Cunninghame Graham; Eden Phillpotts's early Dartmoor novels; the slum fiction associated with Arthur Morrison's *Tales of Mean Streets* (1894) and *A Child of the Jago* (1896) and Somerset Maugham's *Liza of Lambeth*; later novels of Maugham's, *Mrs Craddock* (1902) and *Of Human Bondage* (1915), and closely related *Bildungsromane* such as Compton Mackenzie's *Sinister Street* (1913) and J. D. Beresford's *Jacob Stahl* trilogy (1911–15). It enters Scottish fiction through Stevenson's later work, notably *The Beach of Falesá* (1893) and *The Ebb Tide* (1894), and provided the literary inspiration for George Douglas Brown to blast the complacency of the 'Kailyarders' in *The House with the Green Shutters* (1901). Not that the Kailyard novelists were always sentimental: the tone of *Auld Licht Idylls* (1888) occasionally suggests that J. M. Barrie, one of Brown's targets, was not entirely unfamiliar with French naturalism. Apart from Moore the most enthusiastic convert was Bennett whose serious work, in spite of a markedly English vein of irony, was always to recall naturalistic models, though in the manner of Balzac and the Goncourts rather than Maupassant and Zola. Like James,

Bennett stood for a new kind of 'artistic interest in form and treatment', for a passionate commitment to 'the *science* of construction', but unlike James he retained in his mind French ideals of fictional form that he was never to move completely beyond.[72] The carefully plotted phases of life, detailed descriptions of environments and physical states, distanced narrative tone, and the conditioning effects of family life in Bennett's fiction proclaim an inescapable debt to France. It was qualities such as these that fuelled Woolf's charge against Bennett of insensitive materialism and helped justify Lawrence's telling dismissal of him as 'an old imitator'.[73]

What interest there was in Zola's theory of the novel soon disappeared. In 1887 the news that five young French disciples of Zola had published a manifesto in *Le Figaro* disowning the Master's latest novel, and naturalism along with it, was greeted with some relief in both France and Britain. By 1899 the influential British critic Arthur Symons was describing the naturalistic tradition as dead and finished: revolt was still the order of the day and France remained the land of artistic inspiration, but the new creed was symbolism, 'an attempt to spiritualise literature, to evade the old bondage of rhetoric, the bondage of exteriority. Description is banished that beautiful things may be evoked, magically.'[74] Most of the new writers whose work Symons praised were poets: the only novelist to be included was Huysmans, whose name was frequently invoked as someone who had rebelled successfully against the limitations of naturalism and whose *A Rebours* (1884) became a cult novel for the aesthetes; it was reputed to be the book with which Lord Henry Wotton captivates Dorian Gray's imagination. The most striking indications in Britain that realism was being tempered, if not superseded, by symbolism were to be found in Conrad and James. They provide justification enough for Symons's claim that it was here the future path of fiction lay, though his cavalier dismissal of materialism, description and rhetoric was quite a bit premature. Zola was scornfully dismissed by Symons as having 'tried to build in brick and mortar inside the covers of a book'.[75] Four years later in a characteristically regal summing up of Zola's life and work, Henry James used the same terminology: 'The pyramid had been planned and the site staked out, but the young builder stood there in his sturdy strength, with no equipment save his two hands and, as we may say, his wheelbarrow and his trowel.'[76] Coming at a time when the novel was having claimed for it a new kind of high seriousness, the description of Zola as a bricklayer was a calculated snub, to be added to the other common insults that he was a mere journalist, a reporter without imagination, a materialist, a pessimist, and a peddler of filth. Zola, of course, regarded himself as a surgeon.

It has always been easy to point out the weaknesses in Zola's naturalistic theory, to demonstrate that even his own novels do not conform with it, and to mock the pretentiousness of his scientific analogies. The five French novelists who denounced *La Terre* in *Le Figaro* could sneer confidently at 'the ridiculousness of that so-called *Natural and Social History of a Family under the Second Empire*, the tenuous nature of the thread of heredity, the child-ishness of the famous genealogical tree, and the profound ignorance of the Master in things medical and scientific'.[77] The trouble with such judgments is that it is almost impossible to recognise in them the author of novels as important as *L'Assommoir*, *Germinal*, and *Nana*. No doubt Zola was ill-advised to advance such a comprehensive theory: the novels were, and still are, powerful enough to speak for themselves. The theory – even if as misguided as critics of Zola usually find it to be – does not lessen the impact of the novels. It could have been dismissed as an aberration of a major, if shocking, author, but that was not the line usually taken, and it seems likely that the theory was often seized upon as a means of dissipating the threat posed by the novels. Much of the argument advanced by Zola would have been familiar to informed readers in the 1880s, especially the need for literature to keep in touch with scientific developments:

> The experimental novel is a result of the scientific evolution
> of the age . . . it is the literature of our scientific age, just as
> classic and romantic literature corresponded to an age of
> scholasticism and theology.[78]

True to evolutionary theory, the experimental novel can represent only one stage of a much grander design to be completed by science:

> We shall enter into an age where all-powerful man will have
> mastered nature and will use its laws to make the greatest
> possible sum of justice and liberty reign on this earth. There
> is no goal more noble, more elevated, more grandiose. That
> is the role of intelligence: to penetrate the why of things in

order to become superior to things and reduce them to a
state of obedient mechanisms.[79]

Such claims were not outrageously new. There had been many earlier attempts to try to explain both literature and morality in scientific terms, the most comprehensive of which was Comtean Positivism: it had made a considerable impact on mid-Victorian writers, and although its power was waning by the 1880s it still carried respect in Humanist circles. The deterministic theories of Hippolyte Taine, whose *Histoire de la littérature anglaise* (1863) was translated into English in 1871, were also widely known in Britain, and it was not unusual for natural scientists like T. H. Huxley to talk in similar terms:

> The whole of modern thought is steeped in science: it has
> made its way into the works of the best poets, and even the
> mere man of letters, who affects to ignore and despise
> science, is unconsciously impregnated with her spirit and
> indebted for his best products to her methods. I believe that
> the greatest intellectual revolution mankind has yet seen is
> now taking place by her agency. She is teaching the world
> that the ultimate court of appeal is observation and experi-
> ment, and not authority; she is teaching it to estimate the
> value of evidence; she is creating a firm and living faith in
> the existence of immutable moral and physical laws, perfect
> obedience to which is the highest possible aim of an intelligent
> being.[80]

Faith in a 'perfect obedience' to 'immutable moral and physical laws' was not to survive the First World War, and indeed was to be challenged by major writers and artists long before then, but the optimistic trust in science was a dominant strand of late nineteenth-century thought. In one sense it was an extension of the mid-Victorian concept of progress, though now splintered into a dozen different areas of thought and research. It was democratic in that it rejected arbitrary 'authority' in favour of 'observation and experiment', and at this level lay behind the development of empirical sociology. It was anti-religion in that it dispensed with supernatural explanations of existence and gave, ironically, a new 'creed' or 'faith' to late Victorian humanists. Zola shared both of these aims: he had brought working-class life into fiction more successfully than any other novelist of the nineteenth century, and he set his own art against that of 'idealist novelists' who 'leave

observation and experiment to base their works on the supernatural
and irrational'.[81] His insistence on the determining effects of
environment would not have been thought excessive by almost any
Socialist of the period nor by many Liberal politicians: among
writers his environmentalism becomes pallid when set against that
of William Morris in *News from Nowhere*, H. G. Wells in
Anticipations or Bernard Shaw in *Major Barbara*; while the
'scientific' nature of his claims is humble in comparison with those
made by Engels in *Socialism: Utopian and Scientific* (1892). From
the publication of the *Origin of Species* to the early years of the
present century, the adjective 'scientific' was liable to be attached
to almost any reasonably coherent creed, discipline, or body of
knowledge, and employed with equal confidence whether the
speaker was for or against science: this situation only changed as
scientific research became increasingly specialised, and as biology
gave up its central position in the natural sciences to physics. If
Zola was cavalier in his use of scientific terminology, so were most
thinkers and writers of the time.

Zola's interest in heredity was often regarded more distrustfully
than his environmentalism, though here again he was not out of
touch with central concerns of the age. Towards the close of the
century Lombroso's theory of identifiable criminal types enjoyed a
considerable vogue and is apparent in such novels as Arthur
Morrison's *A Child of the Jago* and Conrad's *The Secret Agent*:
there was also a growing interest in eugenics which was given a
popular dimension in imaginative literature by Wells and Shaw. Of
more lasting importance for fiction was the systematic study of
psychology which developed throughout this period and was
directly related to the new kind of emphasis placed by novelists on
the minute analysis of individual and collective states of mind.
'Novel writing as an art cannot go backward,' Hardy wrote in 1886;
'Having reached the analytic stage it must transcend it by
going still further in the same direction.'[82] One literary sign of this
analytical interest was the entry into fiction of the doctor who is
concerned more with the mind than the body. 'Are you an alienist?'
Marlow asks the doctor who examines him to see if he is fit enough
to descend into the heart of darkness. He is told: 'Every doctor
should be – a little.'[83] Marlow's doctor, like the doctor whose
unorthodox views so impress Jude and Sue in *Jude the Obscure*, is
obviously 'an advanced man'.[84] It was to be some years before the

'alienist' would make way for the psychoanalyst in British fiction, and the process by which this change took place provides a striking illustration of both the vagueness of scientific terminology at the time and the curiously indirect ways that new ideas can sometimes be introduced into literature.

The first of Freud's major works to be translated into English was the *Three Essays on the Theory of Sexuality*. It was translated by Freud's American disciple A. A. Brill and published in 1910 in America by the Journal of Nervous and Mental Diseases Publishing Company. The first translations to appear in Britain were also by Brill, *The Interpretation of Dreams* in 1913 and *The Psychopathology of Everyday Life* in 1914: in Britain, as in America, they were advertised as being primarily of interest to the medical profession. In 1914 there was also published in Britain M. D. Eder's translation *On Dreams* which, true to the spirit of intense rivalry between Freud's various foreign disciples, announced itself as the 'only authorised English translation'. There were a few 'alienists' or specialists in mental diseases, and sexologists like Havelock Ellis, who knew of Freud's work much earlier, but a general awareness of Freud and Freudianism only developed in Britain in the few years before the First World War: the *New Age*, for example, which was influential in the spread of interest in psychoanalysis, began paying attention to Freud in 1912.[85] In the following year a London branch of the International Psycho-Analytical Association was formed, with Eder and Ernest Jones as founder members; and the translations by Brill and Eder opened the subject to a wider audience. Typical of the excitement these translations aroused was the response of Leonard Woolf: 'I am, I think not unreasonably, rather proud of having in 1914 recognised and understood the greatness of Freud and the importance of what he was doing.'[86] That Woolf was not over-exaggerating the sudden impact of Freud at this date is given convincing support by the experience of one of Britain's most respected psychologists, William McDougall. His *Introduction to Social Psychology* (1908) established itself immediately as a standard textbook. It was reprinted in revised editions year after year, sometimes running through more than one impression in a single year. But although McDougall prided himself on his knowledge of European developments in psychology, he did not know of Freud's work when his book was first published in 1908, and it was not until the book's eighth edition in 1914 that this omission was rectified by the addition of an appendix on 'The Sex Instinct'. In earlier editions, McDougall had regarded sexuality as primarily an 'instinct of reproduction' and had related it to parental instincts which 'in all (save debased) natures' are 'in some degree of tender emotion'. He also noted that the sexual instinct tended to direct the 'immense energy of its impulse' to the 'sentiments . . . while its specific character remains submerged and unconscious'. On this particular aspect he felt it was unnecessary to dwell, 'since it has been dealt with exhaustively in many thousands of novels'.[87] By 1914 he realised his earlier views were being superseded:

> Freud proposes to extend very greatly the sphere commonly
> attributed to sexuality in human life, assigning a sexual root
> to mental and nervous disorders of almost every kind, as well
> as to all dreams and to other processes of normal mental life
> that have no obvious connection with sex.[88]

The honesty and edginess of McDougall's discussion of Freudianism marked him down as a partial convert, sufficiently so for Eder and Jones to ask him to join them in the International Psycho-Analytical Association. He declined the invitation.

That a man like McDougall could have been taken so unawares by Freudianism at such a late date tends to confirm the general atmosphere of ignorance in Britain until about 1912, but, as far as fiction is concerned that is somewhat less than half the story. In a rather special sense, it can be argued that great writers of the past had long understood the essential message of Freudianism without the benefit of Freudian terminology: Freud himself recognised the justice of this argument and was always generous in his acknowledgment of the help given by imaginative literature in the formulation of his ideas. More specifically, Freud's own investigations were part of the re-orientation of 'scientific' enquiry taking place in every area of this post-Darwinian world: they were one further manifestation of the late nineteenth-century conviction that rational and physiological explanations of human behaviour were proving totally inadequate.[89] In a passage of *The Way of All Flesh* that was probably written around 1880 Butler drew attention to just this kind of change: 'I fancy that there is some truth in the view which is being put forward nowadays, that it is our less conscious thoughts and our less conscious actions which mainly mould our own lives and the lives of those who spring from us.'[90]

Some fifteen years later, Gustave Le Bon was accepting as axiomatic that 'the part played by the unconscious in all our acts is immense, and that played by reason very small'.[91] Le Bon was interested primarily in collective expressions of that unconscious life: other psychologists focused on the working of the individual consciousness. As far as the future of fiction was concerned, nobody was indirectly more influential in this endeavour than William James, who in 1890, searching for a metaphor to describe how consciousness functions, discarded the too mechanical-sounding 'chain' and 'train' in favour of 'river' or 'stream': 'In talking of it hereafter, let us call it the stream of thought, of consciousness, or of subjective life.'[92] Twenty-eight years later, May Sinclair applied the term 'stream of consciousness' to the work of Dorothy Richardson, thus categorising a type of subjective modernist fiction.[93] It was yet another psychologist, Graham Wallas, who in 1910 indicated (with the aid of recent technology) one of the major ways in which the modernist novel was eventually to draw most successfully on the findings of psychology:

> If . . . a man were followed through one ordinary day,
> without his knowing it, by a cinematographic camera and a
> phonograph, and if all his acts and sayings were reproduced
> before him next day, he would be astonished to find how few
> of them were the result of a deliberate search for the means
> of attaining ends.[94]

Although psychologists and film directors – both of whom had learnt much from fiction – seemed in certain crucial respects technically in advance of British novelists in the early years of this century, it was a branch of popular fiction that created the missing link between the alienist and the psychoanalyst. This was the 'psychic doctor' who was introduced by Sheridan Le Fanu in his story 'Green Tea' (1869) and taken up by many later writers on the supernatural.[95] The real-life psychic doctors were the members of the Society for Psychical Research which was founded in 1882. Their investigations into what they called 'the mass of obscure phenomena commonly known as Spiritualistic' were undertaken not because they believed in such phenomena, but in order to discover a 'scientific' explanation of them.[96] Frederick W. H. Myers, one of the founder-members of the SPR, coined the term 'subliminal' to define the powerful forces at work 'beneath the threshold' of consciousness. He also published the first sustained

discussion in Britain of the experimental work being carried out by
Breuer and Freud into the treatment of hysteria. These experiments,
Myers announced enthusiastically in 1893, gave 'emphatic support' to
his own theories which had been reached by 'mere analogical
reasoning'. He proceeded: 'That extraordinary potency of subliminal
action, which [Breuer and Freud] frankly present as insoluble by pure
physiology, is part and parcel of my scheme of man.'[97] Myers was not
being fanciful in claiming this kind of kinship with Freud. Ironically,
it was the eventual triumph of Freudianism that sealed the public
image of the Society for Psychical Research as a gathering of cranks,
but in the 1890s this view was by no means appropriate. Myers's
excitement when he read of Freud's treatment of now legendary
patients like Miss Lucy R. and Fraulein Anna O. was perfectly
understandable: the files of the SPR were crammed with similarly
detailed case studies. Nor was there any lack of professional
recognition for Myers's importance, either in his own right or as a
populariser of Freud. Ernest Jones praised Myers for making
accessible to English readers the 'first discoveries of what later became
psycho-analysis . . . within six months of their being announced'.[98]
There can be no doubt that among those readers there would have
been a number of British novelists. William James was a close friend
and great admirer of Myers: he was also an active supporter of the
SPR and served as its president in 1894.[99] In 1911 Freud himself
became an honorary member of the Society for Psychical Research.

Although Freudianism would eventually provide a focal point for
public indignation in much the same way as Zola's novels had done
in the 1880s, that was still some time in the future. As the furore
over Zola began to fade away, moral outrage turned its attention to
Ibsen, with the first performances in London of *A Doll's House* and
The Pillars of Society in 1889, and *Rosmersholm*, *Ghosts* and *Hedda
Gabler* in 1891. The lessons Ibsen's plays offered were similar to
those already being assimilated from the French realists, notably
tautness of structure, authorial objectivity, and (following Flaubert's
example in *Madame Bovary*) the subdued poetry of mundane,
everyday speech. Most of all Ibsen demonstrated, by the blending
of realism and symbolism, a way out of Zolaesque documentary
squalor, and he did so without retreating from the major moral and
social issues raised by contemporary life. This was something that
the young Joyce particularly admired:

> But the naked drama – either the perception of a great truth,
> or the opening up of a great question, or a great conflict
> which is almost independent of the conflicting actors, and has
> been and is of far-reaching importance – this is what primarily
> rivets our attention.[100]

It was precisely the issue of how 'great' or 'true' were the questions raised by Ibsen that brought his plays such virulent abuse and made it inevitable that more attention would be paid to his social message than to his art.

To his critics Ibsen was the man who had encouraged married women to desert their husbands and children, portrayed middle-class family life as riddled not only with hypocrisy but with venereal disease as well, and whose plays, it was claimed, were being promoted by a 'claque' made up of 'the socialistic and the sexless'.[101] To his admirers he was a great moralist, stripping away the repressive conventions of life in the cause of individual freedom: that his individualism encompassed women as much as men ensured, in the early 1890s, that the participants in the debate would confront each other with particular ferocity, as they also did, for similar reasons, over Hardy's last novels. Not only was Ibsen frequently described as a spokesman for women's rights (which he wasn't) he was also frequently accused of being a Socialist, when, as far as his own political views were concerned, he was probably not even a democrat.[102] As in the case of Zola, the intensity of the press attacks on Ibsen soon faded away and were replaced by semi-official recognition. In 1897, as part of the Jubilee celebrations, Queen Victoria and the Archbishop of Canterbury attended a performance of *Ghosts*, though the play was still not technically licensed. The event produced, as Shaw pointed out, a bizarre contrast: 'The Jubilee represents the nineteenth century proud of itself. *Ghosts* represents it loathing itself.'[103]

It is not easy to explain why Ibsen's plays should have provoked as much outrage and shock as the translations of Zola's novels. The sensational aspects of Ibsen were rarely lurid or overwhelmingly physical as they could be in Zola, and mingled with the abuse were repeated complaints that Ibsen was boring. That the setting of the plays, and therefore the target of the social criticism, was inescapably middle-class counted for much. As James said, in-imitably: 'His people are of inexpensive race: they give us essentially the *bourgeois* impression.'[104] There was also, in the response to Ibsen, a far greater degree of polarisation, typified by the theatrical confrontation between Queen Victoria and Mrs Alving, than there had been with Zola. Of course, Zola's supporters were embattled and committed, and they were often the same people who were to speak publicly for Ibsen, but the issues at stake seemed more serious: the iconography of prophet and acolytes that soon became widely applied to Ibsen was rather special. To be dubbed or to call oneself an Ibsenite in 1890 was like adopting the label of Wagnerite ten years earlier when 'the Master's' works were all being performed in London. To speak for Zola meant approving a greater degree of frankness in literature without anything else being necessarily involved, and it very soon became just as fashionable to denounce the nature of that frankness. But to speak for Wagner or Ibsen meant allying oneself with the 'new', a popular word of the 1890s that was for a while synonymous with 'modern' and was quickly to be superseded by it. If there was not exactly a definable creed or party programme attached to being an Ibsenite, there was something very like it, and both sides were agreed on what was at stake: often tone or emphasis was the only discernible difference between the statements of the pro-Ibsenites and the anti-Ibsenites. When the *Saturday Review* described *Hedda Gabler* sarcastically as the 'latest golden calf of the Freethinking community', it was saying much the same as Edmund Gosse – a great admirer of Ibsen and the critic who had introduced Ibsen's name to British readers as early as 1872 – when he described the plays as 'inspired by an intensely modern spirit, all rigorously divested of everything ideal, lyrical, or conventional, whether in form or in spirit'.[105] It is characteristic that this praise of 'the modern spirit' should be expressed in what at any earlier time would have been considered bleakly negative terms: even so, Gosse's approval of Ibsen's lack of ideals strikes an odd note. It was not, however, a usage peculiar to Gosse. During the final two decades of the century it was widespread and became associated with Nietzsche, though he does not seem to have been the source: nor was Zola who, as we have seen, described 'idealist novelists' as concerned with 'the supernatural and irrational' in comparison with the clear-eyed observation of the realists. In 1887 Matthew Arnold quoted Sainte-Beuve on Flaubert in terms almost identical to those of Gosse on Ibsen: 'The ideal has ceased, the lyric vein is dried up; the new men are cured of lyricism and the ideal; "a severe and pitiless truth has made its entry, as the last word of experience, even into art itself".'[106] The meaning of the change was made clear by Shaw who placed it at the centre of *The Quintessence of Ibsenism* (1891). Shaw acknowledged that he was using the words 'ideals' and 'idealist' in a way that might be unfamiliar to his readers, and explained that an idealist is someone who supports outworn conventions: his opponent is the realist who exposes the falsity of middle-class idealism.[107] Shaw's argument was, as usual, moving in more than one direction, but revealingly so in this instance. No doubt he was logically correct to see Nora leaving Helmer as enhancing the movement for women's rights, but Ibsen's play gives greater support to Shaw's inverted interpretation of idealism. When Nora leaves Helmer she has no idea what she will do or what will become of her. She has become a 'realist', driven to it by the 'idealism' of her husband.

As part of this kind of linguistic change, adjectives like 'realistic' and 'analytical' began to be used by supporters and opponents of modern literature in contradictory ways. To describe a work of literature as 'realistic' or 'analytical' constituted praise if the speaker approved the destruction of older forms of idealism, and abuse if he didn't. Like Zola, Ibsen was frequently described as a surgeon dissecting modern life, and the force of the metaphor lay at exactly the point where it broke down. The ruthless analysis would invariably expose a terrible disease, but it seemed incapable of recommending the operation that could bring the patient back to health. 'The modern spirit is vivisective,' announces Stephen Dedalus in *Stephen Hero*, 'vivisection itself is the most modern process one can conceive'.[108] The conviction that all moral and societal values were being swept away often led to novelists accepting negativism as the only attitude possible to someone in their situation at that particular moment in time, though the longing for some kind of positive answer to the problem is hardly less apparent in their work. James and Conrad are classic examples of such novelists, and so is Hardy. In *Jude the Obscure* he explained why positivism had been rendered impossible, separating himself from Jude to do so:

> [Jude] perceived that at best only copying, patching and
> imitating went on here; which he fancied to be owing to
> some temporary and local cause. He did not at that time see
> that mediaevalism was as dead as a fern leaf in a lump of

coal; that other developments were shaping in the world
around him, in which Gothic architecture and its associations
had no place. The deadly animosity of contemporary logic
and vision towards so much of what he held in reverence was
not yet revealed.[109]

Jude recognises that Gothic restoration provides the main work of
the yard, and puts this down to a local cause. What Hardy is
pointing out is that the Victorian concern with medieval ornamenta-
tion represents a blindness to modern forces, a refusal or inability
to confront a totally different world that is emerging. The striking
sentence 'He did not at that time see that mediaevalism was as dead
as a fern leaf in a lump of coal' expresses this blindness perfectly
by enforcing a contrast between two dominant, inter-related
Victorian concerns – medievalism (the spiritually complete world
now irretrievably lost) and evolution (the terrifying alternative of a
Godless future). Jude, at this point in his life, is still trying to hold
on to values which have already been destroyed by the 'deadly
animosity of contemporary logic and vision'.

Jude's tragedy comes from his unawareness of this fact. It is his
'form of the modern vice of unrest', as, at a lesser degree of
consciousness, it is Tess's tragedy to feel, but to be unable to
conceptualise, those 'feelings which might almost have been called
those of the age – the ache of modernism'.[110] To be modern is to
experience lost positives and to have no idea what can possibly
replace them. But beyond this, there is the imperative need to face
the loss, otherwise the final result is too distressing to contemplate:
'You behold in me, Stephen said with grim displeasure, a horrible
example of free thought.'[111] For the opponents of writers like
Hardy, Ibsen, Zola and James, only the negativism mattered: the
'deadly animosity' of the logic that had created it meant next to
nothing. The classic example of such criticism is Max Nordau's
Degeneration (1895) which enjoyed a considerable vogue in Britain
and America when it was translated from its original German.
Taking inspiration from his fellow alienist Lombroso, Nordau
claimed that virtually every modern novelist, composer, painter, or
dramatist worth mentioning could be shown to be suffering from
degeneracy or hysteria. Nordau's views, then as now, have
understandably not been taken seriously. Shaw claimed that he
could 'prove Nordau to be an elephant on more evidence than he
has brought to prove that our greatest men are degenerate lunatics',

and no doubt could have done just that.[112] Yet Nordau's wild denunciations, which usually display more 'emotionalism' than he was able to find in modern art, did contain moments of genuine insight. He warned repeatedly of the folly of believing that artistic change is somehow the same thing as social reform, and while his alienist terminology was crazily misguided, he was as aware as Stephen Dedalus that much modern thought and art was bleakly negative. The 'degenerate', he noted, 'is tormented by doubts, seeks for the basis of all phenomena, especially those whose first causes are completely inaccessible to us, and is unhappy when his enquiries and ruminations lead, as is natural, to no result'.[113] The fullest reply to Nordau came from A. E. Hake whose argument could have done little to change Nordau's mind. Hake described the 'moral state of the civilised world' as like 'a nation preparing for revolt against a tyrant', with 'gloomy, discontented and excited men . . . encouraging one another with secret signs and pass-words, mustering and drilling in secret places', and all preparing for 'a higher philosophy, nobler arts, a loftier literature, sounder principles of legislation, a purer religion'.[114] In place of Nordau's degenerate, Hake presented the modern artist as a cultural terrorist.

Considering the ferocity of the response to Zola and Ibsen it is strange that English translations of the Russian novelists provoked little opposition. Dostoevsky's *Crime and Punishment* was included in Vizetelly's 1887 list (together with *The Idiot* and several of the shorter works) and was proudly advertised as 'A Russian Realistic Novel', but it escaped the charge of being an 'obscene libel' that was levelled at works by Zola, Flaubert, Maupassant, Bourget and other French novelists. This unexpected liberality on the part of the moral protesters tends to confirm that it was France, rather than simply her fiction, that was regarded as the great moral danger to British purity. It is also relevant that the most widely known Russian novelist in Britain before the 1880s was Turgenev. His *Sportsman's Sketches* had been published in an English translation as early as 1855 and several of his novels from the late 1860s onwards. Praised highly for the formal perfection of his work, he tended to be treated in this respect as an honorary Frenchman, though without the unpleasantness usually associated with that label. Not only was the subject matter of Turgenev's fiction not sordid, it was informatively Russian, and Royal

Gettmann has noted that in the 1870s and early 1880s Turgenev's novels were often valued for what they revealed about political conditions in Russia.[115] Similar factors were apparent in the early reception of Tolstoy. He was even given the distinction of an approving article by Matthew Arnold who rarely wrote about fiction, British or foreign. Arnold found *Anna Karenina* to be 'all palpitating with modernity', but morally superior to French fiction which was no longer attractive to 'the cultivated classes'.[116] There is often observable in late Victorian book-reviewing a sense of relief when French licentiousness was found not to be passing like a disease to novelists of other countries. In these circumstances 'realism' itself became more acceptable, and Tolstoy's and Dostoevsky's reputations benefited from the attitude. In 1886 the *Spectator* pronounced that *Crime and Punishment* was not 'Zolaesque', and in the following year the same periodical assured its readers that while Tolstoy was a realist, he was 'not realistic with the repulsive realism of the modern French school'.[117]

It was not only conservative periodicals, however, that took this kind of welcoming approach to the Russian novelists. In Britain, as we have seen, novelists were generally admiring of the greater frankness and artistry of French fiction but at the same time unwilling to commit themselves fully to discipleship. For some novelists Ibsen provided an alternative model: for others a similar liberating function was served by Tolstoy and Dostoevsky. The great fluidity of Russian realism was closer to the mid-Victorians than the tight narrative frames of the French, but it escaped the taint of Victorianism by virtue of its moral daring, modernity of theme, and startling psychological insights. The way that late Victorian novelists tended to line up in favour of either the French or Russians was well observed by Stevenson:

> Raskolnikoff is easily the greatest book I have read in ten
> years; I am glad you took to it. Many find it dull: Henry
> James could not finish it: all I can say is, it nearly finished
> me. It was like having an illness. James did not care for it
> because the character of Raskolnikoff was not objective; and
> at that I divined a great gulf between us, and, on further
> reflection, the existence of a certain impotence in many
> minds of to-day, which prevents them from living *in* a book or
> a character, and keeps them standing afar off, spectators of a
> puppet show.[118]

Another reason why it was some time before the full impact of Dostoevsky came to be felt on British fiction was that relatively few of his works (unlike those of Zola and Tolstoy) were available in English translation. Stevenson read Dostoevsky in French, as did Gissing, another early admirer, while Arnold, giving a touch of cultural snobbery to the act, read Tolstoy's *Anna Karenina* in French even though a perfectly acceptable English translation was readily available, because, 'as I long ago said, work of this kind is better done in France than in England'.[119] As late as 1910 Galsworthy was telling Edward Garnett that Maurice Baring's *Landmarks in Russian Literature* had made him 'desire to read Dostoevsky's *The Idiot* and *The Brothers Karamazov* and *The Possessed*, but *what translations are there*?'[120] There were none available at that moment except for *Crime and Punishment* which was by far the best-known of Dostoevsky's novels, though the situation changed almost at once with translations of the other major novels appearing in various editions, including Dent's recently established Everyman's Library. In 1912 Constance Garnett's translation of *The Brothers Karamazov* was published, the first of a twelve-volume edition of Dostoevsky. Chekhov's short stories began attracting attention in 1903 with R. E. C. Long's translation *Black Monk and other Stories*, to be followed by the same translator's *The Kiss and other Stories* (1908), but Chekhov only became truly established for English readers with the publication of Constance Garnett's *The Tales of Chekhov* (13 vols, 1916–22).

It can be seen that there were two main phases of foreign influence on British novelists during this period. In the 1880s and 1890s the scene was dominated by French realism, naturalism, and to a lesser extent symbolism, by Ibsen and the Russian novelists, notably Turgenev and Tolstoy. Then in the few years immediately preceding the First World War there was a further astonishing influx of ideas and artistic inspiration from Europe. However, unlike the earlier period, there was not a prominent emphasis on European fiction. Much of the experimental excitement focused on other forms of art – on Post-Impressionist and Cubist painting; the Russian ballet; Strauss, Debussy, and Stravinsky; French symbolist poetry; Marinetti and the Futurists. British novelists were influenced by these new styles and movements in a variety of ways, but immediately they experienced just as great an impact from the delayed arrival in Britain of the work of a slightly older generation of writers, philosophers, and dramatists. Dostoevsky and Freud have already been mentioned. More surprising in some respects was the case of Strindberg, who might have been expected to follow Ibsen onto the London stage in the early 1890s. But *The Father*, written in 1887, was not translated into English until 1899, while *Miss Julie* (1888) had to wait for translation until 1912. Then, as with Chekhov, Dostoevsky and Freud, there was a rush of enthusiasm and translations.[121] Henri Bergson's theory of time and consciousness which was to be so influential on the modernist movement had been published in France as long ago as 1889. It waited until 1910 before being translated into English as *Time and Free Will*: further translations of Bergson's work followed immediately.[122] The case of Nietzsche, a translation of whose complete works was published in eighteen volumes, 1909–1913, is slightly different. His name, notoriety, and to some extent his ideas, had been known much earlier. He had featured in Max Nordau's gallery of degenerates as the theorist of 'ego-mania'; 'From the first to the last page of Nietzsche's writings the careful reader seems to hear a madman, with flashing eyes, wild gestures, and foaming mouth, spouting forth deafening bombast.'[123] In the same year, 1895, *The Case of Wagner*, the first of Nietzsche's works to be translated into English, appeared in the *Fortnightly Review*. *Thus Spake Zarathustra* was translated in 1896 and *A Genealogy of Morals* in 1899.

David Thatcher has suggested that Nordau's hysterical treatment of Nietzsche 'effectively short-circuited any chance the English reader might have had of looking at Nietzsche with unprejudiced eyes', but that seems an exaggeration.[124] Nordau was prejudiced against all modern writers of any value and this had little effect on the reputations of, say, Ibsen or Tolstoy: and, as Thatcher goes on to point out, at this time Nietzsche tended to be placed together with writers like Ibsen as one of the destructive analysts of nineteenth-century social stasis.[125] Havelock Ellis's inconoclastic view of Nietzsche as 'above all a freethinker, emancipated from every law save that of sincerity', is representative of the anti-Nordau camp, though even Ellis, who was exceptionally open to new ideas, held back from approving the 'extravagant, almost reckless' morality that emerged 'post-Zarathustra'.[126] Nietzsche's reputation was similar to that of Carlyle – a fairly common comparison of the time and one that Nietzsche himself disowned – in that it was possible to admire the insight and be disgusted by

some of the conclusions at one and the same time. Few British
writers in the 1880s and 1890s needed Nietzsche to inform them
that God was dead – Butler had been one of the pall-bearers at the
funeral organised by Darwin some years earlier – and there were
other writers to hand who, like Nietzsche, were courageous enough
to spell out what exactly was involved in accepting that the world
would, in future, be God-less. It is not easy to imagine anyone
being more fiercely to the point on this issue than Winwood Reade
in *The Martyrdom of Man* (1872):

> The following facts result from our investigations – Super-
> natural Christianity is false. God-worship is idolatry. Prayer
> is useless. The soul is not immortal. There are no rewards
> and there are no punishments in a future state . . . I undertake
> to show that the destruction of Christianity is essential to the
> interests of civilisation; and also that man will never attain
> his full powers as a moral being until he has ceased to believe
> in a personal God and in the immortality of the soul.[127]

The Martyrdom of Man was widely read in the late Victorian
period. It was frequently reprinted, and became an indispensable
text for Humanists. In comparison, *Thus Spake Zarathustra* was of
minority interest. Both Reade and Nietzsche called for the
elimination of Christianity as the first crucial step to a new world,
but while Reade painted a vision of the future that was rather like
an ideal Christian community, Nietzsche called for a completely
different scale of moral and ethical values. This was the freethinking
'sincerity' that Ellis admired. Some of the political implications of
Nietzsche's views were taken up by Shaw and Wells; references to
the *Ubermensch*, 'Superman', or 'blond beast', occur with some
frequency from the mid-1890s; and there were real enthusiasts, like
John Davidson. But it was only with the rise of the *New Age* under
the editorship of Orage, and the call for a new aristocracy to lead
the way out of supposed democratic stagnation, that Nietzsche
gained a firm intellectual following in Britain.[128] Even then there
were writers warning that this flirtation with a new élite might not
have quite the beneficial results the Nietzscheans expected. In 1909
Edward Thomas noted:

> Unless we of the middle classes take him into our tender
> bosoms and charming parlours and stifle him there, it will
> perhaps be not with the aristocracy so-called which is dead or

dying but with the brutal unspoilt multitude that his hope of
life or resurrection will lie.[129]

Thomas was right that this kind of political faith would prove only
temporary, though Nietzsche was not stifled by comfortable middle-
class bosoms. When interest in his thought began to revive a few years
later it was to place him as part of the new concern with irrationality
associated with writers like Dostoevsky, Strindberg and Freud.

As young British novelists looked increasingly to Europe for
inspiration the reputation of mid-Victorian fiction slumped. It
stood accused, as the Victorians did generally, of philistinism,
insincerity, hypocrisy and smugness: it made up a good part of that
'clipped and limited literature' that, according to Wells's Remington, had satisfied Victorian souls. In 1899, jotting down an idea
for a book to be called *Our Novelists*, Bennett decided, in all
seriousness, that he would have to clear the ground before writing
on the influence of Turgenev and the importance of George Moore
and Eden Philpotts: 'There would be chapters on "conscious
pleasure in technique", which was apparently unknown to the earlier
generation; illiteracy among our leading writers; the real position of
Dickens, Thackeray, George Eliot and others whom everyone has
(ridiculously) agreed are above criticism.'[130] Once Bennett's
generation had finished with them they would be considered
beneath criticism, as *Punch*, seizing the changing mood, realised:

> I cannot read the old books!
>   They always bore me so.
> I *never* read the old books,
>   They are so dull and slow.
> DICKENS and SCOTT are awful rot
>   LYTTON's pure fiddlededee.
> I cannot read the old books
>   They give the hump to me.[131]

Perhaps Gissing best expresses the changing attitude to mid-
Victorian fiction, if only because he acknowledged the regret he felt
at having to jettison many aspects of the books that had meant so
much to him. In the first full-length critical study of Dickens to be
published, Gissing apologised for having to speak of 'the master's
work' in 'disparaging phrase', but: 'So great a change has come
over the theory and practice of fiction in the England of our times

that we must needs treat of Dickens as, in many respects, antiquated.'[132] The history of literary reputations is not quite as neat as that suggests, and the great Victorian novelists were never to be without faithful admirers. But for the next thirty or forty years antiquated Dickens and antiquated Thackeray, Eliot, Gaskell, Trollope and the Brontës were relegated to the schoolroom where they were often read, with unconscious irony, in abbreviated or truncated editions.

The terminology of revolt so widely used to express late Victorian discontent with Victorianism evokes, inevitably, a picture of the younger generation assailing the unyielding, repressive, and largely unified ideology of their elders in the cause of greater freedom. In one sense that is what the late Victorians thought they were doing, though there was no agreement of what function the new freedom was to serve and the two fundamental changes that created the ethos of modernism were not brought about by them at all: they came from the despised Victorians. In the intellectual sphere it was Darwin who had finally made possible the discussion and application of a morality that did not look necessarily to religion for its justification, while in the social and political spheres (where Darwin's influence was also strongly felt) late Victorian attitudes were determined by the decision, taken by parliament in the 1860s, to turn Britain into some kind of democracy.

The 1867 Reform Act did not leap into existence overnight, and Richard Shannon is probably right to warn against regarding the extension of the franchise as a deliberately forward-looking move: 'The 1860s were not consciously straining to make themselves the 1890s. The debate of 1866 and 1867 looked back rather than forward.'[133] Since 1832 there had been several attempts to revive the issue of electoral reform, and in the early 1860s there was certainly a feeling among politicians and pressure groups that they were dealing with unfinished business. But the way in which these crucial democratic changes took place and the lack of agreement on the principles underlying them suggest that hardly anyone involved was quite sure of what he was doing. Even Gladstone, the politician most immediately responsible for initiating the reform, seemed at times to be calling for full manhood suffrage and at others for the vote to be given as a reward to those members of the working class who had proved their social responsibility. When the architects of reform were confident they tended to regard limited electoral reform as strengthening rather than undermining the existing social structure, as Disraeli made clear in a speech at the Merchant Taylors' banquet on 11 June 1867, after the bill had been passed:

> It is said we are on the verge of a great democratic change.
> My lords and gentlemen, believe me the elements of
> democracy do not exist in England (cheers). England is a
> country of classes and the change impending in the country
> will only make those classes more united, more content, more
> complete and more cordial (cheers).[134]

The newness of the situation is observable in Disraeli's political language which already sounds archaic, though the view advanced here was widely shared, and not only by Conservative politicians. If the 'classes' could be controlled, and deference – a key concept in the 1860s – maintained, then 'democracy' would be frustrated: in other words, the extension of the franchise would not change the tone or power structure of Britain. The trouble with this argument was that while a surprising degree of deference did survive and the classes overwhelmingly supported the principle of further democratic change through parliamentary representation, the forces released by the 1867 Reform Act went far beyond anything that could be effectively controlled by parliament. This fear had been voiced by those opponents of reform who had called for either gradual change or no change at all. It was what both Robert Lowe and Matthew Arnold referred to despairingly as rule by 'numbers'; what Gladstone, confident in his role as the people's champion, called admiringly 'masses' rather than 'classes'; and what everyone would eventually call a 'mass society'.[135] The 1860s may not have been 'consciously straining' to become the 1890s, but that is what happened.

Nor was the process, once it had begun, unconscious or backward-looking. From whatever point of view it was possible to regard the 1867 Act, it was immediately clear that such a reform could not stand by itself, as H. J. Hanham notes: 'For the seventeen years after 1867 there was scarcely a break in the catalogue of reforms, even during the Conservative parliament of 1874 to 1880.'[136] Not all of these reforms were electoral, though most of them were in one way or another responses to the demands

posed by the new kind of society created by the extension of the
franchise. They also produced an accumulative effect that accelerated the pace of change, always leading forward to the next
inevitable instalment, with the uncertain principles underlying the
original reform constantly in a state of redefinition. The 1867 Act
itself is a prime example of this. The size of the electorate in
Britain was virtually doubled, with $2\frac{1}{2}$ million men now eligible to
vote: in the accompanying redistribution of seats, some corrupt
boroughs were abolished and a stronger representation given to the
large industrial towns. In 1872 the Ballot Act introduced secret
voting: in 1883 the Corrupt Practices Act restricted the amount of
money that candidates could spend on an election. When the
franchise was again extended in 1884, giving the vote to the
agricultural working class and increasing the size of the electorate to
$5\frac{1}{2}$ million, it was not accompanied by the passionate debate that
had distinguished 1867. In 1885 a Registration Act made further
attacks on corrupt practices, and in the same year a Redistribution
Bill established a more equal division of constituencies together
with an extension of the principle of single-member constituencies.
The extensions of the franchise and the impetus to clean up the
system went hand in hand. By the mid-1880s the principle of one
man one vote had been established, together with the method of
returning a government in Britain that has been followed ever
since.

Also well on the way to being established was the basic structure
of the two-party system, with its opposing political programmes,
election agents, systematic study of constituencies, charismatic
competing leaders pioneered by the verbal duels between Gladstone
and Disraeli, and most important of all the dramatic nation-wide
appeals to 'numbers'.[137] If Disraeli's sudden conversion to electoral
reform shocked political commentators by its apparently blatant
opportunism, they were no less shocked by Gladstone 'stumping'
the country in the 1879 Midlothian campaign, whipping up moral
fervour over the Bulgarian atrocities, counting heads to get the
Liberals back into power.[138] This was exactly the kind of
emotional manipulation that opponents of electoral reform had
feared, except that they had looked to the newly enfranchised
working-class voter as likely to be seduced by radical demagogy.
How wrong they had been is further demonstrated by the peaceful
establishment of the Labour Party and its swift absorption into

the Liberal–Conservative party system. The Independent Labour Party was formed in 1893 and replaced seven years later by the Labour Representation Committee which brought together the various Socialist groups – the trade unions, ILP, Fabians, and Social Democratic Federation. The title Labour Party was only adopted after the 1906 general election when twenty-nine Labour MPs were returned. The more extreme of the socialist groups like the SDF broke away from the main body of the party which gradually consolidated its position within parliament. By 1914 there were forty-two Labour MPs.[139]

The major outstanding electoral reform was the enfranchisement of women. John Stuart Mill had not only argued that women should be included in the 1867 Act, he even suggested that the word 'person' be substituted for 'man' in the definitions of suffrage.[140] He was derided by most of his parliamentary colleagues, but with the principle of manhood suffrage accepted it was inevitable that it would be extended to women: it is only surprising that it was delayed for so long. Throughout the second half of the nineteenth century the anomaly of women not having the vote was challenged in the courts, raised repeatedly in parliament, and perhaps just as effectively, surfaced whenever any other legislation relating primarily to women was debated and whenever individual women achieved any kind of publicity or distinction. But it was not until 1903 with the formation of the Women's Social and Political Union that an effective, nationally co-ordinated campaign for women's suffrage was established.[141] One particularly galling aspect of the anomaly was captured by a *Punch* cartoon in 1905. A 'qualified voter' stands on the steps of a polling station: he is dressed like a navvy, with heavy boots, dirty hands, and from the evidence of his bleary eyes, probably drunk. He is jabbing a finger towards a smartly-dressed, middle-aged woman, and saying to her: 'Ah, you may pay rates an' taxes, an' you may 'ave responserbilities an' all; but when it comes to *votin'*, you must leave it to us men.'[142]

The main point of the cartoon was not one of class or even of injustice to women: it had to do with intelligence. Throughout the parliamentary debates of the mid-1860s a recurrent theme had been the need for the government to be free to take decisions on issues which could only be understood by the intelligent or educated. This had not been the case in 1832 when the qualified voter had been the man who could prove his social responsibility by the possession of minimum property (the £10 householder). Much of the detailed discussion of the 1867 Act was concerned with how far this kind of qualification could be lowered, and various 'fancy franchises' were suggested, including the payment of rates, rent, the amount of savings a man might have accumulated, and education. As long as some kind of property qualification obtained then the individual would have a stake in society, the Disraelian notion of the 'classes' as a hierarchy of property would hold firm, and deference could be left to do the rest. Walter Bagehot, the great constitutional theorist, explained the way that a deferential nation, as compared with a democratic nation, functions:

> It has been thought strange, but there *are* nations in which
> the numerous unwiser part wishes to be ruled by the less
> numerous wiser part. The numerical majority – whether by
> custom or by choice, is immaterial – is ready, is eager to
> delegate its power of choosing its ruler to a certain select
> minority. It abdicates in favour of its *élite*, and consents to
> obey whoever that *élite* may confide in.[143]

This comforting theory was undermined as the Reform Bill lurched through parliament, with the Conservatives and Liberals outbidding each other and slowly whittling away the principle of property ownership. Once the principle, if not the immediate practice, of manhood suffrage had been accepted, as it was in 1867, the vote would go to the working man whether he owned property or not, whether he was educated or not; numbers would rule and political power would go to whoever was capable of swaying the greatest number of individual opinions. The unmarried woman who owned substantial property and was intelligent or educated did not have the vote: nor did a married woman, even when the Married Women's Property Act of 1882 finally allowed her to own property independently of her husband. The drunken and barely literate *Punch* navvy, on the other hand, was a 'qualified' voter. In many respects this kind of contrast recalls Robert Lowe's notorious claim during the reform debates that the bottom of the social structure was typified by 'venality, ignorance, drunkenness and facility for being intimidated'.[144] It is impossible to know how many MPs shared that view but felt unable to express it openly. Bagehot thought that the number was high and announced on their behalf that he was 'exceedingly afraid of the ignorant multitude of the new constituencies'.[145] There can be no doubt that just as many MPs did share Lowe's more temperately expressed fear that the working classes were making a bid to 'pass from the position of non-electors to the position of sovereign arbiters in the last resort of the destinies of the nation'.[146] The truth was that no one involved in the passing of the Reform Act wanted the franchise to be extended as far as it was, not even the Radicals, and nobody was at all clear what kind of society it would lead to: in the common phrase of the time, it was a 'leap in the dark'.[147] With the leap taken, efforts began immediately to influence, control and direct the new, largely unknown, electorate. In the second edition of *The English Constitution* published in 1872, Bagehot took the opportunity to rethink his theories of deference in the light of recent changes:

> We have not enfranchised a class less needing to be guided
> by their betters than the old class; on the contrary, the new
> class need it more than the old. The real question is, Will
> they submit to it, will they defer in the same way to wealth
> and rank, and to the higher qualities of which these are the
> rough symbols and the common accompaniments?[148]

The mass of legislation that now began to be rushed through parliament suggested that no one involved in government was willing to run the risk that the answer to Bagehot's 'real question' might be No.

The crucial legislative issue was outlined in the Queen's Speech, 1868: 'The general question of the education of the people requires your most serious attention, and I have no doubt you will approach the subject with a full appreciation both of its vital importance, and of its acknowledged difficulty.'[149] Education was of 'vital import-ance' if the new electorate was to be sufficiently literate to reach an informed political decision, or, if Bagehot was proved right, to understand what their 'betters' told them. It was an issue of 'acknowledged difficulty' because it meant taking on both of the two main agencies for elementary education then existing – the Church of England and the Nonconformists. The profound mid-Victorian distrust of central government control seemed to pose insurmountable problems for any coherent national system of education. If education was free it would destroy personal initiative and philanthropic effort; if run by the government, it threatened political freedom; if placed in the hands of the Church of England, then religious choice was put at risk. Forster's 1870 Education Act had to be a compromise, but the mood of urgency created by the extension of the franchise enabled the compromise to be a courageous one.[150] Like the 1867 Act it established a principle which it could not put immediately into practice and was therefore an instalment of a more comprehensive reform that would only emerge in piecemeal fashion. Under the Act, provision was to be made for the elementary education of all children in those districts where voluntary systems were inadequate. The schools were administered by elected Boards, and financed by a mixture of goverment grants, local rates, and fees which were not to exceed 9d per week. Two important results of the administration of the Act were that women could be, and were, elected to the School Boards, and that the basis for a widespread restructuring of local government was laid down. The Boards also had powers to clarify the provisions of the Act: they could levy a rate, determine the age to which children in their district should be educated, and regulate fees to help the poorer parents who were not at first obliged to send their children to school.

In 1876 further legislation allowed action to be taken against those districts which had not yet set up School Boards: in 1880 education was made compulsory for children between the ages of five and ten; in 1891 the school leaving age was raised to eleven and most fees, which were running at an average level of 3d per week, were abolished. However impressive the steady movement towards the principle of free compulsory education for all, serious weaknesses remained. Syllabuses were often limited to very basic reading and writing skills; school attendance was poor and varied considerably, as did the quality of schools, from district to district; and, most seriously, there was no national system of secondary education that would allow the child who was gifted or intelligent and poor to develop beyond the age of ten. In this last respect, Scotland was in advance of England, having ensured that its own Education Act of 1872 covered secondary as well as elementary education: Wales and then England took up the issue only with the passing of the Technical Instruction Act of 1889, though once again there were local variations, with some School Boards encouraging education beyond the compulsory age limit and even running continuation evening classes.[151] By 1900 there were nearly five million children in elementary schools: they were divided almost equally between the Board and voluntary systems. In 1902 a new Education Act, the passing of which was far more fiercely contested than had been the case in 1870, abolished the School Boards; placed elementary education in the care of newly-established Local Education Authorities; made the County Councils responsible for secondary education; and, the cause of much of the controversy, began to withdraw State aid from the voluntary, denominational schools.

Out of these educational reforms we can see gradually emerging not only the acknowledgement that the State needed to be responsible for elementary education, regardless of the ability of parents to pay and whether the parents wanted their children educated or not, but also the establishment of a quite new pattern of social mobility. It had always been possible for a child from a poor or working-class family who displayed outstanding intellectual or artistic ability to move up the social scale by means of education: this could be achieved through the ancient grammar schools, the church, upper-class or aristocratic patronage, mechanics' institutes, working-men's colleges, and various other agencies.[152] It was possible and it did happen, though not as often as one might suppose from a reading of Victorian self-help tracts and romantic novelettes. Nor was it part of the intention of the 1870 Education Act to make this kind of social mobility more accessible. Those who spoke for the creation of a meritocracy were well outnumbered by those who believed that elementary education should be kept elementary. As we have seen, the provision for secondary education was little more than an afterthought. Earlier in the century elementary education for the poor had been restricted out of the fear that if people were literate they would read subversive books. Now, in a complete reversal of attitude, the poor were to be taught to read so that they would be less easily swayed by radical or socialistic oratory. In its crudest form, this assumption did not survive at a policy level for very long, though it was profoundly to influence modern cultural values. It was transformed into a system of social mobility partly because of the unstoppable process of change that has already been noted; partly because of the need which began to be felt strongly in the 1880s for more skilled and technical workers to help counter the threat to Britain's industrial supremacy posed by Germany and America; and partly through the dedicated stand on educational issues taken by members of the

School Boards and their allies in local government and the civil service. Where educational reforms most immediately accelerated social mobility was through some of the teachers rather than the children. In the same year as the Education Act they took the classically late Victorian decisions to form themselves into the National Union of Elementary Teachers, found their own journal, and consolidate their professional status. In February 1872 the *Schoolmaster* urged teachers to 'awake to a sense of their power. Few classes of the community could exert more influence in a contested election than teachers, if they only chose to exert themselves.'[153] The political response to that call came in 1895 when two schoolteachers were returned to parliament, but of far greater significance was the growth in numbers of teachers as training colleges and universities expanded to meet the new educational demands. Nothing is more characteristic of the fundamental social changes taking place at the end of the nineteenth century than this new class of meritocrats and the neat, brick buildings, surrounded by gravel playgrounds, in which they worked.[154] As far as the future of literature was concerned, their taste and judgment were to be vital.

To the crucial role of the teacher in this process of social reconstruction was added that of the public librarian. In 1891, Thomas Greenwood prophesied:

> In another fifteen or twenty years, when some millions more
> children have passed through the Board Schools, and Public
> Libraries and other similar institutions have been established
> all over the kingdom, then we shall become a cultivated
> people.[155]

It did not seem an impossible dream. Only a few years after Greenwood's prophecy, T. H. S. Escott described the cultural transformation of Britain as already well under way. He noted that areas of cities which were once considered 'unsafe' were now 'covered by a mass of buildings in red brick or stone, of aspect rather more academic than the new quarter of Victorian Oxford', and he teased the reader to guess what purposes these new urban landmarks served:

> If it chance to be Saturday night, hundreds of working men,
> decently clad, with parcels under their arms will be seen
> passing to and fro near these buildings. They are not going

to the public house. The packages they carry do not imply a
negotiation with the pawnbroker. The men are, in fact,
returning to the library the books which, taken out some days
earlier, have given them their reading during the week after
the day's work has been done.[156]

Idealised as Escott's description obviously is, it memorialises the
pride felt by many of the new teachers and librarians in their work,
and it recognises, in the changing urban landscape, the visible
symbols of that pride.

As the debate on the extension of the franchise and its possible
consequences intensified in the early 1860s, the attitudes of leading
mid-Victorian writers can be observed re-adjusting to a new state of
crisis. Like the politicians, few of them were ardent supporters of
the changes about to take place: like the politicians, their responses
ranged from the conviction that chaos would descend on Britain,
through a last-minute determination to salvage something positive
from the mess, to a muted belief that actual events might not be
quite as catastrophic as was being predicted. What these writers
shared was the feeling that a relatively peaceful period of social
harmony was about to be disrupted, and that that disruption could
well return Britain to the divisive atmosphere of the 1830s and
1840s. There were sound reasons for their fear. Once again the
central political issue was electoral reform; there were mass
demonstrations in the streets, and increasingly clamorous reports of
terrible poverty in the cities. There were also deep personal reasons
why mid-Victorian writers should have feared a return to the class-
conflict of the 1840s. Arnold, Carlyle, Dickens and Eliot all carried
painful memories of their individual readjustments to the time
which J. A. Froude characterised as 'an open spiritual ocean' in
which young intellectuals had been forced to learn to swim by
themselves.[157] Carlyle and Eliot had both lost the religious faith
that had meant so much to them in their youth; Arnold had seen
his dream of becoming a great poet destroyed by the fragmentation
of the age; the young Dickens had felt his exuberant delight in the
world slip away from him as social problems forced themselves
increasingly on his attention. All four writers had survived by
committing themselves not nostalgically to the worlds they had
lost, but positively to the uncertain values of the new world coming
into being: they were its critics and its spokesmen. None of them

could have been totally surprised by the resurgent demands for reform in the 1860s: the nature of their early commitment to a 'progressing' society made that impossible. But, like Trollope sitting down to write his autobiography in 1875, they were all conscious of entering the last phases of their careers and worried that the society they had helped to pull out of the threatened turmoil of thirty years ago was about to sink back.

Arnold was the least challenged of these writers by the events of the 1860s, just as he was the only one of them whose work at this time offered a sustained attempt to understand the new forces at work. In 'My Countrymen' (1866), *Culture and Anarchy* (1869) and *Friendship's Garland* (1871) he portrayed a rigid class-divided society, with each class motivated by its own narrow interests, listening to its own politicians, reading its own newspapers, all serving to create further fragmentation when what was needed was social and cultural unity. He was not in principle opposed to the extension of franchise, his relativist view of life having long ago convinced him that democracy was inevitable. He said again and again that the 'populace' (or working class) was the only part of British society susceptible to current, relevant 'ideas', and in 1884 he supported the extension of the franchise to agricultural workers on the grounds that it was better for them to speak for themselves than to have someone else do it.[158] But accepting social changes is not the same as approving them, though it may involve, as it did in Arnold's case, a new dedication to making them work. In that sense Arnold reasserted the lesson he had learnt in the 1840s: he acknowledged the signs of the times and set about helping them to move in the right direction. This meant above all educational reform; support, as always, for popular elementary education; and even more urgently, improved education for the middle classes. Meanwhile the main problem was how to maintain cultural standards in the age of democratic mediocrity that Arnold (together with many contemporary politicians) was convinced had already begun. As the mood of anti-Victorianism became increasingly fierce towards the end of the century, Arnold was one of the very few mid-Victorian writers whose reputation and influence continued to grow.

The reputations of Carlyle, Eliot and Dickens were to move, in varying degrees, into temporary eclipse. While this was not caused simply by their attitudes to events of the 1860s, the way in which they tended to look back rather than forward did reinforce the widespread feeling that they had little to teach the late Victorians. Carlyle's was the most extreme case. In 1893 George Saintsbury noted that an 'ardent admiration' for Carlyle was now generally taken as the surest sign of 'a man's having reached the fogey, and of his approaching the fossil, stage of intellectual existence'.[159] In fact, by that date Carlyle's active influence on literature was long over: the publication in 1867 of *Shooting Niagara: And After?*, with its virulent slating of the Reform Act, had effectively announced that he was finished. He would continue to be read and praised by people of various political persuasions, but that was mainly for his brilliant social analysis of the 1830s and not for the implications of those early insights which were now made unavoidably plain. Even the later cult of Nietzschean élitism tended to work to Carlyle's disadvantage.[160] Carlyle professed to believe that the extension of the franchise was being hailed on all sides as a universal panacea, though nobody at all seems to have thought anything of the sort. Appalled at the possibility of 'Count of Heads to be the Divine Court of Appeal on every question and interest of mankind', he derided the 'swarmery', took his now customary swipe at the 'settlement of the Nigger Question', praised Prussian militarism, pondered the advantages of what 'might be done in the way of military drill' for 'the entire population', yearned for a true Hero to emerge, and with an unexpected flash of his old knock-about humour wondered whether 'Manhood Suffrage' would be followed by 'Horsehood' or 'Doghood' suffrage.[161] It is curious that 'womanhood' suffrage as the next step appears not to have entered his mind.

   Great Expectations (1861), *Our Mutual Friend* (1864), *Felix Holt the Radical* (1866) and *Middlemarch* (1871) all, in slightly different ways, reflect the concern of the 1860s with electoral reform, and all of them convey a weary mood of lost ideals. Felix Holt's ambition to be a 'demagogue of a new sort; an honest one if possible' and to help extend the franchise to those working men excluded from the 1832 Act leads to a drunken riot, prison, and the opportunity to step out of the pages of the novel in order to give a topical 'Address to Working Men' who were demonstrating for that same right: 'If there's anything our people want convincing of, it is, that there's some dignity and happiness for a man other than changing his station.'[162] In spite of Eliot's firm humanism, the thwarted ambitions of Will and Dorothea in *Middlemarch* are also seen as leading to social stasis. Dorothea is 'absorbed in the life of another' and while this is regarded as a terrible waste by her friends, 'no one stated exactly what else that was in her power she ought rather to have done'. The link between the high political hopes of 1832 and later disillusionment is made explicit in the male career that absorbs Dorothea:

> Will became an ardent public man, working well in those
> times when reforms were begun with a young hopefulness of
> immediate good which has been much checked in our days,
> and getting at last returned to Parliament by a constituency
> who paid his expenses.[163]

Great Expectations looks even further back to the world that Victorianism was to replace. The violence, injustice, snobbery and aristocratic patronage of Georgian England are survived by Pip who becomes a representative type of early Victorian – hardworking, self-made, honest, respectable, and a little smug: 'We were not in a grand way of business, but we had a good name and worked for our profits and did very well.'[164] What happened to those fine Victorian values Dickens explored four years later in *Our Mutual Friend* which is aggressively up-to-date, with its middle-class philistinism, worthy slum priest, organised police force, schoolteachers, 'shares', self-reflecting politicians, ruthless working-class ambition spurred on by education, and its Arnoldian analysis of each of the classes apeing the manners of the one above. Unlike Eliot, Dickens does not point warningly to an enfranchised working class as a debilitating element in society, though he does not speak on its behalf either: in *Our Mutual Friend* no one escapes criticism.

Outside his novels, the evidence suggests that Dickens approved of the new working-class voters. In 1868 he wrote: 'The greater part of the new voters will in the main be wiser as to their electoral responsibilities and more seriously desirous to discharge them for the common good than the bumptious singers of "Rule Britannia", "Our dear old Church of England", and the rest of it.'[165] If that kind of positive endorsement was not made in *Our Mutual Friend*, the contempt for cheap patriotism that it also expresses was presented in the satirical portrait of Mr Podsnap who, in one fleeting moment, reveals another aspect of Dickens's thinking on these issues. When a 'stray personage of a meek demeanour' tries to get Mr Podsnap to acknowledge that the condition of the poor in

Britain demonstrates that 'there must be something appallingly wrong somewhere', he is told: 'Easy to say somewhere; not so easy to say where! But I see what you are driving at. I knew it from the first. Centralisation. No. Never with my consent. Not English.'[166]

Mr Podsnap was right that centralisation was not English, but he was not to be right for long. More government intervention in the social welfare of the people was the logical conclusion to draw from repeated attacks by Victorian writers on *laissez-faire* economics, whether it was openly advocated, as by Arnold and Ruskin, or implied in the manner of Dickens. The inevitability of more centralisation was recognised as the electoral reforms of 1867 led to the Education Act three years later, and from there through legislation on housing, local government, higher education, health, 'sweating', trade unions, the poor law, town planning, old-age pensions, and virtually every other aspect of the national life. By 1914 responsibility for finding solutions to social problems rested on the central government to a degree that would have flattened poor Mr Podsnap. Nor was this massive growth of centralisation the result of any one party political programme. Liberal and Conservative administrations both contributed to it: and while the fear of Socialism was an important goad to reform throughout the period, and while the Labour Party did exert an influence on the social policies of the Liberal government that came to power in 1905, centralisation in Britain at this time can be described as Socialist only in a very general sense. The connection was, however, frequently made, most persuasively by A. V. Dicey in his 'lectures' on *Law and Public Opinion in England during the Nineteenth Century* (1905). Taking the 1870 Education Act as a turning-point, Dicey argued that the dominant political philosophy in Britain had changed from *laissez-faire* Liberalism to collectivism which he defines as:

> The school of opinion often termed (and generally by more
> or less hostile critics) socialism, which favours the intervention
> of the State, even at some sacrifice of individual freedom, for
> the purpose of conferring benefit upon the mass of the
> people.[167]

Although Dicey himself was one of those 'more or less hostile critics' he did not fully accept the equation between collectivism and socialism, mainly because he regarded collectivism as 'a sentiment rather than a doctrine': it is a 'hope of social regeneration' that has its source in Benthamism and its more recent expansion in the combined humanitarianism of mid-Victorian writers and the extension of the franchise.[168] He is also careful to discriminate between democracy and Socialism: 'The government of England is far less democratic than is the government of the United States, but the legislation of Congress is less socialistic than the legislation of the Imperial Parliament.'[169] What Dicey deplored in collectivism, and what by the time of the second edition of his book in 1914 he saw as having ominously increased, was the erosion of individual effort under the pressure of 'the democratic idea that the people, or any large number of people, ought to have what they desire simply because they desire it, and ought to have it quickly'.[170]

Dicey was concerned to define a broad pattern of change, and his interpretation of events has been criticised by historians as an oversimplification, which it clearly is.[171] Yet, Dicey's analysis is highly relevant in the present context. It was, for a start, representative in that Dicey identified a process of social change which was coming to be felt as true to the everyday experience of large numbers of people. His analysis was also representative, in a different sense, in that its frame of reference was almost exclusively Anglo-American: at this late date, 1905, Dicey could discuss the rise of collectivism without taking into account either Marxism or the wider debate – often inspired by Marxism – that had long been argued out in Europe. One of the key factors seen by Dicey as having contributed to the 'sentiment of goodwill' which had helped prepare the path for collectivism, was the early and mid-Victorian novel.[172] In this attitude too, Dicey was representative: by the turn of the century the great Victorian novelists were often criticised for allowing their art to be corrupted by utilitarian considerations, and it was not uncommon for Dickens especially to be regarded as an inchoate Socialist or Marxist.[173] In his skilful blend of broad political trends and highly specific social instances, Dicey's method was closer to that of fiction than the law (his own profession) or history (the profession on which he was trespassing). In terms of his own political values he had little affinity with Victorian novelists: he did, however, have a good deal in common with emergent modernists. The general lack of interest in European political theories shown by most British novelists at this time, stands in marked contrast to their eagerness, in other respects, to

follow the artistic example of Europe. It was part of the foreignness
often remarked in Conrad that he had experienced European
revolutionary politics at first hand, something he shared with few
British writers, but an important element in his friendship with the
Socialist Cunninghame Graham, whose political beliefs Conrad
would normally have viewed unsympathetically.

In so far as British writers announced themselves as politically
committed they tended to bear out Dicey's worry that the rise of
collectivism had eclipsed not only mid-Victorian Liberalism, but
most other shades of political belief as well. 'There is no future for
men, however brimming with crude vitality,' Shaw proclaimed in
1903, 'who are neither intelligent nor politically educated enough
to be socialists.'[174] Chesterton made the same point, just as pithily
and with the benefit of hindsight:

> I called myself a Socialist; because the only alternative to
> being a Socialist was not being a Socialist. And not being a
> Socialist was a perfectly ghastly thing. It meant being a
> small-headed and sneering snob, who grumbled at the rates
> and the working-classes; or some hoary horrible old Darwinian
> who said the weakest must go to the wall.[175]

It is here that we can see being formulated the familiar twentieth-
century assumption that Socialism (however vaguely conceived) is
the only acceptable or possible political creed for an intelligent (or
young) person.[176] The important irony is that relatively few of the
major writers of the time, and hardly any of the great pioneers of
literary modernism, shared that assumption or even had much
positive interest in the political changes taking place around
them.[177] The broken connection with writers of the immediate
past did not go unremarked. 'In those days,' James Bryce observed
ruefully, 'literary men were mostly Liberals.'[178] They weren't any
longer. Nor were they united by any other broadly-based political
philosophy. They were gripped by the 'vivisective' nature of the
modern spirit, by the modern vice of unrest. 'The doctor says there
are such boys springing up amongst us,' Jude tells Sue, 'boys of a
sort unknown in the last generation – the outcome of new views of
life.'[179]

Late Victorian interest in the way that one generation succeeds
to another was obsessive. It owed much to Darwinism, as did the
related fascination with the nature of time: it was further precipi-

tated by the electoral reforms which had created a political and
social climate quite different from that of mid-Victorian Britain.
Bagehot tried to argue that the 1867 Reform Act was itself
explicable in terms of a new generation of politicians who were
discontented with the ageing 'pre-'32' statesmen.[180] More convincingly, he warned that the full effect of these changes would
not be felt for something like a generation:

> A new Constitution does not produce its full effect as long as
> all its subjects were reared under an old Constitution, as long
> as its statesmen were trained by that old Constitution. It is
> not really tested till it comes to be worked by statesmen and
> among a people neither of whom are guided by a different ex-
> perience.[181]

Dicey, taking a similar starting point to Bagehot, settled on 1880 as
the moment when the trend towards collectivism became dominant,
and more recently historians have tended to confirm that kind of
date, though not necessarily the analysis.[182] If there is a period of
'transition' here, it can perhaps be identified as from the introduction
of electoral reforms in 1867 to about the mid-1880s when the
effects of those reforms began to be widely felt and recognised.
This moment in time can also be taken as marking the decisive
separation from the mid-Victorians of the two generations with
which the present study is primarily concerned. They correspond
roughly to Woolf's classification of Edwardians and Georgians –
those who were born in the late 1850s or early 1860s and began
their writing careers some twenty or twenty-five years later, and
those, like Woolf herself, who were born in the early 1880s. These
two generations were, however, not as distinct as Woolf tried to
make out: neither of them, to use Bagehot's phrase, was reared
under the old Constitution, and few of them were happy with the
new Constitution they had inherited. Scornful of the mid-
Victorians, and desperately concerned with fixing identities of their
own, their discontent focused, appropriately enough, on the family.

Chapter Three

Parents and Children

The question of Christianity is virtually settled – or if not settled there
is no lack of those engaged in settling it – the question of the day now
is marriage and the family system.

Samuel Butler, *The Way of All Flesh* (1903)

I confess myself altogether feminist. I have no doubts in the matter. I
want this coddling and browbeating of women to cease.

H. G. Wells, *The New Machiavelli* (1911)

One of the most telling arguments in G. M. Young's attempt to
show that the Victorians were questing, doubting, energetic beings
rather than the smug, prudish hypocrites of popular imagination,
was his claim that there were only two areas of life they regarded as
inviolable: representative institutions and the family.[1] Both came
under strong attack in the late Victorian period. Representative
government, as we have seen, survived by adapting itself to new
democratic demands and accepting, often without enthusiasm,
responsibility for a far greater range of social needs than ever
before. The family would seem to be a quite different matter, not
directly subject to the kind of parliamentary control that could
extend the franchise or order compulsory education, and therefore
less susceptible to dramatic change. It is certainly the case that in
early modern fiction the changing nature of family relationships
was often made to serve symbolic rather than sociological purposes,
but the principal source of that symbolism was the growing
involvement of the State with family life in a wide variety of
unprecedented ways. Legislation relating to education, the rights of
women, separation and divorce, employment and social welfare, all

helped to modify the autonomy of the family whether or not that
was part of the original intention.

There was, for example, nothing fanciful about the awe-inspiring,
stern, dominant, often violent father who haunted the imaginations
of so many late Victorian novelists. The power of his fictional
image grew strongest towards the end of the century as his actual
powers declined or were taken from him and a youthful generation
prepared for his overthrow. Even then he was to prove a daunting
opponent, and understandably so given the virtually absolute
power he once possessed. At the beginning of the nineteenth
century a man's wife and children had no legal rights which were
independent of his authority. While alive he was free to exercise
despotic control over his family and he could even extend this
beyond the grave. If he chose to appoint a guardian, in preference
to his widow, to bring up his children, then he could do so. No
distinction was drawn in this respect between happy and unhappy
marriages, and where there was marital discord, the scope for
vindictiveness on the part of the husband was endless, for in
matters relating to the family he was literally beyond the law. As
Ivy Pinchbeck and Margaret Hewitt point out: 'The rights of the
father as against the mother were so absolute that the courts did
not in fact have the power to grant a right of access to her children
to a mother whose husband had not granted it himself.'[2] Nor did
the courts have any right to intervene on behalf of children in cases
of the most extreme parental cruelty. As late as 1871 when Lord
Shaftesbury was asked to support a movement to change the law on
this issue, he expressed his sympathy but felt that the problems
were 'of so private, internal and domestic a character as to be
beyond the reach of legislation'.[3]

The process by which the power of the father was brought
within 'the reach of legislation' can be traced through a series of
parliamentary Acts which gradually conferred independent rights
on married women and children. This was largely achieved by
transferring responsibility from the father to the courts. In 1839
the Custody of Infants Act which was precipitated by Caroline
Norton's struggle for custody of her children, and was later the
inspiration for Meredith's *Diana of the Crossways* (1885), allowed
the courts for the first time to intervene on behalf of the mother:
in 1873 these powers were extended by allowing a mother who had
committed adultery to petition for access to her children and by the

Court reserving the right to act in what it considered the best interests of the child. In 1886 the Infants Bill recognised that a mother was the natural guardian of her children on the death of her husband and further strengthened the power of the courts to overrule parental considerations if the well-being of the children was at stake. The shift of control away from the husband and father was also enhanced by the discretionary powers allowed to divorce courts in the Matrimonial Causes Acts of 1857 and 1878; the Summary Jurisdiction (Separation and Maintenance) Act of 1895, which made it possible for a magistrate to grant custody to a wife rather than the husband; and the Prevention of Cruelty Act and the Poor Law Adoption Act, both of 1889, which began the process of transferring responsibility for neglected children from the parents to the State. The same year saw the various pressure groups which had worked for this legislation formed into the National Society for the Prevention of Cruelty to Children. Further legislation in the early years of the present century, culminating in the Children's Act of 1908, established the principle of probation for child criminals, and separated adult and juvenile courts.

The opposition view that such legislation was an unjustifiable intrusion on individual rights had been stated repeatedly throughout the Victorian period, and the fears were now felt to be confirmed as the State took more and more powers upon itself. The voices of the objectors were not easily silenced. In 1884 it was still being argued in parliament that a woman legally separated from her husband should not be allowed access to her children because it is 'laid down in Holy Scripture as the law of God that the husband should be supreme over the wife': it was to be another seven years before a Court of Appeal finally ruled that a husband could not legally detain his wife in his home.[4] It is no wonder that Sue Bridehead looked with despair on 'the barbarous customs and superstitions of the times that we have the unhappiness to live in' and viewed marriage with dread.[5] The sweeping away of 'barbarous customs and superstitions' was taking place all around her, and as an enthusiastic reader of John Stuart Mill, Sue would have known that the main agent of change would have to be the State: from her own unconventional relationships with men she also learns that changes in law do not bring with them automatic changes in attitude, either in the self or in society as a whole. Sue and Jude are ahead of their time, pioneering 'experiments' in personal rela-

tionships, acting out the logical conclusion of late Victorian
legislative reform which would, as many commentators at the time
understood, mean the transformation, even perhaps the death, of
the Victorian family. It was, however, to be a long and painful
struggle, as H. G. Wells warned – though personally joyful at the
prospect of the traditional family disappearing:

> I think the prophet is inclined to overestimate the number of
> people who will reach this condition of affairs in a generation
> or so, and to underestimate the conflicting tendencies that
> will make its attainment difficult to all, and impossible to
> many, and that will for many years tint and blotch the
> achievements of those who succeed with patches of un-
> sympathetic colour.[6]

The patches of unsympathetic colour used to discredit the
'achievements' of those brave enough to establish unconventional
sexual and familial bonds would, Wells estimated, have faded away
by about 1950. His argument was that by that time society could be
expected to comprise so many different kinds of relationships that
any surviving 'moral censor' would have difficulty finding a
'congenial following to gather stones'.[7]

Well's confidence on this and similar social prophecies was made
possible by his belief, shared generally by Socialists and by some
Liberals at the turn of the century, that State centralisation was the
path to increased individual freedom: the opposing ideological
argument was that the State would eventually destroy freedom by
making it unnecessary for the individual to act or think for
himself. The battle over family rights was a classic instance of the
clash between old individualism and new individuality that is so
characteristic of the whole period. What was often regarded as the
type of interfering legislation was the Education (Provision of
Meals) Act of 1906 which allowed local authorities to use the rates
to provide free school meals for children from poor families. The
need for some such provision had long been acknowledged, and
indeed was already being met in some areas by voluntary
organisations. But however cogent the arguments in favour – and
they ranged from the waste of educational resources if children
were hungry in school, to the military and imperial desirability of
Britain having a fit working class – the horror of encroaching on
parental authority often seemed greater. When the Act was finally

passed many local authorities did not implement it, and continued
to rely on voluntary organisations to see that school children were
properly fed. In 1907 Arnold Bennett, returning home from
France, noted sentimentally that England was still the same even
though 'old-age pensions and war balloons may be in the air' and
'the strange notion may have sprouted that school children must be
fed before they are taught'.[8] Bennett was being ironic: A. V. Dicey on
the other hand was genuinely concerned that the provision of free
school meals marked the virtual triumph of the new collectivism.[9]
His concern was shared by many Liberals, especially those who
carried personal memories of the mid-Victorian period. Socialism,
John Morley noted in 1907, had become 'the key' to Liberal
policies: it was 'the catchword of the hour'.[10] As far as the family
was concerned, the decline of mid-Victorian individualism meant the
constant erosion of the authority of the father or husband over his
wife, sons and daughters. That such changes were made in the name
of the increased freedom or well-being of wives and children hardly
lessened the feeling of crisis they invariably provoked as the old
individualism clashed with the new individuality. No doubt there
never had been a time when all was well with family relationships,
and it is significant that modern historical studies of the family –
inspired by the growth of interest in anthropology and sociology –
begin at this point of time.[11] But whatever the nature and status of
the family in the more distant past, from the 1870 Education Act
onwards family life was to be regarded as under constant threat.

The reason why all of this mattered so much to the novelist was
noted by Sidney Webb as he prepared his campaign to create an
'apotheosis of the vote' in British society:

> Neither Dickens nor Thackeray, neither Tennyson nor
> Browning, ever thinks of man as a citizen. He is a lover,
> husband, father, friend – but never a voter, town councillor or
> vestryman. George Eliot is a little better but not much. Surely
> it would be well if our novelists were to emphasise more
> the *public* duties of life.[12]

Webb was exaggerating slightly. Dickens, Thackeray, Eliot, Trollope, Disraeli, Gaskell – Fielding too, if we go back further in time
– were not indifferent to the 'public duties of life', their own and
those of their readers, though not quite in the way that Webb
meant or, generally, in terms of political philosophies he would

have approved, and this distinction was even more pronounced among novelists who were Webb's contemporaries. But if novelists continued to ignore man as 'voter, town councillor or vestryman', they remained fascinated by him as 'lover, husband, father, friend'. Ernest Pontifex announces to Overton that 'marriage and the family system' was the question of the day.[13] It must have seemed to many observers, as it did to Sidney Webb, that it always had been the question of the day and that British novelists rarely wrote about anything else. The mid-Victorians especially had given the family an almost mystical significance. In so far as any coherent theory lay behind their reverent attitude it focused on the family as a microcosm of the nation, and later the Empire: the family was a potent symbol of unity and selflessness in an age threatened by the newness of industrialism and the divisiveness of class warfare. It also united religious belief and an hierarchical society by means of a familial scale descending from the Holy Family, through the Royal Family and the Clerical Family, down to the poorest slum inhabitants, whose outcast state, as many social explorers were to testify, was confirmed by their supposedly lax views on marriage. Perhaps few people believed in the absolute, eternal nature of this scale, but it is clear that a very large number subscribed to the ideal, while many may even have regarded it as having been attained. Enough certainly to make it seem at times, as W. L. Burn observed, 'that the home and the family were the invention of the age, like the telegraph, and that until, say, 1837, the people of England had lived in a sort of nomadic promiscuity'.[14]

More than any other institution the family could serve as visible justification of a progressing middle-class society, with the materialism of the age qualified by its religiosity: for those lower on the social scale religiosity alone had to do. It was a fatal combination that would fuel the later charges of hypocrisy. Even Dickens, the least self-satisfied of Victorians, in *Our Mutual Friend*, one of the most satirical of his novels, was unable or unwilling to break with the ideal of the middle-class family. While the Veneerings, the Podsnaps and the Lammles show clearly enough that all is far from well with this sacred institution, Bella Harmon is used to glorify it. 'You will naturally want to know,' she says to her mother and sister, 'how we live, and what we have got to live on.' As she gushingly provides the information, she also advances an image of her self that within the space of twenty years was to become notoriously a complaint rather than a boast:

> Well! And so we live on Blackheath, in the charm-ingest of
> dolls' houses, de-light-fully furnished, and we have a clever
> little servant, who is de-cidedly pretty, and we are economical
> and orderly, and do everything by clockwork, and we have a
> hundred and fifty pounds a year, and we have all we want,
> and more.[15]

That describes relatively hard times. Once Bella has learnt how to
be truly economical and orderly she will also learn that she is a
very rich doll indeed. She has been lucky enough to have a
husband who can educate her morally: he is not a Veneering or a
Lammle, and he will not turn into a Podsnap. The family is safe in
his hands, even though Bella does warn him (not ominously in this
particular context) that she wants to be 'something so much
worthier than the doll in the doll's house'.[16]

W. L. Burn was surely correct to single out Queen Victoria's
accession as a crucial moment in the sanctification of the family.
When she died sixty-four years later the obituaries praised her for
having rescued the monarchy from disrepute: it was widely
regarded as her greatest single achievement. Coming to the throne
at a moment of political crisis, the argument ran, she had helped
prevent the collapse of British society by strengthening the weakest
link in the hierarchy. This she did by epitomising qualities which
were already coming strongly into favour, the same qualities that
old George Pontifex in *The Way of All Flesh* hoped to instil into
his young grandson by naming him Ernest. The alternative
proposed by Ernest's father Theobald is George, an obvious act of
filial submission on his part, though Butler realises (and old Mr
Pontifex senses intuitively) that the emerging society would prefer
to forget all about the Georges.[17] The youthful Queen Victoria,
once joined with her consort Albert, had earnestness in plenty.
Together they also represented stable family life, moral seriousness,
religious faith, and social concern – everything, in fact, that Ernest
Pontifex was not to have or want, even though he did have the
right Christian name and had been baptised with water from the
river Jordan. It was not, of course, simply a matter of Queen
Victoria possessing the right personality and attitudes: just as
important was the fact that the country she ruled over witnessed
during her reign a revolutionary transformation in every aspect of
communications, without the support of which the iconography of
a respectable, rather dour, bourgeois monarchy giving a lead to

British and Imperial society would have been impossible.[18] The same bourgeoning communications industry publicised the Prince of Wales's apparent reversion to the licentiousness of the Georges, and it is an indication of the firm hold that the sacrosanct image of the family had in the popular imagination that Edward's behaviour did not blow it up as effectively as Samuel Butler was later to do. This was partly because by the 1870s and 1880s Prince Edward's rebellious spirit was less likely to be condemned by a younger generation that was itself tired of hypocrisy and eager to reject Victorianism; and partly because of the less often expressed belief that Edward served as a kind of safety-valve for the Regency sensuality that it was convenient to believe had been eliminated by the accession of Victoria. It had actually been driven underground where it flourished, known and connived at by many men, and tolerated by many women who were expected to feign ignorance of such areas of life.[19] With a double standard on sexual morality operating widely in Victorian society, it was possible for Edward to be seen as no worse than other men, even as comparatively and commendably honest, especially in that part of upper-class Society where public and private morals were wildly, and at the same time often systematically, at odds.[20] Radical and republican criticism of the Prince of Wales was overpowered by the daunting respectability of his mother and, later in the century, by the even more daunting power of the popular press.

When the voice of middle-class morality was heard on this topic it expressed not outrage but rather a longing that the Victorian model be continued. This was the view that Marie Corelli took in her obituary tribute to the dead Queen. She urged Britain to give thanks for the way that Victoria had upheld the family virtues at a time of generally declining values, and to pray that Edward would be strong enough to resist his sycophantic friends.[21] Corelli could not seriously have believed in the sudden transformation of the rakish Prince of Wales into a King Edward who would epitomise the desired image of a devoted father and husband: ever since her first published novel *A Romance of Two Worlds* (1886) she had denounced, with far more moral fervour than the newspapers, Britain's growing decadence and is, therefore, in a rather special sense, an invaluable chronicler of late Victorian discontent. What she now feared was that with the death of Queen Victoria there would also die the temporal symbol of the family that had served

Britain so well. If the family broke up, so would everything else. Henry James privately expressed much the same conviction:

> I feel as if her death will have consequences in and for this country that no man can foresee, the Prince of Wales is an arch-vulgarian (don't repeat this from me) . . . the Queen's magnificent duration has held things magnificently – beneficently – together and prevented all sorts of accidents . . . the Prince of Wales in sight of the throne, and nearly sixty, and after all he has done besides of the same sort, is 'carrying on' with Mrs George Keppel . . . in a manner of the worst omen for the dignity of things. His accession in short is ugly and makes all for vulgarity and frivolity.[22]

It was not the family itself that needed to be defended, but the wider stability it represented, that holding of things 'magnificently – beneficently – together' as both James and Corelli realised. The Prince of Wales posed a threat to the familial hierarchy not merely because his accession to the throne seemed a throwback to the Regency, but because it was a kind of blasphemy after the pure symbolism of Victoria. She herself (as every good Victorian knew) had surrendered domestic authority to the man who had captured her heart, and rightly so. It was, after all, God or Jesus who occupied the top place in the hierarchy, and made the father of a family, in theory (and in law) the clergyman, monarch, even God, in his own home. It was a central and flexible enough belief to affect virtually every aspect of Victorian life, not least that of the novelist whose fictional creations were his children. When Dickens was obliged to kill Paul Dombey, he did so, fallen being that he was, with deep personal emotion at this unnatural act.[23] The artistic justification was totally consistent with religious faith. The novelist exercised full control over his creations, just as God had full control over him. The omniscience of the novelist, and therefore the characteristically Victorian form of realism, was only possible because the existence was assumed of a higher form of omniscience. The popular image of Dickens seated in his writing chair surrounded by the shades of characters from his novels expresses this belief, as does Thackeray's view of himself as a parson and Trollope's of himself as a clergyman. It was to be George Eliot, the non-believer, who would self-consciously introduce into her work the shifting point of view, a hint to be taken up eagerly by future novelists who were to deny the paternity (or maternity) of their fictional children and thrust upon them an autonomous existence, just as God had denied his paternal responsibility and cast them loose in the world.

That there are relatively few complete or harmonious families to be found in Victorian fiction is not a repudiation of the importance attached to the idea. The broken family units – widows and sons, widowers and daughters, guardians and wards, aunts and nephews, lonely and endangered orphans – all serve to emphasise the precariousness of the social fabric and point forward to the stable unity that only marriage and children can convincingly represent. It often reads like the impossible dream it was. There were a few dissenting mid-Victorian voices. J. S. Mill, the supporter of the vote for women and the great advocate of Liberal individualism, compared the public image of the family ('a school of sympathy, tenderness, and loving forgetfulness of self') with its more common reality ('a school of wilfulness, over-bearingness, unbounded self-indulgence, and a double-dyed and idealised selfishness').[24] By the turn of the century, and in spite of the fact that many of the legal reforms to which Mill was drawing attention had been enacted, Mill's reality had almost entirely overthrown the ideal. The 'school of sympathy' became a prison-house of tyranny; 'tenderness' was transformed into harsh possessiveness; and 'loving forgetfulness of self' had been changed into internecine selfishness. It was still possible to find the family eulogised. In 1906 Helen Bosanquet described it as 'greater than love itself, for it includes, ennobles, makes permanent all that is best in love. The pain of life is hallowed by it, the drudgery sweetened, its pleasures con-secrated.'[25] But such claims were now defensive, insisted upon in this particular case by Bosanquet's awareness of the modern view, backed by reputable historians and sociologists, that the family is a 'merely temporary form of organisation'.[26] For the mid-Victorian novelist, marriage, a family and home, were ideals to strive for, rewards paid for surviving the dangers of a perilous world, an attained condition of stability. For the late Victorian novelist, marriage, family and home, were more commonly symbols of repression, to be treated warily at best and if necessary to be avoided entirely by desperate flight. 'Do you know what you're a proof of, all you hard, hollow people together?' the self-centred Mr Croy asks his no less self-centred daughter Kate in *The Wings of the Dove* (1902): 'Of the deplorably superficial morality of the age.

The family sentiment, in our vulgarised, brutalised life, has gone utterly to pot.'[27]

There is no simple or single explanation why the family became such a focal point of discontent for the late Victorians. To some extent its representation in fiction changed because it was changing in reality, but the main cause was the comprehensive idealism with which the family had been regarded by the previous generation. The late Victorian attack on the family was the most widespread and potent manifestation of anti-Victorianism. Criticism, scorn and contempt were flung at it from every conceivable ideological angle. Its abolition had been enshrined as an ultimate aim in *The Communist Manifesto* (1848) by Marx and Engels who were convinced that the modern family was a middle-class creation:

> On what foundation is the present family, the bourgeois
> family, based? On capital, on private gain. In its completely
> developed form this family exists only among the bourgeoisie.
> But this state of things finds its complement in the practical
> absence of the family among the proletarians, and in public
> prostitution . . . The bourgeois family will vanish as a matter
> of course when its complement vanishes, and both will vanish
> with the vanishing of capital.[28]

What this means is made clearer in Engels's *The Origin of the Family: Private Property and the State* (1884) in which the form of the 'individual family', the 'molecule' of modern society, is claimed to have evolved as an instrument of class domination. Like industrialism, the family is patriarchical, with the father representing the bourgeoisie and his wife the proletariat. Women will only achieve emancipation with 'the reintroduction of the entire female sex into public industry', and for this to take place it is necessary that 'the quality possessed by the individual family of being the economic unit of society be abolished'.[29]

Marxism does not enter strongly into British political thought or imaginative literature until after the First World War, though when it did attract earlier writers the abolition of the family was treated prominently. In the Utopia of *News from Nowhere* Morris's traveller to the future is informed about the current state of the family in words that seem to have been learned by heart from the *Communist Manifesto*:

> Another cognate cause of crimes of violence was the family

tyranny, which was the subject of so many novels and stories of the past, and which once more was the result of private property. Of course that is all ended, since families are held together by no bond of coercion, legal or social, but by mutual liking and affection, and everybody is free to come or go as he or she pleases.[30]

Like Marx and Engels, Morris has no interest in blaming the family as such for the unhappiness and pain suffered by its individual members. The family was created by modern capitalism and has vanished with it: gone also (or at least surviving now so faintly that they can be treated as merely quaint) are all human feelings founded on competitiveness, possession and sexual jealousy. Not only has capitalism been eliminated, but, as Morris observes, the traditional relevance of most literature as well.[31] Wells's time-traveller is not so convinced a Marxist, but when he catches his first glimpse of a future landscape in which 'apparently the single house, and possibly even the household, had vanished', he sums up the situation in one word – 'Communism'.[32] He then sees the Eloi deceptively calm and happy, the men barely distinguishable from the women, and again he finds no difficulty in explaining to himself the changes that have taken place, 'for the strength of a man and the softness of a woman, the institution of the family, and the differentiation of occupations are mere militant necessities of an age of physical force'.[33] The time-traveller is soon to learn that his conjectures are wrong, but as he points out it was quite natural for a late Victorian to think as he did: 'We see some beginnings of this even in our own time, and in this future age it was complete.'[34] The time-traveller's disillusionment about future developments in human relationships was not shared by Wells himself. In the epilogue to *In the Days of the Comet* (1906) he portrayed a future society in which the words 'wife' and 'home' were understood only as barely remembered customs of the 'old world': they have been replaced by 'friends, helpers, personal lovers in a world of lovers'.[35] Advocacy of free love was the logical culmination of Wells's futuristic writing up to this time: *In the Days of the Comet*, together with his Fabian pamphlet *Socialism and the Family* in the same year, made his views explicit. It helped precipitate his break with the Fabian Society, encouraged in him a new phase of rebelliousness, and provided an opportunity for a Conservative candidate campaigning for election in Lancashire to claim that it was the Socialist policy to 'separate husband and wife and subject every woman to communal prostitution.'[36] The orthodox Marxist claim, followed here by Wells and supported by many feminists, was that middle-class marriage itself was a state of prostitution and bondage.

While travel into the future provided an opportunity to speculate on the long-term future of the family, the study of the past created a different kind of challenge. Engels's *Origin of the Family* was made possible by the expansion of anthropological research in the 1860s and 1870s, notably that of the American Lewis Morgan whose *Ancient Society* (1877) was much admired by Marx and Engels. There had been an Ethnological Society in England since the 1840s, but in 1863 a breakaway group formed the Anthropological Society of London and three years later the *Popular Magazine of Anthropology* was founded, its aim being to keep the general reading public in touch with scientific developments. The growth of interest in the comparative study of ancient and primitive peoples was given impetus by Darwinism and popular appeal by the increasingly strident mood of late Victorian imperialism. As Brian Street has demonstrated, there was a close connection between the views of popular anthropologists like E. B. Tyler, Max Müller and Andrew Lang, and the even more popular novel of Empire, that was to hold until discredited by the development of sophisticated field-work techniques.[37] Much of this literature was as conjectural as science fiction: it served primarily to reinforce racial stereotypes and white superiority. But its influence was not simply limiting or negative. Anthropology introduced into the debates on the family and marriage the possibility of a comparative method, abundant historical evidence which (whether right or wrong) appeared to prove that the mid-Victorian family was not God-given, and gave powerful support to the relativism that is so characteristic of the period.

It was the historical evidence that excited Marx and Engels; the comparative religion of Sir James Frazer's *The Golden Bough* (12 vols. 1890–1915) that was later to fascinate T. S. Eliot.[38] The debates on polygamy and monogamy, patriarchal and matriarchical societies, provided feminists not only with a necessary historical and comparative method but a 'scientific' terminology that drew on Darwinism, anthropology and the related new discipline of sociology. It made possible world-wide studies like Annette Meakin's

Women in Transition (1907) and, more forcefully, Mona Caird's series of essays on the morality of marriage. As Caird pointed out, 'history and science' were rapidly undermining beliefs that were not founded in truth but merely justified in terms like 'the will of God' and 'the ordinance of Nature'.[39] The fiction of Empire, even when serving the imperial dream, was also capable of popularising the new relativism. Kipling's view of Anglo-India in *Plain Tales from the Hills* (1888) with its trivial flirtations and adulteries, hardly amounted to a vote of confidence in the sanctity of married life, while his stories and ballads of Indian and barrack life constantly emphasise the meaninglessness of moral judgments which are not related to particular conditions.[40] Even Rider Haggard, whose novels abound with handsome, supernaturally strong Englishmen, made a serious attempt in one of his best novels *Nada the Lily* (1892) to portray an African world in which polygamy was the norm; and in *She* (1887) he created an immensely popular symbol of a matriarchal society. Ayesha did not exactly represent the kind of feminist assertion that Mona Caird advocated, but the basic idea being advanced by Haggard is not unrelated. When Ustane steps up to the beautiful, athletic Leo and publicly kisses him, the travellers prepare themselves for instant death. 'The hussy! – well, I never!' gasps Job, the lovable Cockney servant. But Ustane is acting in accordance with the customs of her people, and Haggard points the moral:

> It is very curious to observe how the customs of mankind on
> this question vary in different countries, making morality an
> affair of latitude and religion, and what is right in one place
> wrong and improper in another.

That could still be taken to mean that however much customs may vary the English are right and the Amahaggers wrong. The conclusion, however, deliberately shuts off this possible escape:

> There is, even according to our canons, nothing immoral
> about this Amahagger custom, seeing that the interchange of
> the embrace answers to our ceremony of marriage which, as
> we know, justifies most things.[41]

Haggard did genuinely believe in this kind of moral relativism, but the tone and atmosphere of *She*, with its blatant eroticism, violence and white superiority, nullify any serious challenge to the reader's ingrained assumptions. A striking contrast to *She* is offered by Stevenson's *The Beach of Falesá* (1892) which expresses his horror at the attempts by missionaries to impose Christianity on the South Sea Islanders and at the shabby tricks played on the native girls by white traders. The original version of the marriage contract treasured by Uma would have told her, if she could have read it, that she is 'illegally married to *Mr John Wiltshire* for one night, and *Mr John Wiltshire* is at liberty to send her to hell next morning'. When the story was serialised in the *Illustrated London News* the passage describing the marriage contract was omitted by the editor Clement Shorter in spite of Stevenson's protests.[42] The strip-teases in which Ayesha periodically indulges, and Ustane's public choice of Leo as her husband were acceptable: Stevenson's blunt, sympathetic realism was not.

That the British reader was not to be allowed too much reality in such fiction was a lesson fully learnt, and applied, by Conrad. In the greatest of all novels of Empire, European moral absolutes collapse into savagery and Marlow himself is only prevented from going ashore for 'a howl and a dance' by his need to prevent the steamer he commands from sinking. The heart of darkness beats not only in the Congo but beneath the fragile pavements of Europe as well. That is a perception that Kurtz's fiancée could not possibly live with. Instead she is told a lie so that her romanticism can survive intact. It was precisely this kind of protection that feminists were increasingly determined to reject. With Mona Caird they insisted that if the truth was discernible, then they should have access to it, uncluttered by the comforting euphemisms coined for their benefit. The same point was made scornfully by Olive Schreiner:

> Men do not say God sends the books, or the newspaper
> articles, or the machines they make; and then sigh, and shrug
> their shoulders and say that they can't help it. Why do they
> say so about other things? Liars! 'God sends the little babies!'[43]

Schreiner's pioneering attempt to introduce the woman's point of view into a world of fiction dominated by men was to be taken up most directly by the 'New Woman' novelists of the 1890s, and her narrative method which mingles a dramatic story with heavy discussion of the wrongs suffered by women was also to be widely adopted. These concerns, however, were felt by men as well as women. It is not difficult to see why. The general reaction against Victorianism and the doctrine of realism both pointed to the overthrow of mid-Victorian fictional stereotypes, and those of women were prominent. The angelic ideal did not disappear overnight: it can be seen, struggling against less conventional portraits of women in fiction throughout the 1880s and 1890s, sometimes employed positively (by both men and women novelists) for purposes of ideological or sexual contrast, but nearly always acknowledged, in one way or another, as an anachronism. By the time of *The Old Wives' Tale* Bennett could turn the description of Daniel Povey's murdered wife, who for years has been a secret drinker, into a virtuoso exercise in iconoclasm:

> In a room as dishevelled and filthy as the bedroom, Mrs
> Daniel Povey lay stretched awkwardly on a worn horse-hair
> sofa, her head thrown back, her face discoloured, her eyes
> bulging, her mouth wet and yawning: a sight horribly offen-
> sive. Samuel was frightened; he was struck with fear and
> with disgust. The singing gas beat down ruthlessly on that
> dreadful figure. A wife and a mother! The lady of the house!
> The centre of order! The fount of healing! The balm for
> worry, and the refuge of distress! She was vile.[44]

The French example contributed in this respect to the subject matter as well as to the form of late Victorian fiction, the central characters of so many admired French novels being women. The names and personalities of Eugénie Grandet, Emma Bovary, Germinie Lacerteux, and Gervaise Coupeau, were generally more familiar to late Victorian novelists than those of Emma Wood-house, Catherine Earnshaw, or Dorothea Brooke. Nora Helmer should be added to that list, though the Christian name alone would be sufficient. Excepting Queen Victoria, Ibsen's heroine was probably the most famous woman in late Victorian Britain, within literary and intellectual circles at least. An important aspect of her fame, like that of Tess, was that she was admired or loathed by women as much as men, by feminists and non-feminists. She was an inspiration or a warning, according to one's point of view, but always an instance to be taken into account. On the other hand, the doomed tragic heroines of French fiction – sexually exploited, their romantic ideals crushed, their physical decline charted in loving detail – may have aroused pity in the British feminist or served as a frightening indication of a powerful literary tradition that would have to be confronted, but they could not be expected to provide the inspirational model that men found in them. Not that literary influence by itself is a completely satisfying explanation. The drive towards greater individual freedom now to be found everywhere in fiction led men inevitably to the relative lack of freedom allowed to women: it became their problem as well. Hardy's obsession in his novels with the desirability of divorce reform and with sexual double standards, the class-based torments experienced by Gissing's male characters, and the personal agony of James's and Meredith's manipulated heroines, all express the conviction that there could be no freedom for men until 'the woman question', as it was commonly called, was settled. The hesitancy and uncertainty apparent in novels of the late 1870s and the 1880s gave way not to a solution – that was, and is, clearly impossible – but to the remarkable experimentation of the next decade.

Until then the characteristic fictional pattern was of a woman making a bid to challenge the traditional assumptions about what her role in life should be and either failing completely or accepting a modification of her rebellion that is distinguishable from the traditional role only because it is shown to be of her own choosing. While the resolutions are often customary, the challenges to convention can be startling. Bathsheba Everdene in *Far from the Madding Crowd* (1874) is a flamboyant example of the new daring. She is 'a girl on horseback', a 'woman farmer', a 'mistress' not a 'master', who is presented in a series of masculine roles – hiring and paying the farm labourers, outlined by sheets of lightning as she helps Gabriel Oak cover the barley stacks while her husband lies drunk and useless. The extent of her unconventionality is spelt out in Oak's first proposal of marriage. All that a farmer's wife could possibly want she is offered: a piano, ten-pound gig, cucumber frame, the births of babies – 'every man jack of 'em' –announced in the newspaper. It is not enough:

> What I mean is that I shouldn't mind being a bride at a
> wedding if I could be one without having a husband. But
> since a woman can't show off in that way by herself, I shan't
> marry – at least yet.[45]

There is no one on the novels that follow *Far from the Madding Crowd* in a situation quite like that faced by Bathsheba who has the possibility of choosing between an independent career and a marriage that will hand that career over to her husband. Married life itself now becomes central to the novels and with it, as Penny Boumelha points out, 'sexual discord and marital breakdown, which had previously only hovered impendingly on the periphery of Hardy's fiction'.[46] Like so much else in Hardy the mismatches and adulteries that feature in *The Return of the Native* (1878), *The Mayor of Casterbridge* (1886) and *The Woodlanders* (1887) are seen sometimes as the result of modern restlessness and at other times as the eternal, perverse order of things. While Fitzpiers pleads with Grace Melbury to marry him, two birds that had 'either been roosting above their heads or nesting there', suddenly tumble into the fire 'apparently engrossed in a desperate quarrel that prevented the use of their wings'. They fly apart, leaving a scorched smell behind. 'That's the end of what is called love,' observes Marty South.[47] The symbolism is obvious but effective. In *The Mayor of Casterbridge* Michael Henchard marks the ending of his love by resorting to the age-old custom of selling his wife: in *The Woodlanders* Grace marks the ending of hers by consulting the recently-passed Matrimonial Causes Act of 1857 which, she is told, 'enables ill-assorted husbands and wives to part in a way they could not formerly do without an Act of Parliament'.[48] The information is only partly correct. In spite of his repeated adultery, 'Fitzpiers's conduct had not been sufficiently cruel to Grace to enable her to snap the bond.'[49] Hardy does not spell out the crucial distinction, but under the terms of the act a wife could be divorced for simple adultery while a husband could only be divorced if it was possible to prove some additional cruelty on his part (such as rape, sodomy or incest). It was also now possible to cite desertion without cause for more than two years in addition to adultery and cruelty as grounds for divorce, and decrees were introduced for judicial separation. In spite of the way that talk of divorce is casually bandied about in late Victorian and early twentieth-century popular fiction, it was still a fairly unusual, cumbersome and expensive procedure. In the late 1870s the average number of divorce petitions filed each year in England and Wales was 460: by 1915 it had increased to 1033.[50] Of far more significance in fiction and in life for the loosening of marital relationships was the greater ease with which judicial separation could be obtained, especially after 1878 when magistrates were empowered to grant separation orders with maintenance. 'How can any woman who is not a mere man's creature live with him after what has taken place?' Grace Melbury asks despairingly.[51] In the end she is won back by Fitzpiers and neither she nor Hardy has to answer her pertinent question.

A very different challenge to Victorian convention came from the young Henry James with his introduction into British fiction of the pretty, charming, naive, intelligent and (when set within a European context) shockingly liberated American girl, a phenomenon already familiar to real-life European Society when *Daisy Miller* was first published in 1878. Her introduction is calculated and theatrical. 'Here comes my sister!' Randolph shouts at Winterbourne, 'She's an American girl.'[52] It might almost be a line from the music-hall where American girl artistes were also featured as a well-defined national type. One line of opposition came from upper-class women who regarded any wealthy young American girl in Britain as bent on marrying into the aristocracy, and their fear was well-founded. There was no shortage of American parents eager to send their eligible daughters as 'paying guests' of impoverished aristocratic families. This is how Florence Dowell in Ford's *The Good Soldier* first visits Britain. Florence does not marry into the British upper class, though she becomes Ashburnham's mistress, and always insists that 'her ideal husband would be one who could get her received at the British Court'.[53] The desire to unite old-world tradition and new-world money was so great that even the desperate method of newspaper advertisements was tried, on both sides of the Atlantic: it has been estimated that by 1915 a total of four hundred and fifty-four American women had married into the European aristocracy.[54] The success rate was so high that American girls in British popular fiction could be shown as blandly triumphant:

> 'In my country we should call it real mean to laugh at people
> who had been our guests and performed in our houses.'
>   'In your country, my dear,' said Myra Ingleby, 'you have
> no duchesses.'
>   'Well, we supply you with quite a good few,' replied the
> American girl calmly, and went on with her ice.[55]

The theme was explored most bitingly by James in 'An International Episode', and most pathetically by Marie Corelli in *The Sorrows of Satan* where Miss Diana Chesney, financed by her parents, sits in the country home of Lord Elton waiting for his sick wife to die. She becomes a tourist attraction:

> We've got a young lady staying with us – an American,
> dollars, accent and all – and by Jove, I believe she wants to
> marry me, ha ha ha! and is waiting for Lady Elton to go to a

better world first, ha ha! Come along – come and see the
little American, eh? Thursday shall it be? [56]

But a greater threat came with the American girl's freedom from
the strict conventions of European Society and her refusal to be
bound by them. 'Why should I suffer the restrictions of a society
of which I enjoy none of the privileges?' Bessie Alden asks.[57]
Bessie receives the coveted proposal of marriage and having tasted
British aristocratic manners has the dignity to turn it down: Daisy
Miller cares for nothing but her own freedom – to talk with
whoever she likes, see the Colosseum by moonlight, become
engaged, be entertained. It is her freshness, spontaneity and
'innocence' that draw European men to her, and the same qualities,
given a different emphasis, that alienate the women. James's own
view was ambivalent. Leon Edel sees Daisy Miller as an expression
of James's 'unerring vision . . . of the total abdication, by the mass
of American parents, of all authority over their children', and there
is clearly an element of national distrust in James's attitude.[58] The
Europeans who meet Daisy Miller believe she is so liberated that
sexual promiscuity as well as naivety simply must be involved in
the new freedom, and James, while eventually judging Daisy
'innocent', was enough of a realist to share that view. But he was
also aware that whether innocent or designing, the American girl in
Europe was entering a class of Society where sexual behaviour was
often notoriously loose and the marriage market ruthlessly organised. Corelli's Lord Elton was very much a part of the scene. So
were the Duke and Duchess of Plaza-Toro:

> I present any lady
> Whose conduct is shady
>   Or smacking of doubtful propriety.
> When Virtue would quash her,
> I take and whitewash her,
>   And launch her in first-rate society.[59]

Daisy Miller's flirtatiousness and candid chatter were genuinely
refreshing in such a world: they could be casually accepted as long
as she did not also possess social poise and wealth. In the complex,
sordid manoeuvres that developed out of this clash between the old
and the new worlds James found his greatest theme which receives
its first major treatment in *The Portrait of a Lady* (1881). Isabel
Archer has none of Daisy Miller's pert charm, but through the

well-meaning interference of Ralph Touchett she inherits money, and that gives her market value which is just as fatal. So rare is Isabel's American freshness and so intense her longing for self-fulfilment that all the men in the novel are in love with her and none of them able to help in the attainment of her quest. The European marriage market absorbs her effortlessly. If James could see only death or renunciation as women's destiny – and the conviction hardly lessens in his later novels – he was at the same time able to convey, more convincingly than any of his con-temporaries, the desperate longing of late Victorian women to break free, to assert their independence, or, to use the bird imagery that he himself often favoured, to spread their wings, to fly. He was also unequalled in his understanding of the social and sexual structures that could break their spirits and hold them earthbound.

There are close similarities in this respect with the novels that Meredith published in the 1880s, though unlike James his view of life was avowedly optimistic. It was this, together with Meredith's occasional pronouncements on the subject, that gave him in his lifetime his reputation as a semi-official spokesman for women. Today the happy marriages which are eventually granted to Clara Middleton in *The Egoist* (1879) and Diana Warwick in *Diana of the Crossways* (1885) seem as much an acknowledgment of Meredith's uncertainty about what else an intelligent sensitive woman could do as Jamesian renunciation, though there is too great a striving for independence on the part of both Clara Middleton and Diana Warwick for their eventual marriages to be fairly described, in Kate Millet's phrase, as 'mere matings'.[60] The satire of *The Egoist* works entirely to arouse sympathy for Clara's attempt not only to break away from Sir Willoughby Patterne, but also to break through the incomprehension of his relatives and of her own father. Without the aid of satire Diana Warwick has to fight the even more insidious forces of press innuendo, Society gossip, and the sexual advances of her best friend's husband. Like James, Meredith at this stage of his career portrays women as rather precious, wonderful creatures, full of unrealised potential, restricted by a man-controlled world. If neither novelist could see how freedom might be attained, they did strongly acknowledge that the issue of sexual liberation had to be examined in relation to marriage and the family. As so often in these novels about women written by men, awareness of the difficulties involved emerges in the form of questions put by or on behalf of the women characters, and the question that Clara Middleton asks herself is perhaps the most important. It hovers over a great deal of the fiction of the period, and the various attempts to answer it in the 1890s indicate a break with the general avoidance of the 1880s: 'Can a woman have an inner life apart from him she is yoked to?'[61]

Expressed simply in those terms the problem remains frustratingly theoretical. An 'inner life' preserved and nurtured under the 'yoke' of marriage was the most traditional of solutions: it was a balance between inner and outer lives that was now being sought, and if this was to exist only as a theoretical ideal, with little satisfaction in reality, then the yoke had to be discarded. This was the brilliantly simple conclusion dramatised by Ibsen in *A Doll's House* which had its first, complete and public British production in London in June 1889:

> HELMER: To forsake your home, your husband, and your
> children! You don't consider what the world will say?
> NORA: I can pay no heed to that! I only know that I must
> do it.
> HELMER: It's exasperating! Can you forsake your holiest duties
> in this way?
> NORA: What do you call my holiest duties?
> HELMER: Do you ask me that? Your duties to your husband
> and your children.
> NORA: I have other duties equally sacred.
> HELMER: Impossible! What duties do you mean?

And Nora answers, as figures in literature were increasingly to answer similar challenges, 'My duties to myself.' When Helmer insists that she is before all else a wife and mother, Nora replies: 'That I no longer believe. I think that before all else I am a human being, just as much as you are – or at least I will try to become one.'[62] Nora accepts the essential selfishness of her action as necessary if she is to become a complete human being, and Ibsen is careful not to lessen the courage of the decision by supplying her with any extenuating motive: she is not in love with another man and she is not inspired by feminist theory. She acts in the name of personal liberation, of the right to try to bring her inner and outer lives into some kind of harmony, and that can only be attempted if she abandons her family. What the future may hold is irrelevant to her.

It was not irrelevant to London audiences who debated what had happened to Nora once the door closed behind her. That she would have to return, in some state or other, seemed inevitable. 'Throughout Europe,' Michael Egan observes, 'the dispute over Nora's return and the consequences of her departure had become a key issue in the Ibsen debate.'[63] Walter Besant rushed to publish a melodramatic sequel to *A Doll's House* in which Nora, now an 'advanced thinker' and successful, cold-hearted feminist novelist, returns home after many years to find her family in a condition of irretrievable moral collapse.[64] Bernard Shaw responded by writing a 'sequel to Besant's sequel' in which Nora, far from cold-hearted, returns to convert the now wealthy Krogstad to her feminist beliefs.[65] In America it was revealed that after leaving home Nora had devoted herself to philanthropic work: she returns just in time to nurse Helmer through a cholera epidemic.[66] It is even possible that Conrad's short story 'The Return' was an attempt to re-write *A Doll's House* from the man's point of view.[67] So great was the disbelief that a wife and mother could behave so unnaturally that Ibsen wrote an alternative, ambiguous ending for the German production of *A Doll's House* rather than have censors mutilate the play, though this particular 'happy ending' was never performed in Britain.[68] Ibsen took revenge on his critics in *Ghosts* which was first produced in London in February 1891. Mrs Alving had listened to the argument that a wife's most sacred duty is to her home and stayed with her debauched husband: now she nurses her son as he dies from inherited disease. For the Ibsenites, Nora's slamming of the door came to symbolise what Shaw called 'the revolt of the daughters'.[69] For British novelists, it seemed to point a way out of the dilemmas that they, and their fictional heroines, had been struggling to resolve for the previous decade.

Daisy Miller dies of the fever; Eustacia Vye drowns in the weir; Isabel Archer returns to Osmond, Grace Melbury to Fitzpiers; Bathsheba Everdene does eventually marry Gabriel Oak, and Thomasin Yeobright does eventually marry Diggory Venn; Clara Middleton and Diana Warwick escape from bondage to new loves; Marty South dedicates her life to the memory of Giles Winterbourne who had loved not her but Grace Melbury. In complete contrast, Nora walks out of the doll's house and takes her chance on what comes next. In one sense the writers and critics who conjectured about what would happen to Nora afterwards were more in tune with the new mood than the ardent Ibsenites, who tended to assume that the slamming of the door meant that victory had been won. In fact everything was still to be fought for. The family might have been abandoned, but there was no agreement on what could replace it. Conjecture had become, and was to remain, the norm.

The problem was being stated by men, but often in ways that acknowledged their own limitations. They seemed constantly to be urging women to take up the issue, as though convinced that the questions posed in their novels could only be answered by women. 'Do you like me, or do you respect me?' Boldwood asks Bathsheba. She replies:

> I don't know – at least, I cannot tell you. It is difficult for a
> woman to define her feelings in language which is chiefly
> made by men to express theirs.[70]

This was the challenge picked up by the 'New Woman' novelists.

Discussion of the attempt to develop a woman's point of view in British fiction of this period is complicated by the simple fact there were no women novelists of a literary stature remotely comparable to that of James, Conrad, Hardy, Meredith, Bennett, Wells, Gissing, or a dozen other men. This situation was itself a specifically late Victorian phenomenon. It is especially curious because while it had long been recognised that there were few women painters, poets or composers who could challenge the achievements of men, the same was not true for fiction. From the eighteenth century onwards in Britain women had excelled as novelists. With the examples ready to hand of Jane Austen, Fanny Burney, Emily and Charlotte Brontë, Elizabeth Gaskell and George Eliot, the line was continuous and might well have been considered as irreversible. Yet from the death of George Eliot in 1880 until the publication of Virginia Woolf's first novel *The Voyage Out* (1915), there was a break in this great tradition. It was to re-assert itself. Katherine Mansfield's first collection of short stories *In a German Pension* was published in 1911; *The Three Sisters* (1914) marked a change in May Sinclair's narrative method with her attempt to apply to fiction lessons learnt from theories of psychoanalysis; in *Pointed Roofs* (1915) Dorothy Richardson began experimenting with the stream-of-consciousness techniques that were to become so influential. With Woolf's emergence in the post-

war years as a major force in modernist fiction the line of
innovative women novelists was firmly re-established, and has been
maintained ever since: but this was only after a gap in time
equivalent to a whole generation. As these were the years during
which the foundations of modern fiction in Britain were laid, the
process can be described as almost entirely man-made, even though
there were more women publishing fiction and earning a good
living from it than ever before.

Women writers like Ouida, Rhoda Broughton, Mrs Henry
Wood, M. E. Braddon, Marie Corelli, Emma Jane Worboise,
Annie S. Swan, and slightly later Florence Barclay, Elinor Glyn
and Ethel M. Dell, dominated the field of best-selling fiction. Not
all of their work was as laughably romantic as modern critics often
suppose. Ouida, Rhoda Broughton and M. E. Braddon especially
never lacked admirers among critical readers, and although much
of their fiction followed romantic formulas it was by no means
vapid. When *A Modern Lover* and *A Mummer's Wife* ran into
censorship troubles with the circulating libraries, George Moore
based his defence on the argument that many of the popular novels
in the libraries were more sexually daring than realistic fiction, and
Moore was right.[71] Whatever the approved public image of the
Victorian woman, if she was reading Ouida and M. E. Braddon she
would not be likely to believe that strong sexual passion was
unwomanly or that all was well with the family: she would also
have been exceptionally well informed on the marriage market and
the decadence of aristocratic life. But the collective reputation of
these novelists was fixed inescapably by the advent of realism in
the 1880s and the new self-consciousness of the Artist-Novelist.
Generally treated with far more critical respect were Mrs Oliphant
and Mrs Humphry Ward. Mrs Oliphant's writing career had
begun as long ago as 1849, and her most characteristic fiction
belongs to the mid-Victorian period, though she was still to
produce one of the best supernatural tales of the age, *A Beleaguered
City* (1880), while her remarkable *Autobiography and Letters*
(published posthumously in 1899) struck a topical note with its
record of a life of unremitting literary labour that in some respects
surpassed that of Trollope.[72] Mrs Humphry Ward was very much
of the late Victorian period, and all the signs seemed to favour the
possibility, as reviewers quickly pointed out, of her becoming a
modern George Eliot. She was related to Matthew Arnold, had

lived in Oxford during the intellectual crises of the 1870s, was impressively self-educated in theology and modern languages, knew as personal friends influential men like Pater and T. H. Green, and was aggressively determined to succeed. The sensational reception of *Robert Elsemere* (1888) appeared to vindicate the prophecies of Mrs Ward's greatness, and the novels that followed consolidated her fame. *The History of David Grieve* (1892), *Marcella* (1894), *Sir George Tressady* (1896) and *Helbeck of Bannisdale* (1898), revealed an author in touch with some of the most disturbing areas of British life – religious doubt, philanthropy, urban slum conditions, the decay of rural communities – but they also showed so little sensitivity to the changes taking place in the theory and practice of fiction that they might have been written a generation earlier. The unintentional irony of the comparison with George Eliot was soon clear; in spite of the modernity of her subject-matter Mrs Ward became for many younger writers the type of staid Victorian, the strange phenomenon of a late Victorian who was a regular target of anti-Victorianism.[73] What tends to be remembered most about Mrs Ward today is her anti-feminism, though that in itself would not necessarily have placed her at any great disadvantage in late Victorian Britain.[74] Eliza Lynn Linton, for example, who apart from being a respected novelist had married into Radical circles, led a strikingly independent life, was a pioneering woman journalist, and formed a close friendship with the much younger feminist writer Beatrice Harraden, is also most often referred to today for her anti-feminism.[75] Nor would this particular stance account for Mrs Ward's failure to develop as a novelist: on many other issues she was a passionate reformer. More to the point is an ambivalence in her work defined by Vineta Colby as 'the desire to see England as simultaneously the guardian of a proud old aristocratic tradition and the leader of vigorous progressive reform. Her most sympathetic characters are crusaders but not rebels.'[76] Mrs Ward's unfulfilled promise was re-enacted, less spectacularly, in the careers of many other women novelists of the time, some of whom – Olive Schreiner, Beatrice Harraden, Ella D'Arcy, E. L. Voynich and George Egerton, for example – were strongly aware of the changing nature of fiction, and not easily willing to settle for being crusaders rather than rebels.

It was certainly rebels the age demanded, and the opposition they invariably provoked could be fierce, as the cases of Zola,

Ibsen, Wilde, Hardy, Gissing and many others demonstrate. There
was no intrinsic reason why a woman with sufficient talent and
determination should not have faced and overcome the abuse that
would be hurled at her: George Eliot had not had an easy time
establishing herself. But there are indications that hostility increased
rather than decreased as the century neared its close. Public
concern, now centred on democracy and the growing power of
Socialism, displayed an ideological touchiness similar to that shown
towards industrialism and Chartism in the 1840s, and this was
reinforced by the massive expansion of the periodical and newspaper market: publicity was more widespread, insidious and
personal. One aspect of this was a new version of the double
standard, with the press lauding the greater freedom and opportunities being opened to women in matters of education, dress,
sport, and employment, but swiftly closing ranks whenever the new
freedom began to concern sex, feminism or the family. A woman
novelist who ventured, however tentatively into these controversial
subjects could expect to be branded as a follower of Ibsen or Zola,
have her work regarded with horrified disbelief, and see herself
described as an unnatural being who had surrendered all right to
the respect traditionally due to women. The journalistic passion for
catchy tags and labels – given respectability in this case by the
pseudo-alienist Max Nordau – was directed with great enthusiasm at
the New Woman novelists. They were 'revolting women', members
of the 'Ibsenite neuropathic school' or the 'physiological-porno-
graphic school'; they were 'diseased', 'morbid', 'pathological'; they
suffered from 'tommyrotics', 'sex-mania', 'erotomania'.[77] Most
commonly they were said to suffer from 'nerves', which now enters
fiction as the type of modern condition.

These kinds of criticism came just as readily from women as
from men. Eliza Lynn Linton had led the way as early as 1868 in
her 'Girl of the Period' articles. 'The net result of her present
manner of life,' Linton concluded about the modern woman, 'is to
assimilate her as nearly as possible to a class of women whom we
must not call by their proper – or improper – name'; Marie Corelli
has a publisher advise a would-be novelist to follow public taste
and then add: 'Understand me – I don't suggest that you should
write a book on any positively indecent subject – that can be safely
left to the "New" woman'; and while focusing on Hardy and Grant
Allen together with some of the New Woman novelists, Mrs

Oliphant deplored the 'complete and extraordinary transformation' of the 'pure woman' in British fiction, noted that women were becoming the 'active agents' in fictional seductions, and described the modern trend as 'an assault on the stronghold of marriage, which is now beleaguered on all sides'.[78] Even men with generations of hardened public experience behind them were shocked by the force of late Victorian resistance to literary freedom. Women writers were particularly susceptible to these pressures, though only partly because of the dispiriting hostility accorded to any work that tried to deal frankly with sexuality or the family. Formal experimentation was liable to be treated with similar abuse and insensitivity. The most innovative novelists of the period – Meredith, James, Conrad, Joyce and Lawrence – all lived creative lives which were isolated, embattled, in many respects consciously opposed to the main social developments of their age, and dominated by an obsessive concern to redefine the long traditions of fiction. The ways in which women were connected with those traditions made it especially difficult even to react against them. They may have been exhilarated by the new possibilities of sexual explicitness pioneered by the French but, as has already been mentioned, in so far as this related to the lives of women in fiction it offered only negative help. And so changed was the intellectual climate that the women novelists of earlier in the century were also a limited inspiration: the example of their individual lives continued, but their work could seem annoyingly contained by younger writers who were constantly urging that inhibitions be cast off. There was also a rather special sense in which earlier women novelists had been claimed by the enemy. The new illustrated periodicals were busily romanticising the Brontës, and late Victorian belletristic critics were inclined to laud them, George Eliot, Jane Austen and Elizabeth Gaskell as great women novelists who had achieved classic literary status without indulging in modern salaciousness. The mythologising was so intense that it is now often difficult even to identify the writers being described:

> Then, a little later, when no one had paid the slightest
> attention to the slender trio of maiden voices, 'Something like
> the chill of despair began to invade their hearts.' With a less
> powerful inspiration, they must have ceased to make the
> effort; they must have succumbed in a melancholy oblivion.
> But they were saved by the instinct of a mission. It was not

> their private grief which primarily stirred them. What urged
> them on was the dim consciousness that they gave voice to a
> dumb sense of the suffering of all the world.

That is Edmund Gosse, the introducer of Ibsen's name to the English-speaking world and the author of *Father and Son*, talking in 1903 on 'The Challenge of the Brontës'.[79] The Brontës' rebelliousness and anger have been canonised, their individual ambitions transformed into a collective desire to serve the world.

The difficulties facing an aspiring woman novelist were great, but there still remains the objection that a real literary talent backed by determination could have succeeded, and the main reason why it didn't is probably that the energies of some women who in an earlier period might have dedicated themselves to fiction as one of the few outlets for intelligence and sensitivity were now being absorbed elsewhere.[80] Feminist activity itself, whether campaigning for political and legal rights or arguing the woman's case through journalism, demanded a commitment that could seem at odds with the ideological compromises accepted by the popular women novelists who were satisfying, and often creating, market demand. Mona Caird managed to succeed in both activities, though her fiction now reads like a weighty extension of the still fresh journalism. That she could earn money by journalism was itself an indication of an expanding job market for women largely created by the emerging democratic, consumer society. The 'decayed gentlewoman' who had missed out on marriage and was no longer suitable as a governess or companion was a continuing feature of late Victorian society, but her days were numbered. 'Why Be a Lady?' Ménie Muriel Dowie asked in a characteristically forthright article. 'Gentlehood,' she pointed out, 'is a drug on the market': it was far more sensible and dignified to be a 'woman' and drop once and for all the convenient pretence that a 'lady' lost her social status once she admitted to actually earning her living.[81] Somewhat surprisingly for a periodical that habitually glorified marriage and motherhood, the *Girl's Own Paper* would have agreed with Dowie on this point. In 1892 the author of an article on 'How to Secure a Situation' observed:

> Too often ladies hide the fact that they have to work for
> their living, as if it were an everlasting disgrace and could
> never be forgotten . . . Only this week an elderly spinster,

who has lived in highly-genteel poverty for the best part of
her life, remarked to me, 'My grandmother was a perfect
lady – she *never did anything*'. May future years be preserved
from such nonentities.[82]

The *Girl's Own Paper* gave regular advice on the kinds of
employment opening up for young women – nursing, teaching,
typewriting, shorthand, journalism, photography, midwifery and
clerical work, though definitely not acting, because 'once on the
stage, those wishing to leave it and live religious lives find much
prejudice from prospective employers'. The attention of readers
was also drawn to the advantages to women of pursuing higher
education; to the greater opportunities for women's work and
higher education in America; and to the importance of joining a
trade union. The paper's main emphasis was on middle-class
women, though their working-class 'sisters' were not forgotten:
the low wages paid to women in labouring occupations (estimated
as averaging ten shillings per week) were deplored, and detailed
advice was offered on working conditions for domestic servants,
shop-girls, and barmaids.[83] In 1861 there were already nearly
80,000 women employed as teachers in England and Wales: by
1911 that figure had more than doubled to 183,000. Over the same
period the number of women clerical workers increased from 279
to more than 124,000.[84] The rapid growth in numbers of middle-
class working women, especially in public services and commerce,
was one of the most notable features of late Victorian social life. It
was a visible and remarkable phenomenon. When Mina Murray,
who is an assistant schoolmistress, begins to keep one of the most
famous journals in the whole of popular literature, she is inspired
by the example of other working women: 'I shall try to do what I
see lady journalists do: interviewing and writing descriptions and
trying to remember conversations.'[85]

If she was willing to fight social prejudice, and often her parents,
it was now possible for a young woman to live independently, on
very small earnings, in rooms or in the small 'flats' that figure
prominently in fiction of this time. 'Flats house a flashy type of
person,' Mrs Munt announces crushingly in *Howards End*.[86] Her
view was widely shared, though not necessarily by the working
women of the 1880s and 1890s who suddenly found themselves
with the means of liberation from their parents' homes. It was a
development that fascinated sociologically-minded novelists like

Gissing, Wells and Bennett. The short stories that Lawrence wrote while a schoolteacher in Croydon also explore the freer social and sexual relationships made possible by lodgings and flats.[87] Sherlock Holmes estimated that 'a single lady can get on very nicely upon an income of about sixty pounds', and is gently corrected by the single lady in question who says she 'could do with much less than that'.[88] Less perhaps, but not much less if she wished to avoid genteel poverty: a qualified elementary-school teacher could expect to earn £50 per annum, and a skilled clerical worker ten or twenty pounds more than that. Many middle-class women would have had their earnings supplemented by an allowance from their parents or by their own capital. This was particularly necessary if they were using their independence to try to establish themselves as writers: there were increasing possibilities of earning money from freelance journalism while they wrote the novel that might just bring them financial success, but such work was no substitute for a regular income, as we have already seen in the case of Cosima Chubleigh in George Paston's *A Writer of Books*.

Of particular importance in this context was the development of higher education. The 1870s saw women's colleges established at Cambridge (Newnham in 1871, Girton in 1872) and Oxford (Lady Margaret Hall in 1878, and Somerville the following year): women would not be allowed to obtain degrees from either Oxford or Cambridge for some years to come, though they were admitted to examinations and awarded certificates. Other universities adopted more consistent policies. In 1878 the regulations governing the constituent colleges of London University were changed to allow women to take degree courses equally with men, while the Victoria University, which comprised what would eventually become the separate universities of Liverpool, Manchester and Leeds, admitted women under its charter of 1880. The universities of Wales and Scotland followed in the 1890s and the new provincial universities in England admitted women equally with men from the beginning. The 1890s also saw an expansion of specialised teacher-training colleges. When residential and run by religious denominations (as they had traditionally been) they were hardly centres of sexual or social liberation: an austere daily routine often made them closer to the 'species of nunnery' that Sue Bridehead attends, and is expelled from.[89] But by the turn of the century, they had been joined by the day colleges which were often attached to the Education

Departments being enthusiastically established by the universities.[90] In addition, there was a wide variety of business and commercial schools offering professional qualifications; evening classes of various kinds were beginning; and there were the nationwide lecture series provided by the University Extension Movement, which were often aimed at, and particularly popular with, women.[91] Like flats, these various educational and training institutions were recognised by novelists as epitomising the new freedom of young people from their parents. H. G. Wells claimed, in one of his early short stories, that the science colleges were the freest of all the educational institutions in that they even anticipated America in encouraging classes which were socially and sexually 'mixed': 'The prestige of the College is high, and its scholarships, free of any age limit, dredge deeper even than do those of the Scotch universities . . . Of the nine who had come into the laboratory three were girls.'[92] Attendance at a day business college could mean renting a nearby flat, as it does in Oliver Onions's psychological thriller *In Accordance with the Evidence* (1912), and that meant in turn that both home and parents were distanced from everyday life. Even if the student returned home in the evening an unprecedented degree of freedom was still possible, especially for women. Not all the opportunities it afforded were necessarily connected with education, as Lady Bracknell realises when she learns that Gwendolen has engaged herself to Jack Worthing: 'Her unhappy father is, I am glad to say, under the impression that she is attending a more than usually lengthy lecture by the University Extension Scheme on the Influence of a permanent income on Thought. I do not propose to undeceive him.'[93] More seriously, though with just as little benefit to her intellectual development, Nancy Lord in Gissing's *In the Year of Jubilee* has attended a day school until the age of eighteen and, 'since then she had pursued "courses" of independent reading, had attended lectures, had thought of preparing for examinations – only thought of it'.[94] Her friend Jessica Morgan – one of Gissing's sourest portraits of women – does more than think about examinations: she bores eveyone talking about them and finally collapses under the strain of trying to gain entrance to a London university BA course. The central characters in New Woman novels are often Oxbridge-educated, and there is more than a hint that the 'nerves' they frequently suffer from and the complicated sexual relationships they enter into have their origins in education. It certainly sets them apart. When we first meet Herminia Barton in Grant Allen's *The Woman Who Did* (1895) she has just come down from Girton and has 'the face of a free woman'.[95]

It is not surprising that the important place given to formal education in fiction was most fully expressed by Joyce and Lawrence who, like Wells, had benefited from scholarships and prizes to take them out of their lower-middle or working-class backgrounds. In *Stephen Hero* and *A Portrait of the Artist as a Young Man* Stephen's education, at both school and university, serves to cut him off from his parents, arrogantly and consciously so for much of the time: the re-education in life by Leopold Bloom, that Stephen later submits himself to, reinforces as much as it symbolically corrects the disruption that education brings to the family. In the final chapter of *A Portrait* Joyce created the prototypical hero or anti-hero of hundreds of twentieth-century novels of undergraduate life. 'It's a poor case,' his mother says to him as she scrubs his neck at the kitchen sink, 'when a university student is so dirty that his mother has to wash him.' When his father calls angrily down stairs to ask if Stephen has left for university he is assured that he has, and Stephen slips cockily out of the house:

> – Ah, it's a scandalous shame for you, Stephen, said his
> mother, and you'll live to rue the day you set your foot in
> that place. I know how it has changed you. – Good morning,
> everybody, said Stephen, smiling and kissing the tips of his
> fingers in adieu.[96]

Stephen is set slightly apart from the social context of education examined here as he attends Jesuit colleges and one of the older universities: women play no direct part in his educational world. Lawrence's circumstances were very different. He had been a student at the University College of Nottingham and his first full-time teaching post took him away from his home in Eastwood to Croydon in South London where he lived for just over three years, from October 1908 to January 1912. The poems, short stories, letters and novels that he wrote at this time, together with the memoirs written by friends and acquaintances, make up what must be a unique record of the social lives of intelligent young people, many of them connected with education, in the few years before the First World War.[97] In addition, it provided the experience and information that Lawrence was to draw on in the memorable description of how Ursula Brangwyn obtains a job teaching in a Board School. The chapter in *The Rainbow* is called, aptly, 'The Man's World'.

Each stage of Ursula's educational development is meticulously documented. Together with Gudrun, she first attends the local village school and then, partly to escape the 'common people', is transferred to Nottingham Grammar School. She is seventeen when she passes her matriculation examination and returns home 'to face that empty period between school and possible marriage'. The date is 1899, or perhaps exactly the turn of the century. Her father is absorbed in a new phase of his life, evening classes in woodcarving and metalwork having brought him 'into contact with state education'. Bored with home, Ursula seeks advice from the mistress at the High School and is told that she might be able to obtain a post as an 'uncertificated teacher' in an elementary school 'at a salary of about fifty pounds a year'. Her father is appalled at the thought of his daughters working – 'Fifty pound a year was a pound a week ... enough for her to live on independently': already acting independently, Ursula goes to the Free Library where she copies out addresses from advertisements in *The Schoolmistress*. She is first offered a job at Kingston-on-Thames, but her father refuses to let her leave home entirely and she settles for a nearby Board School where she will have to teach the 'common children of Ilkeston' who had once 'shouted after her and thrown stones'. On her first pay-day she receives 'four pounds two shillings and one penny', and immediately gives fifty shillings of it for 'board' to her mother who sulkily leaves it lying on the table: 'Ursula was hurt. Yet she had paid her scot. She was free. She paid for what she had.' It describes a pattern of experience common to many young men and women at the turn of the century. The scenes which portray Ursula surviving as a teacher only by becoming part of a brutal educational machine carry too much of Lawrence's own hatred of mechanistic education to be fully effective, though they are no doubt faithful to the atmosphere of many large Board Schools in slum areas, and also to the further ambitions they inspire in Ursula:

> She could not see her future, but a little way off, was college, and to the thought of this she clung fixedly. She would go to college, and get her two or three years' training, free of cost. Already she had applied and had her place appointed for the

coming year . . . So she continued to study for her degree.
She would take French, Latin, English, mathematics and
botany. She went to classes in Ilkeston, she studied at
evening. For there was this world to conquer, this knowledge
to acquire, this qualification to attain.[98]

The world waiting ready to be conquered was an entirely new one,
created consciously by the State. It was to be serviced by young
'qualified' people like Ursula Brangwyn whose 'training' would be
'free of cost' and who would take upon themselves, as a result of
their qualifications, new kinds of independence and responsibility
that become central concerns of the modern novel.

Just as the Married Women's Property Acts rendered inoperable
one of the standard plots of eighteenth and nineteenth-century
fiction by making the financial manipulation of women no longer a
sinister (and legal) motive for marriage, so, in a more general sense,
the expanding democratic institutions of the 1880s and 1890s – of
which education can be taken as the type – created freer forms of
social and sexual relationships which destroyed the novelist's
traditional reliance on home-based courtship and marriage. This is
most apparent in the fraught relationships between parents and
children, but it also affects every other aspect of fiction. In, for
example, the ways that characters in novels move around the city
streets, whether going to work, college, restaurant, pub, or just
taking a walk. In the novels of Gissing, Wells, Bennett, Joyce and
Lawrence, there is a degree of individual freedom – of movement
and choice – which simply does not exist in fiction of an earlier
period, and indeed could not exist because the social conditions
which provide the novelist's raw material did not themselves exist.
The increasing openness of society at the close of the nineteenth
century and the increasingly open narrative forms of early modern
fiction go hand in hand.

To what extent these various changes and developments might
have deflected women from a dedicated experimental career in
fiction it is impossible to estimate. Different factors would have
counted in individual cases, while there would also have been a
general accumulative effect. Nor should work opportunities for
women be exaggerated: the principal career was still marrriage and
family. But there were more opportunities than before; it was now
sometimes possible to choose between options; and feminist
awareness served to publicise the alternatives available. 'Why be a

Lady?' Ménie Muriel Dowie had asked, and the question could be
reworded to ask 'Why be a novelist?' A woman interested in
writing – whether she was formally or informally educated – would
not now immediately think of fiction as the literary form she
should turn to. Apart from the possibilities offered by journalism,
education, and feminism, the growth of academic studies led
during these years to a proliferation of separate 'disciplines' –
anthropology, sociology, politics, literary history and criticism,
social psychology, and education itself – all of which attracted
women writers as well as men. In popular fiction of the period, the
woman who is portrayed as sitting at her desk 'writing a book' is
still most likely to have the fiction market in mind, though it is
now not unusual for her to be 'working on' some learned topic or
heavy social question of the day. There is at least one well-
documented example of a woman writer's career which adds
support to these generalisations. Throughout her life, in spite of
the fame that came to her as a social scientist and historian,
Beatrice Webb was never quite able to rid her mind of the belief
that, to use the words of the editors of her diaries, 'she was a talent
lost to literature'.[99] She had a deep and sensitive appreciation of
George Eliot, read Zola with enthusiasm, kept a professional eye
open for young novelists whose work might serve the Fabian cause,
and more than once seriously considered writing fiction: in 1889
she even began to collaborate with Auberon Herbert on a futuristic
answer to Edward Bellamy's *Looking Backward*, the novel that was
also to provoke William Morris's *News from Nowhere*. She was
haunted by 'a longing to create characters and to move them to and
fro among fictitious circumstances – to put the matter plainly, by
the vulgar wish to write a novel'![100] If she had ever succumbed to
the temptation, the result might have been 'vulgar', or dull pastiche
Eliot: it might, on the other hand, have been as vivid and
perceptive as her diaries and *My Apprenticeship*. There is no way
of knowing. The career she settled for was social science rather
than fiction. To succeed in that she nurtured, with obsessive
dedication, the professional expertise now being demanded by an
age of specialists. In this career specialisation there are close
similarities with Virginia Woolf who was as much the new kind of
dedicated Artist-Novelist as James and Conrad.

In contrast, the New Woman novelists were little concerned with artistic perfection. A good deal of their work is harmfully dated, and some of it intense in ways that now seen funny, but two claims can be made for its historical interest. It dramatised the woman's point of view with a frankness found only very occasionally in earlier British fiction, and, through the enormous publicity it received in the first half of the 1890s, helped break the convention – dominant, as we have seen, in the previous decade – that fiction was unavoidably marriage-oriented. The principal writers usually classified as New Woman novelists were Sarah Grand, George Egerton, Iota, Mona Caird and Ménie Muriel Dowie: it was on them that most of the criticism and outrage focused, though other women writers like Emma Brooke, Ella Hepworth Dixon, Beatrice Harradan and Ella D'Arcy were also sometimes included. Penny Boumelha points out that these novelists 'often claim to be writing with female readers in mind, and to be making a political or moral statement on behalf of their sex', and she instances Ella Hepworth Dixon saying of her novel *The Story of a Modern Woman* (1894) that it was intended as 'a plea for a kind of moral and social trades-unionism among women'.[101] The example is an interesting one, demonstrating as it does the surprising lack of concern by the New Woman novelists with direct political action: the issue of votes for women appears as part of the general discontent, but it arouses no special anger. Only Emma Brooke, who was a member of the Fabian Society, seems to have attempted, in *Transition* (1895), to relate the position of women to the conflicting strands of Socialism at this time. The attitude of Mary Erle, the central character in *The Story of a Modern Woman*, on the other hand, is, as Ella Hepworth Dixon implies, attracted to 'moral and social' rather than political 'trades-unionism' among women. Her moment of realisation comes when she breaks off the affair she is having with a married man because she feels sorry for his wife: 'All we modern women mean to help each other now. We have a bad enough time as it is . . . Surely we needn't make it worse by our own deliberate acts.'[102] It is, however, more common for the call for a modern sisterhood to be provoked by hostility to other women, especially conventional wives who do not share the New Woman's liberated views, and the mothers of New Women heroines who are blamed, in classic late Victorian manner, for their conventionality, selfishness and lack of feminist awareness. One of the most vitriolic of these attacks comes in George Egerton's short story 'Virgin Soil', the pun contained in the title carrying the essential message. Florence has been married at the age of eighteen to a man who is portrayed as disgustingly sensual. After five years of his infidelities she leaves him and pays a brief visit to her mother simply to hurl accusations at her:

> I say it is your fault, because you reared me a fool, an idiot,
> ignorant of everything I ought to have known, everything
> that concerned me and the life I was bound to lead as a wife;
> my physical needs, my coming passion, the very meaning of
> my sex, my wifehood and motherhood to follow. . . . You
> sent me out to fight the biggest battle of a woman's life, the
> one in which she ought to know every turn of the game, with
> a white gauze . . . of maiden purity as a shield.[103]

In Mona Caird's *The Daughters of Danaus* (1894) the mother of Hadria Fullerton is more actively selfish, helping to destroy her daughter's career ambitions and provoking the final longing for a 'sisterhood' made up of women who will support each other: 'They have always been trained to think of men, and of Heaven, and their souls. That training accounts for their attitudes towards their own sex.'[104] Other writers tried to show relationships between women in a more positive light, especially George Egerton in stories like 'A Cross Line' and 'The Regeneration of Two', where, as Martha Vicinus has argued, there is an attempt to blend fantasy and realism, with the call for sisterhood being presented more as a future dream than a present reality.[105]

This issue is complicated since the New Woman novelists did not constitute a school of writers in any formal sense, and, once reviewers and critics had given them a collective image, it was not necessary to be a woman to write a New Woman novel. Hardy was a frequent point of reference, so were novels like William Barry's *The New Antigone* (1887) and Frank Frankfort Moore's *I Forbid the Banns* (1893), while Grant Allen's *The Woman Who Did* was probably the most famous of all New Woman novels. Allen also took upon himself the role of spokesman for what he called 'The New Hedonism' and 'Hill-top' purity, much-debated and short-lived catch-phrases which were meant to indicate that only through total openness in sexual relationships could true purity be attained:

> The New Hedonism . . . will cry out with a trumpet voice, in
> spite of detraction, that whatever makes for race preservation
> is pure and holy, whatever makes for race-extinction or race-
> degradation is vile and harmful.[106]

It was a reformulation of the conviction that conventional marriage is a form of prostitution in which the purity and innocence of young women are offered up to the sensuality of men, the view of Egerton's 'Virgin Soil', Emma Brooke's *A Superfluous Woman* (1894) and, with the dramatic addition of venereal disease transmitted by the degenerate husband to his pure wife, of Sarah Grand's *The Heavenly Twins* (1893). There were, as always, both men and women novelists who rushed to follow the fashionable trend in fiction, and the New Woman theme was highly profitable as well as fashionable: it was the large sales of such novels, as much as their moral daring, that really disturbed critics. Allen has sometimes been seen as cashing in on a trend, but there is little real evidence to suggest that he wasn't just as sincere as, say, Sarah Grand or Iota: his novels certainly share the same kinds of confusion and ambiguity. This is worth emphasising not because of any lasting value possessed by Allen's novels, but because of the important reciprocal influence between men and women novelists at this particular moment in the early 1890s. Sarah Grand sent a copy of *The Heavenly Twins* to Hardy as 'a very inadequate acknowledgment of all she owes to his genius'.[107] Gissing received an admiring letter from Ménie Muriel Dowie telling him that she possessed all of his books and ranked him as 'one of the *three* first novelists'. He had already read *A Girl in the Karpathians* (1891) and now bought *Gallia* (1893) and spent an afternoon reading it: 'Not at all a bad book,' he noted in his diary.[108] In both cases correspondence led to meetings, personal friendships and literary influence. The admiration for Hardy is particularly just, though it was not shared by all women writers.[109]

But, with the exception of Ibsen (and in George Egerton's special case other Scandinavian writers like Strindberg and Hamsun who were little-known in Britain at this time), there was no single work of literature more influential than *Tess of the D'Urbervilles*. Its defiant subtitle 'A Pure Woman' provoked Mrs Oliphant to ask despairingly how anyone who had 'twice fallen from the woman's code of honour and purity' could be called 'pure'?[110] It also gave Grant Allen his rallying cry, and focused on the immorality and indignity of sexual double standards that was to be the main preoccupation of New Woman fiction. To the influences of Ibsen and Hardy, there should be added that of Josephine Butler whose long campaign against the Contagious Diseases Act of 1869 also publicised the double standard, made venereal disease a topic of public discussion and led to the repeal of the Act in 1883.[111] An additional influential factor was the late Victorian phase of the century-long debate on birth-control which began in 1877 with the prosecution of Charles Bradlaugh and Annie Besant for publishing *The Fruits of Philosophy*; became a major, if largely secret, element in changing attitudes to sexual relationships in this period; and developed into the sexological studies pioneered in Britain by Havelock Ellis and Edward Carpenter which emphasised the pleasurable rather than the procreative role of sex.[112]

It was freedom that the New Woman novelists demanded and wrote about, freedom from social conventions which did not allow them to express themselves openly on certain topics, and from a double standard that encouraged pre-marital sexual experience in men while preparing women to serve as dolls in dolls' houses. Parodists were quick to draw the logical conclusion to such arguments:

> ENID: And *I* say that a man reeking with infamy, ought
> not to be allowed to marry a pure girl.
> VICTORIA: Certainly not! *She* ought to reek with infamy as
> well.[113]

In fact, none of the New Woman heroines 'reek with infamy'. It is the men who do that, and either make hideous victims of their pure wives, or provoke in them a spirit of revolt. What often counted as infamy was the frank expression by women of their own sexuality and their refusal to accept that it should be acted upon only within the confines of marriage. The heroine of George Egerton's 'A Cross Line' argues for women as essentially lawless, witchlike, untameable, seen truly by Strindberg and Nietzsche, and fantasises about herself as a modern Salome:

> She can see herself with parted lips and panting, rounded
> breasts, and a dancing devil in each glowing eye, sway
> voluptuously to the wild music that rises, now slow, now fast,
> now deliriously wild, seductive, intoxicating, with a human
> note of passion in its strain.[114]

In mid-Victorian fiction any woman who could even be suspected of such thoughts or feelings would be either an adventuress like Becky Sharp or end up a social outcast like Little Emily. But the New Woman is neither: she is simply being honest about herself,

and the men she admires accept this, though not without a degree
of understandable perplexity. 'By Jove, you're a rum 'un!' responds
the husband in 'A Cross Line'.[115] Theodora in the short story by
Victoria Cross published in the *Yellow Book*, January 1895, called
'Theodora: A Fragment', is similarly seductive. She has been left a
large sum of money which remains hers as long as she does not
marry: her admirers conjecture whether they are willing to risk
marrying her and losing the money, but it soon becomes clear that
Theodora has more straightforward ways of solving the problem. It
is difficult not to believe that Victoria Cross was casting at least one
cynical eye back to the tortuous soul-searching created by a
similarly vindictive legacy in *Middlemarch*, Theodora being a
perfect anagram of Dorothea: any woman who could choose the
pseudonym Victoria Cross to write under might well have had that
kind of word-play in mind. She was also the author of *The Woman
Who Didn't*, one of several fictional replies to Grant Allen, in
which the unhappily married heroine refuses to leave her husband
for the man she loves, because: 'To me marriage is the holiest of
Sacraments and divorce is a sacrilege.'[116] The attitude is unusual
for a New Woman novel, though the disappointment in love is
characteristic. Jessima Halliday, the type of victimised wife in *A
Superfluous Woman*, during a happy Highland interlude in her
generally harrowing life, tries to seduce a handsome 'Scottish
peasant': in a neat ideological turn-about, he refuses to think of
anything but conventional courtship and marriage.[117]

   The use of shock-tactics both dramatically within a story and to
assert the need for women to speak out as bluntly as men is the
favoured device of Ménie Muriel Dowie in *Gallia*. The novel opens
with Gallia, down from Oxford, reading the newspaper at breakfast
and announcing to her shocked family: 'There is an agitation about
the State regulation of vice.'[118] Later, during a tea-party conversation one of the women remarks on the ease with which household
services can now be 'got in'. Another suggests that 'getting all the
cooking in' would be useful. Gallia has more adventurous ideas:

> It would indeed. We may live to see that, but we shan't live
> to see the real advance; which will be the getting in of fathers
> and mothers, or rather husbands and wives to be fathers and
> mothers.
>   Gertrude shrieked: Margaret was startled and silent.[119]

When a man tries to compliment her by saying that she isn't the kind of woman to be satisfied with marriage and bringing up children, she replies: 'I certainly hope to bring up a child. I think that is all I do want.'[120] Having clarified her views on the importance of selective breeding, she does marry, after thoughtfully telling the chosen man that he will not need to suffer the 'unfairness of the average proposal scene':

> We'll try and be more honest. So it is my turn now. I have
> thought for some little time of marrying you, and to spare
> you any further anxiety, I may tell you that I had decided to
> if you spoke of it.[121]

It is irresistibly reminiscent of another great proposal scene of 1895 when Gwendolen Fairfax objects to being taken for granted by Jack Worthing:

> GWENDOLEN: I adore you. But you haven't proposed to me
> yet. Nothing has been said at all about marriage.
> The subject has not even been touched on.
> JACK: Well . . . may I propose to you now?
> GWENDOLEN: I think it would be an admirable opportunity.
> And to spare you any possible disappointment,
> Mr Worthing, I think it only fair to tell you
> frankly beforehand that I am fully determined to
> accept you.[122]

There is quite a bit of the New Woman about Gwendolen Fairfax, though the New Woman novelists had none of Wilde's wit and verbal ingenuity, and they were not interested in comic resolutions to the problems they wrote about. They were unrelentingly serious.

Gwendolen Fairfax demonstrates the new daring and independence in the way she takes control of the marriage proposal, but if she had been a genuine New Woman heroine she would have gone further and either spelt out the precise terms of the marriage relationship, with a cancellation clause prominently insisted on, or, more probably, she would have suggested a trial marriage or a free union to see how things worked out. Either way, marriage ceases to be a sacred act of commitment and becomes an experiment. This idea is present in all New Woman novels and it was made central in two of the most notorious, Iota's *A Yellow Aster* (1894) and Allen's *The Woman Who Did*. The subject tackled by Iota was controversial even by the standards of this type of fiction. Brought up by parents who are austerely rational and unworldly, Gwen Waring is exceedingly beautiful, socially popular, frequently proposed to, and, as she herself admits, 'sexless'. When she does meet a man she is willing to marry, she explains her condition to him and he asks – and how else could he know? – whether this is their 'betrothal':

> She bowed her head.
> 'Oh, my darling!' he said suddenly.
> 'Will he often say it?' she thought curiously. 'Can I stand this?'
> 'My darling, you have no idea how I shall enjoy giving you lessons in love.'
> Will you?' she said grimly, 'I doubt it; I tell you I have no taste for the cult.'

She agrees to the marriage as long as it is only 'a preliminary experiment as to how life together goes; if it did not do, we might each go our own way and bury the past'.[123] The 'lessons in love' lead to Gwen becoming pregnant, though still without any feelings of sexual pleasure, and for much of the novel, and the pregnancy, her husband is away in Africa sublimating his passion and fighting the fever while Gwen is struggling to cope with motherhood. Eventually in some mysterious, unexplained way the couple are united literally, and presumably sexually, by the baby grasping their hands. *The Woman Who Did* contains yet another startling proposal scene. Herminia Barton hears her father, the Dean of Dunwich, preach a sermon on the theme 'The Truth shall make you Free' and swears to live her life according to that teaching.[124] When she falls in love she announces to the man: 'I am yours this moment. You may do what you would with me.' He replies: 'Then how soon can we be married?':

> At sound of these unexpected words from such lips as his, a flush of shame and horror overspread Herminia's cheek.
> 'Never!' she cried firmly, drawing away. 'O Alan, what can you mean by it?'[125]

Herminia does remain true to her belief that marriage is a 'still deeper and more loathsome slavery' than free love.[126] When her lover dies she brings up their daughter by herself, refusing other offers of marriage, and when the daughter shows herself determined to marry conventionally, Herminia commits suicide. Betrayal of the new ideals is also the theme of a bizarre story by Francis Gribble called 'A Shattered Doll's House'. Eleanor and Walter are married, but live immaculately intellectual, unemotional lives. When Eleanor learns that her husband is having an affair she is interested only in finding out what sort of woman he is attracted to. It turns out to be bohemian, pretty, unintelligent Dora, and Eleanor collapses on the floor crying: 'Walter likes doll women – Walter likes doll women.' She locks up her 'advanced books'; reads Ouida instead of Ibsen; goes to comic opera rather than 'literary plays', and 'burns the manuscript of the new psychological novel which she had just begun to write'. When none of this makes any impression on Walter she accepts that he loves the kind of women 'who could sink her individuality in his' and kills herself.[127] The literary and fashionable allusions are so neatly up-to-date in 'A Shattered Doll's House' that the story may have been intended as a skit, though it may also be perfectly serious comment: as in the case of 'Theodora' it is impossible to tell for sure.

New Woman fiction amounted, ultimately, to a series of defiant gestures, and there was little that the writers most committed to it could do other than go on repeating the defiance. They were limited by their self-conscious intensity, narrow social range, and a general lack of interest in any political or feminist ideology that might have given a wider inspiration to their work. The personal rebellions tended to remain strictly personal, and the occasional call for the development of a new kind of feminist awareness is never strong enough to counterbalance the suicides, lonely deaths and crushed ambitions that feature in several of the novels. Yet, in spite of its obvious weaknesses, the influence of the New Woman novelists was considerable. Out of their work, and the public discussion provoked by it, there emerged into the open a large number of human relationships and attitudes which British fiction had been traditionally obliged to ignore or justify and which had been responsible for bringing upon the New Woman novelists charges of 'erotomania' and 'neurosis'. They recognised, for example, the unmarried mother who is content to remain unmarried; the single woman whose lack of marital status does not condemn her to celibacy; the married couple who make a conscious decision not to have children or decide not to marry at all but live in a 'free union'; the woman, married or single, who dislikes babies; the right of a woman to make a sexual advance or proposal of marriage; the feelings of sexual disgust experienced by some women sold on the marriage market; the existence of established sexual relationships between married men and single women in which the mistress may be financially dependent upon the man or financially independent of him. Most of these relationships and attitudes were reasonably familiar aspects of earlier Victorian life, though concealed by the holistic image of the family. From the mid-1890s – inspired by Hardy, Meredith, and the New Woman novelists, and by the social reality of more easily available separation, divorce, and birth-control methods – irregular sexual relationships moved to a central place in British fiction.

Although it was to be men writers who, over the next twenty years, would most fully exploit the fictional possibilities of sexual liberation, it mattered greatly to them that many of the novelists proclaiming the new frankness were women. Like Nora Helmer, such women had rejected the protection that went along with being an angel or doll even though they were uncertain of what would follow. The real struggle was only beginning, but it was easy for men to mistake the gesture for a solution. As early as 1897 Shaw was using the occasion of a revival of *A Doll's House* to call, semi-seriously, for sympathy for Helmer because the problem of the 'awakening of women' had been solved by Ibsen, 'just as it is being solved in real life'. Nora's revolt was now seen as marking not the start but the 'end of a chapter of human history' because, as Shaw pointed out, 'when she comes back, it will not be to the old home; for when the patriarch no longer rules, and the "breadwinner" acknowledges his dependence, there is an end of the old order'.[128] It seems never to have occurred to Shaw, or the other writers who produced sequels to *A Doll's House*, that Helmer might start enjoying his independence and not want Nora back. It was, however, apparent to some writers that the emergence of the New Woman represented not a general shift in society as a whole but the formation of a vanguard of sexual and moral liberation by the standards of which all other women were to be judged. Pointing to the generally 'admirable' qualities of 'our English emancipated women' and looking hopefully towards a world 'reconstituted on a basis of *intellectual aristocracy*', Gissing confided to Bertz:

I am driven frantic by the cfass imbecility of the typical

woman. That type must disappear, or at all events become altogether subordinate. And I believe that the only way of effecting this is to go through a period of what many people will call sexual anarchy. Nothing good will perish; we can trust the forces of nature, which tend to conservation.[129]

Among the novelists of the time perhaps only Meredith could have seconded Gissing's view that the 'forces of nature' tend to conserve the 'good' in humanity, but none of them would have disagreed that Britain was entering what 'many people' were to see as a period of 'sexual anarchy', as the caution of the 1880s gave way to a widespread experimentation in which the regular or conventional marriage seemed odd. 'Nobody thought o' being afeared o' matrimony in my time ... Why when I and my poor man were married we thought no more o't than of a game o' dibs!' says Widow Edlin scornfully, and she can be taken as the choral voice of the age, not just of *Jude the Obscure*.[130] In *Jude* marriage is merely a temporary arrangement, one choice among several possibilities, and as Mrs Oliphant noted it is the women who are actively challenging convention: Jude, like many men in the new fiction, is comparatively passive. There could hardly be a cruder expression of the new liberation than Arabella initiating her relationship with Jude by flinging a pig's pizzle at him: when she is tired of the marriage, she goes off to Australia. Sue refuses to be married at all or, as she defines it, 'licenced to be loved on the premises', though as a further aspect of the torment of modern restlessness she is unwilling to be 'loved' with or without a license and eventually collapses back into an 'enslavement to forms'.[131] The principle of divorce and separation is openly accepted, and in contrast to Widow Edlin's stolid acceptance of marriage as nothing to make a fuss about, the almost equally conventional Phillotson is converted to a belief in matriarchy, while Jude comes to despise 'the excessive regard of parents for their own children', suggesting instead a kind of collective parental concern for all children.[132] Meredith was less eager than Hardy to enter conjectually into the forms that sexual relationships might take in the future: the principal women characters in *One of Our Conquerors* (1891), *Lord Ormont and his Aminta* (1894) and *The Amazing Marriage* (1895) are models of quiet dignity compared with Sue Bridehead or Arabella, but they are also subject to victimisation by men in ways that are more pervasive and more puzzling than in Meredith's own earlier novels. Conceal-

ment becomes both theme and method. The egotism of Victor
Radnor and Lord Ormont is no longer presented in high satirical
style, as that of Sir Willoughby Patterne had been: instead it
functions unchecked as a destructive, and (in *Lord Ormont*
especially) a motiveless, sinister force. In *One of Our Conquerors*
and *Lord Ormont* there are moments when Meredith's own voice
breaks angrily and awkwardly through the complicated plots to
denounce the human misery caused by Society's hypocritical
attitudes to marriage. Meredith's anger is most effective in the scene in
One of Our Conquerors following Dudley Sowerby's proposal of
marriage to Nesta. He is informed, calmly, by Nataly that she is not
legally married to Victor Radnor and that Nesta is therefore
illegitimate. As Dudley Sowerby rides away we follow his thoughts:

> Who would have imagined Mr Radnor a private sinner
> flaunting for one of the righteous? And she, the mother, a
> lady – quite a lady . . . How had it been concealed? In
> Dudley's upper sphere, everything was exposed: Scandal
> walked naked and unashamed – figurante of the polite
> world.[133]

At a comparable moment in *Lord Ormont*, Meredith is more
urgently intrusive. Aminta, left isolated by her husband, and offered
(deliberately it is assumed) as prey for one of the notorious upper-class
womanisers who feature in many of Meredith's novels, tries to make
sense of her life:

> That Institution of Marriage was eyed. Is it not a halting
> step to happiness? It is the step of a cripple; and one leg or
> other poses for the feebler sex – small is the matter which!
> And is happiness our cry? Our cry is rather for circumstance
> and occasion to use our functions, and the conditions are
> denied to women by Marriage – denied to the luckless of
> women, who are many, very many.[134]

If that kind of protectiveness of women was becoming rare, it was
even rarer to find unorthodox sexual relationships treated with
authorial calmness, though this was achieved by Mark Rutherford
in *Clara Hopgood* (1896) which also provides a striking example of
old and new conventions blending successfully together. The
suffering caused by the indissolubility of marriage had been a
constant theme of Rutherford's fiction: his usual answer to the
problem was renunciation and endurance. But in *Clara Hopgood* he

took an approach which, while not inconsistent with the Radical philosophy of his earlier books, was more in tune with the mood of the 1890s. He had certainly read George Egerton's *Keynotes* which he described sarcastically as one of the modern books 'praised by "culture"', and no doubt some other examples of New Woman fiction.[135] It is possible that he regarded *Clara Hopgood* as a defence of an older type of liberal thinking that had faced up to Philistine opposition without the clangorous self-advertisement of the late Victorian revolt. The novel is set in the 1840s: Clara and Madge Hopgood are the daughters of free-thinking parents who believe, to the horror of their neighbours, that girls should receive the same education as boys. Rutherford allows no concession to the new sexual explicitness: Madge Hopgood and Frank Palmer make love in the kind of thunderstorm – complete with lightning and splintered elm tree – that descends directly from *Jane Eyre* and was soon to be taken over by Hollywood. But the calm refusal of Madge to marry Frank Palmer because whatever wrong they may have done, marriage would make the situation even worse; the decision to bring up their child by herself; the moral support she is given by her mother, sister and Mrs Caffyn; the subtlety of the relationship with her sister; even her eventual marriage, all contribute to make *Clara Hopgood* one of the most unusual and convincing fictional explorations of the new morality.

The moral confidence of *Clara Hopgood* is particularly notable in comparison with the frenetic nervousness that was now the hallmark of relationships between young people in fiction, yet even so, this late in his career Rutherford, like Hardy and Meredith, can be seen responding to a domestic world that was facing a devastating challenge to earlier sexual values. A very similar response is observable in James's later fiction. In his case the influence of Ibsen was paramount; the novels he wrote after his failure to become a successful dramatist are quite different from the earlier work in their social analysis as well as their artistic form.[136] From *What Maisie Knew* (1897), *The Turn of the Screw* (1898) and *The Awkward Age* (1899) through to *The Sacred Fount* (1901), *The Wings of the Dove* (1902), *The Ambassadors* (1903) and *The Golden Bowl* (1904), Jamesian renunciation and moral certainty are constantly disrupted by a frenzied sexuality which is equally disturbing whether it is casually acknowledged by characters or elaborately concealed. The notorious obliquity of James's later

narrative method has much to do with the mysterious controlling
and threatening power of sex that runs as an obsessive theme
throughout these novels. It was initiated, in a relatively straightforward manner, by *The Spoils of Poynton* (1897). Fleda Vetch is
not, in feeling or outlook, one of the New Women: indeed, her
alliance with Mrs Gereth against modern vulgarity places her
firmly in an opposing camp. Yet in his portrayal of Fleda, James
acknowledges some of the standard trappings of New Woman
fiction and uses them to dissociate Fleda from what he regards as
the moral coarseness they can lead to. It is not simply a matter of
Fleda having spent a year 'with several hundred other young
women' in a Paris studio studying Impressionist painting, or her
father leaving her free to come and go by herself for much of the
time, though both of these observations are representative of
James's great care with social detail.[137] More pertinent are the
long, edgy conversations she has with Owen Gereth in which it
seems as though she is constantly being urged to take some kind of
sexual lead in the relationship. Mrs Brigstock, interrupting them,
clearly thinks this is what Fleda could well have been doing, and
Fleda's poor joke that she is being treated like 'one of those bad
women in a play' confirms the fear.[138] Returned to Mona
Brigstock, who has nothing of Fleda's conscience in such matters,
Owen is rushed off to the registry office and lost to Fleda. How
exactly Mona does succeed in trapping Owen is left open to
interpretation by James's conscious obscurity, but there is no
doubt about her ruthlessness. She is representative of a new kind of
modern woman – as, in slightly different ways, are Mrs Beale in
What Maisie Knew and Kate Croy in *The Wings of the Dove* –
criticised by James, though glorified by some other writers, who
achieved popular recognition in fiction through E. F. Benson's
Dodo (1894) and Anthony Hope's *The Dolly Dialogues* (1896).

Dodo particularly is offered as a prevalent modern type: her
story is subtitled 'A Detail of the Day'. She is extremely beautiful,
married to money and social position, and interested only in
pursuing whatever she considers 'shocking' or 'chic': the appropriate activities include frantic smoking and requests to her
philanthropic friends to be taken to one of 'those darling little
slums'.[139] She is hard, callous, and indifferent to the sufferings of
others. When her baby dies, Dodo asks: 'Why was the baby ever
born? I wish it never had been. What good does it do to anyone

that I should suffer?'[140] Her husband is given all the decent
qualities that she conspicuously lacks, being sensitive, baby-loving,
and sexually faithful. Some of the more traditional masculine
qualities are transferred to Dodo's close friend Edith Staines who
when she is not composing a symphony or a Mass is riding,
shooting, playing tennis, or calling for 'brandy-and-soda and a
grilled bone' to keep up her strength.[141] *Dodo* epitomises an extreme
though not uncommon response to New Woman fiction. The intense
idealism and defiant actions have been absorbed into bland amorality.
Women have won the battle and been granted independence: what
they do after the victory is up to them. There are no more dolls or
angels: they have become comic imitation men like Edith Staines or
selfish sensation-seekers like Dodo. They have everything they could
possibly need and can be left to look after, and look out for, themselves.

It was in Gissing and Wells that the changing attitude to women
in fiction (and therefore the changing nature of sexual relationships)
was most pronounced. A central theme in the work of both novelists
is the search by a male protagonist for a suitable partner. This, of
course, was an old-age preoccupation of novelists, part of the
perennial fictional view of man as 'lover, husband, father, friend'
that irritated Sidney Webb. The radical change in the 1890s is to be
found in the assumption that the questing man has set before him
not simply a choice between this particular woman or that – a
choice traditonally decided on the grounds of love, material gain, or
social status – but a wide range of options or types which have
somehow been categorised and approved by women themselves. In
neither Gissing nor Wells is love, in any conventional sense, the
motivating force. For Gissing the desired compatibility is primarily
cultural: for Wells it is primarily sexual. Not that the quest is as
cold-blooded as that makes it sound. On the contrary, the urgency
of the need to find the right partner is so intense that the
possibility of success can justify, in high romantic style, the
metaphoric annihilation of the material world. This is particularly
the case in Wells, as it was also to be in Lawrence, who took over
many of these assumptions and attitudes. But if the quest is not
cold-blooded, it can be ruthless, and there now enters into British
fiction yet another group of women characters to set against the
courageous pioneers established by the New Woman novelists. It is
made up of discarded girlfriends, abandoned wives, angry mistresses, and former lovers of one kind or another.

Gissing, as we have seen, was already an established novelist when the New Woman novels began to appear: he knew some of the writers personally, and the changes that have been noted as taking place in fiction between the 1880s and the 1890s are as apparent in his work as in that of Hardy, James, Meredith and Rutherford. He was, however, significantly younger than these other novelists. His view of life was less curtailed than theirs by mid-Victorianism, and his response to the promised new sexual liberation was more excited and comprehensive. Throughout his novels in the 1890s there are repeated acknowledgments of the openness with which unorthodox sexual relationships can now exist in life and be treated in fiction, at least within certain easily definable areas of society. Sometimes these acknowledgments are sly, as in *In the Year of Jubilee* when Beatrice French shows off her new flat to Nancy Lord. Looking into the bedroom, 'Beatrice remarked on the smallness of the chamber, adding archly, "But I sleep single."'[142] Sometimes they are challengingly direct, as in *The Whirlpool* when Alma Frothingham is propositioned by Felix Dymes. Alma is at first puzzled, and then amused:

> Yes, it was a proposal of marriage – marriage on the new
> plan, without cares or encumbrance; a suggestion rather than
> a petition; off-hand, unsentimental, yet perfectly serious, as
> look and tone proclaimed.[143]

Whether small or central, hinted at or fully explored, the various sexual relationships in Gissing's novels function as separate case-studies which achieve their desired effect only in accumulation: taken together, they make up a compendium of the new sexual possibilities. These range from the archetypal Victorian long engagement in which a frustrating celibacy is enforced by a mixture of genteel poverty and cloying sentiment, through experimental marriages and one-parent families, to idealised images of totally contented motherhood: 'Into her pure and healthy mind had never entered a thought at conflict with motherhood. Her breasts were the fountain of life; her babies clung to them, and grew large of limb.'[144]

Gissing's rapidly changing analysis of sexual relationships is observable in the roles he allots to the questing male protagonists of his four remarkable novels published between 1891 and 1894. In *New Grub Street* the qualities Jasper Milvain looks for in a wife are unequivocal: she must possess money, good looks, and sufficient personality to help him advance his career. Reardon's widow Amy has all the necessary qualities, plus an appropriate touch of hard materialism. Marian Yule – one of Gissing's finest portraits of the faithful, decent, discarded career girl who now begins to feature in fiction – has to be sacrificed, but in Milvain's moral scheme that doesn't matter. The fictional pattern is fairly traditonal. Godwin Peak in *Born in Exile* is also set on getting to the top through marriage. He is more devious, more fastidious, and less successful than Milvain. Peak could never be satisfied with an Amy Reardon: the quality he seeks in a wife is 'refinement'. *The Odd Women* and *In the Year of Jubilee* show Gissing making a sharp change of emphasis, with the men suddenly being given the upper hand in their unconventional courtships. No longer is the woman expected to provide money or social status: instead she is called upon to prove, through an elaborate test of her unconventionality, her worthiness for marriage to this particular, equally unconventional, man. *The Odd Women* is clearly indebted to New Woman attitudes, and the sexual test between Everard Barfoot and Rhoda Nunn is offered as a contest between two like-minded independent people, though that is not quite the final impression left by the novel. Even pretence of this kind is dropped in *In the Year of Jubilee*. Lionel Tarrant and Nancy Lord are forced, by one of the tortuous plots that Gissing could never rid himself of, to keep their marriage secret. For much of the novel Nancy appears to be an unmarried mother, while Tarrant pursues a bachelor life. When it is no longer necessary to maintain the deception, Tarrant decides that as he and Nancy already have the ideal relationship/marriage, they should continue as they are. Nancy is not convinced, but there is little she can do about it. She is, as it were, forced to appear to be a New Woman while being, in fact, a doubly-trapped wife.

In spite of Lionel Tarrant's triumphant manipulation of Nancy Lord, there is generally in Gissing's work considerably more talk than action: as Virginia Woolf observed, he is 'one of the extremely rare novelists who believes in the power of mind, who makes his people think'.[145] In this phase of his career what his male characters think mostly about, and debate endlessly among themselves, is the difficulty of finding a suitable woman to share their lives. It is widely assumed that conventional marriage has become unthinkable and that celibacy is unbearable, but it is not at all clear to them how both of these agonising conditions can be avoided.

Lionel Tarrant finds a solution to the problem by marrying a woman who is allowed to be strong-willed and excessively compliant at one and the same time. No other Gissing character has this degree of luck, and the blame is placed firmly on women. Godwin Peak divides women into three distinct groups. First, the 'daughters of the people' ('repulsive'); secondly, 'the average emancipated girl' ('unsatisfying'); and thirdly, 'the lady as England has perfected her towards the close of this nineteenth century. A being of marvellous delicacy, of purest instincts, of unsurpassable sweetness.'[146] He makes a further distinction between the unsatisfactory 'average emancipated girl' and the 'truly emancipated girl' who is 'almost always asexual' and therefore, to him, 'utterly repugnant'.[147] A very different option is offered by Malkin who proposes to avoid marital incompatibility by selecting a schoolgirl and training her as his future wife.[148] It is also accepted that working-class girls are not so 'repulsive' that they cannot serve as temporary sexual partners. In *The Odd Women*, Everard Barfoot explains the situation to Rhoda Nunn, whose name is a partial indication of her decision to sublimate her own sexual feelings in order to devote her full energy to the feminist cause. There are, he points out, 'a million or so of us very intelligent and highly educated' men and only a 'few thousands' of comparable women. With not enough intelligent women to go round, the 'mass of women ... contemptible', and working-class women 'mere lumps of human flesh', it is inevitable that 'the vast majority of men must make a marriage that is doomed to be a dismal failure'. Rhoda Nunn listens calmly to this analysis, admits to Barfoot that there is something in his way of putting things that she doesn't like, but agrees with his main point that before the marriage problem can be solved 'women must first be civilised'.[149] Until that comes about, the Gissing hero is tormented by the hopeless inadequacy of every type of woman, except one. The ideal is described by Godwin Peak:

> Were it but possible to win the love of a woman who looked
> forth with eyes thoroughly purged from all mist of tradition
> and conventionalism, who was at home among arts and
> sciences, who, like himself, acknowledged no class and bowed
> to no authority but that of the supreme human mind.[150]

There is an element of irony here directed at the self-deceiving Peak, but not much of it needs to be stripped away to encounter Gissing's own view of the perfect woman.

This 'idealised "noble" woman' was one of the features of Gissing's novels that H. G. Wells disapproved of, and he found the same fault in other writers of the time. In what Wells himself described as a 'slating' review of *The Woman Who Did* he attacked Grant Allen for appearing to believe that 'real women . . . have spotless souls and a physical beauty that is invariably overpowering'. Correcting that misguided view, Wells insisted: 'Real women are things of dietary and secretions, of subtle desires and mental intricacy; even the purest among them have at least beauty spots upon their souls.'[151] The desire to right this kind of false idealism was an important element in Wells's inconoclastic approach to fiction. Much of the blame for the social waste and inefficiency that he observed all around him he placed on repressed sexuality. Liberation, he believed, was possible, even easy to achieve. All that was required was for knowledge to replace ignorance, and idealism to give way to realism. As Arthur and Ann Kipps lie unhappily in bed after a trivial quarrel, Wells pictures as hovering over them 'a monster, a lumpish monster, like some great clumsy griffin thing . . . It is the anti-soul, it is the ruling power of this land, Stupidity.'[152] Looking back on his failed marriage, George Ponderovo is astonished 'by the ignorant, unguided way in which we two entangled ourselves with each other', and decides that 'Love is . . . the most important concern of the community; after all, the way in which the young people of this generation pair off determines the fate of the nation; all the other affairs of the State are subsidiary to that.'[153] It is not surprising that the young D. H. Lawrence, struggling to complete *The White Peacock*, was excited by *Tono-Bungay* and urged his friends to read it.[154]

Wells's theory and practice of fiction were not, however, always in harmony. He may have known what constitutes a 'real woman' and have possessed the secret of sexual happiness once liberation has been achieved, but the information is never successfully conveyed in his novels. Always in Wells there is an unresolved conflict between iconoclasm and reconstruction, with the desire to break free from limiting conventions felt so strongly that it can often make the need to reconstruct irrelevant. Like Gissing, Wells, classified women into easily defined types, though his classification was simpler and cruder than that of the older novelist. The three principal types – pretty young girl, unsatisfactory wife, and liberated mistress – mark the main stages of the male protagonist's quest for self-fulfilment. In novel after novel, gauche, jaunty courtships conducted in sexual ignorance slide into marriages which are narrow, repressive and frustrated. Mr Polly, after trying with comic lack of success to burn down his house, learns that 'if the world does not please you, *you can change it*', and decides to 'Clear out.'[155] Remington suppresses his sexuality to his wife's ambition so that they can dedicate their joint energies – in the manner of the Webbs – to social service. George Ponderovo's wife Marion has a 'disgust and dread of maternity. All that was fruition and quintessence of the "horrid" elements in life, a disgusting thing, a last indignity that overtook unwary women.'[156] Both Remington and Ponderovo escape the frustration of their marriages by affairs with sexually liberated women, a pattern that is given a slightly more subtle variation in *Ann Veronica*; Mr Polly settles for the Potswell Inn and its 'agreeable plump' landlady, while his wife, happy enough to see him go, runs a tea-shop; the marriage of Arthur and Ann Kipps survives in spite of the shadow of Stupidity hovering over them; Remington abandons his political career for the sake of Isabel and leaves England, not totally convinced that he has the right to choose private satisfaction rather than public duty. 'What is one life against the State?' he ponders, and he and Isabel cling to each other more like the babes in the wood than passionate lovers.[157] Wells's fiction never carried with it the inward, lonely, isolated air that is typical of Gissing's; that sense – however profound the social analysis – of the novels serving as the means to work out some deeply personal problems. Wells's own experiences of life are constantly re-enacted in his fiction, but the novels themselves seem always to be at the service of some larger cause which has sprung from Wells's socialism or, more generally, his compulsive need to predict trends and events. However unstable the ideology (and it could veer crazily between extremes) the novels are involved, committed, outward-looking; they seek to exert influence, provoke debate, and inspire discipleship. Virginia Woolf described them as 'incomplete' and claimed that 'in order to complete them it seems necessary to do something'.[158] That is surely right, but it is not necessarily a negative quality: the activism encouraged by Wells's novels was one of their most important characteristics.

After three or four years of the new century it was beginning to

seem as though fiction had given up on the question of sexual
liberation. Gissing was dead; the New Woman experiment had
fizzled out; and although Wells's predictions and speculations grew
more and more daring they did not transfer easily to *Love and Mr
Lewisham* (1900), his one novel of contemporary social life written
at this time. For some feminists the lack of interest was ominous
and Lucas Malet was not alone in warning that although the
committed New Woman would be likely to resist the trend, many
other women were in danger of being charmed 'back to the store-
closet and the nursery'.[159] That fear was somewhat lessened by the
formation of the Women's Social and Political Union in 1903, but
even the suffragette movement had surprisingly little impact on
fiction.[160] The militant suffragette is to be found frequently in
popular fiction of the day, but rarely as more than social detail.
The fictional case for stronger representation was pioneered by
Elizabeth Robins with *The Convert* (1907), which was successful as
both novel and play. This was followed by Wells's *Ann Veronica*
(1909) and a handful of minor works of which Evelyn Sharp's
collection of realistic sketches *Rebel Women* (1910), G. Colmore's
sympathetic novel *Suffragette Sally* (1911), and Mrs Humphry
Ward's unsympathetic *Delia Blanchflower* (1914) are representative.
As the campaign for women's suffrage intensified, Wells began to
lose much of the feminist admiration he had once held. The strain
of protective domesticity that was never entirely absent from his
novels steadily increased, and *Marriage* (1912) provoked a furiously
angry review from Rebecca West who insisted that all 'women
ought to have a chance of being sifted clean through the sieve of
work'.[161] The feeling that Wells had betrayed the cause was
particularly bitter because so much had been expected of him.
Nothing comparable could have been expected from E. F. Benson,
but even so the resurrection of his great hit of the 1890s as *Dodo
the Second* (1914) was an audaciously bland expression of the belief
that the woman question (on its domestic side at least) was now a
thing of the past. Dodo, miraculously transformed into a doting
wife and mother, sits surrounded by her daughter's bright young
friends: 'Oh, do tell us,' they beg her, 'about those delicious
Victorian days of 1890 when you were a girl and people thought
you fast and were shocked.'[162]

In fact, the theme of sexual liberation had not disappeared from
fiction, the lessons of the 1890s were not forgotten, and the quiet

beginning to the new century was deceptive. From about 1905 literary journalists and moral reformers began drawing attention to what they called the 'sex novel' or the 'sex problem' novel. The two terms were used indiscriminately and applied by hostile critics to almost any novel which contained a sexual element. The phenomenon they were coined to describe, however, was real enough, and the vagueness of the terminology inevitable, perhaps even necessary, for a development in fiction that embraced many different approaches and methods and denoted a widespread trend rather than any particular school. What the term 'sex novel' referred to was the preoccupation of early twentieth-century novelists with questions of sexual psychology once the constraints of Victorianism had been cast away. Wells was a major influence, through his non-fictional speculative works as much as the novels, but he was in no sense the initiator of the trend. Edwardian feminists, reformers and Socialists were involved in it, and so were some best-selling novelists who in every other respect shared nothing with feminism or socialism, and little more with social reform. It was clearly a natural extension of the various fictional experiments with sexual relationships already discussed in this chapter: Hardy, Gissing, Meredith and the New Woman novelists were the sex-novel's immediate precursors, though not quite its progenitors. To readers and critics of the time it certainly felt as though a drastic change had taken place, even though the sex 'problems' remained largely what they had been in the 1890s and sexual explicitness was often less an issue than it had been in the 1880s. The crucial change lay in tone and attitude. Quite suddenly the time for defensive experimentation appeared to be over, and attention began to switch to a close analysis of the proven results of those experiments. It could now be assumed that there was no such thing as normal or orthodox sexuality; no single generally acceptable pattern for family life; no one kind of sexuality that was attributable to all women and all men. There were still problems in plenty, and still novelists who used their work to draw attention to the change of heart or legislation that they believed would bring a solution. But even these novelists – excepting the most ardently propagandist of them – now understood that sex itself was the key problem.

The new mood was signalled by such works as Maugham's *Mrs Craddock* (1902) and Bennett's *Leonora* (1903), but its wider significance was only revealed with the publication in 1905 of

Wells's *Kipps*, E. M. Forster's *Where Angels Fear to Tread*, Elizabeth Robins's *A Dark Lantern*, and Bennett's *Sacred and Profane Love*. The following year saw the publication of Galsworthy's *The Man of Property*, Bennett's *Whom God Hath Joined*, and Violet Hunt's *The Workaday Woman*. The trend was now clear and throughout 1907 and 1908 the sex-novel consolidated its position. Its dominant mood could be gently persistent (Galsworthy's *The Country House*, Forster's *A Room with a View*); bewilderingly analytical (May Sinclair's *The Helpmate*); solemnly assertive (Hubert Wales's *The Yoke*); or sensationally erotic (Elinor Glyn's *Three Weeks*, Horace de Vere Stacpoole's *The Blue Lagoon*). It did much to pave the way for the controversial reception of *Ann Veronica*; further provoked Wells into writing his best social novels – *Mr Polly*, *Tono-Bungay* and *The New Machiavelli*; and made an important contribution to the psychological context of such varied early modern works as Lawrence's *The White Peacock*, *The Trespasser*, *Sons and Lovers*, and 'The Daughters of the Vicar'; John Masefield's *The Street of Today*; May Sinclair's *The Three Sisters*; Compton Mackenzie's *Sinister Street*; Gilbert Cannan's *Round the Corner*; Maugham's *Of Human Bondage*; and Ford's *A Call* and *The Good Soldier*.

The sex-novel marked a distinctive phase in the growing interest of novelists in psychology. It could be silly, serious, or sensational, but always it focused on the need to rid the self of sexual repression and honestly face the consequences. Mr Emerson's advice to Lucy Honeychurch in *A Room with a View* is characteristic:

> You are inclined to get muddled, if I may judge from last
> night. Let yourself go. Pull out from the depths those
> thoughts that you do not understand, and spread them out in
> the sunlight and know the meaning of them.[163]

Katherine in *A Dark Lantern* has no Mr Emerson to advise her, but learns for herself a similar lesson – that the answer to her problem lies in the unconscious. Apparently tricked into a 'private marriage' she forces herself to face the truth: 'Deep down in my heart, fathoms below admission even to myself, *I have been conscious of it all*. No innocent maiden trapped. His accomplice, I.'[164] Carlotta Peel in *Sacred and Profane Love* offers herself to a famous concert pianist, and then analyses her situation: 'I had always a sort of fierce courage; and as I had proved the courage of

my passion in the night, so I proved the courage of my . . .
intellectual honesty in the morning.'[165] She is not only courageously passionate and intellectually honest, but sensible as well: she
is probably the first woman in fiction to be shown going to a doctor
for a pregnancy test.[166] It was a cardinal doctrine of the sex-novel
that true morality lay not in any particular action but rather in the
nature of the protagonist's response to that action. Elinor Glyn's
lurid description of the three weeks of passion enjoyed by the
handsome young Englishman Paul Verdayne and a mysterious East
European 'Lady', was, the author insisted, profoundly moral.[167]
That was not, however, why millions of readers rushed to buy
Three Weeks, or *The Blue Lagoon*, which was in some respects the
ultimate sex-novel. Taking one of the most revered plots in the
history of fiction – castaways on a desert island – de Vere
Stacpoole dispensed with virtually all the conventional adventure-
tale trappings and concentrated on the gradual growth of two
young children from total innocence, through puberty and teenage
self-conscious, to sexual awareness and fulfilment in parenthood. It
was a fable for its time, illustrating the natural sexuality that had
become merely a dream in corrupt modern society.

For several feminist writers the psychology of sexuality took on a
rather special significance. Violet Hunt, May Sinclair and Cicely
Hamilton were all active supporters of the suffragette movement:
they were also members of the Women Writers Suffrage League,
and published polemical books or pamphlets on suffragism. But
unlike Elizabeth Robins, they did not write fiction which dealt
directly wth this aspect of their lives. Perhaps they feared that
concentration on so specific an issue would lead them into a trap
similar to that which had already dated New Woman fiction. Nor
were they interested in the sexual fantasies of Elinor Glyn or de
Vere Stacpoole: rather, they looked to sexual psychology to give to
their work a deeper sense of reality. Of the three writers, Violet
Hunt's approach was the most straightforward. The social world of
The Workaday Woman is that of 'hardworking girls in flats' and
much of the story is conveyed through dialogue, a technique that
Hunt had been consciously developing for some years. Details of the
girls' love affairs, jobs and different social circles, emerge in a
matter-of-fact tone and are given a slight twist at the end of the novel
by the insistence that this is the story not of exceptional, but of
'everyday' women. May Sinclair's *The Helpmate* and Cicely

Hamilton's *Just to Get Married* are more intensely focused than *The Workaday Woman*, but they also rely on a twist of fictional convention to make their point. *The Helpmate* tells the story of a woman who just after being married learns that her husband has earlier had an affair with another woman, an act which she persists in regarding as infidelity to herself. In a New Woman novel the woman would have been pure and the husband a drunkard or syphilitic: here the husband is portrayed as fairly normal and the wife mentally tormented by her own excessive emphasis on purity. Cicely Hamilton's *Just to Get Married* (1911) is a neatly-turned fictional illustration of ideas that she had advanced two years earlier in her polemical book *Marriage as a Trade*. Georgina Vicary sets out on a determined campaign to win a husband. When the chosen man does eventually propose, Georgina is shocked to find that he is passionately in love with her. Convinced that her own motives were dishonest and acknowledging that she had been willing to prostitute herself 'just to get married', she breaks off her engagement. Then, the couple accidentally meeting, she proposes to him, demonstrating that 'a woman's love is not free as a man's is'.[168] The twists and turnabouts of what is basically one of the most common of all novel plots are teasingly ironic. They make the point that Georgina's lack of genuine sexual response to her future husband is created by the hypocritical role that women are expected to play in courtship: once that role is challenged, Georgina's sexual inhibitions are released. The proposal refers back to a familiar gesture of New Woman fiction, but Cicely Hamilton gives it a deeper psychological and feminist significance.

Whether written by women or men, most of the sex-novels made the sexuality of women a central theme. This was one of the aspects of Hubert Wales's *The Yoke* that attracted the attention of the National Vigilance Association who succeeded in getting it withdrawn from circulation. The 'yoke' of the novel's title refers not to the traditional union of marriage, but to the unbearable sexual constraints placed upon single men and women: the only people excluded from Wales's generalisation are those 'who appear to have been given a special temperamental adaptation for an ascetic and abstinent life'.[169] The principal characters in his novel are not blessed with this gift. Angelica Jenour is an attractive, respectable unmarried woman of forty who has been largely responsible for bringing up twenty-two-year-old Maurice Heelas.

When she realises that he has been going with prostitutes she offers herself to him. They live together happily, and secretly, as lovers until Maurice falls in love with a younger girl. Angelica then relinquishes her claim on Maurice, after explaining to the girl the reason for her behaviour. In spite of Wales's moralising tone, *The Yoke* was a genuinely daring novel which brought together several important sexual concerns of the time. Society's double standard on sexual behaviour means that Maurice's use of prostitutes is condoned, while Angelica, 'a maid at forty!', is expected to be ignorant of, and uninterested in, sex. The argument that the double standard leads to a high incidence of venereal disease among young men is forcefully put: Maurice's close friend commits suicide after contracting syphilis, and it is Angelica's wish to save Maurice from this kind of fate that gives her the courage to act as she does. But at least as powerful a motive is her own sexual frustration. The 'yoke' is on her as well as Maurice. The mental agony she experiences when she overhears a married couple making love in the next room is one of the frankest, and most psychologically convincing, scenes in any of the sex-novels.[170]

Although it was a recurring conviction of these novels that responsibility for release from sexual repression lies mainly with the individual, legislative help was repeatedly called for in the crucial area of divorce reform. The expense and difficulty of obtaining a divorce, and the different standards applied by the law to men and women, were seen by novelists as cruel and unnecessary barriers to the attainment of individual happiness. It was not, however, only the personal experiences of many of the novelists that drew them to this subject. Roughly coinciding with the popularity of the sex-novel, there was a wider campaign for a reform of the divorce laws that culminated in the setting up of a Royal Commission of Inquiry in 1909. The expectation of substantial reforms developing out of the inquiry was a strong influence on the way that adulterous relationships are treated in these novels, and, of course, the influence was reciprocated, with novelists carrying the subject to a wider audience. Wells and Bennett gave a prominent place to the need for divorce reform in several of their novels, but it was Galsworthy who put the case most forcefully with *The Man of Property* and *The Country House*. 'An unhappy marriage!' young Jolyon muses, 'No ill-treatment – only that indefinable malaise, that terrible blight which killed all sweetness

under Heaven.'[171] The terrible blight of an unhappy marriage is
personified in Irene Forsyte, and the vindictive power the law gave
to husbands in Soames: the relationship between them is an
exemplary demonstration of the view of marriage as a property
transaction that feminists and Marxists had been proclaiming for
the previous thirty years. The high hopes and aspirations raised by
the Royal Commission on divorce are revealed by Stephen Torre's
only novel *The Blot* (1910). Unashamedly propagandist, it traces
the campaign of an unhappily married solicitor, Romandy Watson,
to repeal the 'one English law' which is a 'blot' on the country's
legislation. In spite of the opposition of the Church, Watson's
campaign is a succcess and the novel ends with a new divorce law
being passed by the Lords. The triumphant celebrations of *The
Blot* were, however, quite a bit premature. The Royal Commission
Report published in 1912 did everything expected of it, recommending that men and women should be treated equally before the
law, that no one should be excluded from the possibility of divorce
through poverty, and that the grounds for divorce be widened.[172]
But the legislation that might have turned these recommendations
into reality was postponed by the outbreak of war, and the social
and sexual unhappiness caused by an unreformed divorce law
remained a major subject of fiction for years to come.

In spite of the determination by the more talented of the 'sex-
novelists' not to allow their work to run into the kinds of restrictive
stereotypes associated with New Woman fiction, there was one
aspect of the earlier pattern that was now repeated. During the
years 1905 to 1908 when the journalistic label 'sex-novel' was most
often applied, there was, as we have seen, a sympathetic attempt in
many of these novels to communicate a deeper understanding of
the psychology and sexuality of women. This concern gradually
faded away. The centre of fictional interest once again became the
questing man, and the narrow type-casting of women re-emerged.
The part played in this process by H. G. Wells has already been
noted: to it there needs to be added that of D. H. Lawrence. Lettie
Beardsall in *The White Peacock* is presented as a distinct type of
modern woman. By turns she is flirtatious, edgy, seductive,
unobtainable, neurotic, off-hand, never satisfied:

> Difficult to please in every circumstance; she, who had
> always been so rippling in thoughtless life, sat down in the
> window-sill to think, and her strong teeth bit at her handker-

chief till it was torn in holes. She would say nothing to me;
she read all things that dealt with modern woman.[173]

The idealised contrast to Lettie is Emily Renshaw who at the close
of the novel is introduced 'rich as always with her large beauty, and
stately now with the stateliness of a strong woman six months gone
with child'. She is not only gloriously pregnant, but intensely
happy baking a pie: 'Emily had at last found her place, and had
escaped from the torture of strange, complex modern life.'[174] The
clear choice is between neurosis brought on by the attempt to come
to terms with modern conditions, and happy domesticity achieved
by rejecting any involvement with modernity. There is no such
contrast offered in *The Trespasser*, but although the story is
essentially Helena's – and based on the real-life experiences of
Lawrence's friend Helen Corke – the movement of sympathy in
the novel is strongly towards Siegmund who is caught between the
'dreamy', 'swooning', Helena, and his nagging wife. With *Sons and
Lovers* Lawrence overcame the narrative problems he had failed to
solve in the previous two novels, and Paul Morel, now placed
triumphantly at the centre of the book, succeeds in escaping the
clutches of all three of the women who dominate his life – a
clinging, soulful, sexually-repressed girlfriend; a jealous mother;
and a sexually liberated, married feminist. *Sons and Lovers* contains
one strange echo of the belief expressed in *The White Peacock* that
for a woman domesticity is the way out of self-torturing modernity.
When Paul manipulates Clara and Baxter Dawes into a possible
reunion, Clara is understandably angry and thinks Paul 'a mean
fellow . . . to take what he wanted and then give her back'. But
Lawrence corrects her: 'She did not remember that she herself had had
what she wanted, and really, at the bottom of her heart, wished to be
given back.'[175]

That is not simply Lawrence being characteristically confident
about what everyone else 'really' wants: it also represents a wider
shift of novelists' interest from the sexuality of women to the
sexuality of men. In the years immediately preceding the First
World War the growing fascination with minute psychological
analysis and the determination of younger novelists to assert their
independence combined to produce a large number of what
Somerset Maugham called 'autobiographical novels of immense
length'.[176] It was not necessary for these novels to be 'immense',

though many of them were: the newness lay in their relatively undiluted autobiographical or confessional nature. Samuel Butler was a principal English influence on this modern variation of the *Bildungsroman* or *Künstlerroman*: other novelists who were drawn to it included Lawrence, Joyce, Maugham, J. D. Beresford, Gilbert Cannan, Bennett, Wells, Compton Mackenzie and Dorothy Richardson, who was well aware of the overwhelmingly masculine nature of this branch of fiction.[177] In all of these novels prominent attention was given to the yoing protagonists' sexual initiation. Ernest Pontifex in *The Way of All Flesh* makes a mess of this, as of most other aspects of his young life: unable to tell the difference between a respectable girl and a prostitute, his confusion lands him in prison. The more knowing Stephen Dedalus in *A Portrait of the Artist* learns about sex in the brothels of Dublin. Prostitutes or, similarly commercial in their motives, girls (often working-class) picked up casually, serve the same initiatory function in several of the novels. But given greater prominence was the initiation conducted by a slightly older woman whose sexual experience is sometimes associated with feminism, but more usually has come to her through marriage: she is often divorced or separated from her husband. Clara Dawes in *Sons and Lovers* qualifies for the role on several of these counts. The mysterious and sexually willing Englishwoman encountered by Remington in *The New Machiavelli* is sufficiently knowledgeable about the function she is to fulfil that she even describes herself in terms of one of its literary archetypes: 'She said she was the Woman of Thirty, "George Moore's Woman of Thirty." I had not read George Moore at the time, but I pretended to understand.'[178] Miss Wilkinson in *Of Human Bondage* is not married, a feminist, or particularly attractive, but she starts Philip Carey on the path to his later, even more disastrous sexual relationships:

> She wore a camisole of white calico with short arms. She
> looked grotesque. Philip's heart sank as he stared at her; she
> had never seemed so unattractive; but it was too late now.
> He closed the door behind him and locked it.[179]

Here, as in many of the sexual experiences described in fiction of the period, there is remarkably little concern at the possibility of pregnancy. The most obvious reason for this was the widespread assumption that some form of birth-control method was available and functioning successfully, though it was still rare for a novelist to mention such things.[180] An important part of the appeal of the sexually mature, older or married woman was that she could be expected to be in possession of his kind of knowledge: a similar assumption runs through much of the New Woman fiction. But with regard to the pre-war *Bildungsroman* and *Künstlerroman*, an additional factor has to be taken into account. To the young, predominantly male protagonists of these novels, sexual experience may be of crucial importance to their development, but none of them regards it as leading naturally to fatherhood. It is not simply their awareness that the pleasurable and the procreative aspects of sex can now be separated: it is, rather, that they are not much interested in children, and considerably less interested in becoming fathers. They are, however, wholehearedly interested in themselves, and – as the representatives of the generation that finally emerged from thirty years of furious debate on marriage and the family system – in seeking revenge.

According to the mythology of the Erewhonians, the unborn are constantly pestering humans to accept them as children. These unborn children have displayed before them the essential emptiness of life, and in a further attempt to dissuade them from 'suicide', the conditions for being born are made exceptionally strict so that only 'the most foolish of the unborn will consent to them': it is from these 'that our own ranks are recruited'. Once the decision is taken there can be no return for birth/suicide is a 'capital crime'. The child has no rights, no chance to choose its parents. In exchange for insisting that he is born he submits to parental resentment, ingratitude, viciousness. He becomes the parents' property, their chattel.[181] Hardy also envisaged children as emerging from a 'Cave of the Unborn'. Like the Erewhonians they come into the world full of 'artless trust' and are immediately:

> Driven forward like a rabble rout
> Into the world they had so desired,
> By the all-immanent Will.[182]

These agonised, suffering children, disillusioned from birth, prematurely aged like little Father Time, knowing instinctively that there is no pleasure to be had from life and that 'rightly looked at there is no laughable thing under the sun', are the late Victorian heirs of all those mid-Victorian fictional orphans who struggled out of their own loneliness and isolation to attain a position of societal or familial stability.[183] There are exceptions to the generalisation: the late Victorian generation of doomed children looks back to the baby in Blake who leaps into a dangerous world only to be repressed by swaddling bands, and to Paul Dombey, who is in many respects the fictional prototype of the unnaturally mature child. What goes, generally, is not simply the concept of childhood innocence, but the belief that childhood is primarily a natural stage on the way to a desired and desirable adulthood. Little Father Time knows that modern conditions make it not worth being an adult, and to demonstrate this perception he kills his brothers and sisters and then kills himself.

Readers have always felt that Father Time is too obviously serving a symbolic function to be acceptable as a psychologically convincing portrait of a child, however unusual. Even so, Hardy stresses that his mother conceived him in the old world, and, changing her identity in the new world, where he is born, launches him back to the old. He moves, alone, across vast areas of space and time to join his actual father and a step-mother who is apparently, but not actually, a wife. In accepting Father Time, Jude queries the 'beggarly question of parentage' and proposes a radical solution to what was becoming an obsessive issue in fiction: 'All the little ones of our time are collectively the children of us adults of the time, and entitled to our collective care.'[184] Father Time, however, perceives the impracticability of such a view and regards himself as the cause of his father and step-mother's despair. He understands what Sue and Jude do not – that they are far more concerned with maintaining their own precarious relationship than with what their children are thinking about. With parents increasingly self-absorbed, their 'natural' instincts deflected by either modern analytical theories or the pursuit of sexual freedom, the child is forced into a state of premature adulthood. In Iota's *The Yellow Aster* and Corelli's *The Mighty Atom* this is brought about by the imposition upon children of false, ultimately corrupting, educational theories, as it had also been many years earlier in Meredith's *Richard Feverel*: in Corelli's *Boy* the child's life is morally ruined by the more conventional devices of a slatternly mother and a drunken father. For Henry James, parental neglect was a constant theme. In his early work he saw the relative freedom of American children from parental control as one of the less welcome of the New World's contributions to Western civilisation, a theme that reaches its most scathing denunciation in the death of Morgan Moreen in 'The Pupil'. But here, as with other aspects of James's work, national contrasts are rarely straightforward. Pansy Osmond, kept locked in a convent, safely away from the temptations of the world, by her Europeanised American father in *The Portait of a Lady*, and Jeanne de Vionnet in *The Ambassadors*, who is similarly guarded so that her purity can eventually receive its full market value in a marriage not of her own choosing, are clearly not offered as satisfactory alternatives to American freedom, while in *What Maisie Knew* and *The Awkward Age* James turned his attention fully, and critically, to parental neglect and indifference in Britain. Maisie Farange and Nanda Brookenham are cast loose in an adult world of casual sexual relationships and easily-obtained divorces, of constantly changing partners and uncertain identities, of allegiances, settlements, of friends and acquaintances divided into conflicting parties: it is all, Maisie thinks at first, like a game of 'puss-in-the-corner'.[185] In such a situation where the child is simply 'a ready vessel for bitterness, a deep little porcelain cup in which biting acids could be mixed', truth and lies are indistinguishable, moral guidance is impossible.[186] Maisie and Nanda must both make what they can of this ever-shifting feckless world: they are obliged to become older than their years and are expected at one and the same time to be ignorant of and to 'know' what is going on. Just how much these children do 'know' is, James insists, impossible for the outsider to determine. At least Maisie and Nanda carry their knowledge on into their own adult lives: they do not hang themselves like little Father Time, or drop dead like Morgan Moreen, nor do they meet the still more dreadful fate of two of James's other fictional children. One of the many mysteries of *The Turn of the Screw* is whose children Miles and Flora are. They are given no surnames, and their guardian (who is given no name at all) has inherited their charge from his own parents. The guardian is generous with money to provide a luxurious house and various surrogate parent figures for the children, but he wants no personal contact and is even unwilling to hear news of them. According to how one reads the story, Miles and Flora are abandoned to decadent servants, to a dangerously neurotic governess, or to evil spirits. Whether metaphorically or literally, they are sent to the devil by an uncaring adult world.

James, Hardy, Butler and Corelli are representative of one strand of late Victorian fiction in which children are portrayed as the victims of modern intellectual and moral restlessness. They are forced by parental indifference to come to terms with patterns of adult behaviour which their inexperience of life makes incomprehensible. If they do survive to reach some degree of understanding, it is paid for by the brutal destruction of childhood innocence. Only in *Jude the Obscure* are the adults themselves portrayed sympathetically as the victims of modern forces, yet *Jude* still shares with the rest of these novels the assumptions that the various parents or surrogate parents are unfit to be in charge of children and that the children are totally dependent for their well-being on those same irresponsible adults. The children are trapped: they are the Erewhonian unborn who foolishly sign away all their personal rights in order to become suffering human beings.

Powerful as this view of the child is, it was neither the most characteristic late Victorian response nor, ultimately, the most influential in fiction. Related to it, though often regarded as sufficiently different to constitute a quite separate tradition, was the neo-Romantic attempt to convey the child's own point of view and way of life.[187] In *What Maisie Knew* James succeeds in filtering through Maisie's awakening consciousness the grotesque manipulations of the adults who surround her, but the centre of the novel's concern remains the relationship between the child and the adult world. In contrast, there was a growing body of fiction about, and largely for, children, which accepted that adults were the enemy, but was quite unwilling to believe that childhood was doom-laden or that adulthood represented a desirable alternative.

The new fiction for children, like so much other literature of the period, established itself by publicly annihilating its predecessors. That meant Victorian moralism generally, and the exemplary children of religious tracts in particular:

> 'Let's begin by looking out for something useful to do –
> something like mending things or cleaning them, not just
> showing off.'
>   'The boys in books chop kindling wood and save their
> pennies to buy tea and tracts.'
>   'Little beasts,' said Dick. 'I say, let's talk about something
> else.' And Oswald was glad to, for he was beginning to feel
> jolly uncomfortable.[188]

By the time that exchange took place, the 'little beasts' who had played so prominent a part in children's books since at least the eighteenth century were in full retreat. They continued to appear in volumes presented as Sunday School prizes, and, curiously, one of their most hated manifestations – Frances Hodgson Burnett's *Little Lord Fauntleroy* (1886) – was a contemporary. But even the principal sponsors of the little beasts, the RTS and the SPCK, were losing faith in them, while the very thought of a boy in a tract could make turn-of-the-century Oswald Bastable 'feel jolly uncomfortable'. Children were suddenly to be allowed to be themselves in fiction. No longer were they praised for being pious, industrious, and well-mannered: instead the admired child was likely to be seen as imaginative, inventive, self-reliant and constantly in trouble. For the writers who were most responsible for bringing this new breed of fictional children into being (Helen Mathers, F. Anstey, Kipling, Kenneth Grahame, S. R. Crockett, E. Nesbit and J. M. Barrie) any child who was polite, clean, neatly dressed, respectful to adults or well-behaved carried with him or her a whiff of the hated religious tracts and was therefore distrusted by all normal children. Lewis Carroll's Alice, although slightly too passive to qualify as one of the new breed of naughty children, has great trouble trying to remember the improving poems she has been made to learn, and instead recites inspired nonsensical parodies. Carroll's implicit criticism is directed at the unnaturalness of a moralistic child, a point taken up by Anstey in 'The Good Little Girl'. Priscilla Prodgers remembers her lessons only too well and is determined to bring the various members of her family in line with her own high standards, which include Sabbatarianism: 'Don't you think, dear papa, don't you *think* you could write your newspaper article on some *other* day – is it a work of *real* necessity?' She is, Anstey acknowledges, 'an unusually good child', but for some reason she was not 'loved or respected as she ought to have been'.[189] The distrust of Victorian moralism is typified by the lengthy sub-title Crockett gave to *The Surprising Adventures of Sir Toady Lion* (1897). It read: 'An Improving History for Old Boys, Young Boys, Good Boys, Bad Boys, Big Boys, Little Boys, Cow Boys, and Tom-Boys.' The good boy of Victorian 'improving' literature is included, though now flanked by the old boys who know they never were good, the young boys and the bad boys who do not want to be good, the cowboy (already well-established as an ideal wandering, adventurous, free spirit of boyhood dreams), and even girls, as long as they are willing to be transformed into tom-boys.

Although the good boy was the enemy within, it was obvious to other children that he could not be held personally responsible for his unpleasant condition. The fault lay with his indispensable and powerful allies, the parents: here were the real enemies, and the new children's fiction attacked them ruthlessly. The changing mood was signalled by Helen Mathers's *Comin' Thro' the Rye* (1875) and Flora Shaw's *Castle Blair* (1877). Both authors rejected overt didacticism, sentimentality and adult models of behaviour, portraying children instead as rebellious and irreverent, their natural exuberance curbed by unsympathetic parents. Mathers was especially successful, at least in the early chapters of her very long novel, in portraying the father of the household more as a brooding, tyrannous presence than an actual living being, and there were good thematic reasons for doing this, as the children spend much of their time trying to keep out of his way. When he is in one of his 'furies' there is 'no safety for any one from garret to coal cellar', and the news that he is to be out all day is greeted with cheers. 'I can't think what fathers were invented for,' one of the children sighs, 'I am sure we would have got on much better without ours.'[190] The assumption that children are not merely incipient adults, but a separate species, with their own way of life, codes, values and patterns of behaviour, underlies many of these books. Colin Manlove has noted of E. Nesbit that she 'hardly ever writes about the solitary child, but about the interactions of brothers and sisters, and always from a position of involvement'.[191] This observation can be applied more generally to the literary movement in which Nesbit played so important a part. It is, in one respect, a manifestation of the anthropological and sociological obsessions of the age, the recognition that modern society is made up of interdependent communities and groupings, each of which has allegiances within and beyond its own boundaries. The solitary child, usually the orphan, of Victorian fiction becomes late in the century the prematurely aged Maisie Farange or little Father Time, children who have no affinity with their community of peers and therefore seem not to have experienced the specialness of childhood.

It was not necessary at first for the specialness to be presented as idyllic: the most urgent task was to separate it off from adulthood.

As influential as any single novel in achieving this was Anstey's *Vice Versa* (1882) in which a father and son magically change places. Secure in his position as a father Mr Bultitude can confidently inform his son Dick that the 'hours passed at school' will be looked back upon as the 'very happiest time' of his life, but a brief spell as a schoolboy during which the same platitude is quoted at him changes his mind decisively.[192] Anstey does not attempt to follow the difficulties Dick might have to face as an adult: it is fathers who need re-educating in the closed world of sarcastic schoolmasters, boring lessons, insufficient pocket-money, and the complex lore of schoolboys, all of which they had once experienced and have now conveniently forgotten. One of the most salutary lessons learnt by Mr Bultitude is provided by a letter from his daughter Barbara, sent, she believes, to her adored brother. She can't wait for Dick to see the transformation in their father. He now stays at home much more, plays games with baby on the dining-room floor, 'seems to quite like to have us all about him', and has even given permission for them to hold a party: 'No one but children invited, and everyone to do exactly what they like.'[193] Long before he returns to his normal position, Mr Bultitude has come to wish that he 'had let the moralising alone': once back to adulthood he does just that, with the result that he sees in Barbara 'a girlish freshness and grace he had never looked for or cared to see before' and 'with the graceless Dick there was a warmer and more natural feeling on both sides'.[194] *Vice Versa* is itself an improving tale, albeit one that reverses the traditional emphasis: it offers, as its sub-title promises, 'a lesson to fathers'.

A few other fictional fathers were allowed to benefit from this process of re-education by their children, notably Mr Craven in Frances Hodgson Burnett's *The Secret Garden* (1911) whose only son is neglected so completely that he has to be rescued from the verge of death by other children before the reconciliation between father and son can take place. But most fathers are not shown as capable of learning the lesson their children have to offer: they are rarely ever given the chance to try. When not described as surly, sarcastic or tyrannical, adults are generally seen by children as having no other function than to wield their arbitrary power in order to stop real life going on. They are best when out of the way 'at the office' or on those occasions when children are home-based but free to wander, school holidays being now a favoured plot

device. While parents are clearly impossible as friends or com-
panions, a special place is found for those rare adults willing to side
with the children, see their point of view, and if necessary help
them out of trouble. They are usually bachelor-uncles or spinster-
aunts, people who remember what it was like being a child but
who, for one reason or another, are sensible enough never to have
become parents: if they are not actually related, then the children
adopt them. Ernest Pontifex in *The Way of All Flesh* has both
Overton and Aunt Alethea to help him survive the battle with his
parents. In *Boy* Miss Letitia (single, wealthy and middle-aged)
struggles unsuccessfully to be allowed to take over the education of
'boy' who is totally neglected by his parents: 'They accepted him as
a natural result of marriage, and took no more heed of him than a
pair of monkeys casually observant of their first offspring.'[195] The
ideal adult friend is the 'lady poet' whom the Bastable children meet in
a train. Not only does she understand children, she can demonstrate
her understanding by writing a satirical poem about 'grown-ups':

> They like you best to play with tops
> And toys in boxes, bought in shops;
> They do not even know the names
> Of really interesting games.[196]

For Kenneth Grahame such games were so interesting and so real
that he begrudged the granting of concessions even to aunts and
uncles. All adults are 'Olympians', treating children with a godlike
indifference that comes from 'stupidity': they are bland, pompous,
'void of interests'. As the adults talk over the dinner-table, the
children eat silently, absorbed in their superior understanding of
what 'real life' is and desperate to get back to it. They realise
sullenly the futility of even trying to communicate their views, and
regard with relish their own separateness:

> One in thought and purpose, linked by the necessity of
> combating one hostile fate, a power antagonistic ever – a
> power we lived to evade – we had no confidants save our-
> selves.[197]

The apotheosis of this separate world of childhood, and the logical
conclusion of at least one of its separate strands, is *Stalky & Co.*
(1899). 'In summer all right-minded boys built huts in the furze-
hill behind the College,' it begins: the huts are uncomfortable but
'since they were strictly forbidden, palaces of delight'. Stalky,

M'Turk and Beetle make sure their hut is safe, forbidden as it is, by skilfully setting the local Squire and the College masters against each other: they are then free to smoke, read, talk to each other in their private slang, pursue their individual interests, and to emerge collectively from their hideaway to wage brutal war on Authority. In *Stalky & Co.* childhood innocence is pronounced stone-dead and deeply buried, but, as M'Turk, adopting a mock tone of 'bland patronage' on the occasion of the trio's 'last term', sums up their experiences: 'A trifle immoral, but then – boys will be boys.'[198]

Boys were being considerably more than simply boys in the adventure stories which were increasingly popular from the 1860s onwards. Once again, there is observable a rejection of the moralism that was rarely absent from earlier examples of the genre and a conscious diminution of the part in such adventures played by adults. Taking inspiration from British imperial expansion and the opening up of the American West, the rebellious children of Kenneth Grahame and E. Nesbit play at being cowboys and Indians, pirates, African explorers, and jungle animals. The most sustained instance of this aspect of children's lives is Richard Jefferies' *Bevis: The Story of a Boy* (1882) which is hardly more than a compendium of the new games. *Bevis* was clearly influenced by Mark Twain's *The Adventures of Tom Sawyer* (1876) which together with *Huckleberry Finn* (1884) provided a model of the adventurous, free-roaming adolescent boy, cut loose from familial ties to explore an ever-expanding world. Although these fictional heroes are usually befriended or helped by adults, it is their youthful independence that distinguishes them most strikingly from their earlier equivalents and from the picaresque tradition to which in many respects they belong. The specifically British context was established by Stevenson and Kipling. Jim Hawkins does not just dream of finding buried treasure, he goes off to search for it, fighting real pirates on the way: if Alan Breck is the truly dashing romantic hero of *Kidnapped*, David Balfour is courageously at his side in the siege of the roundhouse and the flight through the heather. Kim's oriental wisdom almost places him among the prematurely-aged children of late Victorian fiction, except that he exudes a delight in all that the world has to offer. He switches languages and nationalities effortlessly, chaperones his innocent Holy Man along the Great Trunk Road in his search for the River of the Arrow, and serves the Empire well as a secret agent. Mowgli, twice orphaned but guarded by Baloo and Bagheera, masters the law of the jungle to become the conqueror of Shere Khan and the Red Dog.

The mid-Victorian ideal of family life held out longest in literature directed at girls. To the author of the popular series of books 'Confidential Talks' it was obvious that, 'a girl who in physical development, mental training and moral character does not become fitted for healthful, successful, happy wifehood and motherhood fails at her highest mission in this world'.[199] That attitude informs much of the fiction of the period written especially to be read by girls. As we have seen, it lay behind the policy of the *Girl's Own Paper* which was adventurous in urging girls to seek careers in real life, but when commissioning appropriate fiction tended to rely on the domestic stories produced by highly professional writers like Rosa Nouchette Carey, Evelyn Everett Green and L. T. Meade, who knew what was expected of them. Much the same is true of the fiction contained in other girls' papers and magazines, and also, with a little qualification, of the work of Juliana Horatia Ewing, the talented author of two late Victorian children's favourites, *Six to Sixteen* (1875) and *Jackanapes* (1883). Of course, some of the authors already discussed (especially Nesbit and Burnett) wrote as much for, and as much about, girls as boys; while Lewis Carroll's Alice had in certain respects pioneered the new mood of freedom and exploratory play in children's books. But generally girls had to be contented with secondary roles in the remarkable number of adventure novels that characterised the period, and often to be satisfied with considerably less than secondary roles in the equally remarkable spate of school novels, at least until Angela Brazil began to pick up the challenge with *The Fortunes of Philippa* (1906).[200] Otherwise, in fiction girls were acceptable as 'tom-boys', and in real life they shared with their brothers the pleasures and excitement offered by Stevenson, Anstey, Kipling, Reed and Haggard. These various attitudes must explain in part the great popularity in Britain of American and Canadian authors whose novels, though still carrying an improving element, gave a freer and more central role to girls. Louisa M. Alcott led the way with *Little Women* (1868). She was followed by Susan Coolidge, *What Katy Did* (1872) and its many sequels: Katy Douglas Wiggin, *Rebecca of Sunnybrook Farm* (1903); and Lucy M. Montgomery, *Anna of Green Gables* (1908). Frances

Hodgson Burnett lived in Britain for some time and wrote on British themes, but she too was American. The comparable British novel for girls was Anna Sewell's *Black Beauty* (1877), significantly an animal fable, a type of children's fiction that was later to find popular expression in Kipling's *Jungle Books* (1894–5) and *Just So Stories* (1902); Beatrix Potter's picture books, which began with *Peter Rabbit* in 1900; and Kenneth Grahame's *The Wind in the Willows* (1908).[201]

There is no single or simple explanation why so much independence was being granted at this time to fictional children. In addition to its links with anthropology and sociology, the change can be related to the greater independence being given to children by legislation, the pervasive mood of anti-Victorianism, the new demands for youthful heroes being made by Empire, and to a resurgence of interest in the education of young children, whether inspired by Education Acts or the educational value of *Kindergarten* play being advocated by the English followers of Froebel. Gillian Avery has noted as significant 'the applause that Crockett's and Grahame's rebellious children received from middle-aged reviewers' and suggests that this response was itself 'an act of rebellion' by adults who had experienced a stricter mid-Victorian upbringing.[202] The enthusiasm with which many of these books were received certainly indicates a society ready and waiting for such a change, though it took some publishers by surprise. *Vice Versa* was turned down by two before being accepted by Smith, Elder on the strong recommendation of their reader James Payn. Even so, the publisher thought the book too slight to succeed and would pay Anstey only a small sum for the copyright.[203] It was phenomenally popular, attracting laudatory reviews and a leading article in the *Daily News*. Not only the reviewers, but, of course, the authors also were adults, and it is easy to forget such an obvious point in all the praise that is often given to the creation of 'real' children and the child's point of view. The evidence offered by that rare instance of a child's novel, Daisy Ashford's *The Young Visiters*, which was written at this time though published some years later, suggests that a fascinated, half-comprehending, intensely close observation of grown-up life was as characteristic of a nine-year old child as rebelliousness or indifference.[204] And, although mid-Victorian moralism was overthrown, its place was not usually taken by moral anarchy. Nesbit was very careful to inculcate patterns of decent behaviour and good manners,

and, often, a Socialist message; Mowgli lives by the 'law' of the
jungle; Kim returns to white society; Mr Bultitude finds school to
be hideously codified when compared with the relative freedom of
adult life; while Stalky and Co., apparently so anarchic, are
preparing for a life of imperial service. There is, however, a
contrasting attitude in some of these books, with childhood being
regarded less as a distinctive transitory stage to adulthood than as a
superior state of innocence which will be left behind only
grudgingly and forever looked back upon with nostalgia. It is not
quite a Wordsworthian notion that the child is spiritually the father
of the man, though Jefferies and Burnett come close to this. It is
rather a resentment that life will never again be as good as when
sailing imaginatively on a raft down a back-garden Mississippi or
playing cowboys and Indians in the undergrowth. For Kenneth
Grahame childhood really was a 'golden age' made up of 'dream
days': and when J. M. Barrie claimed that 'nothing that happens
after we are twelve matters very much', he meant it.[205] This
nostalgic, escapist strain was given mythic status in the figure of
Peter Pan, 'the boy who wouldn't grow up'. Barrie's play was first
produced in 1904 and drew on all of the new children's games for
its effects. Here was a world of pirates, wolves, crocodiles, fairies,
Red Indians and gangs of boys, within which the central moral
dilemma to be resolved was whether to grow up into an adult or
remain in the ranks of the eternally young.[206] For the many
Edwardian parents who made a cult of Peter Pan and Wendy it
must have been an extremely persuasive, and comforting, fantasy,
not least because their adolescent children (who now knew there
was no alternative to growing up) had not only rejected *Peter Pan*
but were beginning to read novels which offered very different
ideas about the way to settle problems between parents and
children. Indeed, by the time that *Peter Pan* was first produced in
London it was becoming difficult to find any author who was
willing to speak confidently and convincingly on behalf of the
family.

While the family was subjected to a wide range of specific late
Victorian criticisms, its fundamental importance for novelists was
that it symbolised more comprehensively than any other institution
the social stasis of Victorianism. It proclaimed itself impervious to
change or development in an age of evolutionary theory and

technological miracles; insisted on unswerving loyalty at a time
when all absolutes were held in doubt; offered stability and security
when social mobility and sexual freedom had never been greater;
clung to love and tenderness as its ultimate justification while these
qualities were being constantly revealed as subterfuges for physical
violence and financial control. The Victorian family was not just an
important institution: it was the age itself. Rebellion against
Victorianism meant, unavoidably, rebellion against the family; and the
enemy, just as unavoidably, was the father of the house.

The theme of intergenerational conflict was very far from new to
literature. 'The younger riseth when the old doth fall,' Edmund
announces in *King Lear*: the experience was age-old and confirmed
as such for late Victorians by the theories of kingship described in
Frazer's *The Golden Bough*. But never before had it played so
central a part in fiction, and no longer was a straightforward
transfer of power at stake, with the younger generation seizing its
natural right to a governing place, asserting its strength, legally or
by usurpation, as the old weaken. It was the nature of power itself
as manifested within the family that was now challenged. With the
public image of family life felt as constantly at odds with inner
reality, the ideal condition of modern existence was transformed
into one in which financial independence is a law of nature,
separated (except for the inconvenient necessity of being born)
from any parental authority:

> Why should the generations overlap one another at all? Why
> cannot we be buried as eggs in neat little cells with ten or
> twenty thousands pounds each wrapped round us in Bank of
> England notes, and wake up, as the sphex wasp does, to find
> that its papa and mamma have not only left ample provision
> at its elbow but have been eaten by sparrows some weeks
> before we began to live consciously on our own accounts.[207]

Butler was unusual in presenting the Pontifex attitude to children
as motivated by hostility rather than incomprehension or indifference. Clearly in this case, the papa and mamma sphex wasps do not
leave their young to fend for themselves out of any progressive
belief in independence: 'Theobald had never liked children. He
had always got away from them as soon as he could, and so had
they from him.'[208] Even more unusually, Theobald's cowed wife
Christina becomes a partner in the tyranny: 'She was fond of her

boy, which Theobald never was, and it was long before she could destroy all affection for herself in the mind of her first-born. But she persevered.'[209]

As men are not sphex wasps, there was no alternative to a long, painful struggle for freedom during which the values and attitudes of the parents are challenged, assailed, parodied, and gradually undermined, though not totally defeated. They are too strongly entrenched for this: they are presented as normative in their grotesqueness and therefore still vividly present in the everyday world; but, having suffered and learned under the old regime, the younger generation had no wish to replace one repressive institution by another. In taking the family as a microcosm of Victorianism and giving urgent priority to the need to escape from it, the traditional pattern of the *Bildungsroman* was overturned and a state of semi-permanent transition installed. The new pattern of oppression, reaction and escape, and the way that this represents a sundering of the late Victorian from the mid-Victorian age, was made explicit by Edmund Gosse. *Father and Son* is, he states: 'A record of a struggle between two temperaments, two consciences, and almost two epochs. It ended, as was inevitable, in disruption. Of the two human beings here described, one was born to fly backward, the other could not help being carried forward.'[210]

Nothing is told the reader of Gosse's life after the final break with his father. Having won 'the human being's privilege to fashion his inner life for himself' he walks away from the family and out of the book just like so many protagonists of the new novel.[211] Ernest Pontifex, however, has children of his own, and his relationship with them is used by Butler to indicate that one phase in the evolution of the family is over. He is no more certain than Gosse about what the future holds, but he does see a way out of the tyrannical violence of the family. When his marriage is conveniently dissolved, he farms the children out to 'kindly decent people . . . in a healthy neighbourhood'. Overton remonstrates with him, but Ernest explains:

> I shall be just as unkind to my children as my grandfather
> was to my father, or my father to me. If they did not
> succeed in making their children love them, neither shall I.

That is not quite the surrender to heredity it sounds, nor is it intended to be callous. As Ernest explains further: 'I want to put the children where they will be well and happy, and where they will not be betrayed into the misery of false expectations.'[212] Whether or not those last words carry an intentional echo of Dickens, the comparison is unavoidable. Ernest's children are to be removed from their natural parents or relatives in order to avoid any risk of unhappiness, They will not have a childhood like Ernest's or Pip Gargery's: instead, they will have to make their own way in the world, though supported from a distance by Ernest's money. They have become just like the eggs of the sphex wasp. Their father, however, is not eaten by sparrows. Once he has deposited his children, he returns 'to civilisation'.[213] Ernest benefits on all sides. He has had children, but avoided the danger of becoming a harsh father: he remains financially responsible for their upbringing while not having to endure constant personal contact with them. They will enjoy similar advantages, plus the kind of freedom that Ernest has had to fight to attain. Having given that gift to his children Ernest liberates himself and heads straight for the city. However neat the theory, there can be little doubt that the reader's response tends to be that the children have been pushed out of the way so that Ernest can seek some form of self-expression. It is *his* childhood that really matters: he is the one who has been beaten, lied to, kept in ignorance of sex, and fooled by a false religion. He has ensured that the next generation will not need to go through the same experiences. Like Nora Helmer he has earned the right to claim that the most sacred duties are to the self.

This attitude was taken up in the many 'autobiographical' novels which, as was pointed out earlier, were published in the few years before the First World War. Not all of these novels were as ferociously personal as *The Way of All Flesh*, but they did share a common concern with sundering the generations and escaping from family ties. Only *Of Human Bondage* ends with a conventional happy marriage, and, a notable sign of changing values, reviewers complained at this falsification: Maugham was later to agree with them.[214] There was also at this time a new kind of interest in the family-saga novel that would eventually develop into one of the most popular of all forms of twentieth-century entertainment, in film and television as well as fiction. Among the major Victorian novelists only Trollope had favoured this fictional form, and while there are, in the Palliser novels especially, some perceptive glances forward to late Victorian preoccupations, Trollope was sufficiently of his age to employ the changing generations and the various branches of his fictional families to mark inter-connectedness as much as contrast, gradual change as well as sudden disruption. In this respect, as in so many others, it was consciousness of evolutionary ideas that separated the later novelists from their predecessors. The main attraction of the family-saga novel lay in the possibility it offered of using the changing generations to dramatise and explain a very special moment of disruption. Out of it there emerges a group of young people whose beliefs and values are quite alien to those of their parents. It was noted earlier that *The Way of All Flesh* is unusual in that while it is justly regarded as archetypally late Victorian in mood, its author belonged firmly to the mid-Victorian period. The same is true of the hero of that novel, Ernest Pontifex: he was born in 1835 and his rebellion takes place in the 1860s. But for the novelists who came after Butler, and who had in varying degrees learned from him, the equivalent decade of crisis was the 1880s, as can be seen from the two most important family-saga novels of the period. For Lawrence in *The Rainbow* and *Women in Love*, the moment of change is placed within the long transformation of Britain from a rural to an industrial society, a process that Lawrence deplores as signalling a victory of the mechanical over the organic. The gradual weakening of traditional values is por-trayed through the Brangwyn family line, with the break marked by Ursula and Gudrun, both of whom are born in the early 1880s. Gudrun plays little part in *The Rainbow* and it is Ursula who fights against mechanistic tendencies to achieve a desolating individuality:

> Repeatedly, in an ache of utter weariness she repeated: 'I
> have no father nor mother nor lover, I have no allocated
> place in the world of things, I do not belong to Beldover nor
> to Nottingham nor to England nor to this world, they none
> of them exist, I am trammelled and entangled in them, but
> they are all unreal. I must break out of it, like a nut from its
> shell which is an unreality.'[215]

Galsworthy, in the first of the Forsyte novels *The Man of Property* (1906), shared this interest in the 1880s and even matched Lawrence's precise dating of events, but instead of tracing the development of the Forsyte family to a moment of crisis he concentrated exclusively on its decline. *The Man of Property* opens on 15 June 1886 with 'that charming and instructive sight – an

upper middle-class family in full plumage', offered as evidence of
the 'mysterious concrete tenacity which renders a family so
formidable a unit of society, so clear a reproduction of society in
miniature'.[216] The purpose of the gathering is to celebrate the
engagement of June Forsyte to Philip Bosinney, the highest point
of the Forsytes' power which will be broken by Bosinney's affair
with Irene Soames. Galsworthy foreshadows the dissolution with
another family gathering just three months after the engagement
party. This time the Forstytes mourn the death of Aunt Ann and
wonder collectively who will be next:

> It was cold, too; the wind, like some slow, disintegrating
> force, blowing up the hill over the graves, struck them with
> its chilly breath; they began to split into groups, and as
> quickly as possible to fill the waiting carriages.[217]

There is no Ursula Brangwyn in *The Man of Property* to assert the
total importance of self in a world that is felt as destructive of
individuality. The Forsytes may be in a state of disintegration, but
they retain much of their power and guard their property with
increased brutality: the rebellions are crushed and Irene is caged
like a wild animal in Soames's house.

Lawrence said of *The Man of Property* that its 'satire', its 'noble
touch', soon fizzled out, and left only 'Galsworthian "rebels" who
are, like the rest of the modern middle-class rebels, not in rebellion
at all. They are merely social beings behaving in an anti-social
manner.'[218] It is a telling observation, the truth of which could
already be tested in the role allotted to 'young' Jolyon in *The Man
of Property*. His personal rebellion is well in the past when the
novel opens: it has made him an outcast from the centre of Forsyte
power and allows him to view with sympathy the relationship
between Irene and Bosinney. But young Jolyon being an observer
of what amounts to a repetition of his own crime against the
Forsytes – the sacrifice of respectability to passion – provides
Galsworthy with the opportunity to bring about a reunion between
the generations and the sentimentality this involves does serve to
weaken, as Lawrence realised, the satirical potential of *The Forsyte
Saga*. The sentimentality is particularly apparent when compared
with the murderous relationship between fathers and children that
were becoming the norm in fiction. 'No compromise ... was
offered: no proposal of a truce would have been acceptable,' Gosse

wrote of his own moment of liberation from paternal domination, and the military image is appropriate.[219] With Victorian pride in the family being eroded on all sides, the focal point of resistance became the father. Mothers were usually exempted from similarly harsh treatment. Sometimes they were shown as joining with their husbands in the household reign of terror (as Christina Pontifex does), and there was a developing tendency to present the mother as an adored contrast to the relatively unimportant father (classically so in such works as Barrie's *Margaret Ogilvy* and Lawrence's *Sons and Lovers*). But it was far more common for mothers themselves to appear as victims, and therefore as allies, even if passively, of their frustrated and violent children. This uneasy coalition had its parallel in the late Victorian legislation which was concerned primarily with freeing the mother and children from the autocratic control of the father, though in fiction it is the children themselves rather than the courts who fight out the final battle.

Anna Tellwright's father Ephraim sits brooding in the front parlour 'unseen but felt, like an angry god behind a cloud ... unappeased and dangerous'.[220] Anna's great moment of personal challenge to his authority comes when she burns Willie Price's forged bill of exchange. Ephraim's response is characteristically violent: 'If thou breathes a word o' this to Henry Mynors, or any other man, I'll cut thy tongue out.'[221] It is a triumph of sorts. Until then Anna has believed that her father might well be capable of carrying out his terrifying threats, but 'she survived; she continued to breathe, eat, drink, and sleep; her father's power stopped short of annihilation'.[222] Her consolation is that 'things could not be worse', but nor perhaps do they greatly improve. Her future husband, Henry Mynors, will not be violent to her or their children – the generations, in this respect as in so many others, are changing as Bennett is pointing out – but the marriage will be loveless. Her rebellion has only taught her how to endure. The father's job has been done. She is tamed, broken, habituated to the belief that 'a woman's life is always a renunciation, greater or less'.[223] By virtue of his sex alone Edwin Clayhanger is freer than Anna Tellwright and the portrait of his father Darius is psychologically more credible than that of Ephraim Tellwright, yet the principal relationship between father and son is still one of mutual resentment, repression and conflict. To Edwin, Darius had 'always been old, generally harsh, often truculent, and seldom indulgent'.[224] Even a moment of heroism on Edwin's part which arouses pride in his father serves a repressive function. His action is interpreted as a sign that 'the old breed was not after all dying out in those newfangled days. Edwin could not escape from the universal assumption.'[225] His own individuality, the distinctive presence of his own generation, is denied by that assumption: like Stephen Dedalus he feels it 'round him as a net which somehow he had to cut'.[226] Cut it will certainly need to be: no less drastic method could have any effect on Darius's 'moral brute-force'. All Edwin can look forward to is the time when old age will place the father in the son's power: '"When you're old, and I've *got* you" – he clenched his fist and his teeth – "When I've *got* you and you can't help yourself, by God it'll be my turn!"'[227] His turn does come, but it is too late: revenge carried out on an ageing senile father seems petty, and the appropriate moment for Edwin to cut through the entangling net has gone.

Like many other fictional fathers of the time, Ephraim Tellwright and Darius Clayhanger are the 'survivals' of apparently extinct cultures revealed by late Victorian anthropologists:

> He did as his father and uncles had done. He still thought of
> his father as a grim customer, infinitely more redoubtable
> than himself. He really believed that parents spoiled their
> children nowadays: to be knocked down by a single blow was
> one of the punishments of his own generation. He could
> recall the fearful timidity of his mother's eyes without a trace
> of compassion.[228]

Ernest Pontifex's children had been farmed out so that they might break just such a chain of violence: Anna and Edwin have less luck. They experience a harsh upbringing, and are also denied the satisfaction of a victory over their fathers devastating enough to turn them into pioneering members of the modernist generation. In these particular cases, the relative weakness of the children was a conscious decision on Bennett's part, justified by his artistic obsession with ordinariness, but they also embodied a wider problem faced by many other novelists: how to set any viable contrast against the overwhelming physical presence of the father. Butler had run into the difficulty in *The Way of All Flesh*, and so did May Sinclair in *The Three Sisters* where the daughters can appear undifferentiated in comparison with James Carteret, their self-pitying, bullying, sexually-frustrated father. It seems reasonably clear that in writing *The Three Sisters* Sinclair had in mind the family atmosphere (though not the historical facts) of the Brontës, and her remarkable novel neatly blends what was now a very substantial tradition of anti-Victorianism with a contemporary feminist moral.[229] The sisters' mother has succeeded in breaking away from Carteret, but the daughters are trapped with him and their victories must take place largely in their minds. Gwenda sits waiting impatiently for her father's death, the 'hour of her deliverance', while Alice takes a more devious, and active, approach to the problem.[230] Ill with anaemia, she pulls out of her yearning for death and decides to live: 'It served all her purposes. If she had tried she could not have hit on anything that would have annoyed her father more or put him more conspicuously in the wrong.'[231]

Not all of the angry emotions provoked by fathers were so exquisitely refined: there were swifter and bloodier ways of getting rid of the hated parental obstacle. Virginia Woolf in *To the Lighthouse* – a novel that drew extensively on her memories of a late Victorian childhood – suggests one: 'Had there been an axe handy, a poker, or any weapon that would have gashed a hole in his father's breast and killed him, there and then, James would have seized it.'[232] That is what John Gourlay in *The House with the Green Shutters* not only dreams of doing, but actually does: 'As Gourlay leapt, John brought the huge poker with a crash on the descending brow. The fiercest joy of his life was the dirl that went up his arm as the steel thrilled to its own hard impact on the bone.'[233] This wholesale destruction of a Scottish family brought about by the pitiless selfishness of the father is repeated with an even greater sense of tragic inevitability in J. MacDougall Hay's *Gillespie* (1914), though the final triumph of patricide is denied Gillespie's sons. By this time Hay might well have read an English translation of *The Brothers Karamazov*, the mood of which would have blended naturally with the violent Scottish families that came more directly to *Gillespie* through *The House with the Green Shutters* and Stevenson's *Weir of Hermiston*. The theme of conflict between parents and children was present in Stevenson's work from the very beginning.[234] It found its most savage expression in his uncompleted last novel, with the legendary figure of the hanging judge carrying his fierce sense of justice from the public to the private domain. The portrait of Hermiston is all the stronger because he is not guided by the mean-minded motives of John Gourlay or Gillespie Strang. He is rather the type of implacable, relentless father, insensitive to moral values or beliefs which are not his own, and therefore representative of the deadening force that so many late Victorian novelists were convinced should be got rid of whatever the cost. In his son Archie, Hermiston's harshness provokes personal disgust and a public denunciation: 'This is my father . . . I draw my life from him; the flesh upon my bones is his, the bread I am fed with is the wages of these horrors.'[235] According to one report, had Stevenson lived to complete the novel he intended that Archie should be brought to court and sentenced to death by his father.[236] If that intention had been carried out it would have been an appropriate comment on a problem that had come to be seen as soluble only by a violent struggle to the death between the generations.

This assumption was carried effortlessly into the work of those novelists who are usually classified as the founders of fictional modernism in Britain and who, in the process, are often misleadingly separated off from their immediate predecessors. There was, as has been shown, a long complex preparation for the importance attached in modern fiction to both irregular sexual relationships and the break-up of the family, typified by intergenerational conflict. There are also, however, important shifts of emphasis and modifications to the desperate solutions proposed by the earlier novelists. In *Sons and Lovers* Paul Morel's reaction against his father is given a new kind of class dimension, a recognition that late Victorian educational reforms were serving to create divisions between parents and children which were self-consciously cultural: it was a phenomenon that Hardy had already begun to explore in several of his novels, and was to receive its classic modern expression in Joyce's *A Portrait of the Artist* and *Ulysses*. Once divided from his parents by a superior education the son must either go forward, leaving the class of his birth behind him, or, when he later feels a sense of loss, consciously set out to rediscover and re-create his working-class or lower-middle-class background: it is a paradigm not only of countless twentieth-century novels but of much academic and sociological writing as well. *Sons and Lovers* is also especially interesting in this context in that the parent who is seen as exercising a restricting influence on the son is the mother rather than the father. The intense relationship between Mrs

Morel and Paul places Lawrence firmly within the context of the pre-war British interest in Freudianism, whether or not he had read Freud at this time, just as the final nature of Paul's release from the dominant parent marks a new ruthless determination on the part of protagonists of fiction to assert their independence. Helped by his sister Annie, Paul gives to Mrs Morel the morphia pills that end her suffering, and he and Annie 'laughed together like two conspiring children'.[237] That they kill their mother out of love rather than hatred does not lessen the urgent need for release from parental ties:

> Beyond the town the country, little smouldering spots for
> more towns – the sea – the night – on and on! And he had
> no place in it! Whatever spot he stood on, there he stood
> alone.

Still, only the thought of his mother holds him back: 'But no, he would not give in ... He would not take that direction, to the darkness, to follow her.'[238] Like Ernest Pontifex before him, he heads, unencumbered, for the city. Stephen Dedalus takes a similar journey, vowing, as he leaves for Paris, that he no longer believes in 'my home, my fatherland or my church'.[239] Stephen does not feed morphia pills to his mother on her death-bed, but he refuses her dying wish that he should take communion and kills her symbolically. Dublin gossip puts the blame on him, and, haunted by the image of his mother, he half-believes it himself: 'In a dream, silently, she had come to him, her wasted body within its loose graveclothes giving off an odour of wax and rosewood, her breath bent over him with mute secret words, a faint odour of wetted ashes.'[240]

It was only when the longed-for total independence had been attained, the generations finally sundered, the inhibiting parents literally or symbolically killed, that the question of what comes next was absorbed radically into the form as well as the content of fiction. Paul Morel, the young Stephen Dedalus, and the young Ursula Brangwyn, leave that problem behind them: personal freedom is all that can be allowed to matter. But there was a growing awareness that freedom can never be total, that old structures (societal and fictional) once finally rejected must be replaced, and as the family had for forty years past been the focus of attack so now it began to be tentatively reconstructed. Rupert Birkin in *Women in Love* in many respects embodies all the tendencies examined here. He rejects marriage, family, a home, even a settled place to live, as impossible, a 'habit of cowardice'.[241] His dismissal of 'marriage in the old sense' seems crushingly decisive:

> It's a sort of tacit hunting in couples: the world all in couples, each couple in its own little house, watching its own little interests, and stewing in its own little privacy – it's the most repulsive thing on earth.[242]

Yet Birkin's deepest impulse, precariously maintained, is re-creative rather than destructive. His longing to establish a special kind of permanent relationship (the 'pure unison' as he calls it when trying unsuccessfully to explain his ideas to Ursula) is part of the quest to find an acceptable replacement for the discredited family. 'It is the old dead morality,' Ursula responds scornfully.[243] It is not quite that, though it does sound as though it might be, and Birkin is unable to offer a more satisfying or convincing definition: the issue is left open. Elsewhere there are related attempts to piece together the shattered reputation of the family, to offer symbolic reconciliation without returning to the 'old dead morality'. James Ramsay does not pick up a poker and gash a hole in his father's breast. Both survive to journey to the lighthouse together, and James at last receives the coveted words of praise from his father: 'Well done!' [244] There is no suggestion that Simon and Stephen Dedalus will reach a similar understanding, yet more than any other novel *Ulysses* dramatises the modern need for it. As Leopold Bloom and Stephen move through Dublin, narrowly missing each other during the day and then finally coming together for their late-night communion, they reveal a whole world of disillusioned fathers and disinherited sons – ancient and modern, theological and secular, mythical and literary, actual and surrogate – all desperately in search of each other.

Part Three

BREAKING UP

Chapter Four

An End to Reticence

On 8 May 1888 the House of Commons debated a motion put by Mr
Samuel Smith, MP for Flintshire. It read: 'This House deplores the
rapid spread of demoralising literature in this country, and is of
opinion that the law against obscene publications and indecent
pictures and prints should be vigorously enforced, and, if necessary,
strengthened.' Smith explained that he could be persuaded to bring
so 'disagreeable a subject' before the House only from an 'imperative
sense of duty' forced upon him by the knowledge 'that there had of
late years been an immense increase of vile literature in London and
throughout the country, and that this literature was working terrible
effects upon the morals of the young.' It soon became clear that
Smith was talking primarily about the English translations of Zola
published by Henry Vizetelly. 'Nothing more diabolical,' he
proclaimed 'had ever been written by the pen of man. These novels
were only fit for swine, and their constant perusal must turn the
mind into something akin to a sty.' In addition to his concern for the
morals of the young, Smith expressed his fear at the wider contagion
theatened by French decadence:

> Now . . . were they to stand still while the country was
> wholly corrupted by literature of this kind. Were they to wait
> until the moral fibre of the English race was eaten out, as that
> of the French was almost. Look what such literature had
> done for France. It overspread that country like a torrent,
> and its poison was destroying the whole national life. France,
> today, was rapidly approaching the condition of Rome in the
> time of the Caesars.

Speaking for the Government in the debate, the Home Secretary, Henry Matthews, joined Smith in condemning indecent literature, but saw no case for strengthening the law. He claimed that existing legislation was sufficient for the purpose and that 'public judgment was a safer guide than that of any official'. Far from being put down by this apparent rejection, Smith 'heartily' thanked the Home Secretary: 'Nothing could be more satisfactory.' He called for the 'unanimous judgment of the House' as this would have a 'very useful effect out-of-doors', and, in the language of *Hansard*, the Question was put and agreed to.[1]

The existing legislation referred to by the Home Secretary was the Obscene Publications Act of 1857 which was usually known as Lord Campbell's Act, and the important interpretation of that act by Chief Justice Cockburn in 1868 in the case of *Regina* v *Hicklin*. The bill had been passed by the House of Lords only after a vigorous debate. Campbell's sole target was, in his own words, 'works written for the single purpose of corrupting the morals of youth, and of a nature calculated to shock the common feelings of decency in any well regulated mind'.[2] Books which it was felt came under this category were usually described as 'obscene' or as 'Holywell Street literature': the term 'pornography', if used at all at this time, had a more specific medical meaning.[3] In the Lords' debate the question as to how it would be possible to distinguish legally between Holywell Street and other kinds of literature was raised repeatedly. One speaker drew attention specially to French fiction – 'nothing can be more unchaste, nothing more immodest' – and asked how nevertheless it could be protected. Lord Campbell rejected this 'analogy' as irrelevant to the 'publications' he was concerned with.[4] It was Campbell's confidence that works of serious literary or artistic merit would not be vulnerable under the Act that allowed legislation to be passed without any clear guideline on how to define what was or was not 'obscene'. This was to be left to local magistrates who, if they decided a book was obscene, were now given the power to order its destruction. The much-needed 'test' of obscenity was eventually formulated by Cockburn in what came to be called the 'Hicklin Judgment' of 1868, and to that judgment can be traced most of the legal problems that were to plague modern fiction:

> I think the test of obscenity is this, whether the tendency of
> the matter charged as obscenity is to deprave and corrupt
> those whose minds are open to such immoral influences, and
> into whose hands a publication of this sort may fall.[5]

Like Campbell, Cockburn seems to have believed that imaginative literature would not be challenged by this ruling, and the famous test was actually not inspired by a work of fiction. But by placing the entire emphasis on a conjectured effect on the reader, Cockburn's test allowed concentration on selected passages of a book without any wider reference to their context and therefore made a defence on literary or artistic grounds virtually impossible. As opponents never tired of pointing out, this procedure would mean that the Bible, Shakespeare, and much other established literature could be pronounced obscene and destroyed. Cockburn's test was not only influential in Britain: it was also adopted by the American courts. It survived in America until 1933 when *Ulysses* was declared to be not obscene, and in Britain until 1959 when a new Obscene Publications Act was passed, clearing the way for the test 'trial' of *Lady Chatterley* the following year. In both countries emphasis now came to be placed on the total effect of any given work, thus making possible a defence on literary or artistic grounds. But, throughout the second half of the nineteenth and much of the present century it was not inconsistent, in strictly legal terms, for a book to be regarded at one and the same time as a literary masterpiece and an obscene publication. When Oscar Wilde included among the epigraphs to *Dorian Gray*, 'There is no such thing as a moral or an immoral book. Books are well written or badly written. That is all,' he was not only proclaiming aesthetic doctrine, he was openly mocking the law. It was a position that Edward Carson, in cross-examination, was to draw on constantly, forcing Wilde to attempt the impossible by explaining how an 'immoral' or a 'perverted' book could be described as a 'good' book just because someone thought it 'well written'.[6] Carson was asking the questions and therefore not obliged to explain how the law had little difficulty in accepting that a 'good' book could also be a 'perverted' book. The only defence possible for Wilde – that it was pointless to talk about a work of 'art' in these terms – was not to be acceptable in a British court for another sixty years.

With the late Victorian novelist so vulnerable to a strict interpretation of the law, it is understandable that Samuel Smith should have been well satisfied with the response he received from the Home Secretary, and why he welcomed the unanimous endorsement of the House as liable to have a 'useful effect out-of-doors'. Although he did not reveal the fact in the Commons debate, Smith was speaking on behalf of the National Vigilance Association. He was a member of the Council of that organisation and it was at his suggestion that the NVA turned its attention to Zola. The NVA's main concern was with the white slave traffic. Its formation in 1885 had been inspired by Josephine Butler's campaign against the Contagious Diseases Act and W. T. Stead's revelations about child-prostitution in the 'Maiden Tribute of Modern Babylon' articles, but the NVA's interests soon expanded to cover any activity which it saw as corrupting the morals of young people – music-hall acts, sex manuals, covert advertisements for birth control and abortion, penny dreadfuls, and indecent or 'pernicious' literature.[7] It was the latest of a number of pressure groups stretching back to the Proclamation Society, founded in 1787, and The Society for the Suppression of Vice, founded in 1801.[8] Such groups continue to the present day, and their aims and methods have hardly changed since William Wilberforce urged that the Proclamation Society should be a voluntary association, function outside government, and aspire to become 'like the ancient censorship, the guardian of the religion and morals of the people'.[9] It is the circumstances and manifestations of censorship that change. The NVA enters literary history because of the conjunction of democratic reform, Board School education, an expanding market for books and periodicals, and French naturalism.

Shortly after the Commons debate on demoralising literature (and probably urged on by Samuel Smith) William Coote, the Secretary of the NVA, brought a private action against Henry Vizetelly for having 'published an obscene libel' (i.e. an English translation of Zola's novel La Terre, called The Soil). The prosecution was conducted by the Solicitor-General who based his case on the Hicklin judgment and went to some lengths to justify the use of passages from a book for purposes of prosecution. He admitted that there could be special circumstances which allowed for the existence in a book of 'one isolated passage of an immoral tendency' and also that some great literature of the past – especially, he added with dramatic naivety, that 'of two or three hundred years ago' – contained 'certain immoral and indecent expressions', but none of this could apply in the present instance because Zola's novel was 'filthy from beginning to end'. He then proceeded to read selected extracts from *The Soil* and when the jury intervened to say they had heard enough Vizetelly changed his plea to guilty and undertook 'at once to withdraw all those translations of M. Zola's works from circulation'. The Solicitor-General expressed himself satisfied with this undertaking, noted that it meant that 'Mr Vizetelly would be no party to the circulation of other works of M. Zola', and agreed with the Defence that 'imprisonment should not be inflicted'. In his summing up the Magistrate found that *The Soil* had been published 'for the sake of gain' and 'deliberately done in order to deprave the minds of persons' who might read it. Vizetelly was fined one hundred pounds and ordered to 'keep the peace and be of good behaviour for twelve months'.[10] The following May a second action against Vizetelly was brought by the NVA. There was an attempt to have Flaubert's *Madame Bovary* and Zola's *L'Assommoir* and *Germinal* named in the indictment, but these were dropped and the 'obscene libels' Vizetelly was eventually charged with having published included Zola's *La Faute de l'abbé Mouret* and *La Joie de vivre*, and Maupassant's *Bel Ami* and *Une Vie*.[11] Vizetelly's son Ernest appeared in court to explain the difficulties involved in expurgating their Zola translations in such a short period of time, but he was not convincing. Even Vizetelly's lawyer had no answer to the prosecution case that Vizetelly had promised to withdraw the translations and had not done so. Vizetelly pleaded guilty and was jailed for three months: it was recommended that he be treated as a 'first-class misdemeanant' on account of his advanced age and poor health.[12]

There is little in the affair that reflects credit on any of the participants. If the NVA made an unpleasant spectacle, gloating over a great victory in its campaign to improve the moral health of the nation, Vizetelly was not a particularly attractive candidate for literary martyrdom, the role usually allotted him by modern commentators.[13] It was ludicrous to say that Vizetelly had published Zola's novels in order to deprave the minds of readers, but it was not so ludicrous to claim that his main motive was commercial: he was certainly not consciously pioneering new artistic standards in fiction. He had started his publishing house in 1884 after having spent much of his life in France as a special correspondent, and it was from France that he brought the idea of marketing cheap one-volume novels which would be sold direct to the public and thus bypass the circulating-library system. It was also France that provided him with the material to publish, though his first author was E. C. Grenville-Murray whose sensational-sounding yet extremely innocent novels like *Imprisoned in a Spanish Convent: An English Girl's Experience* were prominently displayed in Vizetelly's advertisements. His first French translations were of Daudet and George Sand, and when these were unsuccessful he turned to Gaboriau's detective stories out of the conviction, in his son's words, 'that if French fiction was to be offered to English readers at all it must at least be sensational'.[14] Gaboriau's sensationalism, like Grenville-Murray's, was of an old-fashioned variety, and Vizetelly moved on to translations of Zola, Maupassant and other European novelists whose work was sensational in a very different sense. Some of the business transactions with Zola were carried out by George Moore who saw in Vizetelly a sympathiser in his campaign to fight the circulating libraries and bring English fiction up to date by injecting it with a strong dose of French naturalism. Vizetelly published Moore's *A Mummer's Wife* (1885), *A Drama in Muslin* (1886) and *A Mere Accident* (1887) in one-volume editions – all defiantly advertised as 'realistic' novels – and became, willingly or unwillingly, a partner in Moore's self-seeking publicity. Every time Moore boasted that he was selling to the public the kind of novels that circulating libraries had tried to ban, attention was drawn to Vizetelly. The relationship between the two men was close, with Moore probably the dominant partner. In his polemical pamphlet *Literature at Nurse, or Circulating Morals* (1885) Moore had skilfully selected passages from popular novels to argue that the circulating libraries made their profit from books which were pornographic while at the same time refusing to stock supposedly obscene naturalistic fiction. Three years later in an attempt to defend himself against prosecution Vizetelly submitted to the Government a collection of *Extracts Principally from*

English Classics by which he claimed to demonstrate that if Zola was obscene then so were many acknowledged English masters of the past. Both pamphlets demonstrate the crucial role that 'passages' took throughout the long debate on censorship. The writers quoted included Shakespeare, Defoe, Dryden and Fielding. Vizetelly was helped to make the selection by Moore, and when he was imprisoned, Moore spoke out publicly on his behalf.[15]

Vizetelly's advertising methods constantly drew attention to the daring or risqué nature of many of his publications. In the 1880s the word 'realistic' itself was suggestive enough, and so were allusions to France which in another context would be taken as totally innocuous. The translations were grouped into series such as 'Zola's Realistic Novels'; 'Maupassant's Boulevard Novels'; and 'Vizetelly's Popular French Novels' which promised 'translations of the best examples of recent French Fiction of an Unobjectionable Character', implying perhaps that some of the books in the other series were not so 'unobjectionable'. Translations were announced to be 'without abridgement', and Zola's novels cost 6s, or 5s 'without engravings'. When the first prosecution took place Vizetelly was planning new editions of Rabelais, the *Decameron* and the *Heptameron*, the standard wares of 'specialist' book publishers. He seems to have made no serious attempt to comply with the court order which he himself had volunteered – that he would 'at once withdraw all those translations of Zola's works from circulation' – and claimed to understand only that he could publish further Zola novels as long as they were expurgated. Even Ernest Vizetelly, when explaining the problems involved in re-setting the novels, had to admit that his father continued to advertise *Soil* and *Nana* accompanied by a note saying they were 'undergoing revision', a characteristic example of Vizetelly's salesmanship.[16]

To insist that Vizetelly's motives were largely commercial is not to condone the way he was hounded by the NVA. His crime against morality was that the books he published were translations, relatively cheap, and unabridged. There was no attempt to prevent the free circulation of the same books in their original language, nor was there talk of prosecution in 1894 when the Lutetian Society published expensive 'unmutilated' limited editions of twelve of Zola's novels translated by such writers as Victor Parr, Havelock Ellis, Ernest Dowson and Arthur Symons. Vizetelly made French realism available to any non-French speaking man or woman, and it was only when a substantial number of English readers began to show an interest that moral reformers turned to the courts for help. The irony is, that if the readership had been exceptionally large then there was very little that the NVA, magistrates, or circulating libraries could do. This was the basis of Moore's justifiable charge that circulating-library policies were hypocritical, and the point has a wider significance. For example, once Hardy's *Tess of the D'Urbervilles* had become the subject of heated public discussion, and was selling in large numbers, it is inconceivable that a private pressure group like the NVA would have tried to intervene to suppress it. With more courage and determination on the part of some of the defendants – publishers especially – the anti-literature activities of the NVA might have been repelled early on. As it was, the fiction attacked by the NVA tended to be vulnerable because it dealt with controversial topics without the safeguard of a large public interest: the result was the beginning of a trend that lasts well into the present century – the relegation of many modern classics into a market category of dirty books. By 1898 the reader of *Photo Bits*, one of the new, cheap 'naughty' magazines specialising in innuendo and women's legs, and which was itself later to come under the scrutiny of the NVA, could buy a copy of *Nana* for 3s 6d from the seller of 'Rare Books and Curious Photographs' who advertised in the columns of that periodical. No doubt there was a reasonably lucrative market in subterranean or semi-subterranean translations of Zola's novels, but the NVA's claim that Britain was being flooded with French fiction was itself a bit of strategic sensationalism. It was based on Vizetelly's rather foolish boast to W. T. Stead that it was a 'bad week when the sale of Zola translations fell below a thousand volumes': Vizetelly's son did not dispute the total figure, but he pointed out that it covered eighteen Zola titles, and that each novel sold on average approximately three thousand a year.[17] The NVA succeeded in putting an end to those sales and making sure that for some time to come the ordinary reader would confront Zola's novels only in expurgated editions. The Vizetelly titles were bought by Chatto and Windus who began re-issuing them in the late 1890s. The work of abbreviation was done by Ernest Vizetelly whose name as translator stayed on the title page and therefore kept the family link with Zola. In his preface to one of those later translations, Ernest Vizetelly noted that it was 'based on a translation now not generally accessible', and added sadly, 'however, I have made such a vast number of corrections and modifications in the former text that the translation has become almost entirely my own'.[18] It was certainly some way removed from both Zola's original novel and the reasonably faithful English translation that Ernest's father had pioneered.

It has become common to support the argument that Vizetelly was a literary martyr by referring to the fact that he was seventy years old when the sentence was passed on him and, as the court acknowledged, not in good health. But these personal factors – which have always aroused some understandable sympathy for him – are less important than the largely isolated position he held throughout the whole affair, and the blame for this lies on the literary Establishment that refused to come to his help. As we have seen, George Moore stood by him, as did a number of other writers who petitioned the Home Secretary to reduce Vizetelly's sentence.[19] The *Bookseller*, though not approving of Zola, took an exceptionally strong line against the NVA, describing it as 'a society supported by the subscriptions of enthusiastic prudes' and endorsing a letter it had received from 'A Publisher and Bookseller' which condemned British publishers for allowing Vizetelly to stand alone and criticised Vizetelly himself for pleading guilty and thereby failing to seize the chance to clarify the legal definition of obscenity.[20] In retrospect, it does seem unfortunate that Vizetelly gave up the legal battle so easily. Although the NVA was backed unofficially by the government and numbered influential and skilled publicists among its members, its preferred method was to work by threatening individual publishers and booksellers. It took its 'vigilante' role very seriously, claiming to have representatives throughout the country constantly on the look-out for booksellers who could be persuaded to withdraw a particular book from circulation under the threat of prosecution. They achieved a good deal of local success by this method. and whenever possible gleefully acted as the destroyers as well as the censors of books:

> A large number of one of Guy de Maupassant's novels were
> recently sold under the hammer by a firm of good standing,
> who were unaware of the nature of the books. At our
> suggestion, these were afterwards recalled at some expense,
> and handed over to our police for destruction.[21]

They liked to boast about the 'expense' such actions cost them, but

lack of funds was a major reason why they did not stage more
public prosecutions and went for private pressure instead. Another
reason was that magistrates were not always sufficiently impressed
by the NVA:

> The Association are not letting the matter rest. They find the
> magistrates timid, but hope to get aid from the police: for it
> has sometimes been found that the magistrates violate the
> principles of law by refusing to a private prosecutor what
> they will grant to the police authorities.[22]

While a local bookseller or a national publisher might have
dismissed an approach by a representative of the NVA, a visit from
the police was a far more intimidating and potentially damaging
experience. A threat that if action was not taken then the case
would be referred to the police would have brought many
booksellers and publishers into line, and, as Samuel Hynes has
shown, the police were more directly involved in the prosecution of
Havelock Ellis's work, as they were also later to be in seizure of
The Rainbow.[23] All of these cases, however, were made possible by
the relative ease with which pressure could be exerted or a prosecution
brought under the terms of Lord Campbell's Act. A full-scale literary
test-case was not something that the NVA wanted, but nobody else
seemed to want it either. In Vizetelly's case, his commercial motives
would have rendered him vulnerable to a defence on literary grounds,
and, if he had pleaded not guilty, translations of Zola were about the
worst possible novels to build a case on. Even the *Bookseller* separated
itself from Zola when defending Vizetelly, and the press was also
generally hostile, so much so that Ernest Vizetelly argued it was press
outrage that was responsible for his father's second prosecution.[24]
British publishers were invariably timid when confronted by the
NVA, and in the late 1880s the Society of Authors was still struggling
to establish itself. Vizetelly might have turned himself into a genuine
martyr in the cause of the greater frankness of literature if he had defied
the NVA, but he probably knew better than anyone how little support
he would have got.

  The real significance of the Vizetelly affair is that it presented in
the form of a dramatic public demonstration a challenge to mid-
Victorian literary assumptions which custom had made to seem
inviolable. Zola was the perfect catalyst: even the critics and
novelists who did not particularly admire his work were still able to

praise its iconoclastic, liberating effect. Henry James epitomises this tendency in that while withholding praise for Zola's artistry he announced of the Rougon-Macquart: 'No finer act of courage and confidence is recorded in the history of letters.'[25] And the comments of other critics and newspapers at the time show that there was a widespread realisation of what Zola's 'courage and confidence' would lead to. For *The Times*, commenting on the Vizetelly trial, the message for the future was: 'If the line is not to be drawn so as to exclude translations of such works of Zola as *La Terre* . . . it is plain that it cannot be drawn at all.'[26] It was also understood that the reader was to be liberated along with the novelist. 'The public has eaten of the apple of knowledge,' Edmund Gosse warned, 'and will not be satisfied with mere marionettes.'[27] Giving a very different emphasis, and observing that 'Zola sinks to a lower depth than any English writer ever touched,' the *Western Morning News* noted perceptively: 'It is the shame of Zola that he has put an end to reticence.'[28]

For the average reader there was certainly nothing in earlier British fiction to prepare him for the shock of Zola. Mid-Victorian novelists especially had written in accordance with an unformulated code that governed what was and was not permissible in fiction, and their adherence to that code was surprisingly firm: their descent can also be traced from the reform of manners movement of the late eighteenth century, though a very different branch of the movement than that occupied by the NVA. External constraints were involved – notably a combination of commercial and moral pressure from the circulating libraries, and sympathy for the common practice of family readings – but the most important factor was the sense of social responsibility felt by novelists themselves about the part they could play in shaping a new and fragile industrial society. They became adept in the use of allusions and symbols which would communicate obliquely what they hesitated to express openly, and expert at criticising society without removing themselves from it. It was all very well for Dickens in *Our Mutual Friend* to mock the archetypal philistine Mr Podsnap for believing that nothing should be written or spoken that might bring a blush to the cheek of a young girl, but Dickens was careful to put nothing in his own novels that would be likely to bring a blush to anyone's cheek. Among the major mid-Victorian novelists, only Thackeray objected openly to 'a society that will not tolerate

the Natural in our Art'.[29] Most of his contemporaries did not
seem to feel that the unwritten code was an artistic restriction. They
acquiesced in what amounted to a gigantic moral conspiracy with
publishers, libraries, reviewers, editors, and easily-shocked readers.
As long as the system was not directly and seriously challenged by
any one of the participants it remained flexible enough to allow
apparent contradictions and hypocrisies without the threat of the
whole structure collapsing. There were always reviewers or readers
who were ready to pronounce novels like *Jane Eyre* and *The Mill on
the Floss* immoral, but the praise such novels also received
counterbalanced the criticism, and there was never any attempt to
ban them. The circulating libraries could exert pressure on
publishers and authors by refusing to stock a particular book, but
would happily distribute the enormously popular and, for the time,
daring novels of Ouida or Rhoda Broughton. When Thackeray
became editor of the *Cornhill* in 1860 he did not seize the opportunity
to bring the 'Natural' back into Victorian fiction, but took the
'squeamishness' of his readers so much to heart that he turned down
as unfit for his family magazine 'Mrs General Talboys', one of
Trollope's best short stories.[30] Trollope wrote a dignified defence of
his work, but he remained a friend and admirer of Thackeray and
had no trouble placing the story elsewhere.[31] In the Commons
debate on demoralising literature, Samuel Smith claimed: 'Twenty
years ago no London publisher dared to print and put into
circulation such books as are now published: they would have been
indicted at once, and sharply and severely punished.'[32] For Smith
this meant that the law had become flabby, but it really indicates
what little understanding he had of the true situation. Serious-
minded mid-Victorian publishers, editors and novelists were capable
of being terrified by the infamous maiden ladies living in the country
who ordered novels in bulk from Mudie's, but they did not seriously
consider the possibility of being 'severely punished' by the law
courts. Meredith, who had more cause than most novelists to distrust
the mid-Victorian system, knew very well where the danger lay:

> I find I have offended Mudie and the British Matron . . . He
> will not, or haply, dare not put me in his advertised catalogue.
> Because of the immoralities I depict! O Canting Age! I
> predict a Deluge.[33]

That prediction was to prove accurate enough, though the deluge was brought about not by a determined opposition to 'Cant', but rather by a gradual undignified breakdown of consensus.

In 1866 when an American periodical described Charles Reade's novel *Griffith Gaunt* as immoral, Reade responded by taking legal action. Wilkie Collins agreed to speak on Reade's behalf and he asked Dickens to do likewise, but after reading the novel Dickens said he was unable to do so. He explained that in court he would certainly be asked as the editor of 'a periodical of large circulation' whether he personally was willing to publish certain passages of *Griffith Gaunt* and he would be obliged to say that he was not.[34] Ten years later Reade was eager to publish his latest novel *A Woman Hater* in the ultra-Conservative *Blackwood's*. He agreed to submit the manuscript to John Blackwood for scrutiny and to 'excise' any 'lines . . . it would give him pain to publish . . . before the copy goes to the printer'. Blackwood kept a careful watch on what he described as Reade's 'love of plain-speaking and warm flesh-tints', and asked for changes which Reade carried out in the most grovelling manner:

> I have struck out Rhoda's prayer, and corrected the matter;
> also, with much pleasure, the word seduction, substituting a
> vague sentence that will convey no distinct idea to the
> reader.[35]

This was the society that would shortly be confronted with translations of *L'Assommoir* and *La Terre*, a society in which a leading periodical could be worried by printing the very word 'seduction' and be contented with a substituted phrase that 'would carry no distinct idea to the reader', a society also in which Reade was regarded as a daring and rebellious writer, which is why Blackwood was wary of him in the first place. The agreement between Blackwood and Reade is in many respects symptomatic of the distrust and unease that was now being felt between novelists, on the one hand, and publishers, editors and librarians, on the other. No longer were their interests seen to be of the same kind, and no longer was there an implicit agreement between them on what was allowable in fiction. The situation has changed to a form of negotiation, with the author seeing what he can get away with and the publisher looking for what he can prevent. The once-rebellious Reade surrendered his independence even before a contract was signed: younger novelists, just beginning their careers

at this time, were to be notably less pliant, though they too were to
be forced repeatedly into damaging compromises.

The fate of Gissing's early novel *Mrs Grundy's Enemies* is a
striking example of this. The novel was completed in September
1882, offered to Smith, Elder and quickly rejected as being 'too
painful to please the ordinary novel reader' and because it
contained 'scenes that can never attract the subscribers to Mr
Mudie's Library'.[36] It was then sent to George Bentley who
offered Gissing fifty pounds for it: the sum was ridiculously low,
but gratefully accepted. At proof stage Bentley began asking
Gissing to 'soften certain of the features in some of the description
and dialogue'.[37] Gissing at first refused, then consulted Frederick
Harrison who advised him to give way. He did so, though in a
mood of defiance, determined to turn the experience to his own
advantage. To his brother he announced that he would 'fight these
prejudices to the end, come what may', and planned a preface to
the novel in which his defiance would be given heroic status:

> This book is addressed to those to whom Art is dear for its
> own sake. Also to those who, possessing their own Ideal of
> social and personal morality, find themselves able to allow
> the relativity of all Ideals whatsoever.[38]

It is a classically late Victorian statement, unimaginable as coming
from Dickens, Trollope, Eliot, Thackeray or Gaskell. In spite of
the concessions Gissing had made, Bentley was still not satisfied
and asked Evelyn Abbott (a Fellow of Balliol College, Oxford, and
one of Bentley's literary advisers) to revise the whole manuscript:
'If you will put a mark against anything of which you disapprove,
as likely to shock the public by its too great reality, it will help me.'
Abbott genuinely admired the book, though he agreed with Bentley
that its 'power' needed to be 'properly disciplined'.[39] Gissing
probably did not know about the part being played by Abbott: he
was puzzled by the unnatural delay in proofs coming to him, and
once revisions had been made, by the failure to publish the book.
Late in 1884 in response to a 'moralising' letter from Bentley,
Gissing was making still further alterations to the proofs.[40] By then
he had offered Bentley his next novel *The Unclassed* which was
turned down because: 'It does not appear to me wholesome to hold
up the idea that a life of vice can be lived without loss of purity and
womanly virtue.'[41] *Mrs Grundy's Enemies* was never published: the

manuscript and proofs are lost, presumably destroyed. It is notable in this particular case that the publisher actually accepted the manuscript before he became nervous at handling it: his adviser made it clear again and again that he admired the book, and the author was willing to make concessions. Yet, publisher and adviser felt it their moral duty to truncate the book, and the publisher exercised his legal right not to publish what was now his property. That Bentley blamed his own timidity on the possibility of the circulating libraries objecting to *Mrs Grundy's Enemies* does not alter his own position as a moral censor. The writer was gradually being driven into a position of isolation in which he had ranged against him a large number of middlemen who, if they were not capable of actually banning his work, could delay its publication, deny it outlets in periodicals or circulation through the libraries, and by these means influence the moral tone of fiction, intimidate a young writer, and even discourage him from writing.

At this early stage in his career, while mocking the prudery of publishers and librarians, Gissing tended to place responsibility mainly on the cowardice of novelists. While struggling with publishers over *Mrs Grundy's Enemies* and *The Unclassed*, he wrote a letter to the *Pall Mall Gazette* about the stand taken by George Moore against the circulating libraries. He suggested that instead of criticising the 'circulator of books' who after all is a 'tradesman', it would be more to the point to blame novelists: 'English novels are miserable stuff for a very miserable reason, simply because English novelists fear to do their best lest they should damage their popularity, and consequently their income.' The only way out of the problem, he argued, was 'to find literary men with power and courage to produce original books'.[42] Though unfair to Moore, who hardly lacked courage on this particular issue, Gissing was perceptive in seeing that the new fiction would establish itself only after a long, bitter and exhausting battle. It was not to be his generation that would carry the cause to victory – that was to be achieved by Joyce and Lawrence – but Gissing and his contemporaries spent their lives in the crucial preparatory skirmishes. The touchiness of the opposition, in the 1880s especially, can be seen from one unexpected result of Gissing's letter to the *Pall Mall Gazette*. In his call for novelists of 'courage and power' he made the mistake of referring to Thackeray's 'painful confession' in the preface to *Pendennis* that since Fielding 'no writer of fiction among us has been permitted to depict to his utmost power a man' – on penalty, Gissing added, 'of a temporary diminution of receipts. If this be not a tradesman's attitude, what is?'[43] Gissing's letter provoked a virulent response from *Punch*. If he had criticised Trollope – the recent publication of whose *Autobiography* was still fresh in the mind – then perhaps no one would have objected, but Thackeray had been a valued early contributor to *Punch* and, more generally during the late Victorian period, was greatly admired by the literary Establishment. The *Punch* journalist admitted that he had never read anything by Gissing or even heard his name before, but still launched a heavily satirical attack on him as a purveyor of literary 'dirt', and concluded:

> We will do all we can to help you to your desired celebrity,
> Gissing, though we care not to be gissing who can have
> brought you up. Praised be the gods for thy foulness,
> GISSING! but also that, as we fondly hope, that there are
> not very many like thee.[44]

Gissing dismissed the attack, informing his brother that, 'it did not interrupt my work for an hour. I am getting very used to abuse in the place of criticism.'[45]

Perhaps Gissing was speaking the truth, but it is more likely that he was offering a stoical flourish for his younger brother to admire. In spite of his defiance and his call for courage on the part of authors, Gissing was learning that it was hardly possible to make a decent living from writing fiction without compromising the new artistic ideals. Temperamentally he was perfectly fitted to be a literary martyr: he was proud of having experienced bohemian poverty; his contempt for the average reader was, even in late Victorian terms, impressive; and anyone capable of selling an original three-volume novel for fifty pounds must have had an almost outrageous faith in his own future ability to succeed. Yet, even so, he was forced to modify and expurgate his work if he wished to see it in print. Ranged against him were the circulating libraries (on whose purchases the commercial viability of a novel rested); the publishers (whose judgment of the worth of a novel was largely decided by their conviction that the circulating libraries would promote it); and the editors of family and publishers' periodicals (who were influential in deciding the form in which a novel was first presented to readers). This was the network that had created mid-Victorian stability and was now beginning to fall apart because it no longer carried the agreement of all the participants. Thackeray, as Gissing rightly said, had felt the restriction of the system and given way. Gissing also gave way, but minimally and resentfully; Charles Reade surrendered; Moore and Vizetelly stepped outside the system to challenge the paramountcy of the circulating libraries, the publishers' steadiest source of income. Few other authors followed Moore's example, and Vizetelly was crushed. The rebellious author could survive in these conditions, as long as he was willing to accept constant abuse and a low income, but beyond the level of survival his best chance of rising above the system was, as we have seen, to write a commercially successful novel, and this he was unlikely to do when all the main channels of communication would be swiftly closed to him. The only alternative was to play the system, to accommodate the prejudices of publishers and editors, and then gradually, as success came, write more honestly. This was the plan adopted, and to a considerable extent carried out, by Hardy.

Although it took Hardy several years to get his first novel into print, his talent was recognised from the beginning, and he received sympathetic encouragement from publishers and their readers, notably Meredith, Alexander Macmillan, John Morley and Leslie Stephen. Hardy was ambitious for his work to achieve both artistic and financial success: he was confident in his own ability, though often insecure socially and intellectually. It was clear from the beginning that his temperament as a writer would lead him to deal more frankly with sexual relationships than was common or generally acceptable in the late 1860s. The professional advice he now began to receive focused mainly on his inexperience in constructing a novel and on the crudeness of his social satire. Together with the desire that he should correct these faults there were strong hints that he should delete sexual references and descriptions. In 1868 Macmillan turned down Hardy's first novel *The Poor Man and the Lady*, after it had been carefully read by himself and Morley. Macmillan's unease over the decision is apparent in the exceptionally long letter he wrote to Hardy, much of which discusses Hardy's portrayal of fashionable life before the principal objection is approached, and then only obliquely:

> The fault of the book, as it seems to me, is that it lacks the *modesty of nature* of fact. *Romeo and Juliet* and *Hamlet* have

many unnatural scenes, but Shakespeare put them in foreign
countries, and took the stories from old books. When he was
nearer home and his own time you don't find such things in
his writing.[46]

Although Macmillan felt unable to publish *The Poor Man and the
Lady* he did recommend it to Chapman and Hall, where Meredith,
the firm's chief reader, told Hardy that while they were willing to
publish he personally advised against it. No doubt with his own
experience of *Richard Feverel* in mind, he warned Hardy that 'if he
printed so pronounced a thing he would be attacked on all sides by
the conventional reviewers, and his future injured'. He added that it
could be re-written, 'softening it down considerably', or why
shouldn't Hardy try his hand at a novel with a 'more complicated
plot'?[47] Hardy decided on the second option, *The Poor Man and the
Lady* remained unpublished, and in 1870 he sent the manuscript of
his sensation novel, *Desperate Remedies*, to Macmillan. Morley's
report drew Macmillan's attention to the 'highly extravagant' scene
which describes 'Miss Aldclyffe and her new maid in bed', and
insisted: 'The story is ruined by the disgusting and absurd outrage
which is the key to its mystery. The violation of a young lady at an
evening party, and the subsequent birth of a child, is too abominable
to be tolerated as a central incident.'[48] The novel was turned down,
and an agreement was signed with William Tinsley under which
Hardy paid for the publication of *Desperate Remedies*. Even so,
Tinsley insisted on changes to the text, though he seems to have
passed without comment the overtly lesbian scene between Miss
Aldclyffe and her maid which Morley had found so 'extravagant'.

Hardy's next novel was the unobjectionable pastoral *Under the
Greenwood Tree* which he sold outright to Tinsley. It was admired
by Leslie Stephen, who invited Hardy to contribute a serial to the
Cornhill. Hardy was already busy writing another novel, but the
prestige of appearing in the *Cornhill* was irresistible, and in October
1873 he submitted the first chapters of *Far from the Madding
Crowd*. They were accepted and Stephen began suggesting changes
to the manuscript. Many of these were structural, and it has been
claimed that they helped Hardy achieve a greater sense of narrative
compression.[49] Certainly Hardy did not object: nor did he seem to
mind when Stephen deleted on his own initiative passages which
he felt were too frank and warned Hardy in advance that 'Troy's
seduction of the young woman will require to be treated in a

gingerly fashion.'[50] Stephen's editorial actions were not ususual, but his apologetic tone was. He admitted that he was motivated by 'an excessive prudery of which I am ashamed', and then described himself as powerless: 'Excuse this wretched shred of concession to popular taste; but I am a slave.'[51] Hardy quickly reassured him:

> The truth is that I am willing, and indeed anxious, to give
> up any points which may be desirable in a story when read
> as a whole, for the sake of others which shall please those
> who read it in numbers. Perhaps I may have higher aims
> some day, and be a great stickler for the proper artistic
> balance of the completed work, but for the present circum-
> stances lead me to wish merely to be considered a good
> hand at a serial.[52]

These famous words, which Hardy allowed to be printed in the 'biography' compiled by his second wife, have been variously interpreted as demonstrating Hardy's hypocrisy, mercenariness, common-sense, and lack of genuine interest in the art of fiction. His own reference in that letter to Stephen of 'higher aims' in the future suggests that once his popularity was established he might be able to abandon the tactics of indirection and write as he wished, while his comments in the *Life* indicate that his ultimate ambition lay in poetry rather than fiction.[53] Whatever the precise nature of Hardy's motives, his reply to Stephen outlined the strategy he followed as a novelist for the rest of his career. If he was to earn money from his fiction and attain popularity, then periodical serialisation was crucial: the editors could have their 'shred of concession to popular taste'. In 1877 he wrote to John Blackwood about the serialisation of *The Return of the Native* in terms remarkably similar to those Charles Reade was using to the same editor at roughly the same time: 'Should there accidentally occur any word or reflection not in harmony with the general tone of the magazine, you would be quite at liberty to strike it out if you chose. I always mention this to my editors, as it simplifies matters.'[54] Although the wording is similar to Reade's, the attitudes revealed are not at all the same. Reade abased himself: Hardy affected an air of complete indifference. With the conception of a novel firmly in his mind, and the copyright carefully retained or re-purchased where necessary, Hardy gradually, as edition followed edition in book form, restored the omitted passages.

What is so striking about these early experiences of Hardy's is that while all the distinguished literary men who read his work recognised a talent of exceptional power and originality, not one of them urged him to pursue, expand, develop or remain true to that special talent. Instead, they advised him to tone everything down, present life obliquely rather than directly, to conform to standards which they themselves often professed not to believe in. Alexander Macmillan was a publisher in the staid safe mid-Victorian mould, but none of the others would have been thought of as excessively cautious. They were Liberals, and inclined to the radical, free-thinking wing of their party. Leslie Stephen and Meredith (who, like Gissing, was later to call for 'gallant pens' to restore artistic ideals to British fiction) had both faced up to crises in their lives which brought them into conflict with Victorian convention: Morley was the editor of the *Fortnightly Review* and author of *On Compromise* (1874), a classic exposition of Liberal principles. That men such as these became frightened when dealing with the question of what was permissible in fiction indicates how pervasive moral censorship was in the closing decades of the century. Most young authors would not have had the fortune to deal with editors and readers as influential as Stephen, Meredith and Morley, and to overcome the insensitivity they now habitually met was beginning to require exceptional determination. For his part, Hardy was not ungrateful to his advisers. Stephen and Meredith retained his respect, and he continued to think of Macmillan's as possible publishers of his fiction. For their part, Macmillan's were eager to keep in contact with Hardy. They even accepted for publication *The Woodlanders* (1887), one of Hardy's most sexually daring novels, and serialised it, in the customary heavily abridged form, in their house magazine.[55] In 1902 Hardy negotiated terms with Frederick Macmillan to publish cheap editions of all of his novels, a transaction that was to lead ten years later to the Wessex Edition. By then the texts had been gradually revised and fully restored: they also carried the prefaces Hardy had written for various earlier editions in which he pointed wryly to the history of the novels' publication.

The personal cost to Hardy of playing the system can never be assessed: nor is it possible to know the way his career might have developed if conditions of publication in Britain had been different or if his temperament had led him to take an early stand against compromise. But there is no doubt that much of his indifference was affected rather than real, and that his resentment at being obliged to say one thing when he meant another became increasingly difficult to hide. By the late 1880s he was one of the most admired authors in Britain, yet still he was subjected to the same kind of editorial pressure he had succumbed to twenty years earlier, as the curious negotiations over the serialisation of *Tess of the D'Urbervilles* illustrate. In 1887 Hardy signed a contract with the Tillotsons newspaper syndicate under which he agreed to let them have by June 1889 a novel of the same length as *The Woodlanders* for a fee of one thousand guineas. He submitted the first portion of the novel and at proof stage Tillotsons claimed to be 'taken aback' by the story and demanded changes.[56] Hardy, who, as we have seen, usually caused no trouble over such requests, refused, and the contract was cancelled in what appears to have been a fairly amicable manner. It was also turned down by two leading periodicals, *Murray's* and *Macmillan's*. The comments of the editors give a frank insight into both the reasoning that lay behind the moral pressure of the age and the arrogance with which a writer of Hardy's distinction could be treated. Edward Arnold for *Murray's Magazine* explained in part:

> When I had the pleasure of seeing you here some time ago, I
> told you my views about publishing stories where the plot
> involves frequent and detailed reference to immoral situations:
> I know well enough that these tragedies are being played out
> every day in our midst, but I believe the less publicity they
> have the better, and it is quite possible and very desirable to
> grow up and pass through life without knowledge of them. I
> know your views are different, and I honour your motive.[57]

Mowbray Morris, the editor of *Macmillan's Magazine*, pointing out that there were things in the novel 'which might give offence, and, as I must frankly own to think, not altogether unreasonably', made the following observation:

> You use the word *succulent* more than once to describe the
> general appearance & condition of the Frome Valley. Perhaps
> I might say that the general impression left on me by reading
> your story – so far as it has gone – is one of rather too much
> succulence. All this, I know, makes the story 'entirely
> modern', & will therefore, I have no doubt, bring it plenty of
> praise. I must confess, however, to being rather too old-

fashioned – as I suppose I must call it – to quite relish the
entirely modern style of fiction.[58]

Neither editor would touch the novel: it was too honest, too true to
life, too 'succulent' and therefore 'too modern'. It was eventually
serialised in a notoriously distorted form in the *Graphic* newspaper. When *Tess* was published in book form in 1891, Hardy
acknowledged the *Graphic* serialisation and the publication of some
'other chapters, more especially addressed to adult readers' in the
Fortnightly Review and the *National Observer*, and commented tartly:

> My thanks are tendered to the editors and proprietors of
> those periodicals for enabling me now to piece the trunk and
> limbs of the novel together, and print it complete, as originally
> written two years ago.[59]

Hardy's refusal to make changes to the novel for Tillotsons is
puzzling. It seems likely that he regarded the publication of *Tess* as
the moment when he would stand against the degrading dismember-
ment of his work that he had accepted for so long: the negotiations
with several periodicals, sometimes simultaneously, over the novel's
serialisation are uncharacteristic of his usual businesslike manner,
and it has recently been suggested that he may have been 'inviting
rejections from the two magazine editors who he had best reason to
believe would provide them'.[60] The firmest evidence for Hardy's
mood at this time is the contribution he made to a symposium on
'Candour in English Fiction', which appeared while he was writing
Tess. In it he wrote bitterly of the 'Grundyist and subscriber'
forcing the 'true artist' to 'belie his literary conscience' and falsify
his 'best imaginative instincts', this being 'the fearful price that he
has to pay for the privilege of writing in the English language'.[61] If
Hardy had decided that with *Tess* he would make an attempt not to
pay this 'fearful price' for serialisation, then he failed; but the
immediate publication in book form, with the trunk and limbs put
together again, brought the issue of sexual frankness in fiction to
public attention as never before, and the immense popularity of
Tess played a crucial part in the easing of moral pressure in the
1890s. It was noted earlier that the New Woman novelists
benefited directly from this change, and so did other novelists. In
March 1892 Gissing recorded with amazement that the *Saturday
Review* had said of his recent novel *Denzil Quarrier* that, 'A bolder
subject would better suit this writer. That would have been

extraordinary a few years ago . . . Indeed, after Hardy's *Tess*, one can scarcely see the limits of artistic freedom.'[62] Gissing for once was being over-optimistic, though the breakthrough he observed was real enough. For Hardy, the praise and admiration that came to him for *Tess*, and a few years later for *Jude the Obscure*, was insufficient compensation for the furious hostility these novels also received. When his next novel *The Well-Beloved* (1897) was criticised in the press for its immorality, he observed bitterly: 'What foul cess-pits some men's minds must be, and what a Night-cart would be required to empty them.'[63] He published no further novels. The scandalous success of *Tess* and *Jude*, together with the growing public interest in his earlier novels, made him wealthy enough to devote the rest of his long life to poetry.

When Mowbray Morris informed Hardy that the 'succulence' of *Tess* made it 'entirely modern' he was not simply allowing his judgment to be swayed by personal prejudice or philistinism. Like many of the opponents of the new artistic freedom, he understood perfectly well what was at stake. The modern novel was to emerge only when Victorian conventions and compromises had been demolished, and the major court battles were to be fought on the question of 'succulence' in fiction. Morris wanted compromise to continue which, in effect, meant late Victorian novelists continuing to behave like their mid-Victorian predecessors. That British society had moved decisively towards democracy made compromise on such a dangerous area of life as sexual passion all the more necessary, and this fear was compounded by the admiration with which French fiction was regarded by British novelists, it being axiomatic to many Victorians that France had notoriously not followed the path of social compromise and had not enjoyed mid-Victorian stability. The connection was obvious. 'Look what such literature has done for France,' Samuel Smith commanded his fellow MPs in the 1888 Commons debate, and no one objected.[64] The atmosphere was now totally different from that of the 1857 Lords debate on the Obscene Publications Act when, as we have seen, the specific example of French literature had been raised and cleared as not being in danger of prosecution. The kind of compromise sought by men like Mowbray Morris and Samuel Smith was possible only if it was willingly entered into by all the parties concerned, and that was no longer the case. Novelists now

demanded the artistic and democratic right to deal openly with
whatever topic they wished, subject only to the limits of their own
ability: with Henry James they believed in 'the perfect dependence
of the "moral" sense of a work of art on the amount of felt life
concerned in producing it'.[65] Given such a view, there could not
be, as Wilde insisted, any such thing as 'a moral or an immoral
book. Books are well written or badly written. That is all.'[66]
Nobody, however, was going to be brought into court and publicly
humiliated for having published a badly-written book or one in
which the amount of 'felt life' was notably deficient. Questions of
morality were becoming increasingly restricted to sexual behaviour,
the area of human experience more than any other which Victorian
novelists had agreed to keep out of their work, and with the
breakdown of compromise it was inevitable that this would provide
a main point of focus. There could be no easy way out, as the blunt
physicality of Zola's novels made clear. The kind of shock involved
was well described by James: 'Our various senses, sight, smell,
sound, touch, are, as with Zola always, more or less convinced.'[67]
In Zola's novels, women menstruate, men and women urinate; they
sweat, smell, fight and swear; sex is portrayed as an overwhelmingly,
often uncontrollably, natural force. And the artistic justification
was based firmly on realism or naturalism. The claims for the
novels' realism – the insistence that this is what life *is* – caused as
much perturbation as what was actually portrayed. If *La Terre*
really was what agricultural life *was* in France, then in comparison
the novels by daring Thomas Hardy of life in agricultural Wessex
were positively pastoral, while the timidity of a George Eliot,
Dickens or Trollope hardly bore thinking about. That the extreme
hostility to Zola lasted for only a relatively short period of time did
not mean that the campaign to cleanse literature had been given
up. There are three main reasons for the change of attitude.

First, the action by the NVA against Vizetelly had to a
considerable extent succeeded. It was still possible to buy complete
translations of Zola's novels in expensive editions or through
specialist bookshops, but the new translations provided for the
general reader were substantially abridged. No one was eager to
make a test case of the issue, and the real victory by the NVA lay
in reinforcing the already strong conservatism of publishers and
editors who, as is apparent in the cases of Hardy and Gissing, were
themselves skilled in the techniques of moral pressure. Secondly, in

the early 1890s the public outrage against the importation of
decadent foreign literature began to switch to Ibsen, who in some
respects seemed even more subversive than Zola. Thirdly, and
perhaps most important of all, there was almost no serious attempt
by British novelists to follow the example of French naturalism.
British fiction was becoming franker than it had been for a century
past, but the treatment of sex was still generally not explicit and
had little of Zola's physicality. The feared collapse of moral
standards didn't happen, the flood of Zola-inspired indecent
literature that the moral protesters announced was about to engulf
Britain never occurred. In 1888, referring to the seduction of first
Mme Walter and then her daughter in Maupassant's *Bel Ami*,
Henry James said that he knew of no English or American novelist
who 'could' have written this part of Bel Ami's history, and then
added that he found it impossible to think of an English or
American novelist 'who would have written it if he could'.[68] The
distinction is important, and its relevance stretches beyond the
1880s to the whole of the period. Which British novelist might
have been able and interested enough to portray this kind of sexual
experience, the 'taste' of which James found so 'atrocious'?[69]

Certainly Hardy; Moore in the early novels which were imitative
of French naturalism; and Kipling, whose portrayal of sexuality in
such works as 'Love o' Women' and *The Light that Failed*, suffers
from imposed restraint. Gissing would have liked to write more
explicitly about sex and felt himself prevented from doing so, but
the powerful element of idealism in his work was as much a
restraining influence as circumstances of publication, and where he
does come close to the tone of French naturalism the differences are
striking. *New Grub Street* is in many ways an English *Bel Ami*. Both
novels chart the rise to power in journalism of a young man from an
obscure provincial background. In both novels cynicism triumphs
over honesty, and the way to the top is only possible because of the
ambitious hero's sexual attractiveness. In *New Grub Street* Jasper
Milvain dishonourably breaks off his relationship with Marian
Yule to give himself the chance of marrying Reardon's wealthy
widow. Gissing makes it clear that the Reardons' marriage has been
sexually unsatisfactory and links this with the husband's lack of
status as an unsuccessful novelist, but in order to show the way
that Milvain benefits from this situation Gissing committed
himself to a rather clumsy and unexplicit plot, while Maupassant

makes it clear that Bel Ami achieves his ambitions by seducing the wives, widows and daughters of men who are wealthier and more influential than himself. There is little to choose between the cynicism attributed to the two men, but a comparison between *New Grub Street* and *Bel Ami* supports James's contention that there were very few British novelists of the time who would have wanted to emulate Maupassant even if they had been able to do so. An illustration of the discrepancy between how novelists tended to speak of the limitations imposed upon them and the relatively innocuous nature of the work they produced is available in the activities of the Rabelais Club. It was founded in 1880 by Walter Besant as, according to Hardy, 'a declaration for virility in literature' and would today be totally forgotten were it not for Hardy's claim that James's membership application was turned down because of the lack of 'virility' in his work and that he was allowed in only as a guest.[70] Richard Taylor has shown that these comments were written for publication after Hardy had read some offensive remarks about his own work in an edition of James's letters published in 1920.[71] Indeed, they may have been not only spiteful, but untrue, as James was listed as one of the 'original members' of the Club.[72] The main interest of the anecdote, however, is that as far as the Club's avowed aim is concerned it could have applied to almost all of the members. Although many of James's greatest novels centre upon sexual relationships, his narrative method when dealing with such matters was invariably indirect, and much the same can be said of Meredith. Of the other novelists who at one time or another were members of the Rabelais Club, Edward Bellamy and Bret Harte were not interested in pioneering the frank treatment of sex in fiction; Stevenson was often criticised by reviewers for his weak portrayal of women; and it would be difficult to imagine a novelist less 'Rabelaisian' than Besant who, in matters of censorship, subscribed to the principle that 'he who works for pay must respect the prejudices of his customers'.[73] Hardy, again, is the notable exception. No doubt there was some enjoyable fun over dinner or drinks, but it had little to do with the introduction of greater virility into literature. In France any comparable group of novelists gathered together under such a banner would have argued out the literary principles involved, published at least one manifesto, prepared to present collectively their most combative work, and then split up after bitter public disagreements. The Rabelais Club toasted 'the Master', made slightly risqué jokes over passages in French and Latin, and published their 'recreations' in handsome limited editions. It was all probably not much more daring than the debate held by St Dominic's sixth-form Literary Society on the motion, 'That the present age is degenerate.'[74]

Even with slightly later British novelists who were continuing to write within the French tradition there was not necessarily a shared feeling that their books would have been radically different if the publishing climate had been freer. Somerset Maugham in *Mrs Craddock* and *Of Human Bondage* was clearly conscious of the kind of prohibition defined by James. Yet Bennett managed to write successful novels in which every characteristic of French fiction was emulated, with the notable exception of sex. He made a revealing observation on this aspect of his work when describing, half-ironically, the 'scenes of gilded vice' to be found in Ouida's novels: 'She it was who inspired me with that taste for liaisons under pink lampshades which I shall always have, but which, owing to a puritanical ancestry and upbringing, I shall never be able to satisfy.'[75] It sounds as though he is referring to his life, but it applies just as well to his fiction. When he did try to write about sexual passion in *Sacred and Profane Love* (1905) he slipped naturally into the 'liaisons under pink lampshades' style of writing and, though handled more successfully, the scenes in the Restaurant Sylvain in *The Old Wives' Tale* are also indebted to Ouida, even though this was an aspect of Parisian life that Bennett must have long known at first hand and from French fiction. Nor is it particularly surprising that a novelist like Bennett, with his 'puritanical ancestry and upbringing', should have turned stylistically to popular women novelists when writing about sex: after all, that, in the topsy-turvy world of Victorian fiction, was where it was most readily to be found. Bennett might refer ironically to his youthful admiration for Ouida, and, from a more mature standpoint, mock Elinor Glyn, but in this particular area of life they were not the less adventurous writers.[76]

The most unlikely surrender to sexual romanticism was that of H. G. Wells. Renowned throughout the world as a spokesman for free-love, and the most perceptive sociological prophet in Britain, he was virtually incapable of describing sexual passion without sounding like Rhoda Broughton:

'Ann Veronica,' he said, 'I tell you this is love. I love the
soles of your feet. I love your very breath. I have tried not to
tell you – tried to be simply your friend. It is no good. I
want you. I worship you. I would do anything – I would
give anything to make you mine.'[77]

That most British novelists of the late nineteenth and early
twentieth centuries were either unable or unwilling to break
decisively with the sexual traditions bequeathed them by the
Victorians did not totally remove the fear that they might at any
moment be ready to do so. There was a brief respite when it
became apparent that Zola was not inspiring hosts of imitators in
Britain, then the moral protest started up again. It is an indication
of how irrational this kind of literary censorship can be that what
was to become one of the most notorious cases in early modern
literature – that of James Joyce's *Dubliners* – was also one of the
most genuinely innocent.

Joyce sent the manuscript of *Dubliners* to the publisher Grant
Richards on 3 December 1905. Richards accepted it for publication
very quickly and a contract was signed at the end of February
1906. In April Richards notified Joyce that the printer had refused
to handle one of the stories, 'Two Gallants', and certain passages in
'Counterparts': in addition, Richards asked Joyce to remove the
word 'bloody' from another story, 'Grace'.[78] Joyce's first response
was incredulity, then anger that a printer should be able to take
upon himself the right to serve as 'the barometer of English
opinion': it was a point he returned to several times in the
correspondence.[79] The 'right', however rested on the English law
of libel which, as Samuel Hynes has noted, made the printer as
open to prosecution as the author or publisher and therefore was an
encouragement to him to play the role of censor out of self-
protection.[80] In the correspondence that followed, Joyce pointed
out, rightly, that the views of Richards and his printer were
inconsistent, and he detailed other stories and passages which, on
the same reasoning, could be regarded as objectionable. Richards
agreed and demanded that these also be deleted. The more Joyce
protested, the more concessions Richards demanded, with the
material to be omitted developing from the initial passages and
words to entire stories. Joyce gradually began to give way. He
agreed to modify his use of the word 'bloody' in some instances
and even to leave two of the stories out of the collection, but

Richards had had enough. Joyce consulted a lawyer and the Society of Authors to see if he had any legal redress against Richards: he was advised to keep out of court.[81]

Joyce's experience with Richards repeats, in many respects, Gissing's negotiations with Bentley over *The Unclassed*, twenty years earlier, and it is remembered, of course, because Joyce was at the time an unknown writer of genius and because *Ulysses* would eventually provide (in both Britain and America) a key test-case for changing legal attitudes to obscenity in literature. Yet these factors apart, the Joyce–Richards confrontation was typical of the uneasy relationship between authors and publishers on the question of what was permissible in fiction. Joyce at first took a firm aesthetic line, refusing to delete or modify anything on the grounds that the passages objected to were integral parts of a work of art. Legally he seemed secure, with an agreed and signed contract. The subjects of some of the stories, and more importantly their non-moralistic treatment, were unusual, but there were no explicit sexual descriptions involved and similar words and passages to those which offended Richards were to be found in readily-available published fiction: even the expurgated editions of Zola now on sale everywhere in Britain were more sexually daring than *Dubliners*. Joyce was clearly right to accuse Richards of being 'unduly timid' and 'intimidated by imaginary terrors' and also probably right to conjecture: 'The worse that will happen, I suppose, is that some critic will allude to me as the "Irish Zola"!'[82] Yet in spite of all of this Joyce was powerless to change Richards's mind on any of the major issues at stake and felt himself forced to compromise. Richards expressed great admiration for Joyce's work and hoped, once the problems over *Dubliners* were cleared away, that he could publish other work by him: he was, however, careful to stress that his admiration was to be regarded as quite distinct from his 'conviction as to what is wise or not wise for us to publish'.[83] His support for his printer led to a classic defence of the Victorian publishing network:

> If a printer takes that view you can be quite sure that the
> booksellers will take it, that the libraries will take it, and that
> an inconveniently large section of the general public will take
> it.[84]

In 1906 it was by no means 'sure' that this chain reaction would occur: it was only clear that Richards was not willing to take a moral or a commercial risk. He held out to Joyce the possibility (if he agreed to make the desired alterations) of a commercial success or (if he refused to comply) degrading anonymity: 'You won't get a publisher – a real publisher – to issue it as it stands. I won't say you won't get somebody to bring it out, but it would be brought out obscurely.'[85] Built into Richards's warnings there was an added hint that obscure publication would bring Joyce cheap notoriety. In many respects it was a fairly accurate prophecy of Joyce's subsequent career. In all of this, Richards could only adopt the tone he did towards Joyce because he knew that in spite of the signed contract the power of decision was finally his. When he grew tired of Joyce's painstaking defence of his art, Richards simply returned the manuscript.

Over the next four years *Dubliners* was offered to, and rejected by, several English publishers, before Joyce turned to the Dublin publisher Maunsel & Co. where he had personal connections with the managing director George Roberts and the literary adviser Joseph Hone. The book was accepted, a contract signed in August 1909, and there began a re-run of Joyce's experiences with Grant Richards. As the proofs were being set up Roberts started to raise objections. This time they centred on comments by a character in 'Ivy Day in the Committee Room' on King Edward, who had recently died, and his 'bloody old bitch of a mother': there was also concern that libel cases could arise out of Joyce's use in the stories of identifiable Dublin places and people. Joyce softened the offending reference to Queen Victoria, making it 'old mother', but Roberts was still not satisfied, publication was delayed, and the objections multiplied. Joyce threatened legal action, petitioned George V in an unsuccessful attempt to get the new king to say that the references to his father and grandmother were not offensive to him, and wrote up the story of his dealings with Richards and Maunsel in the form of a letter which was published in the newspaper *Sinn Fein* and several years later as an article in the *Egoist* entitled 'A Curious History'. The advice he received from the Dublin solicitor was that there was a Vigilance Committee active in the city 'whose object was to seek out and suppress all writing of immoral tendency' and that the best thing for Joyce to do was to 'take no risks and . . . either delete or entirely alter the paragraph in question'.[86] Although Joyce was willing to make exclusions and alterations, Roberts, like Richards before him, had lost interest in the book. Joyce's last desperate act was to try to buy up the proof copies of *Dubliners* and publish it himself. He managed to save one set of proofs out of the thousand: the rest were destroyed. In November 1913 he turned once again to Grant Richards and after a reasonably friendly exchange of letters in which it was agreed that the original terms of the contract should still apply, *Dubliners* was at last published in 1914.

The stories which Joyce had once agreed to omit were there in the first edition, so were most of the uses of 'bloody' to which Richards had originally objected. The reference to Queen Victoria had changed from 'bloody owl' mother' (1906) to 'bloody old bitch of a mother' (1909) and then to 'old mother' (1914). Three passages in the story 'Counterparts' had originally been blue-pencilled for alteration.[87] The first ('a man with two establishments to keep up, of course, he couldn't') survived unchanged in 1914: the second ('Farrington said he wouldn't mind having the far one and began to smile at her') had gone. The third passage read originally:

> She continued to cast bold glances at him and changed the
> position of her legs often; and when she was going out she
> brushed against his chair and said 'Pardon!' in a Cockney
> accent.

By 1914 it had become:

> She glanced at him once or twice and, when the party was
> leaving the room, she brushed against his chair and said '*O
> pardon!*' in a London accent.

It was largely for the sake of changes such as these that nine years had passed since Joyce first submitted the manuscript of *Dubliners* to Richards: in that time it had been rejected by an estimated ten publishers.[88] Even in 1914 the text wasn't left alone. As a final act of indifference to the author's wishes, Richards announced that he was inserting speech marks (or 'perverted commas' as Joyce liked to call them) in place of the dash which Joyce himself favoured.[89] The reviews of *Dubliners* were generally favourable. There was no moral outburst against the book – or indeed much general interest at all: by May 1915 only 379 copies had been sold.

The brief appearance of the NVA in the 'curious history' of *Dubliners* is a perfect illustration of how that organisation worked.

It had played no direct part in the book's long-delayed publication and, until Joyce sent his open letter to the Irish press, would almost certainly have known nothing whatever about *Dubliners*. In this particular case, as in the vast majority of such cases throughout the period, the nervousness of publishers was a more potent agency of moral control than externally-organised protest. Some publishers simply shared the kinds of concern expressed by the moral campaigners. It did not, for example, require the intervention of the NVA to persuade Frederick Macmillan to turn down the opportunity of publishing *Ann Veronica*, as his explanatory letter to Wells makes clear:

> The plot develops on lines that would be exceedingly distaste-
> ful to the public which buys books published by our firm . . .
> When Ann Veronica begins her pursuit of the Professor at
> the International college, offers herself to him as a mistress
> and almost forces herself into his arms, the story ceases to be
> amusing and is certainly not edifying.[90]

But most publishers were closer to Grant Richards in blaming external forces. William Heinemann's refusal in 1912 to publish *Sons and Lovers* is a classic instance:

> Its want of reticence makes it unfit, I fear, altogether for
> publication in England as things are. The tyranny of the
> Libraries is such that a book far less out-spoken would
> certainly be damned (and there is practically no market for
> fiction outside of them).[91]

In spite of the decline of the three-decker, the event that Moore and Vizetelly had hoped would break the tyranny of the libraries, little had changed since Reade, Hardy and Gissing had faced similarly unsympathetic publishers: the arguments in favour of reticence remained what they had been thirty years earlier. The attitudes of younger novelists, however, were changing: to them, the fears expressed by publishers were almost incomprehensible. The circumstances of the prosecutions which haunted the minds of the literary Establishment at the end of the nineteenth century – those of Vizetelly and Wilde – could now seem too specific to carry any general threat, while the moral protesters were easily dismissed as unimportant philistines, lingering die-hard remnants of out-dated Victorianism. Joyce was no doubt right to accuse Grant Richards of being 'intimidated by imaginary terrors'. But as the

campaign being fought out was largely psychological such reasoning
carried little weight. Publishers *did* feel intimidated, and they did not
believe that their 'terrors' were 'imaginary'. That the mere rumour
of a branch of the NVA being active in Dublin could make a
solicitor advise Joyce to move carefully was not, from the point of
view of publishers, entirely ridiculous, for the period of time
covered by the protracted negotiations over *Dubliners* was marked
by the most determined attempt to impose literary censorship since
the 1880s. It was the last vain attempt by libraries, publishers,
moral campaigners, and their legendary allies the spinster ladies
living in the country, to re-assert mid-Victorian control. Zolaism
had not triumphed in Britain, and there was a brief spell of
relaxation: then the new enemy emerged. It was the 'sex-problem
novel' or simply the 'sex-novel', or, in the primmer language of
The Times, 'improper books'.

As in earlier campaigns by the NVA, fiction in itself was not the
main target of the protesters: it was, however, regarded as a major
symptom of a much wider national degeneracy, an attitude which
has been traced to disillusionment over Britain's performance in
the Boer War and an increasing concern with the possibility of war
in Europe.[92] The most prominent of the new pressure groups, the
National Social Purity Crusade, was formed in 1901, though it was
not until 1908 that it began to achieve nation-wide publicity. By
then it had been joined by various other organisations. Some of
them – the 'White Cross Movement' and the NVA, for example –
were already well established and others, like the Salvation Army,
were not at all interested in questions of literary censorship. What
was new was the banding together of these diverse organisations in
order to make their point more effectively. They courted publicity
by well-organised headline-catching conferences, and published
their proceedings in volumes which were given titles – *The
Cleansing of a City* (1908), *The Nation's Morals* (1910) – calculated
to awaken public interest. The pronouncements of the moral
protesters on fiction were rarely more than vague generalisations.
William Barry, a long-term critic of the modern spirit and
exceptionally well informed on British and European literature,
told one of the conferences that 'romantic literature is yielding
place before a kind which dispenses with drapery on the score of
artistic intention', but named no names.[93] The Rev. R. F. Horton
was equally vague, though far more dramatic, in his denunciation

of a recent translation of a German novel: 'Written (O monstrum
infandum!) by a woman ... Before I had skimmed fifty pages I
found my brain swimming: I nearly swooned.'[94] It was an
experience that made him thankful for British novelists like Marie
Corelli and Hall Caine: ironically he did not seem to be aware that
both of these novelists had attracted the attention of the reformers.
Most of the speakers failed to display even this degree of familiarity
with modern fiction. They concentrated on the damage being done
to the morals of modern youth – especially the immature products
of the Board Schools – by penny-dreadfuls (an extremely hoary
topic at this late date) and more recent developments in comics and
pin-up magazines.

It is important not to exaggerate the direct power that the moral
reformers had, and wrong to believe that they spoke in one loudly-
concerted voice. Nor did they all come from outside the literary
world: publishers, authors, newsagents, librarians and booksellers
were represented at the conferences, and not all of them were there
to speak out against literary censorship. Some did, however, try to
instil common-sense into the proceedings, as when Arthur Spur-
geon, Chairman of the Publishers' Circle, told one audience:

> In the year 1909 there were 10,000 new books and new
> editions published in this country, and of that number I am
> informed the Libraries Association did not consider there
> were more than seven as being unfit for publication.[95]

At this same conference in 1910 W. T. Stead gave a thoughtful talk
on the moral problems created by the modern mass entertainment
industry, and John St Loe Strachey, editor of the *Spectator* and a
renowned moral reformer, spoke strongly against using the law to
control fiction. Even the hard-line campaigners were aware that
more could be lost than gained by censorship. Once he had
recovered from the swoon induced by the German woman novelist,
the Rev. Horton advised:

> We must look rather to the moral culture of readers than to
> the control of writers. The liberty to write what one wishes is
> a liberty too valuable and too hardly won to be lightly sacri-
> ficed.[96]

And James Marchant, a leading figure in the morality campaigns,
admitted that, 'the ultimate test when all is said and done, must be
what the public tolerates'.[97] Not all of these statements can be

taken at face value. At the Caxton Hall meeting in July 1910, in spite of Stead's protests, a motion was carried to urge the government to strengthen the law against the publication of 'noxious literature', and a deputation waited on the Home Secretary. But no official action was taken, and it seems unlikely that the moral reformers really expected it to be. The power they sought was indirect. Like the NVA in the 1880s they were happier working behind the scenes. It was one thing to give stirring speeches at public conferences, but taking legal action was quite a different matter. It was expensive, and even a successful prosecution would not necessarily function as an overall deterrent. Instead they directed their message at publishers, editors, librarians and booksellers. If there had not been many individuals willing to listen or capable of being intimidated, then all of the huffing and puffing would have had no effect whatsoever.

In December 1908 the NVA, encouraged by the resurgence of moral protest, and appalled by, 'an epidemic of what has been called the sex novel' or what the NVA itself preferred to call 'literary filth', took legal action against John Long for having published Hubert Wales's novel *The Yoke*.[98] It had been in print for about eighteen months and there was sufficient public interest in it for a cheap edition to have been published. The time gap between the novel's publication and prosecution was probably because the NVA wanted to find a representative example of the sex-problem novel and surveyed the market before deciding on *The Yoke*. The prosecution would cost them an estimated £1,000 and they had to be sure they had not made a mistake.[99] For reasons already discussed, *The Yoke* was, from the NVA's point of view, a good choice. It was important that Wales did not have an established reputation as a novelist. That would have made a defence more likely and a prosecution more difficult to sustain. The need to avoid the wrong kind of publicity probably explains why the NVA did not select a woman novelist to prosecute, even though women were regarded as being 'the chief offenders in this direction'.[100] Three hundred copies of *The Yoke* were destroyed, and John Long agreed to withdraw the novel from circulation and publish no future editions of it. There was then a lull in the activities of the protesters for nearly a year. When they restarted they attacked from so many different angles that it is difficult not to see it as in some way a co-ordinated effort. It began with a denunciation in the *Spectator* of the 'considerable portion of modern fiction . . . concerned with the apotheosis of successful caddishness, and the acquiescence of decent people in its triumph'.[101] Two weeks later the same periodical published a review by the editor John St Loe Strachey of *Ann Veronica* under the title 'A Poisonous Book', which was clearly intended as a rallying-cry. Strachey himself admitted that it was usually a foolish policy to call attention to an immoral book, but felt that in this instance the risk should be taken because of the threat posed by Wells's views to the stability of the family and therefore 'to a sound and healthy State'.[102] The following week the *Spectator* printed a letter from Herbert Bull, who was a supporter of the NVA, proposing that a 'guarantee fund' be set up and used to prosecute the publishers of immoral books; a leading article in the same number pledged the *Spectator*'s support.[103] Wells also wrote to the *Spectator* defending the ideas expressed in *Ann Veronica*.[104] But in the correspondence that followed his letter was swamped by others from anonymous individuals ('a bookseller' and 'a public librarian') and organisations (the Girls' Friendly Society and the Head-Masters' Association) approving Bull's guarantee fund. Once again, this incident is particularly interesting for the way it reveals both the type of influence exerted by the moral reformers and their ultimate lack of real power. The influence is seen in what must have been a very substantial amount of unpublicised pressure. The 'public librarian' who wrote to the *Spectator* claimed that 'on several occasions' he had reported books as unfit for circulation and 'as a rule they have, after examination, been condemned to be burnt'.[105] There is every reason to believe he was speaking the truth; and though Bull himself may have been exaggerating when he claimed to have 'a list of ninety-eight books which a single firm [presumably a bookseller] has placed under ban', it is possible that he too was speaking the truth.[106] How little effective support there was beneath all the noise is apparent from the fate of the guarantee fund which was, in Bull's words, to be used to preserve 'our English homes from needless contamination'. In just over a month donations amounted to £720, not enough to launch one cut-price prosecution against a little-known author.[107] And this was the case even though in the same week that Bull proposed setting up his fund the wider attack on the sex-problem novel was strengthened by the decision of the principal circulating libraries to form a

Libraries Association in order to take a collective stand against books 'which are regarded as transgressing the dictates of good taste in subject or treatment'.[108]

The announcement by the circulating libraries – W. H. Smith, Boots, Day's, Mudie's, Cawthorn and Hutt, *The Times* and the Booksellers' Association – was made on 31 November 1909. Acting on behalf of their subscribers, they agreed 'not to place in circulation any book which, by reason of the personally scandalous, libellous, immoral, or otherwise disagreeable nature of its contents, is in our opinion likely to prove offensive to any considerable section of our subscribers'. They also drafted a set of resolutions to be sent to publishers. All published books were to be classified by the new Association under one of three headings: (*a*) satisfactory (*b*) doubtful (*c*) objectionable. In order to carry out this policy the libraries stated that:

1. They will not circulate any novel until it has been submitted for reading at least one week.
2. They will at once advise the other members of any doubtful or objectionable book.
3. They will not circulate or sell any book considered objectionable by any three members of the Association.
4. They will do their best to make the distribution of any book considered doubtful by three members of the Association as small as possible.[109]

In one sense the circulating libraries were only bringing into the open policies of control which they had long operated. The major changes were that they now publicly acknowledged this role and arrogantly proposed to extend it by making publishers submit for the libraries' approval before circulation all novels or perhaps all 'books', a confusion that was to cause a good deal of trouble in the ensuing debate. It was, in effect, blatant pre-publication censorship; the threat against the distribution of any book classified by three members of the Association as 'doubtful' was felt as particularly offensive. No longer did the proposed censorship rest on the tacit agreement of other members of the literary community; it did not have a scapegoat like Zola; and although the main target was the sex-problem novel, this was not actually stated, leaving the impression that all books would depend for their existence on the approval of the circulating libraries. Nor was it possible to localise the issue. Everyone was involved, and the alignments that followed cut across professional boundaries.

At first the Publishers' Association gave a guarded welcome to the proposal, a response that can be explained partly by the fact that several influential publishers were supporters of moral control and, more generally, because of the threat to their commercial interests, though they reserved a final judgment until the Society of Authors had been consulted.[110] As there was no possibility that authors (or ultimately publishers) would be able to act collectively on such an issue it was a wise precaution. The Society of Authors was in a similar predicament. The line that had descended to them from Besant was that they should not intervene in what was a financial contract between the libraries and their subscribers, but this was no longer a policy they could sensibly endorse, since it was their members who would be discriminated against.[111] Censorship of one kind or another was becoming one of the matters on which the Society's advice was most regularly sought, and its first response was to try to satisfy internal divisions by condemning that part of the circulating libraries' ultimatum that would delay publication of books, while at the same time upholding the libraries' right to buy, on behalf of their subscribers, whichever books they wished. With the professional associations divided, it was left to individual members to argue the issue out, and this they did in every periodical and newspaper of the day.

The uncompromising case against censorship was put by Edmund Gosse who accused the libraries of setting up a 'secret tribunal against which there is no appeal' and invoked the example of Milton who had stood against the Star Chamber, 'the circulating library of his day'.[112] At the other extreme there was the publisher John Murray arguing that it was 'worth surrendering a little liberty to gain decent publications', there being no doubt that 'many books have been published this year which ought never to have been published', and William Barry airily pointing to piles of immoral books that 'deserve simply to be burnt'.[113] The *Spectator* quickly applauded the action of the circulating libraries, as did the representatives of the organisations that could now be expected to support any movement towards censorship. Notable in this case was the President of the Central Council of the Mothers' Union who wrote to *The Times* pledging the support of 300,000 members to the circulating libraries' attempt to bring about a 'permanent

improvement in tone of modern literature'.[114] Individual enthusiasts for moral control seized the chance to give a contemporary
polish to the most hallowed of censorship clichés:

> There is surely no reason why libraries should continue to
> annoy the bulk of their subscribers by supplying them with
> 'literature' that disgusts a healthy-minded man and brings the
> blush of shame to the cheek of all but unsexed women.[115]

Most novelists stood firm and followed the unyielding example of
William de Morgan who simply objected 'without any reserves, to
the proposed censorship of novels by the libraries'.[116] The clearest
statement of the dangers inherent in the controversy came from
Anthony Hope. He warned that were it to be accepted that books
be classified as 'improper' and 'objectionable' those words would
soon be construed as meaning 'unorthodox' and 'anti-conventional',
and then 'we have a censorship and an "Index"'.[117] As usual, the
discontent of authors mattered little to the circulating libraries, and
in the event it was the publishers' refusal to submit books for the
prior approval of the libraries that made it impossible for the
scheme to operate in any co-ordinated way. Instead, the lingering
determination to impose moral censorship functioned at the level of
skirmishes rather than full-scale war, constantly irritating authors
and publishers alike.

There were two factors that eventually undermined the power of
the circulating libraries to carry through their repressive policies.
Unwilling to participate in the kinds of compromise demanded in
the past, and generally contemptuous of the social changes taking
place around them, the more adventurous or experimental younger
novelists were being driven increasingly into forms of publication
which could bring them into contact with a small number of
admirers. Private presses and little magazines were now regular
parts of the literary scene. Completely independent of the circulating libraries, they were often backed financially by a new type of
literary patron, and at their best they aimed to create a network of
like-minded readers that transcended national boundaries. Initially
the link was Anglo-American, though it was no longer necessarily
centred on London. With the growing assumption that the
experimental writer was cut off from the land of his birth, the
temporary centre of the movement could be Paris, or Zurich, or
Mexico. And, with the gradual shift away from the stifling

repression of commercial publishing to the less demanding patronage of universities and other educational institutions, the advanced novelist was already beginning to realise that he could get more money from selling or mortgaging the manuscript or work-sheets of a novel than from the royalties that might come to him once he had managed to get it published. By 1914 these tendencies were apparent if still not highly developed. Most novelists con-tinued to look to commercial publishers as their main hope, and though they were sometimes let down (as Joyce was by Richards over *Dubliners* and Lawrence by Methuen over *The Rainbow*) they were being joined by younger publishers who accepted the need to stand with their authors against irrational moral pressure. When the circulating libraries raised objections to Gilbert Cannan's *Round the Corner* (1913), Martin Secker immediately counter-attacked with advertisements proclaiming it '*Not* an immoral book', one that he was 'proud to have issued', and urging the public to insist on the right to decide the matter for itself.[118]

The second factor which weakened the power of the circulating libraries was the rapid growth of public libraries in the early years of the present century. Such a claim can appear paradoxical, for in theory the public libraries were even more susceptible to moral pressure than the circulating libraries, financed as they were by ratepayers' money and answerable for their book-buying policies to committees appointed by local councils. They were central targets of the moral protesters and frequently forced to yield to demands that 'doubtful' or 'immoral' books should not be purchased, or should be removed from the library shelves, or placed in a reserved category. Supporters of the NVA and other protest groups were prominent members of library committees, and their influence could extend beyond the suppression of sex-problem novels. The practice of 'blacking-out' of newspapers details of horse-race meetings in order to discourage people from using library reading rooms to write out bets was widespread, and in 1911 Alderman Plummer of Manchester could announce openly that 'certain kinds of extreme socialist literature' were banned from the city's public libraries.[119] There must have been a good deal of re-pressive activity of this kind throughout the country. In the early days of the public library movement, control was exercised by the libraries simply not buying controversial books, as Thomas Greenwood noted in 1891:

> After a search through a large number of catalogues there has
> been found not a single case of a library having in its
> catalogue the works of two or three modern Continental
> writers whose productions are notoriously vicious in taste and
> demoralising in tendency.[120]

During the later years public libraries, like their circulating rivals, sometimes operated local schemes of classification by which specified books could only be issued on request or after the approval of the chief librarian had been given, and they also (either willingly or under pressure from their book-buying committees) took informal action against the same kinds of fiction that the circulating libraries were trying to have formally banned. It was by no means only innovative or experimental fiction that attracted local attention. At one time or another, and in various parts of the country, there were reports that the libraries (public or circulating) had refused to issue, or had withdrawn from stock, novels by Wells, Bennett, Lawrence, W. B. Maxwell, 'a Peer', Hall Caine, Victoria Cross, Elinor Glyn, Eden Phillpotts, Gilbert Cannan, Compton Mackenzie, E. L. Voynich, Charles Garvice, John Trevena, and Neil Lyons; and there was similarly sporadic and local action against foreign translations, earlier British fiction (*Tom Jones* being a favoured target) and the increasing number of sexological studies. Serious as the underlying principles were, there was often present an element of farce in the whole proceedings, typified by the claim of one reader that a circulating library had refused to send him a copy of Henry James's *Italian Hours* because the distribution of such a book 'would be detrimental to the good name our library holds for the circulation of thoroughly wholesome literature'.[121] The Circulating Libraries Association denied that this incident ever took place, but it (or something very like it) might well have done. The sniffing of book titles to catch a possible whiff of salaciousness was becoming part of the job of at least some librarians, circulating and public.

Yet it remains the case that the spread of public libraries had, on balance, a liberating rather than repressive influence on literary censorship. It would have been a very different matter if the State had intervened and imposed stricter legal controls, but this was not done or even seriously considered by a succession of different governments. The circulating libraries, with or without State action on 'obscene literature', would continue to limit the distribution of novels they disapproved of by acting in the name of their predominantly middle-class subscribers. The public libraries had greater freedom in this respect, simply because the local control they were subject to varied greatly throughout the country. If Hull decided to ban *Ann Veronica* and Manchester tried to keep socialist periodicals out of library reading rooms, those were decisions which needed to be challenged at local level. But there was no requirement for libraries in other parts of the country to follow suit, and the localisation of repressive action served to heighten its often arbitrary and irrational nature. The principal liberating force, however, lay in the public librarians themselves. Like elementary and secondary schoolteachers (and unlike circulating librarians) they were intensely conscious of both their newly attained professional status and the social role they were being called upon to fulfil. The hard-line moral reformers among them were vocal but made up only a small minority. The professional organisation of the public librarians, the Library Association, was understandably annoyed when the circulating libraries, combining, as we have seen, late in the day and with the avowed intention of combating immoral literature, chose as the title of their organisation the barely distinguishable Libraries Association. There was little the two groups had in common to justify the similar names. During the public controversy that followed, the Library Association, through its journal the *Library World*, maintained an exceptionally level-headed attitude. Reporting the Public Morals Conference of 1910, it noted that, 'an amusing feature of the conference was the anxiety of most of the speakers to transfer the responsibility to the shoulders of someone else', and insisted: 'There is no possible means of limiting literature by police regulations, Acts of Parliament, or Vigilance Societies. Every case must be taken by itself, and on its own merits or demerits.'[122] In the following year, reporting the annual Library Association meeting at Perth where moral reformers had raised the topic of pernicious literature, the *Library World* described the whole issue as one of 'a few recent novels', noting ironically how 'the discussion shambled along, and all the old arguments, *pro* and *con*, were trundled out without a particle of variety, and practically no humour'.[123] It even printed an article by an American librarian called 'What makes a Novel Immoral?' and warmly applauded her conclusion that it matters little what the novelist writes about as long as he is 'true to the finer possibilities in human nature'.[124]

The determination of public librarians not to be rushed into hasty damaging action gave a welcome touch of common-sense to what was generally a very shabby affair. The failure of moral pressure groups to strengthen the terms of the Obscene Publications Act was some kind of victory for the new democracy, though the ambiguity of the original legislation was to continue to allow interpretations which were against originality or daring in literature for many years to come, and there were other areas of modern art that did not escape as lightly as fiction. Official censorship of drama continued far beyond this period, in spite of constant agitation for reform by dramatists and the Society of Authors. The emergent film industry, beginning to be harried by watch committees and with the chaotic experience of drama and fiction before it, decided to establish its own form of control rather than have something worse imposed from outside and the British Board of Film Censors began work on 1 January 1913.[125] In spite of the strident anti-Victorianism of younger writers, they did not succeed in carrying the vast majority of middle-class readers with them, and it could often seem to them that little had changed except themselves. 'In matters of hypocrisy,' Arnold Bennett wrote in 1910, 'there is really something very wrong with this island, and the atmosphere of this island is thick enough to choke all artists dead.'[126] It is a mistake to leap too quickly from such observations to the belief that Britain was uniquely repressive in this respect. The contrast with other countries often seemed greater because of Britain's dominant position in the world. There may have been less hypocrisy and more receptiveness to artistic innovation elsewhere – and France was still the automatic point of reference – but in fact there was no artistic Eldorado for modern writers to flee to: not America, or Germany, or Spain, or Sweden or Norway. The cause lay less in the peculiar quirks of any one nation than in the special demands made by modernism, which, as Ortega y Gasset was to point out, had little chance of converting 'the masses', it being not only 'not popular' and 'unpopular', but 'anti-popular' as well.[127] Just as we can see the signs already in this period of an international network of readers and admirers, so the modern writer was beginning to accept rootlessness as part of his natural condition, an alienation that could obtain whether he wandered the world like Lawrence or largely stayed at home like Woolf. The repeated attempts to impose moral control on fiction were symptomatic of much deeper struggles taking place throughout Europe and America on the questions of what form modern mass democracy should take and whether literature was to have a significant place in whatever kind of democratic society eventually emerged. Within Britain, the complex battles over literary censorship played a large part in creating the intellectual and sexual timidity that characterises a good deal of late nineteenth- and early twentieth-century fiction; it encouraged in some writers obscurity, obliqueness and a contempt for the values and intelligence of the ordinary reader, and thus contributed to the alienation of the major writers of the time from the mass reading-public, making it inevitable that when innovatory modern novelists were attempting to establish themselves the atmosphere in which they worked was one of conflict and aggression rather than sympathy and understanding. Again and again there was the assumption by writers that nothing else could be expected. 'Our great event has been that [Edward] Arnold has taken Leonard's novel with great praise,' Virginia Woolf wrote in 1914. 'Of course he makes it a condition that certain passages are to go out – which, we don't yet know.'[128] Of course!

Chapter Five

The Pride of Documentary History

'The business of a novelist is not ethical principle, but facts.'

H. G. Wells, *Kipps* (1904)

'It is art that *makes* life, makes interest . . . and I know of no substitute whatever for the force and beauty of its process.'

Henry James to H. G. Wells, 10 July 1915

Modernist fiction has associated itself so completely with fractured time, with relativity, with the epiphany which claims to encapsulate the very essence of life, that the realistic novel dealing in a fairly uncomplicated way with present social conditions now has little chance of being regarded as literature at all: its allotted place, when it is allowed one, is within a sub-category of fiction labelled 'social history' or 'documentary'. This twentieth-century preference for a fictional reality achieved by going beyond realism reversed the central trend of British fiction as it had developed from the early eighteenth century. The crucial moment of change came in the 1890s with the reaction against naturalism, which, in spite of the liberating effect it had had on British novelists, was seen increasingly as leading to a literary dead end. The main complaints were, that naturalism reduced the art of fiction to mere reportage or documentation; that it was destructively obsessed with moral and physical squalor; and that it had replaced idealism with a spurious scientific objectivity. As already noted, innovative novelists who were to be accepted as the founders of modernism in Britain can be seen as part of what Arthur Symons described as 'a revolt against exteriority, against rhetoric, against a materialistic tradition'.[1] This

applies whether they were (like James, Joyce and Lawrence) at first
strongly inspired by realism or naturalism, or whether (like Conrad
and Woolf) they regarded such doctrines as not really for them
from the start of their careers. One sign of the widespread
objection to naturalism's scientific pretensions was the insistence
by several novelists that a novel is an 'impression' of life and that
its artistic quality is dependent upon the 'temperament' of the writer.[2]
Closely allied was the growing conviction that chronological time is not
the most natural means of conveying fictional experience. Conrad's
rhetorical definition of the novel combines all of these concerns:

> What is a novel if not a conviction of our fellow-men's
> existence strong enough to take upon itself a form of imagined
> life clearer than reality and whose accumulated verisimilitude
> of selected episodes puts to shame the pride of documentary
> history?[3]

In distinguishing between two kinds of fictional method Conrad
was not rejecting reality as the novelist's aim: he was simply
asserting that unimaginative documentation is not the way to
achieve it. Zola himself would hardly have disagreed, though his
theoretical statements could make it sound as though he saw little
essential difference between the roles of the novelist and the
perceptive reporter: even Charles Reade, who was often regarded
by British critics as anticipating Zola's obsession with documentation, did not regard this as an end in itself and placed his
scrupulously gathered material at the service of a sensational plot.
Such examples and qualifications made little impact on those late
Victorian novelists who were convinced that the final effect of
naturalism was reductive. This is the point made by Gissing in his
affectionate portrait of Harold Biffen who is dedicated to what he
calls 'absolute realism in the sphere of the ignobly decent', his
artistic task being to capture 'ordinary vulgar life with fidelity and
seriousness'. Dickens is rejected as a model because he treated such
material with humour: Zola because he turned it into tragedy.
Correcting the balance, Biffen commits himself to the reproduction
of everyday conversation 'verbatim' and describes the imposition of
any point of view except 'honest reporting' as 'impertinent'. To the
charge that a novel written in compliance with his theory would be
'unutterably tedious' he replies: 'Precisely . . . If it were anything
but tedious it would be untrue.' In contrast, Edwin Reardon is

described by Biffen as 'a psychological realist in the realm of culture', a label that can be applied equally well to Gissing.[4]

Biffen's extreme ideas epitomise the late Victorian dilemma over realism. The mid-Victorian example – triumphantly successful in its way – was felt to be limited by its utilitarianism, idealism or moralism; while the French example – equally triumphant and in many respects felt as superior to its British counterpart – was regarded as trapped within its own distancing techniques. The way out that was to prove most acceptable to the twentieth century was the blend of realism and symbolism pioneered by James and Conrad, and the problem they faced was how to continue to convey a sense of reality without being drawn into the unimaginative documentation that realism now seemed to involve. They were, of course, far from alone in this concern. The uneasy, discontented movement between different literary modes is characteristic of much of the best fiction of the period, and so is the intense awareness of what would be lost if realism should be overthrown in the name of a higher reality. The case of Gissing, Harold Biffen's gentle satirist, is relevant here. Gissing was not to follow James and Conrad in their move towards symbolism. Like them he was concerned about the limitations of realism, but he remained to a great extent the type of late Victorian realistic novelist. His fullest statement on the importance of realism, written very late in his career, comes in the fourth chapter of *Charles Dickens*: it is called, significantly, 'Art, Veracity and Moral Purpose'. Although Gissing acknowledges that 'had the word been in use' Dickens must have described himself as a 'realist' and even at one point sees Dickens as taking a 'bold step towards naturalism (had he known the word)', the qualifications that need to be made about his work are regarded as too great to accept him, in late Victorian terms, as a realist, or even an Artist. Dickens's close relationship with his readers led him too often into compromising and refining the social truth of his fiction. He disguised facts, modified circumstances, never believed it his task to offer a 'literal transcript' of characters, and 'had a moral purpose; the thing above all others scornfully forbidden in our schools of rigid art'. In comparison, the modern realist believes that his 'sole reason for existing' is to perceive the truth and 'set it down without compromise'. He must never modify his work to please or entertain readers, and never refine the speech and behaviour of coarse lower-class characters: 'This kind of thing

is permissible to no artist who deals with the actual world.' [5]
Perhaps it was Gissing's determination to be fair to Dickens by
placing him within a drastically changed historical context that
makes the modern realist in the discussion nearer to Harold Biffen
than Edwin Reardon – and therefore somewhat removed from
Gissing himself, though not really much removed. It is apparent
that what Gissing is defining is not only close to his own art but
exactly the type of realism that Conrad and James regarded with
distrust. Emphasis is placed on 'truth', 'literal transcript', 'veracity',
'facts', the 'actual world', and absence of 'moral purpose' as the
distinguishing marks of the modern Artist. It calls to mind the joke
that H. G. Wells has at the expense of the dramatist Harry
Chitterlow in *Kipps*: 'I don't believe in made-up names. As I told
you. I'm all with Zola in that. Documents whenever you can. I like
'em hot and real.' [6] The joke, however, is not without point. Later
in the same novel Wells observes in his own voice: 'The business of
a novelist is not ethical principle, but facts.' [7] In other words, life
as it is, without the distorting presence of Victorian moralism.
Wells himself was far from being 'all with Zola' on this issue, but
like Gissing he was disturbed at the thought of novelists losing
direct contact with the actual world. Unlike Gissing, Wells would
turn his concern at the new trends in fiction into an active
opposition, initiating in the process an important anti-experi-
mentalist line in twentieth-century British fiction.

By the mid-1920s the victory of modernism was so complete,
and the reaction against realism in the ways foreseen by James and
Conrad so pronounced, that it had obliterated its own cultural
roots. In an obvious sense this is what happens in any major shift
of literary sensibility: the tools of one generation, to return to Woolf's
dismissal of the Edwardians, become 'useless for the next'. The
essential difference at the turn of the century was that literary
sensibility did not so much change as fragment. If traditional
realism was routed and deemed out of date it nonetheless survived
(and continues to the present day to survive) with surprising
vigour. Frank Swinnerton, who was actively committed to a
slightly later phase of realistic fiction, could even argue, against
Symons's view, that realism rather than symbolism was 'the new
trend in 1901 ... It grew out of a perception that, even if one
disliked them, one could not and should not ignore facts.' [8] It
seems fairer to say that neither realism nor symbolism by itself is

an adequate term to cover the complex changes taking place and that Swinnerton's partiality is as apparent and restricted as Symons's. But he was undoubtedly right to place 'facts' at the centre of the problem; both the opposing camps agreed on this. For Swinnerton, symbolism was too 'ethereal': it served to divorce the novelist from actuality. For Woolf, documentary realism destroyed 'reality', and the fiercest satire in 'Mr Bennett and Mrs Brown' is aimed at the Edwardian love of facts:

> Begin by saying that her father kept a shop in Harrogate.
> Ascertain the rent. Ascertain the wages of shop assistants in
> the year 1878. Discover what her mother died of. Describe
> cancer. Describe calico, Describe –' But I cried: 'Stop! Stop!
> And I regret to say that I threw that ugly, that clumsy, that
> incongruous tool out of the window.[9]

Woolf never makes it clear whether the world of shops, rent, shop assistants, cancer and calico, is to be thrown out of the window along with the 'incongruous tool' of realism. Instead she insists that the true work of fictional art should be 'complete', as *Tristram Shandy* and *Pride and Prejudice* are complete: 'The Edwardians were never interested in character in itself; or the book in itself. They were interested in something outside.'[10] The reference to Sterne and Austen takes something of the chill away from that statement, but not enough to remove the cultural solipsism from the assertion that there is something wrong with a novel that reaches out beyond itself. It recalls Flaubert's desire to write 'a book about nothing, a book dependent on nothing external' and looks forward to *The Waves, Finnegans Wake* and the post-modernist literature of silence.[11] It was the early stages of this tendency that forced Wells into opposition: his principal target was the later fiction of Henry James.

Leon Edel and Gordon N. Ray have shown how the parody of James in *Boon* (1915) that led to a complete break between the two novelists was precipitated by resentment on Wells's part: it was only inserted in the manuscript after Wells had read James's ornate and condescending survey of contemporary novelists, 'The Younger Generation', in the *Times Literary Supplement* (19 March and 2 April 1914). But if the decision to write the parody was sudden, the resentment was long-standing and into *Boon* Wells 'packed all the things about James and his work that had irritated and amused him during the past seventeen years'.[12] An element of genuine respect for James should be added to the irritation and amusement, otherwise Wells's part in the exchange can be too easily portrayed as merely a cheeky gesture. In his final letter to James, Wells apologised for the lack of 'grace' in *Boon*, but he made no attempt to retract his criticism. There was between them, he wrote, a 'profound and incurable difference and contrast' and James's influence was becoming so great that 'there was no other antagonist possible'.[13] Always sensitive to the low sales of his novels, James replied indignantly that there was no evidence whatsoever that his 'view of life and literature, or what you impute to me as such, is carrying everything before it and becoming a public menace'.[14] As James had spent most of his life following the example of Matthew Arnold in calling for the development of a rigorously critical frame of mind in Britain, and as, at this date, his call was being taken up seriously by a new generation of writers, James's indignation was a little naive. It was, however, understandable. Arnold had argued that while the creative faculty is superior to the critical faculty, there are moments in a society's growth when criticism will take priority in order to prepare the ground for an epoch of creative expansion.[15] In 1914 when James wrote the *TLS* article that angered Wells, he was, in Arnoldian terms, at the very point when an epoch of concentration or criticism was giving way to one of expansion. During that period James himself had played a central critical role, taken over in many respects from Arnold. But whereas Arnold had surrendered his ambitions as a poet to the criticism demanded by an epoch of concentration, James had succeeded in writing fiction which embodied and exemplified his critical ideals. It was inevitable that he would not be sufficiently honoured by his contemporaries for this effort, and as inevitable that in time he would become an admired point of reference for many of the younger modernists. As far as British fiction was concerned there were, as James surveyed the field for the *TLS*, few signs that great changes were taking place and he indicated this by referring slyly to 'the new, or at least the young novel'.[16] James's criticism foreshadows Woolf's attack on the Edwardians – even to the extent of dividing the authors covered into older and younger generations – and it supports, in a striking manner, Swinnerton's claim that most young British novelists of the early twentieth century were fascinated by realism rather than symbolism: they included Maurice

Hewlett, Galsworthy, Bennett, Wells, Compton Mackenzie, Hugh Walpole, Gilbert Cannan, and D. H. Lawrence for *Sons and Lovers*, in which James might have been expected to recognise a talent not bound by its general acceptance of realism. There was certainly little in these authors to comfort James that his lifetime's dedication to the Art of Fiction was inspiring emulation or discipleship, and they were rebuked for not having learnt the lesson James had given them, for relying for effect on 'saturation', a massive accumulation of detail with no attempt to structure it into an artistic whole:

> They squeeze out to the utmost the plump and more or less
> juicy orange of a particular acquainted state and let this
> affirmation of energy, however directed or undirected, consti-
> tute for them the 'treatment' of the theme.[17]

Bennett is described as an author who puts 'down upon the table, in dense unconfused array, every fact required to make the life of the Five Towns press upon us'.[18] Only Conrad escaped the charge of unimaginative documentation: his *Chance* 'places the author absolutely alone as the votary of the way to do a thing that shall make it undergo most doing'.[19]

The implication that in his social novels Wells was offering the public slices of unstructured life rather than things properly 'done' was not new. Time and again in the years of his friendship with James, Wells had received, in response to complimentary copies of his books, elegant variations on exactly that point: Wells had graciously acknowledged the justice of the criticism and deprecated his habitual carelessness and rush. But while Wells's artistic carelessness is undeniable, it is quite wrong to see it as unconscious or lacking purpose. He had begun his career as a serious student of the Art of Fiction: his early admiration for James and Conrad was sincere, though it did not last for long.[20] What Wells feared was that an excessive concentration on the 'treatment' or 'doing' of fiction would eventually obliterate the novel's social function and isolate the novelist at a time when exhilarating changes were taking place in virtually every area of British life. It was to combat this tendency that Wells called on novelists to participate fully in the new kind of society that was emerging and to reject the example of the 'artist' who 'lives angrily in a stuffy little corner of pure technique'.[21] In 1911, in a much-publicised lecture 'The Con-temporary Novel' given at the Times Book Club, Wells turned his back stubbornly on the formal experimentation of modern fiction. He did not speak in the name of any particular doctrine of realism (though some kind of realism was implied) and he was not obliged to recant his anti-Victorianism (though some earlier targets were now viewed more favourably). He praised the long tradition of the 'discursive' English novel; denounced the 'narrowing and restriction', the 'exacting and cramping conceptions of artistic perfection' that had replaced Dickensian discursiveness; and closed by presenting himself as a spokesman for the collective views of contemporary British novelists: 'We are going to write, subject only to our limitations, about the whole of human life. We are going to deal with political questions and religious questions and social questions. We cannot present people unless we have this free hand, this unrestricted field.'[22] James also had always insisted that no restriction could be placed on the subject-matter of fiction, but he differed from Wells in believing that justification lay solely in the artistry of the chosen subject's treatment. When Wells was attacking 'exacting and cramping conceptions of artistic perfection' at the Times Book Club there were very few readers in Britain who were not convinced that the author of symbolic masterpieces like *The Wings of the Dove* and *The Golden Bowl*, the author who had written prefaces to the New York edition of his collected works pointing out the technical difficulties confronted and overcome in his novels, had lost all sense of social reality in his obsession with artistic technique. If this kind of dedication was to be attacked, there was 'no other antagonist possible'. The 'bad manners of *Boon*', to use James's own words, were directed to demonstrating the social uselessness of a Jamesian novel.[23] If Wells was right, then James really was a 'public menace':

> His people nose out suspicions, hint by hint, link by link.
> Have you ever known living human beings do that? The
> thing his novel is *about* is always there. It is like a church lit
> but without a congregation to distract you, with every light
> and line focused on the high altar. And on the altar, very
> reverently placed, intensely there, is a dead kitten, an egg-
> shell, a bit of string.[24]

The quiet dignity of James's response is justly famous, as also is its extreme aestheticism: 'It is art that *makes* life, makes interest, makes importance, for our consideration and application of these things, and I know of no substitute whatever for the force and beauty of its process.'[25] Wells was hardly less dignified and just as extreme. Confessing his 'natural horror of dignity, finish and perfection', and his conviction that literature was a means rather than an end in itself, he announced: 'I had rather be called a journalist than an artist, that is the essence of it.'[26]

In describing himself as a journalist and implying that the vitality of the modern novel would be more secure if it allied itself with journalism rather than Art, Wells was being deliberately provocative. James, like Wells, was a journalist as well as a novelist in that he wrote prolifically for an exceptionally wide range of periodicals and magazines, but he would not have described that part of his writing life as the work of a journalist. As this exchange indicates, 'journalist' and 'journalism' rank among the most emotive words of the period. The older usage simply described someone who wrote for the journals, a relatively respectable activity and one that James would not have found unacceptable. But by the 1880s a journalist was someone who wrote primarily for the newspapers: journalism was a booming profession, its high status marked by official recognition. In 1889 a charter was granted to the Institute of Journalists, placing the profession, it was often claimed, on a par with those of the law and medicine: one of Gladstone's final public acts before retiring was to confer knighthoods on six journalists.[27] 'Every year sees the power of the Press increasing,' a newspaper editor wrote in 1896; 'Its influence on the national life is incalculable: With its rapid progress the responsibility of all associated with journalism increases.'[28] Few observers would have denied that the power of the press was increasing and that its influence on the national life was incalculable: it was the question of how responsibly it was handling its great power that caused concern. For many 'writers' (a word that was now frequently used to dissociate the activity it describes from that of the journalist) journalism was tainted by its mission to entertain and instruct the newly-enfranchised 'masses'; it also drew its characteristic mode of communication from America, which, for many critics, ensured its vulgarity. The power it had suddenly attained was viewed with a mixture of disgust and awe:

Somebody – was it Burke? – called Journalism the fourth estate. That was true at the time, no doubt. But at the

present moment it really is the only estate. It has eaten up
the other three . . . We are dominated by Journalism. In
America the President reigns for four years, and Journalism
governs for ever and ever.[29]

In telling James that he would rather be called a journalist than an
Artist Wells was deliberately associating himself with what he knew
James would regard as one of the most corrupting cultural forces of
modern life. It could be taken as his approval of *Answers* and *Tit-Bits*, the *Daily Mail*, the Northcliffe Empire, and the whole
paraphernalia of competitions, personal interviews, sneaked photo-
graphs and frothy paragraphs of gossip and non-information that
by the time of the break between Wells and James was often seen
as journalism's chosen province. In his novels James had repeatedly
stressed the need for any writer with serious artistic aspirations to
keep himself clean of contact with modern journalism, even if it
meant, as it invariably did, sacrificing much-needed publicity for
the sake of genuine work. John Delavoy, the novelist in one of the best
of those short stories, is described as 'the most unadvertised,
unreported, uninterviewed, unphotographed, uncriticised of all
originals', and that counts as very high praise indeed.[30] It is not
difficult to find similar sensitivity on this point in real life. 'A criticism
of the book is all right,' Conrad explained, on turning down a request
for a photograph and interview, 'but my face has nothing to do with my
writing. If I were a pretty actress or a first-rate athelete I wouldn't
deprive an aching democracy of a legitimate satisfaction.'[31]

Scorn for the debasing power of the new journalism was a
common response among novelists, even among those who were
willing enough to take a portion of their earnings from it, and the
memorable hostile portrayals by writers such as James and Gissing
have ensured that it is the most remembered response today.
Arnold led the way. He had been an early critic of the *Daily
Telegraph* during the 1860s when it was able to boast of having
'The Largest Circulation in the World', and in the early 1880s he
was quick to denounce the 'new journalism' as 'featherbrained'.[32]
The criticism was almost always based on the assumption that a
once proud and dignified press had succumbed to cheap vulgarisa-
tion. Gissing, who for much of his career refused to earn money by
writing for newspapers or magazines, described the new journalism
as having 'abolished the sense of reverence'; Bennett, who was a
compulsive journalist and had been for a while editor of *Woman*,

deplored 'its growing tendency to pander unduly to the prejudices and intellectual laziness of the average man'; while some years before placing himself on the side of the journalists against the Artists, Wells had decided that 'criticism, discussion, and high responsibility pass out of journalism, and the press comes more and more to be a dramatic and emotional power, the power to cry "Fire" in the theatre'.[33]

Not all journalism, however, was sensational, and not all journalistic sensationalism was irresponsible. Nor was it particularly appropriate for novelists to be superior on this point. The novel and journalism had developed simultaneously in Britain from the beginning of the eighteenth century: they had shared a common concern in the realistic portrayal of social life, and comparisons between them were commonplace. Major novelists from Defoe to Dickens had not felt it culturally lowering to move between the two activities: they had no compunction about using in their fiction a sensational incident or plot to make a valid point of social criticism, and they were as aware as the late Victorians that the manipulation of a reader's emotions for the sake of easy thrills was poor writing, whether in fiction or journalism. Where the method of the novelist appeared to differ most obviously from that of the journalist was his reliance on a sustained story to convey social truth, but even this placed him at no great disadvantage to the journalist as long as the circulation of newspapers was small, the price high, and communication slow. In the second half of the nineteenth century these restrictions swiftly disappeared, and journalism and fiction moved gradually apart. The widespread use by the expanding newspaper industry of serial fiction further served to heighten rather than lessen this division, with the serial now nearly always being seen simply as 'story' or 'entertainment', light relief from the more serious business of hard news, whether national or provincial. While novelists were tending to look down on professional journalists as purveyors of trivia, newspaper editors were coming to regard novelists with interest only if they were capable of providing the limited kinds of fiction that were reputed to help sell newspapers or if their private lives could be turned into saleable copy.

What lay behind this mutual distrust was not simply the 'featherbrained' content of the new journalism: more worrying was the realisation that newspapers were beginning to challenge some of the novel's traditional functions. It was convenient for novelists

to point contemptuously to the newspapers' increasing preoccupation with 'pretty actresses' and 'first-rate athletes', with
personalised interviews and typographical experiments, but the
threat to novelists was more fundamental. Whatever the rights and
wrongs of the new journalism, it could never be accused of not
having responded positively to changed social circumstances. It
was deeply involved in meeting market demand (as its apologists
claimed) or creating it (as its critics feared): from its start
exhilaration and cynicism jostled each other for supremacy, but
both assumed that the power journalism now wielded was real.
Even James's irony could not quite conceal the genuine excitement
generated by a journalist's attempt to expand the scope of his paper:

> The society news of every quarter of the globe, furnished by
> the prominent members themselves (oh *they* can be fixed,
> you'll see!) from day to day and from hour to hour and
> served up at every breakfast table in the United States –
> that's what the American people want and that's what the
> American people are going to have.[34]

As major novelists pointed despairingly to a society that appeared
ever more hostile to the full expression of individuality, complained
bitterly at their lack of readers, and consoled themselves with the
belief that true Art had always appealed only to the few, the new
journalists gloried in their accession. 'There is no calling that is so
full of interest,' W. T. Stead announced in 1899: 'In the theatre of
life, the journalist occupies the front stalls, and instead of paying
for his ticket, he is paid for attending the performance.'[35] T. P.
O'Connor, like Stead an editor in the 1880s of an influential
London evening newspaper, displayed a similar evangelising fervour. His first editorial for the *Star* he even called a 'Confession of
Faith': 'In our reporting columns we shall do away with the
hackneyed style of obsolete journalism; and the men and women
who figure in the forum or the pulpit or the law court shall be
presented as they are – living, breathing, in blushes or in tears – and not
merely by the dead words they utter.'[36] It is a sure sign of the changing
relationships between fiction and journalism that while many mid-
Victorian novelists would have used terms similar to O'Connor's to
describe the range of emotions they wished their work to provoke,
almost every serious-minded late Victorian novelist would have
regarded both the language and the ambition as distressingly vulgar.

Equally significant is the emphasis placed on the urgency of communication, the need to find new ways of breathing life into the 'dead words' of 'obsolete journalism'. O'Connor and Stead were self-confessed importers of American journalistic methods – personal interviews, aggressive campaigning, eye-catching presentation, the elimination of the solid black columns of mid-Victorian newspapers, and an expansion of the domain of journalism into topical areas of everyday life. O'Connor, picking up, as many other newspaper editors were to do, the example offered by Newnes's *Tit-Bits*, made greater ease of reading a central concern: 'We shall have daily but one article of any length, and it will usually be confined within half a column. The other items of the day will be dealt with in notes terse, pointed and plain-spoken.'[37] This was probably the model, combined again with *Tit-Bits*, for Whelpdale's scheme in *New Grub Street* to be found a new-style magazine called *Chit-Chat:* 'No article in the paper is to measure more than two inches in length, and every inch must be broken into at least two paragraphs.' Dora Milvain's response is to ask Whelpdale if he is joking. He replies: 'No, I am perfectly serious.'[38] Gissing was recording a contemporary phenomenon and expressing his own horror at the cultural debasement it represented. Whelpdale *is* serious, and so were O'Connor and Stead, neither of whom wholly deserved the cynical motivation often attributed to them. At the *Star* O'Connor gathered together journalists and reviewers of outstanding ability: at the *Pall Mall Gazette* Stead led the way into a new era of outspoken investigatory journalism. It was their abrasiveness that aroused hostility: 'For the great public, the journalist must print in great capitals, or his warning is unheard. Possibly it has always been so.'[39] In one sense it had, and the new journalism can be seen drawing not simply on the American example but also on various indigenous forms, ranging from broadside ballads and the Sunday press to informative journals like the *Penny Magazine* which has been claimed as 'the first mass-market publication in Britain'.[40] What, however, was different, and gave force to the lessons to be learnt from democratic America, was the conviction that the extension of the franchise had created in Britain a totally new kind of reading public which made older forms of communication irrelevant.

In spite of their pioneering efforts, Stead and O'Connor were not commercially successful editors. They lacked the financial backing for the nation-wide distribution and advertising that would enable Harmsworth to establish the first truly mass-market newspapers in Britain: they also, together with George Newnes, formulated the basic assumptions that dominated journalism well into the twentieth century and provided novelists with a focus for their discontent that was eagerly accepted. From them came the message that the 1867 Reform Act and the 1870 Education Act had produced a generation of young men and women who were sufficiently literate to read and vote but who did not have any solid educational grounding and were incapable of sustained thought. If the attention of these new readers was to be attracted, a loud voice, or large type, was necessary. Undeveloped powers of concentration would be serviced by short paragraphs, crisp sentences and constant changes of topic; the reader's lack of interest in the finer details of politics, art, public affairs and literature would be countered by greater emphasis on sport, personalities, puzzles and competitions. It was an immensely persuasive collective image, though somewhat misleading in its bland assumption that the 1870 Education Act had been called into being to transform a largely illiterate working class. Like many institutional relationships in a mass society, it was also uncertain whether it was the creator or the creation of market demand. Stead suffered from no doubts about this problem. While denouncing sensationalism used for its own sake, he argued that the sensationalism of the new journalism was a direct reflection of the excitement of modern life:

> The ideal of much modern existence is a life of 'thrills', a
> rapid succession of varied sensations, an ideal of life which is
> symbolised by the switchback railway. For that kind of thing
> there is nothing like journalism.[41]

It was precisely such assertions that led James to portray admired writers in his work as 'blessedly unadvertised' and added to the disenchantment many novelists felt towards realism: if this was really what modern life was and what reporting it entailed, then it was better left alone. It is no accident that the most common derogatory words that Zola's documentary passion earned him were 'journalist' and 'reporter'. George Moore, recovering from his youthful enthusiasm, observed scornfully: 'What I reproach Zola with is that he has no style; there is nothing you won't find in Zola from Chateaubriand to the reporting in the *Figaro*. He seeks immortality in an exact description of a linendraper's shop.'[42]

The handing over of description to the inferior literary skills of journalism was, however, not quite the matter of lofty indifference that Moore makes it sound. It was more in the nature of a surrender, an acknowledgment that fiction could no longer even pretend to match the immediacy and coverage of the modern newspaper, and perhaps of modern life itself: in certain areas of Stead's 'theatre of life' the journalist really did occupy 'the front stalls'. The revolution in transport and communication that did so much in the nineteenth century to change everyday conceptions of space and time was particularly marked in journalism. The electric telegraph had been used for the transmission of news as early as the 1840s and the close of that decade saw the founding of Reuter's, the first professional news-gathering agency. As so often, technological development was hastened by war – in the Crimea, America, France and South Africa – and by a new phase of late Victorian imperial expansion. The international demand for news made public heroes of the special war correspondents: they were dashing, adventurous, competitive, desperate to be first to reach their paper with a news story, and they were personally named. In Britain, special correspondents like William Howard Russell of *The Times*, George Augustus Sala of the *Daily Telegraph*, and Archibald Forbes of the *Daily News* were celebrated romantic figures. Their reports were soon supplemented by the work of photographers like Roger Fenton in the Crimean War and George N. Barnard and Matthew Brady in the American Civil War, though it was to be some time before journalism and photography were to be directly, and naturally, joined together. The first newspaper to reproduce a half-tone photograph was the New York *Daily Graphic* in 1880, and the practice did not become widespread for a further twenty years, but the potential of photography's challenge to fictional realism was already apparent: the realisation that a camera would soon be able to record a sensational moment more precisely than the written word long antedated the new journalism. When the villainous Levison in *East Lynne* (1861) is dumped in the village pond, Mrs Henry Wood has Lord Vane comment: 'I'd give all my tin for six months to come to have his photograph as he looked then.' Little more than thirty years later Lord Vane might well have had his snap-shot camera handy to capture the scene, at a cost substantially less than his 'tin for six months to come'.[43] The development of small portable cameras and their widespread marketing in the 1890s held out the promise that anyone – man, woman or child – could be a realist. There was nothing to it. In the words of Kodak's advertising slogan: 'You press the button, we do the rest.'[44]

By 1914 domestic journalism was well established as a subject for fiction, with the journalist (or reporter) appearing not simply as the peripheral, largely distrusted figure that he is in James and Gissing, but as an accepted and recognisable social type. In novels like Philip Gibbs's *The Street of Adventure* (1909) and C. E. Montague's *A Hind Let Loose* (1910), the world of the newspaper office, soon to serve as the dramatic setting for countless films, was already full formed. It was a world with its own scale of romantic values, but the romanticism was now tinged with seediness and disillusionment, and stood in marked contrast to the heroic exploits of the war correspondents and their fictional counterparts created by Kipling in the 1880s. Not that the Indian newspaper office of Kipling's early stories is always full of excitement: the heat, boredom, pressure from government officials, and the long months when there is nothing to write about but 'amusements in the Hill-stations or obituary notices', are frequently acknowledged.[45] Nor is the journalist-narrator of many of the stories particularly daring or courageous. His job – like that of James's Artist-Novelists, with whom he has much in common – is to write about life rather than live it, and he buys adventures from his soldier friends: 'The tale was cheap at a gallon and a half.'[46] But despite the spells of lassitude and physical hardship, what Kipling is more often concerned to convey is the honour, the privilege even, that being a journalist entails: 'Once a priest, always a priest; once a Mason, always a Mason; but once a journalist, always and forever a journalist.'[47] In addition to the Indian stories, Kipling centred *The Light that Failed* (1891) on the lives of war correspondents and artists; published a two-volume collection of travel journalism, *From Sea to Sea* (1900), which celebrates the free, wandering life of the journalist; and in many of his later stories continued to experiment with the technique of the observer-narrator that he had developed on the *Civil and Military Gazette* in Lahore. Like Zola, he was soon being referred to sneeringly as a 'journalist' rather than an 'Artist'.

Although Kipling and the war correspondents were influential in romanticising the image of the journalist, their subject-matter clearly had more in common with the boys' adventure story than with the realistic novel of social life, and it was the rise of the social exposé, with 'special correspondents' turning their attention to conditions at home while maintaining the pose of the distant traveller, that proved to be journalism's most forceful challenge to fictional realism. The late Victorian prototype was James Greenwood's *A Night in a Workhouse*, first published in 1866 in the *Pall Mall Gazette* which at that time was edited by Greenwood's brother Frederick. The idea was simple and dramatic. Instead of relying on official reports for information about workhouse conditions, Greenwood disguised himself as a down-and-out and spent a night in a workhouse in order to learn the truth at first-hand. He was, as his pseudonym proclaimed, an 'Amateur Casual' who had undergone temporary privation and danger to carry the reality of poverty into the homes of his paper's middle-class readers. It was a method and attitude later taken up by many other writers, notably Jack London in *The People of the Abyss* (1903) and George Orwell in *Down and Out in Paris and London* (1933).[48] Greenwood went on to make a successful career out of his forays into lower-class life, and in 1874 once again achieved notoriety for an article in the *Daily Telegraph* describing an organised fight between a man and a dog in Hanley. The truth of the matter was never established, though it was widely believed that Greenwood had invented the story, and according to Arnold Bennett, its memory rankled for many years in the Five Towns.[49] W. T. Stead described the man-and-dog fight report as 'bad sensationalism', a piece of journalistic writing that functioned only as an 'exhibition of brutality', but *A Night in a Workhouse* he regarded as 'sensationalism of the best kind' and praised its realism and social purpose:

> His narrative was carefully written up, and no pains spared
> to make every detail stand out in as life-like and real a
> fashion as was possible, and the object of its publication was
> the attainment of a definite improvement in the treatment of
> the poorest of the poor. It secured, as it deserved, a brilliant
> success, both social and journalistic.[50]

Twenty years after Greenwood's workhouse adventure Stead himself was working for the *Pall Mall Gazette* and surpassed the success of *A Night in a Workhouse* with *The Maiden Tribute of Modern Babylon* in which he revealed (in a similarly life-like and more sensational manner than Greenwood) that it was perfectly easy to buy a thirteen-year-old virgin in a London brothel for five pounds. For demonstrating his claim rather than simply making it Stead was sentenced to jail for three months. It did his reputation as a campaigning journalist little harm and played its part in persuading Parliament to raise the age of consent to sixteen.[51]

In both of these cases it was a newspaper that initiated the campaign, or at least staged a sensational dramatisation of the central issue, and then watched the publicity spread throughout the country's press. On other occasions newspapers took up an issue they regarded as deserving public support and gave to it a breadth of coverage it could not otherwise have attained. This is what happened with Andrew Mearns's revelations about the appalling conditions of working-class housing, *The Bitter Cry of Outcast London* (1883) which was published originally as a penny pamphlet. Stead again was instrumental in drawing public attention to the *Bitter Cry*, though the controversy it aroused soon spread beyond London, provoking the publication of 'bitter cries' from many other cities and leading to the setting up of a Royal Commission on the Housing of the Working Classes in 1884.[52] Complementing *The Bitter Cry* in its focus on working-class living conditions was the publication, also in 1883, of George R. Sims's *How the Poor Live* in the *Pictorial World* together with graphic illustrations by Frederick Burnard. At this level the new campaigning journalism was neither trivial nor frothy. In its detailed descriptions of environments, individual case-studies, and emotional appeals for government action to alleviate social problems, it took on some of the characteristic qualities of the Condition of England fiction of the 1840s and 1850s; it also connected with earlier Victorian works of non-fictional social exploration – notably Henry Mayhew's *London Labour and the London Poor* (4 vols, 1861) which had begun publication in the *Morning Chronicle* in 1849 – and with the official publications of Royal Commissions or 'blue books'. It quickly became the late Victorian equivalent of the Disraelian concept of the two nations, with the socially conscious middle-class explorer entering the unknown world of the poor and reporting back on what he finds there, though now without the aid of story to enhance what he insists must be accepted as a true representation. The similarities between this documentary journalism and the late Victorian theory of realism as outlined by Gissing in his study of Dickens are obvious enough. Now, however, it was the journalist who was expressing the reformist passion and social conscience of earlier fiction, while the late Victorian novelist either rejected all concern with 'moral purpose' or, in Conrad's revealing phrase, tried to move beyond 'the pride of documentary history'.

What finally dislodged realism from the most innovative fiction of the day and gave 'documentary' its distinctive twentieth-century form (in literature, film, radio and television) was the late Victorian professionalisation of empirical sociology, the indisputable case for its relevance to modern society being made by the publication in 1889 and 1891 of the first two volumes of Charles Booth's *Life and Labour of the People in London* (17 vols, 1902). Sociology shared with campaigning journalism a central concern with social conditions, and it drew on similarly diverse antecedents – the statistical societies which had flourished since the 1830s, Royal Commissions, the occupational classification pioneered by Mayhew, Comtean Positivism, the moving if unscientific accounts by novelists and social explorers, and the language and inspiration of evolutionary and anthropological theory. With these forerunners it placed its faith in the attainment of an objective truth free from personal impressionism or political bias: as the National Association for the Promotion of Social Science explained in 1858, it had been founded 'to collect facts, to diffuse knowledge, to stimulate enquiry' and to 'elicit truth, not to propound dogmas'.[53] Booth subscribed fully to these ideals; his principal contribution to their realisation was the construction of a methodology that made it possible for the first time to measure the extent of poverty in a great modern city.

The new journalism took to sociology from the start, recognising in it an incomparable source of up-to-date information about contemporary society, and, in turn, Booth's survey benefited greatly from this interest: 'Every type of newspaper – daily and weekly, serious or sensational, at home and abroad – carried reviews and articles.'[54] But apart from utilising the power of the press to disseminate his findings, the sociologist did not return the journalist's respect: nor did he look with much more favour on fiction. Booth acknowledged that something useful might be 'gleaned' from a 'few' novelists, and mentioned approvingly Mark Rutherford, Gissing and Margaret Wood, but warned that most descriptions of working-class life in novels were 'as unlike the truth as are descriptions of aristocratic life'.[55] In this respect Booth was

far less perceptive than Beatrice Webb, one of his assistants on the
survey, who, as was noted earlier, remained deeply interested in the
sociological possibilities of fiction. It seems that Booth was even
unwilling to draw any distinction between realism and sensationalism. The two terms he used interchangeably:

> The materials for sensational stories lie plentifully in every
> book of our notes: but even if I had the skill to use my
> material in this way – that gift of the imagination which is
> called 'realistic' – I should not wish to use it here.[56]

The kind of imagination characterised by fiction, whether of the
sensational or realistic variety, is felt to be out of place in this
context. The sociological method is scientific, objective, quantifi-
able: it demonstrates 'the numerical relation which poverty, misery
and depravity bear to regular earnings and comparative comfort'
and describes 'the general conditions under which each class
lives'.[57] Booth is by no means as cold as his methodological
statements can make him sound. He was aware that in 'the
arithmetic of woe' it was often 'intensity of feeling' that had the
'power to move the world', and in his descriptions of working-class
life he often reveals an imaginative stylistic flair, but he was
sufficiently committed a social scientist to insist that 'by statistics
must this power be guided if it would move the world aright'.[58]

In spite of criticisms of the way Booth's information had been
gathered, the importance of his survey was recognised immediately.
What Beatrice Webb defined as a 'method of observation, reasoning
and verification' made it possible to dispense with hazy guesswork
and speak with statistical confidence about the nature and extent of
poverty in the largest city in the world.[59] It boosted the hopes of
those who had long called for the establishment of a science of
humanity: it promised to displace sentiment in favour of reason, to
elevate fact above fiction. Booth described his intention as like
raising the painted curtain of a fairground in order to discover
whether the hideous pictures outside fairly represented the reality
within.[60] Novelists and journalists were prominent among such
showmen. So were Socialists whose claim that twenty-five per cent
of London's population lived in poverty Booth had at first regarded
as an exaggeration: his survey showed it to be an underestimate.
That finding had to be accepted: it was hard evidence, the result of
a sociological method dedicated to 'showing how things are'.[61]

Booth's findings were catalytic as well as revelatory: they demanded that they be acted upon. In this respect Booth was, unconsciously at first, a spokesman for collectivism, and his empiricism set up a forceful counter-blast to Spencerian individualism, even though, ironically, Herbert Spencer was already legendary for his fact-gathering. So strong was the statistical, factual content of this kind of approach, and so closely was it to be related to the implementation of government policy, that it has been fixed as a major cause of the slow growth in Britain of sociology as an academic discipline: the first Professor of Sociology in Britain was L. T. Hobhouse, appointed at the London School of Economics in 1907. It has been blamed also for the relative lack of British interest in the more theoretical work of the great European sociologists – Tonnies, Durkheim, Weber – which was roughly contemporary with that of Booth.[62]

The most important work to develop directly from *Life and Labour* was B. S. Rowntree's *Poverty: A Study of Town Life* (1901). Basing his investigation on the relatively small town of York, Rowntree confirmed that Booth's poverty statistics for London were generally applicable to the country as a whole, and he proposed a more refined working definition of poverty than Booth had been able to establish.[63] Following the examples of Booth and Rowntree were such works as Lady Florence Bell's study of Middlesbrough *At the Works* (1907); Edward Howarth and Mona Wilson, *West Ham* (1907); Maude F. Davies, *Life in an English Village* (1909); C. B. Hawkins, *Norwich: A Social Survey* (1910); Mrs Pember Reeves, *Life on a Pound a Week* (1912), a Fabian pamphlet on family life in South London expanded into *Round About a Pound a Week* the following year; and Rowntree and May Kendall, *How the Labourer Lives* (1913). In 1915 A. L. Bowley and A. R. Burnett-Hurst's *Livelihood and Poverty* devised the method of random sampling which enabled them to make a comparative study of different towns. These various books were among the more rigorously sociological of the many hundreds that now came from authors eager to explore, document, chart and tell the truth about what James Milne described perceptively in 1906 as 'the condition-of-ourselves question'. Milne also noted the way that sociological studies were beginning to replace fiction as the layman's educational guide to political and economic issues: 'Bring either of these subjects under the sign of "Sociology" and we are willing to read about it in place of the latest novel.'[64]

The comparison with fiction was heightened because many of the new 'sociological' books were stronger on human interest than scientific method, and while the gathering of 'facts' or 'statistics' allowed an attitude of impartiality to be struck there was nothing impartial about the causes which the evidence was called upon to support. Quickest off the mark, and aided by the ubiquitous Stead, was William Booth, the founder of the Salvation Army, with *In Darkest England and the Way Out* (1890) which contained a passionate denunciation of a country as rich as England failing to provide the 'submerged tenth' of its population with the living standard of the London cab-horse; statistics culled from *Life and Labour*; and a mass of evidence in the form of moving life stories and letters gathered by Salvation Army officers. This combination of qualities – social message, statistical evidence, and personal involvement creating human interest – now firmly characterised the documentary. The proportions varied according to the individual author's commitment or the degree of statistical seriousness involved, but what distinguished it most tellingly from roughly similar work published earlier was the sociological awareness employed to justify the claim of objectivity. This is observable in the changes that take place between Greenwood's *A Night in a Workhouse* and London's *The People of the Abyss*, even though, in many other respects, London's is the coarser interpretation; it is strikingly present in the distancing effect attempted by C. F. G. Masterman in *From the Abyss* (1902) and *The Condition of England* (1909); and it is also important for Rider Haggard, a writer not usually credited with this kind of social interest, whose *Rural England* (1902) is a classic example of turn-of-the-century social exploration, though out into the depopulated countryside rather than the more common descent into the overcrowded city.

As the methods and concerns of journalism, empirical sociology and fiction intermingled, it became increasingly difficult to distinguish between them. Stead was the dramatised self-hero of his adventures among the brothels of the modern Babylon, Jack London a special correspondent heading not for the front-line of an imperial war but into the darker reaches of the East End. The reports sent back from their travels drew extensively on narrative techniques traditionally associated with fiction, although, like Booth contemplating his notebooks, they denied the role of imagination in their work. What they presented to their readers was authentic, life as it is, the authenticity being confirmed by their own direct participation, and sometimes little more than that. The book of personal experience ranged through working-class life in London presented from the inside by writers such as Olive Malvery, *The Soul Market* (1906) and M. E. Loane, *The Next Street But One* (1907) and *From their Point of View* (1908); through workhouses and lodging-houses in Mary Higgs, *Three Nights in Women's Lodging Houses* (1905) and Everard Wyvall, *'The Spike'* (1909) and some of the hidden corners of industrialism in Robert Sherard's *The White Slaves of England* (1897) and *The Child Slaves of Britain* (1905); to the whole sub-genre of tramping literature, epitomised by James Greenwood, *On Tramp* (1883), Josiah Flynt, *Tramping with Tramps* (1900), Mary Higgs, *The Tramp Ward* (1904), and the book which gave literary respectability to tramping, W. H. Davies, *The Autobiography of a Super-Tramp* (1908). In a preface to the last of these books Bernard Shaw neatly expressed the socio-educational appeal they possessed: 'Where does the man with sixpence in his pocket stay? Mr Davies knows. Read and learn.'[65]

At its most extreme the fictional element was so completely absorbed in these books of social exploration that without a public disclaimer they could easily have been accepted as fiction. Clarence Rook's *The Hooligan Nights* (1899) recorded a social phenomenon much discussed in the 1890s by means of a series of sketches or stories of the type established by Arthur Morrison's *Mean Streets*. It was Morrison more than any other author who had picked up the new sociological objectivity and applied it to fiction. He adopted a point of view that was at one and the same time distanced and familiar, and a descriptive method that might have come straight from Booth's notebooks:

> Of this street there are about one hundred and fifty yards –
> on the same pattern all. It is not pretty to look at. A dingy
> little brick house twenty feet high, with three square holes to
> carry the windows, and an oblong hole to carry the door, is
> not a pleasing object; and each side of this street is formed
> by two or three score of such houses in a row, with one front
> wall in common. And the effect is as of stables.[66]

In line with the principles of late Victorian realism, Morrison refused to write with a moral purpose or, as he expressed it in a striking phrase, to act as 'a sort of emotional bedesman' for the reader.[67] Rook went much further than this, claiming that *The Hooligan Nights* was 'neither a novel, nor in any sense a work of imagination . . . Whatever value or interest the following chapters possess must come from the fact that their hero has a real existence'.[68] The origin of the book was supposed to be some 'confessions and revelations' written by Alf the Hooligan which led to a meeting with Rook who felt that the reader 'would not be unwilling to have a photograph of the young man who walks to and fro in your midst, ready to pick your pocket, rifle your house, and even bash you in a dark corner if it is made worth his while'.[69] The contrived nature of some of the situations Rook describes and the uneasy relationship between the narrator and the hooligan-hero undermine the insistence that this is a straightforward transcript from life, but the best of the stories have a hard, dry quality that enables them still to carry a convincing documentary authenticity. The most disturbing aspect of the book is the air of cold detachment with which Alf's actions are presented, so much so that one recent admirer of Rook's work has said: 'It would take a moral imbecile not to be repelled by much of this sort of business, yet Rook offers us no sign that he is shocked or angry.'[70] No doubt Rook would have replied that objectivity justifies anything; no imagination is involved, it is life *The Hooligan Nights* offers, a human document, 'hot and real' as Harry Chitterlow would have claimed.

The problems caused by blending fiction and journalistic documentary which Rook dismissed so casually were treated with greater respect by another largely forgotten writer of the time, Stephen Reynolds. He was born into a comfortable middle-class family and public-school educated; following a quarrel with his father he went to Paris determined to become a novelist. In 1903 he visited Sidmouth and based himself there for the remainder of his life, finding in the lives of Devon fishermen the emotional and cultural security that had hitherto eluded him. His own description of these events has what would eventually come to be known as a characteristically Orwellian flourish: 'Made my home with a fisherman's family and, as a general thing, threw up middle-class society. Can't say I feel much loss.'[71] The material he gathered in Sidmouth was intended at first to be used for a novel:

> Fiction, however, showed itself an inappropriate medium. I
> was unwilling to cut about the material, to modify the

characters, in order to meet the exigencies of plot, and so on.
I felt that the life and the people were so much better than
anything I could invent.[72]

His method he described as inductive, the only trustworthy way of
capturing the truth about people being to begin always with the
individual. Sociology he seems to have regarded as deductive, and
in contrast to his own personal approach he offered a list of the
modern officials who were incapable of understanding working-
class life because they approached it with reformist intentions: they
were the 'parson, philanthropist, politician, inspector, sociologist,
statistician'.[73] The novelist is probably excluded from the list only
because Reynolds himself still had ambitions in that direction, even
though he was already arguing cogently that fiction was incapable
of doing justice to the kind of life he most wanted to write about.
When John Lane accepted *A Poor Man's House* (1909) for
publication Reynolds insisted that he also take *The Holy Mountain*,
the long satirical novel on which he had lavished years of attention.
The novel aroused little interest, while the documentary record of
life with a fisherman's family was recognised as a unique work and
established Reynolds as both a literary celebrity and an authority
on the fishing industry. It was followed in 1911 by *Seems So! A
Working-Class View of Politics* written in conjunction with two of
Reynolds' fisherman friends.

Reynolds was not only a practitioner of what was a relatively
new and experimental form of writing: he became its theorist as
well. Pointing out that a number of recent books had shown
authors exploring a border territory between fiction, the essay and
autobiography, he coined the term 'autobiografiction' to describe
the phenomenon. He admitted the 'rather dreadful portmanteau'
quality of the word, but felt that nothing else could adequately
cover such diverse, yet generically similar, works as Mark Rutherford, *Autobiography* and *Deliverance*; Richard Jefferies, *The Story
of My Heart*; Gissing, *The Private Papers of Henry Ryecroft*; A. C.
Benson, *The House of Quiet*; J. H. Shorthouse, *John Inglesant*; and,
one should add, Reynolds's own *A Poor Man's House* together with
many of the books of social exploration already mentioned. For
Reynolds, the distinguishing quality of autobiografiction was its
ability to offer readers personal aid in an age that had fallen into
spiritual sickness. The need for 'story' remained as strong as ever,
and as this requirement was not now being met by 'fiction' there

had emerged a literary hybrid that blended 'genuine spiritual experience' and a 'more or less fictitious autobiographical narrative'.[74] The recognition by Reynolds that novelists were increasingly attracted to the use of relatively undiluted, though slightly fictionalised, autobiographical experience in their work was to remain as true for Joyce and Lawrence as for Gissing, Butler and Wells. Where Reynolds was especially perceptive, was in relating this trend to the development of new ways of describing society which were encroaching on, and to some extent supplanting, the traditional domains of fiction. This places Reynolds's analysis very close to that of Wells. Both feared that major novelists were now so introspective and obsessed with narrative technique that their work was becoming socially exclusive. But while Wells called for fiction to explore the complex interactions of the pluralistic ideologies underlying modern society, Reynolds trapped himself in the impossible position of arguing for a kind of writing which would be free from sociological quantification while at the same time he acknowledged that the advent of sociology had created the need, even perhaps made possible, the kind of writing he most wanted to do. In Wellsian terms Reynolds was retrogressive, though his personal dilemma was to become a familiar one for many twentieth-century intellectuals and writers. Convinced that working-class life was culturally superior to that of the middle and upper classes, he could not bring himself to countenance social or political reforms in case materialism should obliterate the working-class qualities – bred, after all, in conditions of economic hardship – which he so admired.[75] It was a ruthlessly logical position to hold, and it carried within it the unavoidable dangers of nostalgia and idealisation. The most serious problem was one of communication. How was it possible to write about a way of life which Reynolds regarded as 'so much' better than anything he could 'invent', without imposing upon it a pseudo-scientific method or the distortions of plot and story? Neither sociology nor fiction was adequate to meet Reynolds's ambition, and while he did find a successful solution in the autobiographical *A Poor Man's House*, it was not in a form that could be repeated unless a new stage in his spiritual autobiography should be opened up by a change of heart, and that was not likely to happen. Reynolds did not really want working-class life to be brought into the twentieth century at all. He longed for it to remain untainted by sociology, journalism,

education, facts, politics, fictional realism, social reform, technological invention, aesthetic doctrine, middle-class manners or any other
aspect of the social transformation that Wells found so exciting.
Yet, like Wells, he believed that if fiction was not to collapse into
itself and lose all direct contact with the changing world outside,
then it had to expand into new forms and structures, and speak on
behalf of proliferation and variety rather than artistic exclusiveness: Reynolds's contribution to this literary pluralism was
autobiografiction.

That the realistic novel really was losing ground to literary
symbolism, amateur social explorers, and the new professional
specialists – sociologists, journalists and academics – was most
apparent in its failure to come to terms in any convincing way with
either modern politics or working-class life. The day-to-day
experience of government had never played a prominent part in
British fiction, though some novelists – notably Disraeli, Trollope
and Meredith – had indicated how such a topic might be
approached. Working-class representation in fiction was similarly
sparse. In the 'Condition of England' fiction of the 1840s leading
novelists of the time had responded actively to the political
challenge of Chartism and Trade Unionism. Their humane
sympathy for the suffering of industrial workers did not extend to
political support of the wider working-class movement, but within
their fiction they did identify and confront the symbols of new
industrial power – the northern city, factory, machine and
organised working class. There were very obvious reasons why the
later novelists might have been expected to respond with similar
urgency. Under the reformed electoral system, with numbers all-
important, the working class *was* the new democracy, something
known (theoretically at least) to all late Victorians. It was also clear
that the precise way in which the reconstruction of British society
would take place was still undetermined. In *Beauchamp's Career*
(1876) Meredith offered a bitingly sharp analysis of the powerful
reactionary forces that political radicalism would need to face, and
in *The Princess Casamassima* (1886) James turned aside from his
usual subject-matter to explore the anarchism that was very much
part of the London political scene in the 1880s. But the political
involvement of these novelists – even the limited degree displayed by
James – was exceptional. Nor did the situation change much in

the early years of the present century. Only Hilaire Belloc in *Mr Clutterbuck's Election* (1908) and *A Change in the Cabinet* (1909) tried to write directly about the working lives of politicians. Belloc's novels express his distrust of the parliamentary system that he knew at first hand, but as fiction they are insignificant, with little of the considerable interest that his non-fictional study of modern politics, *The Servile State* (1912), still retains. More characteristic of novelists in general was the disillusionment with both politics and the working class expressed by Gissing. Early in his career it seemed he might well become a novelist of acute political awareness. He felt temperamentally allied with the poor, was a committed realist, and in his first novel *Workers in the Dawn* (1880) presented himself as 'a mouthpiece of the advanced Radical party': among his ambitions he listed the intention 'to show the hideous injustice of our whole system' and 'to give light upon the plan of altering it'.[76] By the time of *Demos* six years later the radicalism had become a scornful distancing from working-class political aspirations. The commitment to realism remained as strong as ever, and he was still to publish *Thyrza* (1887) and *The Nether World* (1889), the best of his novels of working-class life, but the political message of his work was now one of containment, retrenchment, or simply retreat. Gissing's refusal to allow any political credit to democratic change was shared by Conrad. The profound analysis of revolutionary politics in *Nostromo* (1904) is directed to a demonstration of a profoundly anti-revolutionary belief: 'There was something inherent in the necessities of successful action which carried with it the moral degradation of the idea.'[77] His separation of the dignity of labour and political responsibility is clearly shown in his authorial farewell to Donkin, the worthless layabout in *The Nigger of the 'Narcissus'* (1897): 'And Donkin, who never did a decent day's work in his life, no doubt earns his living by discoursing with filthy eloquence upon the right of labour to live. So be it!'[78]

Yet, from the mid-1880s there were more British novelists writing about working-class life than ever before. Ten years later, the working-class or 'slum' novel, as it was often more properly called, was a recognised feature of the publishing scene. In spite of some notable achievements – by Gissing, Morrison, Kipling and Maugham – this fiction was severely limited in scope and understanding. The writing of fiction was still an overwhelmingly middle-class profession, and those novelists who did come from working-class homes – Thomas Wright, Robert Blatchford, Edwin Pugh, Joseph Keating and Patrick MacGill – generally worked more effectively in various kinds of non-fictional prose, a tendency supported by the strong tradition of working-class autobiography in the nineteenth century.[79] Morrison's experience of the East End of London was first-hand, though complicated by his refusal to acknowledge his working-class background.[80] Until the emergence of D. H. Lawrence there was no outstanding novelist who could write from an intimate and confident knowledge of the everyday life of the great majority of British people. Most of the best working-class novels of the period came from middle-class authors whose experience of the lives they described was the result of relatively brief personal or professional contact – Kipling as a journalist in India, Maugham as a hospital doctor, Gissing as a lodger and then through marriage. Even Robert Tressell, whose *The Ragged-Trousered Philanthropists* (1914) gives a unique insight into the painting and decorating trade, was probably working-class by adoption rather than birth.[81] Inevitably, in an age of self-conscious democracy, emergent Socialism, and Board School education, there were frequent claims that within the working class there was a large, dormant literary talent that universal literacy would awaken. 'The current literature of the next generation will, I am quite certain, be written by the Board School boy,' announces a well-informed character in one of Besant's novels.[82] It would have seemed to many people that that prediction was if anything a little too qualified. Once liberated by literacy the working classes would not only meet the market demand for 'current literature' but give expression to experiences which had been neglected for centuries: here was the 'secret people', in Chesterton's words, 'that never has spoken yet'.[83] Neither claim, in this period at least, was to be justified. In fiction the secret people remained largely silent, their point of view advanced by upper- or middle-class spokesmen. And there were other kinds of restriction. With the exception of a few long-forgotten novels like W. E. Tirebuck's *Miss Grace of All-Souls* (1895) and Joseph Keating's *Son of Judith* (1900), both of which portray the lives of coal-miners, the industrial working class was entirely absent from fiction: this again was a situation that only began to change with Lawrence's early stories and novels. Nor were there many convincing attempts to unite the realistic working-class novel and socialist or Marxist ideology. *The Ragged-Trousered Philanthropists* is the major exception, even though the first edition of 1914 was abridged in ways that weakened its political message.[84] Other novels with a similarly militant socialist point-of-view are, H. J. Bramsbury, *A Working-Class Tragedy* (serialised in *Justice*, 1888–9); Constance Howell, *A More Excellent Way* (1888); and the novels written by Margaret Harkness and published under the pseudonym John Law – *A City Girl* (1887); *Out of Work* (1888); *In Darkest London* (1890) and *A Manchester Shirtmaker* (1890). In neither quantity nor quality is it an impressive response, and the way that this particular branch of the socialist novel is pushed to the sidelines of fictional concern in the 1880s and 1890s – a time which saw an unprecedented growth of trade unionism, the emotional appeal of Trafalgar Square's 'Bloody Sunday', dramatic large-scale strikes, the formation of the Labour Party, and the growing intellectual attraction of Fabianism – is a startling illustration of the way that fictional realism was proving itself incapable of handling many of the formative events of public life.

The dominant focus of late Victorian working-class fiction was on the undifferentiated mass of the urban poor, typified by the image of the dreary monotonous wasteland of the East End of London that became so important a part of the public consciousness of poverty in the 1880s. By the time of Morrison's *Mean Streets* in 1894 the familiarity of London's East End as a shorthand identification for the working class was such that it had obliterated all other areas of working-class life and the east-ends of all other cities as well: 'This street is in the East End. There is no need to say the East End of what. The East End is a vast city, as famous in its way as any the hand of man has made.'[85] It is not difficult to sense behind much of the mythologising of the East End a horrified awareness that the massed poor were the actual or potential new electors, and the contrast between East End and West End was a frequent device to draw attention to the class polarisation of society. In these senses the slum novel was political, though the cause it served was reform rather than revolution and it did this by carefully separating the poor from the working class and anticipating a cultural rather than a political transformation. It is best seen as part of a widespread changing attitude to poverty that Beatrice Webb (following Samuel Barnett, the influential vicar of

St Jude's Whitechapel) described as 'a new consciousness of sin among men of intellect and men of property'.[86] The inspirational idealists of the movement were Ruskin, T. H. Green, Arnold Toynbee, and, putting the theory into practice, Barnett himself, who, with the founding of Toynbee Hall in 1885, had initiated the settlement movement which brought university graduates to live and work in the London slums.[87] The visible presence of 'settlers' was only one of many factors that drew public attention to the East End at this time. Others included the debate on working-class housing provoked by *The Bitter Cry of Outcast London*; the popularity of Besant's novel *All Sorts and Conditions of Men* in 1882 and, associated with this, the founding of the People's Palace five years later; the Jack the Ripper murders; strikes by the Bryant and May matchgirls in 1888 and the dockers in the following year; and the publication of Booth's *East London*, the first volume of *Life and Labour*, in 1889. The concept of the 'consciousness of sin' was not solely or even primarily philanthropic. For Beatrice Webb and many other socialists and reformers it was merely a welcome stage in the gradual transition of society from capitalistic individualism to State centralisation. Little of this wider meaning was apparent in the slum novelists. In such representative works as Morrison's *Tales of Mean Streets* and *A Child of the Jago*, Maugham's *Liza of Lambeth*, Henry Nevinson's *Neighbours of Ours*, Edwin Pugh's *Mother-Sister*, William Pett Ridge's *Mord Em'ly* and Richard Whiteing's *No 5 John Street*, there are genuine attempts to recreate the spirit and language of slum life, though the imaginative freedom of the novelist is invariably curtailed by the assumptions of the sociologist or anthropologist. Paradoxically, this is far less the case with Kipling's early stories and ballads about British soldiers in India: with *Barrack Room Ballads*, *Soldiers Three*, *Life's Handicap* and *Many Inventions*, working-class values and language entered fiction with a vigorous comprehension that had been absent since the death of Dickens.

The principal attraction of the public image of the East End for novelists was that it provided them with an entry to a way of life that was otherwise closed to most of them. It also supplied them with a terminology and narrative method – shared with journalists and sociologists – that were to continue influential beyond the local popularity of the slum novel. The influence was not entirely one-way. As we have seen, the journalist and the realistic novelist were increasingly feeding upon each other, while the empirical sociologist, quantitatively aloof in a theoretical sense, had more in common with naturalistic documentation than he would normally have cared to acknowledge. Just as the home-based journalist had taken over the characteristic language of his more exotic colleagues – the explorer of empire and the war correspondent – so the working-class novelist travelled to far-flung corners of the East End or peeped into the social abyss to record the behaviour of alien inhabitants. Earlier in the nineteenth century a traveller in the slums would have been accompanied by a policeman or a minder: the unknown world was presumed, sometimes rightly, to be dangerous. The late Victorian explorer was more likely to be accompanied by a settler, slum priest, or upper-class philanthropist. The world of the slums remained unknown, but passive rather than dangerous. The journey would also now commonly contain an element of self-exploration, not in this particular context as devastatingly revealing as Marlow's double-journey into his own and Africa's heart of darkness, but with a closely related understanding that the slum inhabitants are neighbours as well as aliens.

The impact on novelists of sociological distancing and analysis also functioned in more subtle ways than the simple device of signposting class divisions by an East/West contrast. For example, *Esther Waters* is usually, and rightly, regarded as one of the finest examples of naturalism in British fiction, albeit one in which the French doctrine is modified by British idealism. The French influence is clear in the largely impersonal narration; the way that the fortunes of all of the characters are determined by the central theme of gambling; the detailed descriptions of physical and pathological states; and the circular nature of Esther's rise, fall, and recovery, to which Moore draws attention by repeating the opening paragraphs of the first chapter as part of the novel's coda. Yet Esther's progress through society also involves experiences which seem not to develop naturally out of the special circumstances of her situation, but rather are used self-consciously by Moore as sociological atmosphere. When Esther goes to stay with her family in London the reader is presented with a cluster of images taken straight from the journalism and social-exploration literature of the day. Her stepfather is a type of urban working man made familiar by *Punch* cartoonists like E. J. Milliken and Phil May: 'Jim Saunders was a stout dark man about forty. He had not shaved for some days ... Around his short, bull neck he wore a ragged comforter.'[88] Later the other essential props, a jug of beer and a clay pipe are added. He is also lazy, a wife-beater and a sponger, bullying money for drinks out of Esther and his wife: Esther's two younger sisters contribute to the family income by making toy dogs at home. A similar documentary reliance is apparent in the portrayal of Esther's Salvation Army lover; baby-farming; the conditions of employment of domestic servants; the problems involved in obtaining admission to a maternity ward without a letter of introduction from a hospital subscriber; and, most successfully as far as the plot of the novel is concerned, the greater availability of legal separation and divorce. All of these familiar aspects of late Victorian life were coming to provide a library of sociological reference that could be drawn on by a socially-concerned novelist, or, to put the point less sympathetically, by a novelist who simply wanted to make sure that his work was sociologically up to date.

In this respect Gissing provides a valuable contrast to Moore. Like Moore he was strongly attracted to French naturalism and retained to the end of his life the belief that a major function of the modern novelist was to portray life as it is, without compromise. In conformity with this belief, he was an ardent note-taker, carefully researching the subjects he was preparing to portray in his novels. He was proud of being selected by Charles Booth as one of the few novelists from whom a trustworthy picture of working-class life could be obtained, and he returned the admiration by studying *Life and Labour* in the British Museum reading room.[89] It was not only empirical sociology he was in touch with. Early in his career he had gone through a relatively brief enthusiasm for positivism, was well read in Herbert Spencer, and through his reading of Gustave Le Bon's *La Psychologie des foules* (1895) he was familiar with a major work of modern social psychology. He would have recognised in Le Bon similar views to those which he himself had expressed in *Demos* and *The Nether World*, though his interest in this new field of academic study was by no means self-justifying. The plot of one of his last novels, *Our Friend the Charlatan* (1901), centres on the attempt by the ambitious Dyce Lashmar to pass off as his own some modern social theories which he has taken from an un-translated French book. As Gissing acknowledged in a prefatory note to his novel, the book referred to was *La Cité moderne* (1894) by Jean Izoulet, a professor of sociology at the Collège de France. In another of the later novels, *The Whirlpool*, Gissing has Harvey Rolfe respond to correspondence received in reply to an advertisement for domestic servants by announcing that it 'would have made a printed volume of higher sociological interest than anything yet published'.[90] That kind of documentary awareness belongs to Gissing as much as to Rolfe: it is crucial to the effect of his most characteristic fiction. The titles of many of the novels announce a subject to be explored in the manner of Zola – women (*The Odd Women*), writers (*New Grub Street*), classlessness (*Born in Exile*), slum life (*The Nether World*), though his kind of exploration is different from that of Zola. It rests on a social classification closer to that being established by Booth and Rowntree. At its most subtle this method undermines the collective images of the novels' titles and contradicts the sweeping generalisations about life that Gissing was fond of making. So, in a novel like *The Odd Women*, the 'oddity' referred to is of a particular kind: those women who do not marry. But Gissing's extremely fine classification, by which the situation of each of the many women in the novel is portrayed as slightly different from that of all of the others, challenges the very concept of oddity. Instead, it records the complex pluralism of modern life that sociology was called into being to explain. The importance of this aspect of Gissing's work was recognised and admired by H. G. Wells. Noting its similarity to European fiction and its difference from most British 'novels of persons', Wells defined Gissing's novels as 'neither studies of character essentially, nor essentially series of incidents, but deliberate attempts to present in typical groupings distinct phases of our social order'.[91]

Although realism continued to hold a central place in British fiction, there was a marked change in its tone at the turn of the century. Gissing's particular form of sociological documentation was not taken up directly by other novelists; Moore and Kipling, in their very different ways, were drawn increasingly to non-realistic narrative forms; Maugham remained loyal to the earlier French example. So did Bennett, though the tragic inevitability of naturalism tended to become in his work a pervasive, melancholic acceptance of life as it is. Relentlessly unheroic and theoretically committed to an almost Biffen-like evocation of ordinariness, the realism of Bennett's fiction was constantly modified by irony and broad humour. The temporary truce in the controversial progress of realism that was also apparent in the vein of social comedy which Wells first displayed in *The Wheels of Chance* (1896), developed in *Love and Mr Lewisham* (1906) and *Kipps* (1905), and, as controversy began to surround him once again, re-activated in *Mr Polly* (1910). Wells had not surrendered his political message: these novels were written at the time of his most intense involvement with the Fabians, and they reveal the fact. Nor, in spite of their strong element of romanticism, was there any diminution of the democratic conviction that the novel should involve itself with phases of modern life often omitted from fiction: like Bennett, Wells was, in this side of his work, committed to ordinariness. The combination of gentle humour, precise social observation, and a realism kept firmly in check, was both popular and influential. To the reading public it announced that realism was no longer threatening, and to many novelists of the time it provided a similarly welcome breathing-space. A related relaxation of mood can be seen in the social comedy of such various writers as G. K. Chesterton, Oliver Onions, Leonard Merrick, Anthony Hope, W. J. Locke, and, more substantially, in the early novels of E. M. Forster.

The most important factor in this changing mood of realism was a shift in the class emphasis of fiction. Gissing had turned away from working-class life as a suitable subject for his work as early as 1889 with *The Nether World*, and Moore did the same with *Esther Waters* five years later. Morrison's final working-class novel was *The Hole in the Wall* (1902), and it is significant that, in the years that followed, the most popular of his working-class stories, in anthologies and as a stage adaptation, was the farcical 'That Brute Simmons'. The East End was still a point of automatic reference in hundreds of popular novels, but the brief phase of the slum novel was effectively over. Of the writers who had been connected with it, or followed shortly after, it was those who were drawn to a more light-hearted portrayal of working-class life – W. W. Jacobs, William Pett-Ridge, Barry Pain, Arthur St John Adcock and Arthur Neil Lyons – who kept the tradition going. Symptomatic of the kind of working-class fiction that was now welcomed by readers was the debut as a novelist of the sixty-seven year old William de Morgan with *Joseph Vance* (1906) and *Alice for Short* (1907), rambling old-fashioned romances that were instantly successful.

The centre of class concern for the realistic novel – in Wells,

Bennett, Galsworthy, Forster, and many other novelists, including
the young James Joyce – was now the broad heterogeneous band of
the middle classes, ranging from clerks, typists, and shop assistants,
through school teachers, owners of small businesses, civil servants,
managers, journalists and novelists, to relatively small-scale rentiers
and members of the long-established professions. The corresponding topographical shift was from the slum to the suburb. As C. F.
G. Masterman noted in 1909, the suburbs were 'practically the
product of the past half-century' and 'the creations not of the
industrial, but of the business and commercial activities of
London'.[92] The same kinds of building development were also
taking place on the outskirts of other large urban centres and many
seaside towns. While the demand for suburban homes came from
an expanding middle class, the setting of those homes was decided
by a massive expansion of railway branch-lines and by the invention of
the motor car. The new pattern of housing rendered inadequate as a
symbol of class relationships the traditional East/West contrast, with
its stark connotations of wealth set against poverty, culture against
ignorance, the spacious homes and public buildings of the West
End of London against the endless, narrow monotonous streets of
the East End. Masterman offered a memorable alternative image:

> Every day, swung high upon embankments or buried deep in
> tubes underground, [suburban man] hurries through the area
> where the creature lives. He gazes darkly from his pleasant
> hill villa upon the huge and smoky area of tumbled tenements
> which stretches at his feet.[93]

The 'creature' is the urban working-man who inhabits the 'abyss'
of modern society. He is distanced, objectified, merely glimpsed
with a shudder of fear by his suburban counterpart as the train
carrying him home from the office passes over or under the slum.

The growing interest of early twentieth-century novelists in
suburban life was in part a fairly straightforward recognition of a
contemporary phenomenon, but it also embodied a determination
to reverse the class bias of the slum novel, and, as the Labour Party
became increasingly the official spokesman for Masterman's 'creature' of the abyss, to re-assert the right of the middle classes to
more sympathetic consideration. For years it had been customary
to talk of the working classes and the poor as leading lives which
were closed off from, or unknown to, the upper and middle classes,

even though no other section of British society had been so
minutely studied, analysed, reported upon, and written up. It was
at least arguable that far more was generally 'known' about the
inhabitants of city slums than about the relatively comfortable, and
less publicised, skilled artisan, lower-middle-class office worker, or
suburban housewife. Nobody could reasonably claim that novelists
had traditionally ignored the middle classes: indeed, it would be
more common to argue that since its beginnings in the early
eighteenth century the novel had been, pre-eminently, a middle-
class art form. That argument, however, could not apply in any
direct sense to the new commuter class, made up largely of office
workers (men and women) and the recently professionalised, which
had been created by late Victorian commercial and educational
expansion. Their homes were in the suburbs, and to write about
suburbia was for most novelists as adventurous and self-conscious
an undertaking as to write about the mean streets of the East End.
As Keble Howard, the author of *The Smiths of Surbiton* (1906) and
its sequel *The Smiths of Valley View* (1909), complained, to write
about suburban life was often regarded as a 'confession of mediocrity' by those who believed there was 'no scope for artistic work
between Mayfair and Whitechapel'.[94] This attitude was particularly
surprising because the concept and terminology of suburbia were
ancient, and even its literary usage was long-established.[95] What
was different for the late Victorians was the apparently sudden
emergence of a large and distinctive class of people who not merely
lived beyond the city walls but descended daily upon the city and
then returned every evening to their curious, and unknown, tribal
rites and customs. They were in some respects more terrifying than
the creatures of the abyss. Marx and the Labour Party insisted that
the future of civilisation lay there in the abyss, but the suburbanites,
apart from their occasional troubled glances downwards from the
commuter train, seemed to insist that though the message was
getting through to them, they were certainly not going to believe it.
Masterman recognised the confidence as well as the fear, and
asked: 'Is this to be the type of all civilisations, when the whole
Western world is to become comfortable and tranquil, and progress
finds its grave in a universal suburb?'[96] If the suburbanites had
been given the chance to answer they would have said, 'Why not?'

Masterman's horrified assumption that progress along suburban
lines would turn the Western world into a comfortable graveyard

was characteristic of the condescension that the suburbanites had
repeatedly to endure. They were claiming for themselves a
property stake in the new society – ideally a detached house, or
failing that a terraced 'villa', with a small garden at the front to
separate them from the street, and a larger and more private 'back
garden'. Their equivalent of the horse-drawn carriage was the
motor car. Their most important local building was the railway
station; their social centre was the modern 'village' made up of
shops, school, church and public library. They carried from their
Victorian ancestors much of the adulation of home and family; the
need for at least one servant; and a pride in property ownership
that was typified, as every commentator on the suburbs noted, by
the naming of houses. Suburban home was 'Belle Vue', 'Buona
Vista', 'Sunnyhurst', or 'The Laurels'.[97] The main complaint
against the suburb was not its materialism or even its pretentiousness, but its stifling philistine uniformity. It was this that
promised to turn the civilised world into a graveyard, though
Masterman, with his usual perceptiveness, fully understood that
there were also more positive developments fermenting in suburbia.
In contrast, T. W. H. Crosland could find no good in it at all:
'Whatever . . . strikes the superior mind as being deficient in
completeness, excellence, and distinction may with absolute safety
be called suburban.'[98] That particular 'superior' mind also noted,
with something less than historical accuracy, that the complaint
about servants being 'So dreadful, my dear' was 'a purely suburban
one', and explained that 'nine times out of ten' suburban servants
'belong to the same class as their mistresses, who were born to
wrestle not to reign'.[99] Gissing shared the view that suburbs
attracted the uncultured people who were doing well out of the
new consumer society, a theme he explored with gentle humour in
The Town Traveller and with ferocity in *In the Year of Jubilee*
where the 'mistresses' prove their unfitness to reign by literally
wrestling with each other:

> Now indeed the last trace of veneer was gone, the last rag of
> pseudo-civilisation was rent off these young women; in physical
> conflict, vilifying each other like the female spawn of
> Whitechapel, they revealed themselves as born – raw material
> which the mill of education is supposed to convert into
> middle-class ladyhood.[100]

Ouida viewed suburbia from the other end of the social scale, and more sympathetically. When the upstart Massarenes move into a large town house where they are completely out of place, Ouida observes how much happier they would have been living 'in splendour on Clapham Common, near Epping Forest, or out by Sydenham and Dulwich': there they would have been with people who, like Mr Masserene, earned their living 'in the City' and were perfectly content 'with their fine houses, their good dinners, their solid wealth, their cordial company'.[101]

Some writers accommodated suburbia in their work with no fuss at all: E. Nesbit's Bastable family are classically suburban, and Sherlock Holmes and Dr Watson, though not themselves inhabitants of suburbia, were perfectly familiar with its tree-lined streets and semi-detached villas. Such natural acceptance did not, however, make the criticism of a Gissing or a Crosland any less irritating. Keble Howard expressed himself astonished that reviewers of *The Smiths of Surbiton* should have described it as satirical, but his treatment of the Smiths was certainly humorous, and at times facetious.[102] In this he was following the lead given by two of the suburban comic masterpieces of the age – Jerome's *Three Men in a Boat* (1889) and the Grossmiths' *The Diary of a Nobody* (1892). So also was William Pett Ridge in books such as *Outside the Radius* (1899) and *Nine to Six-Thirty* (1910), and less facetiously so, Shan Bullock in *Robert Thorne: The Story of a London Clerk* (1907). Even Bennett and Wells, both of whom wrote naturally about suburban life, found it difficult not to be satirical. Of the two, Wells's response was the more complex. From suburbia there came shocked criticism of Wells's sexual and political theories, though it was also suburbia that supplied many of the young men and women who were keen to follow Wells and learn more about free love, feminism, or socialism. Ann Veronica lives in Morningside Park, 'a suburb that had not altogether, as people say, come off'.[103] It is a place of stalwart Philistinism, where businessmen complain knowingly to each other about the disgraceful nature of modern fiction, and where a disobedient twenty-one-year-old daughter can still be forcibly prevented from doing something disapproved of by her father. But new ideas are seeping into Morningside Park and, tempted by them, Ann Veronica bursts out of the suburb. Wells's relationship with suburbia had, however, an additional and rather different side to it. Much of his work

celebrated the rise of the self-made man, the meritocrat who
through his knowledge of science would simplify, rationalise and
eventually rule the world. It was a message that – in spite of its
risky connections with free-love and socialism – could expect to go
down well in at least some parts of suburbia, and this possibility
did not go unremarked. T. W. H. Crosland decided that 'the ideal
comic author of Suburbia is Jerome K. Jerome, and when pathos is
required J. M. Barrie'. That judgment amounted to little more
than the conventional sneer at suburban bad taste, but with an
unexpected flash of imagination Crosland added that Wells's *A
Modern Utopia* (1905) was a classically suburban book.[104] That
also was meant as a sneer, though in retrospect it sounds more like
a compliment.

By using suburbia as a starting-place for the challenging
exploration of new ideas (in his science-fiction tales as well as *Ann
Veronica*) Wells managed to avoid the danger of allowing the
realistic portrayal of suburban ordinariness to sound inevitably like
satire or facetiousness. But he achieved this by focusing on the
escape from dull conformity to romantic adventure; it amounted to
neither an enthusiastic endorsement of the suburban way of life nor
a serious recognition of its social importance. It was, respectively,
Chesterton and Forster who carried these attitudes decisively into
twentieth-century fiction. Chesterton celebrated suburbia by turning all the customary views of it upside down. The main question
one could ask of life, he claimed, was: 'How can we contrive to be
at once astonished at the world and yet at home in it?' This
question he immediately related to the modern city: 'How can this
world give us at once the fascination of a strange town and the
comfort and honour of being our own town?'[105] The temporal city
was a place not of dullness but wonder, not of uniformity but of
startling unexpected activity. When members of the Browning
Society tried to explain their poet's exoticism by searching through his
family background for foreign blood, Chesterton informed them that
Browning was exotic because he was born in Camberwell:

> It is in the middle classes that we find the poetry of
> genealogy; it is the suburban grocer standing at his shop door
> whom some wild dash of Eastern or Celtic blood may drive
> suddenly to a whole holiday or a crime.[106]

In *The Napoleon of Notting Hill* (1904) the suburbs are 'glorious', as colourful and individual as a medieval walled city or a Greek *polis*: they stand for a 'mode of life, a manner of living, which shall renew the youth of the world ... like Nazareth'.[107] In the paradoxes which Chesterton needed to express his religious belief, suburbia is extraordinary (as only the truly ordinary can be) and eternally young (as only the the very oldest of things can be). It is also romantic, because romanticism is the truest form of realism.

In *Howards End* Forster was unable to view suburbia as either fantastic or romantic: nor could he regard the rapid urbanisation of England as a sign of mankind's eternal youth. The self-concious symbolism and the strain of mysticism in the novel demonstrates his additional distrust of realism, but Forster clung to realism with a desperation that makes *Howards End* one of the great representative novels of the age. When Mrs Munt goes on her mission to rescue Helen from a hasty engagement at Howards End she travels into an unknown land, one hour's train journey north of London:

> The station, like the scenery, like Helen's letters, struck an
> indeterminate note. Into which country will it lead, England
> or Suburbia? It was new, it had island platforms and a
> subway, and the superficial comfort exacted by businessmen.
> But it held hints of local life, personal intercourse, as even
> Mrs Munt was to discover.[108]

The 'indeterminate' is the keynote not only of suburbia but of *Howards End* as well. 'Everyone moving!' says Mr Wilcox, and Margaret expands the literal meaning of his words into a sad awareness of a 'continual flux even in the hearts of men'.[109] One of the most important of the many patterns of movement in this 'nomadic civilisation' is around the edge of the abyss. Leonard Bast is 'not in the abyss, but he could see it' and he knows of the degradation it represents from his wife Jacky who 'had risen out of the abyss, like a faint smell'.[110] When Leonard visits Margaret and Helen immediately after they first meet his wife, he too now carries with him 'odours from the abyss'.[111] As good Liberal-Socialists Margaret and Helen constantly debate what should be done for the inhabitants of the abyss, but they are incapable of translating their well-meaning words into effective social action. The Wilcoxes, on the other hand, turn their backs on the abyss and drive ever further out into the country, accumulating houses as they go, carrying suburbia with them. Trying to follow the

romantic examples of Borrow, Jefferies and Stevenson, Leonard
Bast has difficulty finding the countryside. He takes an underground train to Wimbledon and has to suffer 'gas-lamps for
hours' before 'he gets into woods'. Even then his great adventure is
only possible because Surrey's 'amenities' are covered by darkness:
its 'cosy villas had re-entered ancient night'.[112]

Although Forster's Liberal spirit forces him to acknowledge that
without the commercial wealth of the Wilcoxes the leisured culture
of the Schlegels could not exist in the form it does, *Howards End*
remains a novel of bewildered, highly pertinent questions rather
than answers, except in so far as the novel's thin symbolism
manipulates a possible future solution. Like *Jude the Obscure*,
Howards End functions by establishing multiple contrasts, comparisons and conflicts, but whereas Hardy had portrayed a painful
state of transition with only the faintest glimmer of hope that some
time in the distant future contrasts might become connections,
Forster was driven by the urgency of the situation to insist that
connections be made here and now before everything collapses.
'Only connect the prose and the passion,' the reader is exhorted,
'Only connect . . . the beast and the monk.'[113] Within these
metaphorical connections there are subsumed abyss and suburb,
town and country, commerce and culture, Britain and Germany,
materialism and mysticism, mechanism and nature, employer and
employee, men and women, leisure and work. The alternative to
connection is to continue to 'live in fragments'.[114] It was the fear
of desolating fragmentation that made Forster (like Wells and
Gissing before him) cling, with at least one hand, to realism, as it
was the conviction that fragmentation had already triumphed that
led James and Conrad to abandon the realist cause. The panoramic
sweep of the Victorian novel that had allowed Dickens, Eliot and
Trollope to lay claim, whatever the actual social omissions, to a
comprehensive representation of the entire country, is clearly
under strain in *Howards End*, though a similar ambition is no less
clearly at work, as it is also in other realistic novels of the time.

As the novel separated itself off into easily definable and socially
limiting sub-genres, and as, in the years immediately preceding the
First World War, some of the most urgent of the public issues left
unsettled by the Victorians (notably, suffragism, labour relations,
and Ireland) re-emerged explosively into the open, so realism made
one last desperate attempt to prove itself relevant to contemporary

life. It looked back self-consciously to the Victorian panoramic solution, as the title of Masterman's influential *The Condition of England* sufficiently indicates, and it took up as its characteristic pose the social explorer image which was now substantially modified by journalistic and sociological example. Its necessary task was to examine the many different aspects of British society and, as in *Howards End*, to insist on the urgency of establishing connections between them. The social exploration method was employed most straightforwardly by Galsworthy in *The Island Pharisees*, with its protagonist literally journeying throughout Britain in an attempt to understand a society that he feels is falling apart. Using a technique that was to recur in the fiction of this time, Galsworthy employed chapter titles to signify both the stages of Shelton's pilgrimage and distinct phases of British social life: 'Marriage Settlement', 'The Club', 'Rotten Row', 'A Parson', 'Academic'. Bennett used a similar technique in *The Old Wives' Tale* to compare French and British social life. In *Round the Corner*, Gilbert Cannan used as his starting point the removal of a clerical family from the comfortable South of England to the unknown industrial North, a device taken directly from Elizabeth Gaskell which served to link in a variety of ways the old and new 'condition of England'. A variation on this method was to make one social institution central and allow the exploration to radiate outwards: a common focal point of this kind was the country house – Howards End, Worsted Skeynes in Galsworthy's *The Country House*, Bladesover in *Tono-Bungay*.[115] Many of the novels took the form of the *Bildungsroman* or *Künstlerroman* which, as was pointed out in Chapter Three, linked realism with the growing interest in psychology, and, in the present context, served the additional function of dramatising an individual's discontent with the progress of society.

While all of these various novels were deeply critical of the Britain they portrayed, relatively few of them were explicitly reformist: too much was felt to be wrong for the advocacy of specific reforms to be worthwhile. What they did all share was the understanding that if realism was to survive and continue to strive for a comprehensive portrayal of society, then new ways had to be found to make sense of the bewildering fragmentation that now seemed to typify both social and literary forms. Just as Forster's call in *Howards End* for connections to be made in order that

people should 'live in fragments no longer' effectively heightens the
disconnection that made the exhortation necessary in the first
place, so a similar despair is apparent in many other contemporary
novels. The stages of Richard Shelton's journey help to educate
him, but offer no hope of a wider unity; in *Tono-Bungay* George
Ponderovo presents an 'agglomeration' of different aspects of
society that he can finally only stand aside from; while Michael
Fane in Compton Mackenzie's *Sinister Street*, like the protagonists
of several of the *Bildungsromane*, undergoes simultaneously a self-
exploration and a social exploration, moving steadily down from a
comfortable (if unconventional) upper-class life to mix with
prostitutes and criminals at the bottom of the social hierarchy, and
then, with comprehensiveness achieved, out into exile. Again and
again that kind of withdrawal from ways of life which have been
painstakingly examined and experienced is repeated in fiction, and
often it carries with it the inevitable surrender of realism. As far as
the immediate future of fiction was concerned, Joyce and Lawrence
were the major exponents of this pattern. As *Stephen Hero* evolved
into *A Portrait of the Artist*, the social context of Stephen's life was
pared ruthlessly away, leaving his final rejection of 'home',
'fatherland' and 'church' as an exile from what has become for the
reader little more than abstractions: only with that destruction
achieved was it felt possible to attempt the supra-realistic comprehensiveness of *Ulysses*. Lawrence's reaction against realism was
less extreme than Joyce's, though in certain repects just as decisive.
Like Stephen Dedalus, Paul Morel leaves behind him all societal
and familial ties, but for Lawrence that did not involve the
temporary obliteration of the material world, in spite of his famous
avowal to Edward Garnett that he would not 'write in the same
manner as *Sons and Lovers* again . . . that hard, violent style full of
sensation and presentation'.[116] The reason why his change of
method could not be total had been given to the same correspondent
a few months earlier: 'I do write because I want folk – English folk
– to alter, and have more sense.'[117] These words were prompted by
Lawrence's dislike of Wells's *The New Machiavelli* which had just
been published, but the social purpose they express might have
come from Wells himself. The novels that Lawrence went on to
write, *The Rainbow* and *Women in Love*, represent a culmination of,
and perhaps, a farewell to early twentieth-century realism, rather
than an overthrow of it. *The Rainbow* is the most sustained of all

attempts in fiction to explain how the 'condition of England' came to be what it is, and an attempt that rejects, on the way, the alternative analyses of Wells, Bennett and Galsworthy. *Women in Love*, with the distinct phases of social life it examines labelled in the same way as that pioneered by those same rejected novelists, is the most explicit insistence we have in British fiction that the time for even trying to make connections between phases of life is finished: everything has to start all over again.

Chapter Six

A Woven Tapestry of Interests

'Is that you?' she said, 'from the other side of the county?'

Rudyard Kipling, 'They', *Traffics and Discoveries* (1904)

'And Rogers came back with a bump and a start to what is called real life.'

Algernon Blackwood, *A Prisoner in Fairyland* (1913)

One particularly complex aspect of the various attempts by early twentieth-century novelists to contain within their work contrasting phases of contemporary life can be seen in the growth of a new kind of self-conscious regionalism in fiction. The recurrent pattern of social exploration and rejection in novelists like Lawrence, Wells, Mackenzie, Joyce and Bennett was enacted in their lives as well as their novels. The sense of exile that they and their protagonists endorse was not, however, as total as many accounts of 'modernism' tend to assume. There can hardly ever have been a novelist with a more developed commitment to one topographical place than Joyce: in spite of his, and Stephen Dedalus's, dismissal of Dublin as a possible home base, it nonetheless provided Joyce with an inspirational focal point for the whole of his creative life. And in a similar, if less exclusive manner, Lawrence turned repeatedly to Nottinghamshire, Bennett to the Five Towns, Wells to the Home Counties and Mackenzie to Scotland. It was far from uncommon for earlier novelists to become associated in this way with specific areas of the country, as the major examples of Scott, Austen, Eliot and the Brontës demonstrate. Even important novelists such as these experienced something of the age-old

condescension of metropolitan critics towards outsiders, but the
opposing view – that the value of their work depended little on
whether it was set in Midlothian, Hampshire, Warwickshire or
Yorkshire – served as an emphatic corrective. For slightly later
novelists this line of defence became irrelevant, not least because
they themselves were often contributing to the distinctly pejorative
connotations that were now habitually attached to the words
'regional', 'provincial', and 'local'.[1] The rhetoric of exile, of flight
from home environments which were denounced as narrow,
restricted, repressive, and destructive of the modern artistic spirit,
triumphantly established an image of the rootless artist even when
his work was still centrally, and often humanely, focused on the
home environment which he claimed to be leaving behind him. It
is not difficult to identify factors which helped bring about this
change of attitude. Matthew Arnold's constant denigration of
'provincial' values made a powerful contribution to it. So did the
ever-increasing business and commercial appeal of London as
publishing houses and newspaper offices became more centralised.[2]
For the young aspiring writer, London offered not only the
promise of ultimate fame, but in the meantime many opportunties
to earn money from writing. 'There grows in the North Country,'
states the opening sentence of Bennett's *A Man from the North*, 'a
certain kind of youth of whom it may be said that he is born to be a
Londoner,' and the assumption recurs in dozens of novels. In this
respect, even French fiction, through its scathing portraits of the
meanness of provincial life, was a socially limiting as well as an
artistically liberating force. It was all part of the vivisective nature
of modernism. If the family, nation and church were on the way
out, there was little chance that the regions would be allowed to
survive. But, as is usual in such battles, it was the winning side
which dictated the terms for the future and created the most
persuasive myths. Regional fiction was not only *not* dead, it was
actually flourishing.[3] The buoyant fiction market in books and
periodicals offered unprecedented opportunities for 'local' authors;
and as the publishing industry became centred on London, it was
easy to forget that there were active publishers in other English
cities, and in Scotland, Wales and Ireland. Regional fiction was
often very popular both within the area of the country it portrayed
and nationally as well. In 1898 *Literature* devoted a leading article
to what it saw as the 'current passion for local colour' among

novelists: 'A tendency has already been displayed to divide the map
of the United Kingdom amongst them – to every man a parish or
two – and to threaten trespassers with all the terrors of the Society
of Authors.'[4] *Literature* regarded this trend as epitomising the
spread of realism, and it certainly is the case that while many of
the leading novelists of the day were turning away from realism, at
least one of its several strands found a welcome home in the regions
where it survives contentedly to the present day, and is still usually
ignored by academic and metropolitan critics.

Not all regional fiction, however, was realistic: nor was the
realism of regional fiction all of the same kind. *Literature* had in
mind a British version of French naturalism. There was also a far
gentler evocation of local manners and customs that looked back to
Our Village and *Cranford* and, largely because it was not a British
version of French naturalism, was greatly enjoyed by large
numbers of readers and often dismissed by critics as whimsical or
quaint rather than realistic. Falling into either (or neither) of these
categories there was, in addition, a considerable body of dialect
fiction that attracted a devoted local following while rarely
receiving any attention nationally.[5] And although it was becoming
common to regard 'regional' as virtually a synonym for 'rural', it
was not necessarily the case that regional fiction should deal with
country life: in their day, *Dubliners* and *Sons and Lovers* were both
regarded as 'regional'. A further problem of classification arises
with the late Victorian assumption that realism was concerned pre-
eminently with contemporary life. This had not necessarily been
the case for the mid-Victorians whose work was often set in the
recent past: nor did it apply to a great deal of late Victorian
regional fiction where the 'local colour' came from historical
research rather than direct observation. While Scott remained the
model of an historical-regional novelist, the immediate late Victorian inspiration was provided by R. D. Blackmore's *Lorna Doone*
(1869), a rambling, episodic adventure story set in the seventeenth
century. *Lorna Doone* was subtitled 'A romance of Exmoor', and
Blackmore used the same kind of topographical signposting for his
subsequent novels: *Kit and Kitty* (1890), was a 'story of West
Middlesex'; *Darvil* (1897) 'A romance of Surrey'. The technique
was not exactly new, but Blackmore brought it back into fashion.
The huge success of *Lorna Doone* also played a significant part in
inspiring a whole school of West Country novelists which

included Eden Phillpotts, Sabine Baring-Gould, John Trevena, 'Zack', Quiller-Couch, and, most prominently, Hardy who swiftly took over from Blackmore as the major influence on regional fiction.

Hardy's ambiguous position in this context is an indication of how restrictive the regional label has become. However just the assumption that the work of a writer of major status transcends its local interest, one result of that assumption is to turn the regions into a string of rest-homes for minor literary talents. Addressing this kind of problem, Raymond Williams notes that while 'the Hardy country is of course Wessex', the 'real Hardy country, we soon come to see, is that border country so many of us have been living in: between customs and education, between work and ideas, between love of place and an experience of change'.[6] That is in one sense clearly correct: it defines the transitional experience between rural and urban ways of life that Hardy shares with George Eliot and the Brontës on the one hand, and Lawrence on the other. But the assumption that this is a more 'real' side of Hardy than regional Wessex is somewhat misleading. By birth and background Hardy might well have been expected to live out the career-pattern of flight and exile from the provinces that was characteristic of so many other novelists of the time. In fact his career was a conscious rejection of that possibility. He did not move out to London or Paris, but back into Wessex. Far from restricting his work, this served to heighten the border experience that Williams identifies. It also entailed a commitment to a specific region and culture that found expression in a wide variety of different ways: most strikingly of all, it served to unite a view of life that was disquietingly sensitive to 'the new' and an ancient trust in the communicative power of a strong story. It was a combination that drew patronising comments from a self-conscious modernist like James, though not, significantly, from Woolf, who shared with Hardy the psychological need to belong to a particular place.[7] In one sense, of course, Hardy did not simply write about or from within the area in which he lived: he invented the area because, as he himself explained, the novels he intended to write 'being mainly of the kind called local' they seemed 'to require a territorial definition of some sort to lend unity to their scene'.[8] Wessex was introduced to the reading public in *Far from the Madding Crowd* (1874), and Hardy was soon aware of the opportunity it provided to explore the clash between old and new – or 'the anachronism of imagining a Wessex population living under Queen Victoria' as he described it – and of the way his invented region seemed to take upon itself a heightened air of reality:

> The appellation which I had thought to reserve to the
> horizons and landscapes of a partly real, partly dream-
> country, has become more and more popular as a physical
> provincial definition; and the dream-country has, by degrees,
> solidified into a utilitarian region which people can go to,
> take a house in, and write to the papers from.[9]

Outside the novels Hardy contributed actively to the creation of this 'physical provincial definition', not only by public pronouncements on 'Wessex' life and language, but also by his willing support of popularising and commercialising schemes advanced by admirers of the novels. Wessex was featured in exhibitions and books of etchings, paintings and photographs: it also provided the subject for a series of picture-postcards. Hardy was consulted, and often gave very detailed advice, on all of these projects. To the photographer Herman Lea he suggested that it would be worth sending his Wessex photographs to some of the more popular illustrated magazines, adding that if the magazines were American then they might like a title like 'A Fair in Old England': Lea used the title for an article in *Country Life*.[10] By the end of the nineteenth century Hardy was already well on the way to joining novelists like Scott, Dickens and the Brontës who had made specific areas of Britain distinctively their own, and like them his national fame was enhanced by the romanticisation of his 'regionalism', a type of image-making that attracted not only the illustrated periodicals but the growing late Victorian tourist industry as well.

Richard Jefferies stands in marked contrast to Hardy's regional success story, though there are similarities between the two writers. Like Hardy, Jefferies was at first tempted to try his hand at the melodramatic novel of fashionable life before turning to the countryside that he knew so well. He was, in much of his work, a chronicler of the late Victorian agricultural depression, writing about it from the kind of radical viewpoint that is also often present in Hardy. He shared the need to lay literary claim to a region. As he explained in a letter: 'I have worked in many of the traditions of Wiltshire, endeavouring, in fact, in a humble manner to do for that

county what Whyte Melville has done for Northampton and Miss
Braddon for Yorkshire.'[11] The 'humble' comparisons drawn there
are to the point, for while Jefferies continues to be remembered as
a writer *of* Wiltshire, he was never able to take possession of it in
the way that Hardy possessed Wessex, or Scott the Borders. The
best of his novels, *Greene Ferne Farm* (1880), *Bevis* (1882), *After
London* (1885) and *Amaryllis at the Fair* (1887) all possess skilfully
evoked rural scenes but little development. They are barely novels
at all, and their episodic nature emphasises not simply Jefferies's
weaknesses, but also his strengths. In Chapter Five there were
quoted two admiring contemporary references to Jefferies, neither
of them to his fiction. Stephen Reynolds saw him as a leading
exponent of autobiografiction, and he was one of the writers who
inspired Leonard Bast to spend his uninspiring night under the
stars. Through his many collections of journalistic essays and
personal reminiscences – of which *The Gamekeeper at Home* (1878),
Wild Life in a Southern County (1879), *Hodge and his Masters*
(1880), *Wood Magic* (1882) and *The Story of my Heart* (1883) are
representative – Jefferies contributed two distinctive, and in some
senses contradictory, qualities to late Victorian regionalism. On the
one hand, there was his loving, detailed exploration of human and
animal life in Wiltshire which ranged in tone from the radical to
the sentimental; and, on the other hand, a mystical communion
with nature that invoked a post-Darwinian despair at mankind's
ephemerality in order to heighten the individual's spiritual union
with the whole of natural life. The first of these qualities was
regional in that it concerned itself with the recreation of the very
special conditions of a particular time and place: the second is
better described as an expression of ruralism because it exalted the
experience of country life above anything that modern science,
technology, or the city, could offer.

Jefferies' presence is felt in a good deal of late nineteenth- and
early twentieth-century literature. Elements of his lyrical ruralism
are observable in writers as diverse as Lawrence, Forster, Edward
Carpenter and Kenneth Grahame: the documentary aspect of his
studies of village life was further developed by George Bourne in
The Bettesworth Book (1901), *Memoirs of a Surrey Labourer* (1917),
and *Change in the Village* (1912); while W. H. Hudson, in such
works as *Nature in Downland* (1900), *Hampshire Days* (1903) and *A
Shepherd's Life* (1910), seems often to be following directly in

Jefferies' footsteps. Hudson's one outstanding novel, *Green Mansions* (1904), is set in a South American tropical forest, and the story it tells of the explorer Abel's love for the bird-girl Rima may seem to have little in common with British regionalism. Yet in certain important respects *Green Mansions* captures the cult of ruralism more effectively than any other novel of the time. Just as Abel inhabits a personal 'world of nature and of the spirit', so Rima has both the 'beautiful physical brightness' of a wild animal and the 'spiritualising light of mind' that pronounces her human.[12] The 'vast green world' of the novel is both a realistically evoked forest and a symbolic Eden, in which man's fallen state is brought about not by disobedience to God, but by the Darwinian revelation of nature's indifference to man. It is a mythic, romantic variation on the literature of life under the stars or on the open road that Leonard Bast, along with many other Edwardians, longed to experience for himself. Underlying much of this ruralism there is the assumption that modern man needs contact with nature, or with 'the country', or, failing either, with a garden, if he is to live his life to the full, because only in nature will he be able to rediscover the animism that urbanisation and the decline of organised religion have taken away from him.[13] Leonard Bast, yearning for the open road, epitomises in a subdued way the stirring of Pan that is found everywhere in Forster's – and Lawrence's – early fiction. At this level, ruralism and regionalism both actively employ the imagery of exploration that is more readily associated with city literature. Hudson was literally an explorer who reversed the imperial pattern by journeying from South America to discover the neglected wonders of the southern counties of England, and Kipling shared that image. In 1902, just after his move to Bateman's in Sussex, Kipling wrote to Charles Eliot Norton: 'Then we discovered England which we had never done before ... England is a wonderful land. It is the most marvellous of all foreign countries that I have ever been in.'[14] It was characteristic of Kipling's multi-faceted genius that his literary exploration of this newly discovered country of England (or more specifically, Sussex) should have taken many different forms. In stories like 'My Son's Wife' and 'An Habitation Enforced', he examined the theme of outsiders trying to become assimilated into the complex class structure of rural society; in 'Friendly Brook', the lives and superstitions of agricultural labourers; in 'They', county lines are employed supernaturally to denote the uncertain boundaries between life and death; while *Puck of Pook's Hill* (1906) and *Rewards and Fairies* (1910) examine the ways in which a region continues to express the spirit of all the long generations of people – the 'mere uncounted folk' as much as the 'great' and 'well-bespoke' – who have contributed to its specialness.[15]

While the South West of England dominated the late Victorian regional novel, and the southern counties of England were most often the setting for ruralism, it was Scotland that came for a few years at the close of the century to typify regionalism in fiction. What Margaret Oliphant described as the 'field of amusing and picturesque observation first opened by Sir Walter', had been popular throughout the Victorian period.[16] In addition to Oliphant herself, and Stevenson, some notable late Victorian practitioners were William Black, George MacDonald, Jane and Mary Findlater, and Annie S. Swan. Most of these novelists moved easily between Scottish and English subjects, or between local-colour regional fiction and historical or supernatural tales. Not all of their work is adequately covered by the classification 'amusing and picturesque', but at least one strand of it pointed towards the whimsical, sentimental, image of Scotland that was purveyed with spectacular commercial success by 'Kailyard' fiction. The phenomenon was sharply noted by a *Punch* cartoon in 1895. A publisher, on being offered a volume of short stories, asks 'if they are written in any unintelligible Scotch dialect'. 'Certainly not,' responds the indignant author. 'Then,' says the publisher, 'I'm afraid they're not of the slightest use to me.'[17] The label 'Kailyard' – or cabbage-patch – had been coined in the same year as the *Punch* cartoon.[18] It covered such works as J. M. Barrie's *Auld Licht Idylls* (1888), *A Window in Thrums* (1889) and *The Little Minister* (1891); S. R. Crockett's *The Stickit Minister* (1893) and *The Lilac Sunbonnet* (1894); and Ian Maclaren's *Beside the Bonnie Briar Bush* (1894) and *The Days of Auld Langsyne* (1895). The apotheosis of the kailyard came in 1896 with the publication of *Margaret Ogilvy*, Barrie's biographical study of his mother: it was, the *British Weekly* announced, 'a book which it is almost too sacrilegious to criticise'.[19] In that same book, Barrie told how when nine years earlier he had tried to collect his journalistic 'Auld Licht' sketches into a volume, no publisher 'Scotch or English' would accept it 'as a gift'.[20] By 1896 he must have been enjoying *Punch*'s joke that publishers now seemed interested in handling little else. The Kailyard novels were immensely popular not only in Scotland and England, but in America as well where they appeared regularly on best-seller lists. Their success was due in part to skilful publicity engineered by William Robertson Nicoll who was editor of both the *British Weekly*, where much of the Kailyard fiction was first published, and the *Bookman*, the most widely read literary periodical in Britain. The extent of Kailyard popularity cannot, however, be explained solely in terms of the booming activities of one editor, even someone as influential as Nicoll. The real reason lay once again in the public reaction to realism. Barrie's stories, backed by Nicoll's advocacy, began to attract attention shortly after the Vizetelly trial, and the works of Crockett and Maclaren that followed were exactly contemporary with the bowdlerisation of Zola's novels, the hysterical press attacks on Ibsen, Moore and Hardy, and Wilde's trial. Many of the regional novels centred on the South-West of England were also associated with the less acceptable side of realism. There were a few faint hints in *Auld Licht Idylls* that Barrie might be drawn in the same direction, but once that fear was shown to be false, all was well. The Kailyarders were not only harmless, they were notoriously safe.

In true regional style, each of the Kailyard novelists laid claim to a particular part of Scotland – Barrie to Kirriemuir, Maclaren to Perthshire, Crockett to Galloway – but what emerged from their work was not so much regional difference as a collective Scottish image. The Kailyard world was largely rural, backward-looking, sentimental, nostalgic, and essentially domestic, though with a strong bitter-sweet element that was conveyed through the recurrent theme of exile from the beloved home. The Kailyard label was particularly appropriate for the way it designated a type of fiction that relied for its effect entirely on local domestic props, something well understood by Crockett: 'To every Scot, his own house, his own gate-end, his own ingle-nook is always the best, the most interesting, the only thing domestic worth singing about and talking about.'[21] It is no accident that Crockett might have been describing a stereotypical music-hall backcloth for a character sketch by Harry Lauder, who was to carry Kailyard sentimentality into as many English-speaking homes as the novelists themselves. What Nicoll treasured in Kailyard fiction was its gentle yet firm attachment to the moral certainties – epitomised by family, church and community – that were subject to increasingly bitter attacks in other types of fiction. The criticism that the Kailyarders presented a misleadingly unrealistic picture of Scottish life meant nothing at all to Nicoll. In his view realism was morbidly unhealthy, and he spent so much energy promoting the Kailyard precisely because it was not realistic: Kailyard fiction was to serve, in Thomas D. Knowles's words, as 'a bastion against the ungodly aspects of literature'.[22] The very large numbers of readers who rushed to buy the Kailyard novels would not perhaps have shared Nicoll's militant denunciation of realism, but they did share his relief that there were still stories available which assured them that however hard the world may seem there is always more good than bad to be found in it, and that tears are enjoyable when mingled with smiles. It was a long-established best-selling formula that was gathering new life in the late Victorian commercial market.

What the Scottish opponents of Kailyard fiction lacked in numbers, they made up for in the ferocity of their attacks. George Douglas Brown's *The House with the Green Shutters* (1901) was written, at least in part, as a rebuttal of what he described as 'the sentimental slop of Barrie, and Crockett, and Maclaren'.[23] His small Scottish community is mean, squalid, full of gossip, envy and barely-suppressed violence, as also is that of J. MacDougall Hay's *Gillespie* (1914). T. W. H. Crosland in a characteristic piece of facetious debunking, *The Unspeakable Scot* (1902), derided the Kailyard communities as 'little bits of heaven dropped on the map of Scotland', and praised *The House with the Green Shutters* for giving the world a true picture of the modern Scot.[24] But the response of J. H. Millar, who had originally coined the Kailyard label, was more perceptive. Writing in 1903, he noted sadly that Scottish writers now seemed incapable of being 'amusing without being jocose' or 'sympathetic without being maudlin', and looked forward to the day when someone would 'write of Scottish life and character with a minimum of the dreary old wit about ministers and whisky'. Before his book was published Millar rushed to add a footnote to this passage saying that his 'not very lofty ideal had to some extent been realised . . . in an unpretending, but excellent, brochure' published in Glasgow.[25] He was referring to John Joy Bell's *Wee Macgreegor* (1902) which was soon joined by two books by Neil Munro, published under his journalistic pen-name of Hugh Foulis, *Erchie* (1904) and *The Vital Spark and Her Queer*

Crew (1907). All three books were collections of sketches which had appeared originally in Glasgow newspapers. As Millar noted, they are 'unpretending', but manage to convey genuine, rather folksy humour without excessive resort to either the sentimentality of the Kailyard or the squalid meanness of George Douglas Brown. But, in the emphasis they placed on exactly reproduced accents, national or regional characteristics, and personal idiosyncracies, they also functioned at the level of stereotypes. They were the Scottish equivalent of the tough but good-hearted Cockney popularised by writers such as William Pett Ridge, Edwin Pugh, and W. W. Jacobs.

The relentless fragmentation and categorisation of fiction that typifies the last two decades of the nineteenth century resists any simple explanation. 'Our society has ceased to be homogeneous,' Wells announced in 1903, 'and it has become a heterogeneous confusion, without any secure common grounds of action.'[26] Wells, as usual, was uncertain whether to commit his personal support to collectivism or to pluralism, and at what was usually a less conscious level, his dilemma was one of the main dilemmas of the age. If collectivism had won the struggle for control of the new democracy, then absolutes – though not, certainly, the same absolutes – might have been re-established, but it didn't, and they weren't. Pluralism, or 'heterogeneous confusion', was the triumphant victor. Like most other aspects of British life at the turn of the century, fiction began to splinter into a variety of different forms which were often mutually, and culturally, incompatible, at least according to earlier systems of categorisation: it had become what Wells, in his lecture at The Times Book Club, was to describe memorably as 'a woven tapestry of interests'.[27]

The proliferation of magazines, newspapers and periodicals, directed at very clearly defined groups of readers, encouraged novelists either to specialise in one particular kind of fiction, or, if the writer was exceptionally talented (or facile) to move between different kinds, thus profiting from (or taking advantage of) several sectors of the fragmenting market. One of the best-informed of the literary manuals advised young authors to begin by establishing 'a reputation in the magazines for a special kind of story', and added in support of this advice: 'Mr Kipling is identified with Indian life, Mrs Stannard ("John Strange Winter") with cavalry life, Mr G. R.

Sims with London life (of a sort), while Mr Anthony Hope, Mr Machen, and others are all *specialists* in fiction.'[28] The short story played a prominent part in this specialisation, as also did the growing popularity of the one-volume novel, at first in competition with the three-decker and then later in the century as its official replacement. Mid-Victorian novelists, grudgingly concocting the second volume of their three-deckers, had constantly predicted that once this artificial form of publication was got rid of, then formal artistry, based on the natural or inevitable length of a story, would flourish. They were right, but only to the extent of the number of authors available who were capable of striving for artistic perfection, and in that particular sense the prescribed length of a story made little difference. Indeed, for many lesser novelists the one-volume novel served to restrict both social range and literary ambition, with a corresponding loss rather than gain of artistry. It was now all too tempting to focus exclusively on the slum or the suburb, on the lovable Cockney or dour Kailyard Scot, on the city clerk or the New Woman: as we have seen, the reaction against this kind of journalistic and sociological labelling was a major factor in the resurgence of wide-ranging, socially-panoramic realistic fiction in the few years immediately before 1914. There was, however, a more positive result of the commercial tendency towards shorter fiction. A good deal of children's, horror, and adventure fiction had long been published in the one-volume format, for the obvious reason that neither the reader's attention nor narrative suspense could expect to be effectively sustained over a long period of time. This lesson was taken to heart by the late Victorians as literary specialisation began to divide popular fiction into distinctive sub-genres.

With a little critical ingenuity it is possible to trace the ancestry of all of these sub-genres – science fiction, ghost stories, adventure tales, fantasy, detective novels, and horror – back beyond the existence of the printed word. So much and so popular a part were they of late Victorian fiction that they often seemed to be inventions of the age, though their archetypal nature was just as important in that popularity. They functioned by bringing age-old fears, longings and aspirations firmly into a modern context through the revivification of myth. The short story or short novel was their natural medium: it provided writers with a limited space within which they could sustain suspense, move swiftly to an horrific climax, or work out an ingenious puzzle. As all of these sub-genres began to establish their own traditions and inspirational texts, the narrative skills became more self-consciously adventurous: they were able to exist within a frame of reference created by their own conventions. No longer were they one element in a large-scale fictional examination of society: instead, they demanded that their exploration of social issues should take place entirely in their own terms. Here again there are losses and gains to record as the size of novels quite visibly shrank. The mid-Victorian 'sensation' novel of M. E. Braddon or Mrs Henry Wood, which was written in the three-decker format and employed the sensational to make larger claims of social portrayal and criticism, was transformed into the brief one-volume 'shocker' like Hugh Conway's *Called Back* (1884) and *Dark Days* (1885), or Richard Marsh's *The Beetle* (1897), which functioned purely at a sensational level, or into works which made more substantial moral demands on the reader but were still clearly part of the new tradition, like Stevenson's *Dr Jekyll and Mr Hyde* and Wilde's *The Picture of Dorian Gray*. In similar fashion mid-Victorian novels such as Dickens's *Bleak House* and Collins's *The Woman in White*, which pioneered the fictional detective but cannot be described adequately as 'detective novels', were rendered down into the tightly controlled solution-solving adventures of a Sherlock Holmes or Father Brown: this trend was initiated by the combined force of Poe's much earlier Dupin stories and Collins's *The Moonstone* (1868). Although strongly pronounced, the appeal of shorter fiction, even in the new sub-genres, was not absolute. The greatest horror novel of the age, Bram Stoker's *Dracula* (1897), is almost as long as many of the older Gothic novels that inspired its creation; and while M. E. Braddon switched effortlessly from three-deckers to the one-volume novel and showed herself perfectly capable of writing up-to-date detective stories, Marie Corelli, taking over something of Braddon's earlier reputation, continued to write massive up-to-date sensation novels. As with almost every other aspect of the late Victorian literary market, the response of novelists was varied and eclectic, but the trend towards shorter fiction was an inspiration as well as a snare to the popular writer.

It was a snare partly because it provided a relatively easy way into the fiction market for any writer who was willing to pander to regional or class stereotypes, or who simply set out to imitate popular literary forms, and partly because once entry had been achieved, the market was reluctant to let any writer deviate from the image of him or her that its own publicity machine had created. Once fixed as a 'slum', 'suburban', 'New Woman', or 'Dartmoor' novelist, an exceptional creative effort was required ever to be regarded as anything else. One of the remarkable features of Stevenson's career is the way that he moved over so many different kinds of fiction, proving a commercial success in most of them, functioning as a powerful influence on their subsequent development, and ignoring the advice of friendly admirers that he should sit still and concentrate on being an Artist. Henry James gave similar advice, for much the same reason, to H. G. Wells. Stevenson and Wells were in effect, being invited to join the 'modernists', the most exclusive of all the specialists. Both declined the invitations and have never been forgiven. Their literary eclecticism was a conscious decision, backed by sufficient talent for them to carry the public with them through various changes of image. Other novelists became inextricably trapped by their success in one particular kind of fiction. The self-consciousness with which these popular literary forms was regarded is apparent at every level of late Victorian fiction. Ray Limbert in Henry James's 'The Next Time', weary of writing highly regarded but commercially unsuccessful novels, decides that the 'next time' he will make a bid for popularity. He writes what he thinks is an '"adventure-story" on approved lines. It was the way they all did the adventure-story that he tried most dauntlessly to emulate.' It turns out to be a 'superb little composition, the shortest of his novels but perhaps the loveliest', and of course, uncommercial.[29] In acknowledging that an 'approved' type of fiction can transcend limiting conventions if the right kind of artistic mind sets to work on it, James was perhaps thinking of Stevenson. Viewed from another angle, the moral of 'The Next Time' is also relevant to Conrad. Throughout his early career Conrad was touchily conscious of sharing the subject-matter of much of his work with the writers of popular adventure fiction. He constantly acknowledged the relationship in order to disown it. *Youth*, he insisted proudly was made out of 'the material of a boys' story', while not being a story written for boys; more bitingly, he points out in *Lord Jim* that Jim's unfulfilled dream of personal heroism can be traced to his adolescent love of 'the sea life of light literature'.[30] Unlike James's

Ray Limbert, Conrad wanted popularity only on his own terms. He was determined that it would not be achieved by writing 'approved' adventure stories or 'light literature' of the kind devoured by Jim, but that fact should not be allowed to conceal the irony that *Lord Jim* was serialised in *Blackwood's*, a major purveyor of conventional adventure fiction. In spite of their very different responses to the fragmentation of fiction, both James and Conrad were disturbed by the threat it posed to their own positions as Artists. Other novelists viewed the situation quite differently: the contrasting attitudes of Wells and Stevenson have been mentioned, and their example inspired in turn the work of novelists who were totally uninterested in the idealism and achievement of a James or Conrad. For example, Max Pemberton was a frankly commercial writer. University-educated, though with no definite profession in mind, he studied 'the reading tastes of the masses' and turned to Fleet Street to earn his living. Paragraphs and stories for various magazines led to the editorship of *Chums*: the next inevitable step was a novel. The authors of the day he most admired were Stevenson and Haggard, so he followed their example with *The Iron Pirate* (1893), the first of many commercially successful adventure stories.[31] Haggard himself had nothing of Pemberton's literary opportunism, though the way that he achieved commercial success was not entirely dissimilar. In 1884 he was the author of two unsuccessful novels. Hearing the recently-published *Treasure Island* highly praised, he spoke slightingly of it and was challenged by his brother 'to write anything half so good'.[32] He responded with *King Solomon's Mines*, which shared with *Treasure Island*, a string of exciting adventures and instant mythic appeal. Although Haggard's tone and view of life were totally unlike those of Stevenson, it was on these two authors more than any others that responsibility fell for saving the country's fiction from the threat of realism. The semi-official doctrine of opposition was labelled 'romance'. It was in many respects an unfortunate choice.

Although the term realism was of relatively recent coinage, its essential meaning had long been understood and used as a standard comparison with romance. The term 'romance' itself, however, had an even more complicated lexical history than realism, and complications were to multiply into total confusion as late Victorian critics and novelists set to work on it. Meredith was a major influence through his opposition to realism, which he described scathingly as 'a conscientious transcription of all the visible, and a repetition of all the audible'; and also through his call for an alternative method which would instil 'philosophy' or 'brainstuff' into fiction by means of sophisticated comedy.[33] A related influence was J. H. Shorthouse, the success of whose historical novel *John Inglesant* in 1881 encouraged him to add a preface to the second edition in which, like Meredith, he called for fiction and philosophy to be united so that eternal truths about mankind could be conveyed effectively to a 'prosaic age'. It was not, however, high comedy that Shorthouse wanted, but a new branch of historical fiction: this literary hybrid he called 'Philosophical Romance'.[34] He was not opposed to realism as the novelist's fundamental method as long as it was imbued with a romantic spirit. 'Yes, it is only a Romance,' he announced, in rhetorical anticipation of his critics, and in the heightened language that was to feature so often in subsequent discussions of the subject: 'It is only the ivory gate falling back at the fairy touch. It is only the leaden sky breaking for a moment above the bowed and weary head, revealing the fathomless Infinite through the gloom.'[35] Kenneth Graham fixes 1887 as 'the year of recognition for the new romance' because in that year George Saintsbury, Rider Haggard and Andrew Lang – the writers who, with the addition of Stevenson, were the major propagandists for romance – issued 'manifestos on its behalf'.[36] All of these writers saw romance as serving to deflect attention away from the dangerous unpleasantness of realism, a classification that in this context allowed for no distinction between Zolaesque documentation and Jamesian psychological analysis: both types of realism were seen as equally guilty of fostering introspection, unmanliness and morbidity, and of favouring a literary method that was mechanical and monotonous. Lang professed to believe that 'any clever man or woman may elaborate a realistic novel according to the rules', while 'romance bloweth where she listeth'.[37] The socially undesirable qualities associated with realism, and its narrow conception of art, are well, if cryptically, expressed there. The fresh wind of romance not only blows away morbidity and brings a return to health, it does this by liberating the imagination, thus making great art possible again. Saintsbury was similarly drawn to imagery of health and cleansing to convey his enthusiasm for romance. The current *malaise* in fiction will not be cured, he announced, 'till we have bathed once more long and well in the romance of adventure and of passion'.[38] There was some talk, by Lang especially, of the battle between realism and romance being fought out to 'the bitter end', but Lang's confidence that romance and realism could be kept apart, that they represented respectively the 'golden' and the 'silver' sides of the 'shield of fiction', was soon undermined.[39] W. E. Henley, a close friend of Stevenson's and a leading spokesman for the 'romance' of imperialism, was also, in his own poetry and as editor of the *National Observer* and the *New Review*, a supporter of certain kinds of realism; while Kipling, who hated literary cliques, and whose early work was predominantly realistic, was immediately enlisted (against his will and approval) into the anti-realist camp because he had introduced the 'romance' of India to the British reading public. Claims for the superior healthiness of romance were further weakened when reviewers began to complain about the lurid descriptions of violence in Haggard's novels.[40] Lang's faith in romance survived not only all of this, but the apparent defection of Stevenson as well. Of *The Ebb-Tide* he observed: 'There is little pleasure in voyaging with such a crew . . . But it is not long since Mr Stevenson gave us *Catriona*. May he soon listen to the muir-cocks crying "Come back!" across the heather!'[41]

The conjunction of Lang and Stevenson is of some importance to an understanding of how romance came to carry such high hopes towards the close of the century. Like Kailyard fiction, much of the publicity that surrounded it was skilfully engineered, though Lang, the major publicist, was a far more substantial literary figure than Robertson Nicoll. He was a talented scholar, and regarded respectfully for his contributions to folklore, anthropology and the occult: he was also a leading exponent of the flowery, allusive affected style of writing that was becoming the trademark of literary journalism. He published volumes of graceful poetry; several historical novels under his own name, notably *A Monk of Fife* (1896); a collaborative novel *The World's Desire* (1890) with Rider Haggard; and the collections of fairy stories for which he is probably best remembered today. His prolific output, however, was nothing compared with the energy which went into the advocacy of romance: like Nicoll, Gosse and Clement Shorter, Lang was at heart a literary middleman. His public pulpit was a regular column 'At the Sign of the Ship' in *Longman's Magazine* which he employed to denigrate French realism and any British fiction influenced by it, and to praise the increasingly popular novels of adventure. The same preferences were pursued in his semi-public or anonymous roles as publisher's reader, literary adviser and book reviewer. A book or manuscript that met with his approval might be recommended for publication in England or for serialisation in America, where he was the English editor of *Harper's*, and once published it would receive additional publicity in 'At the Sign of the Ship', and possibly several reviews, signed or anonymous but all by Lang, in different periodicals and newspapers.[42] The influence that a man like Lang could exert was very considerable indeed, but it would remain only temporary or local unless it could focus on a writer of genius who would serve to exemplify and justify the extravagant theory. This was where Stevenson came in.

The attractiveness of Stevenson rested on his possession of two highly-developed qualities which are rarely found together. He was an Aesthete and a writer of exciting stories. In an age which was becoming obsessed with the need to separate Art from Entertainment, Stevenson spoke and acted on behalf of both. If the experimental range of his work worried his admirers, there was still at the heart of it *Treasure Island*, *Kidnapped*, *The Black Arrow* and *The Master of Ballantrae*. They were the perfect antidote to naturalism. They were absorbing for children and adults; committed to action rather than analysis; at first, they barely acknowledged that sexuality existed; offered no disturbing analogies with modernity; linked late Victorian fiction with Scott on the one hand and with the acceptable French tradition of Dumas on the other; and, most important of all, since these various qualities could have been found elsewhere, they were brilliantly written. Stevenson's theories on the art of fiction were just as acceptable as his practice. Like Wells after him, Stevenson took public issue with Henry James's claim that art 'competes with life', but unlike Wells he did not call for fiction to involve itself directly in life, or for it to reflect the chaotic unorganised quality of life. On the contrary, he displayed a dedicated belief in organicism:

> From all its chapters, from all its pages, from all its sentences,
> the well-written novel echoes and re-echoes its one creative
> and controlling thought; to this must every incident and
> character contribute; the style must have been pitched in
> unison with this; and if there is anywhere a word that looks

another way, the book would be stronger, clearer, and (I
had almost said) fuller without it.[43]

Such views may have been reassuring to those critics who wanted
to believe that realism was not carrying all before it, but they were
unlikely to convince anyone else. Although Stevenson acknowledged
in his early critical essays that realism and romance were essentially
different 'technical methods', artistic precedence was given repeatedly to romance, usually by denigrating realism. The novel of
'incident' was set unjustly against a type of fiction that concerned
itself with 'the clink of teaspoons and the accent of the curate': the
'great creative writer' was described as someone whose 'stories
may be nourished with the realities of life', and then qualified
by the insistence that the 'true mark' of those stories was 'to
satisfy the nameless longings of the reader, and to obey the ideal
laws of the day-dream'. Fiction, he claimed, in a definition that
appeared to eliminate any serious adult interest, 'is to the grown
man what play is to the child ... when it pleases him with
every turn, when he loves to recall it and dwells upon its
recollection with entire delight, fiction is called romance'.[44] It
was statements such as these that were later to provoke the
charges that Stevenson's criticism was mere belletristic chat and
his fiction nothing but tales about pirates written for schoolboys,
but they were accepted gratefully by Lang and his followers. In
spite of Stevenson's more considered critical judgments, it was
largely under his influence that 'romance' lost whatever specific
meaning it might once have had and became, in effect, almost
anything that wasn't realism.

It was the historical novel that Lang and Stevenson had
primarily in mind, though, as they understood, not all historical
novels were romances, and not all romances historical: furthermore,
an historical novel might well be realistic in its method or, in
Shorthouse's sense, 'philosophical'. The 'adventure story on approved lines' written by James's Ray Limbert was probably
historical and romantic, though, in the late Victorian literary
market, it could just as well have been near-contemporary and
reasonably realistic. Many romances were fantastic, but 'fantasy'
was beginning to insist that it was distinct from other kinds of
'romance'; and in much the same way the 'horror' story was often
classified as a romance because it was not 'realistic' and not quite

'supernatural', though, obviously enough, it could be historical or contemporary, and its treatment could be romantic or realistic.[45] The tales of scientific experiment and exploration pioneered by Jules Verne and H. G. Wells were known throughout this period as scientific 'romances' (the term 'science fiction' did not come into general use until the 1920s); tales of ghosts and poltergeists and other supernatural phenomena were often described as 'psychical romances'; and there were few late Victorian fictional heroes as truly romantic and a part of their age as the private detective, except perhaps when that dual role was undertaken by the imperial explorer or soldier in an 'adventure' story.

Whereas many reviewers, critics and readers welcomed the new forms of romance as an antidote to the pernicious influence of realism, the novelists themselves were more often motivated by a distrust of realism's scientific and documentary pretensions. 'We have in our police reports realism pushed to its extreme limits,' observes Conan Doyle's surrogate author Dr Watson, 'and yet the result is, it must be confessed, neither fascinating nor artistic.' Holmes agrees with him: 'A certain selection and discretion must be used in producing a realistic effect.'[46] Select and discreet the details may be, but both Holmes and Watson do see the need for the narration of their adventures to remain broadly within the scope of realism. In complete contrast, Walter de la Mare's Henry Brocken rejects realism as in any sense capable of conveying the nature and flavour of his adventures, and apologises to the reader for standing against so powerful a tradition:

> Most travellers, that he ever heard of, were the happy
> possessors of audacity and vigour, a zeal for facts a zeal for
> Science, a vivid faith in powder and gold. Who, then, will
> bear for a moment with an ignorant, pacific adventurer,
> without even a gun?

For the regions he is to explore, Brocken can 'present neither map nor chart . . . latitude nor longitude; can affirm only that their frontier stretches just this side of Dream.'[47] The assumption that facts and modern science have obscured rather than revealed the truth about life is fundamental to much of this fiction. The really worthwhile studies undertaken by the protagonist of George MacDonald's *Lilith* (1895) only begin when he comes down from university: 'Ptolemy, Dante, the two Bacons, and Boyle were even more to me than Darwin or Maxwell, as so much nearer the vanished van breaking into the dark of ignorance.'[48] True knowledge is attained not by marching doggedly forward with each scientific discovery, but by moving further and further back to a point where the mind is no longer corrupted by modern scientific reasoning. Having watched Count Dracula leave his castle by crawling lizard-fashion down the wall, Jonathan Harker feels safe enough to enter details of this latest chilling episode in his diary. As a safeguard he writes in shorthand: 'It is nineteenth century up-to-date with a vengeance. And yet, unless my senses deceive me, the old centuries had, and have, powers of their own which mere "modernity" cannot kill.'[49]

The imagery of exploration was clearly as important to the romance as to the realistic novel and social documentary, and here also it functioned on both a literal and a metaphorical level, though its emphasis was totally different. The realist, the journalist and the sociologist employed exploration imagery to dramatise present social conditions, to draw the reader's attention to neglected areas of contemporary life. In contrast, the writer of romance employed the same imagery in order to escape from the present, or, if he had a point to make of direct contemporary relevance, to set up a process of extrapolation that the reader was expected to follow through. Of the four major kinds of late Victorian romance examined here – historical, scientific, supernatural, detective – only the writer of detective fiction shared the social explorers' preoccupation with present time and conditions. The other three were interested in the present only in so far as it could be placed within the huge vistas of space and time of which it was, if truly understood, merely an insignificant speck. In the process, they divided among themselves not merely types of fiction, but time as well. The historical novelist took as his special province the whole of time past; the writer of science fiction took the whole of time future; while the writer of the supernatural and occult embraced or ignored both time future and time past in his exploration of states of consciousness which were beyond any concept of time available to human understanding.

It was here that the obsession of twentieth-century fiction with the need to find a replacement for linear time can be said to begin. The structural connections between changing concepts of time and the form of fiction did not go unremarked by the writers of the new sub-genres. In many instances time future and time past were used as fairly mechanical means of getting a story under way, but in the hands of such writers as Stevenson, Kipling, MacDonald, Machen and Stoker, formal experiments with multiple narration, radically shifting points of view, and unreliable or misleading narrators, were also being pursued. The modernists were to be too absorbed with the artistic potential of the work itself and too scornful of the literary market-place to give more than an oblique recognition of the popular resurgence and redirection of romance, though James, as we have seen, was fully aware of Stevenson's achievement: he was also fascinated by the artistic possibilities of the supernatural tale. Conrad too was probably more influenced by Stevenson than he cared to admit, though he openly acknowledged the affinities his work had with that of Kipling.[50] The main case to be made out is not, however, one of direct influence, but rather of the complex pattern of interrelationships and separations out of which literary modernism was born. What is to the point, is that while these sub-genres continued to strengthen their independent identities and flourished apart from, and often scorned by modernism, many post-modernist writers, inspired and frustrated by their great modernist predecessors, have turned increasingly, and with experimental admiration, to the alternative forms of popular fiction pioneered by the late Victorians.

It was the historical novel that initiated the late Victorian debate on the spiritually and socially cleansing power of romance, and it was to be the historical novel that proved, ultimately, the greatest literary disappointment. One problem was that among the various forms of late Victorian romance, only historical fiction had to compete with long-established and vital literary traditions. At this time, Scott still provided the virtually automatic standard of comparison for any new historical novel; not far behind was the much-admired Dumas; Dickens, Thackeray and Eliot had all temporarily turned aside from the general mid-Victorian preference for the recent past as the setting for fiction to write historical novels; and, daunting as comparison with these past masters was, the translation into English of Tolstoy's *War and Peace* in 1886 established a contemporary model that no British novelist could begin to challenge. Even so, in the wake of *Lorna Doone*, *John Inglesant*, *Treasure Island* and *Kidnapped*, historical fiction achieved

a phenomenal new popularity in Britain. So many historical novels
were published that they provoked the compilation of descriptive
guides, bibliographies and library handbooks, making the historical
novel probably the first type of popular fiction to be treated
extensively in this classifying manner.[51] That it was possible to
make a comfortable living by writing mainly historical fiction was
demonstrated in the 1870s by the successful partnership of Walter
Besant and James Rice, and subsequently by a very large number
of individual novelists, including Edna Lyall, Stanley Weyman, H.
S. Merriman, Quiller-Couch, S. R. Crockett, Neil Munro, Baroness
Orczy, Marjorie Bowen and Rafael Sabatini. James, Wells and
Bennett held aloof from the trend, but Hardy, Gissing, Morrison,
Moore, Ford, and even Conrad eventually, wrote historical novels,
while writers like Ouida, Corelli, Caine, Haggard, Doyle and
Hewlett alternated between historical and contemporary subjects.
The sheer quantity of historical fiction, its variety, and its eclectic
use of elements from many different literary genres, make any
very precise classification virtually impossible, but in the light of
the generalisations already made, certain distinctinve groupings of
historical novels can be indicated.

The kind of 'philosophical romance' defined by J. H. Shorthouse
made up one strand. Apart from Shorthouse's own *John Inglesant*,
the most distinguished contributions were Walter Pater's *Marius
the Epicurean* (1885) and *Imaginary Portraits* (1887), and William
Morris's late romances or Socialist fables: *A Dream of John Ball*
(1988), *The House of the Wolfings* (1889), *News from Nowhere*
(1891), *The Wood Beyond the World* (1895) and *The Well at the
World's End* (1896). Meredith's example was too idiosyncratic to
provide a safe model for other writers, though his stylistic influence
can be seen in Stevenson's *Prince Otto* (1885), and, mingling with
the pastiche Malory that tempted too many historical novelists of
the time, in Maurice Hewlett's *The Forest Lovers* (1898) and
Richard Yea-and-Nay (1900). It was common, if not always
correct, to set against these kinds of historical 'romances' the
'realistic' historical novel: this could mean analytical or true-to-life,
though it often only meant carefully-researched. The type of the
late Victorian researcher-novelist was Conan Doyle, with *Micah
Clarke* (1889), *The White Company* (1890), *The Exploits of
Brigadier Gerard* (1895) and *Sir Nigel* (1906). Doyle's own reason
for thinking *The White Company* and *Sir Nigel*, both of which are

set in the fifteenth century, to be the very best of his fiction was that they 'made an accurate picture of that great age'.[52] Among the more successful examples of the 'analytical' historical novel were Maurice Hewlett's *The Queen's Quair* (1904), and Ford Madox Ford's trilogy *The Fifth Queen* (1906), *Privy Seal* (1907) and *The Fifth Queen Crowned* (1908).

The dominant type of historical 'romance' was, however, not primarily 'philosophical', 'analytical', 'accurate', or 'realistic': it was, rather, the loosely-structured collection of exciting episodes and incidents that descended from Stevenson, through Doyle – in spite of his large claims of historical portraiture – and Rider Haggard. The gradual debasement of the high hopes for romance held out by Meredith and Shorthouse can also be traced back to Stevenson's unguarded critical assertions that the greatness of romance lay in its appeal to the 'nameless longings' and 'day-dreams' of the reader, and that it was the adult's version of a child's 'play'. Stevenson could not, however, be held personally responsible for the increasingly strident political tone of this fiction. His historical novels were essentially non-nationalistic, except in so far as they spoke for a lost Scottishness. Furthermore, much of his later work was anti-imperialistic, and it was imperial expansion that created the receptive atmosphere for historical romance, including Stevenson's. It was also imperial expansion that made it increasingly difficult to distinguish in any clear-cut way between an historical and an adventure novel. In one sense, novels like Haggard's *King Solomon's Mines* (1885), A. E. W. Mason's *The Four Feathers* (1902), John Buchan's *Prester John* (1910) and Edgar Wallace's *Sanders of the River* (1911) were firmly contemporary in that the opening up of Africa by Western powers, a subject with which all of these novels dealt, was a familiar daily issue for British readers. But that issue also involved the ancient rights and customs of Africa peoples as well as the constant restructuring of 'tradition' that was so important a part of the mythos of the British Empire: it was frequently difficult (in fiction and in life) to determine where 'history' ended and 'contemporary' adventure began. Ernest Baker said of Flora Annie Steel's novel about the Indian Mutiny *On the Face of the Waters* (1896) that it epitomised 'fiction never interfering with facts', and then added that it also 'pays much attention to sex problems, Ibsenism, and other modern fashions'.[53] The blend of past and present was an inevitable expression of the Empire as history in the making. Nowhere was this more apparent than in the fiction directed at boys, whether in periodicals like the *Union Jack* and *Boy's Own Paper*, or in the adventurous games which featured in fiction that was not ostensibly imperialistic, or, most blatantly, in the novels of writers like W. H. G. Kingston, Gordon Stables, and G. A. Henty, where the message that all boys should be ready to answer the call of Empire was essentially the same whether those boys were expected, to use the evocative titles of Henty's novels, to sail *Under Drake's Flag* (1883) or march *With Roberts to Pretoria* (1902). Although, largely under the influence of Kipling's Indian tales, novelists were beginning to give more attention in their work to the soldier than the sailor and more to war on land than at sea, the traditional British fiction of life at sea – whether experienced by sailors, pirates or fishermen – also saw a revival with such novels as Henry Newbolt's *Taken by the Enemy* (1892), Kipling's *Captains Courageous* (1892) and most interestingly, John Masefield's *Captain Margaret* (1908). The popular apotheosis of historical romance came with Anthony Hope's *The Prisoner of Zenda* (1894), another novel which though contemporary in setting appeared historical because of the quaintness of the Ruritania it portrayed, and with a batch of swashbuckling cloak-and-dagger novels, the most prominent being: Stanley Weyman, *A Gentleman of France* (1893), *Under the Red Robe* (1894), and *The Red Cockade* (1895); Baroness Orczy, *The Scarlet Pimpernel* (1905) and its many sequels; and Jeffrey Farnol's *The Broad Highway* (1910) and *The Amateur Gentleman* (1913). Day-dream and adult play really had taken over.

The social function of a great deal of this historical fiction was perfectly well understood by its authors.[54] First, it had to sustain the mood of adventurous exploration that was necessary for the expansion and maintenance of the British Empire. Secondly, it took upon itself the task of instilling into the new and unformed democracy an appreciation of the long years of progress that had turned Britain into the greatest imperial power the world had ever known. Any period of history, from the Stone Age to the Boer War, could serve these functions. At an individual level the call was for everyone to nurture the qualities of courage, justice and fair play that had made, and would keep, Britain great, and be willing to die for those ideals. Doyle's Sir Nigel Loring expresses the approved sentiment as the Middle Ages are shown drawing to a close:

> If the end be now come, I have had great fortune in having
> lived in times when so much glory was to be won, and in
> knowing so many valiant gentlemen and knights.[55]

Sir Nigel's gallantry and patriotism are a tribute to both his own class, that has for centuries carried the traditions of Britain, and the new democracy that must now take up those traditions. Precisely the same qualities were required because now, as then, the age was one of adventure, excitement and challenge. The code of manliness was, of course, expressed not only in historical fiction, but was also cultivated in schools (both public and board) and in the various youth organisations that were characteristic products of the age.[56] The novelist most commonly associated with the propagation of these attitudes is Kipling; he, certainly, played a conscious part in the process, but the cult of manliness was central in his work for only a short period of time, and there was often little that was truly 'romantic' in his portrayal of the servants of Empire. The more appropriate fictional comparisons are with such characters as Leo Vincey, Sir Henry Curtis, Rudolf Rassendyll and Sir Percy Blakeney, none of whom have equivalents in Kipling. Nor was Kipling's confidence about the ultimate triumph of British imperialism generally as all-embracing as that of many other writers, among them Conan Doyle, whose Lady Tiphaine foresees a future world that is totally Anglicised:

> On I go, and onwards over seas where man hath never yet
> sailed, and I see a great land under new stars and a stranger
> sky, and still the land is England. Where have her children
> not gone? What have they not done? Her banner is planted
> on ice. Her banner is scorched in the sun. She lies athwart
> the lands, and her shadow is over the seas.[57]

England's enemy at the time of that fifteenth-century vision was France, and, as far as most late Victorian historical fiction was concerned, France was still the main threat, even though in certain other types of fiction Germany was beginning to take on a new prominence. It was not so much the fear of direct war with France that attracted the attention of novelists as the example that France's more recent history could be made to yield for British readers. The year 1889 marked the centenary of the fall of the Bastille, and over the next twenty or so years hundreds of novels, exploring every possible aspect of France's revolutionary past, were published. Here was everything that late Victorian Britain and the British Empire should learn to avoid – a poverty-stricken maltreated populace, an arrogant aristocracy, violent revolt, a reign of terror, sexual licence, war, dictatorship, and then, with the lesson not learned, a similar pattern repeated over again. Fictional salvation was provided only by dashing debonair Englishmen and the few remnants of the French aristrocracy who had remained true to the principles of justice and honour that most of their fellow-aristocrats had forgotten.

In placing itself so abjectly at the service of dominant late Victorian domestic and imperial ideologies, historical fiction surrended the literary advantages held out to it by radically changing concepts of space and time: it played safe in an age that demanded experiment and speculation. Few novelists understood these demands better than Hardy. As Henry Knight clings desperately to the cliff-face in *A Pair of Blue Eyes* (1873), time closes up 'like a fan before him. He saw himself at one extremity of the years, face to face with the beginning and all the intermediate centuries simultaneously.'[58] In *Two on a Tower* (1882) Hardy has Swithin St Cleeve gazing not at the fossilised remains of long-dead creatures, but at the unknown 'horror' of the sky: 'You would hardly think, at first, that horrid monsters lie up there waiting to be discovered by any moderately penetrating mind – monsters to which those of the oceans bear no sort of comparison.'[59] Hardy's own fictional explorations of these phenomena remained within the contemporary world. For him, such perceptions expressed the torment of modern man, forced constantly to contrast his own ephemerality with the mocking stolidity of the physical world. The scientific romance acknowledged the contemporary crisis posed by Hardy, but focused its attention on the unlimited possibilities of future change. The revival of interest in Utopian and dystopian fiction established fabular forms which enabled writers to speculate freely on the possible ramifications of present social and political developments, and settled, virtually at a stroke, the apparent inability of the realistic novel to deal convincingly with political issues.[60] It was not surprising that the scientific romance should have accepted politics as a natural part of its concerns: it could, after all, trace the necessary connections back to Plato's *Republic*, something that H. G. Wells was particularly conscious of. Its more immediate literary context was provided by Bulwer Lytton's *The Coming Race* (1871), Samuel Butler's *Erewhon* (1872) and a large number of now largely forgotten novels inspired by evolutionary theory; Jules Verne's scientific tales, which in Britain were often regarded as boys' adventure books, and confirmed as such by the serialisation of many of the later ones in the *Boy's Own Paper*; and, from America, Edward Bellamy's *Looking Backward* (1887). It was Bellamy's vision of a future Boston made functionally beautiful by the technological miracles of science that prompted William Morris to offer a very different vision of the future in *News from Nowhere* (1891), while much of Wells's early work – especially *The Time Machine* (1895) and *When the Sleeper Wakes* (1899) – was motivated in part by his opposition to both Bellamy and Morris. The debate initiated here continues to the present day. It was not concerned primarily with fictional form, though nothing exactly comparable to these books had appeared before, but rather with the questions, how will modern democratic society develop, and will it survive at all? Bellamy stepped confidently into the future and announced that the machine would save mankind; Morris acknowledged the importance of the machine, but packed it out of sight so that it could do all the dirty work of life and leave people free to live as near to the ideal, and as beautifully, as his visionary view of the Middle Ages allowed. Wells placed his Time Traveller on an adapted bicycle – one of the most common symbols of social liberation in the 1890s – and sent him pedalling through time and space to a confrontation with a black, round, tentacled 'thing' which he finds 'hopping fitfully' about on a beach, framed against 'the red water of the sea'.[61]

For Bellamy and Morris the potential future of democracy was Utopian, created on the one hand by technological capitalism and on the other by a Marxist-Ruskinian revolution. Wells, attracted as he was by aspects of both of these ideologies, regarded the fate of democracy as being, like the fate of man himself, clothed in impenetrable darkness. There could, in his view, be no single, completed, attainable Utopia, but only stages of progression (or possibly regression) stretching out further into the future than it was possible for the puny mind of man to comprehend.[62] In Wells's hands, the scientific romance became an imaginative exploration of possible options, with futuristic prophecies usually functioning as extrapolations from observable contemporary trends: the claim for immediate relevance was enhanced by the domestic Home Counties setting or starting-point of the stories. No British realist of the time could match Wells's imaginative portrayal of the conflict between Capital and Labour in *The Time Machine*; or the dangers involved in the modern scientist becoming a new kind of God in *The Island of Dr Moreau*; or the nature of mass control in a totalitarian regime in *When the Sleeper Wakes*, a novel which points directly forward to such works as *We*, *Brave New World*, and *Nineteen Eighty-Four*. In a few years of frenzied activity, as the nineteenth century drew to a close, Wells created, or gave memorable modern form to, many of the images and themes that were to be repeated endlessly throughout the twentieth century, in both fiction and film – time travel; interplanetary war; the vast, glass-domed, self-contained city; mass frenzy; the invisible man; voyage to the moon; the morally corrupt or 'mad' scientist; everyday transportation by aeroplane and helicopter; the bombing of metropolitan populations; and, a few years later, atomic warfare. 'Where is *life* in all this, life as I feel it and know it?' Henry James asked of *Anticipations* (1902), demonstrating, in the saddest possible way, that the modernist novel was ruthlessly determined to be about nothing but itself.[63]

In contrast, the scientific romance at the turn of the century, although on its way to establishing a separate identity, was still a very flexible term. Wells's short stories and romances drew indiscriminately on elements of horror, supernatural, psychological, fantastic and adventure fiction: in his later novels he turned increasingly to the Dialogue, reducing the role of story in order to give greater attention to speculation and prophecy. Certain kinds of narrative which involved journeys into the past rather than the future – Haggard's *She* (1887), Wells's 'The Country of the Blind' (1904), and Doyle's *The Lost World* (1912) – have clear affinities with science-fiction, as also do some of the novels which explored the *Doppelgänger* theme made popular by *Dr Jekyll and Mr Hyde* (1886). Science provides the means of character transformation in Stevenson's fable, and although it has little direct importance apart from that, the ethical and psychological conjecture it indirectly provokes does have a scientific rather than a miraculous origin; at a less imaginative level the mesmerism of du Maurier's *Trilby* (1894) and the drug addiction of the protagonist of Katherine Thurston's *John Chilcote MP* (1904) serve similar purposes. Much closer to later developments in science fiction were Kipling's experiments

with non-realistic literary forms. His fascinated interest in technology could be anthropomorphic, as in '.007' and 'The Ship that
Found Herself'; mysterious, in 'Mrs Bathurst'; or supernatural, in
'Wireless'. His two stories about the Aerial Board of Control –
'With the Night Mail' and 'As Easy as ABC' – are futuristic in the
manner of Wells and similarly speculative about the way the world
is going. A related experimentation is observable in Kipling's
revival of the animal fable. The two *Jungle Books* can be read as
exciting tales, an exercise in Darwinism, or as allegorical representations of the type of hierarchical society that must be retained if the
lawlessness of the bandar-log is to be controlled: while fables like
'Below the Mill Dam', 'The Mother Hive' and 'Little Foxes'
follow the more obvious science-fiction tales in the use of non-
realistic forms to voice explicit social criticism.

Both Kipling and Wells drew on the 'invasion novels' which
were published in very large numbers throughout this period, and
out of which there emerged one of the twentieth century's most
characteristic types of formula fiction. Credit for initiating the
'invasion' trend is usually given to Sir George Chesney's *The
Battle of Dorking* (1871). As I. F. Clarke has shown, late Victorian
interest in fiction that prophesied the nature of future warfare and
showed Britain over-run by, or successfully resisting, invading
foreign forces, was a direct product of the changing balance of
power in Europe – the Franco-Prussian war in 1870; the gradual
displacement of France by Germany as Britain's likeliest military
foe; the rapid technological developments that led to a naval arms
race between Britain and Germany; and the urgent diplomatic
manoeuvres in the early years of the present century that took
Britain out of 'splendid isolation' and into new kinds of national
alignments.[64] The invasion novels ranged from works with an
informed interest in military strategy, like *The Battle of Dorking*;
through M. P. Shiel's sensational *The Yellow Wave* (1905), and the
anti-German propaganda fiction commissioned and serialised by
Alfred Harmsworth; to the young P. G. Wodehouse's boy-scout
proof *The Swoop! or How Clarence Saved England* (1909). In *The
War of the Worlds* (1898) Wells took an imaginative leap –
characteristic of him but beyond most authors of invasion novels –
and made the enemy not France, Germany, China or Japan, but
Mars. The conviction that a European war involving Britain was
inevitable sooner or later meant that diplomacy alone could not be

trusted. An Army Intelligence Department was formed as early as 1873; it was followed by a Naval Intelligence Board in 1887, the first Official Secrets Act in 1889, the more rigorous Official Secrets Act of 1911, and, in the same year, the formation of MI5 and MI6. Popular novelists like E. Phillips Oppenheim, and especially William Le Queux (who had written invasion novels for Harmsworth's newspapers), were quick to recognise the fictional potential offered by this latest version of the ancient profession of the undercover agent, and with works like Oppenheim's *Mysterious Mr Sabin* (1898) and Le Queux's *Secrets of the Foreign Office* (1903) and *The Man From Downing Street* (1904), the modern spy novel began to take shape. The foreign agent – treacherous, dishonourable and mercenary, of course – was already a familiar figure in invasion fiction: his British counterpart – who was, just as naturally, patriotic, honourable and selfless – made his appearance a little later. David Stafford fixes Duckworth Drew in Le Queux's *Secrets of the Foreign Office* as 'probably . . . the first in a long tradition of gentlemanly secret agents' in British fiction.[65] A close relation, and ultimately of more literary significance, was the patriot who gets caught unwillingly and at first uncomprehendingly in intelligence activities. Erskine Childers led the way with *The Riddle of the Sands* (1903), and was followed by John Buchan's *The Thirty-Nine Steps* (1915).

The ghosts, phantasms, and spirits of various kinds that feature so prominently in the fiction of the period were far older phenomena than even spies and undercover agents: they, however, also seemed new. As one commentator noted in 1900: 'The old spectre of our childhood with his clanking chains has faded into nothingness in this age of inquiry. If he appears again it is in a new character and he must at least be civil to the Society for Psychical Research.'[66] Henry James, the author of several outstanding tales of the supernatural in addition to the incomparable *The Turn of the Screw* (1898) also recognised, in order to dismiss it, 'the new type . . . the mere modern "psychical" case . . . equipped with credentials' which he saw as destroying 'the dear old sacred terror'.[67] Certainly, the influence was not all in one direction, or all of one kind. F. W. H. Myers was so fascinated by *Dr Jekyll and Mr Hyde* that he sent Stevenson detailed comments on the story, together with suggestions for its possible improvement.[68] The appearances of the devil in Stevenson's 'Thrawn Janet' and Corelli's *The Sorrows of*

Satan were clearly not prompted by the Society for Psychical Research. Nor did the Society play any part in the development of several branches of supernatural fiction at this time – the semi-playful horror story, for example, that descends from Stevenson's *New Arabian Nights* (1882), to, most notably, Arthur Machen's *The Great God Pan* (1894) and *The Three Impostors* (1895); or the fantasy, fairy, and 'celtic twilight' tales that attracted such diverse writers as George MacDonald, Lord Dunsany, 'Fiona Macleod', J. M. Barrie, Kipling, G. K. Chesterton, Walter de la Mare, E. Nesbit (with novels like *Five Children and It*, 1902, *The Phoenix and the Carpet*, 1904, and *The Enchanted Castle*, 1907), and the side of Algernon Blackwood's neglected talent that found expression in *Jimbo* (1909), *The Human Chord* (1910), *The Centaur* (1911) and *The Prisoner in Fairyland* (1913). The areas of experience covered by the general term 'supernatural' are many and varied, and their fictional representations almost as unclassifiable as the possible types of historical fiction. Yet the impact made by the Society for Psychical Research was immediate and observable. The young Kipling, in India and fascinated by the ancient spiritual and supernatural beliefs he found all around him, would seem to have had no need to refer to the certified case-studies being compiled in London, though in one of the earliest of his Indian stories he has the narrator comment: 'That was more than enough! I had my ghost – a first-hand authenticated article. I would write to the Society for Psychical Research – I would paralyse the Empire with the news!' [69] The narrator is being ironic, and the ghost in question is not really a ghost at all, but already Kipling's later, more serious involvement with psychical phenomena can be seen establishing itself. Henry James, like Stevenson, corresponded with Myers, and would have had still closer knowledge of the SPR through his brother William James. *The Turn of the Screw* took the form of a classically unverifiable ghost story in order that it should not fall into the trap of being a 'psychical case': even so, for some of the details of his story James probably drew on material in the published papers of the SPR. [70]

It was pointed out in Chapter Two that some of the investigations of the SPR had much in common with early developments in psychoanalysis, and it can be added that the detailed case-studies published in the Society's *Proceedings*, in books by members of the Society like Frank Podmore's *Phantasms of the Living* (1886) and

Modern Spiritualism (1902), and Myers's *Human Personality* (1903), and in many related books such as Andrew Lang's *Dreams and Ghosts* (1887) and *Cock Lane and Common Sense* (1894), not only read like ghost stories, but also provided many novelists with their raw material. Here were ghosts and hallucinations, *Doppelgängers*, dreams and nightmares, poltergeists and table-rappings, automatic-writing, precognition, hypnotism, materialisations of every conceivable form, and, as was noted earlier, Freud, Breuer, hysteria, and incipient theories of the sub-conscious. There can be little doubt that the new sophistication of the ghost story owed a considerable debt to the SPR, though the wider growth of interest in supernatural phenomena, at least during the Victorian age, had its origins, as did the SPR itself, in the undermining of religious faith by historical and scientific criticism.[71] The popularity of the ghost story increased as the authority of organised religion declined. The responses of SPR investigators and novelists were not, however, identical, with each other or between themselves. For some, the existence of states of consciousness that were not subject to man's control created a challenge that scientific knowledge would ultimately come to understand, if not actually master: for others, it provided evidence that the much-vaunted concept of Victorian progress was finally breaking down, revealing the emptiness of the material world, and with it the vulnerability of fictional realism. Either way, the supernatural provided a means for many writers to come to terms with areas of experience which the destructively analytical tenor of the age appeared to be closing off: in the common language of supernatural fiction, doors were opened, veils raised, and hitherto unsuspected levels of awareness revealed.

There were mysterious Christian allegories (Mrs Oliphant, *A Beleaguered City*, 1979); 'primitive survivals', of the kind identified by anthropologists, masquerading as 'bogles' in the Scottish Highlands (John Buchan, 'No-Man's-Land', 1898); whimsical spirits (Richard Middleton, *The Ghost Ship*, 1912); spirits wreaking revenge from distant parts of the Empire (W. W. Jacobs, 'The Monkey's Paw', 1902); the dead taking over the bodies of the living (Walter de la Mare, *The Return*, 1908); and some highly convincing erotic ghosts (Robert Hichens, 'How Love Came to Professor Guildea', in *Tongues of Conscience* (1900); Oliver Onions, 'The Beckoning Fair One', *Widdershins*, 1911). Algernon Blackwood's lasting contribution to supernatural fiction came in 1908 with *John*

Silence, a collection of five stories which reintroduced the idea of the Psychic Doctor and initiated a distinguished series of stories from Blackwood which he described as studies 'of extended or expanded consciousness'.[72] M. R. James had nothing of Blackwood's fascination with the possible causes of supernatural manifestations: he was concerned solely with effects. If there is to be left 'a loophole for a natural explanation', James advised, 'let the loophole be so narrow as not to be quite practicable'.[73] In some ways, that assumption turns his *Ghost Stories of an Antiquary* (1904) and *More Ghost Stories* (1911) into exercises in horror rather than supernatural explorations. But the blend that James achieved of quiet scholarly atmosphere, old towns and flat landscapes (often East Anglia), and inexplicable malevolent forces, has become, for many modern readers, the very type of 'English' ghost story. Kipling too became associated with a particular kind of Englishness, in this area of his work as in so many others, but the range of his interests, stretched always by his linguistic and narrative daring, kept him constantly present as the epitome of the changing nature of consciousness discussed here. The animism of rural England in 'A Friendly Brook' has to be set against the inexplicable horror of 'At the End of the Passage' and 'The Mark of the Beast'; the spiritualistic pathos of 'They'; the telepathy of 'The Dog Hervey'; the metempsychosis of 'The Finest Story in the World'; the Christian benediction of 'The Gardener'; the power of transforming love granted by the wraith in 'The Wish House'; and, ultimately, after two decades of exploring nervous disorder as the type of modern illness, the explicit Freudianism of 'In the Same Boat'.

Of all the romantic specialists of the age – whether scientist, sociologist, psychic doctor, journalist, space traveller, alienist, imperial explorer, spy, modernist, town-planner or psychoanalyst – none offered so specialised, and yet so comprehensive, a service as the private detective as personified by Sherlock Holmes. Holmes was by no means the first detective in fiction.[74] Nor did he lead the way, in any chronological sense, among late Victorian fictional detectives: throughout the 1870s and 1880s the detective had been a familiar character in books, penny-dreadfuls, and periodicals. Holmes first made his appearance in two short novels, *A Study in Scarlet* (1887) and *The Sign of Four* (1890), but it was not until the publication of the first of the short stories, 'A Scandal in Bohemia' in the *Strand* in July 1891 that his remarkable popularity began.

He became almost immediately the most famous detective in the
world – though challenged for much of this century, it has been
claimed, by another late Victorian creation Sexton Blake – and he
remains so to the present day.[75] When Conan Doyle sent Holmes
to his apparent death with Moriarty over the Reichenbach Falls,
there were many other writers eager to produce a replacement, but
while there were enough readers of detective fiction around to
support the work of, among others, Arthur Morrison, Baroness
Orczy, Ernest Bramah and R. Austin Freeman, there could be no
satisfactory substitute for Holmes. Of his most serious rivals at this
time only G. K. Chesterton with *The Innocence of Father Brown*
(1911) and *The Wisdom of Father Brown* (1913) came near to
creating a detective with the mythic stature of Holmes. Among his
other worthwhile challengers were Inspector Hanaud of A. E. W.
Mason's *At the Villa Rosa* (1910), and E. W. Hornung's inverted
crime stories which feature the criminal rather than the detective,
Raffles: The Amateur Cracksman (1899) and *Raffles: The Black
Mask* (1901). By 1913 the detective story was sufficiently established for E. C. Bentley to publish an enjoyable spoof of the genre,
Trent's Last Case. Bentley hit many of his targets effectively
enough, but not Holmes, who had placed himself beyond the reach
of harmful satire or parody.

That the police force had a special and urgent role to play in
modern urban society was a mid-Victorian rather than a late
Victorian perception: its fictional expression is to be found in
Dickens's *Bleak House* and Collins's *The Moonstone*. These detectives are in some respects already the solitary, wide-roaming,
tight-lipped unravellers of riddles familiar to twentieth-century
readers and film-goers, except that they are also policemen, and,
for Dickens especially, their centre of operations is the police
station, a spotlessly clean, well-lighted centre of authority and calm
in a chaotic urban world.[76] In contrast, Holmes is a 'consulting
detective', who only takes up crimes that the police cannot solve
and, at his best, succeeds 'where the police of three countries had
failed'.[77] This separation of the police and the detective in fiction
can to some extent be explained historically. As Ian Ousby has
noted, the formation of the Criminal Investigation Department in
1878 gave detectives an expanded role within the police force, and
in the 1880s there was a good deal of public disillusionment with
the police, especially over the Fenian bomb outrages and the Jack

the Ripper murders.[78] Additional contributory factors to the atmosphere of the Holmes stories were the growing tenseness of European diplomatic relations and the increasing use by nations of undercover agents. Holmes was fully aware of the fraught state of international diplomacy, and Watson liked to hint that certain cases he was involved in were diplomatically too sensitive to be revealed to the readers of the *Strand* for some years to come. Not that Holmes himself could ever be identified with anything as limited as an undercover agent: there are some doubts whether he was even human. 'All emotions . . . were abhorrent to his cold, precise, but admirably balanced mind,' Watson comments chillingly; 'He was, I take it, the most perfect reasoning and observing machine that the world has seen.'[79] That is, surely, going quite a bit too far: if Holmes were so totally a machine then he could never have served the double role that Julian Symons has well described as a Nietzschean 'Superman' who is simultaneously 'the Great Outsider'.[80] The vision of an Anglicised world given to Lady Tiphaine in *The White Company* would have counted as prophecy within the fifteenth-century setting of that novel, but to the late Victorian Doyle it had become all but a fact. Sherlock Holmes embodied Doyle's own dream that with a good deal of care the world might just stay that way.

Like so many other protagonists of late Victorian fiction, Holmes is an explorer: the greatest of them all. One of the first things that Watson notices about him is his occasional habit of taking long walks 'into the lowest portions of the city'.[81] From those walks he gains his substantial knowledge of Darkest London and recruits the street urchins who serve him as the Baker Street 'irregulars'. His principle area of exploration is, however, his own mind. Most cases he can solve without leaving his room, just as he can recognise someone who has come from Afghanistan without having been there himself. It is sometimes said of Holmes that he is the all-round man in an age of specialists, but that is surely not correct: he is the supreme specialist. He believes that 'a man should possess all knowledge which is likely to be useful to him in his work', and take little notice of anything else. He is exceptionally well-informed on 'sensational literature' but not other kinds of literature: he is also a first-class scientist, actor, boxer, and swordsman.[82] One of the things he is not interested in is politics, but that hardly matters as he is an ardent supporter of established governments and the royal families of Europe. The specialism to which all of his formidable knowledge is directed is, of course, the scientific investigation of crime, the activity which more than any other threatens to upset the established order he represents. If he is attracted only to the more arcane and complex crimes, that does not mean that lesser criminals are getting away with anything. On the contrary, his power spreads omnipotently over the modern city: 'He loved to lie in the very centre of five millions of people, with his filaments stretching out and running through them, responsive to every little rumour or suspicion of unsolved crime.'[83] If anyone should get past the police, he is picked up by Sherlock Holmes. 'I am,' he announces, 'the last court of appeal.'[84] When, eventually, the criminal evil he has to confront is so great that it can be defeated in no other way, he willingly sacrifices his own life. In dying with the 'Napoleon of Crime' he vanquishes not only the 'organiser of half that is evil and of nearly all that is undetected in this great city', but the great representative of Britain's traditional national enemy as well.[85]

Shortly before his final battle with Moriarty, Holmes reveals a side of himself that had hitherto been given little prominence. Travelling with Watson on a train high over South London, Holmes gazes down into the working-class abyss, exactly as Masterman was to do a few years later. Holmes, however, finds the sight of 'big, isolated clumps of buildings' rising out of a 'lead-coloured sea' cheering. Watson thinks them 'sordid', and explains that they are Board Schools. As on so many previous occasions, Holmes forcefully corrects his companion: 'Lighthouses, my boy! Beacons of the future! Capsules, with hundreds of bright little seeds in each, out of which will spring the wiser, better England of the future.'[86] It is difficult to imagine that those little English boys could turn out to be wiser or brighter than Holmes, but if that should happen it would be because Holmes had been there to watch over their formative years.

Part Four

TAKING OVER

Chapter Seven

Readers and Novelists

BRUTUS: There's no more to be said, but he is banished,
An enemy to the people and his country.
It shall be so.
PLEBEIANS: It shall be so, it shall be so.
CORIOLANUS: You common cry of curs, whose breath I hate
As reek o' th' rotten fens, whose loves I prize
As the dead carcasses of unburied men
That do corrupt my air – I banish you.

William Shakespeare, *Coriolanus*

'You're a terrible man, Stevie, said Davin, taking the short pipe from
his mouth. Always alone.'

James Joyce, *A Portrait of the Artist as a Young Man*

In 1882 Matthew Arnold took the opportunity provided by an
invitation to lecture at the recently-founded University College of
Liverpool to survey his life's work. He decided that however
misunderstood he may have been and in spite of the scant public
success he had achieved, his message was the right one. 'I wish I
could promise to change my old phrases for new ones, and to pass
from my one practical suggestion to some other,' he told his
audience, 'But I fear that there is no chance of this happening.
What has been the burden of my song hitherto, will probably have,
as far as I can at present see, to be the burden of it till the end.' [1]
The 'one practical suggestion' was education for the middle classes,
the 'Philistines'. It really had been at the centre of his thought and

writing about society for the previous thirty years, and it did remain
so until the end. In 1887, just one year before his death, he
published a survey 'Schools in the Reign of Queen Victoria' in
which he pointed out that while the principle of education for the
working class had now been accepted, as he had always insisted it
must be, the middle class still suffered from its 'peculiar disadvantage', or, in other words, its 'markedly inferior' educational system.[2]
But while Arnold's thinking about education and society did not
change during these last few years of his life it did have to be
reformulated, and this reformulation was undertaken during his visit
to America in 1883. The interest in America was far from new.[3] Like
many writers and thinkers in the first half of the nineteenth century
he had looked to America as a democratic model which would
eventually exercise a decisive influence on Britain, for good or ill.
For John Bright, to whom Arnold was still referring in the 1882
lecture, American democracy and republicanism epitomised the
welcome overthrow of the old world by the new. On the other hand,
commentators such as de Tocqueville, John Stuart Mill and Arnold,
warned that American ideals could only triumph by sacrificing social
and cultural standards to the needs of the 'average man' which
would lead to a general levelling down. This attitude was not the
result of simple-minded political reaction. Arnold fully recognised
that democratic change in Britain was inevitable and he constantly
acknowledged that the most vital political ideas were to be found in
the working classes or 'the masses', terms which early in his career
he tended to use as synonyms: later he was to exercise a more careful
discrimination. Accepting that the French Revolution had been the
most important event in modern life, Arnold looked for a democratic
model to emerge not from America but from 'the intelligence of the
idea-moved masses' of France which, even in 1848, as nationalistic
revolutions spread through Europe, he still insisted was superior to
that of 'the *insensible masses* of England'. Worse than either was the
threat posed to the 'educated world' by the 'intolerable *laideur* of the
well-fed American masses'.[4] Arnold was never to change this
view of America in any fundamental way. What had changed by
the 1880s was his belief that France – whose idea-moved masses
were now absorbed in worshipping the 'great goddess Lubricity'
– could provide a satisfactory alternative.[5] The American experience forced itself back upon his attention with a new kind of
urgency.

Of the lectures Arnold prepared especially for America it was the one given the significant title 'Numbers' in which he took up these concerns. Its purpose was to convince his audience that in any society, ancient or modern, the majority of people are unreliable and that only from the few (the 'remnant' as they are labelled) can we expect sound judgment and true wisdom. Arnold justified his rudeness in telling his hosts that the majority of them lacked taste and judgment by assurances that he had been just as blunt with his own countrymen. And so he had. In the celebrated analysis of *Culture and Anarchy* he had examined and dismissed the claims of each of the three classes to possess the qualities of leadership necessary for modern society: hope for the future he placed on a small number of classless individuals whom he called 'aliens'.[6] It was not one of his inspired catch-phrases and never shared in the popularity achieved by 'Barbarians' and 'Philistines', though there were deeper reasons at work than linguistic currency in Arnold's transformation of the 'aliens' into the 'remnant'. France had let him down and in America he now saw the type of modern democratic society which he had spent much of his life proclaiming as natural and inevitable for Britain. There was no aristocracy and no class structure, of the European varieties at least, but the absence of these elements had led in America not to the greater influence of the wise few (whether aliens or remnant) but to an ever-increasing expansion of philistinism. Here was the justification for the constant reiteration of his 'one practical suggestion'. Without it British democracy would either become dominated by the 'raw' working class, or follow the American example of bland, classless, uncultured materialism. Arnold's use of the word 'numbers' referred mainly to the mass, the total of individuals making up democracy, but also in a more specific sense to the 'remnant', for if 'the majority is and must be in general unsound everywhere', then 'to enable the remnant to succeed, a large strengthening of its numbers is everything'.[7] Arnold therefore returned yet again to his one practical suggestion, though now removed slightly from its earlier association with the middle class and adapted to the American situation. Numbers are held to be everything in America and in democracy, he told his audience; was it not then possible, given the Americans' pride in doing things on a large scale, that they could bring this ability to bear on the remnant and increase its numbers so that it might become 'incomparable, all-transforming'?[8]

There are many reasons why it is worth giving so much attention to Arnold at this point. His direct influence on the development of higher education in Britain, on the way that English literature especially was to be studied, and more generally on cultural attitudes, was enormous. For a man so often criticised by his contemporaries for being, supposedly, detached from real life, he was remarkably successful in keeping his attention focused on 'the way the world was going'.[9] To speak for culture, he said again and again, is not enough without acting to make it prevail, and he followed his own advice: he was both analyst and activist, a combination by no means characteristic of all important thinkers. While his New York lecture could be dismissed angrily as the unsought advice of yet another snooty Englishman, there were many American writers at the time (and there were to be more in the near future) no less patriotic than their outraged compatriots, who would have approved Arnold's comments. Henry James, firmly settled in England and already convinced of Arnold's importance as a critic, went so far as to publish an article on Arnold while his visit to 'the great country of the Philistines' was actually in progress. He hoped that Arnold would find things to admire, but thought more was to be gained from him being disappointed, 'for such disappointments . . . are inspiring, and any record he should make of them would have a high value'.[10] Arnold was too sure of what he would find to be disappointed, though he may have been surprised at the receptiveness of many young Americans to both his analysis and the proposed solution. The emergence of modernism is bound, inextricably, to the concept and nature of the remnant, and the American response is particularly important.

It has often been pointed out that, of the writers making up Anglo-American modernism, considerably more were American than English: it is also the case that few of those writers made their pioneering contributions in America, but moved instead to Europe, mainly to London at first, and then, after the First World War, to Paris. Some lived permanently in exile, some took British nationality, though neither decision was necessarily allowed to eclipse their Americanism; others, increasingly, returned home. Many of the individual stories involved nationalistic hostility, whether directed by or at the writer, and the fiercest criticism came from the American whom James once typified as being 'a provincial who is terribly bent upon taking, in the fullness of ages, his revenge'.[11]

The complexity of the issue can be seen in W. D. Howells, who was one of the writers who stayed in America. Although his own fiction was decisively influenced by European models he refused to follow the example of James and move to Europe, arguing instead that a genuine American literature would never be established if writers rejected the challenge and inspiration of their own society. Related to this conviction was a streak of Anglophobia that surfaced whenever British critics took a high line with American writers: Arnold was a prominent target among these critics. Yet, prickly as Howells could be, he did not collapse into insularity. A perceptive and broad-minded critic, he was throughout the 1880s and 1890s a leading spokesman in America for the revolutionary artistic changes taking place in Europe.

Nor did his disagreement with James lead to any lessening of his admiration for this greatest of all American novelists. By arranging the American serialisation of James's novels he was helping to make it financially possible for his compatriot to continue living in England, and when American critics attacked James as unpatriotic it was the response of Howells rather than that of James himself they learned to fear. Edwin Cady has noted that in the later years of his life Howells's attitude to Britain softened: he 'was not conquered but he was reconciled: the war was over'.[12] In so far as that war had to do with the novel, Howells was satisfied that American fiction had proved its ability to break from the long dominance by Britain: a still deeper satisfaction came with the realisation that British and American fiction were now subject to the same influences. Both had been Europeanised:

> Our fiction so far as it really exists is of the European and
> not the English make and the newer English fiction, so far as
> it really exists, is not of the English, but of the European
> make, the American make.[13]

The final clause of that observation seems to imply that American novelists had now moved so far beyond British fiction that they had actively reversed the burden of influence, but in 1912 there was no substantial justification for such a claim, and it is possible that Howells was making the subtler point that because American novelists had been more open to the European example they would be better able to benefit from it. That Howells was probably not fully informed at this point in his life about recent developments in literature (and he was, after all, seventy-five years old) can be seen in his belief that Britain had retained its ascendancy over America in poetry, precisely the area of early modern literature in which young American writers were beginning to make themselves most powerfully felt.[14] More curious is the fact that Howells's understandable pride in the growing stature of American literature was not sufficiently shared by younger writers to make them want to stay in America, to follow his example rather than that of James. The number of American writers who came to Britain and stayed for varying periods of time was very substantial. They included Bret Harte, Stephen Crane, Gertrude Atherton, Harold Frederic, Henry Harland, Robert Frost, Conrad Aiken, Hilda Doolittle, John Oliver Hobbes; together with influential figures in the business of literature; the great photographer Alvin Langdon Coburn; and painters such as Whistler and Sargent. The most important of the young writers who moved to Britain before the First World War were, of course, Ezra Pound in 1908, and T. S. Eliot in 1914.

None of these writers was drawn to Britain by illusions about the modernity of its literature. Indeed, James and Pound, covering between them the late Victorian and modern periods, were very similar in adopting iconoclastic rather than admiring roles. Both constantly complained at the philistinism of most British writers and urged them to look to Europe for artistic education: they also both maintained close connections with developments in America. In his obituary article on James, T. S. Eliot described their cultural situation in terms that recall Howell's comments on the changing relationship between English and American literature, though with a different kind of emphasis: 'It is the final perfection, the consummation of an American to become, not an Englishman but a European – something which no born European, no person of any European nationality can become.'[15] Why they should have been drawn to London at all rather than Paris, Vienna or Berlin – all of which were more vital centres of cosmopolitan modernism – has to be explained by the dominance of American by British literature until late in the nineteenth century, as Howells willingly acknowledged: 'American literature was not derived from the folk-lore of the Red Indians, but was . . . a condition of English literature.'[16] As part of that 'condition', and in spite of the tone of critical superiority which Howells resented, there was a warm appreciation of American literature by British readers that stretched back to at least the start of Victoria's reign, while the assumption that a writer could be recognised in Britain though neglected in America lasted well into the present century. When her novels were turned down by New York publishers Gertrude Atherton decided that if she 'made a reputation in the literary headquarters of the world, America would be forced to acknowledge me'.[17] Pound, looking back on his early career, made the same point more colourfully and egotistically: 'The U.S. thirty years ago was still a colony of London so far as culture was concerned . . . the only way I could educate the educatable minority in the United States was to come to London.'[18] British novelists and poets had long been a central part of the literary consciousness of Americans, and when young American writers moved to Britain in the late nineteenth and early twentieth centuries their mood was less one of emulation than of reaction. Like British writers of their respective generations they were determined to bury Victorianism, and that determination was sharpened by their being, in certain other respects, outsiders. But they did not urge British writers to bring themselves up to date by looking to America: like Howells, they pointed to the shared culture of Europe. Where they differed from Howells, and allied themselves more comfortably with James, was in their conviction that Europe rather than America was the place to be.

The argument against America was put most forcefully by James in his study of Hawthorne published in 1879, and in his replies to criticism of the book, most notably a review by Howells. James argued that Hawthorne had suffered as an artist because he was writing in a country that lacked tradition: compared with Europe, America was 'provincial'. It has since been pointed out by many critics that similar views were expressed by Hawthorne himself, but even so the list compiled by James of the European blessings not available to Americans might have been deliberately calculated to arouse republican, democratic fury. It ranged from monarchy, court and aristocracy, through country houses and thatched cottages, to Eton, Harrow, Oxford and Ascot. What is left to the American novelist, James asked, when all this is removed?[19] In his review of *Hawthorne*, Howells answered: 'We have the whole of human life remaining, and a social structure presenting the only fresh and novel opportunities left to fiction, opportunities manifold and inexhaustible. No man would have known less what to do with that dreary and worn-out paraphernalia than Hawthorne.'[20] James replied to Howells in his firmest manner:

> I sympathise even less with your protest against the idea that
> it takes an old civilisation to set a novelist in motion – a
> proposition that seems to me so true as to be a truism. It is
> on manners, customs, usages, habits, forms, upon all these
> things matured and established, that a novelist lives – they
> are the very stuff his work is made of; and in saying that in
> the absence of those 'dreary and worn-out paraphernalia'
> which I enumerate as being wanting in American society, 'we
> have simply the whole of human life left', you beg (to my
> sense) the question.[21]

Either James was being deliberately unfair to Howells or he did not
see the main point of the criticism. The question is 'begged'
because, for James, nothing is left of life for the novelist to write
about once the traditions of an 'old civilisation' are removed. But
Howells had given a perfectly straight answer to the question. The
novelist has left confronting him 'a social structure presenting the
only fresh and novel opportunities left to fiction', or in other words
modern democratic society.

   James did not, of course, turn his back on modern life: nor did
he write uncritically of his adopted country. While his novels drew
extensively on the customs and forms of old Europe they also
demonstrated his conviction that much of this European 'paraphernalia' was 'worn-out', an attitude to be shared and taken much
further by Pound and Eliot. It can even be argued that by
pioneering the 'international theme' James was confronting the
changing orientation of modern life in ways that were beyond
Howells's imagination; here, after all, was not simply glorification
of old civilisation but a wonderfully subtle exploration of the old in
continuous and ambivalent conflict with the new. Yet what James
rejected as a possible concern of his art was exactly what Howells
accused him of rejecting – the challenge of many of the most
characteristic features of democratic society; and it is fair to talk of
rejection because James was conscious of the problem. In his
preface to *The Princess Casamassima* he explains the process by
which he considered and discarded the possibility of placing a
genuinely working-class character at the centre of his novel. 'There
are degrees of feeling,' he pointed out, 'the muffled, the faint, the
just sufficient, the barely intelligent, as we may say; and the acute,
the intense, the complete, in a word – the power to be finely aware
and richly responsible.'[22] For James it was the possessor of the

second set of qualities alone who was capable of providing interest in the new art of fiction. What was rejected in such a selection James made clear in his criticism of Zola, an author who had attempted to make central to his work the kind of modern experience James himself largely avoided. What James admired in Zola was his 'courage and confidence': what he disliked, or feared, was Zola's concern with 'numbers':

> It was the fortune, it was in a manner the doom, of *Les Rougon-Macquart* to deal with things almost always in gregarious form, to be a picture of *numbers*, of classes, crowds, confusions, movements, industries . . . The individual life is, if not wholly absent, reflected in coarse and common, in generalised terms . . . It produces the effect of a mass of imagery in which shades are sacrificed, the effect of character and passion in a lump or by the ton. The fullest, the most characteristic episodes affect us like a sounding chorus or procession, as with a hubbub of voices and a multitudinous tread of feet.[23]

In a particularly neat summarising phrase James points to how in Zola 'breadth and energy supply the place of penetration'.[24] The two methods are seen as antithetical, with psychological penetration attaining such centrality that the outer, material world comes to exist only through the individual consciousness. In this criticism of Zola we can see rehearsed the polarisation of critical attitudes in James's break with Wells over the irreconcilable demands of Life and Art and also Woolf's dismissal of the materialistic base of fiction in the name of an art that centres on the inner consciousness as the only possible reality.

It is not necessary to disagree with James's belief that the novelist's prime concern must be with the 'individual life' to recognise the comprehensive nature of what he himself excludes by this kind of emphasis – classes, crowds, industries, multitudes, masses, numbers; together with the characteristic sounds, noise and coarseness that accompany these phenomena of any industrial, urbanised society. None of them features in the list of the necessary institutions of an old civilisation he offered in *Hawthorne*, even though, ironically, the particular civilisation invoked was also the most industrialised country in the world. England was preferred to America because a choice between old and new was still possible. America was all new, all industries, crowds, and loud democratic assertion, an unavoidable portent of things to come. 'Henrietta . . . does smell of the Future,' Ralph Touchett observes in *The Portrait of a Lady*; 'It almost knocks one down.'[25] Ralph is himself one of the 'alienated Americans' who are to provide the 'human interest' for Henrietta Stackpole's newspaper articles, and the contrast between his kind of Europeanised sensitivity and Henrietta's American brashness runs throughout James's novels. The satirical tone is not unaffectionate, and not all of the American expatriates who seek European refinement are admired, but there is a firm tendency to leave America to those who are committed to its social modernity and treat it as a place of banishment for those who are not. Madame Merle's farewell line in *The Portrait of a Lady* is, 'I shall go to America,' and as her fellow-American Mrs Touchett observes on hearing the news: 'To America? She must have done something very bad.'[26] The reader is also clearly meant to mark up to Henrietta Stackpole's credit her decision 'to marry Mr Bantling and locate right here in London'.[27]

In James's later novels these kinds of contrasting attitudes to Europe take a sharper and more specific form. The very title of *The Ambassadors* indicates that cultural relations between Europe and America have become so complex that diplomatic negotiations are needed to sort them out. Strether is an unusual figure in James's work in that while sensitive to the pull of Europe he chooses to return to America: the sadness of what that involves is heightened by the financial manipulation of Mrs Newsome, the bustling noisiness of the Pococks, and Waymarsh's grumpy dissatisfaction with Europe. The source of American power is fixed more firmly than ever by James in industrial wealth, and while this is given a slightly comic touch there is nothing lighthearted in the way that Chad's moral coarseness is finally demonstrated. He returns to America to devote his future to the science of advertising: very little in James's scheme of things could be worse than that. Europe is either ceasing to perform its transforming magic or the power of money is now regarded as the greater force. James's next novel *The Golden Bowl* provides some evidence for the second of these alternatives. Like Madame Merle before her, Charlotte Verver acknowledges personal defeat in Europe by self-imposed banishment to America. She does not want to go, but at least she takes with her the works of art that her husband's hard-earned money has been devoted to accumulating. Adam Verver's dream is to release his hometown from its 'bondage of ugliness' by building a museum:

> It hadn't merely, his plan, all the sanctions of civilization: it was positively civilization condensed, concrete, consummate, set down by his hands as a house on a rock – a house from whose open doors and windows, open to grateful, to thirsty millions, the higher, the highest knowledge would shine out to bless the land.

Verver does not live in Europe, but makes periodic visits to take advantage of 'changes and chances', to refresh his 'sensibility to the currents of the market', and transport civilisation to America. He is a missionary, an evangel. The museum will 'propagate' his 'religion', his 'passion for perfection at any price'.[28]

Perhaps James was simply recording a gathering trend that would eventually take Europeans across the Atlantic in order to see or study many of the artistic masterpieces of their own civilisation; perhaps he was approving the preservation of art often neglected in Europe. What he certainly did not believe was that millions of Americans were thirsting for the experience of artistic perfection. Nor did he believe this about Europeans. If America typified for him the materialism and vulgarity of modern life, he soon observed the same qualities all around him in his adopted country. As he became more critical of England he also became more and more determined that his own art should epitomise the refinement and subtlety that were being crushed out of existence by mass society. He shared with Verver a 'passion for perfection' and he was also willing to pursue it at 'any price', but he was closer to Mrs Gereth in *The Spoils of Poynton* (1897) in seeing his personal dilemma as a fight for survival against rampant philistinism: 'The world is full of cheap gimcracks, in this awful age, and they're thrust in at one at every turn. They'd be thrust in here, on top of my treasures, my own. Who would save *them* for me – I ask you who *would*?'[29] Who is to save the nation's literary treasures in such an awful age, and the related question who they are to be saved for, reverberate obsessively throughout the period.

The clearest indication that not many people shared James's concern with the pursuit of artistic perfection was the failure of virtually every novelist of any innovative importance at the turn of the century to earn a living by writing fiction. In his series of short

stories about the artistic life, James portrayed the modern novelist as a
lonely, isolated figure, forced to live in solitude by his Flaubertian
dedication to artistic form. For this kind of Artist-Novelist, life seems
hardly to exist except as the subject for Art: he is a 'disfranchised
monk'.[30] In return for his total dedication he can expect to receive
reassurance from a small number of sensitive readers that his Art will
outlive his body, and critical scorn from everyone else. His recurrent
nightmare is that he is unworthy of the task he has set himself, that his
life has been thrown away, like that of Max Beerbohm's Enoch
Soames who, tormented by critical neglect, sells his soul to the
devil for a glimpse of the British Museum catalogue one hundred
years hence, only to find that his books have remained unread.[31]
Like Enoch Soames, many of James's fictional novelists console
themselves with the belief that their long years of suffering and
neglect will be rewarded by eventual recognition: it will be belated,
necessarily, and perhaps posthumous. Philip Vincent, whose collected works are being illustrated by the unnamed artist in 'The Real
Thing', is the fortunate type of such a novelist. He is:

> One of the writers of our day – the rarest of the novelists –
> who, long neglected by the multitudinous vulgar and dearly
> prized by the attentive . . . had had the happy fortune of
> seeing, late in life, the dawn and then the full light of a
> higher criticism – an estimate in which, on the part of the
> public, there was something really of expiation.[32]

To most major mid-Victorian novelists, Philip Vincent's career
would have meant little, though it does describe, unerringly, what
was to be the experience of many early modern novelists. The
career graph charting early neglect, years of critical scorn sweetened
only by the praise of a few discerning critics, discouraging sales,
and an eventual adulation that came almost too late to affect the
life, was to recur in varying degrees with James, Meredith, Conrad,
Joyce, Lawrence and Woolf.

The Victorian prototype was not a novelist but the poet Robert
Browning, with whom, as G. K. Chesterton pointed out, there
entered into modern literary history a new phenomenon: 'the author
whom it is fashionable to boast of not understanding'.[33] The
notorious difficulty of Browning's poetry dominates every phase of
his career: there was hardly a mid-Victorian critic or reviewer who
did not have ready to hand some witticism about it. He was

not infrequently thought of as mad or at least unbalanced. The publication of several of his early books had to be financed by his father and commercial distrust was fully justified: the first of his books failed to sell a single copy. He had a small number of loyal supporters in the early difficult years, but even Elizabeth Barrett told him during their famous courtship that his poetry was too difficult to understand and urged him to write more clearly.[34] He took little notice. The immense popularity that came to him fairly late in life marked a change in the attitude of readers rather than any compromise on his part. It was now the obscurity of his poems that made them the objects of extravagant devotion. He regarded with wry tolerance the Societies founded to honour his work, and, anticipating Chesterton, noted that 'readers' were being transformed into 'students':

> I write, airily, 'Quoth Tom to Jack, one New Year's Day,'
> and one 'Student' wants to know who Jack was, – another
> sees no difficulty there, but much in Tom's entity, – while a
> third, getting easily over both stumbling blocks, says, 'But –
> *which* New Year's Day?'[35]

In spite of the comic side of the Browning Societies, there was much in this transformed reputation of Browning in the 1880s that has to be seen as symptomatic of wider changes taking place in the attitudes of writers towards their audiences and in what certain groups of readers were beginning to expect from literature. It was, for example, to Browning's credit that he had for so long been unpopular as well as difficult. This served to dissociate him from conventional Victorianism, as also did the element of sexual frankness in his poetry. What worked to his disadvantage among some other readers and younger writers was his unshakeable religious belief or optimism which could be regarded as fixing him as very conventionally Victorian, and the bluff unartistic image he often cultivated in his personal life. He was at times a little more like Trollope than his late Victorian admirers cared to admit.

This could matter, because as novelists were insisting more forcefully than ever before that their work demanded the same kind of artistic dedication as that of the poet or painter, it was becoming important for every aspect of their lives (including dress) to reflect that dedication. It was pointed out earlier that the extreme manifestations of French bohemianism were never really taken up by late Victorian novelists, and after the Wilde trial there was, even

among many aesthetes, a marked reaction against styles of dress
and manners that offered too flamboyant a means of artistic
identification: among some novelists it even became a matter of
care that they should not look 'literary'.[36] But for the writer to look
the part it wasn't necessary to be a genuine dandy (like Wilde), or
wear a velvet jacket (like the young Stevenson), or knickerbocker
suits (like Richard Le Gallienne). There were subtler, more manly,
fashions that could be adopted. From the 1890s onwards the
slightly baggy suit, broad or bow tie (cloth or velvet), soft hat and
hair worn slightly longer than usual, became recognisable indicators
of an 'artistic' temperament, while the bohemianism of France still
allowed for (in some senses insisted on) an appropriate eclecticism,
typified by the photograph of himself that Joyce had taken before
he left Paris in 1902. He is shown wearing a black knee-length
overcoat, a black broad-brimmed hat, and what Richard Ellmann
describes as a 'long-suffering look'.[37] That the sensitivity of the
artist is observable from his face, hands or general posture, was
part of the neo-romantic image, as also was the pride of being able
to boast of having spent at least part of one's early years in a garret.
The pervasiveness and youthfulness of this view of the artist were
acknowledged and given a dash of bitter reality by Conrad. 'I
presume bohemianism has no terrors for you,' he wrote to
Cunninghame Graham in 1897. 'It isn't pretty at my age but it's
one of those facts one must face – with concealed disgust.'[38] The
local and temporary aspects of these various assertions of artistic
identity were often trivial, but the underlying assumptions of
specialness, separateness, and superiority, were not.

The clothes worn by a novelist could, for example, signify
success to the public at large and, at the same time, failure to the
insider. The most potent image of this kind was that of the writer
who looked like a businessman. If the image was justified then it
meant that the writer had sold out artistically: if it wasn't then it
meant he was an enigma. Either way, it was a difficult perception
to convey in fiction without it revealing the bitterness or envy
created by unpopularity. In *New Grub Street* Biffen risks his life to
save the manuscript of his novel from the fire that destroys his
lodgings. Asked by a sympathetic neighbour, who 'kept an oil
shop', whether he has lost anything valuable, Biffen replies: 'All
my books burnt!' The neighbour thinks he means his account
books until, 'the author' corrects 'this misapprehension'.[39] Biffen

lives in poverty to write a novel that is, in money terms, worthless: his reverse image was the successful author whose novels were indistinguishable from account books and therefore worthless in artistic terms. It was this aspect of the literary world that James explored in 'The Lesson of the Master', one of the most ironic and ambiguous of his short stories. Paul Overt, the young aspiring novelist and 'student of fine prose', notices on his return to England that he can no longer recognise 'the artist and man of letters by his personal "type", the mould of his face, the character of his head and even the indications of his dress'. In England, novelists have developed the habit of 'sinking the profession instead of advertising it'. When he first meets Henry St George – the 'master' of the story's title and named to epitomise the successful English novelist – his outward image is of someone who 'might have passed for a lucky stockbroker – a gentleman driving eastward every morning from a sanitary suburb in a smart dog-cart'. St George's prosperity is a certain indication that he has sold out his considerable artistic talent. How otherwise could such material comfort come to a serious novelist? The 'lesson', brutally demonstrated to the young idealist, is that he should not follow the Master. The way that St George's public image is gradually revealed as a true reflection of his artistic corruption was reversed by James in 'The Private Life', the story in which he tried to capture the bewilderment that Browning inspired in him. The trivialised social behaviour of Clare Vawdrey is so completely false to the genius of his writing that it can be explained only by acknowledging that there are two Vawdreys: his real self sits in a darkened room writing while his *Doppelgänger* goes off to socialise. Leon Edel has argued that James's preoccupation with Browning's character came from 'a dichotomy which he envisaged in his own life', and it does seem clear that James was responding to similarities in their literary careers.[41] But beyond this he was analysing a developing trend in the literary life that is best appreciated by taking Meredith into account as well.

The originality and the difficulty of Meredith's work were acknowledged by reviewers from the start, though his earliest books were not received with the blank indifference that Browning experienced. His equivalent moment of personal shock came in 1859 with the banning of *Richard Feverel*, which provoked in Meredith a scorn for the intelligence and taste of the reading public that he was never to lose. 'Oh heaven!' he wrote to Samuel Lucas in 1859 'Why have you advertised me as a "popular" author? Isn't that almost a fraud on the public?'[42] The public responded by largely ignoring Meredith's novels. During the 1860s and early 1870s much of his regular income came from anonymous political journalism and an influential part-time job as a reader for Chapman and Hall: neither activity served to correct his conviction that the reading public was both obtuse and hypocritical. Then in the later 1870s, beginning with *Beauchamp's Career* (1876) and reaching a peak with *The Egoist* (1879) and *Diana of the Crossways* (1885), there was a startling change in his reputation. It coincided with the period of Browning's greatest fame, and comparisons were frequently drawn between the two writers by reviewers. Like Browning, Meredith was difficult, incomprehensible to the general reader. He was, Arabella Shore claimed in 1879, 'the private delight of those who can discover genius for themselves – a choice if a somewhat isolated, ground'. She was not, however, content to keep the 'private delight' to herself: Meredith could and should be more widely read. All that was needed was for 'some great critic' to explain why readers should admire him. The only reason he had not already been sufficiently recognised was that his books were weighted with too much 'subtle and profound thought' for the 'popular reader': perhaps Meredith is difficult at times but 'the indirect expressions embody so much wit, or sense or fancy, that we love the work the more for the trouble it has given us'.[43]

If this article by Arabella Shore was merely a freak response then it could be sensibly ignored, but it was actually mild in comparison with what was to come. Meredith was hailed as 'a giant' among English novelists, a prose Shakespeare, he had 'pondered on man and his destiny till his insight has perceived whole regions and vistas of human possibility that as yet are untenanted'.[44] In 1885 Gissing recommended to his brother that he should read Meredith because 'George Eliot never did such work, and Thackeray is shallow in comparison'.[45] A few days later, helping to educate his sister this time, Gissing explained why she too should read Meredith:

> For the last thirty years he has been producing work un-
> speakably above the best of any living writer and yet no one
> reads him outside a small circle of highly cultured people.
> Perhaps that is better than being popular, a hateful word.[46]

In one sense Meredith's late Victorian admirers were not really saying anything that had not been said about him for years past. W. E. Henley who played an important part in the shift in Meredith's reputation hailed him as an 'artist' of 'genius' and called for *The Egoist* to be 'read and studied as it deserves', but at the same time he placed at least some of the blame for public indifference on Meredith himself: 'The better half of his genius is always suffering eclipse from the worse half. He writes with the pen of a great artist in his left hand, and the razor of a spiritual suicide in his right.'[47] But if the sentiments were not new, there were more people uttering them in louder voices, and the points of emphasis had changed drastically.

What might happen to an unpopular author who after a lifetime spent quietly dedicated to his art suddenly finds himself at the centre of public interest, is the subject of James's short story 'The Death of the Lion'. Neil Paraday is 'discovered' by a 'big blundering newspaper' and is 'proclaimed and anointed'. Wearied by years of isolation and tempted by public recognition he convinces himself that 'the phantasmagoric town was probably after all less of a battlefield than the haunted study' and moves into Society.[48] He enters a world that really is phantasmagoric, where he is lionised by fashionable hostesses, smart literary journalists, trivial party-goers and self-seeking popular novelists, none of whom has any interest in his work. His excursion from the haunted study leads to the loss of the manuscript of his latest, and finest, book, and to his own death. The story is told by Paraday's literary executor, a loyal and genuine admirer. As with James's other stories of the artistic life, what we have in 'The Death of the Lion' is a parable compounded of wish-fulfilment and fear that offers finally an unresolvable paradox: in this case, the artist is unable to live without recognition and is destroyed by the only kind of recognition possible in such an age.

Meredith was wiser, or perhaps more cynical, than Neil Paraday, though he assigned to himself a slightly different quality: 'A Stoic habit of taking hostile opinions smilingly has hardened me somewhat to smile in the same manner at praise.'[49] In fact he never had accepted hostile criticism 'smilingly', but as the great theorist of comedy he could now well afford to grin at the praise. If the financial terms and the size of print runs on his new novels were still not high by late Victorian popular standards, they were considerably better than anything Meredith had previously enjoyed. For *Lord Ormont and his Aminta* (1894) he received £17 per thousand words for its serialisation in *The Pall Mall Magazine*, a $22\frac{1}{2}\%$ royalty on the three-volume edition of 1500 copies, and a 25% royalty on the one-volume edition.[50] He had always been careful to keep a personal interest in his copyrights, usually by leasing them for a specified number of years, and he now benefited greatly from the uniform and collected editions of his works that publishers were eager to produce. Less tangible, though no less gratifying honours were also forthcoming. In 1892 Meredith succeeded Tennyson as President of the Society of Authors, ten years later he was awarded the Order of Merit, while his house at Box Hill in Surrey became a literary shrine where young writers could talk with the ageing author whose first books had been published in the despised mid-Victorian period and who, indifferent to public taste and untainted by popularity, had worked on to achieve success at last. In spite of the many parallels with Browning's career, there were also important differences that worked to Meredith's advantage. He was not plagued by some of the sillier admirers that Browning had to endure: it was often the younger writers and critics who looked to Meredith for guidance and who had sometimes been helped by him during his years as a publisher's reader; and although he was a self-proclaimed optimist – in itself a curious phenomenon amidst so much youthful pessimism – Meredith's Nature worship and faith in the potential of women were more acceptable than Browning's religious beliefs. Meredith also looked the part to perfection: no one would ever mistake him for a businessman. When, in 1928, Virginia Woolf praised the now virtually forgotten Meredith as 'a great innovator' who had helped prepare the way for the modern novel, she remembered also the legend, 'the fame of George Meredith, who sat with the head of a Greek poet on his shoulders in a suburban villa beneath Box Hill'.[51]

In all of these real and fictional literary careers there are certain recurrent values and attitudes. 'Popular' has clearly become a very dirty word indeed unless it is used to indicate a certain level of success attained after years of neglect: to describe oneself as an 'unpopular author' has ceased to be simply a factual statement of poor market expectations (though that may still be involved) and has become a boast. Neither Meredith nor James – nor Gissing and Conrad who should also be included here – set out with the intention of being unpopular. On the contrary, they all yearned for commercial success: James even conscientiously studied popular novels to see where he was going wrong.[52] They were not so eager for fame that they could have considered lowering their artistic standards to achieve it, and if the constant urging by reviewers that they should write more clearly in order to display their genius to its best advantage didn't mean that, then it was difficult to imagine what it did mean. The standard of commercial success they carried with them was that attained by their mid-Victorian equivalents, and they had no doubt that their own generation had not only maintained but improved the artistic stature of the novel. Gone was the formal naivety of the Victorians; and prudery, if still far from banished, was on its way out. The novel was no longer entertainment that might become Art. It now had a theory behind it. It was *discutable*, fully conscious of itself, highly wrought, philosophical, challenging, subtle, teasingly intellectual. The novelist had metamorphosed himself into an Artist, and described himself proudly as such. His novels were works of art and hailed as works of art by discriminating critics but, for the vast majority of readers, entertainment they certainly were not. It was the age that took the blame, and that meant democracy.

The precedents for regarding democracy as inherently hostile to cultural excellence were so long established that considered in relation to them the mid-Victorian period seemed merely a fleeting phase. In his New York lecture Arnold called on Plato and Isaiah to support his contention that 'the majority is and must be in general unsound everywhere'.[53] He was unusual in drawing on the Old Testament, though classical analogies were often favoured, for the reason put by George Moore:

> Democratic art! Art is the direct antithesis to democracy . . .
> Athens! a few thousand citizens who owned many thousand
> slaves, call that democracy! No! What I am speaking of is
> modern democracy – the mass. The mass can only appreciate
> simple and *naive* emotions, puerile prettiness, above all conven-
> tionalities.[54]

Gissing fully shared this conviction. His novel of failed working-class aspirations he called *Demos*, and to the chapter in *The Nether World* which describes an August Bank Holiday he gave the title 'Io Saturnalia', the day when 'the slaves of industrialism don the *pileus*', the cap of temporary freedom. Following some heavy irony about what the 'philosophical mind' could make of fairground games and contests, he observes: 'How characteristic of a high-spirited people that nowhere could be found any amusement appealing to the mere mind.'[55] In an early article called 'The Day of the Rabblement' James Joyce quoted with approval Giordano Bruno's statement: 'No man can be a lover of the true or the good unless he abhors the multitude.'[56] In a similarly uncompromising mood in *Diana of the Crossways* Meredith pointed to the 'unfailing aboriginal democratic old monster' who, hostile to 'brainstuff', lies in wait ready to 'pull down' the philosophic novelist, and made explicit the link with political change:

> You are acutely conscious of yonder old monster when he is
> mouthing at you in politics. Be wary of him in the heart:
> especially be wary of the disrelish of brainstuff. You must
> feed on something. Matter that is not nourishing to brains
> can help to constitute nothing but the bodies which are
> pitched on rubbish heaps.[57]

Blame is allotted primarily to the naive taste of a reading public that corrupts the finer instincts of novelists, tempting them to become suppliers of rubbish. Given a lead – and Meredith's long diatribe is advanced as a battle-cry – some novelists at least would be eager to produce better work:

> Dozens of writers will be in at yawning breach [i.e. posterity]
> if only perusers will rally to the philosophic standard. They
> are sick of the woodeny puppetry they dispense as on a race-
> course to the roaring frivolous. Well, if not dozens, half-
> dozens; gallant pens are alive; one can speak of them in the
> plural.[58]

The talent is available, so is the will to break away from the degrading occupation of dispensing 'woodeny puppetry' to the 'roaring frivolous', but high courage is also required, for the 'half-dozens' of novelists who take Meredith's advice can expect to have only 'a dozen for an audience, for a commencement'.[59] It was a reflection of Meredith's own experience, and the adulation of the younger writers who were now paying him homage helped justify the moral he offered: 'The example is the thing; sacrifices must be expected. The example might, one hopes, create a taste.'[60] Diana Warwick, whose writing career is so unconvincingly portrayed in

Diana of the Crossways, soon learns to develop the approved Meredithean attitudes. Convinced that what she writes is 'doomed to unpopularity', she resolves that it shall therefore represent 'a victory in style', and in moods of 'angry cynicism' she even composes 'phrases as baits for the critics to quote, condemnatory of the attractiveness of the work'.[61] That seems rather foolish when one considers that a handful of those critics are likely to be the only readers she has, but her scorn, and Meredith's, for the intelligence of the general reader was shared by many real and imaginary novelists of the time. Like Egremont in Gissing's *Thyrza* they believe: 'If one goes on the assumption that the ill word of the mob is equivalent to high praise, one will not, as a rule, be far wrong, in matters of literature.'[62]

Although the mob, the mass, democracy, tended to have the blame allotted to them for their insensitivity and ignorance, the novelist should not be accepted too easily as a passive victim. The cynical enjoyment Diana Warwick derives from laying stylistic traps for hostile reviewers has its real-life counterpart in the wilful resolution to write solely for the self that typifies the later works of James and Meredith. Satisfied as he was with his new-found admirers, Meredith took his revenge for the long years of neglect by writing his final novels in his most obscure and convoluted manner. When reviewers attacked the opening of *One of Our Conquerers* as virtually incomprehensible – which it is – Meredith responded by pretending to believe that 'literary playfulness in description is antipathetic to our present taste'.[63] James said of *Lord Ormont and his Aminta* that it filled him with a 'critical rage, an artistic fury ... I doubt if any equal quantity of extravagant verbiage, of airs and graces, of phrases and attitudes, of obscurities and alembications, ever *started* less their subject, ever contributed less of a statement – told the reader less of what the reader needs to know.'[64] There is an irony built into these comments that James could not have foreseen at the time. Early in the following year, 1895, the failure of *Guy Domville* – 'hooted at, as I was hooted at myself, by a brutal mob, and fruitless of any of the consequences for which I have striven' – brought an end to James's attempt to make money and win public esteem as a dramatist.[65] It confirmed his contempt for what popularity could involve, and, as he turned away from the theatre, inaugurated the period of his late fiction, the complexity of which was to provoke precisely the kind of 'critical rage' that *Lord Ormont* had provoked in him. Reviewers would soon point to the 'extravagant verbiage', 'airs and graces', 'obscurities and alembications' of novels like *The Awkward Age* (1899), *The Wings of the Dove* (1902) and *The Golden Bowl* (1904) and ask whether such work ever 'told the reader less of what the reader needs to know'. In May 1899 James wrote bitterly to Howard Sturgis:

> That's right – *be* one of the few! I greatly applaud the tact
> with which you tell me that scarce a human being will
> understand a word, or an intention, or an artistic element or
> glimmer of any sort, of my book. I tell *myself* – and the
> 'reviews' tell me – such truths in much cruder fashion.[66]

The most fundamental cause of discontent was the apparent refusal by modern novelists to offer a straightforward narrative. As early as 1886 W. L. Courtney had pointed out that only at this particular moment in time could a novelist like Meredith be 'acceptable, for only in such an age could his peculiar gifts win for themselves recognition or even tolerance'.[67] In this respect, Meredith is clearly seen as representative of a trend rather than an individual oddity. The reason why 'so many novels are such hard reading' was given by Courtney as the 'conscious and wilful neglect' of story.[68] It was easy to respond to a complaint of this kind by pointing out that no novelist of any value was a 'mere' story-teller, and still be able to deplore the strong narratives and moral naivety of popular fiction where it was axiomatically assumed that the story was virtually everything. As a writer in *Literature* observed a few years later: 'The fact is the average English reader demands above all things a good story – quocumque modo a good story – and one which ends happily.'[69] If that really was what the average reader demanded, he wasn't getting it from some of the most important novelists of the day. The obsession with psychological analysis and narrative techniques was rendering the strong story-line suspect, while endings were not only not happy but were ceasing to exist at all in any traditional sense. From Isabel Archer's unexplained decision to return to Osmond at the close of *The Portrait of a Lady*, through the uncertainty in *Lord Jim* whether Jim has redeemed his lost honour, to the inconclusive discussion between Birkin and Ursula in *Women in Love*, we find the refusal to round off stories that was to appear to frustrated readers an abdication of the novelist's responsibility, and to students of modernism an expression of necessary, unavoidable

relativism.[70] The changing nature of fictional endings was important, as Wilde's Miss Prism understood to perfection, and the
epigrammatic firmness of her realisation of what 'fiction means'
also served to heighten the seriousness of the wider social issues at
stake. For Dickens it had been an unshakeable law that 'a story-
teller and a story-reader should establish a mutual understanding
as soon as possible'.[71] But the new novelists had hardly anyone to
tell their stories to, and it is difficult to see how a mutual
understanding can be established when no one is listening. The
novelist was now an Artist and simple storytelling was as vulgar as the
kind of reader who needed to be entertained by that simple a story.

The changing attitudes were parodied with breath-taking brilli-
ance by James in *The Turn of the Screw*, a ghost story, the most
traditional of tales, placed in the most traditional of settings, 'as, on
Christmas eve in an old house, a strange tale should essentially be'.
The narrator asks who will provide the audience for a tale even
more gruesome than the last? Who will stay to hear it?:

> 'Everybody will stay!'
> '*I* will – and *I* will!' cried the ladies whose departure had
> been fixed.
> Mrs Griffin, however, expressed the need for a little more
> light. 'Who was it she was in love with?'
> 'The story will tell,' I took upon myself to reply.
> 'Oh, I can't wait for the story!'
> 'The story *won't* tell,' said Douglas; 'not in any literal,
> vulgar way.'
> 'More's the pity then. That's the only way I ever under-
> stand.'[72]

'The ladies', who do *not* stay to hear what the story will *not* tell
them, are the conventional devourers of sensation novels who
demand that all shall be explained: Mrs Griffin is the romantic
reader who requires a love element to bring a story to life. Douglas
is the modern storyteller who rejects such narrative crudities and
tells stories of a kind that most readers do not 'understand'. Those
who remain to listen are the select few, readers concerned not with
'vulgar' literalism, but with the subtleties of narration. They are
rewarded with a story that, after more than eighty years of critical
scrutiny, refuses to divulge exactly what kind of story it is.

Conrad, too, restructured traditional narrative forms, and although he did not usually do this with the kind of sustained critical

playfulness demonstrated by James in *The Turn of the Screw*, he
was similarly prompted, by doubts about the existence of his
audience, to pioneer new effects from ancient methods. No
narratives could be more straightforward than a seaman's yarns:
'they have a direct simplicity', we are told in *Heart of Darkness*,
'the whole meaning of which lies within the shell of a cracked nut'.
But Conrad's narrator Marlow is no ordinary seaman, and the
'yarns' he tells, though often dealing with the material of boys'
adventure stories, are far from simple and never direct. 'The
meaning of an episode' for Marlow:

> Was not inside like a kernel but outside, enveloping the tale
> which brought it out only as a glow brings out a haze, in the
> likeness of one of these misty halos that sometimes are made
> visible by the spectral illumination of moonshine.[73]

If it is possible at all to translate those images, they seem to suggest
that the meaning of a story lies entirely in the way it is seen or
interpreted: there is no easily demonstrable moral: truth is relative
and can actually be made less clear by the narrator's struggle to
reconstruct events, the 'glow' bringing out only a 'haze'. In
distancing himself from Marlow and allowing his principal narrator
only restricted knowledge of what occurs, Conrad moves even
further away than James from that mutual understanding between
storyteller and story-reader that Dickens felt to be the indispensable
starting-point of the novelist's art. In place of story we have a
halting struggle towards story, a characteristic shared by Meredith
and James and referred to frequently by reviewers. 'He *has* a story
... but it will not let itself be told,' the *Saturday Review* noted
tartly of Meredith's *One of Our Conquerors*.[74] Conrad's awareness
of the irritation this could cause his readers did allow him
occasionally to indulge in a kind of Jamesian irony, though directed
against himself as much as his frustrated readers. At moments when
Marlow attempts to formulate some philosophical explanation of the
events he is piecing together he cannot resist the temptation to abuse
his audience for not following his thoughts, or perhaps he just wants
to discover if they are still there. The two concerns are indivisible:

> When you have to attend to things of that sort, to the mere
> incidents of the surface, the reality – the reality, I tell you –
> fades. The inner truth is hidden – luckily, luckily. But I felt
> it all the same; I felt often its mysterious stillness watching

> me at my monkey tricks, just as it watches you fellows
> performing on your respective tight-ropes for – what is it?
> half-a-crown a tumble –
>   'Try to be civil, Marlow,' growled a voice, and I knew
> there was at least one listener awake besides myself.[75]

As long as there is one person making an effort to understand, communication has not failed entirely.

Even that limited success does not lessen the doubts about what, given these particular narrative techniques, there is ultimately to be communicated. 'Then there we are,' says Strether at the end of *The Ambassadors*, challenging the reader to ask where 'there' is, and provoking the now familiar criticism that in James's later novels so total an emphasis is placed on the attainment of consciousness that consciousness itself becomes the sole, and uncommunicable, object. The reader is forced to participate actively in the process, even at times to finish the story for himself. In *Lord Jim*, as Marlow brings his narrative to as much of a close as he can reach, his listeners drift away 'in pairs or alone without loss of time, without offering a remark'.[76] Like so many references to audiences in early modern fiction, the mood is disturbingly unsettled. In this case their disquiet is caused by Marlow's description of his last sight of Jim – 'a tiny white speck, that seemed to catch all the light left in a darkened world ... And, suddenly, I lost him ...' It is that 'last image of that incomplete story, its incompleteness itself, and the very tone of the speaker' that makes 'discussion vain and comment impossible'. Each of the listeners carries away his own 'impression', like a 'secret'.[77] In fact it is not the end of Jim's story, only the stopping-point of Marlow's direct contact with him. What remains to be told is communicated to just one of the listeners who had drifted discontentedly away at the close of Marlow's narrative. He is a 'privileged man' who is given the chance to link together the scraps of evidence, first-hand reports, letters and rumours that constitute Conradian reality.

The shift of emphasis from story itself to the way that story is told assumes the existence of sophisticated, intelligent, 'privileged' readers, and, if such readers do not already exist in sufficient numbers, it takes upon itself the responsibility for bringing them into being. The process was painful. 'Sacrifices must be expected,' as Meredith insisted, in order that 'a taste' might be created. The didacticism of the mid-Victorians had been employed to inculcate

moral and social values, and this moralism was mocked by later
novelists as epitomising a utilitarian, rather than artistic, attitude to
fiction. They themselves, however, were no less didactic: it was
simply that their teaching was now directed not outwards into
society, but inwards onto their own art. It did not necessarily
involve a lessening concern with the morality of their characters'
actions – nobody could read James or Conrad for ten minutes and
believe this – but it did mean that before moral judgments could be
made the reader had to be educated in the new fictional techniques.
It was as though the modern novelist was leaping back across the
occasional statements about their art by George Eliot, Dickens and
Jane Austen, to the position of Fielding who found it necessary to
build into *Tom Jones* both story and explanation of what he was
doing with the story. It was like starting up the history of the novel
all over again. The prefaces James wrote for the New York edition
of his novels were, he told Howells, 'A sort of plea for Criticism,
for Discrimination, for Appreciation on other than infantile lines –
as against the so almost universal Anglo-Saxon absence of these
things.' He added, perhaps ironically, that the time might come
when he would add a preface to the prefaces.[78] The Arnoldian
echoes are unavoidable: 'How little of mind, or anything so worthy
and quickening as mind, comes into the motives which alone, in
general, impel great masses of men.'[79] The minds of readers are to
be made sufficiently critical and discriminating by James's prefaces
to appreciate the 'interesting' and 'beautiful' difficulties of his
narrative techniques, and these will, among other educative
functions, serve to answer the accusation that his novels do not
have enough story.

   Although James and Conrad were the most determined of the
early modern novelists to break with authorial omniscience in
favour of a more purely dramatic method, it is again Browning who
comes to mind as the first Victorian writer to be fully aware of the
essential difference between the two narrative approaches and how
they could affect the writer's relationship with his readers. In a
letter to Elizabeth Barrett he explained: 'You speak out, *you* – I
only make men and women speak – give you truth broken into
prismatic hues, and fear the pure white light, even if it is in me.'[80]
The distinction is between the direct speaking voice ('The pure
white light') and the dramatic creation of characters who, independently of their creator, appear to speak in their own voices

('prismatic hues'). Neither approach holds a monopoly on artistic truth, though they communicate it in opposing ways. The 'pure white light' is immediate, direct, the full expression of an author's personality: the 'prismatic hues' are indirect, oblique, fragmentary, with the author's own personality absorbed within the dramatisation. The mid-Victorian novel falls largely into the first of these two categories, the great exception being *Wuthering Heights* which was, significantly, one of the novels that escaped the early twentieth-century's general distaste for Victorianism. Browning explained his adherence to the prismatic hues not so much in terms of a preference chosen out of possible options, but rather as an unavoidable expression of his temperament. By the end of the century his attempt to portray the truth about the human condition by means of restricted, partial, or false consciousness was very much in tune with an age that felt itself no longer sure about religious and social absolutes, challenged by the confidence of scientists to interpret the world, and threatened by the growing power of an uneducated or half-educated mass society. In 1903 William Hale White ('Mark Rutherford') was deeply shocked by the views of a much younger friend who was writing a novel: 'She propounded a theory to me that in conversation and writing a person's real self should be concealed.' At first he was only willing to believe that she was 'arguing for arguing's sake', but soon realised that she was perfectly serious. He blamed the influence of Browning for this strange theory and urged a mutual friend to 'impress upon' the young author 'that she must write what she feels and thinks'.[81]

It is, however, by no means obvious that the kind of insincerity White feared was involved, or that Browning deserved to be blamed for it. The assumption that a novel was the product of a particular temperament, an 'impression' of life rather than a confident assertion of objective reality, was now widespread: it had been expressed forcefully by Hardy, James and Conrad, and there was no point in accusing them of not having written what they really felt and thought. It was more important to understand that their deepest artistic motives were guided by the conviction that the basis of White's moral confidence had collapsed: their immediate moral concern was how to prevent chaos from taking over. Hardy continued to employ largely traditional forms of storytelling, though the main characters in his last novels are increasingly

alienated from the moral and social certainties of an older
generation. Both James and Conrad were drawn to indirect
narration ('prismatic hues'): no less than Browning they had
sincerely-held views of life, and like him, though for different
reasons, they feared 'the pure white light' as an impossible,
simplistic distortion. The uncertainty that they now constantly
expressed about the motivation of their own characters' actions was
shared by many other authors; by Gissing, for example, in the moral
ambivalence that is a central theme of novels like *Born in Exile* and
Our Friend the Charlatan, and by many writers of the new sub-
genres. At about the same time that William Hale White expressed
his distrust of the author's 'real self' being concealed, Kipling published 'Mrs Bathurst', one of the most radically experimental stories
of the age, in which the uncertain new technology of the cinema
newsreel is employed to convey the impossibility of reconstructing, in
any morally clear way, the motives governing individual behaviour.[82]
Joyce also was experimenting with a method of fictionalising a self-
portrait that would present simultaneously to the reader an
apparently straightforward portrayal of adolescent artistic arrogance
and a distanced ironic commentary on that arrogance. The
changing relationship between an author and his characters was
acknowledged abrasively by Ford in his now neglected novel *A
Call* (1910). British readers always want a 'happy ending', Ford
told his own readers, much as 'foxes have holes' and 'birds of the
air have nests', but they would not get a conventional ending of any
kind from him. He explained why, in words that, many years later,
were to influence one of Graham Greene's greatest novels:

> Since to me a novel is the history of an 'affair' – finality is
> only found at what seems to be the end of that 'affair'. There
> is in life nothing final. So that even 'affairs' never really have
> an end as far as the lives of the actors are concerned.[83]

The unsolved narrative difficulties that weaken the total effect of *A
Call* were overcome by Ford in *The Good Soldier* (1915). 'Who in
this world can give anyone a character? Who in this world knows
anything of any other heart – or of his own?' asks the unreliable
narrator John Dowell.[84] His answer is that nobody does. If he is
asked why his characters behaved as they did, he can only excuse
his retreat from omniscience by claiming, 'It is all a darkness.'[85] If
the creator doesn't understand, there is no logical reason why his

creations should do so. It was becoming the task of the reader to make up his own mind. As Conrad explained, in a statement that developed, interestingly, out of a defence of Kipling: 'One writes only half the book: the other half is with the reader.'[86] In the mid-Victorian age Browning and *Wuthering Heights* were oddities. By the mid-1880s neither seemed quite so strange: by 1914 they didn't seem strange at all.

The growing emphasis throughout the 1880s and 1890s on narrative techniques which were either distanced or oblique marked the decline of one of the most treasured of Victorian conventions – the direct authorial address. 'It is better to make no kind of reference to the Reader, I think,' Gissing advised his brother Algernon in 1883, 'Simply present what you have, and without comment.'[87] The following year Henry James described Trollope's asides to the reader as 'a betrayal of a sacred office': they were seen as part of a conspiracy between author and reader to deny the artistic illusion of fiction and therefore a bar to the attainment of a higher reality represented by the theory of organic form.[88] They were also a constant, irritating reminder of a once close relationship that was on the point of breaking up, and it was perhaps a half-realisation of what would be lost by no longer being able to speak directly to the reader that kept the habit alive for so long. In this respect Gissing never really followed his own advice, and James only gave up addressing the reader when he was finally persuaded that he had almost no readers to address. By the turn of the century it was generally accepted as old-fashioned for a novelist to adopt a tone of personal familiarity with the reader, though there was little consistency of practice. George Moore, in his early naturalistic novels and the symbolist *The Lake* (1905), maintained an impersonal narrative method, while Bennett, striving for a similar effect, was capable of suddenly interpolating a comment on his characters in a manner irresistibly reminiscent of Trollope. In the main, novelists divided over this issue, as over so many others, according to the degree of importance they attached to the social message of their work. Wells remained aggressively present, cajoling, hectoring, bullying the reader to see the potential of the world as he himself wanted it to be seen. Forster was no less determined that connections should not be entirely severed, though his tone was insistent rather than aggressive, and not quite bullying. At the opposite extreme there was the movement that culminated in Stephen Dedalus's deification of the artist who 'remains within or behind or beyond or above his handiwork, invisible, refined out of existence, indifferent, paring his finger-nails'.[89] The direct source was Flaubert – 'The artist in his work must be like God in his creation, invisible and all-powerful: he must be everywhere felt, but never seen' – but in order to reveal Stephen's untested confidence Joyce has him move some way beyond that original definition.[90] Flaubert's artist-god is invisible yet all-pervading: Stephen's is invisible and bored. The danger of the artist making himself so completely a god that he loses all contact with humanity is thus acknowledged, though that in itself solved little as long as the works the artist created remained incomprehensible to the vast majority of readers.

In 1897 James sent Conrad a complimentary copy of *The Spoils of Poynton*. Conrad thought it as good as anything James had ever written. 'The delicacy and tenuity of the thing are amazing,' he told Edward Garnett, and added:

> But I imagine with pain the man in the street trying to read it! And my common humanity revolts at the evoked image of his suffering. One could almost see the globular lobes of his brain painfully revolving and crushing, mangling the delicate thing. As to his exasperation it is a thing impossible to imagine and too horrid to contemplate.[91]

There is a sad desperation in Conrad's attempt to joke his way out of the perception that he and James were writing books for each other and for those few readers whose globular lobes didn't revolve painfully when confronted with artistic delicacy. Like Coriolanus, they had defiantly banished the plebeians who showed no interest in them. If the 'man in the street' could possibly have had any remaining doubts about his irrelevance for the modern novelist they were cleared up by Somerset Maugham: 'Be not deceived, gentle reader, no self-respecting writer cares a twopenny damn for you.'[92]

So, who were these readers and non-readers that the major novelists of the time regarded with such contempt? The quickest way of answering the question would be to accept the view of a Meredith, Gissing, James or Conrad, and say that they comprised approximately 99.9% of the total adult population, though that would tend to be a little too optimistic. Certainly the concept of the 'few' readers, the 'two or three at most', was not simply a convenient myth: its actuality (allowing for a little numerical exaggeration) was borne out again and again in very low sales figures, insensitive reviews, handouts from friends or admirers, and the general inability to earn a decent living from the writing of fiction.[93] The devotion of the few is not in doubt: it is the indifference of the vast majority that is of particular interest, and the relationship between the few and the many that has greatest historical importance. The common late Victorian explanation was that board-school education and mass journalism had created a reading public incapable of sustained thought or intelligent discrimination, the implication being that if compulsory elementary education had been better (or had never been introduced) then the new readers would not have been so easily seduced by cheap journalism (or, alternatively, the quality of the reading public would not have been diluted at all). This argument was often expressed in class terms – the working class or poor being the main recipients of the new education – but novelists soon recognised that the problem was not restricted to any one class. In *New Grub Street* Whelpdale's periodical *Chit-Chat* is addressed to 'the quarter-educated; that is to say, the great new generation that is being turned out by the Board Schools'. When Milvain and Dora are on holiday in Guernsey they see an 'obese and well-dressed man' reading *Chit-Chat*:

> 'Is *he* one of the quarter-educated?' asked Dora, laughing.
> 'Not in Whelpdale's sense of the word. But, strictly speaking, no doubt he *is*. The quarter-educated constitute a very large class indeed.'[94]

In this view of the situation, membership of that 'very large class' was now determined less by dress, occupation or income than by what was read for pleasure. Books, periodicals and newspapers were becoming important social or cultural indicators. In *The Spoils of Poynton* when Mrs Brigstock accompanies her daughter Mona to Poynton she carries with her 'a trophy of her journey, a "lady's magazine" purchased at the station, a horrible thing with patterns for antimacassars, which, as it was quite new, the first number, and seemed so clever, she kindly offered to leave for the house'.[95] Mrs Brigstock is very clearly one of the quarter-educated, though she alone is not James's target. As she and Mona enter their

carriage to leave Poynton, Mrs Gereth flings the 'precious periodical' after them, deliberately throwing it 'higher in the air than
was absolutely needful'.[96] Mona doesn't even recognise the insult.
She leaps up to catch the missile and her agility is warmly
applauded by Owen Gereth. The cultural battle-lines of the book
are drawn up. Mona and Owen join Mrs Brigstock in the ranks of
the quarter-educated: Mrs Gereth and Fleda are placed among the
embattled, sensitive 'few'.

The recognition that readers would be better classified in terms
of 'masses' rather than 'classes' was not, however, sufficient to
explain away the many contradictions contained in the late
Victorian view of a debased reading public. It is now widely
recognised by historians that some of the claims made on behalf of
the 1870 Education Act were exaggerated. Earlier in the century
the skilled working classes especially were far from illiterate, and,
even among the unskilled, literacy was steadily increasing before
the Education Act began to take effect.[97] Even so, its long-term
achievement should not be underestimated. As Richard Altick has
warned, the fact that by the end of the century 97% of men and
women could sign the marriage register should not be taken too
easily to mean that total national literacy had been attained, though
the evidence available does suggest that that target was being
reached, at least by the younger generation.[98] In 1891, for
example, 96.87% of school-children successfully passed their
reading examinations.[99] In her 1907 survey of two hundred
working-class families in Middlesbrough, most of which contained at
least two adults, Lady Florence Bell noted a total of only seventeen
women and eight men who could not read. Many of these would
have been older people who had not had the opportunity of a
Board School education, and it is perhaps significant that although
Lady Bell often refers to the sons and daughters of the households
as being interested or uninterested in reading, she gives no instance
of a child not being able to read.[100] Whatever the precise national
percentage, it is undoubtedly the case that at the turn of the
century a far higher proportion of the population could read and
write than any other time in British history. If by itself that tells us
little about the quality of reading most people were capable of, it
can hardly be said to give very convincing support to the doom-
laden descriptions of a wholesale collapse of national intelligence
and sensitivity that were common at the time, especially when it is

taken into account that never before in British history had the incentives to read and write been so pervasive. There were more books, periodicals and newspapers on the market than ever before, and more talk about books and authors as well; careers in non-manual occupations were expanding, the way into many of them being opened up by the now well-established school and public examinations which in turn had created the boom in educational books which continues to the present day; public libraries were joining the board schools and town halls as recognisable landmarks in many towns and cities, and so were universities, teacher-training colleges, and commercial and business schools.

It is understandable that writers like Conrad, James and Gissing who could rely on only a handful of people to read their novels should have taken a jaundiced view of all of this activity, but they were wrong to interpret it so scathingly as being entirely a matter of rampant philistinism: much of it was nothing of the kind. If they could point with some justice to the new section of the reading public as having its intellectual development stunted by trivia – by the 'pretty actresses' and 'first-rate athletes' with whom Conrad refused to allow his portrait to be associated – and were right to see the 'quarter-educated' as making up a 'very large class indeed', they were still bewildered by what had happened to the rest of their potential readers. Even the prevailing mood of anti-Victorianism and the conviction that the leading mid-Victorian novelists had been entertainers rather than artists could not quite explain why the readers who had been faithful to Dickens, Eliot or Thackeray seemed to have melted away. The situation was all the more depressing because it appeared to contradict a prophetic line that had descended from a number of Victorian novelists who were both successful in their own careers and widely respected for their knowledge of literary business. In 1838 Thackeray had drawn attention to the existence of a vast reading public in working-class areas of cities which was unknown to most upper and middle-class novelists. He noted that in comparison with this audience made up of 'fourteen-fifteenths of the people among whom we live' his own literary circle was merely a 'miserable clique', and he praised both the 'enlightened spirit of the age' that had encouraged the spread of literacy and the producers of penny journals for providing reading material cheap enough for the poor to buy.[101] Twenty years later Wilkie Collins recorded the same phenomenon. He estimated the

size of the unknown reading public as being around three million.
Like Thackeray he was fascinated to learn that the authors of
penny-journal fiction were totally unfamiliar names to readers of
three-volume novels and fashionable periodicals, but he pursued his
sociological exploration further. He observed that although cheap
literature was only available at small local shops, the same material
was available at the same kinds of shops throughout the whole
country: it serviced a nation-wide network of predominantly
working-class readers. He also perceived that cheap literature served
the important function of a community advice service, with
'Answers to Correspondents' columns being particularly useful to
women, both married and single. He closed his article with a
rousing optimistic phophecy:

> The future of English fiction may rest with this Unknown
> Public, which is now waiting to be taught the difference
> between a good book and a bad. It is probably a question of
> time only. The largest audience for periodical literature, in
> this age of periodicals, must obey the universal law of
> progress, and must, sooner or later learn to discriminate.
> When that period comes, the readers who rank by millions,
> will be the readers who give the widest reputations, who
> return the richest rewards, and who will, therefore, command
> the service of the best writers of their time.[102]

Another twenty years on, James Payn took up the issue. He
referred back to Collins's discovery of the Unknown Public and
noted that while the literature it favoured had been 'of considerable
dimensions' then, 'the luxuriance of its growth since has become
tropical'. The size of the 'unknown' reading public Payn now
estimated at four million, and the cause of its recent expansion he
gave as the spread of elementary education. He too was optimistic
about the future relationship between novelists and this huge
reading public, but his interpretation was the opposite to that of
Collins. Whereas Collins had seen a 'universal law of progress' as
functioning to create a sense of literary discrimination in unsophisti-
cated readers so that they would rise to the challenge of (and give
prosperity to) the best writers of the day, Payn argued that the
future prosperity of novelists depended on researching the kinds of
fiction that readers wanted and meeting the demand. The novelist
who, like Payn himself, was satisfied with pursuing a career in
'light literature' could expect financial success, but 'literary persons'

would find that unless they followed Payn's advice and moved with the market their careers would be arduous and financially unrewarding.[103] Besant's commercial attitude to fiction was very close to that of Payn and may have owed something of its formulation to the older writer. Besant too regarded himself, in the world of fiction, as nothing more than a successful purveyor of 'light literature' and held out to his fellow novelists (light and otherwise) the future prospect of a vast reading public that would bring many of them prosperity. But as we have seen, the important difference was that Besant was not willing to allow novelists to remain subject to the uncertain fluctuation of market forces. By combining, establishing common principles and practice, and taking on blood-sucking publishers and American pirates, the market could to some extent be controlled so that all writers (according to their individual abilities and temperaments) would benefit from the millions of readers clamouring for books. Everything depended on the readers' co-operation.

The essays by Thackeray, Collins and James Payn on the 'unknown public' are pioneering exercises in the sociology of literature. Between them they outline the polarised attitudes to readers that were to dominate the emergence of modernism in Britain, and undermine the argument that a mass reading public was only created post-1870. From a slightly different angle, they also confirm that the fiction being read has little direct connection with that favoured by the middle classes. It is even marketed in a different way:

> The literary wares that find such favour . . . do not meet the eye of the ordinary observer. They are to be found neither at the book-seller's nor on the railway stall. But in the back streets, in small dark shops, in the company of cheap tobacco, hardbake (and, at the proper season, valentines), their leaves lie thick as those in Vallombrosa.[104]

In case this picture of mean streets and dark shops should give a false impression of the contents of the fiction being sold, Payn is careful to stress its 'coolness', 'purity', general lack of 'sensationalism', its moral superiority to the once infamous publications of the Minerva Press and, following Collins, how the essentially domestic nature of penny fiction was connected with local advertising which provided much-needed advice on legal and 'matrimonial' matters. Thackeray, Collins, and Payne did not, of course, personally admire this fiction. It would not have provided satisfying reading material for them; they did not regard it as 'literature' at all, except in a debased form. But they were not only fascinated by its commercial potential: they also recognised in it a deeper significance that is relevant to the late Victorian novelists' concern with disappearing readers. Recognition of the existence of this unknown public of four million readers exposed, Payn argued, the pretentiousness of a 'few thousands of persons' imagining themselves to be 'the public' or 'arbiters of popularity', when they were in fact 'nothing of the kind'. The 'favourites' of the 'subscribers to the circulating libraries, the members of book clubs, the purchasers of magazines and railway novels ... were "nowhere" ... in comparison with novelists whose names and works appear in penny journals and nowhere else'.[105] In other words, the stability of mainstream Victorian fiction did not rest on genuine popularity. The overwhelming majority of readers of fiction did not care about, or know of, the major writers of the day whose limited popularity was maintained by a tightly controlled business network and relatively few readers. Payn exaggerates in certain respects the completeness of the separation between these two reading publics. As Louis James has demonstrated, the writers of penny fiction, if not many of its readers, were fully aware of what their more fashionable fellow-novelists (Dickens especially) were doing; and certain types of fiction, both domestic and sensational, which were enormously popular in the circulating libraries had their close equivalents on the counters of those small dark shops in city backstreets.[106] But the general trend of Payn's analysis was proving to be correct. The reading public was increasing year by year and showed not the slightest interest in radically changing its taste in fiction. Commercial organisations, on local and national levels, were now actively courting this lucrative market with cheap newspapers, periodicals and syndicated fiction, but they were not alone in doing so: comparable changes had also taken place in the marketing of fiction. The replacement of the 31/6d three-decker by the 6/- one-volume novel had been welcomed by many novelists and younger publishers precisely because it represented a movement away from their reliance on a book-borrowing to a book-buying public. Not everyone believed in Wilkie Collins's 'universal law of progress' that would ensure the development of literary discrimination alongside the expansion of the reading public, but it was widely felt that the killing-off of the three-decker meant that the sales of fiction would no longer be controlled by the tyrannical circulating libraries. The new appeal would be to the taste and pockets of individual readers. They would decide. While the new, unusual or experimental writer could not expect to establish himself any more easily under the new system than under the old, he would at least be able to make direct contact with the portion of the reading public sympathetic to his work. That was the theory, and in the long run it was to be borne out, though not quite in ways that were anticipated. The immediate result was a commercial and cultural crisis in which the readership for many of the leading novelists of the day virtually collapsed. 'They all read you,' Henry St George says comfortingly to the young artist-novelist in James's 'The Lesson of the Master'. 'Me?' replies Paul Overt, 'I should like to see them! Only two or three at most.'[107]

The first reason why the expanding, increasingly literate late Victorian reading public did not respond to changes in the traditional marketing of fiction was economic. In 1898 Besant estimated that the lowest income on which someone might be expected to be able to buy 'new and expensive' books was £250 p.a. Using Charles Booth's analysis of the 1891 census, Besant conjectured that there were no more than 400,000 families in the whole country (out of a total population of just over 40 million) with such an annual income. This level of income was, however, the 'lowest' possible, and Besant suggested that not 'many families with incomes under £750 spend much upon books, especially when there are children'.[108] The emphasis on children there is significant, for, as Besant observes, a single person with no family responsibilities would be able to buy books regularly on an annual income of £250. As far as fiction is concerned, a 'new and expensive book' refers to the 6/- novel which throughout this period would normally have been purchasable in a book shop, once trade discounts were taken into account, for 4/6d. A necessarily approximate, though reasonably reliable, estimate as to how many potential book buyers there were at Besant's suggested income of £750 can be made from the figures compiled in 1903 by the economist L. G. Chiozza Money covering the distribution of incomes throughout the whole of the United Kingdom. He divided the population into three broad bands – those who were rich (with

incomes over £700 p.a.), those who lived in comfort (with incomes
between £160–£700 p.a.), and those in poverty (with incomes
below £160 p.a.). The figure of £160 features so prominently
because that was the rate at which income tax began to be assessed.
The information gathered by Chiozza Money[109] about different
levels of individual incomes can be presented as follows:

Income per annum	Number of Individuals
Above £700	258,000
£600–700	13,000
£500–600	29,000
£400–500	53,000
£160–400	607,000
Above £160 but escaping income tax	48,000
Below £160: non-manual	3,000,000
Below £160: manual	15,000,000
Total	19,008,000

If Besant was right that not 'many families with incomes under
£750 spend much upon books', we can see that out of a working
population of just over nineteen million there were approximately
258,000 wage-earners, or 1.35% of the total, who could afford to
buy new fiction regularly. Quite apart from the fact that Chiozza
Money was a controversial economist, there are several imponder-
ables in applying such a rough statistic to novel-buying. Many
people, though able to do so, would not have wanted to buy new
novels or books of any kind; others would have been avid
purchasers of non-fiction; some people on incomes considerably
lower than £750 would certainly have been regular buyers of new
fiction; and, as already mentioned, there was the single person on
whatever income whose purchasing power was already proving to
be important to the new consumer economy. Furthermore, then as
now the buying of books tended to be an occasional rather than an
habitual activity, motivated by the need to buy presents or to
satisfy curiosity about a popular or much-discussed work. The value
of this statistic as a starting-point is that it provides an indication of
the *maximum* market potential for new fiction. Actual sales were
substantially lower, but it was on this tiny proportion of the
working population that novelists and publishers would have to

rely if they were to realise their dreams of a prosperous industry based on a book-buying readership.

The low priority given to the purchase of books by middle-class families is strikingly apparent in the large number of household budgets compiled by professional and amateur sociologists at this time. It is unusual to find in them special attention given to books: when books were mentioned at all they tended, as W. Hamish Fraser has noted, to be 'lumped in with other miscellaneous items ... under the heading small expenditure'.[110] When the *Cornhill* commissioned a series of family budgets to be compiled in 1901, it included one for the lower-middle class and one for the upper-middle class. G. S. Layard took as his representative lower-middle-class family a cashier in a solicitor's office, married with two children, and he pointed out that the estimated income of £150–£200 p.a. would cover an unusually wide range of occupations, from a bank clerk and skilled mechanic through to a police inspector and curate. He included an annual sum of £4.10/- for 'newspapers, books etc'.[111] In the budget for someone living on £800 p.a. G. Colmore allowed £18 for 'stationery and postage' but made no mention of books. He did, however, allow for the wages of a cook and a parlourmaid and the annual consumption of four and a half dozen bottles of whisky.[112] Colman's example was followed in the budgets analysing life on £1800 and £10,000 a year.[113] Books were not itemised in either case, though again they may have been assumed to be part of stationery, postage or 'small bills'.

It hardly needs to be said that books were also not listed in the 'workman's budget' which Arthur Morrison contributed to the *Cornhill*. If the expenditure of 4/6d on a new novel by a fairly comfortably-off married clerk or skilled mechanic earning about £3 a week would have been regarded as a rare luxury, it was something inconceivable to the unskilled workmen whose weekly wage was less than half that amount. Morrison deliberately chose as his example someone earning a regular weekly wage of 30/-, and estimated that once the necessities of life were deducted this workman's family would have 1/3d left for 'savings, postage, literature, amusements and all the rest of it'.[114] In their surveys of London and York, Booth and Rowntree had shown that a third of the population of Britain lived in conditions of actual poverty. Rowntree estimated that a minimum weekly income of 21/8d was the lowest required for 'the maintenance of merely physical

efficiency', and in a moving passage of *Poverty* he explained what
was meant in human terms by this scientific-sounding phrase:

> A family living upon the scale allowed for in this estimate
> must never spend a penny on railway fare or omnibus. They
> must never go into the country unless they walk. They must
> never purchase a halfpenny newspaper or spend a penny to
> buy a ticket for a popular concert. They must write no letters
> to absent children, for they cannot afford to pay the postage
> . . . The children must have no pocket money for dolls,
> marbles or sweets. The father must smoke no tobacco, and
> must drink no beer. The mother must never buy any pretty
> clothes for herself or for her family.[115]

In the detailed family budgets published in *Poverty*, new books
were, obviously enough, entirely absent, as they had to be from the
cost-of-living calculations of most people in a country which was
made up, in Chiozza Money's words, of 'a great multitude of poor
people, veneered with a thin layer of the comfortable and the
rich'.[116] It was only possible for consumerism to take off at all in
Britain because for much of the period the real value of earnings
was increasing. Levelling out the years of depression, A. L. Bowley
estimated that from 1880 to 1914 money earnings rose on average
1% p.a., with 'real wages' increasing substantially until 1895 and
then largely stabilising.[117] The average earnings for a male worker
in industry rose from about 24/- (1886) to 29/6d (1906) and to 32/-
(1914).[118] Taking a wider social sample Bowley tried to estimate
the real value of a 'median family' budget based on all wage-
earners: in 1880 the average weekly income was 26/6d, and by 1914
it had increased to 35/6d. Once essential expenditure (on rent,
food, and clothing) was deducted, a sum was left for 'sundries' of
3/5¼d in 1880 and 3/11d in 1914.[119] At no time in the whole of this
period did the small surplus of income over basic expenditure
enjoyed by Bowley's median family rise to the cost of just *one* new
novel.

The fact that there was now a small surplus for many families
was crucial to the growth of consumerism, though in itself this was
insufficient to engineer the late Victorian consumer boom which
was largely financed by a bourgeoning credit system. This ranged
from the traditional pawnshop and tallyman, familiar not only to
the poor but to many of the skilled working class as well, to the

practice of 'hire purchase', which, in one form or another, had long been an accepted and expensive method of borrowing, though the term itself seems only to have begun to be used in the 1890s to describe the credit arrangements offered by the new department and chain stores.[120] Hire purchase was welcomed by both the middle and working classes. For someone with a small amount of money it could mean an immediate rise in social prestige, as Gissing recorded in 1898: 'Mr Nibby had just come in for a little legacy, on the strength of which he took a house in a south-east suburb, and furnished it on the hire system, with a splendour which caused Miss Waghorn to shriek in delight.'[121] For someone with no capital at all, hire purchase provided the means of immediately establishing a home: it also became, if work was unreliable, a cause of personal worry and marital tension. When the young married couple Ruth and William Easton in *The Ragged Trousered Philanthropists* try to sort out their chaotic household budget, the husband (who has left all such matters to his wife) is appalled to learn that although they owe money to everyone, the largest debt, apart from rent, is to 'the furniture people'.[122]

Although new fiction priced itself out of the consideration of very large sections of the reading public, there was certainly no decline in the demand for reading matter, or for fiction: indeed, as the figures given in Chapter One show, there was a large increase in demand. It was catered for by the small rise in real wages, and it is here that the significance of those items in household budgets labelled as 'sundries' or 'miscellaneous expenditure' becomes apparent. Lady Bell noted in Middlesbrough that Sunday was the day on which 'both men and women are likely to read', and explained that 'even in households where each penny is an important item of expenditure, $1d$, $2d$, $3d$, and sometimes as much as $6d$, is set apart for this delectable Sunday reading'.[123] The habit of a relaxed working-class Sunday spent reading the newspapers had by this date become traditional: it stretched back to even before Queen Victoria's accession, and its appeal lay in a journalistic mixture of bloody sensationalism and political radicalism. The newspaper-reading habit carried over into the late Victorian expansion of evening, local and daily papers costing $\frac{1}{2}d$ or $1d$. For those people existing on Rowntree's level of 'merely physical efficiency' even a penny paper was a luxury, but for many working and middle-class readers whose incomes were only slightly higher it became a luxury they were able and willing to afford. Much the same applied to cheap periodicals aimed at other members of the family. *Funny Folks* was often a manageable 1*d* treat for the children, or *Comic Cuts* a ½*d* treat, and though directed at a predominantly middle-class readership the *Boy's Own Paper* and the *Girl's Own Paper* also cost 1*d* weekly. A determined commercial drive at every segment of what Thackeray and Collins had regarded as an 'unknown' public, and what was now very well known indeed and coming to be called the mass market, provided cheap periodicals for the whole family, married women, single women, boys and girls of various ages, and trade, hobby and sporting interests of every conceivable kind. The market was also catered for according to its class or social status. The self-consciously respectable middle-class man who might have shied away from buying a new novel for 4/6*d* and felt, perhaps, that it was demeaning to have a copy of *Tit-Bits* or *Answers* displayed in the house, need not have felt the same about the 6*d* monthly *Strand* or the 1/- monthly *Woman's World*; and fiction, as we have seen, was a strong selling-point for virtually all of these periodicals, ranging from the syndicated serial in a local newspaper to the latest adventure of Sherlock Holmes in the *Strand*. The penny novelette, supplemented now by many fiction magazines, was as flourishing as it had been in the 1870s when James Payn began buying copies as sociological samples, and it still served the important additional function of providing much-needed advice to women, increasingly in the form of discreet advertisements offering help on birth-control or abortion, or what Payn described as 'all questions of propriety in connection with the affections'.[124]

These readily available and cheap forms of reading were the principal though by no means the only competition faced by new fiction. The consumer who was not interested in reading and had the occasional penny, threepence, sixpence or shilling to spend, had ranged before him the options advertised by the ever-growing sports, leisure and entertainment industries.[125] He could go to a music-hall, swimming-pool, or football match; save up for, or buy on credit, a bicycle, piano, pocket camera or tennis racket. By the end of the century the two technological inventions which were shortly to provide the most persistent consumer challenge to book-buying – the gramophone and the cinema – were well-established and on their way to becoming commercially viable. In 1898 American business methods, German technology, and European musical talent united in Hanover to form The Gramophone Company Ltd which produced flat discs seven inches in diameter to be played on a wind-up machine.[126] Like books, the new discs or records could be enjoyed at home, carried, stored, collected and treasured. The Edison Kinetoscope was first demonstrated in London in 1894 and almost immediately replaced by the Cinematographe-Lumière which projected moving pictures onto a screen: it received its British debut at the Marlborough Hall, Regent Street on 20 February 1896.[127] At first 'moving' or 'living' picture shows were presented as sensational novelties at music-halls, circuses and fairgrounds. The great attraction was to see captured on film familiar everyday sights involving spectacular movement. A popular favourite was a train drawing into a station, the effect used by Kipling in 'Mrs Bathurst'. Sporting events were also recorded – the Derby, Boat Race, and boxing matches: in 1898 Henry James went to 'the cinematograph – or whatever they call it' to see the world championship fight between Fitzsimmons and Corbett.[128] The earliest British film to dramatise a 'made-up' story was R. W. Paul's *The Soldier's Courtship* (1896) which lasted for just under one minute, and, like topical and special-effects films, was treasured for its novelty rather than its narrative. This quickly changed as it became possible to extend the running time of a film. Within a few years the length of a film was a matter of artistic choice rather than technical necessity, as can be seen by two popular films by one of the most successful British film-makers, Cecil Hepworth. *Rescued by Rover* and *Falsely Accused* were both made in 1905: the first ran for seven minutes, the second for fourteen.[129] Most film shows were still a collection of short items, but by 1914 the one-and-a-half or two-hour feature film was firmly established; there were some four thousand 'picture theatres' throughout Britain, and a night at the pictures was becoming a regular and familiar experience for a very large number of people indeed: a weekly attendance figure of about five million would probably be a fair estimate.[130] The challenge to the novel of this new form of storytelling was apparent from the start of the industry. 'This film is a complete little series in itself,' stated a synopsis of Hepworth's *The 'Call to Arms'* (1902), 'A veritable novel in a nutshell.'[131]

The irony built into the commercial battle for the threepences and sixpences of the late Victorian mass market is that where the

average working-class or lower-middle-class reader did have access
to new fiction was in the 'free' libraries. Supporters of the
movement objected to libraries being described as 'free' because it
made them sound like charitable institutions and the adjective was
gradually replaced by the more acceptable 'public': its opponents,
however, continued to describe library books as 'unjustly gotten
books' and to insist that 'free' libraries had been 'imposed upon the
public by a number of doctrinaire believers in the superhuman
value of a mere literary education'.[132] Like elementary education,
public libraries were often dismissed as 'socialistic', one more
example of the 'collectivist' tendency of the age, and the hostility
they provoked could be extreme. But while it was commonly
argued that the poor should not be educated at the expense of
ratepayers, few critics seriously believed that if the poor couldn't
pay for their own education they should be left in ignorance: the
changing political system of late Victorian Britain rendered that
argument totally unacceptable. Even so, fees were at first levied on
the parents of children attending board schools. The debate over
the free library movement raised similar concerns about the
undesirability of using ratepayers' money to finance an activity that
should be left to individual effort, and the fear of centralization was
just as strong; but although the free library movement won the
debate in principle, it was if anything more difficult to put into
practice than the policy of elementary education. The legislation
governing the provision of free library facilities preceded late
Victorian electoral and educational reforms, and although it was
frequently up-dated as the century progressed, attitudes towards
public libraries were always to retain a concessive tone inherited
from the social conflict of the 1840s.

The original Act of 1850 allowed large boroughs to levy a $\frac{1}{2}d$
library rate as long as it was approved by two-thirds of the
ratepayers at a special meeting.[133] The money raised could only be
used for library buildings: it could not be spent on books which, it
was assumed, would come from donations, gifts and public
subscription. Further legislation in 1855 increased the permissible
library rate to $1d$ and allowed the purchase of books: the clauses in
the original act restricting libraries according to the size of the local
population were repealed in 1866, and all previous legislation was
consolidated in the Public Libraries Act of 1892. Some large cities
– notably Manchester, Norwich and Birmingham – responded

positively from the start, but they were exceptional. By 1860 only twenty-five towns had taken steps to set up free libraries, and even the electoral and educational upheavals later in the decade brought only a relatively small increase. So great was the distrust of this intrusion on voluntary effort that as late as 1887 'only two parishes in all of Metropolitan London had rate-supported libraries'.[134] That the number of local authorities adopting the Act accelerated sharply towards the close of the century was largely due to the decision of the Scottish-born American millionaire Andrew Carnegie to use the fortune he had made out of the steel industry to endow libraries and educational institutions. He began in 1879 with the offer of £8,000 to his home town of Dunfermline: his conditions were accepted and the first Carnegie Library was opened there in 1883. This was followed by similar grants to other Scottish towns and extended to England and Wales in 1897. By the time of Carnegie's death in 1919, a total of three hundred and ten towns in England, Wales, Scotland and Ireland had received library grants.[135] The money was given solely to pay for the building of a library: the local authority had to provide a site, maintain the library once it was built, and raise money for books through the rates. It was a perfect blend of Victorian philanthropy and civic awareness, yet still it did not win over all doubters. The question of a public library for Edinburgh, the cultural capital of Scotland, was raised as early as 1868 and voted down. It was raised again in 1881 and again rejected. This time in order to draw maximum publicity to their case the opposition employed men to walk through the streets carrying sandwich-boards which read:

RATEPAYERS!
Resist This Free Library Dodge,
And Save Yourselves From the Burden of £6,000
Of Additional Taxation

They resisted until successfully bribed in 1886 by an exceptionally large Carnegie grant of £50,000. Even then the council would only levy a $\frac{1}{2}d$ rate, though it was raised to $\frac{3}{4}d$ after a year. A splendid public library was eventually opened in 1890.[136] The ratepayers of Dover were even more stubborn than those of Edinburgh. In 1903 they rejected a £10,000 Carnegie grant and did without a public library rather than suffer the $1d$ rate.[137] A survey carried out for the Carnegie Trust reported that by 1911 the 'public rate-supported library' had become the major kind of library institution in Britain, but that the service it provided was still restricted. Twenty-two towns with populations exceeding 30,000 had not adopted the Act, and there were many others which had adopted the Act without putting it into practice. People living in rural areas were almost totally neglected, with only 2.5% of them having access to a public library, as compared with 79% of the urban population. In the United Kingdom as a whole 57% of the population lived within public-library areas.[138]

Underlying much of the resentment directed at public libraries, and used frequently to justify the delays in setting them up and the refusals to spend ratepayers' money on them, was the conviction that their main function was to dispense popular novels to the poor and working class which they either would not or could not buy for themselves. This argument placed the public library in a category all on its own. Circulating libraries and the libraries of mechanics' institutes and working-men's clubs were financed by subscribers who were therefore entitled to read whatever they wished; libraries attached to places of work (factories, mills or large stores) were regarded as part of a contract between an employer and his employees; libraries established out of philanthropic motives (Toynbee Hall or The People's Palace) were worthy in themselves and restricted to specific groups of people. Public libraries were nation-wide and indiscriminate; the users were not 'subscribers' but 'borrowers', and what they borrowed (at the expense of the ratepayers) was entertainment. If novels were to be made freely available in this way then why shouldn't visits to a music-hall or the evening paper be paid for out of the rates? The establishment of reading rooms within public libraries, stocked with current newspapers and periodicals, confirmed the fear. Not all of the criticism came from people who suspected any State intervention of being 'socialistic' or 'collectivist'. Just as the public library movement was early Victorian in its origins, so were many of its critics early Victorian (even pre-Victorian) in their insistence that the reading of books should be an educative or morally improving activity: fiction, therefore, was profoundly distrusted. The pervasiveness of these attitudes has already been seen in the attempts to impose a form of literary censorship: their influence on issues relating to public libraries was less obviously dramatic, though ultimately perhaps of wider significance.

The common claim that public libraries catered mainly for the poor and working class was not strictly correct. Evidence is usually based on the occupation which everyone joining a public library was obliged to state, but this is difficult to assess with any accuracy because the terminology varied so much. It is easy to place an 'errand boy' socially, though a 'schoolboy' creates all kinds of problems, as does a 'servant' or 'assistant'; while terms such as 'unknown', 'no occupation: female' were generally taken to mean a 'housewife' which in turn is not easy to interpret with any precision. It seems reasonable to accept Richard Altick's suggestion that the greater part of 'readers and borrowers' came 'between the middle class proper and the labouring population'.[139] The largest single group would have been 'artisans' or skilled workmen, making up as much as 25% of the whole; clerks and 'tradesmen' comprised a similar proportion; housewives (often married to artisans) a further large section; while 'labourers' and 'professionals' or 'employers' made up significant minorities, probably each 7–8%. The great majority of public library borrowers were, therefore, skilled working class or lower-middle class, with a smaller proportion of the poor and the upper-middle or professional classes. This would bear out the observations of many people involved in setting up libraries, or running educational classes in the settlements, that it was skilled and clerical workers who took most advantage of the opportunities offered.[140] But the quality of libraries, and the social position of the borrowers, varied greatly. Although the public library movement was often seen as providing a service for the poorer classes – the aspect that has tended to receive most attention from historians – it was never solely this. The expanding suburbs and commuter areas surrounding London and other large cities also had their 'free' libraries, and the borrowers there were predominantly middle or upper class. The students who were benefiting from the expansion of secondary and higher education would also have been an increasing proportion of public library users, middle as well as working class. The existence of a public library in a district had become a factor in deciding where to live and how to apportion family expenditure. This would be a major reason why the middle-class family budgets discussed earlier did not include expenditure on books. In the only one that did – that of a representative lower middle-class married man – G. S. Layard dismissed the need for the regular purchase of books as unnecessary, unless the 'neighbourhood is scandalously behind the times' and does not have a 'free' library.[141]

The criticism that most public library users were interested only in popular fiction worried the Library Association more than any other issue, not least because the charge often came from its own members. The topic was raised so regularly at the annual meetings of the Association that in 1908 the editor of the *Library World* dubbed it 'The Great Fiction Bore' and urged those members of the Association who could not leave the topic alone to consider the damage they were doing to their profession:

> Every time the subject is discussed in public, the same lofty
> platitudes concerning novels are uttered by the same solemn
> bores, and the newspapermen are utterly misled, both as to
> the quantity and quality of fiction circulated and supplied by
> Public Libraries.[142]

To support his charge he printed four pages of hostile newspaper comments provoked by a talk on 'Fiction Reading in Public Libraries' given at the most recent meeting of the Association. The standard, and perfectly justified, replies to the critics were that public libraries did not stock just fiction but the whole range of books, from scientific and industrial textbooks through to history and biography; that reading and reference rooms were invaluable assets to local communities; libraries were educational not entertainment centres; and that the fiction held by libraries included work by many of the greatest writers in the English language. The *Library World* editor scornfully dismissed the charge that libraries were full of 'literary trash' and 'degenerate novels', and – courageously for the year 1908 – called on library committees not to 'ban Balzac, Fielding, Flaubert, Rabelais, Boccaccio, Apuleius, Zola, or other great classical writers because they are somewhat strong meat for youthful readers', but to restrict availability so that they did not fall into the hands of 'immature borrowers'.[143] He also claimed that only a very small percentage of public library fiction was 'of somewhat weak literary power – such as novels by Yonge, Worboise, Wood, Braddon, Corelli, Crockett, Hocking, Garvice etc.' and that, anyway, everyone knew that the percentage of fiction borrowed was falling year by year.[144] He was reasonably safe to argue that the question of 'degenerate' classical authors was exaggerated because few public libraries would have stocked the most controversial of these. But his position on popular and new fiction was disingenuous. The general touchiness shown by librarians on this issue was really an acknowledgment that their critics were right. There was good reason in 1896 for Mrs Oliphant to describe fiction as 'the despair of the high-minded educationist and those who believed that Free Libraries were to redeem the world'.[145]

The difficulty of the situation was neatly expressed by M. D. O'Brien, one of the public library movement's most virulent opponents: 'It must be admitted that there is something very arbitrary in taxing the general public for a library, and then preventing them from seeing the only books they care to read.'[146] The 'only books' is going too far, but it does not require severe qualification. To support his case that fiction borrowing was declining the *Library World* editor announced a drop from 67% to 63%.[147] Ten years earlier the pioneer library historian Thomas Greenwood, in a similarly defensive mood, estimated that fiction amounted to between 60–65% of books issued. His uneasiness can be seen from his spirited attempt to show that readers of Kipling and Flora Annie Steel could learn a lot about India, while the novels of Mayne Reid, Henty and Kingston 'are positive mines of topographical and scientific information'.[148] The pretence that exciting adventure stories are really historical or geographical studies recurs, and reveals what librarians wished readers would demand. Even the most determined and sympathetic librarians could not get the national average of fiction below about 65% and their opponents, manipulating the same statistics, had no difficulty in displaying startling variations. If children's borrowings were added to the 67% in 1908 the overall total amounted to 90%, it was claimed: surveying the returns for twenty-three libraries for 1887–9, O'Brien pointed to Barrow (48.82%) as the lowest fiction-borrowing town, and Chester (88.02%) as the highest.[149] On this particular topic recent scholarly research supports the public library critics. In his study of rural library services Alec Ellis has shown that in 1917 fiction amounted to 91% of books issued in Westmoreland, 86% in Yorkshire, and that for many municipal areas, similar figures apply: 'Fiction and children's books accounted for over 80% of issues at Bradford, Leeds, Leicester and York.'[150]

There can be little doubt that most of the fiction being read was by a relatively small number of immensely popular, mainly women novelists, or it was contemporary fiction which fell within well-defined sub-genres – adventure stories, thrillers, historical romances: the popularity of some earlier, well-established authors (most

notably Dickens and to a lesser extent Scott) was also retained. It is
also clear that most library users sought entertainment or recreation
rather than education. This was frequently deplored by librarians,
but there was little they could do about it: as Lady Bell explained,
'unambitious' libraries functioned on the 'principle not so much of
directing a course of reading as of providing a course that would be
acceptable to the readers'.[151] The readers of Middlesbrough who
specified favourite authors named 'Mrs Henry Wood seven times,
Shakespeare twice, Dickens twice, Marie Corelli once, Miss
Braddon once, Rider Haggard once'.[152] It seems a fairly representative list, and not simply of a working-class readership like that
at Middlesbrough. When Ernest Baker, himself a librarian as well
as a distinguished literary historian, carried out a survey in 1907 of
the standard of fiction in public libraries he was forced to conclude
that 'there is more in the denunciations of the critics than we
admit'.[153] Baker classified novelists into three groups and checked
on how many copies of their work were held by libraries. He found
a total of 390 volumes for Meredith ('the greatest living English
novelist') and slightly less than that for Henry James, as compared
with 2,296 for Miss Braddon (a Class II novelist) and almost as
many for Mrs Henry Wood and Emma Jane Worboise. Among
Class III novelists, each library held an average of 45 volumes by
Guy Boothby, 28 by William Le Queux and 28 by Rita. Baker
concluded that whatever the claims to the contrary, libraries did
stock large quantities of second-rate and 'ephemeral' fiction, a
policy that discouraged the reading of both non-fiction and quality
fiction. This was not, he insisted, what public libraries were set up
for.[154]

If we look beyond these denunciations of fiction-reading we can
see that a very important change has taken place in the age-old
distrust of fiction and of imaginative literature generally, though at
the turn of the century 'literature' really becomes 'fiction': drama
was developing a new sense of respectability, but it was widely
assumed that virtually nobody read poetry and it usually entered
the debate only to be dismissed. The library critics would have
preferred people to read non-fiction and to use libraries as
educational rather than recreational centres; they were also concerned to prevent modern 'sex', 'pornographic', or 'realistic' novels
being made available on the rates and they did have some success,
through library committees, in restricting the circulation of such

books. In addition, there was a handful of critics, influenced by extreme Spencerian ideas of individualism, who did not want 'free' libraries at all. But the view of fiction-reading as in itself a sinful activity which is common throughout the eighteenth and most of the nineteenth centuries had all but disappeared. It was now widely acknowledged that the reading of fiction could have an educative function: everything depended on what fiction was being read, and the principal charge against the users of public libraries was that the fiction they wanted to read was largely ephemeral, worthless, or trash. As the public libraries were not 'directing a course of reading' their powers of intervention on the quality of fiction read by their borrowers were limited. They were rapidly becoming indistinguishable from the circulating libraries which they had once proudly set out to rival and which they would eventually supersede.

In the early days of the public libraries there were, however, attempts to influence the kinds of borrowers they would attract. This was done by trying to create an atmosphere in the libraries which would encourage the studious and deter the casual reader: in many areas this policy was unconsciously aided by penny-pinching local authorities who provided inadequate buildings, inconvenient opening hours, poor lighting and insufficient money for maintenance. In order to obtain a book it was necessary to consult a catalogue in the form of a ledger or a mechanical contrivance called an 'indicator'. Books were then ordered by giving a number rather than an author or title at a counter, behind which the library assistant and the books were protected by a metal grill. In this way, Ernest Baker observed ironically, the books could be kept 'in working order and unpilfered' and out of the reach of 'the reading proletariat'.[155] A visit to a public library could be a daunting experience, and it is hardly surprising that they were at first used overwhelmingly by the skilled working class and the lower-middle class. The habitual reader of popular novels who simply wanted an entertaining book would often rely on the advice of the library assistant rather than risk the terrors of the catalogue or the indicator. In contrast to the idealised description by T. H. S. Escott which was quoted in Chapter Two, of decently dressed working-men carrying parcels to the library rather than the pawnbroker, and giving to poor areas of large cities a more academic atmosphere than Oxford, there is Lady Bell's greater understanding of what going to a free library could entail:

A woman who lives in a distant part of town, whose outer
garment is probably a ragged shawl fastened with a pin, may
not like going up an imposing flight of stairs, getting a ticket,
giving a name, looking through a catalogue, having the book
entered, etc., whereas many of these would read the book if
it were actually put into their hands.[156]

Librarians were as divided over how to deal with this issue as
they were on the circulation of popular fiction. On the one hand,
there was the argument that the atmosphere of libraries should be
kept studious; that using catalogues or indicators would create a
respect for books and literary discrimination, while the removal of
these restraints would lead simply to a scramble for popular novels.
On the other hand, it was claimed that a studious atmosphere
discouraged the very readers whom libraries should attract; a
borrower who knew what kinds of books he wanted would have no
trouble with a catalogue or indicator, but the general readers of
fiction would simply go for the name of an author known to them,
and that would actually encourage the borrowing of popular
fiction; also, if they had greater access to books then they could
browse among different kinds of fiction, and the reader who had
come to the library for the latest novel by Miss Braddon might well
be attracted to something by James or Meredith and take that
home instead, marking the first step to the possible development of
literary discrimination. The debate led to a decisive victory for the
supporters of 'open access'. Month by month the *Library World*
recorded the names of those libraries which had gone over to open
access as enthusiastically as it recorded the grants coming in from
Andrew Carnegie. Once again a policy profoundly affecting the
book world had been adopted which would rely for its effectiveness
on the taste and common-sense of a mass public, and once again,
the commercial implications were enormous. In 1886 the total
stock held by public libraries amounted to two million books: by
1914 it had increased to nearly eleven and a half million.[157]

The rapid spread of public libraries throughout Britain from the
1890s onwards finally dispelled the late Victorian dream that the
reading public was capable of conversion from its habit of
borrowing novels rather than buying them. The death of the three-
decker had not brought about any noticeable shift in the power of
the circulating libraries: indeed, there were obvious practical gains

for the subscriber in the replacement of the clumsy three-volume novel by an easily portable one-volume, while the financial advantage of subscribing to a circulating library had not been seriously challenged by the drastic fall in the price of novels. If the circulating libraries could no longer boast that for an annual outlay of less than the cost of one new three-decker it was possible for a subscriber to read as many novels as he or she wished, a year's supply of fiction was still available for the cost of three new one-volume novels. It was to take a long time for the public libraries to draw substantial numbers of readers away from the circulating libraries. Some middle-class readers would have recognised and accepted the advantage of not paying at all for fiction, but most of the early middle-class users of public libraries would have been people who did not normally belong to a circulating library. Those who did tended to be the members of the community who could most afford to buy novels. This they would not do as a regular thing. They preferred a library subscription not only for cheapness – it was, no doubt, one of the standard items of 'small expenditure' in those family budgets – but also for the social prestige it gave them in an age of proliferating 'free' libraries, an attitude that was to linger on well into the present century. Although novelists had raged against the circulating libraries throughout the Victorian age, they were slow to realise that the public libraries might work against their interests in similar ways. In Boston in 1876 Gissing noted:

> We have a glorious public library here. It is free to all to use
> and I can assure you it is excellently patronised; for here,
> you know, everybody reads. There are very few books that
> one would be at all likely to want that it does not contain.[158]

Two years later he was back in London, complaining at the 'scandalous' lack of libraries, and still drawing unfavourable comparisons with America: 'There is not a town of the least pretensions in the States, which has not its excellent Free Library.'[159] Gissing's relative poverty, as much as his radical tendencies at this time, made the idea of free libraries particularly attractive to him. He used them whenever they were available, as other writers (especially those of a generation slightly younger than Gissing) were increasingly to do. But his praise for them was not motivated mainly by either personal or ideological reasoning. They were 'glorious' and to be without them was 'scandalous' because their existence presupposed a literate society: they made books available to all and by doing so increased the general interest in books: they were to everyone's advantage. Once the successful establishment of public libraries in Britain was assured, the argument began to be voiced that they were to everyone's advantage except the author's, and denunciations of 'the libraries' now referred collectively to both the circulating and public varieties. The nature of the complaint, if not the precise circumstances, would have been familiar to any mid-Victorian novelist. As a commentator in the *Author* observed on the commercial plight of modern novels: 'They may be read by thousands; they are bought by hundreds. The libraries take nine-tenths of all that are sold, or more.'[160] Two years later another commentator in the *Author* expressed the same feelings more forcefully, and suggested a solution:

> No society, corporate or private, ought to be allowed to purchase a copy of a book and make it the common property of many hundreds of readers. Clearly the author is robbed by such a proceeding. The writer of a modern book ought to be paid a royalty every time a copy of it is lent out of a library – at any rate a public library.[161]

It was to take the Society of Authors more than seventy years to obtain legislation that would put this kind of Public Lending Rights scheme into operation.[162]

For reasonably popular novelists it mattered little, in terms of making a decent living, that the libraries (circulating and/or public) were the main purchasers of fiction, simply because the libraries would buy sufficient numbers of their novels to satisfy borrower demand. It was, of course, obviously the case that if every reader of such a novelist was a buyer and the novelist received a royalty on each copy sold, then his potential income was being held back by the libraries, but neither the Victorian nor the early twentieth-century system worked in quite this straightforward way. As we have seen, the library calculation is important throughout the period because the vast majority of readers in Britain were unable to afford or unwilling to buy new fiction. The difference lay in the changed price of a new novel. The mid-Victorian novelist who could rely on a small initial sale (largely to the circulating libraries) of between five hundred and one thousand copies could live reasonably well on the proceeds because of the artificially high price of a three-decker; his earnings would be increased if he could rely on periodical serialisation and a readership for a cheap edition of a novel (allowing, of course, that he had retained the copy-right).[163] If his novel aroused a great deal of interest and led to an initial sale of, say, three thousand copies, then he would be doing very well indeed. When the price of a new novel fell and the libraries (circulating and public) were still the main purchasers, the number of copies sold had to increase at least threefold (and more often four or fivefold) to make an equivalent profit. With novel-reading holding its own as a major form of entertainment against the emergent leisure industries, and with an unprecedented prestige being given to novels and novelists in the press, there were many writers (especially those willing to write within the newly-established sub-genres of fiction) who could attract the necessary larger number of readers. As far as the level of authors' earnings was concerned, the main issue was how many of those readers were interested enough to be buyers as well. Nobody expected the mid-Victorian reader to go out and buy a three-decker: most readers who admired a three-decker enough to want to own a personal copy would either wait for the cheap one-volume edition or buy a second-hand library copy. Under the new system there were also cheap editions and second-hand copies, but initially the crucial factor was the number of individual buyers who would top-up the basic sales to libraries.

To be a truly commercial success novelists now had to rely on library sales for a good basic income, and, at the same time, provoke those members of the reading public who were able to buy new novels on an occasional if not regular basis, to go out and do so. It was from this situation that the modern 'best-seller' developed, and not, as is still often erroneously assumed, from novelists deliberately writing down for the hard-earned pennies of the newly literate. Recognition of this came swiftly from booksellers. With the argument about the death of the three-decker still active, a writer for the trade journal of booksellers offered a public thanksgiving to Hall Caine and George du Maurier for the success of *The Manxman* (1894) and *Trilby* (1894), both 6/- one-volume novels, the popularity of which had brought a revival of the book trade and 'materially helped the booksellers to pay their rent'. The same writer warned:

It will be futile on the publishers' part to issue novels at 6/-

which are not of the first rank. The second and third rate
novel will never do at 6/-.[164]

The term 'first rank' here refers to both a type of novel and commercial popularity, the two being indistinguishable in this context: it
is the novel which large numbers of people will buy. 'Second and third
rate' does mean less popular, liable to be borrowed rather than
bought, but it also contains within it an assumption of non-com-
mercial literary quality, something not to be trusted. Such books,
the publisher is advised by this bookseller, may find a market at the
lower price of 3/6d or 2/-: less than that would be pointless, for the
'shilling-shocker' has 'had its day'.[165] The question of cheap fiction
is more complex than this allows, but the main point being made is
clear enough – give the reading public a good strong novel at 6/-
and they will buy it, but they are not much interested in anything
else. It is worth noting that one of the legendary writers of these
best-sellers, Marie Corelli, discouraged the publication of cheap
editions of her novels: her commercial instinct was right.[166]

   In terms of sales a best-seller meant anything in excess of about
50,000 copies of a novel and the ability to repeat that sales figure
with subsequent novels. A one-off success was welcome but it did
not bring the regular profits spread over a period of years which
were shared by the publisher and bookseller and made a national
celebrity of the author. Vociferous publicity from the press and
publishers made it sound as though half of the literary world was
made up of best-sellers, but the actual number of such writers was
exceedingly small. Arnold Bennett's computation is probably
reliable: 'There are ten authors in England who can count on
receiving at least four thousand pounds for any long novel they
choose to write, and there are several who have made, and may
again make, £20,000 from a single book.'[167] There were considerably more, though still not a very large number of novelists,
who could regularly sell above 10,000 copies of a novel, which
would bring them a very comfortable living, and a substantial body
of writers, as in the mid-Victorian period, who were the day-by-
day suppliers of fiction to the libraries and periodicals, or, as
Bennett described them, the 'scores of mediocrities who make
upwards of £500 a year from fiction by labour that cannot be called
fatiguing'.[168] All of these writers depended on the circulating and
public libraries for their basic income, with subsequent earnings

rising in proportion to their popularity – bookshop sales, serialisations, colonial editions, the crucially important American market, translations, Tauchnitz continental rights, cheap editions, and, later in the period, film rights. It was often claimed that the general level of new fiction had never been higher or more varied, but the possible truth of that claim was weakened by the concern that the standard of best-selling fiction had probably never been lower and that there were no visible successors to the great masters of the Victorian novel. 'While the crop has been plentiful and of fair quality,' the editor of *Literature* observed in his survey of fiction published in the first year of the new century, 'it is not easy to pick out any works of commanding merit.'[169]

Where the new system was proving markedly inferior to the old was in its apparent inability to do anything materially to help the author whose work did not fall within any of the definable popular categories of fiction or whose talent needed slow growth to mature, the two areas from which fiction of 'commanding merit' was most likely to emerge. Novelists in either of these situations did not have an easy time during the mid-Victorian period, but the circulating libraries were able to offer them a certain amount of protection: it was largely because of this that popular novelists like Besant and Braddon were uneasy about the passing of the three-decker. The fictional type is Edwin Reardon in *New Grub Street*, just as Gissing himself is in most respects the real-life equivalent. Reardon regards the circulating libraries as 'from the commercial point of view . . . indispensable'. He explains that an 'author of moderate repute' can write one three-volume novel a year and sell it outright for 'from one to two hundred pounds'.[170] Trollope, from a more elevated financial position, worked on the same principle, as did many other Victorian novelists. To a later age of royalties and best-sellers, it could seem wasteful and unjust, but its merit was that it bought time to write another, and possibly, better novel. Reardon believes that he would need to write four one-volume novels a year to earn the same as one three-decker. That gloomy prophecy wasn't accurate, but when Milvain objects, rightly, that the libraries will continue to 'circulate novels in one volume', Reardon is also half right in his reply: 'Profits would be less, I suppose. People would take the minimum subscription.'[171] Reardon's financial situation was not enviable in the mid-1880s (the period in which *New Grub Street* is set), though it should be noted that even on his own reckoning his annual income was still higher than that of most wage-earners in Britain. Twenty years later, under the new system, his position would have been untenable. Applying the standard conditions, he would have a contract for his novel bringing him a 10% royalty on the full price of every copy sold. For a sale of one thousand copies he would receive £30: the novel would need to sell five thousand copies for him to make up the average sum of £150 he expected to receive for the copyright of his three-decker.

These figures, of course, comprise only the simplest of calculations, though variations on them do not necessarily work in Reardon's favour. He might have obtained a higher royalty. Although 10% was becoming standard, it was still not uniform practice and could range from 5% to 30%. The higher rates, however, were used only as a bargaining ploy with best-selling novelists, 25% being the point at which the author began to draw profits equivalent to, or slightly higher than, those of the publisher.[172] As an author of 'moderate repute' Reardon has no real bargaining power, and while a publisher who admired his work might have allowed him a royalty of 15% or even 20%, it is unlikely that it would have applied to the first thousand copies sold. It is not even certain that an author in his position could have obtained such a straightforward contract. Some publishers still commonly insisted that royalties should only begin after a specified number of copies had been sold (a deferred royalty as it was commonly called) and continued to charge various costs of production against the author. There were meaner tricks as well. In 1899 Besant drew attention to contracts which paid a 10% royalty on the trade price (about 3/6d) rather than the selling price (6/-), and many authors eager to see their novel in print found themselves tied, at the same terms and to the same publisher, for their next three or four books.[173] Taking these various factors into account, an early twentieth-century Reardon might have considered himself lucky to get £30 for one thousand copies of his novel, but the more important point is that he would have been luckier still to even sell that number, while the five thousand copies which would bring him £150 was barely conceivable. One method by which the author could earn a fairer proportion of the profits on a medium-selling novel was the rising royalty, and the Society of Authors agitated for its general acceptance. It was obviously most profitable for the high or best-selling novel where it mainly functioned, but the Society of Authors wanted it introduced to help writers on much lower incomes, and their suggested plan demonstrates just how low that could be. They argued for a 10% royalty on the first five hundred copies, rising to 15% on the next five hundred, 17.5% for above one thousand, and similar increases for higher sales.[174] This was a typical case where publishers would accuse the Society of greed, but they were really talking about basic survival.

Merely to cover the costs of production, a 6/- novel had to sell five hundred copies: the sum due to the author on such a sale, according to the terms of his contract, was negligible or nil. Bennett estimated that five hundred copies was the likely sale of a first novel: if it sold twice as many as that it was doing well. In other words, a successful first novel would not in itself bring its author anywhere near enough money to reach, say, Rowntree's level of 'merely physical efficiency'. These figures – staying with an author starting his career or one like Reardon with a moderate reputation – are actually optimistic compared with those advanced by contributors to the *Author* where the statement that a 'second-class novel' could rely on sales of seven hundred and fifty copies was aggressively challenged. It was suggested that four hundred was a likelier maximum which meant 'a loss of £10 or £20 to the publisher', and that the only reason why publishers were even willing to consider such novels was because they regarded them as 'a necessary outlay for the maintenance of their "list" and for the capture of an occasional success'.[175] There seems every reason to accept that view as generally correct.[176] Under the Victorian system the 'second-class novel' or the work of a moderately successful novelist was often regarded as 'safe' because of the high price of the three-decker and the agreements between publishers and circulating libraries. Under the new system, with the level of sales crucial, the 'second-class novel' had become a risk, an investment or a gamble. Neither publisher nor author could live on it unless its sales began to climb to a level where profits were very great. For most publishers that meant keeping constant watch for a potential high or best-seller. For most authors, it meant accepting that their basic income had to come from some area of the literary world other than the writing of fiction, and, as we have seen, there were many opportunities to earn this necessary money – from journalism, book-reviewing, reading manuscripts for publishers, writing short stories or articles for the commercial market or even guides advising other literary aspirants of the pitfalls confronting them. This had now become the way that time could be bought to write fiction, but it could just as easily absorb all available time or dissipate energy that should be reserved; and, with the serious novelist increasingly self-conscious about his status as an Artist the literary market-place was usually regarded with disdain. Reardon, in spite of Milvain's urgings, wants nothing to do with it, and when obliged to compromise is a failure. Gissing's own attitude for most of his career was similar. James looked to literary journalism, the American serialisations of his novels, and to short stories, for the money that he could not earn from the sales of the novels themselves; Meredith wrote political journalism and acted as a publisher's reader; Conrad and Joyce steadfastly refused to take advantage of the journalistic opportunities offered them and probably were, anyway, temperamentally incapable of making a financial success of them; Woolf and Lawrence were brilliant book-reviewers and essayists, but unless they were personally involved in such work, resented the distraction it represented. In complete contrast, Bennett gloried in being able to turn his hand to anything, and Wells, though his attitude was very different from Bennett's on this issue, was equally versatile.

The financial difficulties now facing a novelist who needed time to develop his talent or create a following for his work, but who was unwilling to undertake other kinds of short-term writing, can be seen by relating some specific examples to the general situation already described. In the late 1890s when James began writing one-volume novels instead of three-deckers, he was at the height of his career and his lack of sales potential is apparent from the size of the printing his publishers considered appropriate. Heinemann printed two thousand copies of *The Spoils of Poynton*, *What Maisie Knew*, and *The Awkward Age*. It has been claimed that the growing respect with which James was regarded in the literary world led to increased sales of his later novels, and this seems to be correct.[177] Even so, a printing of 3,500 copies of *The Ambassadors* led to 341 of them being remaindered. The sales of Conrad's novels were comparable to those of James, though his habit of borrowing large sums of money as informal advances against royalties meant that for much of his life the income from book sales was irrelevant to his day-to-day expenses. He was treated generously by Blackwood's who paid him £300 for the serialisation of *Lord Jim* (1900), and advanced £200 against a 1/- royalty (about 17%) on book sales. 2,100 copies of the novel were printed and sold, but four years later Blackwood's had still not made enough profit from the book to cover the initial advance.[178] The indirect earnings from the book (its serialisation) were worth considerably more to Conrad than its sales in book form, something well appreciated by both author and publisher. When Conrad, desperate for another loan, offered to sell the copyright of *Lord Jim* at a bargain price to Blackwood's, the offer was turned down: 'He was very kind but told me plainly that I was a loss to the Firm. That's hard enough to hear at any time.'[179] He was to remain a loss to various firms until the commercial success of *Chance* (1913). By 1907 he was well enough regarded for Methuen to print 3,000 copies of *The Secret Agent*: it took five years to dispose of them.[180] E. M. Forster's career also developed slowly and, as Philip Gardner has shown, it was marked by the 'faith of his publishers that increased numbers of his books would sell'.[181] Forster did not need to rely solely on the sales of his novels, which was just as well. Blackwood's printed 1,050 copies of *Where Angels Fear to Tread* (1905) and a further 526 copies almost immediately: for *The Longest Journey* (1907) the same publisher obviously took the sales of the earlier novel as a guide and printed 1,587 copies.[182] *A Room With A View* (1908) went to Edward Arnold who printed 2,000 copies, and increased the imprint to 2,500 for *Howards End* (1910), the popularity of which transformed Forster's earnings.[183] From this point of view, Forster's early career can be considered a success story, at least for a writer of quality fiction: it also illustrates how precarious the path to such a success was. The terms he received for his first novel, *Where Angels Fear to Tread*, were derisory: nothing on the first 300 copies sold, 10% on the next 1,000, 15% up to 2,500.[184] Five years later the terms for *Howards End* were generous: a straight 25% royalty and an advance of £300 against earnings.[185] From the sales of his first novel he could not have earned more than about £40 and not much above that for the second: from the sale of the first printing of *Howards End*, at an excellent royalty, he could not have earned £200. Where Forster's case was different from that of many other authors, and the publishers' investment justified, was his ability with *Howards End* to break through to a sales figure of about 5,000 copies, at which point he began receiving an income from his books which it was possible to live well on; there could be a revived interest in his earlier work and an optimism about the future which generated further earnings; and the publisher also began making a substantial profit. As we have seen, Joyce's first published work of fiction, *Dubliners*, took nine years to get published and sold 379 copies: he received no money for it. In comparison, Lawrence's debut was auspicious. He received just under £50 from Heinemann for royalties on *The White Peacock*, while the terms offered by Duckworth for *Sons and Lovers* were, as Lawrence himself described them, 'quite gorgeous': a 15% royalty on the first 2,500 copies, 17½% on subsequent sales, and an advance of £100.[186] The terms negotiated by the same publisher for Virginia Woolf's first novel, *The Voyage Out*, were not at all gorgeous, though from the publisher's point of view they were to prove realistic. She accepted a 15% royalty on the first 5,000 copies sold, rising to 20% on subsequent sales.[187] It is difficult to believe that anyone involved in this negotiation could have regarded the terms as reasonable: it was to take fifteen years to sell just 2,000 copies of *The Voyage Out* and earn Woolf about £90.[188]

The necessity for a novelist to have a source of income other than that derived from book sales is apparent in all of these various figures, and the situation was much the same for certain novelists who were to develop reputations for being blatantly commercial in their attitudes to the art of fiction. Bennett's substantial earnings from miscellaneous literary and journalistic work, and his own compulsive self-advertisement, have often concealed both the seriousness of much of his fiction and the fact that his income from that fiction accounted for only a small proportion of his total earnings. The terms he obtained for his first novel were actually less attractive than Lawrence's for *The White Peacock* or even Woolf's for *The Voyage Out*. For *A Man from the North* John Lane's terms were 5% on the first 2,000 copies, 10% on the next 3,000 and 15% subsequently: its sale price was 3/6d.[189] It was widely and well reviewed, and his financial return on it 'exceeded the cost of having it typewritten by the sum of one sovereign'.[190] With characteristic bravado Bennett refused to complain: 'Many a first book has cost its author a hundred pounds. I got a new hat out of mine.'[191] No less than Conrad, Lawrence or Woolf, Bennett realised that a first novel was really an investment for the future, but it took him some time to benefit from his investment. The British rights for *Anna of the Five Towns* together with those for three other novels were sold to Chatto and Windus in a kind of job-lot for £250, and as late as 1908 Chapman and Hall were uneasy about advancing Bennett £150 on *The Old Wives' Tale*.[192] The contract allowed for a good royalty of 20% on the first 5,000 copies and 25% for sales above that number: it was negotiated by the literary agent J. B. Pinker. Galsworthy paid for the publication of his first volume of short stories in 1897, negotiated a 'deferred royalty' arrangement for the publication of his first novel the following year – 'so deferred,' he commented 'that nothing came my way' – and published a further two novels and one volume of short stories before the commercial success in 1906 of *The Man of Property* which sold 5,000 copies.[193] As he liked to claim, looking back from his years of prosperous popularity: 'I had been writing nearly eleven years without making a penny, or any name to speak of.'[194] He was only slightly exaggerating. The fact that he was already financially independent of his earnings from writing allowed him to escape both the nervous torment that establishing a reputation provoked in Conrad and the worldly-wise boastfulness of Bennett, but it does not affect the overwhelming evidence that good-quality British fiction was suffering a severe commercial crisis.

To many commentators the solution to the problem was obvious – authors and publishers should abandon the 6/- novel, drastically reduce the price of new fiction, by-pass the libraries, and compete in the mass market: even the regular alternative prices of a new novel, 3/6*d* and to a lesser extent 2/-, were too high. Typical of the optimism with which the advocates of a 'cheap fiction' policy made their case was a correspondent to the *Author* in 1909. Pointing out, rightly, that 6/- was an arbitrary sum, he proposed that new fiction be published in attractive paper covers at 1/6*d*; 'Imagine the effect of such a reform. All the cheap magazines would be swept off the front of the bookstalls, and in their place would be piles of new novels.'[195] 1/6*d*, however, was no more rational a price than 6/-, or 1/- or 4*d* if the cost of production and distribution could not be met and a profit made for publisher and author by a substantial increase of sales. That was exactly what the supporters of cheap fiction wanted to try for and claimed could be achieved, but it was difficult to put a convincing case when the average 6/- novel was having a struggle to sell the necessary five hundred copies to cover costs and enough above that to pay the author a sum that he could

e on. The lower the price of a novel the more copies needed
sold. It took sales of two thousand just to cover the
production costs of a 3/6d novel; three thousand for one at 2/-.[196]
The basic statistics for a 6d book had been set out in the *Author*
some years earlier. An edition of 50,000 copies would cost £340 to
produce, and to cover that 27,000 copies would need to be sold: if
the author received a royalty of $\frac{3}{4}d$ on each copy – and the *Author*
warned, he is often offered as little as $\frac{1}{4}d$ – then it would take
36,000 copies to cover production costs. If the whole edition was
sold the publisher would receive about £128, the author £156. The
bookseller would sell the book at $4\frac{1}{2}d$ and make 1d profit on each
copy.[197] Sales figures of 50,000 and 100,000 and more were
frequently bandied about in discussions of newspapers, periodicals
and best-sellers. Why shouldn't new fiction be able to reach similar
peaks if it was offered at a competitive price?

It was a tempting argument, even allowing that discussions of
the huge sales of periodicals and best-sellers were themselves often
inflated and therefore unreliable guides. The objections to a cheap-
fiction policy were powerful, but not crushingly so. The evidence
was actually uncertain and open to different interpretations, and
there was a good deal of evidence to draw on, for the ideal of cheap
literature stretched back to at least the beginning of the nineteenth
century. It had played a prominent part in the 'popular educator'
and 'march of intellect' debates in the 1820s and 1830s; religious
organisations had distributed and sold a legendary number of
tracts; it was the profusion of penny fiction in working-class city
districts that had fascinated Thackeray, Collins and Payn; in the
1840s and 1850s publishers like Bentley and Routledge had
successfully marketed 'railway novels' or 'yellow-backs' in hard
covers, attractively designed and costing as little as 1/-; even when
the three-decker was at the height of its power there were
publishers tempted to challenge it with cheaper fiction; and certain
kinds of fiction – children's stories, temperance tracts and adventure
tales – had long been issued at lower than standard prices: the
success in this format of *The Time Machine* and *Dr Jekyll and Mr
Hyde* was encouraging. There had also been recent attempts to
publish less sensational new fiction at 1/6d, notably by J. W.
Arrowsmith, the Bristol-based publisher, T. Fisher Unwin in his
'Pseudonym' and 'Autonym' Libraries, and Cassell in their 'Pocket
Library'. There were, however, two areas of publishing more than

any others which attracted the attention of the cheap-fiction advocates. From the early 1890s Chatto and Windus had been publishing paperback reprints of popular novels. They were printed in rather unattractive double-columns in order to squeeze what was originally a three-decker into about two hundred pages, but they cost only 6d and were extremely popular. Andrew Chatto claimed that in twelve years he had sold a total of six million of these paperbacks.[198] Individual novels by Ouida, Charles Reade and Wilkie Collins had each sold as many as 300,000 copies, and although other novelists in the series did not do this well it was still an indication of what could be achieved with cheap fiction in the mass market.

The second influence was the publishing boom in reprints of 'classic' works of literature, ancient and modern. There was again a direct link here with the early nineteenth century but the distinctive late Victorian contribution was the broad expansion of educational opportunities – ranging from elementary schools, through entry into the civil service by competitive examination, to the founding of provincial universities and the university extension movement – out of which there developed a new concept of the 'text' book. The mid-Victorian model was Henry Bohn's 'Standard Library' which began in 1846 at 3/6d a volume, later increased to 5/-. In 1864 the project was taken over by another publisher and expanded to contain more than seven hundred titles, many of them translations of classical and European works.[199] The Bohn policy of publishing at a reasonably low price texts which were difficult to obtain except in expensive editions, or in their original language, and sometimes not at all, was taken up by Henry Morley who was Professor of English Literature at University College, London. Morley also printed translations but his main concentration was on works of English literature, many of which had long been out of print. He lowered the price considerably and for his first large-scale venture – Cassell's 'Library of English Literature' (1875) – he revived the long-established educational practice of publishing in monthly parts, each part costing 7d. This was followed by 'Morley's Universal Library' (1883) for Routledge which was directed more obviously at the examination market: well-produced and hardback, they sold for 1/- or 1/6d per volume. In 1886 he returned to Cassell and went even further down-market with his 'National Library' which offered texts at 3d (paper covers) or 6d (cloth).[200] George Newnes went still further down with his 'Penny Library of Famous Books', and so did W. T. Stead with a series of 'Penny Poets' and 'Penny Popular Novels'. Traditional publishers competed energetically with each other to produce similar, though more respectably priced and attractively presented, reprints.[201] The most successful of these series were Dent's 'Everyman's Library' which began in 1906 and was described by its publisher as 'a democratic library at the democratic price of one shilling', and Oxford University Press's 'World's Classics' which was taken over from the bankrupt Grant Richards and also sold at 1/- in direct competition with Everyman's.[202]

The opponents of a cheap-fiction policy were quick to point out that the great majority of books being published at 1/6d, 1/-, and 6d were either reprints, non-fiction, novels which had already proved their popularity in expensive editions, or they were out of copyright, thus allowing a more attractive level of profit to the publisher. None of these busy areas of publishing activity was relevant to new fiction, and where publishers had been tempted to try issuing new novels at experimental prices they had not met with notable success. As we have seen, the statistical evidence compiled by Besant to show up what he called 'the madness of the sixpenny book' was certainly not encouraging: at a time when it was difficult for many novelists to find a thousand buyers at the standard price, there seemed little reason to believe that a sharp reduction in price would attract the necessary fifty times more buyers. There was also concern expressed that if new fiction was readily available at a low price it would drive away traditional customers, lower the status of the novelist (by equating his work with the price of the entrance to a music-hall), be ignored by the libraries, ruin booksellers, and render the 6/- novel extinct. Strong support for the opponents of cheap fiction came from Andrew Chatto, who warned that the commercial success of his sixpenny paperbacks could be easily mis-interpreted.

> It is only the fiction that lives that can hope for a triumph in this latter-day appeal at sixpence to the masses. Their knowledge extends to the books which cry from the heights, as it were, but it does not yet penetrate into the highways and byways of literature. In other words, the masses want what is of proved interest, the established story – that and that only.[203]

It was quite impossible, Chatto announced, to publish original novels in the same way and at the same price as the heightened established 'stories' demanded by 'the masses'. The argument was of the same circular kind as that employed at every stage of the establishment of the late Victorian mass market, but whether consumers were supplied with what they demanded, or were given what it was assumed they would demand if they were capable of choosing, was, as far as fiction was concerned, never tested in any convincing or whole-hearted way.

Any lingering chance that it might have been was effectively closed off by publishers and authors uniting to preserve the 6/- novel. They were brought together initially by *The Times* 'book war' of 1905. The sale by The Times Book Club of virtually new books at bargain prices convinced both the Publishers' Association and the Society of Authors that they had been tricked into what was in effect a cheap book policy, and one that was seriously detrimental to their interests. In this particular case, there were common causes – notably American business methods and the blatant use of books by *The Times* to boost its circulation – which could be identified and fought in public. The book war was hardly over when a new and equally worrying threat emerged with the announcement by the Edinburgh publishers Thomas Nelson of their plans to issue a series of novels costing 7*d* each. They were hardback, clearly printed, and many of them were still in copyright. It was a carefully planned operation, made possible by a large capital investment in new machinery which had reduced labour costs and enabled the publisher to negotiate terms with living authors. Although the novels were, technically, reprints, only a relatively short period of time had elapsed since their original publication, and they included works by some of the most popular and the most respected novelists of the day. It was the nearest any British publisher came to entering the mass market with cheap new fiction, and it was a commercial success. The response of other publishers was largely hostile. On 21 December 1908 representatives of the Society of Authors were invited to a meeting with five leading publishers and urged to do what they could to dissuade authors from participating in schemes similar to that of the Nelson Library. There was no objection by the publishers to various other cheap editions on the market: 'It was the clothbound book of good appearance at 7*d* that was alleged to be mischievous.'[204] Apart from the commercial argument that profits on such a book were dependent on very large sales, the main worries were that the very existence of the 7*d* book would encourage the public to believe that it was possible to produce all fiction at this price, and, as many people would buy these editions, that there would be a reduced demand from the libraries which would render the 6/- novel unviable. The Society of Authors shared these concerns and proposed that its members should observe a lapse of two years before allowing any novel published originally at 6/- to appear in a cheap edition. Authors were balloted, and a list of those agreeing to abide by the proposal was published in the *Author*.[205] Not all novelists, however, belonged to the Society of Authors, and not all members of the Society agreed to the proposal: it was yet another policy decision that could not be carried out in any truly effective way. But the combined forces of the Authors and Publishers were powerful enough to ensure that the 6/- novel would continue; libraries would remain the principal buyers; sales of popular novels would increase; new fiction would be prevented from competing in the mass market; cheap fiction would be made up of 'classic' non-copyright 'texts', the work of novelists whose popularity was already proven, and novels and novelettes consciously written-down for the quarter-educated; and any new, adventurous or experimental novelist would be shoved to the periphery of the market until he or she could break through to popularity or build up a dedicated following.

The agreement between the Publishers' Association and the Society of Authors, their acknowledged reliance on library sales, and the general approval of the Booksellers of the 6/- novel, represent in certain important respects a return to the mid-Victorian system, though this was the result of innate conservatism rather than a conscious decision, and the essential differences between the two systems are equally important. The mid-Victorians had assumed that there was only one market and acted accordingly to control it. They tended to ignore the much larger 'unknown public' identified by Thackeray and Collins, except for the possibility of raising segments of it into a dominant culture that was financially strong enough to maintain fiction of varying quality. The late Victorians acknowledged the existence of the larger reading public and expanded it. The ideal was now truly of one culture, but in practice it led to still further fragmentation and exposed the pretentiousness of mid-Victorian cultural assumptions. With the novel laid precariously open to the mass market the only major mid-Victorian novelist who continued to be read enthusiastically by large numbers of people was Dickens. Instead of the 'newly literate' poor and working-class readers swelling the traditional audience for major fiction, exactly the opposite happened, with large numbers of upper- and middle-class readers revealing that their taste in fiction was essentially little different from that of the 'unknown public'. It was a secret long known to the circulating libraries – given the choice, most readers, regardless of class, would prefer Ouida to George Eliot, Mrs Henry Wood to Thackeray. There really should have been no surprise early in the twentieth century when readers overwhelmingly plumped for Elinor Glyn rather than Conrad, or Florence Barclay rather than Virginia Woolf.

Although the drive to preserve the 6/- novel was motivated primarily by a concern for commercial safety, other factors were also influential. On the part of many publishers and authors there was a growing distaste at the way the mass market was developing: participation was coming to involve a loss of status for which the money to be made was insufficient compensation. The novelist who was serious about his art was unable to accept the compromises that now seemed inevitable. The publisher who wished to maintain the dignity of one of the most respected of the professions was similarly uneasy, and looked to the admired (if low-selling) author who would uphold the prestige of the house even if this meant subsidising his work from the profits made on more popular fiction. David Meldrum's advice to William Blackwood to publish Conrad's novels simply for the honour they would bring was becoming common practice. A more drastic solution was for likeminded novelists, publishers and editors to ignore the mass market entirely and function through private presses or 'little' magazines. An additional factor in the retreat from cheap books was distrust of America. Throughout the nineteenth century it had been foretold that great prosperity would come to British authors and publishers once the Americans signed an international copyright agreement and reformed their piratical habits. To some extent this view was correct: after 1891 American 'rights' were something to be taken into account in any publishing contract. But there were other factors which tended to be left out of the wider calculations. By the time that British authors were legally entitled to payment for American editions of their books, every area of American industry (including publishing) was in the process of rapid expansion, at home and overseas. W. T. Stead proclaimed it – not too grandly as things were to turn out – 'The Americanisation of the World' and called for a merging of the United States and the British Empire to form a 'Race Union', with Britain as 'the cradle of the race', a solution to the future relative decline of Britain that several other authors, most notably Kipling, also flirted with.[206] Conrad always despised such grandiose schemes and offered his own brilliantly perceptive analysis of American economic imperialism in *Nostromo*: 'We shall run the world's business whether the world likes it or not. The world can't help it – and neither can we, I guess,' the American millionaire Holroyd informs Gould before returning to his San Francisco skyscraper to get on with running the world.[207]

There were early complaints in the *Author* that American piracy had not stopped but only shifted to the British dominions and colonies, and that the publishing industries in Canada and Australia were slipping away from British influence and being taken over by America.[208] The most disturbing feature of Americanisation, for those who didn't share Stead's enthusiasm, was its aggressive pioneering of a mass market. It represented everything that the most conservative British publishers wanted to hold back or restrict, and was a principal cause of them being so rattled by the announcement of the Nelson Library the very moment they had won a victory against the Americanisation of The Times Book Club. It was also, of course, a main reason why many young American writers felt that their ambitions could not be satisfied in their own country. But the majority of British readers did not share these assumptions and prejudices, and not the least unexpected aspect of Americanisation was the ever-growing popularity of American fiction in Britain. Arnold Bennett devoted a section of *Fame and Fiction* (1901) to the phenomenon, and nine years later Gertrude Atherton (herself a firm favourite in Britain) was pointing to Winston Churchill, Kate Douglas Wiggin, Francis Marion Crawford and James Lane Allen as American writers whose novels could expect unusually high British sales.[209] They were not exactly the novelists who would bring about the astonishing achievement of modernist fiction, but then neither were the British authors whose popularity they were challenging. The opened-up American market was refusing to have quite the result that mid-Victorian authors had expected. The vast world-wide English readership had finally emerged, and there was already more than a suspicion of an American accent to its dominant tone. Up until the mid-1890s lists of the most popular novels in America contained a very high proportion of British titles: in 1895 six out of the top ten, according to one account.[210] There were still to be some spectacular British successes, and to the present day the American market remains of great importance to British novelists, but from the mid-1890s onwards the most popular novels in America were increasingly by American authors, and many of those novels were equally popular in Britain.

It was at this time that the term 'best-seller' was coined. The OED Supplement attributes the earliest use of the term to a Kansas newspaper in 1889: 'Kansas City's literary tone is improving. The six best sellers here last week were . . .' The man usually credited with systematising the concept is Harry Thurston Peck, editor of the New York *Bookman* which began publication in 1895 and from the beginning carried a list of 'books in demand' submitted by booksellers in selected American cities. In 1897 these lists were collected into an annual survey called 'Best Selling Books', and in 1903 the monthly lists began to be called 'The Six Best Sellers'.[211] Peck, however, almost certainly took the idea from the London *Bookman* which had been listing 'books on demand' and using the term 'best-selling books' for four years before the New York version of the periodical was even founded. James Milnes's *Book Monthly* listed 'best-selling novels' from October 1903 and was soon referring unselfconsciously to 'best-sellers', probably by this time in imitation of the New York *Bookman*. Whoever was originally responsible for the usage, it began as a fairly neutral trade report and was quickly developed by American literary journalists, at first for its newsworthiness – a best-seller list was itself a selling point – and then by journalists, publishers, booksellers, and occasionally authors, for publicity or commercial reasons. In America there was an early concern to establish some kind of statistical reliability for best-seller lists, especially once they were taken over by the *Publishers' Weekly* in 1912. In Britain there was a generalised vagueness about them, characterised by Milnes's

list of best-selling novels which he simply described as having been
'prepared by a high authority'.[212] As late as 1935 the literary agent
Curtis Brown could refer nostalgically to *Red Pottage* going to 'the
top of what in these days we would call the best-sellers', as though
the concept of a best-seller was a current fad.[213] It was in fact, in
both America and Britain, very much a product of the 1890s.

The problem is that apart from its symptomatic importance and
its original usefulness as a trade indicator – one of the 'books in
demand', or the formulation sometimes used by the London
Bookman, one of the 'books which have sold most freely during the
month' – the term best-seller is virtually meaningless. As James D.
Hart has pointed out it is a linguistic oddity, 'untrustworthy by its
very nature: it indicates a superlative: it is used as a comparative'.[214]
Throughout the period covered here it was rarely used with any
precision, though the concept was well understood. A certain level
of sales was necessary to qualify as a best-seller, and a minimum
number of 50,000 copies has already been suggested as appropriate
for Britain at this time. This level of sales alone was not, however,
sufficient qualification. Just as the idea of the best-seller developed
out of the polarisation of the mass market in the 1890s, so there
was built into the definition assumptions of very specific kinds of
inferiority. Fiction which advocated radical views (*The Woman
Who Did*) or functioned within a clearly defined sub-genre (*The
Adventures of Sherlock Holmes*) or had obvious literary merit (*Tess
of the D'Urbervilles*) would only have been described as a best-
seller in a very general sense; and the same was true for a cheap
novelette and a volume of stories by Kipling, both of which could
often outsell a best-seller. The true best-seller was read and bought
by the 'quarter-educated': it was what in a later, even more socially
divisive, coinage would be called 'middle-brow', which does not,
however, mean that it was not also read by a great many 'low-
brows'. It was directly descended from the great popular favourites
of the circulating libraries: *Lady Audley's Secret* and *East Lynne*
were best-sellers in every sense before the word was invented. In
terms of subject matter best-sellers at the turn-of-the-century can
be divided into a large number of different categories – religious,
sensational, romantic, sentimental, adventure – but what unites
them is a shared sense of fundamental assumptions and values. It is
this that gave best-seller status to such representative works as:
Anthony Hope, *The Prisoner of Zenda* (1894); George du Maurier,

Trilby (1894): Marie Corelli, *The Sorrows of Satan* (1895); Mary Cholmondley, *Red Pottage* (1899); Hall Caine, *The Eternal City* (1901); Guy Thorne, *When it Was Dark* (1902); Robert Hichens, *The Garden of Allah* (1904); Elinor Glyn, *Three Weeks* (1907); Horace de Vere Stacpoole, *The Blue Lagoon* (1908); Maud Diver, *The Great Amulet* (1908); Florence Barclay, *The Rosary* (1909); Ethel M. Dell, *The Way of an Eagle* (1912). It is quite wrong to associate these early best-sellers with 'best-sellerism' which, in Britain at least, is a later phenomenon and has been well described by John Sutherland.[215] Of course, there were already authors who approached the lucrative market of best-selling fiction with business-like efficiency or cynicism – Edgar Wallace and E. Phillips Oppenheim, for example – as there were publishers willing to employ gimmicky advertising methods to get a book talked about and a fair number of envious or disillusioned accusations of 'booming'. But for the most part the 'best-sellers' were as intensely sincere in the value of their work as Conrad or Gissing. When literary critics today even mention best-sellers of this period it is invariably to make the negative and obvious point that they lacked all the qualities of their pioneering modernist contemporaries. But in order to understand the historical importance of the best-sellers it is advisable to reverse that attitude and recognise that they possessed in abundance all the qualities which their great contemporaries either lacked or had jettisoned.

For Lady Bell the novels of Mrs Henry Wood were popular with working-class readers because of their 'admirable compound of the goody and the sensational': she also decided that the necessary ingredients of a successful novelette were 'something about love, with a dash of religion'.[26] These are certainly crucial qualities in the nineteenth- and early twentieth-century best-seller, though to them there must be added the more positive characteristic noted by Q. D. Leavis:

> Even the most critical reader who brings only an ironical appreciation of their work cannot avoid noticing a certain power, the secret of their success with the majority. Bad writing, false sentiment, sheer silliness, and a preposterous narrative are all carried along by the magnificent vitality of their author.[217]

The 'magnificent vitality' of the best-selling author's personality

rested on a moral confidence of such strength that it could make
the dominant trends of modern 'vivisective' thought appear
irrelevant to the normal processes of everyday life. In this sense the
best-seller can be described (as it commonly is) as escapist, as long
as that categorisation does not necessarily indicate a blindness or
indifference to the forces making for change in turn-of-the-century
Britain. Hall Caine, Robert Hichens and Marie Corelli were no less
aware of what was taking place around them than Gissing or
James, and the breakdown of societal and familial values portrayed
in, say, *The Whirlpool* or *The Wings of the Dove* is not as far
removed as is often supposed from that of *The Christian, Bella
Donna,* or *The Sorrows of Satan.* Boredom, cynicism and lassitude
play as central a part in the best-sellers as in other fiction of the
time. Before he sets out on the path to Ruritanian immortality
Rudolf Rassendyll in *The Prisoner of Zenda* lives a life of contented
purposelessness, seeing no reason why he should ever 'do' anything;
Geoffrey Tempest in *The Sorrows of Satan* is one of the self-
seeking egoists to be found everywhere in late Victorian fiction;
while Domini Enfilden in *The Garden of Allah* is the type of 'neurotic'
heroine, 'one of the weak or dissipated sisterhood for whom "rest
cures" are invented'.[218] And although all of the best-selling authors
retained their faith in a fairly straightforward narrative and strong
plot, they were by no means entirely addicted to the conventional
happy ending that is frequently regarded as their hall-mark. Some
were, though the bitter-sweet was just as acceptable. Horace de Vere
Stacpoole even offered a classically ambiguous ending to *The Blue
Lagoon,* leaving it open to the reader to decide whether the castaway
lovers are brought back to corrupt civilisation alive or dead.

   At a time when the most advanced novelists were striving to
refine themselves out of fiction, to subdue their personalities in
favour of dramatic, oblique or impersonal narrative methods, the
best-selling author slid easily into the spot vacated by the mid-
Victorians, berating, denouncing or consoling the reader, and
always telling a strong story. In opposition to the godless relativism
of the age, the best-seller asserted the existence of absolute values.
At its most defiant it presented itself as a coherent philosophy that
was both older and newer than advanced modern thought. As
Satan explains to Geoffrey Tempest:

   My beliefs are too positive to be brought even into contact

with your contradictions – too frightfully real to submit to
your doubts for a moment. You would at once begin to revert
to the puny used-up old arguments of Voltaire, Schopenhauer
and Huxley – little atomic theories like grains of dust in the
whirlpool of My knowledge![219]

This was the kind of assurance that would allow Corelli to portray
in her fiction not only a sorrowful Satan but Christ's crucifixion
and resurrection as well. The importance of 'size' to the best-
selling novel was something that did not escape the professional
understanding of Arnold Bennett: 'The unrivalled vogue of Miss
Marie Corelli is partly due to the fact that her inventive faculty has
always ranged easily and unafraid amid the largest things.'[220] With
When it Was Dark Guy Thorne proved himself even more unafraid
of the largest things than Marie Corelli. He conjured up a human
Anti-Christ who is determined to overthrow 'the Gigantic Fable of
the Cross and the Man God', but is finally defeated by the humble
curate Basil Gartre who combats and defeats 'depths of human
wickedness so abysmal and awful that the mind can hardly
conceive of them'.[221] If not all of the best-sellers were quite that
confident, they still participated with their readers in spiritual
rituals that promised to heal the sufferings of the temporal world
and purge the horror of unbelief. The religious terminology usually
had little to do with any definable theological doctrine. It was the
atmosphere of sanctity or holiness that mattered, and that could be
easily adapted to the sexual passion of Elinor Glyn's *Three Weeks*;
the vast Sahara desert of *The Garden of Allah* where Domini
Enfilden's neurosis is cured; the Indian mountains of *The Way of
an Eagle* ('They stood alone together – above the world – with
their faces to the mountains'); or even the traditional wedding
service which was becoming much less common in fiction than the
Sahara Desert, though it marks the dramatic climax of *The Rosary*:

So they took each other – these two, who were so deeply
each other's already – solemnly, reverently, tenderly in the
sight of God, they took each other, according to God's holy
ordinance; and the wedding ring, type of that eternal love
which has neither beginning nor ending, passed from Garth's
pocket, over the Holy Book, on to Jane's finger.[222]

While the faith in absolute values cut the best-seller irrevocably
loose from more serious fiction of the time and provoked the

mockery of critics – often justifiably so, for the 'sheer silliness' identified by Q. D. Leavis is obviously real enough – it also served to free the author from many of the inhibitions that were now strongly present elsewhere in fiction. Not constrained by modern artistic self-consciousness or the denial of self, the best-seller operated at an extraordinarily high pitch of emotional intensity. It could absorb the death-bed or sick-bed scene loved by the Victorians; squeeze the last drop of emotion out of personal loss, physical mutilation, or ill-fated love; and draw on age-old sensational and melodramatic techniques, an interest shared only with Hardy among the acknowledged masters of early modern fiction. At its most vital the best-seller achieved a mythopoeic status that transferred successfully to the stage and then film, reaching out to ever-increasing audiences and creating its own cultural pantheon of classic characters and moments: 'the lady' reclining on a tiger skin, 'between her red lips was a rose not redder than they – an almost scarlet rose'; Kate Llewellyn raising the crucifix over her dying blasphemous husband; Jane Champion singing 'The Rosary' to a hushed Society gathering; the London opera house chanting a derisory 'Svengali! Svengali! Svengali!' as Trilby snaps out of her trance; Rudolf Rassendyll faithfully mourning his lost Queen and receiving every year a parcel containing a solitary red rose with the message 'Rudolf–Flavia–always.'

As reward for stirring the hearts of so many readers, the best-selling author received not only a large income and constant publicity but also the devoted, distant friendship of what would eventually come to be called 'fans'. Lady Bell recorded the case of 'a poor woman, the widow of a workman, who had gone away to a distant part of the country'. She was being supported by the parish, and wrote to someone in her former town to say that if she had 'that beautiful book *East Lynne* it would be a comfort to her'.[223] The best-seller (author or novel) was a companion, friend, inspiration and spiritual guide. When the authors were willing to give public lectures they were assured of large audiences, and they talked not on the art of fiction or the importance of symbolism in modern literature but on the meaning of life. They received thousands of letters from unknown readers seeking personal advice or merely wishing to record their appreciation for the novels which had meant so much to them at times of loneliness or despair. Publishers too responded with appropriate displays of gratitude.

On the publication day of one of her novels Florence Barclay would present herself at her publisher's office, receive a bouquet of flowers, and distribute autographed copies of the novel to all the members of staff.[224] There were many other popular novelists of the time who received thank-you letters from admirers and could attract curious crowds whenever they spoke in public – Wells, Conan Doyle, Kipling and Haggard. But this was not the same thing at all. The essential quality that distinguished the best-seller was defined with great precision, and little cynicism, by one of the period's least successful authors. Bored with his own books, George Arthur Rose in Baron Corvo's *Hadrian the Seventh* borrows a copy of Edna Lyall's *Donovan* from a neighbour. He is keen to know what kind of author it can be whose books sell in 'tens of thousands while we don't sell ours by tens of hundreds'.[225] His determination to 'dissect and analyse' overcomes his irritation with the book and he sits over it until midnight when the secret is finally revealed to him:

> 'Yes,' he said, 'she's a dear good woman. Her book – well –
> her book is cheap, awkward, vulgar – but it's good. It's
> unpalteringly ugly and simple and good. Evidently it's best to
> be good. It pays.'[226]

The secret, of course, is quite useless to him.

For a James, Conrad, Gissing or Joyce, the adulation given to the best-seller was a final confirmation of Britain's cultural decadence, damning evidence that the majority could not be trusted and that hope for the future lay with the sensitive few. In February 1917, reviewing *A Portrait of the Artist* which had been published at long last in book form, Ezra Pound noted sarcastically that Joyce could not expect 'members of the "Fly-Fishers" and "Royal Automobile" clubs, and of the "Isthmian"' to read his book, but that that no longer mattered, as a new kind of reader was coming into being: 'The last few years have seen the gradual shaping of a party of intelligence, a party not bound by any central doctrine or theory.'[227] The 'party of intelligence' was virtually the same as Arnold's 'remnant', and, in keeping with the collectivist tendency of the age, it was created by the State.

Epilogue

Although a great deal of twentieth-century literary criticism and theory appears to deny the fact, it should be obvious enough that as long as there has been literature there has also been literary criticism. What happened in the second half of the nineteenth century was not the discovery of literary criticism, but its extensive and formal institutionalisation, the start of a shift of critical authority away from the pronouncements of imaginative writers and into the classroom. Throughout the period covered by this book, and for some years beyond, literary criticism maintained its traditional, and, it would generally have been assumed, its symbiotic association with imaginative literature, as the careers of James, Pound, Ford, Lawrence, Eliot and Woolf sufficiently demonstrate. Like many innovative writers of earlier periods, the Modernists knew that they would have to win over a reluctant public and that the process was likely to be a slow one. Their criticism was self-justifying and proselytising: this too they shared with previous generations, both near and distant. Earlier writers in a roughly comparable situation had survived either through aristocratic patronage or by gradually converting the taste of editors, reviewers, publishers and readers. Examples of both of these career patterns can be found in the opening years of the twentieth century, though the patronage was no longer 'aristocratic' in any traditional sense, and, marking a strong break with the immediate past, the little patronage available was now being sought by major novelists as well as poets.

As we have seen, the hardship experienced by many innovative novelists did not come from their inability to find publishers, or indeed readers. Joyce was exceptional in this respect. Other novelists of his generation, together with Joyce, had to experience petty interfering acts of censorship, but they did not have great difficulty getting their work accepted for publication, and the initial sales of their novels would, forty years earlier, have brought them a sufficient income to live on while they established their reputations. What they could not do, in the new commercial conditions, was attract *enough* readers. Although 'numbers' were crucial here, as in every aspect of the age, the issue was not simply numerical. The combative nature of much of the new fiction, whether in its form or content, demanded a particular kind of reader, not a general change of taste or fashion. Converts were found among existing readers and within the Literary Establishment, but they were heavily outnumbered by enthusiasts for formula-fiction, best-sellers, clearly defined sub-genres, or for novelists like Hardy, Wells and Bennett, whose innovative qualities were allied to a strong story. The success of Modernist fiction depended not on the age-old necessity for the writer to create his own readership, but on a new kind of reader being created for him. In welcoming the book publication of *A Portrait of the Artist*, Pound correctly identified the two principal qualities this new reader should have – 'intelligence' and the willingness not to be 'bound by any central doctrine or theory'. Pound also gave special attention to Joyce's 'hard, clear-cut' prose style, and explained why this was important for both the well-being of literature and good government:

> The terror of clarity is not confined to any one people. The
> obstructionist and the provincial are everywhere, and in them
> alone is the permanent danger to civilisation. Clear, hard
> prose is the safeguard and should be valued as such. The
> mind accustomed to it will not be cheated or stampeded by
> national phrases and emotionalities.[1]

Even allowing that Pound was writing during the First World War, his claim that the 'hell of contemporary Europe' was caused in part by the 'non-existence of decent prose in the German language' was extreme.[2] Not, however, all that extreme: the conviction that a sensitive appreciation of literature would save, or at least safeguard, civilisation, had been steadily growing for years.

The idea of a cultural élite being formed in order to prevent the total collapse of civilised values that democracy was expected to bring about, can be traced back to Coleridge who, on the eve of the first Reform Bill, called for the establishment of a 'permanent, nationalised, learned order, a national clerisy or Church'.[3] The term 'clerisy' did not catch on, but the concept did: it can be seen being reworked in response to rapidly changing circumstances by such mainstream Victorian writers as Carlyle, John Stuart Mill, Newman and Arnold, whose 'aliens' and 'remnant' are clearly descended from the Coleridgean 'clerisy', though now invested with the even more urgent task of safeguarding standards in a mass society.[4] Although never lacking admirers, Arnold had, for much of his life, been dismissed as a dilettante; someone who, in his own satirical words, sat in the midst of a hardworking world, indifferent to stern practicality, 'trifling with aesthetics and poetical fancies' and handing round his 'pouncet-box'.[5] By the 1880s his insistence that middle-class education in Britain must be radically improved, and his advice to Americans that they should concentrate on strengthening the 'numbers' of their 'remnant' so that it might become 'incomparable, all-transforming', were being listened to with a new kind of respect. It was no longer his rigorous approach to literary criticism that was being praised: the more important social implications of that critical rigour were also being taken seriously. In 1897, ten years after Arnold's death, Hugh Walker was far from alone in pointing out that 'no criticism was ever less negative' than Arnold's, and that the greatness of Arnold as critic, and the cause of his high reputation, was that his 'purpose' was always 'practical'.[6] Walker was Professor of English Literature at St David's College, Lampeter, and, therefore, a prominent member of the new clerisy: his praise of Arnold's practicality appeared in one of the most popular of the many handbooks and primers which were being hurriedly written to extol the humanising virtues of English literature and to establish its formal study at the centre of university syllabuses.

That responsibility for the clerisy would have to rest on the universities was not apparent to many people until relatively late in the nineteenth century. In 1800 Oxford and Cambridge were the only universities in England. They were small, catering between them for just over one thousand students; fiercely resistant to change; and, as far as the humanities were concerned, dominated by classicism. Nearby, Scotland offered a more progressive model, with twice as many universities as England, seven times more students, a broader syllabus (based on philosophy rather than the classics) and a democratic policy on university entrance. The exclusive Anglicanism of Oxbridge would have made it impossible for the Scottish example to be followed in England, even if there had been any desire to do so on other grounds. The social exclusiveness of Oxbridge – only partly as a result of its religious exclusiveness – was also extreme. Harold Perkin has noted that as late as 1860 there was not one working-class (or 'plebeian') student at Oxford, and that there were few middle-class students at either Oxford or Cambridge.[7] By this time new universities had been established at Durham and London, and Oxford and Cambridge were being slowly brought up to date, but many Englishmen still travelled to Scotland for their higher education. Harold Perkin's gloomy view of the prospects of university education at mid-century does not even make an exception of Scotland: 'The universities of Britain in 1850 could have been abolished with no great loss to the British economy and society.'[8] Certainly, in the 1860s, anyone concerned for the emergence of an English clerisy might justifiably have looked first to the 'higher journalism' of the new monthly and weekly periodicals, staffed largely by discontented Oxbridge graduates.[9] Arnold dubbed these journalists 'the young lions', but his irony did not stop him from joining them and using the same public platforms for the dissemination of his views. That the higher journalism did not go on to establish itself as a principal centre of cultural authority was largely because in the 1880s and 1890s it was rendered peripheral by the 'new' journalism and the frantic activity of emergent consumerism. It was also challenged by the prestigious growth of scientific knowledge. In the mood of destructive euphoria that typified post-Darwinian Britain there was, for a relatively short period, an atmosphere of scientific confidence that appeared to threaten the very existence of humanistic culture. For the disciples of the Victorian cultural prophets, scientific advance provided the final spur to positive action by confirming their already pronounced distrust of industrialism and their contempt for democratic potential.

By the turn of the century there was, in Graham Wallas's words, a widespread conviction that 'our adoption of representative democracy had been a mistake.'[10] Wallas's evidence came from his practical experience in politics and his theoretical interest in social psychology: as a Fabian, he was also fully aware of the growing attraction for many intellectuals of Marxism and various other forms of State Socialism. He drew particular attention to the speculations of his friend and fellow-Fabian H. G. Wells on the need for the creation of a modern 'Samurai' or 'voluntary nobility'.[11] Wells himself acknowledged his debt to Plato's 'Guardians', but the specific influences are less revealing than the symptomatic concern, stretching far beyond Wells, with ruling groups and élites – the Guardians, *Ubermensch*, Samurai, Nobility, Aristocracy, Clerisy, Aliens, Remnant, Few. The related interest in Galtonian eugenics at this time also testifies, as David Thatcher has pointed out, to the 'urgency with which a solution was sought' to the assumed degeneracy of Western society.[12] The case for the failure of representative government advanced by literary spokesmen focused on the numbers and ability of readers. In 1898, prompted by a speech of John Morley's on 'popular culture', *Literature* published a series of leading articles drawing comparisons between the 'enthusiasm' with which 'the academic, scholastic, and other allied classes' greeted the 1870 Education Act, and the disillusionment that had followed.[13] For nearly thirty years, *Literature* noted, 'the schoolmaster has been abroad in the land', cheap reprints had put the masterpieces of English literature within the reach of everyone, the 'children of the artisan or labourer' had been taught to read, and the results were hardly worth the effort:

> The key of knowledge has been handed over to the people.
> What do they unlock with it? To a large extent, no doubt,
> drawers empty or filled with rubbish.

Although it was the lack of literary sensitivity on the part of 'the people' that most upset *Literature*'s leader writer, he found little compensation elsewhere. Both the middle and upper classes were denounced for emerging from their years of expensive schooling 'without any literary or intellectual tastes whatever'.[14] It is worth emphasising the Arnoldian comprehensiveness of this criticism because the development of English Studies is sometimes seen as a weapon used by Capitalism to suppress working-class political aspirations. There was certainly a strong, and a strongly subdued, ideological element in the advocacy of English Studies, but the working class as a class was almost entirely irrelevant to the issue. It was the insensitive 'mass' and the ways in which its stolid philistinism had to be countered by an expanded remnant (drawn from whatever class) that caused most concern.

While it was clear to the editorial staff of *Literature*, and to many other commentators, that sensitive readers of English had to be found somewhere, it was still, even at this late date, by no means obvious that they should be looked for in the universities, even though it was here that the clerisy was already being installed. As far as the future of English literature was concerned, the need was for trained readers, who, as Pound observed, should be 'intelligent' and, ideally, not 'bound by any central doctrine or theory'; or, to use Arnoldian terminology, people who through their contact with 'the best that is known and thought in the world' had become the possessors of 'disinterestedness' or 'culture', the quality that would raise them above the squalid partisanship of class and politics.[15] Thus equipped, they would be able to preserve from the past everything worth preserving, and they would provide (as Pound happily observed) a readership for the best contemporary authors. There were, however, serious problems involved in turning the theory into practice. The clerisy were to be at the top of the educational ladder, but first they had to get there, and in the peculiar circumstances of late Victorian education that meant introducing the reading and appreciation of English literature at every step on the way up, from Board School to Oxbridge College. In the public and grammar schools, from where university students were mainly drawn, emphasis in the humanities was almost entirely on classics: English grammar was studied, but it was unusual for any attention to be given to English literature. In Board School education, English literature was only gradually introduced as an essential subject: ability in 'English' was tested by having children read aloud, parse a sentence, compose a brief letter or 'statement', or recite a specified number of lines of poetry learned by heart. The primers or 'readers' compiled for use in the Board Schools generally assumed a low level of comprehension, even for children in the top grades. Although publishers and editors frequently expressed the hope that these primers would foster a love of literature, the way they were compiled and the way they were used in classrooms would more often have discouraged any kind of continuous reading: they were geared primarily to rote-learning and examination, and consisted of abbreviated, condensed or re-told English classics, together with notes and exercises to help with the attainment of factual knowledge and spelling skills. It was on these primers and methods that the proud claims for near total national literacy were based, and it was at these young readers that the snippets and paragraphs of the mass periodicals were most consciously directed.

Of course, it could happen that an individual child might be inspired by a school primer or a devoted teacher to develop a love of books, but the odds against this happening were high. Until near the end of the century, three-quarters of the teachers in elementary schools had had no formal college training, and the other quarter had usually attended teacher-training colleges where not much more attention was given to English literature than they themselves would eventually try to impart in Board Schools.[16] It was noted by one Board of Education report that until 1890 the English literature element at teacher-training colleges consisted largely of 'paraphrasing and grammar', and that in the examinations set for potential teachers, 'questions designed to test any intelligent appreciation of the substance of the few books read were extremely rare.'[17] Of even more significance in the undeveloped reading potential of Board School children was the stark fact that their elementary education was intended to be and to stay 'elementary': if they showed exceptional ability, they might have aspired to become in their turn a schoolteacher (qualified or unqualified), but they would have needed to be very exceptional indeed to rise much further on the educational ladder. The situation began to change in the 1890s as the universities established Education Departments and took more responsibility for the training of teachers, and as the importance of secondary education became generally acknowledged. It was, however, only after the 1902 Education Act that the old Board School attitudes were replaced by a system that confessed to the pointlessness of an educational ladder that did not allow for natural movement from an elementary to a secondary school, and from there the possibility of a further movement upwards (by means of scholarships) to university. Even so, by 1911 only one child in every twenty-two was transferring from elementary to secondary education, and in many of the secondary schools the teaching of English was still primitive.[18] As late as 1908, a Board of Education Report, strongly critical of the standard of English teaching in secondary schools, concluded: 'In a very large number of schools, the teaching has not yet reached a stage at which criticism begins to be useful or possible.'[19]

Virtually the same words could have been used to describe the study of English literature in British universities. As recent books on the 'rise of English Studies' have demonstrated, pressure for the acceptance of English literature at university level came largely

from outside the Academic Establishment.[20] Its origins are to be
found in mid-eighteenth-century Scotland (where it developed as
an extension of rhetoric or logic) and in the dissenting Academies
in England (where it was cultivated as an alternative to Oxbridge
classicism). A Chair of Rhetoric and Belles Lettres was founded at
Edinburgh in 1762; a Chair of English Language and Literature at
the dissenting University College, London, in 1828; a Chair of
English Literature and History at the Anglican King's College,
London, in 1835; and Chairs of History and English Literature at
the university colleges of Belfast, Cork and Galway in 1845. The
tradition that English Literature was usually studied not so much
for its own sake but as a second-best, alternative or substitute
subject – a 'poor man's classics' as it came to be called – is of long
standing, though it should be noted that in the early stages of this
development the poverty lay in the subject rather than the 'men'
who took it. That emphasis was reversed when the usefulness of
English Literature as either a professional qualification or as a
means to some wider social or ideological goal became apparent. It
flourished in working men's colleges and mechanics' institutes; in
the University Extension Movement from the late 1860s where it
played an important part in the campaign by women for entry to
universities; in slum settlements; in the expansion of public
examinations and the subsequent boom in reprints and textbooks;
and in the 'civic' university colleges which were founded throughout Britain from the 1870s onwards. Oxford and Cambridge were
actively involved in all of these movements as guides, arbiters, or
missionaries, but it was only reluctantly that they themselves
formally acknowledged English Literature as a fit honours subject
for their own students. At Oxford, the Merton Chair of English
Language and Literature was founded in 1885, though full
recognition only came in 1904 with the appointment of Walter Raleigh
to a Chair of English Literature. What the founding of the Merton
Chair did do, however, was provoke a bitter widely-publicised
debate about the role of English Literature in university studies: it
was, in the period of time covered by this book, Oxford's most
important contribution to the issue.[21] Cambridge held out until
1912 when Quiller-Couch was appointed to the newly-founded
King Edward VII Chair of English Literature. In Scotland, the
introduction of more specialised degree courses under the Universities (Scotland) Act of 1889 made it possible for the first time,

and after more than a century of pioneering teaching, for English
Literature to be studied as a degree subject at honours level in
Scottish universities.[22]

The limited involvement of Oxford and Cambridge at this time
meant that they could not match either the number of students
now studying English Literature elsewhere, or the quality of the
teaching those students were receiving. Among the new Professoriate at the turn-of-the-century were George Saintsbury (Edinburgh), Herbert Grierson (Aberdeen), A. C. Bradley (Liverpool
and then Glasgow), W. P. Ker (University College, London), C.
H. Herford (Aberystwyth and Manchester), Oliver Elton (Liverpool), Hugh Walker (Lampeter) and Walter Raleigh (Liverpool
and Glasgow before moving to Oxford). It was in Scottish, Welsh,
London and English provincial universities such as these where the
most rapid development of English Studies was taking place in the
late nineteenth and early twentieth centuries. There remained,
however, a great deal of uncertainty about what kind of academic
subject English Literature was. At first, virtually all of the new
professors were appointed to joint chairs. This reflected, in part,
the fact that most of the professors were coming to the new subject
either from other academic disciplines or from professions outside
the universities: it also imparted a greater sense of intellectual
respectability if English was linked with some other subject –
classics, philosophy, or history, and, increasingly, English Language, which allowed a strong emphasis to be placed on philology
and Anglo-Saxon. The pioneering books written by the new
professoriate reveal a similar state of insecurity. They were
overwhelmingly historical, with every writer included who could
have any possible claim to a place in a history of English
Literature, and the demarcation lines of literary periods, schools
and influences carefully charted. It was essential work, a laying out
of the whole field before the ruthless selectivity of twentieth-
century literary criticism could come into play. It also embodied
the conviction that it was knowledge rather than simply reading
skills that students needed. The logic of this situation was
expressed by Henry Morley in his *Tables of English Literature*
(1870). Taking the years AD 200 to 1869 ('with space for additions
until 1890'), and using a system of black and red lines, Morley
constructed an elaborate chart from which the student could
immediately discover for any given period 'who were the chief

writers then, what were their relative ages, what were their chief
books published, and their relation of date to preceding and
succeeding literature'. He added that he had made 'no attempt to
suggest relative merit of authors': the student, presumably, was
expected to be able to determine that for himself.[23]

Because of the high claims for the special humanising qualities
imparted by the study of English Literature that were to be made
so stridently a little later in the twentieth century, it is easy to forget
that much of what has been said here about the establishment of
English as an academic subject also applies to many other
'disciplines' that were striving to attain recognition – social history,
psychology, sociology, anthropology, engineering, various branches
of the physical sciences, and education. It was an age of professionalisation and specialisation, and the study of English Literature
followed both of these trends. Where the development of English
Literature, however, differed from that of most other disciplines
was in its swift rejection of specialist knowledge as the main reason
for its existence, and in the commandeering of 'criticism' for its
own exclusive use, something that would have appalled Matthew
Arnold. The newly appointed Chairs of English Literature soon
shed their joint subjects – though most of them were to stay united
to English Language for many years to come – and the historical
charts and maps, handbooks and primers, gave way to exercises in
critical appreciation. The change was apparent at every educational
level. As we have seen, after the 1902 Education Act, there was a
concerted effort by the Board of Education to reform English
teaching in both elementary and secondary schools, and from 1906
the new policies were greatly influenced by the proselytising
activities of the English Association, a pressure group whose
members included many of the new English Literature professoriate.[24] In his 1913 inaugural lecture at Cambridge, Quiller-Couch,
using terms and allusions that frequently echoed Arnold, assured
his audience that, in spite of the doubts so frequently expressed,
English Literature was a genuine and worthy academic subject. He
gracefully recognised the scholarly 'activity of many learned
Professors' and the accumulated knowledge that might one day
help the students he was addressing to appreciate English Literature, and then just as gracefully dismissed it all as irrelevant. The
true purpose of the study of English Literature, he announced, was
the 'refining of the critical judgment': it aimed to create 'a man of

unmistakable intellectual breeding, whose trained judgment we can trust to choose the better and reject the worse.'[25]

The connection between the appreciation of the best literature of the past and the best of the present, made explicit by Quiller-Couch, had hovered uneasily over the educational debates of the previous thirty years. In 1895 *Punch* had recorded the hilarious news that Yale University was starting to run courses on 'modern fiction'. Its comment took the form of a sketch portraying a Cambridge tutor, annoyed at having to leave work on his 'Prolegomena to *Three Men in a Boat*' and upbraid lazy students. 'Your acquaintance with modern realism is quite insufficient,' he tells them, 'you will attend the course of anatomy lectures at the hospital please.' He also sets them some essay titles to help them prepare for the Tripos: 'Rewrite the story of *Jack and Jill* – (*a*) in Wessex dialect (*b*) as a "Keynote" (*c*) as a Dolly Dialogue.' Or, alternatively: 'Trace the bearing of the history of Mowgli on the Darwinian Theory.'[26]

That *Punch* satirist no doubt thought he was merely being funny: he was, of course, being prophetic. Inadvertently, and employing points of reference that are themselves now understood only by English Literature specialists, he was sharing with Quiller-Couch the recognition that readers – or at least one crucial group of readers – were being turned into students, and that the survival of the best fiction would now depend, for the first time in its long and popular history, on those students being properly trained to appreciate it.

Notes

Introduction

1 *Victorian England: Portrait of an Age* (Oxford 1936), pp. 154, 165.
2 *Culture and Society 1780–1950* (Harmondsworth 1961), p. 165. For Williams's later change of mind on the term 'interregnum', see his *Politics and Letters* (1979), p. 102.
3 For example: Granville Hicks, *Figures of Transition* (New York 1939); William C. Frierson, *The English Novel in Transition 1885–1940* (Norman, Oklahoma 1942); and the foremost academic periodical devoted to this period, *English Literature in Transition 1880–1920*. Among writers who have argued for various kinds of continuity rather than transition, see: William York Tindall, *Forces in Modern British Literature 1885–1946* (New York 1947); Malcolm Bradbury, *The Social Context of Modern English Literature* (Oxford 1972); Tom Gibbons, *Rooms in the Darwin Hotel: Studies in English Literary Criticism and Ideas 1880–1920* (Nedlands, Western Australia 1973).
4 *Edwardian Occasions* (1972), p. 1, and the same author's *The Edwardian Turn of Mind* (Princeton 1968). See also: John Batchelor, *The Edwardian Novelists* (1982); Jefferson Hunter, *Edwardian Fiction* (Cambridge, Mass. 1982).
5 *Fabian Essays* (1889), p. 173, and the novel *Transition* (1895) by Shaw's fellow-Fabian Emma Brooke.
6 *The Crowd: A Study of the Popular Mind* (1896), pp. xiv–xvii, a significantly speedy translation of *Psychologie des Foules*, first published in Paris the previous year.
7 *The New Machiavelli* (1911), p. 321.
8 This kind of prediction is most familiar from works such as William Morris, *News from Nowhere* (1891); Hardy, *Jude the Obscure* (1896); and Wells, *Anticipations* (1901) and *Mankind in the Making* (1903): it also figures frequently in contemporaneous theories of 'transition'. Very similar views are to be found in the work of European writers of the time. See, for example, Strindberg's preface to *Miss Julie* (1888) for his attempt to portray characters living 'in

an age of transition'; and Chekhov's Astrov in *Uncle Vanya* (1897):
'I wondered whether the people who come after us in a hundred
years' time, the people for whom we are now blasting a trail –
would they remember us and speak kindly of us? No . . . I wager
they won't.' *Chekhov: Plays* translated by Elisaveta Fen
(Harmondsworth 1959), p. 188.

9 'There is a deep-lying struggle in the whole fabric of society; a
boundless grinding collision of the New with the Old.' Carlyle,
'Signs of the Times' (1829), *Critical and Miscellaneous Essays* (5
vols 1899), II, p. 82. For other similar early Victorian views, see
Walter E. Houghton, *The Victorian Frame of Mind* (New Haven
1957), Chapter 1.

10 *The Return of the Native* ('Macmillan's Pocket Hardy' 1912), p. 7.
All quotations from Hardy's novels are from this edition unless
otherwise indicated.

11 *Degeneration* (New York 1895), p. 6, a translation of *Entartung*, first
published in Berlin in 1892.

Chapter One   Novelists and Readers

1 *The Letters of Anthony Trollope*, edited by N. John Hall (2 vols,
Stanford 1983), II, 638–9.

2 Trollope, *An Autobiography*, edited by Frederick Page ('The Oxford
Trollope' 1950), p. 349. All quotations from *An Autobiography* are from
this edition unless otherwise indicated.

3 *Letters*, II, p. 642.

4 *Letters*, II, p. 685; Henry Trollope's preface to *An Autobiography*
(1883).

5 For the decline in Trollope's reputation, see: Michael Sadleir,
Trollope: A Commentary (1927); *Trollope: The Critical Heritage*,
edited by Donald Smalley (1969); David Skilton, *Anthony Trollope
and his Contemporaries* (1972).

6 Introduction to the Fontana Library edition of *An Autobiography*
(1962), p. 11.

7 *An Autobiography*, p. 120.

8 *Ibid.*, p. 118.

9 *Ibid.*, p. 222.

10 *Ibid.*, p. 146.

11 *Ibid.*, p. 365.

12 *Ibid.*, p. 121.

13 *An Autobiography* ('Fontana'), p. 10.

14 Quoted, Philip Collins, *Dickens and Crime* (2nd ed. 1965), p. 216.

15 See: *The Letters and Private Papers of William Makepeace Thackeray*, edited by Gordon N. Ray (4 vols 1945), II, p. 282; C. Brontë, preface to the second edition of *Jane Eyre*, 1847.

16 *The Way We Live Now*, Chapter Seventy-Four.

17 *Ibid.*, Chapters Two, Eighty-Nine.

18 Robin Gilmour, *The Idea of the Gentleman in the Victorian Novel* (1981), p. 173.

19 Henry James, *Letters*, edited by Leon Edel (4 vols 1974–84), I, p. 484.

20 Trollope's personal inclination to discourage young men and women to look to literature for a living was strengthened by his experience as a committee member of the Royal Literary Fund, where he 'heard and saw much of the sufferings of authors'. *An Autobiography*, pp. 211–13.

21 For example, 'The Adventures of Fred Pickering', *Lotte Schmidt and other Stories* (1867): 'Mary Gresley', *An Editor's Tales* (1870).

22 For a detailed discussion of Trollope's business sense, see John Sutherland, *Victorian Novelists and Publishers* (1976), Chapter Six.

23 *Letters*, II, p. 715.

24 James Hepburn sees James Spedding's *Publishers and Authors* (1867) as initiating the late Victorian interest in the American royalty system, *The Author's Empty Purse and the Rise of the Literary Agent* (1968), pp. 13–14. A slightly later American influence was the publisher George Haven Putnam. In his *Authors and Publishers: A Manual of Suggestions for Beginners in Literature* (New York 1883) he outlined the way the royalty system worked in America, and four years later he advised the Society of Authors to adopt the system in order to improve relations between publishers and authors; see, *The Grievances Between Authors and Publishers* (1887). Appendix III. The Society of Authors, however, regarded the royalty as 'a system where all is chaos'. *Author*, I (16 June 1890), p. 38.

25 *Bookman*, III (October 1892), p. 22.

26 Simon Nowell-Smith, *The House of Cassell 1848–1958* (1958), p. 188.

27 *The Letters of Robert Louis Stevenson*, edited by Sidney Colvin ('Tusitala Edition', 5 vols 1924), II, p. 238.

28 *Ibid.*, II, p. 245.

29 Roger Swearingen, *The Prose Writings of Robert Louis Stevenson: A Guide* (1980), p. 67.

30 Morton Cohen, *Rider Haggard: His Life and Work* (2nd ed. 1968), pp. 84–87.

31 *Ibid.*, p. 232.

32 Nowell-Smith, *The House of Cassell*, p. 134.

33 Cohen, *Rider Haggard*, p. 123.

34 Swearingen, *The Prose Writings of Robert Louis Stevenson*, p. 105.
35 Nowell-Smith, *The House of Cassell*, pp. 136–7.
36 *Mankind in the Making* (1903), p. 383.
37 *Letters of George Gissing to Members of his Family*, edited by
    Algernon and Ellen Gissing (1927), p. 312.
38 *My Story* (1908), p. 377.
39 *Ibid*, p. 280–2.
40 *Ibid*, p. 377, and Samuel Norris, *Two Men of Manxland* (1947), pp.
    6–7.
41 Hesketh Pearson, *Conan Doyle: His Life and Art* (1943), p. 77; A.
    Conan Doyle, *Memories and Adventures* (1924), pp. 75–6.
42 Archive of the Society of Authors, British Library, File No. 56694.
43 *The Collected Letters of Joseph Conrad*, Volume I 1861–1897, edited
    by Frederick R. Karl and Lawrence Davies (Cambridge 1983), p.
    180.
44 *Ibid.*, p. 257.
45 Norris, *Two Men of Manxland*, p. 57.
46 Frederic Whyte, *William Heinemann: A Memoir* (1928), p. 104;
    Gillian Kersley, *Darling Madame: Sarah Grand and Devoted Friend*
    (1983), p. 87.
47 *London and the Life of Literature in Late Victorian England: The
    Diary of George Gissing Novelist*, edited by Pierre Coustillas
    (Hassocks 1978), pp. 296–7. Hereafter referred to as *Diary*.
48 Gordon S. Haight, *George Eliot: A Biography* (Oxford 1968), pp.
    318, 436–7.
49 For Dickens's earnings and methods of publication, see: Robert L.
    Patten, *Dickens and his Publishers* (1978); *Dickens: The Critical
    Heritage*, edited by Philip Collins (1971).
50 Gordon N. Ray, *Thackeray: The Age of Wisdom 1847–1863* (1958),
    p. 293.
51 *A Victorian Publisher: A Study of the Bentley Papers* (Cambridge
    1960), pp. 103–8.
52 For the historical development of the three-decker, see: Charles E.
    Lauterbach and Edward S. Lauterbach, 'The Nineteenth Century
    Three-Volume Novel', *Papers of the Bibliographical Society of America*,
    LI (1957); for connections between the three-decker and circulating
    libraries, see Guinevere L. Griest, *Mudie's Circulating Library and
    the Victorian Novel* (Bloomington 1970).
53 A striking example of a publisher forcing a very high price from
    Mudie's is provided by John Blackwood's negotiations over *The
    Mill on the Floss*; see Griest, *Mudie's Circulating Library*, pp. 65–6.
54 Griest, *Mudie's Circulating Library*, p. 24.
55 *Ibid*, p. 56.

56 For mid-Victorian publishing in general, see (in addition to Gettmann and Sutherland): F. A. Mumby and Ian Norrie, *Publishing and Bookselling* (5th ed. 1974); Richard D. Altick, *The English Common Reader: A Social History of the Mass Reading Public 1800–1900* (Chicago 1957); Robin Myers, *The British Book Trade* (1973).

57 *Victorian Novelists and Publishers*, p. 15.

58 *Publishers' Circular*, 7 July 1894, p. 6.

59 Joseph Shaylor, 'The Issue of Fiction,' *Publishers' Circular*, XCIII (15 October 1910), pp. 565–6.

60 *Mudie's Circulating Library*, p. 161.

61 Robert Lee Wolff, *Sensational Victorian: The Life and Fiction of Mary Elizabeth Braddon* (New York 1979), pp. 359–60.

62 Griest, *Mudie's Circulating Library*, p. 75.

63 The first suggested title was 'The Company of Authors'. This was quickly changed to 'The Incorporated Society of Authors'. In 1913 the title was expanded to include Playwrights and Composers.

64 G. H. Thring, 'A History of the Society of Authors', Archives of the Society of Authors, British Library, File No. 56868.

65 Walter Besant, *Autobiography* (1902), p. 217.

66 Thring only became secretary of the Society on a full-time basis in 1892: he held the post until 1930. His business and legal contacts with so many authors make him an important, though generally unacknowledged, influence on literature of the period. For the many other writers and lawyers who helped the Society, with either professional expertise or money, in its early days, see: Besant, *Autobiography*, pp. 221–2, and Victor Bonham-Carter's official history of the Society, *Authors by Profession* (2 vols 1978), I, pp. 129–30.

67 *Autobiography*, p. 218.

68 For the real and symbolic importance of the East End at this time, see: Gareth Stedman Jones, *Outcast London* (1971); P. J. Keating, *The Working Classes in Victorian Fiction* (1971).

69 See, for example, the essays in *As We Are and As We May Be* (1903), and, among his many studies of London, *South London* (1899) and *East London* (1901).

70 See Bonham-Carter, *Authors by Profession*, I, p. 226 n. 35, for a list of earlier authors' societies; also Besant, 'The First Society of Authors (1843)', *Essays and Historiettes* (1903). In 1889 the Society sent a representative to Paris to attend the jubilee celebrations of their French counterpart. S. Squire Sprigge's *The Society of French Authors* (1890) was one of the first pamphlets published by the Society.

71 For the awarding of pensions and grants from the Royal Literary

Fund and the Civil List, see Nigel Cross, *The Common Writer: Life in Nineteenth-Century Grub Street* (1985); and for the Society's early attitude to such awards, William Morris Colles, *Literature and the Pension List* (1889).

72 'A History of the Society of Authors', p. 94. The membership figures given here are also taken from Thring's unpublished manuscript.

73 *England: Its People, Polity, and Pursuits* (1881), p. 517.

74 *Experiment in Autobiography* (2 vols 1934), II, p. 507.

75 *New Grub Street*, edited by Bernard Bergonzi (Harmondsworth 1968), p. 38.

76 *Author*, II (1 June 1891), p. 15.

77 'Realism in Grub Street', *Author*, II (1 July 1891), p. 43.

78 *Publishers' Circular*, XXXVIII (31 December 1875), p. 1238.

79 *Ibid.*, L (31 December 1887), p. 1844.

80 *Ibid.*, LXII (5 January 1895), p. 7.

81 *Ibid.*, XL (31 December 1877), p. 1174.

82 *Bookseller*, CCCLXXXVI (9 January 1890), p. 7.

83 *Ibid.*, p. 5.

84 For this issue, and other current debates on Victorian periodicals, see: Walter Houghton, introduction to *The Wellesley Index to Victorian Periodicals 1824–1900* vol. I (Toronto 1966), and his 'Victorian Periodical Literature and the Articulate Classes', *Victorian Studies*, XXII (Summer 1979); *The Waterloo Directory of Victorian Periodicals 1824–1900*, Phase I, edited by Michael Woolf, John S. North and Dorothy Deering (Waterloo, Ontario, 1976); *Victorian Periodicals: A Guide to Research*, edited by J. Don Vann and Rosemary T. Van Arsdel (New York 1978); *The Victorian Periodical Press: Samplings and Soundings*, edited by Joanne Shattock and Michael Woolf (Leicester 1982).

85 *The Rise and Fall of the Man of Letters* (Harmondsworth 1973), p. 75.

86 Trollope, *An Autobiography*, p. 137.

87 *Autobiography and Letters of Mrs M. O. W. Oliphant*, edited by Mrs Harry Coghill (Edinburgh 1899), p. 311.

88 See, Patrick Dunae, 'The *Boy's Own Paper*: Origins and Editorial Policies', *Private Library*, IX (1976).

89 Wendy Forrester, *Great-Grandmama's Weekly: A Celebration of the Girl's Own Paper 1880–1901* (1980), p. 14.

90 *Review of Reviews* I (January 1890), p. 14.

91 An 'incalculable' number if considering, as here, writers who drew some or all of their earnings from fiction. For attempts to establish numbers of at least some groups of writers, see: Nigel Cross, *The*

Common Writer, p. 3; Raymond Williams, *The Long Revolution* (1961), Part II, Chapter Five; R. D. Altick, 'The Sociology of Authorship', *Bulletin of the New York Public Library*, LXVI (1962), pp. 389–404.

92 Jocelyn Baines, *Joseph Conrad* (1960), p. 84; Quentin Bell, *Virginia Woolf* (2 vols 1976), I, p. 331; Richard Ellmann, *James Joyce* (Oxford Paperbacks 1966), p. 50.

93 Reginald Pound and Geoffrey Harmsworth, *Northcliffe* (1959), pp. 60–1; Hulda Friederichs, *The Life of Sir George Newnes* (1911), p. 93.

94 Wells, *Experiment in Autobiography*, I, pp. 316–17.

95 *Black and White*, I (6 February 1891), p. 2.

96 *Letters*, IV, p. 95. For the development of the short story in nineteenth-century Britain: Wendell V. Harris, 'Engish Short Fiction in the Nineteenth Century', *Studies in Short Fiction*, VI (Newberry College, South Carolina, 1968–9); Valerie Shaw, *The Short Story: A Critical Introduction* (1983); *Ninteteenth-Century Short Stories*, edited by Peter Keating (1981).

97 Introduction to *The Country of the Blind and Other Stories* (1911), p. v.

98 *Diary*, p. 373.

99 *Collected Letters*, I, p. 285.

100 *The Art of the Novel: Critical Prefaces by Henry James*, edited by R. P. Blackmur (New York 1962), p. 219.

101 *Academy*, 18 December 1897, quoted in *Gissing: The Critical Heritage*, edited by Pierre Coustillas and Colin Partridge (1972), p. 316.

102 *How to Become an Author* (1903), p. 110.

103 *Collected Letters*, I, p. 351, and other correspondence with Unwin in this volume.

104 *George Moore in Transition: Letters to T. Fisher Unwin and Lena Milman 1894–1910*, edited by Helmut E. Gerber (Detroit 1968), p. 239.

105 *Ibid.*, p. 247.

106 *Charles Dickens* (1906), p. 85.

107 'They say republished stories do not sell. Well, that is why I am in a hurry to get this out. The public must be educated to buy mine or I shall never make a cent.' Stevenson, *Letters*, II, p. 89.

108 Bret Harte, 'The Rise of the "Short-story"', *Cornhill Magazine*, n.s. VII, (July 1899); Richard O'Connor, *Bret Harte: A Biography* (Boston 1966).

109 *The Short Story: A Critical Introduction*, pp. 105–6.

110 William Westall, 'Newspaper Fiction', *Lippincott's Magazine*, XLV (1890), p. 77.

111 Michael Turner, 'Reading for the Masses: Aspects of the Syndication of Fiction in Great Britain', *Book Selling and Book Buying: Aspects of the Nineteenth-Century British and North American Book Trade*, edited by Richard G. Landon (Chicago 1978), p. 53.

112 Westall, 'Newspaper Fiction', p. 80.

113 *Ibid.*, p. 81.

114 See, Simon Nowell-Smith, 'Firma Tauchnitz 1837–1900', *Book Collector*, XV (1966). Until separate treaties were negotiated with the colonies, the standard practice was to pay authors a *3d* royalty on colonial editions, though this was open to considerable variations; Mumby and Norrie, *Publishing and Bookselling*, p. 249.

115 Turner, 'Reading for the Masses', p. 67; see also, Michael Turner, 'Tillotson's Fiction Bureau: Agreements with Authors', *Studies in the Book Trade in Honour of Graham Pollard* (Oxford 1975), and Frank Singleton, *Tillotsons 1850–1950* (Bolton 1950).

116 *Author*, VI (1 November 1895), p. 138.

117 'The First Principles of Literary Property', *Author*, I (15 May 1890), p. 6.

118 John Goode, *George Gissing: Ideology and Fiction* (1978), p. 125.

119 The ideal of co-operative publishing remained throughout the period. Towards the end of his life, Besant still saw it as 'the method of the future', *The Pen and the Book*, p. 208. There were sporadic attempts to put the theory into practice. On 9 October 1889, the *Bookseller*, p. 985, announced the formation of 'The Authors' Co-operative Publishing Company' which claimed to publish 'according to the Society of Authors' terms'. See also: 'Rules of the Authors' and Booksellers' Co-operative Equitable Publishing Alliance Ltd.' (Manchester 1896); *The Plan: A New Departure in Publishing* (1901); O and A, *The Author as Publisher: Or, Why don't Authors Publish their own Books?* (1912). In 1905 Wells, Shaw, and Doyle planned to set up a co-operative 'Bookshops Ltd', but 'nothing seems to have come of the project'; Mumby and Norrie, *Publishing and Bookselling*, p. 308.

120 For the immediately hostile response of publishers, see the editorial comments and correspondence in the *Publishers' Circular*, L (15 March, 1 April, and 15 April 1887).

121 *Author*, X (1 August 1899), p. 68.

122 'The Literary Handmaid of the Church', *Author*, I (15 July 1890), pp. 64–5. Besant also published his case against the SPCK as a pamphlet, with the same title as this article, in 1890. All details here are taken from the *Author*.

123 *Ibid.*, p. 66.

124 *Author*, I (15 October 1890), p. 139.

125 For the meanness to women authors by organisations like the RTS and SPCK, see: Margaret Nancy Cutt, *Ministering Angels: A Study of Nineteenth-Century Writing for Children* (1979); J. S. Bratton, *The Impact of Victorian Children's Fiction* (1981); Lance Solway, 'Pathetic Simplicity: Hesba Stretton and Her Books for Children', *The Signal Approach to Children's Books*, edited by Nancy Chambers (1980). For the poverty of many women novelists, see Nigel Cross, *The Common Writer*, Chapter Five.

126 Gordon Hewitt, *Let the People Read* (1949), p. 74. In 1897 the SPCK sold four million Bibles and eight and a half million other publications; Mumby and Norrie, *Publishing and Bookselling*, p. 257.

127 *Author*, I (15 October 1890), pp. 139–48.

128 Mrs Henry Wood's first novel *Danesbury House* (1860) was entered in a competition run by the Temperance League. She won £100, her sole earnings from the book. Her second novel, for which she retained the copyright, was the legendary best-seller *East Lynne*.

129 S. Squire Sprigge, *The Methods of Publishing*, pp. 31–2. Describing novelettes as 'the least glorious form of imaginative literature', Bennett estimated the rates of pay as varying from two to thirteen guineas per 25,000 words; *How to Become an Author* (1903), p. 123.

130 *The Princess Novelettes*, I (1886), p. 16.

131 'Rita' [Mrs Desmond Humphreys] *Recollections of a Literary Life* (1936), pp. 43–6.

132 *Ibid.*, p. 68.

133 *Ibid.*, p. 162. This was obviously not the only court case that Rita and the Society of Authors were involved in. See *Author*, XII (1 December 1901), p. 158; XVII (1 June 1908), p. 252.

134 *Author*, I (15 October 1890), p. 139.

135 *Ibid*, VII (1 May 1897), pp. 314–15.

136 Friederichs, *Life of Sir George Newnes*, p. 89.

137 *Joseph Conrad: Letters to William Blackwood and David S. Meldrum*, edited by William Blackburn (Durham, North Carolina, 1958), pp. 69–70.

138 Details of the London Literary Society from the *Publishers' Circular*, LI (1 November 1888), pp. 1342, 1349.

139 *Author*, III (1 October 1892), pp. 154–5.

140 *Ibid.*

141 Leopold Wagner, *How to Publish* (1898), p. 69. Sprigge claimed that three-quarters of the novels published were at the authors' expense, *The Methods of Publishing*, p. 20. That sounds an exaggeration, though Besant agreed with it, *Author*, I (15 July 1890), p. 75.

142 Arthur Hamilton, *The Confessions of a Scribbler* (Merthyr Tydfil 1879), p. 96.

143 'Mr Bennett and Mrs Brown', *Collected essays of Virginia Woolf*, edited by Leonard Woolf (4 vols 1966), I, p. 335.

144 *The Letters of George Gissing to Edward Bertz 1887–1903*, edited by A. C. Young (1961), p. 140.

145 *Publishers' Circular*, 26 October 1895, p. 471.

146 Archives of the Society of Authors, British Library, File No. 56864.

147 *Grievances Between Authors and Publishers*, p. 74.

148 'How to Use the Society', printed regularly in the *Author*.

149 Among the many books on copyright law, see: G. H. Thring, *The Marketing of Literary Property* (1933); Simon Nowell-Smith, *International Copyright and the Publisher in the Reign of Victoria* (Oxford 1968); Bonham-Carter, *Authors by Profession*.

150 *Author*, XI (2 July 1900), pp. 18–20; XVII (1 October 1906), p. 1; XVII (1 November 1906), p. 1; XXV (1 October 1914), pp. 9–10; Anthony Hope Hawkins, 'The Authors' Pension Fund', *Literary Year Book* (1901), pp. 43–5.

151 'A History of the Society of Authors', p. 72; *Author*, XI (1 April 1901), pp. 202–5, and the correspondence the following month, pp. 220–1; XII (1 February 1902), p. 125.

152 See, Samuel Hynes, 'Mr Pember's Academy', *Edwardian Occasions* (1972).

153 W. G. Corp, *Fifty Years: A Brief Account of the Associated Booksellers of Great Britain and Ireland 1895–1945* (1948), pp. 3–8.

154 R. J. L. Kingsford, *The Publishers' Association 1896–1946* (Cambridge 1970), p. 216.

155 For all aspects of this important issue, James J. Barnes, *Free Trade in Books* (1964).

156 Frederick Macmillan, *The Net Book Agreement 1899* (Glasgow 1924); Kingsford, *The Publishers' Association*, pp. 5–17; Barnes, *Free Trade in Books*, pp. 141–67.

157 For *The Times* 'book war', see: *Author*, XVII (1 November 1906), pp. 47–8, and running discussion to XIX (1 October 1908), p. 47; Corp, *Fifty Years*, pp. 18–24; *The History of The Times 1884–1912* (1947), pp. 448–59, 829–34; Kingsford, *The Publishers' Association*, pp. 22–36; Anon, *The Times and the Publishers* (1906); *Canned Literature: The Jungle in London*, edited by R. F. Cholmeley (1907).

158 'The Book Club and the Manager' by D. C. Calthrop, *Canned Literature*, pp. 15–17.

159 Kingsford, *The Publishers' Association*, pp. 11–12.

160 *Author*, IX (1 July 1898), pp. 30–49.
161 Quoted, *Author*, IX (1 August 1898), p. 61.
162 *Ibid.*, p. 59.
163 Kingsford, *The Publishers' Association*, p. 12.
164 *Ibid.*
165 *The Cost of Production*, published by the Society of Authors (2nd ed. 1891), p. 5.
166 See, Bonham-Carter, *Authors By Profession*, I, pp. 166–8; Hepburn, *The Author's Empty Purse*, pp. 55–6.
167 Archives of the Society of Authors, British Library, File No. 56710.
168 *The Letters of D. H. Lawrence*, edited by James T. Boulton (7 vols. in progress, Cambridge 1979), II, p. 434; John Carter, '*The Rainbow* Prosecution', *Times Literary Supplement*, 27 February 1969, p. 216.
169 *The Author's Craft* (1914), p. 123.
170 Garnett published the letters he had received from W. H. Hudson (1923), Conrad (1938), Galsworthy (1934); see also George Jefferson, *Edward Garnett: A Life in Literature* (1982).
171 *Letters to William Blackwood*, p. 86.
172 *Ibid.*, p. 40.
173 Quoted, Zdzislaw Najder, *Joseph Conrad: A Chronicle* (Cambridge 1983), p. 253.
174 Dennis Mackail, *The Story of J.M.B.* (1941), p. 138.
175 The agent was Arthur Addison Bright, see Mackail, *The Story of J.M.B.*, p. 389–90, 421–2, and Hepburn, *The Author's Empty Purse*, p. 66. A. M. Burghes and his son C. M. Burghes were also agents who were prosecuted: Hepburn, pp. 50–1; *Author*, XXIV (1 October 1913), p. 17.
176 *The Author's Empty Purse*, p. 23. Hepburn also gives here many details of the literary manuals issued by early Victorian vanity publishers.
177 Wagner, *How to Publish*, p. 106. E. H. L. Watson argued that the agent was turning the author into a 'mechanical producer of fiction', *Hints to Young Authors* (1902), p. 138; in this context, see Bennett's portrait of a literary agent in *A Great Man* (1904), Chapter Ten.
178 'The Hardships of Publishing', *Athenaeum*, MDCCCXCII (3 December 1892), p. 779; Whyte, *William Heinemann*, p. 122.
179 *Ibid.*, p. 280.
180 'An Interview with A. P. Watt,' *Bookman*, III (October 1892), p. 21. For some of Watt's clients, *Letters Addressed to A. P. Watt* (1893, 1894, 1896).
181 Wolff, *Sensational Victorian*, p. 402.

182 *The Author's Empty Purse*, p. 49.

183 *Author*, I (15 October 1890), p. 158. For the possible connection between Digby Long and vanity publishing, see *Publishers' Circular*, LI (1888), pp. 1349, 1437.

184 *New Grub Street*, p. 195.

185 *Arnold Bennett and H. G. Wells: A Record of a Personal and a Literary Friendship*, edited by Harris Wilson (1960), p. 98.

186 *The Art of Authorship*, edited by George Bainton (1890), pp. vii–x. For criticism of Bainton's methods, see *Author* I (16 June and 15 July 1890), pp. 44–5, 83–4.

187 *The Notebooks of Henry James*, edited by F. O. Matthiessen and Kenneth B. Murdock ('Oxford Paperback' 1961), p. 82.

188 *The Complete Tales of Henry James*, edited by Leon Edel (12 vols 1962–4), VI, p. 279.

189 Conrad, *Letters to William Blackwood*, p. 171; Penelope Dell, *Nettie and Sissie* (1977), pp. 104–5.

190 *One Man's Road* (1931), p. 220.

191 T. H. Darlow, *William Robertson Nicoll: Life and Letters* (1925), p. 98.

192 *The Times*, 19 October 1897, p. 5; *Literature*, I (23 October 1897), p. 2.

193 See Gross, *The Rise and Fall of the Man of Letters*, p. 79.

194 For the range and variety of 'little magazines' at this time, see: J. R. Tye, *Periodicals of the Nineties* (Oxford 1974); *British Literary Magazines: The Victorian and Edwardian Age 1837–1913*, edited by Alvin Sullivan (Westport Conn. 1984); Ian Fletcher, 'Decadence and the Little Magazine', *Decadence and the 1890s*, edited by Ian Fletcher (1979).

195 'The Art of Fiction', *Henry James: Selected Literary Criticism*, edited by Morris Shapira (Harmondsworth 1968), p. 84. Hereafter referred to as *Selected Literary Criticism*.

196 For a sightly different meaning of 'bohemian' during the mid-Victorian period, see Nigel Cross, *The Common Writer*, Chapter Three.

197 *Vanity Fair*, Chapters Sixty-Four and Sixty-Five.

198 *Diary*, p. 214.

199 See, Felix Moscheles, *In Bohemia with Du Maurier* (1896); Leonee Ormond, *George Du Maurier* (1969).

200 'John Delavoy', Edel (ed.), *Complete Tales*, IX, p. 413.

201 Kipling, *Something of Myself* (1937), p. 65; Gissing, *Family Letters*, p. 136.

202 *When a Man's Single: A Tale of Literary Life* (8th ed. 1894), p. 260. This novel, like *All in a Garden Fair*, developed a reputation

as a kind of literary advice book. Bennett urged every literary aspirant to read it, *How to Become an Author*, p. 69.

203 *Gleams of Memory* (1894), p. 186.

204 *A Modern Dick Whittington* (1893), p. 433.

205 *A Great Man* (1904), p. 342.

206 *Letters of Arnold Bennett*, edited by James Hepburn (4 vols Oxford 1966–86), I, p. 50; II, p. 116.

207 *The Light that Failed* ('Uniform Edition' 1899), p. 107.

208 *Cynthia: A Daughter of the Philistines* ('The Works of Leonard Merrick', 1918–22), p. 46.

209 *A Man from the North* (3rd ed. 1912), p. 263.

210 *A Writer of Books* (1898), p. 13.

211 *Ibid.*, p. 126.

212 *Grievances Between Authors and Publishers*, pp. 43–4.

213 *The Private Papers of Henry Ryecroft*, edited by Pierre Coustillas ('Bilingual Edition', Paris 1966), p. 180.

Chapter Two The Prevailing Sound of the Age

1 *Diary*, p. 535.

2 *Books and Myself* (1944), pp. 159–60; *The Passing of Victoria: The Poets' Tribute* (1901), p. 6.

3 'On the Day King Edward Gets his Crown On,' sung by Harry Pleon. *Sixty Years of British Music Hall* edited by John McGarrett (1976), n.p.

4 'Mr Bennett and Mrs Brown'. For the personal implications of the clash between Woolf and Bennett, see Samuel Hynes, 'The Whole Contention Between Mr Bennett and Mrs Woolf', *Edwardian Occasions*.

5 'Mr Bennett and Mrs Brown', pp. 319–37. In addition to the First Post-Impressionist exhibition, Woolf was probably drawing attention to the death of King Edward in May 1910.

6 'Portrait of an Age', *Early Victorian England* edited by G. M. Young (2 vols 1934), and then separately in an expanded form as *Victorian England: Portrait of an Age* (1936).

7 'Mr Bennett and Mrs Brown', p. 326.

8 *Sowing* (1960), pp. 151–65.

9 *The Edwardian Turn of Mind* (1968), p. 5.

10 *James Joyce*, p. 149.

11 *Ibid.*, p. 274.

12 *Letters*, II, p. 20.

13 'Old Bloomsbury', *Moments of Being*, edited by Jeanne Schulkind (rev. ed. 1985), p. 185.

14 'E.T.' [Jessie Chambers] *D. H. Lawrence: A Personal Record* (2nd ed. 1950), p. 184; Joyce, *A Portrait of the Artist as a Young Man*, edited by Chester G. Anderson ('Viking Critical Library' New York 1968), p. 203; Moore, *Confessions of a Young Man*, edited by Susan Dick (Montreal 1972), p. 129.

15 Norman and Jeanne Mackenzie, *The Time Traveller: The Life of H. G. Wells* (1973), p. 57; *The New Machiavelli*, p. 100.

16 *Letters of George Gissing to Eduard Bertz*, p. xx; Yeats, 'The Tragic Generation', *Autobiographies* (1955), pp. 279–349, and his introduction to *The Oxford Book of Modern Verse* (1936), p. ix; *R. L. S.: Stevenson's Letters to Charles Baxter*, edited by DeLancey Ferguson and Marshall Waingraw (New Haven 1956), p. ix.

17 Pater, 'Poems by William Morris', *Westminster Review*, XXXIV (1 October 1868), pp. 311–12: the views expressed in this essay were later incorporated into the famous conclusion of *Studies in the History of the Renaissance* (1873); 'Ralph Iron' [Olive Schreiner], *The Story of an African Farm* (2nd ed. 1883), p. 153.

18 *News from Nowhere*, edited by James Redmond ('Routledge English Texts' 1970), p. 1.

19 N. and J. Mackenzie, *The Time Traveller*, p. 162.

20 Gilbert and Sullivan, *Patience*, Act I; Lawrence, *Women in Love* ('Phoenix edition' 1954), p. 83.

21 *The Letters and Private Papers of William Makepeace Thackeray*, II, p. 282.

22 *Ernest Pontifex or The Way of All Flesh*, edited by Daniel F. Howard (1965), p. 69.

23 *The Importance of Being Earnest*, in *The Works of Oscar Wilde*, edited by G. F. Maine (1948), p. 12.

24 H. Montgomery Hyde, *The Trials of Oscar Wilde* (1948), p. 12.

25 *Women in Love*, p. 120.

26 *The Picture of Dorian Gray*, edited by Isobel Murray ('Oxford English Novels' 1974), p. 179.

27 *The Nether World*, edited by John Goode (Hassocks 1974), p. 392.

28 'Of course the book is all contrasts – or was meant to be in its original conception,' Letter to Edmund Gosse, 20 November 1895. *The Collected Letters of Thomas Hardy*, edited by R. L. Purdy and M. Millgate (8 vols, in progress, 1980), II, p. 99.

29 'Apology', *Late Lyrics and Earlier* (1922).

30 *Jude the Obscure*, p. 270.

31 *The New Machiavelli*, pp. 45–6.

32 Young, *Portrait of an Age*; Briggs, *The Age of Improvement 1783–1867* (1959), Chapter 9, and *Victorian People* (1954); Burns, *The Age of Equipoise* (1964).

33 *The Old Wives' Tale* (1908), *p. 76*.
34 'The Turn of the Wheel', Last Studies (1897), p. 167.
35 Preface to *The Picture of Dorian Gray*. Much the same point about satire can be applied to the 'Aesthetes' and 'Decadents', at least as far as fiction is concerned. Their influence, in rather vague ways, was considerable, but their lasting contribution to fiction rests mainly on Wilde, Pater, a number of short-story writers, and minor prose works by Davidson and Beardsley. The satire they provoked was, however, considerable. In addition to Du Maurier's *Punch* cartoons and Gilbert and Sullivan's *Patience*, see: W. H. Mallock, *The New Republic* (1877); Vernon Lee, *Miss Brown* (1884); Robert Hichens, *The Green Carnation* (1884); G. S. Street, *Autobiography of a Boy*. Henry James's *The Tragic Muse* (1890) also belongs in some respects with the satirical camp. Perhaps, ultimately, the most lasting influence of the Decadents on British fiction is to be found in the line of fantasy or grotesquerie that descends from the 1890s through such neglected novels as Baron Corvo's *Hadrian the Seventh* (1904) and Max Beerbohm's *Zuleika Dobson* (1911). For the British contribution to the Decadent movement, see the various essays and bibliographies in *Decadence and the 1890s*, edited by Ian Fletcher (1979), and Linda C. Dowling, *Aestheticism and Decadence: A Selective Annotated Bibliography* (New York 1977).
36 'The Importance of Being Earnest,' *Works of Oscar Wilde*, p. 367.
37 *Ibid.*, p. 339.
38 *Tradition and Change* (1919), p. 234.
39 *The New Machiavelli*, p. 58; *Dr Jekyll and Mr Hyde* ('Tusitala Edition' 1924), p. 57.
40 *Autobiography* (1936), p. 20.
41 *My Apprenticeship* (Harmondsworth 1971), pp. 33, 40.
42 *Father and Son*, p. 61.
43 *Ibid*, pp. 77, 83–4.
44 'A Victorian Son', *The Living Novel* (1946), p. 102.
45 *Father and Son*, p. 5.
46 *The Way of All Flesh*, pp. 67, 40, 100, 86.
47 *Ibid.*, p. 198.
48 *Rosemary's Letter Book* (1909), p. 212.
49 *Some Eminent Victorians* (1908), pp. v–vi.
50 Preface to *Eminent Victorians* (1918).
51 Preface to *Major Barbara* (1907).
52 *The Victorian Age in Literature* (1913), p. 126.
53 *Darwin and the General Reader: The Reception of Darwin's Theory of Evolution in the British Periodical Press, 1859–1872* (Gothenburg 1958), p. 43. For the impact of Darwin on British fiction, see: Leo

Henkin, *Darwinism in the English Novel, 1860–1910* (New York 1963); Peter Morton, *The Vital Science: Biology and the Literary Imagination 1860–1900* (1984).

54 Preface to the 1911 American edition of *The Old Wives' Tale*.
55 'The Art of Fiction', *Selected Literary Criticism*, p. 78. For the exchange with Besant, see John Goode, 'The Art of Fiction: Walter Besant and Henry James', *Tradition and Tolerance in Nineteenth-Century Fiction*, edited by David Howard, John Lucas and John Goode (1966); Vivien Jones, *James the Critic* (1985).
56 'Guy de Maupassant', *Selected Literary Criticism*, p. 124.
57 'The Art of Fiction', *Ibid.*, p. 88.
58 'Guy de Maupassant', *Ibid.*, p. 131.
59 'Gustave Flaubert', *Ibid.*, p. 262.
60 *Letters*, III, p. 28.
61 'A Humble Remonstrance', *Memories and Portraits* ('Tusitala Edition' 1924), p. 136.
62 *The Unclassed*, edited by Jacob Korg (Hassocks 1976), p. 211.
63 *Letters*, I, pp. 169, 91.
64 *Collected Letters*, I, pp. 184–5.
65 See Wolff, *Sensational Victorian* for Braddon's wide-ranging interest in French fiction.
66 *A Portrait of the Artist*, p. 215.
67 See: Clarence Decker, *The Victorian Conscience* (New York 1952); Richard Stang, *The Theory of the Novel in England 1850–1870* (1955); Patricia Thomson, *George Sand and the Victorians* (1977).
68 'The Experimental Novel', *Documents of Modern Literary Realism*, edited by George J. Becker (Princeton 1963), p. 172.
69 *Confessions of a Young Man*, p. 95.
70 Joseph Hone, *The Life of George Moore* (1936), pp. 101–4.
71 'Mr Bennett and Mrs Brown', p. 333.
72 *The Journals of Arnold Bennett 1896–1910*, edited by Newman Flower (1932), pp. 68–9.
73 *Letters*, II, p. 479.
74 *The Symbolist Movement in Literature* (1895), p. 9.
75 *Ibid.*, p. 7.
76 'Emile Zola', *Selected Literary Criticism*, p. 287.
77 Quoted, Becker (ed.), *Documents of Modern Literary Realism*, p. 346.
78 'The Experimental Novel', *Ibid.*, p. 176.
79 *Ibid*, p. 177.
80 Quoted, Clarence R. Decker, *The Victorian Conscience* (New York 1952), p. 19.
81 'The Experimental Novel', *Documents of Modern Literary Realism*, p. 177.

82 *The Life and Work of Thomas Hardy*, edited by Michael Millgate (1984), p. 183.

83 *Heart of Darkness*, edited by Paul O'Prey (Harmondsworth 1985), p. 38.

84 *Jude the Obscure*, p. 424.

85 Wallace Martin, *'The New Age' under Orage* (Manchester 1967), pp. 139–40; Vincent Brome, *Havelock Ellis: Philosopher of Sex* (1979), pp. 208–24; Frederick J. Hoffmann, *Freudianism and the Literary Mind* (2nd ed. Louisiana 1967).

86 *Beginning Again* (1964), p. 167.

87 *An Introduction to Social Psychology* (14th ed. 1919), p. 82.

88 *Ibid.*, p. 395.

89 See: H. Stuart Hughes, *Consciousness and Society: The Re-Orientation of European Social Thought 1890–1930* (1959); L. L. Whyte, *The Unconscious Before Freud* (1962).

90 *The Way of All Flesh*, p. 22. At about the same time Gissing noted: 'It is evident that the science of Psychology will soon become as definite as that of Physiology,' *Family Letters*, p. 69.

91 *The Crowd*, p. ix.

92 *The Principles of Psychology* (2 vols 1890), I, p. 239.

93 'The Novels of Dorothy Richardson', *Little Review*, V (April 1918), p. 6.

94 *Human Nature in Politics* (1910), p. 23.

95 Julia Briggs, *Night Visitors: The Rise and Fall of the English Ghost Story* (1977), pp. 21–2.

96 *Proceedings of the Society for Psychical Research*, I (1882), pp. 7–8. For details of the Society's work see, Renee Haynes, *The Society for Psychical Research 1882–1982: A History* (1982).

97 Myers, 'The Subliminal Consciousness', *Proceedings of the Society for Psychical Research*, IX (1893–4), pp. 12–15, and Myers, *Human Personality and Its Survival of Bodily Death* (2 vols 1903), I, pp. 50–57.

98 *The Life and Work of Sigmund Freud*, edited by Lionel Trilling and Steven Marcus (Harmondsworth 1964), p. 324.

99 See, *William James on Psychical Research*, edited by Gardner Murphy and Robert O. Ballou (1961).

100 'Ibsen's New Drama', *Ibsen: The Critical Heritage*, edited by Michael Egan (1972), p. 387; first published *Fortnightly Review*, LXVII (1 April 1900).

101 *Ibsen: The Critical Heritage*, p. 180; first published *Truth* (5 March 1891).

102 Michael Meyer, *Henrik Ibsen: The Farewell to Poetry* (1971), pp. 195, 266, 308–9.

103 'Ghosts at the Jubilee', *Ibsen: The Critical Heritage*, p. 380; first published *Saturday Review* (3 July 1897).

104 'On the Occasion of *Hedda Gabler*', *Ibsen: The Critical Heritage*, p. 237; first published *New Review* (June 1891).

105 Quoted, *Ibsen: The Critical Heritage*, p. 278; Gosse's article first published *Fortnightly Review* (1 January 1889).

106 'Count Leo Tolstoi', *The Complete Prose Works of Matthew Arnold*, edited by R. H. Super (11 volumes, Ann Arbor, Michigan 1960–78) XI, p. 282. Sainte-Beuve: 'L'idéal a cessé: le lyrique est tari. On en est revenu. Une vérité sévère et impitoyable est entrée jusque dans l'art comme dernier mot de l'expérience', *Causeries du Lundi* (16 vols Paris 1858), XIII, 348.

107 *The Quintessence of Ibsenism* (1891), pp. 19–30.

108 *Stephen Hero*, edited by Theodore Spencer ('Ace Books' 1961), p. 163.

109 *Jude the Obscure*, p. 101.

110 *Tess of the D'Urbervilles*, p. 162.

111 *Ulysses* (Bodley Head 1960), p. 23.

112 *The Sanity of Art* (1908), p. 92; published originally in 1895 as a review of *Degeneration* in the American periodical *Liberty*.

113 *Degeneration* (1895), p. 21.

114 *Regeneration: A Reply to Max Nordau* (1895), pp. 313–14.

115 *Turgenev in England and America* (Urbana, Illinois 1941), p. 83. See also, *Russian Literature and Modern English Fiction*, edited by D. A. Davie (Chicago 1965).

116 'Count Leo Tolstoi', *Complete Prose Works*, XI, pp. 292–3.

117 Quoted, Dorothy Brewster, *East-West Passage: A Study in Literary Relationships* (1954), p. 151.

118 *Letters*, III, p. 81.

119 'Count Leo Tolstoi', *Complete Prose Works*, XI, p. 284.

120 *Letters from John Galsworthy*, edited by Edward Garnett (1934), p. 177.

121 See, Esther H. Rapp, 'Strindberg's Reception in England', *Scandinavian Studies*, XXIII (Wisconsin, February 1951).

122 Martin, '*The New Age*' Under Orage, pp. 136–8.

123 *Degeneration*, p. 416.

124 *Nietzsche in England 1890–1914* (Toronto 1970), p. 5.

125 *Ibid.*, p. 10.

126 *Affirmations* (1898), p. 35.

127 *The Martyrdom of Man* (Rationalist Press Association Ltd, 1926), p. 430.

128 Martin, '*The New Age*' Under Orage, pp. 212–34; Thatcher, *Nietzsche in England*, pp. 42–58; see also, Patrick Bridgwater,

Nietzsche in Anglo-Saxony (Leicester 1972).

129 *Bookman*, XXXVI (June 1909), p. 140.

130 *Journals*, p. 85.

131 'Song of the New Novel Reader', *Punch*, CX (15 February 1896), p. 81.

132 *Charles Dickens* (Glasgow 1898), p. 63.

133 *The Crisis of Imperialism 1865–1915* (1974), p. 58.

134 Quoted, F. B. Smith, *The Making of the Second Reform Bill* (Melbourne 1966), p. 232.

135 See, Asa Briggs, 'The Language of "Mass" and "Masses" in Nineteenth-Century England', *Ideology and the Labour Movement: Essays Presented to John Saville*, edited by David Martin and David Rubenstein (1979).

136 *Elections and Party Management: Politics in the Time of Disraeli and Gladstone* (1959), p. xiv.

137 For all of these developments, see Hanham, *Elections and Party Management*.

138 See, R. T. Shannon, *Gladstone and the Bulgarian Agitation* (1963).

139 Henry Pelling, *A Short History of the Labour Party* (1961), p. 18.

140 Smith, *The Making of the Second Reform Bill*, p. 204; see also, Roger Fulford, *Votes for Women* (1957).

141 See, Antonia Raeburn, *Militant Suffragettes* (1973).

142 'The Dignity of the Franchise', *Punch*, CXXVIII (10 May 1905), p. 327.

143 *The English Constitution* (1867), repr. in Norman St John-Stevas, *Walter Bagehot: A Study of his Life and Thought together with a Selection from his Political Writings* (1959), p. 385.

144 Quoted, Briggs, *The Age of Improvement*, p. 499.

145 Introduction to the second edition of *The English Constitution*; St John-Stevas, *Walter Bagehot*, p. 205.

146 Robert Lowe, *Speeches and Letters on Reform* (1867), p. 15.

147 Briggs, *The Age of Improvement*, p. 513; Smith, *The Making of the Second Reform Bill*, p. 69.

148 St John-Stevas, *Walter Bagehot*, p. 197.

149 Quoted, Mary Sturt, *The Education of the People* (1967), p. 300.

150 For the immediate impact of Forster's Education Act, see: Sturt, *The Education of the People*; James Murphy, *The Education Act 1870* (1972).

151 For the development of secondary education, see George A. N. Lowndes, *The Silent Social Revolution 1895–1935* (1937).

152 For working-class education, see Brian Simons, *Studies in the History of Education 1780–1870* (1960) and *Education and the Labour Movement* (1965); J. F. C. Harrison, *Learning and Living*

1790–1960 (1961).

153 Quoted, Sturt, *The Education of the People*, p. 341. For the
     development of the teaching profession, see R. W. Rich, *The
     Training of Teachers in England and Wales During the Nineteenth
     Century* (1933); Asher Tropp, *The School Teachers* (1957); H. C.
     Dent, *The Training of Teachers in England and Wales 1800–1975*
     (1977).

154 For the design of the new schools, see Malcolm Seaborne and Ray
     Lowe, *The English School: Its Architecture and Organisation 1870–
     1970* (1977).

155 *Public Libraries* (4th ed. 1891), p. 10.

156 *Social Transformations of the Victorian Age* (1897), p. 363.

157 *Life of Carlyle*, abridged and edited by John Clubbe (1979), p.
     418.

158 'The Future of Liberalism', *Complete Prose Works*, IX, 140; see
     also, Peter Keating, 'Arnold's Social and Political Thought', *Mat-
     thew Arnold*, edited by Kenneth Allott (1975).

159 *Corrected Impressions* (1893), p. 40.

160 Thatcher, *Nietzsche in England*, pp. 74–5; 80–81.

161 'Shooting Niagara: And After?' *Critical and Miscellaneous Essays*,
     v, 1–48.

162 *Felix Holt* ('The Novels of George Eliot', Edinburgh n.d.), p. 390;
     'Address to Working Men', *Blackwood's Magazine*, CIII (January
     1868).

163 *Middlemarch* (Edinburgh 1875), p. 619.

164 *Great Expectations* ('Biographical Edition' 1903), p. 363.

165 Quoted, Edgar Johnson, *Charles Dickens: His Tragedy and Triumph*
     (2 vols. 1953), II, pp. 1112–13.

166 *Our Mutual Friend* ('Biographical Edition' 1903), p. 115.

167 *Lectures on the Relation between Law and Public Opinion in England*
     (1905), p. 64. On this topic, see also Ernest Barker, *Political Thought
     in England from Herbert Spencer to the Present Day* (1915).

168 *Ibid.*, pp. 67–8.

169 *Ibid.*, p. 218.

170 *Law and Public Opinion* (2nd ed. 1914), p. lxxxvii.

171 See, Harold Perkin, 'Individualism Versus Collectivism in
     Nineteenth-Century Britain: A False Antithesis', *Journal of British
     Studies*, XVII (Fall 1977).

172 *Law and Public Opinion* (2nd ed. 1914), p. lxii.

173 For example, Edwin Pugh, *Chales Dickens: The Apostle of the
     People* (1908).

174 Preface to *Man and Superman* (1903).

175 *Autobiography*, p. 111.

176 Socialism 'had taken the Universities with particular force, and any youngster with the slightest intellectual pretension was either actively for or brilliantly against,' Wells, *The New Machiavelli*, p. 314.

177 For the writers who were actively committed to Socialism, see Stephen Ingle, *Socialist Thought in Imaginative Literature* (1979); Ian Britain, *Fabianism and Culture: A Study in British Socialism and the Arts 1884–1918* (1982).

178 *Studies in Contemporary Biography* (1903), p. 120.

179 *Jude the Obscure*, p. 424.

180 Introduction to the second edition of *The English Constitution*, St John-Stevas, *Walter Bagehot*, p. 194.

181 *Ibid.*, p. 193.

182 *Law and Public Opinion* (1905), p. 66. In addition to Hanham and Shannon, see: Harold Perkin, *The Origins of Modern English Society 1780–1880* (1969), Donald Read, *England 1868–1914* (1979).

Chapter Three **Parents and Children**

1 *Early Victorian England*, II, p. 363.

2 *Children in English Society: From the Eighteenth Century to the Children Act 1948* (1973), p. 363.

3 *Ibid.*, p. 622.

4 *Ibid.*, p. 381.

5 *Jude the Obscure*, p. 270.

6 *Anticipations* (1902), p. 112.

7 *Ibid.*, p. 129.

8 'The Gate of Empire', first published in the *Manchester Daily Despatch*, 11 January 1908, repr. *Paris Nights* (1913), p. 243.

9 *Law and Public Opinion* (2nd ed. 1914), p. liii.

10 Quoted, Ian Bradley, *The Optimists* (1980), p. 259.

11 For example: Johan Bachofen, *Das Mutterrecht* (Stuttgart 1861); Frédéric Le Play, *L'Organisation de la Famille* (Paris 1871); Edward Westermarck, *The History of Human Marriage* (1891).

12 *The Letters of Sidney and Beatrice Webb*, edited by Norman Mackenzie (3 vols Cambridge 1978), I, p. 194.

13 *The Way of All Flesh*, p. 337.

14 *The Age of Equipoise*, p. 246.

15 *Our Mutual Friend*, p. 563.

16 *Ibid.*

17 *The Way of All Flesh*, p. 69.

18 For the wider implications of this point, see, David Cannadine, 'The Context, Performance and Meaning of Ritual: The British Monarchy and the "Invention of Tradition" ', *The Invention of*

Tradition, edited by Eric Hobsbawm and Terence Ranger (Cambridge 1983).

19 See: Steven Marcus, *The Other Victorians* (1966); Ronald Pearsall, *The Worm in the Bud* (1969); Eric Trudgill, *Madonnas and Magdalens* (1976); Angus Wilson, *The Naughty Nineties* (1976).

20 Commenting on the 'stupendous hypocrisy of the Edwardian age' that pronounced *Three Weeks* immoral, Elinor Glyn noted: 'It was secretly considered quite normal in society circles for a married woman to have a succession of illicit love affairs, during the interval of which, if not simultaneously, intimate relations with her husband were resumed,' *Romantic Adventure* (1936), p. 136. That was already a main theme of her first novel *The Visits of Elizabeth*, and was also explored by many other novelists, notably Henry James and Ouida. Denunciations of the 'smart set' became frequent in the Edwardian period: see, for example, 'Rita', *The Sin and Scandal of the "Smart" Set* (1904), and Father Bernard Vaughan, *The Sins of Society* (1906). For a different kind of interpretation of flamboyant upper-class life, see: Thorstein Veblen, *The Theory of the Leisure Class* (New York 1899).

21 *The Passing of the Great Queen* (1901), pp. 55–6.

22 *Letters*, IV, p. 181.

23 'Paul is dead. He died on Friday night about 10 o'clock, and as I had no hope of getting to sleep afterwards, I went out and walked about Paris until breakfast time next morning.' Johnson, *Charles Dickens: His Tragedy and Triumph*, II, p. 611.

24 *The Subjection of Women* (1869), pp. 66–7.

25 *The Family* (1906), p. 342.

26 *Ibid.*

27 *The Wings of the Dove* (Harmondsworth 1971), pp. 14–15.

28 Marx and Engels, *Selected Works* (2 vols Moscow 1962), I, p. 50.

29 *Ibid.*, pp. 232–3.

30 *News from Nowhere*, p. 69.

31 *Ibid.*, p. 86–7.

32 'The Time Machine,' *Selected Short Stories* (Harmondsworth 1958), p. 29.

33 *Ibid.*, p. 30.

34 *Ibid.*

35 *In the Days of the Comet* (1906), pp. 304–5.

36 Hynes, *The Edwardian Turn of Mind*, p. 115; N. and J. Mackenzie, *The Time Traveller*, p. 227.

37 *The Savage in Literature* (1975). See also J. W. Burrow, *Evolution and Society* (1968).

38 See, John B. Vickery, *The Literary Impact of The Golden Bough* (1973).

39 *The Morality of Marriage* (1897), p. 58.
40 See: Noel Annan, 'Kipling's Place in the History of Ideas', *Victorian Studies*, III (1959–60); Keating, *The Working Classes in Victorian Fiction*, Chapter Six.
41 *She* (1887), pp. 81–2.
42 Roger Swearingen, *The Prose Writings of Robert Louis Stevenson*, pp. 153–6; for this, other changes, and the original text, see, Barry Menikoff, *Robert Louis Stevenson and 'The Beach of Falesá'* (Stanford 1984).
43 *The Story of an African Farm*, p. 196.
44 *The Old Wives' Tale*, p. 213.
45 *Far from the Madding Crowd*, pp. 32–5.
46 *Thomas Hardy and Women* (1982), p. 48.
47 *The Woodlanders* pp. 179–80.
48 *Ibid.*, p. 354.
49 *Ibid.*, p. 363.
50 O. R. McGregor, *Divorce in England* (1957), p. 36.
51 *The Woodlanders*, p. 408.
52 *Complete Tales*, IV, p. 144.
53 *The Good Soldier* (Harmondsworth 1972), p. 77.
54 Ruth Brandon, *The Dollar Princesses* (1980), pp. 1–5. For two American responses, see: Lizzie W. Champney, *Three Vassar Girls Abroad* (1882); Sara Jeannette Duncan, *An American Girl in London* (1891).
55 Florence L. Barclay, *The Rosary* (1909), p. 19.
56 *The Sorrows of Satan*, p. 91.
57 'An International Episode', *Complete Tales*, IV, p. 290.
58 *Henry James: The Conquest of London 1870–83* (1962), p. 307.
59 Gilbert and Sullivan, *The Gondoliers* (1889), Act II.
60 *Sexual Politics* ('Abacus Books' 1972), p. 139.
61 *The Egoist* ('Standard Edition' 1915), p. 239.
62 *A Doll's House*, 'Authorised English Edition' edited by William Archer (1890), Act III.
63 *Ibsen: The Critical Heritage*, p. 8.
64 'The Doll's House – And After', *English Illustrated Magazine*, VII (January 1890).
65 'Still After the Doll's House', *Time*, I (February 1890).
66 Egan, *Ibsen: The Critical Heritage*, p. 9.
67 See, Peter Keating, 'Conrad's *Doll's House*', *Papers on Language and Literature Presented to Alvar Ellegard and Erik Frykman*, edited by Sven Backman and Gavan Kjellmer (Gothenburg 1985).
68 Meyer, *Henrik Ibsen: The Farewell to Poetry*, pp. 268–9.
69 Preface to the 1913 edition of *The Quintessence of Ibsenism*, repr. *Major Critical Essays* (1932), p. 8.

70 *Far from the Madding Crowd*, p. 415.

71 *Literature at Nurse or Circulating Morals*, edited by Pierre Coustillas
    (Hassocks 1976), pp. 5–16.

72 For Oliphant's career, Robert and Vineta Colby, *The Equivocal
    Virtue: Mrs Oliphant and the Victorian Literary Market Place*
    (Hamden, Conn. 1966).

73 For Ward's career and literary reputation, Mrs G. M. Trevelyan,
    The Life of Mrs Humphry Ward (1923); William S. Peterson, *Victorian
    Heretic: Mrs Humphry Ward's Robert Elsemere* (Leicester 1976); and
    her outstanding autobiography, *A Writer's Recollections* (1918).

74 For the prevalence of late Victorian anti-feminism, see Brian
    Harrison, *Separate Spheres* (1978).

75 See: Eliza Lynn Linton, *My Literary Life* (1899); G. S. Layard,
    Mrs Lynn Linton: Her Life, Letters and Opinions (1901); Herbert
    van Thal, *Eliza Lynn Linton* (1979).

76 *The Singular Anomaly: Women Novelists of the Nineteenth Century*
    (New York 1970), p. 116.

77 'She-Note Series', *Punch*, CVIII (30 March 1895); J. A. Noble, 'The
    Fiction of Sexuality', *Contemporary Review*, LXVII (April 1895); Janet
    Hogarth, 'Literary Degenerates', *Fortnightly Review*, LVII (April
    1895); Hugh E. M. Stutfield, 'Tommyrotics', *Blackwood's Magazine*,
    CLVII (June 1895); 'The Philistine', *The New Fiction: A Protest
    Against Sex-Mania* (1895). For further details of this kind of criticism,
    see Gail Cunningham, *The New Woman and the Victorian Novel* (1978),
    and Penny Boumelha, *Thomas Hardy and Woman*, Chapter Four.

78 Linton, *The Girl of the Period and other Social Essays* (2 vols 1883),
    pp. 491–2; Corelli, *The Sorrows of Satan*, p. 6; Oliphant, 'The Anti-
    Marriage League', *Blackwood's*, CLIX (January 1896), pp. 140–1.

79 *Some Diversions of a Man of Letters* (1920), p. 146.

80 See the distinction drawn by Elaine Showalter between the 'femi-
    nine' and the 'feminist' generations of novelists; *A Literature of
    Their Own* ('Virago Edition' 1978), chapters six and seven.

81 'Why Be a Lady?' *Pall Mall Magazine*, XXVI (1902), p. 116.

82 Forrester, *Great-Grandmama's Weekly: A Celebration of The
    Girl's Own Paper 1880–1901*, p. 27.

83 *Ibid.*, pp. 27–42.

84 Lee Holcombe, *Victorian Ladies at Work: Middle-Class Working
    Women in England and Wales 1850–1914* (1973), pp. 204–10.

85 Bram Stoker, *Dracula* (1897, 8th ed. 1904), p. 55.

86 *Howards End*, edited by Oliver Stallybrass ('Abinger Edition'
    1973), p. 54.

87 See 'The Old Adam' and 'The Witch à la Mode', *The Mortal Coil*,
    edited by Keith Sagar (Harmondsworth 1971).

88 'A Case of Identity,' *The Adventures of Sherlock Holmes* (Pan Books, 1976), p. 45.

89 *Jude the Obscure*, p. 172.

90 By 1900 there were sixteen such departments: they contained 1,150 students, nearly a quarter of the total number (5,200) in teacher-training. H. C. Dent, *The Training of Teachers in England and Wales* (1977), p. 33.

91 For this, and other aspects of adult education, see J. F. C. Harrison, *Learning and Living 1790–1960*.

92 'A Slip Under the Microscope', *The Country of the Blind and other Stories* (1911), pp. 261–2. It was first published in the *Yellow Book*, January 1896.

93 *The Importance of Being Earnest*, *The Works of Oscar Wilde*, p. 360.

94 *In the Year of Jubilee* (Hassocks 1976), p. 14.

95 *The Woman Who Did* (1895), p. 4.

96 *A Portrait of the Artist*, pp. 174–5.

97 See: Edward Nehls, *D.H. Lawrence: A Composite Biography* (3 vols Madison 1957–9), I, pp. 81–155; *Lawrence in Love*, edited by James T. Boulton (1969); Helen Corke, *In Our Infancy* (1975).

98 *The Rainbow* ('Phoenix Edition' 1955), pp. 352–411.

99 *The Diary of Beatrice Webb, Vol. I, 1873–1892*, edited by Norman and Jeanne Mackenzie (1982), p. xvii. See also, Samuel Hynes, 'The Art of Beatrice Webb', *Edwardian Occasions*, and for details of Beatrice Webb's other literary interests, omitted from the published diary, Barbara Caine, 'Beatrice Webb and her Diary', *Victorian Studies*, XXVII (Autumn 1983), pp. 85–6.

100 *Ibid.*, p. 298.

101 *Thomas Hardy and Women*, pp. 64–5.

102 *The Story of a Modern Woman* (1894), p. 255.

103 'Virgin Soil', *Discords* (1894), p. 157.

104 *The Daughters of Danaus* (1894), pp. 472–3.

105 Introduction to George Egerton, *Keynotes and Discords* (Virago 1983), pp. xviii–xix.

106 'The New Hedonism', *Fortnightly Review*, LV (March 1894), p. 185. See also: Grant Allen, 'About the New Hedonism', *The Humanitarian*, V (September 1894); Allen's introduction to *The British Barbarians: A Hill-Top Novel* (1895); and Edward Clodd, *Grant Allen: A Memoir* (1900). 'Hill-top' was the name of Allen's house in Surrey.

107 Gillian Kersley, *Darling Madam: Sarah Grand and Devoted Friend*, p. 74.

108 *Diary*, pp. 281, 365–6.

109 See, for example, Edith Slater, 'Men's Women in Fiction', *Westminster Review*, (May 1898), pp. 575–6.

110 'The Anti-Marriage League', p. 136.
111 See: Josephine Butler, *Personal Reminiscences of a Great Crusade* (1896); Glen Petrie, *A Singular Iniquity: The Campaigns of Josephine Butler* (1971).
112 For birth control at this time, see J. A. Banks, *Prosperity and Parenthood* (1954); J. A. and Olive Banks, *Feminism and Family Planning* (Liverpool 1965); Peter Fryer, *The Birth Controllers* (1965); Angus McLaren, *Birth Control in Nineteenth-Century England* (1978).
113 Quoted Cunningham, *The New Woman and the Victorian Novel*, p. 51.
114 *Keynotes* (1893), p. 20.
115 *Ibid.*, p. 16.
116 *The Woman Who Didn't* (1895), p. 71.
117 Emma Brooke, *A Superfluous Woman* (3 vols 1894), II, pp. 205–6.
118 *Gallia* (1895), p. 57.
119 *Ibid.*, p. 190.
120 *Ibid.*, p. 213.
121 *Ibid.*, p. 310.
122 *The Importance of Being Earnest, The Works of Oscar Wilde*, p. 330.
123 *The Yellow Aster* (1894), pp. 130–1.
124 *The Woman Who Did* (1895), p. 21.
125 *Ibid.*, pp. 34–5.
126 *Ibid.*, p. 181.
127 'A Shattered Doll's House', *The Humanitarian*, V (August 1894), pp. 137–46.
128 'A Doll's House Again', *Saturday Review* 15 May 1897; *Ibsen: The Critical Heritage*, pp. 375–6.
129 *The Letters of George Gissing to Eduard Bertz*, pp. 171–2.
130 *Jude the Obscure*, p. 261.
131 *Ibid.*, pp. 324, 505.
132 *Ibid.*, p. 344.
133 *One of Our Conquerors* ('Standard Edition' 17 vols 1914–20), p. 316. All quotations from Meredith's novels are to this edition.
134 *Lord Ormont and His Aminta*, p. 126.
135 William Hale White [Mark Rutherford] *Letters to Three Friends* (1924), p. 72.
136 For the influence of Ibsen on James, see Michael Egan, *Henry James: The Ibsen Years* (1972).
137 *The Spoils of Poynton* (Harmondsworth 1963), p. 12.
138 *Ibid.*, p. 126.
139 *Dodo* (1894), p. 48.

140 *Ibid.*, p. 181.
141 *Ibid.*, p. 86.
142 *In the Year of Jubilee*, p. 329.
143 *The Whirlpool*, edited by Patrick Parrinder (Hassocks 1977), p. 73.
144 *Ibid.*, p. 324.
145 'George Gissing', *Collected Essays*, I, p. 299.
146 *Born in Exile*, edited by Pierre Coustillas (Hassocks 1978), p. 170.
147 *Ibid.*, p. 247.
148 *Ibid.*, 191.
149 *The Odd Women* ('Doughty Library Edition' 1968), pp. 102–4.
150 *Born in Exile*, p. 247.
151 *Experiment in Autobiography* II, p. 550.
152 *Kipps* (1905), p. 392.
153 *Tono-Bungay* (1909), pp. 199–200.
154 'Read *Kipps, Love and Mr Lewisham*, and read, *read*, *Tono-Bungay*; it is a great book.' *Letters*, I, p. 127.
155 *The History of Mr Polly* (1910), p. 283.
156 *Tono-Bungay*, p. 231.
157 *The New Machiavelli*, pp. 525–8.
158 'Mr Bennett and Mrs Brown', p. 326.
159 'The Threatened Re-Subjection of Women', *Fortnightly Review*, LXXVII (May 1905), p. 186; Cunningham, *The New Woman and the Victorian Novel*, pp. 152–7.
160 There was, of course, a great deal of non-fictional prose writing, but as far as imaginative literature was concerned writers for the Suffragist cause seem to have been drawn to drama rather than fiction. The greater immediacy and the public nature of drama would have given it some obvious advantages over fiction at a time of heightened political agitation. Ibsen, Shaw, and the 'drama of ideas' had also established by this time a theatrical tradition that Suffragist writers could build on. See: Hynes, *The Edwardian Turn of Mind*, Chapters Six and Seven; Showalter, *A Literature of Their Own*, Chapter Eight.
161 *The Freewoman*, 19 September 1912: *The Young Rebecca: Writings of Rebecca West 1911–1917*, edited by Jane Marcus (1982), p. 69. It was this review that initiated the long personal relationship between West and Wells. See, Gordon N. Ray, *H.G. Wells and Rebecca West* (1974).
162 *Dodo the Second* (1914), p. 18.
163 *A Room with a View*, edited by Oliver Stallybrass ('Abinger Edition' 1977), p. 26.
164 *A Dark Lantern* (1905), p. 99.
165 *Sacred and Profane Love* (1905), p. 57.

166 *Ibid.*, p. 90.

167 *Romantic Adventure*, pp. 136–7.

168 *Just to Get Married* (1911), p. 308.

169 *The Yoke* (1907), p. 10.

170 *Ibid.*, pp. 58–67.

171 *The Man of Property* (1906), p. 241.

172 McGregor, *Divorce in England*, pp. 26–7; Edmund Haynes, *Divorce Problems of Today* (1912); and the novel by Philip Gibbs, *The Custody of the Child* (1914).

173 *The White Peacock* ('Phoenix Edition' 1955), p. 74.

174 *Ibid.*, pp. 315–6.

175 *Sons and Lovers* ('Phoenix Edition' 1956), p. 407.

176 'Instead of a Preface', *Of Human Bondage* ('Collected Edition' 1937), p. vii.

177 Jerome Buckley, *Season of Youth: the Bildungsroman from Dickens to Golding* (Cambridge Mass. 1974); Dorothy Richardson, preface to the 1938 edition of *Pilgrimage*.

178 *The New Machiavelli*, p. 152; Moore, *Confessions of a Young Man*, p. 89. Moore himself refers back to Balzac's 'La Femme de Trente Ans'. In *The Woodlanders* p. 291, Hardy says of Mrs Charmond: 'She might almost have been taken for the typical *femme de trente ans.*'

179 *Of Human Bondage*, p. 221.

180 There are, of course, some exceptions. 'I was afraid, man, she'd get in the family way. But she's up to that dodge.' Joyce, 'Two Gallants' *Dubliners*.

181 Samuel Butler, *Erewhon*, Chapter Nineteen.

182 'The Unborn', *Time's Laughingstocks* (1909).

183 *Jude the Obscure*, p. 346.

184 *Ibid.*, p. 344.

185 *What Maisie Knew* (Harmondsworth 1966), p. 76.

186 *Ibid.*, p.18.

187 Among many books, see especially; Gillian Avery, *Nineteenth-Century Children* (1965); David Grylls, *Guardians and Angels* (1978).

188 E. Nesbit, *The Wouldbegoods* (1901), p. 33.

189 'The Good Little Girl', *The Talking Horse and other Tales* (1892), pp. 40–41.

190 Helen Mather, *Comin' Thro the Rye* (3 vols 1875), I, pp. 87–94.

191 'Fantasy as Witty Conceit: E. Nesbit', *Mosaic*, X (Winter 1977), p. 112.

192 *Vice Versa* (Revised Edition 1883), pp. 21, 137.

193 *Ibid.*, pp. 172–4.

194 *Ibid.*, pp. 113, 194.

195 Corelli, *Boy* (1900), p. 19.

196 Nesbit, *The Story of the Treasure Seekers* (1899), p. 59.

197 *The Golden Age* (1895), pp. 1–7.

198 *Stalky and Co.* (1899), p. 245.

199 Lyman B. Sperry, *Confidential Talks with Young Women* (3rd ed. Edinburgh 1901), p. 127.

200 For the impact of Angela Brazil, and her predecessors in fiction for girls, see Mary Cadogan and Patricia Craig, *You're a Brick, Angela! A New Look at Girls' Fiction from 1839 to 1975* (1976).

201 John Rowe Townsend, 'Articulate Animals', *Written for Children* (Harmondsworth 1976).

202 *Nineteenth Century Children* (1965), p. 185.

203 F. Anstey, *A Long Retrospect* (1936), pp. 112–13.

204 See, *The Young Visiters or Mr Salteena's Plan* (1919), with a preface by J. M. Barrie.

205 Barrie, *Margaret Ogilvy* (1896), p. 41.

206 Peter Coveney, *Poor Monkey: The Child in Literature* (1957), pp. 202–10; Andrew Birkin, *J. M. Barrie and the Lost Boys* (1979).

207 *The Way of All Flesh*, p. 71.

208 *Ibid.*, p. 78.

209 *Ibid.*, p. 79.

210 *Father and Son*, p. 7.

211 *Ibid.*, p. 223.

212 *The Way of All Flesh*, pp. 305–6.

213 *Ibid.*

214 Maugham, 'Instead of a Preface', *Of Human Bondage*, p. vii.

215 *The Rainbow*, p. 492.

216 *The Man of Property*, p. 3.

217 *Ibid.*, p. 121.

218 'John Galsworthy', *D.H. Lawrence: Selected Literary Criticism*, edited by Anthony Beal (Heinemann Educational Books 1969), p. 128.

219 *Father and Son*, p. 223.

220 Bennett, *Anna of the Five Towns* (1902), p. 107.

221 *Ibid.*, p. 310.

222 *Ibid.*, p. 311.

223 *Ibid.*, p. 359.

224 Bennett, *Clayhanger* (1910), p. 90.

225 *Ibid.*, p. 115.

226 *Ibid.*

227 *Ibid.*, p. 319.

228 *Anna of the Five Towns*, p. 185.

229 Sinclair wrote introductions to several of the Brontë novels and to Mrs Gaskell's *Life of Charlotte Brontë* for Dent's Everyman's Library in 1908–9.

230 *The Three Sisters* (1914), p. 384.
231 *Ibid.*, p. 54.
232 *To the Lighthouse* (Harmondsworth 1964), p. 6.
233 *The House with the Green Shutters* ('Nelson Library' n.d.), p. 258.
234 See Roger Swearingen's introduction to his edition of Stevenson's *An Old Song* and *Edifying Letters of the Rutherford Family* (Hamden, Conn. 1982).
235 *Weir of Hermiston* ('Tusitala Edition' 1924), p. 25.
236 *Ibid.*, pp. 125–6. Editorial Note by Sir Sidney Colvin.
237 *Sons and Lovers*, p. 394.
238 *Ibid.*, pp. 419–20.
239 *Portrait of the Artist as a Young Man*, p. 247.
240 *Ulysses*, p. 10.
241 *Women in Love*, p. 344.
242 *Ibid.*
243 *Ibid.*, p. 144.
244 *To the Lighthouse*, p. 234.

Chapter Four   An End to Reticence

1 *Hansard*, CCCXXV (1888), columns 1707–25. The NVA published transcripts of this debate and Vizetelly's trial as a pamphlet *Pernicious Literature* (1889), reprinted in *Documents of Modern Literary Realism*.
2 *Hansard*, CXLVI (1857), column 329.
3 Pornography means writing about prostitutes. The OED gives 1850 for 'pornographer'; 1857 for 'pornography' in a medical sense, and 1864 for its modern meaning of obscene or licentious; and 1880 for 'pornographic'. See, H. Montgomery Hyde, *A History of Pornography* (1964).
4 *Hansard*, CXLVI (1857), columns 332–3.
5 Quoted, Alec Craig, *The Banned Books of England and Other Countries* (1962), p. 44.
6 H. Montgomery Hyde, *The Trials of Oscar Wilde* (1948), p. 124.
7 For an inside history of the NVA, William Coote, *A Vision and its Fulfilment* (1910), and *A Romance of Philanthropy* (1916).
8 Donald Thomas, *A Long Time Burning: The History of Literary Censorship in Britain* (1965); Edward J. Bristow, *Vice and Vigilance: Purity Movements in Britain since 1700* (1977).
9 Quoted, Donald Thomas, *A Long Time Burning*, pp. 113–14.
10 *The Times*, 1 November 1888, p. 13.
11 *Ibid.*, 3 May 1889, p. 13.

12 *Ibid.*, 31 May 1889, p. 12. Shortly after the first trial a letter from the Vizetelly office was printed in the *Publishers' Circular*, LI (15 November 1888), p. 1437: 'The undertaking did not apply to the whole of M. Zola's works but only to such as contain passages as objectionable as those that form the subject of the indictment. For the present we have withdrawn the books from circulation until they have been carefully examined and revised.' Whether the Vizetellys were genuinely confused about what had been agreed in court, or whether the letter was an attempt to head off further prosecution, is not clear.

13 One notable exception to this generalisation is Graham Hough, 'George Moore and the Nineties', *Edwardians and Late Victorians*, edited by Richard Ellmann (New York 1959), pp. 4–5.

14 E. A. Vizetelly, *Emile Zola: Novelist and Reformer* (1904), p. 249.

15 Hone, *The Life of George Moore*, pp. 151-8.

16 *The Times*, 31 May 1889, p. 12; E. A. Vizetelly, *Emile Zola: Novelist and Reformer*, pp. 281–5.

17 *Emile Zola: Novelist and Reformer*, p. 256.

18 *The Dram-Shop* (Chatto and Windus 1897).

19 Clarence Decker, *The Victorian Conscience* (New York 1952), p. 99.

20 *Bookseller*, 4 May 1889, p. 445; 5 July 1889, pp. 681, 684.

21 NVA, Fifth Annual Report (1890), p. 22.

22 NVA, Third Annual Report (1888), p. 5.

23 Hynes, *The Edwardian Turn of Mind*, p. 264; John Carter, '*The Rainbow Prosecution*', *TLS*, 27 February 1969, p. 216.

24 *Bookseller*, 5 July 1889, p. 681; E. A. Vizetelly, *Emile Zola: Novelist and Reformer*, p. 270.

25 'Emile Zola', *Selected Literary Criticism*, p. 285.

26 *The Times*, 1 November 1888, p. 9.

27 'The Limits of Realism in Fiction', *Questions at Issue* (1893), p. 153.

28 Quoted, *Documents of Modern Literary Realism*, p. 381.

29 Preface to the 1850 edition of *Pendennis*.

30 *The Letters and Private Papers of William Makepeace Thackeray*, IV, p. 206.

31 *Ibid.* 'Mrs General Talboys' was first published in the *London Review*, February 1861, and then in *Tales of All Countries: Second Series* (1863).

32 *Hansard*, CCCXXV (1888), columns 1715–16.

33 *The Letters of George Meredith*, edited by C. L. Cline (3 vols Oxford 1970), p. 39.

34 Malcolm Elwin, *Charles Reade: A Biography* (1931), pp. 184–9. At this point in his career Reade insisted that his publishing contracts

contained a clause preventing any alterations to his manuscripts, Nowell-Smith, *The House of Cassell*, p. 124.

35 *Ibid.*, pp. 290–311.
36 Gissing, *Family Letters*, p. 119.
37 *Ibid.*, p. 121.
38 *Ibid.*, pp. 121–2.
39 Gettmann, *A Victorian Publisher*, p. 217; see also, Gettmann's 'Gissing and Bentley', *Nineteenth-Century Fiction*.
40 Jacob Korg, *George Gissing: A Critical Biography* (1965), p. 54.
41 Gettmann, *A Victorian Publisher*, p. 220.
42 *Pall Mall Gazette*, 15 December 1884, p. 2.
43 *Ibid.*
44 'Gissing the Rod', *Punch* LXXXVIII (3 January 1885), p. 1.
45 *Family Letters*, p. 151.
46 Charles Morgan, *The House of Macmillan*, p. 90.
47 *The Life and Work of Thomas Hardy*, edited by Michael Millgate (1984), pp. 62–4.
48 Morgan, *The House of Macmillan*, pp. 93–4.
49 Robert Gittings, *Young Thomas Hardy* (1975), p. 189.
50 Quoted, *Ibid.*, p. 195.
51 *Ibid.*
52 *The Life and Work of Thomas Hardy*, p. 102.
53 *Ibid.*
54 *Letters*, I, p. 49.
55 For the publication history of *The Woodlanders*, see Dale Kramer's edition of the novel published by Oxford University Press, 1981.
56 J. T. Laird, *The Shaping of Tess of the D'Urbervilles* (1975), p. 9.
57 *Ibid.*, p. 10.
58 *Ibid.*, pp. 10–11.
59 'Explanatory Note' to 1891 edition of *Tess*.
60 Juliet Grindle and Simon Cotrell, introduction to the Oxford University Press edition of *Tess of the D'Urbervilles* (1983), p. 10.
61 *New Review* II (January 1890), p. 19.
62 *Letters of George Gissing to Eduard Bertz*, p. 149.
63 *Life and Work of Thomas Hardy*, p. 303.
64 *Hansard*, CCCXXV (1888), column 1710.
65 *The Art of the Novel*, p. 45.
66 Preface to *The Picture of Dorian Gray*.
67 'Emile Zola', *Selected Literary Criticism*, p. 299.
68 'Guy de Maupassant', *Ibid.*, p. 138.
69 *Ibid.*
70 *Life and Work of Thomas Hardy*, p. 136.

71 *The Personal Notebooks of Thomas Hardy*, edited by Richard H. Taylor (1978), p. 39.
72 *Recreations of the Rabelais Club 1880–1888* (3 vols 1888), I. Besant also refers to James as being a member of the club, *Autobiography*, p. 241.
73 'Candour in English Fiction', *New Review*, II (January 1890), p. 7.
74 Talbot Baines Reed, *The Fifth Form at St Dominic's* (1887), p. 4.
75 *The Truth About An Author*, p. 28.
76 'Mrs Elinor Glyn', *Books and Persons* (1917), pp. 271–77.
77 *Ann Veronica*, (1909), p. 193.
78 Robert Scholes, 'Grant Richards to James Joyce', *Studies in Bibliography*, XVI (1963), p. 145.
79 *Letters of James Joyce*, edited by Stuart Gilbert and Richard Ellmann (3 vols 1957–1966), II, p. 132.
80 *The Edwardian Turn of Mind*, p. 271.
81 Ellmann, *James Joyce*, p. 325.
82 *Letters*, II, pp. 137, 140.
83 Scholes, 'Grant Richards to James Joyce', p. 146.
84 *Ibid.*, p. 145.
85 *Ibid.*, p. 146.
86 Joyce, *Letters*, I, p. 306; Ellmann, *James Joyce*, pp. 341–6
87 Joyce, *Letters*, II, p. 133.
88 Scholes, 'Grant Richards to James Joyce', p. 153.
89 *Ibid.*, p. 155.
90 Lovat Dickson, *H. G. Wells: His Turbulent Life and Times* (1969), p. 166.
91 Lawrence, *Letters*, I, p. 421, n. 4.
92 Hynes, *The Edwardian Turn of Mind*, p. 282.
93 *The Cleansing of a City*, edited by James Marchant (1908), p. 77.
94 *Ibid.*, p. 87.
95 *The Nation's Morals* (1910), p. 121.
96 *The Cleansing of a City*, p. 94.
97 *Ibid.*, p. 99.
98 NVA, Twenty-Fourth Annual Report (1909), pp. 16–17.
99 Herbert Bull, letter to the *Spectator* CIII (25 December 1909), p. 1100.
100 NVA, Twenty-Fourth Annual Report (1909), pp. 16–17.
101 *Spectator* CIII (6 November 1909), p. 750.
102 *Ibid.*, 22 November, p. 846. This review and Wells' reply are reprinted in *H. G. Wells: The Critical Heritage*, edited by Patrick Parrinder (1972).
103 *Spectator* CIII (27 November 1909), pp. 876, 881–2.
104 *Ibid.*, 4 December 1909, p. 945.
105 *Ibid.*, p. 944.

106 *Ibid.*, 27 November, pp, 881–2.

107 *Ibid.*, 25 December, p. 1100.

108 *The Times*, 2 December 1909, p. 12.

109 *Ibid.*

110 *Ibid.*, 3 December 1909, p. 11.

111 *Ibid.*, 7 December 1909, p. 6.

112 *The Times*, 3 December 1909, p. 11: see also, Gosse's article 'The Censorship of Books', *English Review*, IV (March 1910).

113 Murray, *The Times*, 3 December 1909, p. 11; Barry, 'The Cleansing of Fiction', *Bookman* (January 1910), p. 179, and *Heralds of Revolt: Studies in Modern Literature and Dogma* (1904).

114 *The Times*, 9 December 1909, p. 10.

115 *Ibid.*, 13 December 1909, p. 12.

116 *Ibid.*, 10 December 1909, p. 11.

117 *Ibid.*, 16 December 1909, p. 12.

118 Diana Farr, *Gilbert Cannan: A Georgian Prodigy* (1978), p. 92.

119 On 'blacking out', see Anthony Hugh Thompson, *Censorship in Public Libraries during the Twentieth Century* (1975), pp. 82–91; for Plummer, see *Library World*, XIV (1911–12), pp. 103–4.

120 *Public Libraries*, p. 423.

121 *The Times*, 15 December 1909, p. 12, and subsequent correspondence, 17 and 25 December.

122 *Library World* XIII (1910–11), p. 49.

123 *Ibid.*, XIV (1911–12), p. 100.

124 *Ibid.*, XIII (1910–11), pp. 129–40.

125 Neville M. Hemmings, *Film Censors and the Law* (1967), p. 48.

126 'Censorship by the Libraries', *Books and Persons*, p. 185. First published in the *New Age*, 13 January 1910.

127 *The Dehumanisation of Art*, translated by Helene Weyl (Princeton 1948), p. 5.

128 *The Letters of Virginia Woolf*, edited by Nigel Nicolson (6 vols 1975–80), II, p. 13.

Chapter Five   The Pride of Documentary History

1. *The Symbolist Movement in Literature*, p. 10.

2. See: James, 'The Art of Fiction'; Conrad, Preface to *The Nigger of the 'Narcissus'*; Hardy, Preface to the 1892 edition of *Tess of the D'Urbervilles*.

3 *A Personal Record* ('Medallion Edition' 1925), p. 15.

4 *New Grub Street*, pp. 173–4.

5 *Charles Dickens*, pp. 63–84.

6 *Kipps* (1905), p. 116.
7 *Ibid.*, p. 356.
8 *Background with Chorus* (1956), p. 26.
9 'Mr Bennett and Mrs Brown', p. 332.
10 *Ibid.*, p. 327.
11 *The Letters of Gustave Flaubert*, translated by Francis Steegmuller (2 vols Cambridge, Mass. 1982), I, p. 154.
12 *Henry James and H. G. Wells: A Record of Their Friendship*, edited by Leon Edel and Gordon N. Ray (1959), p. 36.
13 *Ibid.*, p. 264.
14 *Ibid.*, p. 265.
15 'The Function of Criticism at the Present Time', *Complete Prose Works*, III, pp. 266–9.
16 'The Younger Generation', *Henry James and H. G. Wells*, p. 179.
17 *Ibid.*, pp. 182–3.
18 *Ibid.*
19 *Ibid.*, p. 200.
20 See, Gordon N. Ray, 'H. G. Wells Tries to be a Novelist', Richard Ellmann (ed.), *Edwardians and Late Victorians* (1959); Bernard Bergonzi, *The Early H. G. Wells* (1961); *H. G. Wells's Literary Criticism*, edited by Patrick Parrinder and Robert M. Philmus (Brighton 1980).
21 *Mankind in the Making*, p. 360.
22 'The Contemporary Novel', *Henry James and H. G. Wells*, p. 155.
23 *Henry James and H. G. Wells*, p. 265.
24 Wells, *Boon* (1915), p. 100.
25 *Henry James and H. G. Wells*, p. 265.
26 *Ibid.*, p. 264.
27 Anthony Smith, *The Newspaper: An International History* (1979), p. 161.
28 R. H. Dunbar, introduction to Ernest Phillips, *How to Become a Journalist* (1896), p. xviii.
29 'The Soul of Man Under Socialism', *The Works of Oscar Wilde*, p. 1033.
30 'John Delavoy', *Complete Tales*, IX, p. 405.
31 *Letters to William Blackwood*, p. 171.
32 'Up to Easter', *Complete Prose Works*, XI, p. 202.
33 *Letters of George Gissing to Eduard Bertz*, p. 119; Bennett, *How to Become An Author*, p. 64; Wells, *Anticipations*, pp. 160–1.
34 *The Reverberator*, edited by Simon Nowell-Smith (1949), p. 60.
35 *A Journalist on Journalism* (1899), p. 20.
36 'Confession of Faith', repr. Stanley Morison, *The English Newspaper* (Cambridge 1932), pp. 289–90.

37 *Ibid.*
38 *New Grub Street*, p. 496.
39 *A Journalist on Journalism*, pp. 55–6.
40 See: Scott Bennett, 'Revolutions in Thought: serial publication and the mass market for reading', *The Victorian Periodical Press*, edited by Shattock and Wolff; Raymond Williams, *The Long Revolution*, Part II, Chapter Three.
41 *A Journalist on Journalism*, p. 20.
42 *Confessions of a Young Man*, p. 110.
43 *East Lynne*, Part III, Chapter Eight.
44 Brian Coe and Paul Gates, *The Snapshot Photograph: The Rise of Popular Photography 1888–1939* (1977), pp. 16–17.
45 'The Man Who Would Be King', *Wee Willie Winkie and other Stories* ('Uniform Edition' 1899), p. 208. All quotations from Kipling's fiction are to this edition, unless otherwise indicated.
46 'The Three Musketeers', *Plain Tales from the Hills*, p. 69.
47 'A Matter of Fact', *Many Inventions*, p. 163.
48 For this literary tradition, see *Into Unknown England: Selections from the Social Explorers 1866–1913*, edited by Peter Keating (1976).
49 'The Death of Simon Fuge', *The Grim Smile of the Five Towns* (1907), pp. 245–6.
50 *A Journalist on Journalism*, p. 55.
51 See: Michael Pearson, *The Age of Consent: Victorian Prostitution and its Enemies* (1972), Deborah Gorham, 'The "Maiden Tribute of Modern Babylon" Re-examined', *Victorian Studies*, XXI (Spring 1978).
52 See, *The Bitter Cry of Outcast England*, edited by Anthony S. Wohl (Leicester 1970).
53 Quoted, G. Duncan Mitchell, *A Hundred Years of Sociology* (1968), p. 2.
54 T. S. and M. B. Simey, *Charles Booth: Social Scientist* (1960), p. 109.
55 Charles Booth, *Life and Labour*, vol. I, East London (1889), p. 157.
56 *Ibid.*, p. 6.
57 *Ibid.*
58 *Ibid.*, p. 598.
59 *My Apprenticeship*, p. 226.
60 *Life and Labour*, I, p. 591.
61 *Ibid.*, p. 592.
62 See, Philip Abrahams, *The Origins of British Sociology 1834–1914* (Chicago 1968).
63 See, Asa Briggs, *Social Work and Social Action: A Study of the Work of Seebohm Rowntree* (1961).

64 'The Autumn of Books', *The Speaker*, XV (6 October 1906), p. 26.
65 Preface to W. H. Davies, *The Autobiography of a Super-Tramp* (1908), p. xiii.
66 *Tales of Mean Streets* (1894), p. 9.
67 Preface to the third edition of *A Child of the Jago* (1897).
68 Rook, introduction to *The Hooligan Nights* (1899); for the many different manifestations of hooliganism, see Geoffrey Pearson, *Hooligan: A History of Respectable Fears* (1983).
69 Introduction to *The Hooligan Nights* (1899).
70 Benny Green, introduction to *The Hooligan Nights* (Oxford 1979), p. x.
71 *Letters of Stephen Reynolds*, edited by Harold Wright (1923), p. x.
72 *A Poor Man's House* (1908), p. ix.
73 *Ibid.*, p. xi.
74 'Autobiografiction', *The Speaker*, XV (6 October 1906), pp. 28–30. I am grateful to Dr John Osborne of Kingston Polytechnic for this information. Further details are contained in his unpublished Ph.D. thesis, *Stephen Reynolds: A Biographical and Critical Study* (University of London 1977).
75 See Reynolds's introduction to *Seems So! A Working-Class View of Politics* (1911), pp. xxiii–xxv.
76 *Family Letters*, pp. 73, 83.
77 *Nostromo* (Harmondsworth 1982), p. 427.
78 *The Nigger of the 'Narcissus'*, edited by Robert Kimbrough ('Norton Critical Edition,' New York 1979), p. 107.
79 See, *Useful Toil: Autobiographies of Working People from the 1820s to the 1920s*, edited by John Burnett (1974); David Vincent, *Bread, Knowledge and Freedom: A Study of Nineteenth-Century Working-Class Autobiography* (1981).
80 Peter Keating, 'Arthur Morrison: A Biographical Study', introduction to *A Child of the Jago* (1969).
81 For this controversial topic, see F. C. Ball, *One of the Damned: The Life and Times of Robert Tressell* (1973).
82 *All in a Garden Fair* (1888), p. 246.
83 'The Secret People', *Poems* (1917), p. 120. First published in *Neolith*, I (November 1907).
84 Ball, *One of the Damned*, pp. 163–77.
85 *Tales of Mean Streets*, p. 7.
86 *My Apprenticeship*, pp. 191–2.
87 For the Settlement movement, J.A.R. Pimlott, *Toynbee Hall: Fifty Years of Social Progress* (1935); K. S. Inglis, *Churches and the Working Classes in Victorian England* (1963); Asa Briggs and Anne Macartney, *Toynbee Hall: The First Hundred Years* (1984).

88 *Esther Waters* (1894), p. 96.

89 *Diary*, pp. 231–2; *Life and Labour*, I, p. 157.

90 *The Whirlpool*, p. 368.

91 'The Novels of Mr Gissing', *George Gissing and H. G. Wells*, edited by Royal A. Gettmann (1961), p. 245. First published *Contemporary Review*, August, 1897.

92 *The Condition of England* (1909), p. 69. For the historical development of suburbia, H. J. Dyos, *Victorian Suburb: A Study of the growth of Camberwell* (Leicester 1961); Alan A. Jackson, *Semi-Detached London* (1973); *The Rise of Suburbia*, edited by F. M. L. Thompson (1982).

93 *The Condition of England*, p. 72.

94 *The Smiths of Valley View*, preface.

95 ' "Where dwelle ye, if it to telle be?"/"In the suburbes of a toun," quod he.' Chaucer, 'The Canon's Yeoman's Prologue,' *Canterbury Tales*.

96 *The Condition of England*, p. 74.

97 The house names are taken from Masterman, *Condition of England*, p. 89; 'The Laurels', Brickfield Terrace, Holloway, is the address of the Pooters in George Grossmith, *The Diary of a Nobody* (1892).

98 *The Suburbans* (1905), p. 9.

99 *Ibid.*, p. 151.

100 *In the Year of Jubilee*, p. 253.

101 *The Massarenes* (3rd edition 1897), p. 18.

102 Preface to *The Smiths of Valley View*.

103 *Ann Veronica*, p. 8.

104 *The Suburbans*, pp. 163, 203–8.

105 *Orthodoxy* (1908), p. 13.

106 *Robert Browning* (1903), p. 8.

107 *The Napoleon of Notting Hill* (1907), p. 208.

108 *Howards End*, p. 13.

109 *Ibid.*, p. 134.

110 *Ibid.*, pp. 43, 112.

111 *Ibid.*, p. 115.

112 *Ibid.*, pp. 116–18.

113 *Ibid.*, p. 184.

114 *Ibid.*

115 See, Richard Gill, *Happy Rural Seat: The English Country House and the Literary Imagination* (New Haven 1972).

116 *Letters*, II, p. 132.

117 *Ibid.*, I, p. 544.

Chapter Six A Woven Tapestry of Interests

1 See, John Lucas, *The Idea of the Provincial* (Loughborough 1981), and *The Literature of Change: Studies in the Nineteenth-Century Provincial Novel* (Hassocks 1977).
2 See, Asa Briggs, *Victorian Cities*, (1963) Chapter Eight.
3. For the gradual growth of interest in, and the various types of, regional fiction, see Lucien Leclaire, *A General Analytical Bibliography of the British Isles* (Clermant-Ferrand 1954).
4. *Literature* II (23 April 1898), p. 463.
5 See, Martha Vicinus, *The Industrial Muse*, Chapter Five.
6 *The Country and the City* (1973), p. 197.
7 See: James, *Letters*, III, 406–7; Woolf, 'The Novels of Thomas Hardy', *Collected Essays*, I, pp. 256–66.
8 Preface to the 1895 edition of *Far From the Madding Crowd*.
9 *Ibid.*
10 *Collected Letters.*
11 Quoted, Roger Ebbatson, *Lawrence and the Nature Tradition* (Brighton 1980), p. 147.
12 *Green Mansions* (1904), pp. 4, 83.
13 For the various manifestations of ruralism at this time, see: Glen Cavaliero, *The Rural Tradition in the English Novel* (1977); John Alcorn, *The Nature Novel from Hardy to Lawrence* (1977): and the popular books by 'Elizabeth', beginning with *Elizabeth and her German Garden* (1898).
14 Quoted, Charles Carrington, *Rudyard Kipling: His Life and Work* (Harmondsworth 1970), p. 438.
15 'A Charm', *Rewards and Fairies*, p. ix.
16 'Scottish National Character', *Blackwood's Magazine*, LXXXVII (June 1860), p. 722.
17 *Punch*, CIX (7 December 1895), p. 274.
18 J. H. Millar, 'The Literature of the Kailyard', *New Review* XII (1895). More generally for the Kailyard, see George Blake, *Barrie and the Kailyard School* (1951); Eric Anderson, 'The Kailyard School', *Nineteenth-Century Scottish Fiction*, edited by Ian Campbell (Manchester 1979); Thomas D. Knowles, *Ideology, Art and Commerce: Aspects of Literary Sociology in the Late Victorian Scottish Kailyard* (Gothenburg 1983).
19 Quoted, Knowles, *Ideology, Art and Commerce*, p. 24.
20 *Margaret Ogilvy* (1896), pp. 73–4.
21 Quoted, Anderson, 'The Kailyard School', *Nineteenth-Century Scottish Fiction*, p. 145.
22 *Ideology, Art and Commerce*, p. 47.

23 Quoted, Ian Campbell, 'George Douglas Brown', *Nineteenth-Century Scottish Fiction*, p. 149.
24 *The Unspeakable Scot* (1902), pp. 87–94.
25 *A Literary History of Scotland* (1903), p. 680.
26 *Mankind in the Making*, p. 359.
27 *Henry James and H. G. Wells*, p. 136.
28 Wagner, *How to Publish*, p. 43.
29 'The Next Time', *Complete Tales*, IX, 227.
30 *Letters to William Blackwood*, p. 154; *Lord Jim* (Harmondsworth 1982), p. 11.
31 Max Pemberton, *Sixty Years Ago and After* (1936), pp. 94–121.
32 Cohen, *Rider Haggard*, p. 85.
33 *The Egoist*, p. 2; *Diana of the Crossways*, pp. 17–8. See also Meredith's *On the Idea of Comedy and the Uses of the Comic Spirit* (1877).
34 *John Inglesant: A Romance* ('Macmillan Illustrated Pocket Classics', 1905), p. vii.
35 *Ibid.*, ix.
36 *English Criticism of the Novel 1865–1900* (Oxford 1965), p. 66.
37 'Realism and Romance', *Contemporary Review*, LII (November 1887), p. 691.
38 'The Present State of the Novel', *Fortnightly Review* XLII (September 1887) p. 417.
39 'Realism and Romace', pp. 693–4.
40 See, Cohen, *Rider Haggard*, pp. 117, 125.
41 'At the Sign of the Ship', *Longman's Magazine*, XXV (November 1894), p. 103.
42 For Lang in a wider context, see Roger Lancelyn Green, *Andrew Lang: A Critical Biography* (1946), and *Andrew Lang* (1962).
43 'A Humble Remonstrance', p. 136.
44 'A Humble Remonstrance' and 'A Gossip on Romance', *Memories and Portraits* pp. 124, 123, 129. See also, Stevenson's 'A Note on Realism,' *Essays Literary and Critical*.
45 Among many studies, see: Colin Manlove, *Modern Fantasy: Five Studies* (Cambridge 1975); Stephen Prickett, *Victorian Fantasy* (Hassocks 1979); H. P. Lovecraft, *Supernatural Horror in Literature* (1945); David Punter, *The Literature of Terror* (1980).
46 'A Case of Identity,' *The Adventures of Sherlock Holmes* (Pan Books, 1976), p. 41.
47 *Henry Brocken.*
48 Lilith (1895), p. 5.
49 *Dracula*, p. 37.
50 *Collected Letters*, I, pp. 369–70.

51 For example, Jonathan Nield, *A Guide to the Best Historical Novels and Tales* (1902); Ernest Baker, History in Fiction (2 vols 1907) and *A Guide to Historical Fiction* (1914).
52 *Memories and Adventures* (1924), p. 80.
53 *History in Fiction*, I, p. 192.
54 See, Valerie Chancellor, *History for their Masters: Opinion in the English History Textbook* (1970).
55 *The White Company* ('Author's Edition' 1903), p. 419.
56 See, John Springhall, *Youth, Empire and Society: British Youth Movements 1883–1940* (1977).
57 *The White Company*, p. 399.
58 *A Pair of Blue Eyes*, p. 242.
59 *Two on a Tower*, p. 34.
60 See, Michael Wilding, *Political Fictions* (1980). Among the many surveys of science fiction, see: J. O. Bailey, Pilgrims Through Space and Time (New York 1947); Mark R. Hillegas, *The Future as Nightmare* (New York 1967); Brian Aldiss, *Billion Year Spree* (1973); Darko Suvin, *Metamorphoses of Science Fiction* (new Haven 1980).
61 *The Time Machine*, p. 78.
62 For the development of the Wellsian concept of Utopia, see Roslynn Haynes, *H. G. Wells: Discoverer of the Future* (1980), pp. 82–111.
63 *Henry James and H. G. Wells*, p. 76.
64 See, I. F. Clarke, *Voices Prophesying War 1763–1984* (1966), and *The Pattern of Expectation 1644–2001* (1979).
65 'Spies and Gentlemen: The Birth of the British Spy Novel, 1893–1914', *Victorian Studies*, XXIV (Summer 1981), p. 490.
66 *Literature*, VI (13 January 1900), p. 50.
67 *The Art of the Novel*, p. 169.
68 The exchange between Myers and Stevenson is reprinted in *Robert Louis Stevenson: The Critical Heritage*, edited by Paul Maixner (1981), pp. 212–22.
69 'My Own True Ghost Story', *Wee Willie Winkie and Other Stories*, p. 165.
70 See, E. A. Sheppard, *Henry James and The Turn of the Screw* (Oxford 1974), Chapter Eight.
71 See especially, Julia Briggs, *Night Visitors*; also, Dorothy Scarborough, *The Supernatural in Modern English Fiction* (New York 1917), and Peter Penzoldt, *The Supernatural in Fiction* (1952).
72 In his introduction to *The Tales of Algernon Blackwood* (1938), p. xi.
73 Quoted, Briggs, *Night Visitors*, p. 141.

74 For the history of detective fiction, see: *The Development of the Detective Novel* (1958); Julian Symons, *Bloody Murder: From the Detective Story to the Crime Novel* (1972); Ian Ousby, *Bloodhounds of Heaven: The Detective in English Fiction from Godwin to Doyle* (Cambridge, Mass. 1976).
75 E. S. Turner, *Boys will be Boys* (1948), p. 117.
76 See, *Bleak House*, chapter Fifty-Seven, and Collins, *Dickens and Crime*, Chapter 9.
77 *A Study in Scarlet* (1888), p. 21; 'The Reigate Squires', *The Memoirs of Sherlock Holmes* (Harmondsworth 1972), p. 117.
78 *Bloodhounds of Heaven*, pp. 129–32.
79 'A Scandal in Bohemia', *Adventures of Sherlock Holmes*, p. 15.
80 *Bloody Murder* (Harmondsworth 1974), p. 74.
81 *A Study in Scarlet*, p. 13.
82 *Ibid.*, pp. 16–17.
83 'The Resident Patient', *Memoirs*, p. 159.
84 'The Five Orange Pips', *Adventures*, p. 118.
85 'The Final Problem', Memoirs, p. 239.
86 'The Naval Treaty', *Ibid.*, p. 215.

Chapter Seven   Readers and Novelists

1   'A Liverpool Address,' *Complete Prose Works*, X, p. 75.
2   *Complete Prose Works*, XI, pp. 244.
3   See, J. H. Raleigh, *Matthew Arnold and American Culture* (Berkeley 1957).
4   *Letters of Matthew Arnold*, edited by George W. E. Russell (2 vols. 1895), I, pp. 5–6.
5   'Numbers', *Complete Prose Works*, X, p. 155.
6   *Complete Prose Works*, V, p. 146.
7   'Numbers,' *Complete Prose Works*, X, pp. 162–4.
8   *Ibid.*
9   'My Countrymen', *Complete Prose Works*, V, p. 15.
10 *English Illustrated Magazine*, I (January 1884), p. 241.
11 'Americans Abroad,' first published in *Nation*, 3 October 1878, repr. *The Tales of Henry James*, edited by Aqbool Aziz (8 vols, in progress, Oxford 1973), III, 522.
12 *W. D. Howells as Critic* (1973), p. 64. See also Cady's *The Realist at War: The Mature Years 1885–1920 of W. D. Howells* (Syracuse 1960).
13 *Ibid.*, p. 58.
14 *Ibid.*, p. 57.

15 'In Memory of Henry James', *Egoist*, V (January 1918), p. 1.
16 Quoted, Stanley Weintraub, *The London Yankees* (1979), p. 10.
17 *Ibid.*, p. 4.
18 Quoted, Patricia Hutchins, *Ezra Pound's Kensington* (1965), p. 47.
19 *Hawthorne* (1879), p. 43.
20 First published in the *Atlantic Monthly*, February 1880, repr. *W. D. Howells as Critic*, p. 54.
21 *Letters*, II, p. 267.
22 *The Art of the Novel*, p. 62.
23 'Emile Zola', *Selected Literary Criticism*, p. 288.
24 *Ibid.*, p. 289.
25 *The Portrait of a Lady* (Harmondsworth 1974), p. 94.
26 *Ibid.*, pp. 559, 573.
27 *Ibid.*, p. 566.
28 *The Golden Bowl* (Harmondsworth 1966), pp. 124–5.
29 *The Spoils of Poynton*, p. 25.
30 'The Lesson of the Master', *Complete Tales*, VII, p. 269.
31 Max Beerbohm, 'Enoch Soames', *Seven Men* (1919).
32 'The Real Thing', *Complete Tales*, VIII, p. 237.
33 *Robert Browning*, p. 35.
34 *The Letters of Robert Browning and Elizabeth Barrett Barrett 1845–1846* (2 vols. 1899), I, p. 135.
35 Quoted, Maisie Ward, *Robert Browning and his World* (2 vols. 1969), II, 202.
36 Characteristic of many periodical articles of the time: 'There is positively little about Mr Haggard . . . suggestive of the literary man,' 'Illustrated Interviews No. VII', *Strand*, III (January 1982), p. 3.
37 *James Joyce*, p. 119.
38 *Collected Letters*, I, p. 371.
39 *New Grub Street*, p. 470.
40 *Complete Tales*, VII, pp. 221–2.
41 *Henry James: The Middle Years 1884–1894* (1963), p. 215.
42 *Letters*, I, p. 48.
43 *Meredith: The Critical Heritage*, edited by Ioan Williams (1971), pp. 192–3; first published, *British Quarterly Review*, April 1879.
44 Quoted, John Lucas, 'Meredith's Reputation', *Meredith Now: Some Critical Essays*, edited by Ian Fletcher (1971), p. 8.
45 *Family Letters*, p. 170.
46 *Ibid.*, p. 172.
47 *Meredith: The Critical Heritage*, pp. 207–8; first published, *Athenaeum*, November 1879.
48 *Complete Tales*, IX, p. 94.

49 *Letters*, II, p. 1013.
50 Michael Collie, *George Meredith, A Bibliography* (1974), p. 68.
51 'The Novels of George Meredith', *Collected Essays*, I, pp. 224–37.
52 See William Veeder, *Henry James – The Lessons of the Master: Popular Fiction and Personal Style in the Nineteenth Century* (Chicago 1975).
53 'Numbers', *Complete Prose Works*, X, pp. 146–7.
54 *Confessions of a Young Man*, p. 112.
55 *The Nether World*, p. 107.
56 *The Critical Writings of James Joyce*, edited by Ellsworth Mason and Richard Ellmann (1959), p. 69.
57 *Diana of the Crossways*, p. 17.
58 *Ibid.*, p. 18.
59 *Ibid.*
60 *Ibid.*
61 *Ibid.*, p. 314.
62 *Thyrza*, edited by Jacob Korg (Hassocks 1974), p. 423.
63 *Letters*, II, p. 1029.
64 *Letters*, III, p. 485.
65 *Ibid.*, p. 521.
66 *Ibid.*, IV, p. 106.
67 *Meredith: The Critical Heritage*, p. 281; first published, *Fortnightly Review*, June 1886.
68 *Ibid.*
69 *Literature* V (29 July 1899), p. 103.
70 'Modern life is expansion and then effacement. We do not round off, we open out. We do not end with valedictions; we open doors and then stand aside.' H. G. Wells, *Experiment in Autobiography*, II, 782. On the question of endings and modern fiction, see: Alan Friedman, *The Turn of the Novel* (Oxford 1966); Frank Kermode, *The Sense of an Ending* (1967).
71 The first sentence of *The Chimes* (1844).
72 *Complete Tales*, X, p. 18.
73 *Heart of Darkness*, p. 30.
74 *Meredith: The Critical Heritage*, p. 356; first published, *Saturday Review*, 23 May 1891.
75 *Heart of Darkness*, p. 67.
76 *Lord Jim*, p. 253.
77 *Ibid.*
78 Quoted, *The Art of the Novel*, p. viii.
79 'The Function of Criticism at the Present Time', *Complete Prose Works*, III, p. 265.
80 *Letters of Robert Browning and Elizabeth Barrett Barrett*, I, 6.

81 *Letters to Three Friends*, p. 234.
82 'Mrs Bathurst', *Traffics and Discoveries* (1904).
83 *A Call* (1910), pp. 298–9.
84 *The Good Soldier* (Harmondsworth 1972), p. 144.
85 *Ibid.*, p. 18.
86 *Collected Letters*, I, p. 370.
87 *George Gissing on Fiction*, edited by Jacob and Cynthia Korg (1978), p. 26.
88 'The Art of Fiction,' *Selected Literary Criticism*, p. 80.
89 *A Portrait of the Artist*, p. 215.
90 Flaubert, *Letters*, I, p. 230.
91 *Collected Letters*, I, p. 339.
92 *Mrs Craddock* ('Collected Edition' 1955), p. 259.
93 For one important aspect of the hardship of authors in the early twentieth century, see Nigel Cross, 'Civil List Pensions', *Times Literary Supplement*, 19 December 1980, p. 1443.
94 *New Grub Street*, p. 516.
95 *The Spoils of Poynton*, p. 22.
96 *Ibid.*, p. 28.
97 See: R. K. Webb, *The British Working-Class Reader 1790–1848* (1955); Altick, *The English Common Reader*; Williams, *The Long Revolution*; Lawrence Stone, 'Literacy and Education in England 1640–1900', *Past and Present*, XLII (February 1962).
98 *The English Common Reader*, p. 172. Lawrence Stone similarly warns against confusing quantitative and qualitative judgments on this issue. He estimates literacy levels for the male population of England and Wales as 66% in 1840 and 97% in 1900: the comparable figures for Scotland are 89% (1855) and 98% (1900). All commentators agree that the literacy rates for women were slightly lower than those for men.
99 Alec Ellis, *Library Services for Young People in England and Wales 1830–1970* (1971), p. 18.
100 She does, however, observe that the mothers who cannot read are placed 'at a disadvantage with their children'. *At the Works*, p. 167.
101 'Half-A-Crown's Worth of Cheap Knowledge', *Fraser's Magazine*, XVII (March 1838), pp. 279–90.
102 'The Unknown Public', *Household Words*, XVIII (21 August 1858), p. 222.
103 'Penny Fiction', *Nineteenth Century* IX (1881), pp. 145–54. Another interesting contribution to this long-running debate is Thomas Wright, 'Concerning the Unknown Public', *Nineteenth Century*, XIII (February 1883).

104 'Penny Fiction', pp. 145–6.
105 *Ibid.*
106 Louis James, *Fiction for the Working Man 1830–1850* (1963), pp. 45–71; see also James's *Print and the People 1819–1851* (1976).
107 *Complete Tales*, VII, p. 248.
108 *Author*, IX (1 December 1898), p. 156.
109 *Riches and Poverty* (5th ed. 1908), pp. 8–43.
110 *The Coming of the Mass Market* (1981), p. 75.
111 'A Lower-Middle-Class Budget, *Cornhill*, n.s. X (1901), pp. 656–66.
112 'Eight Hundred Pounds a Year', *Ibid.*, pp. 790–800.
113 Mrs Earle, 'Eighteen Hundred a Year', *Ibid.*, XI, pp. 48–61; Lady Agnew, 'Ten Thousand a Year', *Ibid.*, pp. 184–91.
114 'A Workman's Budget,' *Ibid.*, X, pp. 446–56.
115 *Poverty: A Study of Town Life* (1901), pp. 133–4.
116 *Riches and Poverty*, p. 43.
117 *Wages and Income in the United Kingdom Since 1860* (1937), p. xiii.
118 *Ibid.*, p. 49.
119 *Ibid.*, pp. 35–6.
120 For contrasting aspects of these developments, see Alison Adburgham, *Shops and Shopping 1800–1914* (1964); Kenneth Hudson, *Pawnbroking* (1982).
121 *The Town Traveller*, edited by Pierre Coustillas (Hassocks 1981), p. 208.
122 *The Ragged-Trousered Philanthropists* (1955), pp. 54–6.
123 *At the Works*, p. 145.
124 'Penny Fiction', p. 151. This was so important a part of these novelettes' appeal that when Charles Shurey became editor of the *Duchess Novelettes* in September 1894, he promised both 'Lady' and 'servant girl' that there would be nothing 'objectionable' in its pages: 'I shall refuse to insert any of those Announcements of unpleasant character which appear so regularly in the columns of some of my contemporaries.'
125 See, for example: J. A. R. Pimlott, *The Englishman's Holiday* (1947); John Lowerson and John Myerscough, *Time to Spare in Victorian England* (1977); Peter Bailey, *Leisure and Class in Victorian England* (1978); James Walvin, *Leisure and Society 1830–1950* (1978).
126 Brian Rust, 'The Development of the Recording Industry', *Gramophone*, LV (April 1977), p. 1521.
127 John Barnes, *The Beginnings of the Cinema in England* (1976), p. 8.
128 Leon Edel, *Henry James: The Treacherous Years 1895–1901* (1969), p. 166.

129 Rachel Low and Roger Manvell, *The History of the British Film 1896–1906* (1948), p. 100.

130 This estimate is deliberately moderate compared with some early estimates; see Rachel Low, *The History of the British Film 1906–1914* (1948), p. 25.

131 Quoted, Low and Manvell, *The History of the British Film 1896–1906*, p. 95.

132 M. D. O'Brien, 'Free Libraries', *A Plea for Liberty: Argument Against Socialism and Socialistic Legislation*, edited by Thomas Mackay (3rd ed. 1892), p. 261.

133 For the early development of public libraries, see W. A. Munford, *Penny Rate: Aspects of British Public Library History* (1951); Thomas Kelly, *A History of Public Libraries in Great Britain 1845–1975* (2nd ed. 1977).

134 Altick, *The English Common Reader*, p. 227.

135 Munford, *Penny Rate*, pp. 42–3.

136 John Ogle, *The Free Library: Its History and Present Condition* (1897), pp. 48, 187–9.

137 Munford, *Penny Rate*, p. 43.

138 W. G. S. Adams, *Report on Library Provision and Policy to the Carnegie United Kingdom Trustees* (1915), pp. 7–8.

139 Altick, *The English Common Reader*, p. 236.

140 Arthur Morrison, who had worked at the People's Palace, described the main beneficiaries of the educational work of settlements and missions as 'tradesmen's sons, small shopkeepers and their families, and neat clerks, with here and there a smart young artisan of one of the especially respectable trades', *A Child of the Jago*, p. 53.

141 'A Lower-Middle-Class Budget', p. 665.

142 'The Great Fiction Bore', *Library World*, XI (1908), p. 127.

143 *Ibid.*, p. 132.

144 *Ibid.*

145 'The Anti-Marriage League', p. 135.

146 'Free Libraries', p. 274.

147 'The Great Fiction Bore', p. 133.

148 *Greenwood's Library Year Book* (1897), pp. 112–15.

149 A. O. Jennings, 'Fiction in the Public Libraries', *Library Association Record*, X (1908), p. 535; O'Brien, 'Free Libraries', p. 267.

150 'Rural Library Services in England and Wales before 1919', Library History IV (1976–8), p. 77. William Faux of W. H. Smith's Circulating Library claimed that 80% of books read by subscribers were fiction, and that a similar figure applied to all other libraries, 'A Great Warrior', *Book Monthly*, I (October 1903), p. 19.

151 *At the Works*, p. 164.

152 *Ibid.*, p. 165.

153 'The Standard of Fiction in Public Libraries', *Library Association Record*. IX (1907), p. 71.

154 *Ibid.*

155 *The Public Library* (1922), p. 38.

156 *At the Works*, p. 163.

157 Thomas Kelly, *A History of Public Libraries*, p. 125.

158 *Family Letters*, p. 16.

159 *Ibid.*, p. 33.

160 E. H. Lacon Watson, 'Cheap Fiction', *Author* XVII (1 April 1907), p. 182.

161 Paul Fountain, 'Manuscript? or Waste Paper?', *Author*, XIX (1 July 1909) p. 285.

162 See the pamphlet issued by the Society of Authors, *Public Lending Right: A Short History* (1867), where it is noted that John Brophy was 'the first man to propose a practical scheme' in the *Author*, September 1951. The debate on practical schemes, however, goes back much further: see Henry Flowerdew, 'Are Novels too Cheap?' *Author* XXV (1 February 1915), pp. 119–121.

163 The figures given by Gettmann for three-deckers, based on the Bentley papers, are probably applicable generally in the early and mid-Victorian periods: 'Most of the agreements stipulated an edition of 1,000 copies with payments to authors ranging between £200–£300 and averaging perhaps slightly more than £250,' *A Victorian Publisher*, p. 139.

164 'The Six Shilling Novel and the Trade', *Author*, VII (1 July 1896), p. 28.

165 *Ibid.*

166 *Author* XIX (1 April 1909), p. 26.

167 *How to Become an Author*, p. 26.

168 *Ibid.*, p. 27.

169 *Literature* IX (4 January 1902), p. 626.

170 *New Grub Street*, p. 236.

171 *Ibid.*

172 'The Meaning of Royalties,' *Author* XI (1 October 1900), p. 85.

173 *The Pen and the Book*, pp. 173–6. Out of many possible examples, the terms of Joyce's disastrous contract with Grant Richards for *Dubliners* is relevant. He was to receive no royalties until 500 copies were sold, and Richards had the right to refusal on Joyce's other books for a period of four years; Joyce, *Letters*, II, pp. 338–40.

174 Sprigge, *The Methods of Publishing*, p. 60; *Author*, VI (1 August 1895), p. 57.

175 *Author* X (1 September 1899), p. 91.
176 The evidence suggests that a sale of 600 copies was now regarded as good for the average 6/– novel. See: Wagner, *How to Publish*, p. 47; Besant, *The Pen and the Book*, p. 138; and Woolf, *Letters*, II, p. 25, announcing that 600 copies of 'Leonard's book' have been sold, 'which is thought to be very good.'
177 *Henry James: The Critical Heritage*, edited by Roger Gard (1968), p. 554.
178 *Letters to William Blackwood*, pp. 97–8.
179 *Ibid., p. 150.*
180 Najder, *Joseph Conrad*, p. 332.
181 *E. M. Forster: The Critical Heritage*, edited by Philip Gardner (1973), p. 3.
182 *Ibid.*, p. 4.
183 *Ibid.*
184 *Selected Letters of E. M. Forster*, edited by Mary Lago and P. N. Furbank (2 vols 1983), I, p. 71.
185 Archives of the Society of Authors, British Library, File No. 56704.
186 *Letters*, I, p. 482. *Sons and Lovers* did not, however, sell as well as Lawrence had hoped: it was not reprinted until 1922. See, *D. H. Lawrence: The Critical Heritage*, edited by R. P. Draper (1970), pp. 3–5.
187 Leonard Woolf, *Beginning Again*, p. 87.
188 *Ibid.*, p. 150.
189 *Arnold Bennett: The Critical Heritage*, edited by James Hepburn (1981), pp. 13–14.
190 Bennett, *The Truth About an Author*, p. 112.
191 *Ibid.*
192 *Bennett: The Critical Heritage*, p. 21; *Letters*, I, p. 104.
193 Quoted, H. V. Marot, *The Life and Letters of John Galsworthy* (1935), p. 136.
194 *Ibid.*
195 *Author*, XIX (1 April 1909), pp. 287–8.
196 *The Cost of Production*, pp. 29–35.
197 'The Sixpenny Book', *Author*, XI (1 October 1900), p. 83.
198 'The "Sixpenny": Its History and the Reasons for Its Great Popularity', *Book Monthly*, IV (October 1906), p. 17.
199 For Bohn and other mid-Victorian cheap reprints, see: Mumby and Norrie, *Publishing and Bookselling*, pp. 223–30; Altick, *The English Common Reader*, pp. 285–6; Hans Schmoller, 'The Paperback Revolution', *Essays in the History of Publishing*, edited by Asa Briggs (1974); Per Gedin, *Literature in the Market Place* (1975).

200 For Henry Morley's various publishing ventures, see: Nowell-Smith, *The House of Cassell*; F. A. Mumby, *The House of Routledge 1834–1934* (1934); Henry Solly, *The Life of Henry Morley* (1898).

201 The *Literary Year Book* tried to keep a check on cheap reprint series: by 1909 it was listing more than one hundred.

202 See: Peter Sutcliffe, *The Oxford University Press* (1978), pp. 141–4; J. M. Dent, *Memoirs* (1928), pp. 124–6.

203 'The "Sixpenny"', p. 18.

204 'Report on the Sevenpenny Cloth-Bound Copyright Novel', *Author* XIX (1 April 1909), p. 169.

205 *Author*, XIX (1 June 1909), pp. 240–2.

206 See: W. T. Stead, *The Americanisation of the World* (1902); Kipling, 'The White Man's Burden' and other poems in *The Five Nations* (1903).

207 *Nostromo*, p. 75.

208 'English Authors and the Colonial Book Market', *Author*, I (15 September 1890), pp. 111–2.

209 'The American Novel in England', *Bookman* (New York), XXX (February 1910), pp. 633–4.

210 Alice P. Hackett, *Seventy Years of Best Sellers* (New York 1967), p. 91.

211 *Ibid.*, See also: F. L. Mott, *Golden Multitudes: The Story of Best Sellers in the United States* (New York 1947); James Hart, *The Popular Book: A History of American Literary Taste* (Berkeley 1950); Claud Cockburn, *Bestseller: The Books that Everyone Read 1900–1939* (1972); R. C. Terry, *Victorian Popular Fiction 1860–80* (1983).

212 *Book Monthly*, I (October 1903), p. 42.

213 Curtis Brown, *Contacts* (1935), p. 111.

214 *The Popular Book* ('University of California Paperback' 1963), p. 184.

215 *Bestsellers: Popular Fiction of the 1970s* (1981).

216 *At the Works*, pp. 166–7.

217 *Fiction and the Reading Public* (1968), p. 62.

218 *The Garden of Allah* (1904), p. 5.

219 *The Sorrows of Satan*, p. 439.

220 *Fame and Fiction* (1901), p. 83.

221 *When it was Dark* (1903), p. 245.

222 *The Way of An Eagle* (23rd impression, 1914), p. 368; *The Rosary*, p. 376.

223 *At the Works*, p. 166.

224 *The Life of Florence L. Barclay*, 'By One of her Daughters' (1921), p. 251.

225 *Hadrian the Seventh* (Harmondsworth 1963), p. 18.
226 *Ibid.*, p. 19.
227 'At Last the Novel Appears', *Egoist*, IV (February 1917), p. 21.

Epilogue

1 'At Last the Novel Appears', *Egoist*, IV (February 1917), p. 22.
2 *Ibid.*
3 *On the Constitution of the Church and State* (1830), edited by John Colmer; Coleridge, *Collected Works* (1976), X, p. 69.
4 On the wider development of this tradition, see: Raymond Williams, *Culture and Society* (1958); Ben Knights, *The Idea of the Clerisy in the Nineteenth Century* (Cambridge 1978).
5 'Culture and Anarchy', *Complete Prose Works*, V, p. 115.
6 *The Age of Tennyson* ('Bell's Handbooks of English Literature' 1897) p. 204; see also, Walker's *The Literature of the Victorian Age* (Cambridge 1910).
7 'The Pattern of Social Transformation in England', *The Transformation of Higher Learning 1860–1930*, edited by Konrad H. Jarausch (Chicago 1983), p. 208; see also, in the same collection, Roy Lowe, 'The Expansion of Higher Education in England'; and the documents and statistics in *The Universities in the Nineteenth Century*, edited by Michael Sanderson (1975).
8 'The Pattern of Social Transformation in England', p. 209.
9 See: Christopher Harvie, *The Lights of Liberalism: University Liberals and the Challenge of Democracy 1860–86* (1976); Christopher Kent, *Brains and Numbers: Comtism and Democracy in Mid-Victorian England* (Toronto 1978).
10 *Human Nature in Politics*, p. 200.
11 *Ibid*; Wells, *A Modern Utopia* (1905).
12 *Nietzsche in England*, p. 272.
13 'Popular Culture', *Literature* II (26 February 1898), pp. 219–20.
14 'The Labourer and Literature', *Literature*, II (18 June 1898), pp. 687–8. See also the leading articles: 'The Apostle of Culture', 16 April 1898; 'The Teaching of English Literature', 25 June 1898.
15 'The Function of Criticism at the Present Time', *Complete Prose Works*, III, pp. 269–71.
16 H. C. Dent, *The Training of Teachers in England and Wales*, p. 57. For the slow acceptance of English Literature in elementary schools, see: David Shayer, *The Teaching of English in Schools 1900–1970* (1972); Peter Gordon and Dennis Lawton, *Curriculum Change in the Nineteenth and Twentieth Centuries* (1978).

17 *Board of Education Report on the Training of Elementary School Teachers* (1912–13), p. 20.

18 *Board of Education Report* (1911–12), p. 4.

19 *Board of Education Report on the Teaching of English in Secondary Schools* (1908–1909), pp. 135–6.

20 For the development of English Studies, see: D. J. Palmer, *The Rise of English Studies* (1965); John Gross, *The Rise and Fall of the Man of Letters*, Chapter 6; Brian Doyle, 'The Hidden History of English Studies', *Re-Reading English*, edited by Peter Widdowson (1982); Chris Baldick, *The Social Mission of English Criticism 1848–1932* (1938). Stephen Potter's *The Muse in Chains* (1937), in spite of its infuriatingly facetious tone, offers a broader and longer perspective on this issue than any other book. The Board of Education Report *The Teaching of English in England* (1921) also contains a great deal of historical information.

21 See: John Churton Collins, *The Study of English Literature* (1891); Palmer, *The Rise of English Studies*, pp. 78–117; Alan Bacon, 'Attempts to Introduce a School of English Literature at Oxford: the National Debate of 1886 and 1887', *History of Education*, IX (1980), pp. 303–13.

22 For educational developments in Scotland, see: Alexander Morgan, *Scottish University Studies* (1933); James Scotland, *The History of Scottish Education* (2 vols 1969); George Davie, *The Democratic Intellect* (Edinburgh 1961): *Robert Anderson, Education and Opportunity in Victorian Scotland* (1983).

23 *Tables of English Literature* (1870), pp. v–vi.

24 One way that the English Association tried to convey the need for a serious interest in the study of English Literature was through the publication of a series of pamphlets, beginning in 1907 with *Types of English Curricula: Boys' Secondary Schools*; another was the publication annually, from 1910, of *Essays and Studies*.

25 Sir Arthur Quiller-Couch, 'Inaugural Lecture', *Cambridge Lectures* ('Everyman's Library' 1943), pp. 8–9.

26 'A Novel Education', *Punch*, CVIII (30 November 1895), p. 255.

Bibliography

British Fiction 1875–1915

Novels and short stories are listed here year by year to give some indication of the range of fiction being published in Britain at any given moment within the period, and also to chart changing generations of novelists. The listing is not intended to be inclusive. In the case of major novelists representation is reasonably complete: for other novelists I have tried to give either a representative selection of their work or simply a mention of their better-known fiction. The dates of Henry James's earliest volumes refer to American publication, and those of Kipling to Indian publication.

* indicates the author's first significant publication [of prose fiction in volume form]
† indicates short stories.

1875	Ainsworth	The Goldsmith's Wife
	Black	Three Feathers
	Blackmore	Alice Lorraine
	Braddon	Hostages to Fortune
	Collins	The Law and the Lady
	Craik	The Little Lame Prince
	Ewing	Six to Sixteen
	James	Roderick Hudson
		A Passionate Pilgrim †
	Jefferies	Restless Human Hearts
	MacDonald	Malcolm
	Mathers	Comin' thro' the Rye
	Oliphant	Whiteladies
	Trollope	The Way We Live Now
	Wood	Told in the Twilight †

1876	Besant/Rice	The Golden Butterfly
	Braddon	Dead Men's Shoes
	Collins	The Two Destinies
	Eliot	Daniel Deronda
	Hardy	The Hand of Ethelbertha
	Meredith	Beauchamp's Career
	Oliphant	Phoebe Junior
	Ouida	In a Winter City

1877	Ainsworth	The Fall of Somerset
	Blackmore	Erema
	Burnett	That Lass o' Lowrie's
	Craik	Will Denbigh
	James	The American
	Jefferies	The World's End
	MacDonald	The Marquis of Lossie
	Mallock	The New Republic*
	Reade	A Woman Hater
	Sewell	Black Beauty
	Shaw	Castle Blair
	Trollope	The American Senator

1878	Besant/Rice	By Celia's Arbour
	Hardy	The Return of the Native
	James	The Europeans
	Mallock	The New Paul and Virginia
	Ouida	Friendship
	Trollope	Is he Popenjoy?
	Wood	Pomeroy Abbey

1879 Ainsworth   Beau Nash
     Braddon   Vixen
     Collins   A Rogue's Wife
     James   Confidence
     Lyall   Won by Waiting*
     MacDonald   Sir Gibbie
     Meredith   The Egoist
     Oliphant   Within the Precinct
     Trollope   John Caldigate

1880 Baring-Gould Mehalah
     Broughton   Second Thoughts
     Disraeli   Endymion
     Gissing   Workers in the Dawn*
     Hardy   The Trumpet Major
     James   Washington Square
     Jefferies   Greene Ferne Farm
     Meredith   The Tragic Comedians
     Shorthouse   John Inglesant*
     Trollope   The Duke's Children
     Oliphant   A Beleaguered City
     Ouida   Moths

1881 Besant/Rice   The Chaplain of the
                     Fleet
     Collins   The Black Robe
     Hardy   A Laodicean
     Henty   In Times of Peril
     James   The Portrait of a Lady
     Jefferies   Wood Magic
     Mallock   A Romance of the
                     Nineteenth Century
     Ouida   A Village Commune
     Rutherford   Autobiography
     Trollope   Ayala's Angel
     Ward   Milly and Olly*

1882 Anstey   Vice-Versa*
     Besant   All Sorts and Condi-
                     tions of Men
                   The Revolt of Man
     Hardy   Two on a Tower
     Henty   Under Drake's Flag
     Jefferies   Bevis
     Lyall   Donovan
     MacDonald   The Princess and the
                     Curdie
     Malet   Mrs Lorimer*
     Ouida   In Maremma
     Stevenson   The New Arabian
                     Nights†*
     Trollope   Marian Fay

1883 Besant   All in a Garden Fair
     Broughton   Belinda
     Collins   Heart and Science
     Conway   Called Back*
     Ewing   Jackanapes
     Henty   With Clive in India
     Moore   A Modern Lover*
     Reed   The Adventures of a
                     Three-Guinea Watch
     Schreiner   The Story of an
                     African Farm
     Stevenson   Treasure Island
     Trollope   Mr Scarborough's
                     Family

1884 Allen   Philistia*
     Braddon   Ishmael
     Collins   I Say No
     Conway   Dark Days
     Gissing   The Unclassed
     Haggard   Dawn*
                   The Witch's Head
     Jefferies   The Dewy Morn
     Kendall/Lang That Very Mab
     Lyall   We Two
     Lee   Miss Brown
     Reade   A Perilous Secret
     Ward   Miss Bretherton

1885 Anstey   The Tinted Venus
     Caine   The Shadow of a
                     Crime*
     Davidson   The North Wall*
     Ewing   The Story of a Short
                     Life
     Haggard   King Solomon's Mines
     Hudson   The Purple Land*
     Jefferies   After London
     Linton   The Autobiography of
                     Christopher Kirk-
                     land
     Lyall   In the Golden Days
     Meredith   Diana of the Cross-
                     ways
     Moore   A Mummer's Wife
     Oliphant   Stories of the Seen and
                     Unseen†
     Pater   Marius the Epicurean
     Rutherford   Deliverance
     Stevenson   Prince Otto

1886 Besant   Children of Gibeon
     Burnett   Little Lord Fauntleroy

	Conway	Living or Dead	
	Corelli	A Romance of Two Worlds*	
	Gissing	Isabel Clarendon	
		Demos	
	Hardy	The Mayor of Caster-bridge	
	Hichens	The Coastguard's Secret*	
	James	The Bostonians	
		The Princess Casa-massima	
	Mallock	The Old Order Changes	
	Moore	A Drama in Muslin	
	Oliphant	A House Divided Against Itself	
	Q	Dead Man's Rock*	
	G. B. Shaw	Cashel Byron's Profession	
	Stevenson	Dr Jekyll and Mr Hyde	
		Kidnapped	

1887	Barrie	Better Dead*
	Barry	The New Antigone
	Blackmore	Springhaven
	Caine	The Deemster
		A Son of Hagar
	Cholmondely	The Danvers Jewels*
	Corelli	Thelma
	Doyle	A Study in Scarlet*
	Gissing	Thyrza
	Hardy	The Woodlanders
	Haggard	She
		Allan Quartermain
	Hudson	A Crystal Age
	Jefferies	Amaryllis at the Fair
	Law	A City Girl
	Moore	A Mere Accident
	Pater	Imaginary Portraits
	Reed	The Fifth Form at St Dominic's
	Rutherford	The Revolution in Tanner's Lane
	G. B. Shaw	An Unsocial Socialist
	Stevenson	The Merry Men †
	Woods	A Village Tragedy

1888	Barrie	Auld Licht Idylls †
		When a Man's Single
	Garnett	The Twilight of the Gods †
	Gissing	A Life's Morning
	Grand	Ideala*

	Hardy	Wessex Tales †
	Howell	A More Excellent Way
	James	The Reverberator
		The Aspern Papers †
	Kipling	Plain Tales from the Hills †*
		Soldiers Three †
		The Story of the Gadsbys †
		In Black and White †
		Under the Deodars †
		The Phantom Rickshaw †
		Wee Willie Winkie †
	Law	Out of Work
	Merrick	Mr Bazalgette's Legacy*
	Merriman	Young Mistley*
	Moore	Spring Days
	Q	Troy Town
	Stevenson	The Black Arrow
	Ward	Robert Elsemere
	Whiteing	The Island
	Wilde	The Happy Prince †*
	Wood	The Story of Charles Strange
	Zangwill	The Premier and the Painter*

1889	Barrie	A Window in Thrums †
	Carroll	Sylvie and Bruno
	Collins	The Legacy of Cain
	Corelli	Ardath
	Doyle	Micah Clark
	Gissing	The Nether World
	Haggard	Cleopatra
	Harraden	Things Will Take a Turn*
	James	A London Life †
	Jerome	Three Men in a Boat
	Meredith	Sandra Belloni
	Moore	Mike Fletcher
	Ouida	Guilderoy
	Somerville/Ross	An Irish Cousin*
	Stevenson	The Master of Bal-lantrae
	Stevenson/Osbourne	The Wrong Box

1890	Blackmore	Kit and Kitty
	Caine	The Bondman
	Collins	Blind Love
	Corelli	Wormwood
	Davidson	Perfervid
	Doyle	The Sign of Four

		The Captain of the Polestar †
Gissing		The Emancipated
Haggard/Lang		The World's Desire
Hatton		By Order of the Czar
Hope		A Man of Mark *
James		The Tragic Muse
Law		In Darkest London
Lee		Hauntings †
MacDonald		The Light Princess †
Moore		Vain Fortune
Morris		News from Nowhere
Oliphant		Kirsteen
Rutherford		Miriam's Schooling
Weyman		The House of the Wolf *

1891 Baring-Gould Urith
     Barrie   The Little Minister
     Caine   The Scapegoat
     Doyle   The White Company
     Gissing   New Grub Street
     Haggard   Eric Brighteyes
     Hardy   Tess of the D'Urbervilles
                  A Group of Noble Dames †
     Henty   Held Fast for England
     Hobbes   Some Emotions and a Moral *
     Jerome   Told After Supper †
     Kipling   The Light that Failed
                  Life's Handicap †
     MacDonald   There and Back
                  The Flight and the Shadow
     Malet   The Wages of Sin
     Meredith   One of Our Conquerors
     Morrison   The Shadows Around Us †*
     Pain   In a Canadian Canoe †*
     Schreiner   Dreams †
     Wilde   The Picture of Dorian Gray
                  Lord Arthur Savile's Crime †

1892 Anstey   The Talking Horse †
     Doyle   The Adventures of Sherlock Holmes †
     Du Maurier   Peter Ibbetson
     Gissing   Born in Exile
                  Denzil Quarrier

Haggard   Nada the Lily
Hobbes   A Sinner's Comedy
Hudson   Fan
James   The Lesson of the Master †
Kipling/   The Naulahka
Balestier
Lee   Vanitas †
Mallock   A Human Document
Merriman   The Slave of the Lamp
Newbolt   Taken by the Enemy *
Payn   A Modern Dick Whittington
Stevenson/   The Wrecker
Osbourne
Ward   The History of David Grieve
Zangwill   Children of the Ghetto

1893 Benson   Dodo *
     Besant   The Rebel Queen
     Cholmondeley Diana Tempest
     Corelli   Barabbas
     Crackanthorpe Wreckage †*
     Crockett   The Stickit Minister †*
     Dowie   Gallia
     Egerton   Keynotes †*
     Gissing   The Odd Women
     Grand   The Heavenly Twins
     Haggard   Montezuma's Daughter
     Harraden   Ships that Pass in the Night
     James   The Private Life †
                  The Real Thing †
     Kipling   Many Inventions †
     Pemberton   The Iron Pirate *
     Q   The Delectable Duchy
     Reed   The Cockhouse at Fellsgarth
     Rutherford   Catherine Furze
     Schreiner   Dream Life and Real Life †
     Stevenson   Catriona
                  Island Nights Entertainment †
     Wedmore   Renunciations †
     Weyman   A Gentleman of France
     Zangwill   Ghetto Tragedies

1894 Blackmore   Perlycross
     Brooke   A Superfluous Woman
     Caine   The Manxman
     Caird   The Daughters of Danaus
     Crockett   The Lilac Sunbonnet

Dixon   The Story of a Modern
                Woman
Doyle   The Memoirs of Sher-
                lock Holmes
Du Maurier   Trilby
Egerton   Discords †
Gissing   In the Year of Jubilee
Grahame   Pagan Papers †*
Grossmith   The Diary of a
                Nobody
Haggard   The People of the
                Mist
Hardy   Life's Little Ironies †
Harraden   In Varying Moods †
Hichens   The Green Carnation
Hope   The Dolly Dialogues
                The Prisoner of Zenda
Hunt   The Maiden's
                Prologue *
Iota   The Yellow Aster
Kipling   The Jungle Book
Lyall   Doreen
Maclaren   Beside the Bonnie
                Brier Bush †
Macleod   Pharais *
Machen   The Great God Pan †
Meredith   Lord Ormont and his
                Aminta
Merriman   With Edged Tools
Moore   Esther Waters
Morris   The Wood Beyond the
                World
Morrison   Tales of Mean
                Streets †
Reed   Tom, Dick, and Harry
Robins   George Mandeville's
                Husband *
Somerville/   The Real Charlotte
Ross
Stevenson/   The Ebb-Tide
Osbourne
Ward   Marcella
Wedmore   English Episodes †
Weyman   Under the Red Robe

1895 Allen   The Woman Who Did
                The British Barbarians
Braddon   Sons of Fire
Brooke   Transition
Buchan   Sir Quixote of the
                Moors *
Conrad   Almayer's Folly *
Corelli   The Sorrows of Satan
Crackanthorpe   Sentimental Studies †
Cross   The Woman Who
                Didn't

Crockett   The Men of the Moss
                Hags
Davidson   Earl Lavender
Dowson   Dilemmas †
Doyle   The Stark-Munro
                Letters
Falkner   The Lost Stradivarius
Gissing   Eve's Ransom
                The Paying Guest
                Sleeping Fires
Grahame   The Golden Age †
Harris   Elder Conklin †*
Hunt   A Hard Woman
James   Terminations †
Kipling   The Second Jungle
                Book †
Locke   At the Gate of
                Samaria *
MacDonald   Lilith
Machen   The Three Imposters
MacLaren   The Days of Auld
                Langsyne
Macleod   The Mountain Lovers
Mallock   The Heart of Life
Mason   A Romance of Wast-
                dale *
Meredith   The Amazing Marriage
Moore   Celibates †
Nevinson   Neighbours of Ours
Pugh   A Street in Suburbia †*
Shiel   Prince Zaleski †*
Tirebuck   Miss Grace of All
                Souls
Wells   The Time Machine *
                The Wonderful Visit
                The Stolen Bacillus †
Weyman   The Red Cockade
Zangwill   The Master

1896 Barrie   Sentimental Tommy
Baring-Gould   Dartmoor Idylls †
Braddon   London Pride
Conrad   An Outcast of the
                Islands
Corelli   The Mighty Atom
                Cameos †
Crackanthorpe   Vignettes †
Crockett   Cleg Kelly
Doyle   The Exploits of Briga-
                dier Gerard
                Rodney Stone
Du Maurier   The Martian
Hardy   Jude the Obscure
Jacobs   Many Cargoes †*
James   The Other House
                Embarrassments †

Lang	A Monk of Fife	
Le Gallienne	The Quest of the Golden Girl	
Mason	The Courtship of Morrice Buckler	
Merrick	Cynthia	
Merriman	Flotsam	
Morrison	A Child of the Jago	
Munro	The Lost Pibroch *	
Oliphant	The Unjust Steward	
Ouida	Le Selve	
Phillpotts	Down Dartmoor Way	
Pugh	The Man of Straw	
Rutherford	Clara Hopgood	
Steel	On the Face of the Waters	
Stevenson	Weir of Hermiston	
Ward	Sir George Tressady	
Wells	The Island of Dr Moreau	
	The Wheels of Chance	

1897	Adcock	East End Idylls *
	Allen	The Type-Writer Girl
	Beerbohm	The Happy Hypocrite
	Blackmore	Dariel
	Broughton	Dear Faustina
	Caine	The Christian
	Crackanthorpe	Last Studies †
	Crockett	The Surprising Adventures of Sir Toady Lion
	Doyle	Uncle Bernac
	Galsworthy	From the Four Winds †*
	Gissing	The Whirlpool
	Hardy	The Well-Beloved
	Hichens	Flames
	Hobbes	The School for Saints
	Jacobs	The Skipper's Wooing
	James	The Spoils of Poynton
		What Maisie Knew
	Kipling	Captains Courageous
	Marsh	The Beetle
	Maugham	Liza of Lambeth *
	Merriman	In Kedar's Tents
	Ouida	The Massarenes
	Phillpotts	Lying Prophets
	Schreiner	Trooper Peter Halket
	Sinclair	Audrey Craven *
	Stevenson	St Ives
	Stoker	Dracula
	Voynich	The Gadfly
	Wells	The Invisible Man
		The Plattner Story †

1898	Anstey	Paleface and Redskin †
	Bennett	A Man from the North *
	Buchan	John Burnet of Barns
	Conrad	The Nigger of the 'Narcissus'
		Tales of Unrest †
	Corvo	Stories Toto Told Me †*
	Douglas	Love and a Sword *
	Falkner	Moonfleet
	Fowler	Concerning Isabel Carnaby
	Galsworthy	Jocelyn
	Gissing	The Town Traveller
		Human Odds and Ends †
	Grahame	Dream Days †
		The Headswoman †
	Grand	The Beth Book
	Hewlett	The Forest Lovers *
	Hope	Rupert of Hentsau
	Jacobs	Sea Urchins †
	James	In the Cage
		The Two Magics †
	Kipling	The Day's Work †
	Moore	Evelyn Innes
	Munro	John Splendid
	Oppenheim	Mysterious Mr Sabin
	Pett Ridge	Mord Em'ly
	Paston	A Writer of Books
	Phillpotts	Children of the Mist
	Pugh	Tony Drum
	Robins	The Open Question
	Shiel	The Yellow Danger
	Ward	Helbeck of Bannersdale
	Watts-Dunton	Alwyn
	Wells	The War of the Worlds
	Zangwill	Dreamers of the Ghetto

1899	Bannerman	The Story of Little Black Sambo
	Braddon	His Darling Sin
	Cholmondeley	Red Pottage
	Crockett	The Black Douglas
	Cuninghame-Graham	The Ipané †*
	Gissing	The Crown of Life
	Hornung	Raffles: The Amateur Cracksman
	James	The Awkward Age
	Kipling	Stalky & Co.
	Mallock	The Individualist

Mason	Miranda of the Balcony	
Maugham	Orientations †	
Morrison	To London Town	
Nesbit	The Story of the Treasure Seekers	
Pett Ridge	Outside the Radius	
Rook	The Hooligan Nights †*	
Somerville/ Ross	Some Adventures of an Irish R.M.	
Wells	When the Sleeper Wakes	
	Tales of Space and Time †	
Whiteing	No. 5 John Street	

1900
Anstey	The Brass Bottle
Barrie	Tommy and Grizel
Braddon	The Infidel
Bramah	The Wallet of Kai Lung †
Conrad	Lord Jim
Corelli	Boy
	The Master Christian
Cunninghame-Graham	Thirteen Stories †
Doyle	The Green Flag †
Galsworthy	Villa Rubein
Glyn	The Visits of Elizabeth *
Harland	The Cardinal's Snuff-Box
Hewlett	The Life and Death of Richard Yea and Nay
Hichens	Tongues of Conscience †
Hobbes	Robert Orange
James	The Soft Side †
Jerome	Three Men on a Bummel
Morrison	Cunning Murrell
Onions	The Compleat Bachelor
Wells	Love and Mr Lewisham
Zangwill	The Mantle of Elijah

1901
Butler	Erewhon Revisited
Caine	The Eternal City
Conrad/Ford	The Inheritors
Douglas	The House with the Green Shutters
Galsworthy	A Man of Devon †

Gissing	Our Friend the Charlatan
Hobbes	The Serious Wooing
Hornung	Raffles: The Black Mask
Jacobs	Light Freights †
James	The Sacred Fount
Kipling	Kim
Le Gallienne	The Life Romantic
Malet	The History of Sir Richard Calmady
Maugham	The Hero
Moore	Sister Teresa
Munro	Doom Castle
Nesbit	The Would-be-Goods
Wells	The First Men in the Moon

1902
Bell	Wee Macgreegor
Bennett	Anna of the Five Towns
	Grand Babylon Hotel
Buchan	The Watcher by the Threshold †
Childers	The Riddle of the Sands
Conrad	Youth †
	Within the Tides †
Corelli	Temporal Power
Cunninghame-Graham	Success †
Doyle	The Hound of the Baskervilles
Glyn	The Reflections of Ambrosine
Haggard	The Pearl Maiden
Hobbes	Love and the Soul Hunters
Hudson	El Ombu
Jacobs	The Lady of the Barge †
James	The Wings of the Dove
Jerome	Paul Kelver
Kipling	Just So Stories †
Mason	The Four Feathers
Maugham	Mrs Craddock
Morrison	The Hole in the Wall
Nesbit	Five Children and It
Potter	The Tale of Peter Rabbit
Thorne	When it was Dark
Wells	The Sea Lady
Wodehouse	The Pothunters *

1903 Bennett   The Gates of Wrath
                   Leonora
      Butler   The Way of All Flesh
      Conrad/Ford Romance
      Deeping   Uther and Igraine*
      Doyle   The Adventures of
                   Gerard
      Gissing   The Private Papers of
                   Henry Ryecroft
      Henty   With Kitchener in the
                   Sudan
      James   The Ambassadors
                   The Better Sort†
      Le Queux   Secrets of the Foreign
                   Office
      Merrick   Conrad in Search of
                   his Youth
      Merriman   Barlasch of the Guard
      Moore   Untilled Field†
      Ward   Lady Rose's Daughter
      Wells   Twelve Stories and a
                   Dream†

1904 Bennett   A Great Man
                   Teresa of Watling
                   Street
      Belloc   Emmanuel Burden,
                   Merchant*
      Brazil   A Terrible Tomboy*
      Caine   The Prodigal Son
      Chesterton   The Napoleon of
                   Notting Hill*
      Conrad   Nostromo
      Corvo   Hadrian the Seventh
      De La Mare   Henry Brocken*
      Galsworthy   The Island Pharisees
      Gissing   Veranilda
      Harland   My Friend Prospero
      Hewlett   The Queen's Quair
      Hichens   The Garden of Allah
                   The Woman with the
                   Fan
      Hudson   Green Mansions
      James   The Golden Bowl
      M. R. James Ghost Stories of an
                   Antiquary†
      Kipling   Traffics and
                   Discoveries†
      Le Queux   The Man from Down-
                   ing Street
      Munro   Erchie
      Nesbit   The Phoenix and the
                   Carpet
      Reid   The Kingdom of
                   Twilight*
      Saki   Reginald*

      Sinclair   The Divine Fire
      Sturgis   Belchamber
      Thurston   John Chilcote MP
      Wells   The Food of the Gods

1905 Bennett   Sacred and Profane
                   Love
      Birmingham   The Seething Pot*
      Burnett   A Little Princess
      Chesterton   The Club of Queer
                   Trades
      Corvo   Don Tarquinio
      Doyle   The Return of Sher-
                   lock Holmes†
      Dunsany   The Gods of Pegana
      Firbank   Odette d'Antever-
                   ines†*
      Ford   The Benefactor
      Forster   Where Angels Fear to
                   Tread*
      Gissing   Will Warburton
      Glyn   The Vicissitudes of
                   Evangeline
      Haggard   Ayesha
      Locke   The Morals of Marcus
                   Ordeyne
      Masefield   A Mainsail Haul†*
      Morrison   Divers Vanities†
      Moore   The Lake
      Orczy   The Scarlet Pimpernel
      Phillpotts   The Secret Woman
      Robins   A Dark Lantern
      Vachell   The Hill
      Wallace   The Four Just Men
      Wells   A Modern Utopia
                   Kipps

1906 Bennett   Whom God Hath
                   Joined
      Blackwood   The Empty House†*
      Bowen   The Viper of Milan*
      Brazil   The Fortunes of
                   Philippa
      Corelli   The Treasure of
                   Heaven
      Crockett   The White Plumes of
                   Navarre
      De Morgan   Joseph Vance*
      Doyle   Sir Nigel
      Dunsany   Time and the Gods
      Ford   The Fifth Queen
      Galsworthy   The Man of Property
      Gissing   The House of
                   Cobwebs†
      Glyn   Beyond the Rocks

	Howard	The Smiths of Surbiton
	Hunt	The Workaday Woman
	Kipling	Puck of Pook's Hill †
	Macaulay	Abbots Verney *
	Machen	The House of Souls †
	Malet	The Far Horizon
	Munro	The Vital Spark †
	Nesbit	The Story of the Amulet
		The Railway Children
	Wells	In the Days of the Comet
	Weyman	Chippinge
1907	Bennett	The Grim Smile of the Five Towns †
	Blackwood	The Listener †
	Bowen	The Glen of Weeping
	Bullock	Robert Thorne
	Conrad	The Secret Agent
	De Morgan	Alice for Short
	Diver	Captain Desmond V.C. *
	M & J Findlater	Crossrigs
	Ford	Privy Seal
		An English Girl
	Forster	The Longest Journey
	Galsworthy	The Country House
	Glyn	Three Weeks
	Hay	Pip *
	Jerome	The Passing of the Third Floor Back †
	Leverson	The Twelfth Hour *
	Locke	The Beloved Vagabond
	Machen	The Hill of Dreams
	Masefield	A Tarpaulin Muster †
	Mason	The Broken Road
	Munro	Daft Days
	Nesbit	The Enchanted Garden
	Q	The Mayor of Troy Town
	Robins	The Convert
	Sinclair	The Helpmate
	Wales	The Yoke
	Zangwill	Ghetto Comedies
1908	Barclay	Wheels of Time *
	Belloc	Mr Clutterbuck's Election
	Bennett	The Old Wives' Tale
	Birmingham	Spanish Gold
	Blackwood	John Silence †

	Bowen	The Sword Decides
	Chesterton	The Man Who Was Thursday
	Conrad	A Set of Six †
	De Morgan	Somehow Good
	de Vere Stacpoole	The Blue Lagoon
	Diver	The Great Amulet
	Dunsany	The Sword of Welleram
	Ford	The Fifth Queen Crowned
		Mr Apollo
	Forster	A Room with a View
	Galsworthy	A Commentary †
	Gibbs	The Individualist *
	Grahame	The Wind in the Willows
	Hewlett	Half Way House
	Hunt	White Rose of Weary Leaf
	Kaye Smith	The Tramping Methodist *
	Leverson	Love's Shadow
	Lyons	Arthur's
	Masefield	Captain Margaret
	Sinclair	Kitty Tailleur
	Ward	Diana Mallory
	Wells	The War in the Air
1909	Angell	The Grand Illusion
	Belloc	A Change in the Cabinet
	Barclay	The Rosary
	Blackwood	Jimbo
		The Education of Uncle Paul
	Bowen	Black Magic
	Brazil	Bosom Friends
	Caine	The White Prophet
	Cannan	Peter Homunculus *
	Chesterton	The Ball and the Cross
	De Morgan	It Can Never Happen Again
	Diver	Candles in the Wind
	Ford	The Half Moon
	Galsworthy	Fraternity
	Gibbs	The Street of Adventure
	Glyn	Elizabeth Visits America
	Hewlett	Open Country
	Howard	The Smiths of Valley View
	Hichens	Bella Donna

Kipling	Actions and Reactions†	
Masefield	Multitude and Solitude	
Onions	Little Devil Doubt	
Walpole	The Wooden Horse	
Wells	Ann Veronica	
	Tono-Bungay	
Wodehouse	The Swoop	
	Mike	

1910 Belloc — Pongo and the Bull
Bennett — Clayhanger
Helen with the High Hand
Blackwood — The Human Cord
Brazil — The Nicest Girl in the School
Broughton — The Devil and the Deep Sea
Buchan — Prester John
Cannan — Devious
De La Mare — The Return
De Morgan — An Affair of Dishonour
Dunsany — A Dreamer's Tales†
Farnol — The Broad Highway
Ford — A Call
Forster — Howards End
Galsworthy — A Motley†
Glyn — His Hour
Hewlett — Rest Harrow
James — The Finer Grain†
Kipling — Rewards and Faries†
Mason — At the Villa Rosa
Meredith — Celt and Saxon
Montague — A Hind Let Loose*
Munro — Fancy Farm
Nesbit — The Magic City
Pett Ridge — Nine to Six-Thirty
Reynolds — The Holy Mountain
Sharp — Rebel Women†
Torr — The Blot
Wells — The History of Mr Polly
Wodehouse — Psmith in the City

1911 Beerbohm — Zuleika Dobson
Belloc — The Girondin
Bennett — The Card
Hilda Lessways
Beresford — The Early History of Jacob Stahl*
The Hampdenshire Wonder
Blackwood — The Centaur

Braddon — The Green Curtain
Brazil — The New Girl at St Chad's
Burnett — The Secret Garden
Chesterton — The Innocence of Father Brown†
Colmore — Suffragette Sally
Compton-Burnet — Dolores*
Conrad — Under Western Eyes
Corelli — The Life Everlasting
De Morgan — A Likely Story
M & J Findlater — Penny MonyPenny
Forster — The Celestial Omnibus†
Galsworthy — The Patrician
Glyn — The Reason Why
Haggard — Red Eve
Hamilton — Just to Get Married
M. R. James — More Ghost Stories of an Antiquary†
Lawrence — The White Peacock*
Le Queux — Revelations of the Secret Service
Locke — The Glory of Clementine Wing
Lyons — Cottage Pie
Mackenzie — The Passionate Elopement*
Mansfield — In a German Pension*†
Masefield — The Street of Today
Jim Davis
Merrick — The Position of Peggy Harper
Onions — Good Boy Seldom
Widdershins†
Reid — The Bracknels
Saki — The Chronicles of Clovis†
The Unbearable Bassington
Wallace — Sanders of the River
Walpole — Mr Perrin and Mr Traill
Ward — The Case of Richard Meynell
Wells — The Country of the Blind
The New Machiavelli

1912 Belloc — The Green Overcoat
Bennett — The Matador of the Five Towns†
Beresford — A Candidate for Truth

	Blackwood	Pan's Garden †
	Buchan	The Moon Endureth †
	Cannan	Little Brother
	Chesterton	Manalive
	Conrad	Twixt Land and Sea †
	Dell	The Way of an Eagle *
	Doyle	The Lost World
	Lawrence	The Trespasser
	Leverson	Tenterhooks
	Mackenzie	Carnival
	Middleton	The Ghost Ship †
	Onions	In Accordance with the Evidence
	Reid	Following Darkness
	Stephens	The Charwoman's Daughter
		The Crock of Gold
	Wells	Marriage
1913	Bennett	The Regent
	Bentley	Trent's Last Case
	Beresford	Goslings
	Blackwood	A Prisoner in Fairyland
	Braddon	Miranda
	Caine	The Woman Thou Gavest Me
	Cannan	Round the Corner
	Cholmondeley	Notwithstanding
	Conrad	Chance
	Dell	The Knave of Diamonds
	Farnol	The Amateur Gentleman
	Galsworthy	The Dark Flower
	Holme	Crump Folk Going Home *
	Jesse	The Milky Way *
	Lawrence	Sons and Lovers
	Lowndes	The Lodger
	Mackenzie	Sinister Street
	Mason	The Witness for the Defence
	Onions	The Debit Account
		The Story of Louie
	Sinclair	The Combined Maze
	Walpole	Fortitude
	Wells	The Passionate Friends
	Young	Undergrowth

1914	Benson	Dodo the Second
	Beresford	The House in Demetrious Road
	Blackwood	Incredible Adventures †
	Chesterton	The Wisdom of Father Brown †
		The Flying Inn
	Corelli	Innocent
	Dell	The Rocks of Valpre
	De Morgan	When Ghost Meets Ghost
	Gibbs	The Custody of the Child
	Hay (J. M.)	Gillespie
	Holme	The Lonely Plough
	Joyce	Dubliners †
	Lawrence	The Prussian Officer †
	Mackenzie	Guy and Pauline
	Munro	The New Road
	Saki	Beasts and Super-Beasts †
	Sinclair	The Three Sisters
	Tressell	The Ragged-Trousered Philanthropists
	Wells	The World Set Free
		The Wife of Sir Isaac Harmon
	Yates	The Brothers of Daphne *
1915	S. Benson	I Pose *
	Buchan	The Thirty-Nine Steps
	Conrad	Victory
	Doyle	The Valley of Fear
	Evans	My People †*
	Ford	The Good Soldier
	Galsworthy	The Freelands
	Glyn	The Man and the Moment
	Lawrence	The Rainbow
	Maugham	Of Human Bondage
	Richardson	Pointed Roofs*
	Ward	Delia Blanchflower
	Wells	Bealby
		The Research Magnificent
	Woolf	The Voyage Out

Index